IT'S A LONG CLIMB TO THE MIDDLE

The Autobiography of Tad Sisler

FOREWORD
By Edwin (Eddie) Balderama

> **"We can't return, we can only look behind from where we came, and go 'round and 'round and 'round in the circle game."—Joni Mitchell**

My good friend, Tad Sisler, has always possessed a marvelous facility for words. It is, in fact, one of the things about him that drew me to him as a friend some forty years ago. I always found it remarkable how he could so easily articulate his thoughts and feelings, and if you were to now characterize the both of us in our friendship, you would definitely label him the "talker" and me the "listener". It has always been that way between us, but I think that's what's been the "secret sauce" in our friendship—we each brought to the table complementary abilities.

If you didn't already know it, Tad also has an incredibly good memory—and when I say good memory, I really mean "scary good". It always used to amaze me how he could pinpoint the exact week, month and year when we first met—and I bet if I pressed him about it, he could probably come up with what I was wearing that day too. His memory is, of course, a function of his powerful intellect and somewhere in the deepest crevices of his "cloud computer-like" brain are memories yet waiting to be accessed.

The size of Tad's brain is only exceeded by the size of his... heart! (Ahh... you thought I was going somewhere else with that! Shame on you!) I must confess that when I met Tad, I had never known anyone in my life who talked so freely and openly about LOVE. I remember him making references to "the power of Love", "being loving to one another" or simply saying "I love you, man" coupled with the occasional references to a certain Maharishi. In the beginning I used to think "this guy is kind of different" and I jokingly liked to think of it as being the last vestiges of a Beatles album where the needle gets stuck in the groove and what you hear is "All you need is Love, All you need is Love, All you need is Love... (ad infinitum)".

But here is what I found out...the man REALLY MEANS IT and his spirituality is genuine! He truly believes that Love Will Conquer All and if you don't believe me, then just wait long enough and he will show you. He might give you an acknowledging glance, or a sunny smile, or touch you as he walks by, or even put his arms around you in a warm embrace; whatever he does, you never get the sense that it's phony like some Hollywood air kiss. There's always a sincerity that comes across and I've watched people responding positively to it for years, and as good as it works with adults, I've seen it works even better with children.

So, if you take someone with superior communication skills, a memory like an elephant, and a heart as big as the ocean, and this person suddenly feels inspired to write his autobiography, you might expect the results to be fairly good. Well, what Tad has written is nothing short of amazing. Equal parts genealogy, travelogue, confessional and devotional-- he forces himself to take a long hard look back on the path that got him to where he is now.

I don't imagine it's an easy task writing one's autobiography, because in order to do so, if you're honest, you have to come face to face with your dashed hopes, sorrows, disappointments, desperate struggles, failures and personal shortcomings all over again. Moreover, it can't be easy to regurgitate those old ugly feelings—the same ones that wounded you and drove you to your knees all those years ago. And then on top of it all, you have to confess too?

We all have shit in our lives that we have to walk through and some of us just have the misfortune of having to walk through more of the stuff than others. Tad's life is, if anything, a lesson in perseverance. He shows that you just have to scrape the stuff off the bottom of your shoes and keep on steppin'.

In the end, I could tell Tad put a lot of himself into his memoirs. I could tell, not just from its sheer breadth, but also from its depth. From its beginning to its conclusion, he dispenses what wisdom he has gleaned. He assiduously collects it all in one box, gift-wraps it with a pretty bow and then hands it to you, seeming to say "Here! It's free! It's a gift! It's from me!" Oh, and that belief that Love Conquers All? Well, Tad will be happy to tell you that it's absolutely true! He knows because he's lived it!

There's one last thing, though, before I go. I want to share with you a memory because I feel it draws a straight line from the Tad of forty years ago with the Tad we know today. It goes like this:

When I first met Tad, we were both young men in our early twenties serendipitously thrown together at work. It wasn't long, however, before we discovered our mutual love for music. After work I would invite Tad over for a beer and we would unwind by spinning some vinyl on the turntable.

On one such occasion, he tells me he needs to pick something up at the apartment where he was living. At the time, he was staying with his friends Kurt and Janet. It was late in the evening when we arrived and, by that time, the two of them had already gone to bed. He didn't want to awaken them, so he refrained from turning on the lights and we spoke in hushed whispers.

The only illumination came from the porch light outside shining through the curtains in the living room. In the dim light I could see the outline of an upright piano. I asked who it belonged to and he said it was Janet's but that he also played. (This was still early on in our friendship so I didn't yet know of his musical talent and it would still be some time before he became a professional musician.) Before I knew it, he sat down in front of the keyboard and softly began to play an Elton John tune. It was not something I had asked for, but I could tell, he wanted to share something of himself. There in that dark apartment, he began to sing. He sang that song from somewhere deep inside of him…I know because I could feel it.

Now here's the connection: Tad's autobiography is like that intimate performance all those years ago. And I can still hear Tad sing … "My gift is my song… and this one's for you."

Eddie Balderama

•••••

FOREWORD
By Suzanne Ramsey

There are a handful of people in this world who have known Tad Sisler his whole life—a couple of Uncles, a couple of sisters and myself, his oldest sister. I remember the excitement we all felt when we finally had a boy in the family after four girls, (the outcome presented at birth in the days before sonograms.) Daddy celebrated by getting drunk, his reflexive response to good news or tragedy, while Daddy's mother, our grandmother Audrey contained his explosion of joy, "My son! I have a son!" Grandma Sisler was always present when Mother gave birth, arriving three weeks early close to the due date and leaving the week after the baby came home as if she forgot each time that Mother was always late for everything including childbirth.

Daddy begged Mother to name him Maynard Lee Sisler, Jr. which she acquiesced to do. But such a formal name did not fit this small monkey-faced newborn with eyes and ears too large for his face! We all debated his nickname and I, having just studied Abraham Lincoln's life, proposed "Tad". Daddy, still under the influence of his exuberance, exclaimed, "Perfect! I'm in the Navy as physician to the midshipmen at Annapolis, we'll call him TAD for Temporary Additional Duty!" And so it was, although Tad was never a temporary addition to our family but an integral and important addition, the Crown Prince, as we called him affectionately.

Eleven-and-a-half years older than Tad, I assumed many of the Nanny duties although Mother was more involved in caretaking than I remember her being with her girls. In the late 1950's a woman counted herself worthy if she could produce a son. Mother let me be Little Mother to my two younger sisters, Kathy and Betsy, whom I adored. The next older sister, Judy, was my antagonist—only twenty-one months apart--she was always in my world that I could remember, always neater and more "together' than I was, and very opinionated as a young girl, meaning she did not agree with me most of the time or let me take charge as the younger girls did. Tad was doted on by all of us but somehow remained unspoiled. He was extraordinarily precocious--with motor and verbal skills and especially with social skills, becoming early-on the humorist of the family and just fun to be around. He was making little jokes at 3 years old—3-year-old jokes to be sure but still funny! His curiosity and inventive creativity defined him as a toddler and preschooler, and still does. I was so proud of him! I used to push his stroller around the block, past the liquor store and the candy store and the little marketplace, sure people would think he was MY baby. And in many ways, he was.

The things that make Tad unique in his person-package emerge from his writings as well. There is his quick mind and his style of thinking, much like our Daddy's. Perceiving the different ways that people think and thus how they view the world I find intriguing. Mother and Judy, for example, were factual people, basing their core processes on facts and being well-grounded in the here and now. Kathy thinks in putting concepts together—holistic and material; spiritual and mundane. There are reasons why certain things occur together that have greater meaning than each separately. Betsy is an organized thinker, quick and precise and able to discern patterns that others can't see as clearly. And Tad is brilliant and conceptual and best at synthesizing memory and meaning, much as his musical talent harmonizes melody and lyrics, organizing his playlist to fit its own pattern as he chooses and changes it. He has a reverence for words (inarguably the best of us at Words With Friends), whether he's writing the story of his life or playing with puns or "quick with a joke or to light up your smoke", metaphorically. His writings, as you will experience in reading this book, have a depth and insight remarkable.

I left the family unit at 16, pregnant, married on Tad's 5th birthday, the carousel rented for his party blaring carnival music outside my girlhood bedroom as my new husband and I changed clothes and consummated our marriage. Two months later the Navy transported my family a continent away. I would not see Tad or my sisters for 3 ½ years until I visited them, now with two children, for Christmas in Corpus Christi. But in those days before social media and cell phones, when any long-distance phone call had to be budgeted, we had letters, many from Tad I still keep, full of information and brim with curiosity. Later he would come to visit many summers, becoming more a bigger brother to my four kids than Uncle. After all, he and my first-born were only five and a half years apart! These visits, and ones when he was a young adult, afforded me to get to know and appreciate the person he was becoming. Then, as often happens even in families living within driving distance, our own lives and marriages and parenting, put parentheses around our lives, wrapping us within our own cocooned worlds. And Tad was good at dissembling as was I, keeping things superficial and "fine" when asked. Only on rare extended visits would we be able to share and communicate honestly. The honesty and purity of truth-telling develops over time and experience, if it develops at all, evolving from willingness to see through tragedy and suffering and emotional scars to the growth they bring. This too comes through in this book!

I love Tad so much and I really like the guy you will see emerge in this book! He is complex, multifaceted, insightful, and good at putting pieces of the puzzle together. We have shared the passings of our grandparents and parents and paternal Uncles, and cousins who died way too early. We've moved together up the ladder of life as their deaths opened up new places of maturity. I've become the Matriarch (I prefer "Monarch") of our extended families while Tad, way too young, could be considered the Patriarch. He brings a love of history and a respect for ancestry into his life and his writings; a respect for what goes before which translates into what will come after, what defines what we mean by legacy. We've also shared with our siblings the god-awful sudden loss of our sister, Judy, which left us wobbling on our ladders of life, groping to grab the hand of a sister or a brother. Take my brother's hand, too, and walk with him through this remarkable book. You will really like the guy you see emerge!

Tad with Suzanne Ramsey

Suzanne Ramsey

PROLOGUE

It's a long climb to the middle…and, the middle is not just a plateau; it contains peaks and valleys; it is an electrocardiogram of our life stories. Climbing the ladder, I sometimes was knocked back down a few rungs, and other times I fell all the way back to the bottom, but his battle-scarred warrior always used his primary weapon: persistence.

There have been fleeting moments that I experienced how it must feel to reach the pinnacle of success as some define it, but in general, it felt more like a journey to an extraordinary life. What makes an ordinary life extraordinary? It could be argued that achievements or awards contribute to an extraordinary life. More importantly, though, how do we react to triumph and tragedy? In the depths of winter, do we find within ourselves that invincible summer, and continue on?

•••••

When I was young, my father instructed me that one's reach must always exceed one's grasp. Always keep pushing for a greater outcome, and if you keep your expectations low, you might be pleasantly surprised here and there.

I also believe wholeheartedly that attitudes and emotions shape our destinies. It is said that humans are half-god, half-animal (I will elaborate on this later in the book). How much of your god-self do you allow to guide you? Do you allow fear, anger, depression, sorrow, envy or greed to shape your actions? The further we move away from these obstacles, the greater our life experience can be. Holding on to negative thought will only hurt you.

•••••

This chronicle of my journey through my life is extensive; even still, it does not cover every baseball game, every beach trip, every moment of love. More so, it is a large slice of core memories that shaped me and perhaps provided the foundation for my philosophy. In telling my story, I will have succeeded if you walk away from reading this manuscript with some self-reflection and perhaps a greater understanding of circumstances you've experienced.

This book, at times, becomes a recitation of events in snapshots of time. What I learned in writing it was simple: there is always meaning to glean from every day and every experience. The trick is to find it and apply it to your life, and that usually happens much later than the experience itself.

I begin by reaching back the handful of generations that I am aware of in my immediate family. It is well and good to know and remember where we come from. It helps us to know a little more of whom we are as we create our own destinies. Before we get too caught up in our heritage, however, it is good to remember that each one of us is the product of two parents, four grandparents, eight great-grandparents, and so on. Reaching back just ten generations, each of us is the product of over a thousand others, with a little piece of each one (and many more before them) in our DNA.

•••••

At the advent of the twenty-first century, the world became interconnected as never before through the Worldwide Web. For the first time in the history of the world, connecting to the internet and owning a smartphone allowed us all to hold the knowledge of the universe in its entirety, in our pockets.

During the same time period, the human genome was mapped for the first time, and huge DNA databases began to be compiled. It became the rage to send your DNA sample into *ancestry.com* or *twenty-three & me* in order to find out exactly what ethnicity you were, as well as any propensity to certain diseases or habits your DNA structure might reveal. Long-lost relatives were reunited, and one could search their family tree *ad nauseum*.

It was exciting to dream of what nobleman, Queen, or hero we might be linked to as one of our ancestors; equally existed the risk of being related to knaves or scoundrels. Did we <u>really</u> want to know all of that complicated history? Then again, our progeny in future generations could turn out to be heroes or villains, no matter how hard we work to fashion our own children into model citizens. Still, it is fascinating to embrace your own DNA and how it fits into the grand scheme of things. No matter what, your progeny will be unique expressions (or mutations!) of you and many others, all in one, and they may just turn out to be the agreeable, darling people you now can only conjure up in your imagination.

When I started to write my own story, I wondered if it would be wise to reveal myself (warts and all) for my own forebears to judge. Should I paint a picture of myself as more righteous, perhaps, than I am? Should I really reveal ALL of the skeletons in my closet? After all, everyone who has truly lived has held secrets they would rather not tell. My conclusion was simple: to tell the truth, because truly I do have a fascinating story, full of comedy and tragedy, of the highest highs and the lowest of lows. I've loved and lost more than once, endured the whips and scorns of time, experienced triumphs, lived my dreams, cherished my offspring, endured the deepest of sorrows and experienced life on the edge of insanity at times. It's all here and every bit of it is true, I promise.

Life is as much observation as it is experience... and what an experience it is to have a front-row seat to observe history in the making.

I was born on June 28, 1958 in Annapolis, Maryland. My father was a young Navy doctor, stationed at the Naval Academy, but he had already been transferred to St. Albans, New York, when I was born. We moved from Annapolis to Hempstead, on Long Island, New York when I was two weeks old. I was the youngest of five children and the only boy. Growing up, I was told many times that I had "five mothers," between my mom and my four older sisters, Suzanne Elaine, Judith Barbara, Kathleen Patricia, and Mary Elizabeth (Betsy).

CHAPTER ONE
My Father, Maynard, and his Family

My father, Maynard, was born in Massillon, Ohio in 1923. His father, George Turner Sisler, was of German and English ancestry and his mother, Audrey Augusta Athey Sisler, was of Irish, Scottish and Dutch heritage.

When my father, Maynard, passed away in 2012, he was already a great-great grandparent to two living children. This is an interesting statistic in the sense that, first, I didn't even know one of my grandfathers (my mother's father died before I was born), and, more importantly, my great-great grandfather on my father's side was born 169 years before me, in the first year of the advent of our great nation, the United States of America.

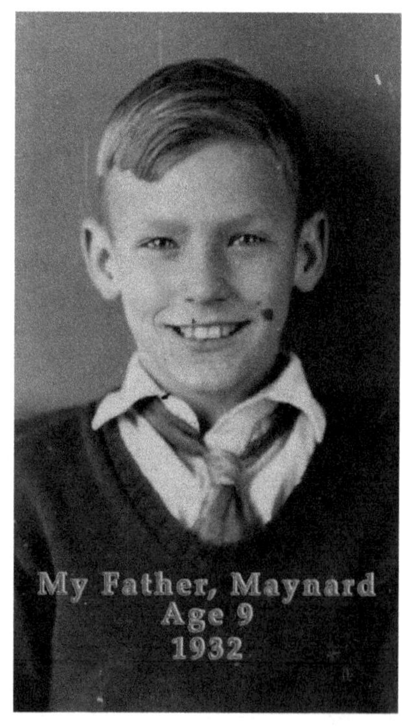
My Father, Maynard
Age 9
1932

My great-great grandfather Abraham was born in 1789. My great grandfather, also named Abraham, was born in 1838. My grandfather, George was born in 1890, my father, Maynard in 1923 and myself in 1958. I am one of very few people alive today who can count only four generations between my birth and the birth of our nation.

•••••

According to genealogy records, the *name Sisler* came to England with the ancestors of the *Sisler* family in the Norman Conquest of 1066. The *Sisler* family lived in Gloucestershire, at the manor of Siston, from whence their *name* was derived.

My father's great-great grandfather was one of two brothers, Johanus Abram (Abraham) Sisler, and George Karl Sisler, born during the 1760's in the German Duchy of Hesse. They were impressed by their Duke into the ranks of a Jaegar Regiment, hired by England's King George as Hessian soldiers to fight against the American colonists in the Revolutionary War. They fought in battle and were surrendered at Yorktown; interred at a prisoner of war camp in Winchester, Virginia and later were paroled as freemen in a free country.

Johanus Abram Sisler took up land in that part of Virginia later to become the State of Michigan. His progeny would later include one George Harold Sisler (not my grandfather George). George was one of the thirteen original members of *Major League Baseball's* Hall of Fame. George Sisler, the baseball player, was primarily the first baseman for the St. Louis Browns. In the 1922 season he batted an unheard-of .420, which would have beat Ted Williams out in the modern era. George's MLB record for most hits in a season held for eighty-five years, until Ichiro Suzuki broke it in the year 2004.

Johanus Abram's brother, George Karl Sisler (my father's great-great grandfather) remained in the Shenandoah Valley of Virginia where he also obtained a land grant and became a farmer. His son, Abraham, born in 1789 (my great-great grandfather), distinguished himself as an American patriot. Abraham served in the War of 1812 and also fought in the Battle of New Orleans, wounding a leg. He belonged to the *German Reform Church,* and he had two children, Abraham and Marie.

•••••

My Great Grandfather Abraham Sisler

George Karl's grandson, Abraham was born in Tilghmanton, Washington County, Maryland On October 15, 1838. He was my great-grandfather. It wasn't until shortly after Abraham became an adult that slavery was abolished in the United States.

Abraham married my great-grandmother, Nancy Ellen Wade of Tilghmanton, Maryland, in 1865. Nancy was the daughter of John Henry and Mary Ellen (McCoy) Wade. Nancy was born near Sharpsburg, Maryland. They parented nine children, named, in the order of their birth, Martha Ellen, born April 10, 1871; Sara Jane, Born March of 1873 (my dad remembered his aunt Sara, growing up, as a puritan, strict but kindly old lady); Mary Eugenia, born May 18, 1876; Charles William, (my grandfather's favorite brother, he named his second-born son after him) born November 11, 1880; John H. Wade, born August 14, 1885; Abraham L., born September 21, 1888; George Turner (my grandfather), born March 23, 1890 and Frank Strother, who died as an infant in May 1892.

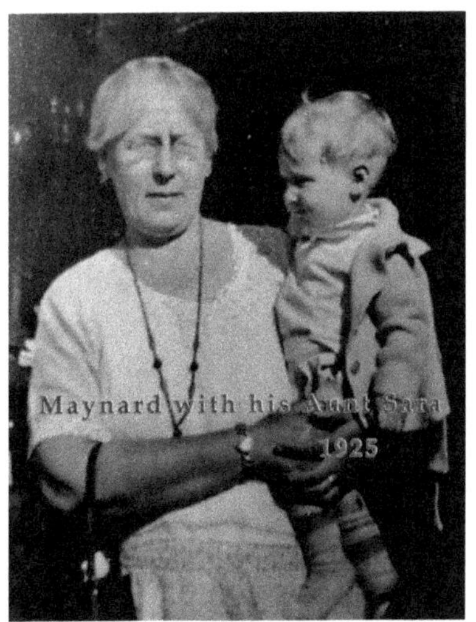
Maynard with his Aunt Sara 1925

As noted above, my father's dad, my grandfather George, was the seventh child of Abraham Sisler and Nancy Ellen Wade Sisler. My great-grandfather Abraham fought in the American Civil War as a Union Soldier. My dad and his brothers remembered their grandfather Abraham as a white-bearded old gentleman with a gruff exterior and a heart of gold.

My great-grandfather Abraham was twenty-three years of age when in September 1862, he rode the three-mile distance between Shepherdstown and Sharpsburg to watch a great smoking battle being fought there. He came to watch, but he remained to serve. A Colonel of the Union Cavalry saw him sitting on his horse and arrested him as a spy. The Colonel offered Abraham the choice between hanging and joining the Union Army. He promptly avoided the noose and wore a blue uniform for the duration of the Civil War, serving with distinction from 1862-1864 in Cole's Cavalry. Abraham Sisler was only twenty-six years old when Abraham Lincoln was assassinated, and the Civil war ended. He saw carnage on an unimaginable scale, and it affected him greatly. He remained stoic throughout his life, yet kind and approachable.

My father, Maynard, relished the memory, as a young boy, of actually sitting on the knees of old Civil War veterans on the town square as they spun their yarns.

Maynard often repeated the story of how his Grandfather Abraham had been wounded in a battle, and subsequently made a poultice from some bark off of a specific tree, as his grandmother had taught him, to treat the wound. This particular bark contained a natural version of an antibiotic, which had yet to be 'discovered', and it worked in healing him.

•••••

Following the Civil War, Abraham owned and operated a string of canal boats on the Chesapeake and Ohio Canal. He also took up farming and carried on his life's work until he retired in 1906. Abraham was a Republican and a member of the *Methodist Episcopal Church.*

When I was very young, my grandfather George recalled how hard his father worked to keep them out of poverty when George was a small boy. His father, Abraham, would take his brother and him into the woods in the wintertime with horses drawing a large wagon with iron wheels. They would spend most of a day cutting huge blocks of ice from the frozen Virginia ponds, load the ice blocks onto a platform attached to the wagon, and then their horses would drag the heavy sleigh with the ice into town to sell to the ice houses for use in ice boxes, the precursors to the modern refrigerator. It was backbreaking work.

My great-grandfather Abraham died in 1917 at age 73. Recalling his misery in life, my uncle Bill told me later that he always believed that his father welcomed death. Abraham had been married for more than a half-century to a woman Bill described as "...a shrew of the first water. Great-grandmother Nancy Sisler was a religious fanatic of the faith-healing *Duncard* persuasion, and was equipped with a violent temper and a vitriolic tongue." I always wondered if my grandfather George's anger, which led to his alcoholism and mistreatment of his own family, came from his mother.

Other than that slight bit of information about my great-grandmother, there is little written I'm aware of about any of the women that preceded me as ancestors. I believe this is largely because women had certain roles in the culture of the times, and rarely deviated from them; homemaker, taking care of the children, active in the church; their role was essential but not seemingly as colorful as their husbands. Their days were long and life was not easy.

•••••

American life in the mid 1800's wasn't much different than life had been centuries before, in the Middle Ages. I always smile when people reminisce about "back when life was simpler and easier." Life was difficult then. Oil lamps and candles delivered artificial light. Someone fortunate enough to own horses needed blacksmiths to shoe them, hay for feed and stables to house them. They needed carriages or buggies, and the tools and supplies to maintain them. Travel was precarious, uncomfortable and slow, for the most part.

Water was gathered from a well or a pump. Plumbing was rare and outhouses had to be maintained. It took all day to wash and dry clothes. Disease was rampant without the blessings of modern remedies. Poverty was out of hand, and many of today's laws that protect the worker were not yet in place. The farmer was more prevalent than the city dweller.

Yet, progress was beginning to make lives easier, and the beginning of the industrial age must have been glorious to view. The cotton gin had been invented. The telegraph (and later, the telephone) began to make information and communication more available to the masses. The completion of the transcontinental railroad made a huge difference in commerce, transportation, expansion and resettlement.

•••••

My father's mother, my grandmother Audrey Augusta Athey, was born On December 11, 1889 to Edward "Cap" Athey and Lillian Lincoln Schell Athey. Her mother, Lillian was born on April 26, 1869 to John and Margaret Schell, in Shepherdstown, Virginia (later, West Virginia). Edward "Cap" Athey was born in 1869 to James Athey and Margaret Woodward, and died in 1947. Cap and Lillian had three other children, Thomas Edward Woodward Athey, Nicholas Strother Athey, and Rosa Belle (Rose) Athey. My great-grandmother Lillian (affectionately called "Lillie") was sweet and kindly, the daughter of a Valley Mill owner and farmer, a testy Dutchman named James (John) Schell. Everyone who knew her adored her.

Lillian Schell Athey

The Atheys were descendants of proud people who fled Ireland's County Clare to escape persecution by Catholic Scottish Monarchs for clinging to the Presbyterian faith. Again, persecuted in Ireland by James I of England, these Scotch-Irish clans migrated once more to the New World and settled in the North Carolina and Virginia mountains and valleys, so very much like the Highlands of their ancestors. They were a fiercely independent race, stubborn, courageous to a fault, devout church goers, and family oriented. My great-grandfather Cap Athey (called "Big Dad" by his grandsons) inherited these traits from his father's side of the family.

From his mother's side, my father inherited the courtliness and courtesy of the Southern gentry; my grandmother Audrey's grandmother was Margaret Woodward, who married Sergeant-Major James Athey of the Confederate Army's *Stonewall Brigade*. Margaret was descended from the Woodwards', Lees' and Bennets' of Virginia; and my grandmother Audrey was well aware of this lineage, which directly linked our family to George and Martha Washington through President Washington's adopted son, George Washington Parke Custis, the father of Mary Custis who married General Robert E. Lee.

•••••

"Cap" Athey, my grandmother Audrey's dad, was a famous U.S. Marshall. He was also a bridge-builder in Virginia. He truly was a great man...a giant of a man, but his unfortunate claim to fame was that he was responsible for the transport of a great train robber, who somehow got away while in my great-grandfather's custody.

Many of the bridges he built around the turn of the twentieth century still stand, well over a hundred years later.

I learned the following from an old newspaper clipping of my great-grandfather Athey's undated obituary, which my grandmother carefully and delicately kept in her large, tattered scrapbook:

> *"Edward W. Athey, aged 78, who as a deputy United States Marshal in 1917 gained nationwide newspaper publicity in connection with the escape and recapture of Henry Grady Webb, a notorious train robber, died yesterday morning in the Kings Daughters hospital at Martinsburg, where he had gone for a minor operation. His death, which was unexpected, resulted from a thrombosis. A native of Jefferson County, he had been a resident of Marion County for nearly thirty years.*
> *Familiarly known here as "Cap" Athey, he had also served as a deputy under Sheriff Andrew West, and at the time of his death, held a position with the State Road Commission.*
> *It was while in the custody of Deputy Athey and other officials, that Webb, the ringleader in the spectacular robbery of a Baltimore & Ohio mail train at Central Station in 1915, made a sensational escape from the train on which he was being escorted to the Atlanta Penitentiary. There had been nation-wide interest in the robbery and in the subsequent capture of the robbers, three in number, and when their leader broke through a Pullman washroom window at Charlotte, NC, and disappeared, every agency of the government was alerted and put upon his trail. Webb's capture a week later and his safe removal to prison closed what probably was the most stirring case in the history of the federal court in this district.*

As deputy marshal, Mr. Athey was an intrepid officer in a period when enforcement of the laws dealing with narcotics, white slavery, and prohibition and of the Espionage Act was largely in the hands of the United States marshals and not delegated to separate agencies, as was subsequently the case. It was while trying to arrest a man charged with white slavery at Martinsburg that Mr. Athey was seriously wounded by a blast from a shotgun. He also figured in numerous other dangerous situations and had several narrow escapes. In government circles he was regarded as a top-notch officer.

Mr. Athey was of a deeply religious nature and for many years was interested in Sunday School work of the Baptist Church...He had a lifelong interest in politics and for many years was a Democratic leader in Jefferson County...but aside from serving as a deputy sheriff, sought no political preferment."

•••••

Audrey Athey 1906

Cap's daughter, my grandmother Audrey, was almost sixty-nine years old when I was born; she truly was one of the greatest gifts of my life. She lived until I was twenty-four years old, and some of the best moments of my childhood were with her.

George Sisler 1935

Audrey, and my grandfather George (whom I called "Pop") were born into an era where there were no automobiles, no airplanes, and no water treatment plants delivering potable water to homes or businesses. The telephone and light bulb had just been invented and were largely unavailable to people just yet except in the larger cities. Through their lives, they experienced all of these amazing inventions, even witnessing men land on the moon! Women were not even allowed to vote in America until my grandmother was a young adult.

My grandfather George attended grade school in Shepherdstown, West Virginia and took courses at Shepherd College for two years. George was a brilliant young man, matriculating to Columbia University and graduating in 1909. For two years after leaving college, George acted as a clerk for *W.P. Licklider* at Shepherdstown. From 1911-1913, he served as Secretary, Treasurer and business manager for *J. N. Zinn & Co., Inc.*, heating and plumbing contractors of Charleston, West Virginia. He also engaged in the business firm of *Athey & Sisler*, heating contractors of Charleston as a junior member of the firm. This is where he learned his craft, working with sheet metal and learning the business side of the trade.

Young George was a Democrat and a member of the *Methodist Episcopal Church.* In fact, George fashioned himself as a shirttail preacher. He was a member of the *Improved Order of the Red Man,* being representative of the grand camp of 1911 and chairman of the committee on state of the order, Grand Camp of West Virginia. He also was a member of the *Independent Order of the Odd Fellows*, of the *Patriotic Order of the Sons of America*, of the *Knights of Pythias*, and the *Royal Order of the Moose.* George was an involved young man, ambitious and interested in politics and civic work.

•••••

My Grandmother Audrey (2nd From Left) circa 1920

Audrey fell in love with George, who was not part or privy to the Southern gentry her family was accustomed to. In fact, George and his family were politically and socially the opposite of Audrey's parents. George and Audrey ran away and eloped on May 30, 1909, when she was nineteen and he was eighteen, against her parent's will. Although Audrey was very close to her father, Cap Athey disowned her for a time after her marriage to George. Even still, she completed High School and attended *Shepherd College.*

A short time after their marriage, my grandfather George drank too much one evening and fell into a platform at a train station into an oncoming train. The train sliced his left leg off above the knee. Nevertheless, he lived until the ripe old age of ninety with a prosthetic leg. In fact, in his young adulthood, he worked with the people who made early modern prosthetics to improve the way prosthetics fit and work.

My Grandfather George Sisler c. 1925

But, most of his life, he utilized the training of his young adulthood, working with sheet metal, building roofs and ducts with his giant, strong hands. He was also an itinerant preacher, and apparently a pretty bad drunk and a womanizer as well for much of his life.

George secured a lucrative job in Ohio, and moved his family to Crystal Springs, a suburb of Massillon, where my father was born.

BOY KILLED ON HIGHWAY

(Continued from Page One)

A youth walking along the McDonaldsville rd., just north of the corporate limits, was struck and fatally injured by an auto and a number of other cars were damaged in traffic mishaps in and near the city over the week-end.

Walking on Highway

Funeral Wednesday

Other Accidents

•••••

George and Audrey had six sons. My father, Maynard was the fifth son, born on August 12, 1923. The fourth son, Maynard's older brother Norman, died as a toddler from an illness that a modern antibiotic would have cured. It was one of many tragedies my grandparents endured. Their third son, Bennett, was hit and killed by a drunk driver at the age of fifteen while trying to run home late for dinner in fear that his father might beat him for being late. Maynard loved his older brothers, and he missed Bennett terribly.

If there was a silver lining to Bennett's death, it might be this: As a child, my grandmother implored me to always walk on the side of the road of the oncoming traffic so I could see what was coming. I was taught to never be in so much of a hurry that you get in trouble or get hurt. Years later, I passed the same concept on to my own children and grandchildren.

Always be aware of what is going on around you. Keep your eyes open and stay safe.

Maynard had a younger brother, Jack. He watched over his kid brother, and they remained very close until Jack's unfortunate death in the 1960's. George and Audrey's oldest son, George Edward, was quite the authoritarian and somewhat of a bully, patronizing, much like his father. The second son, Bill, was thoughtful and protective over my father when the oldest would be too brutal towards him. Bill took Maynard under his wing, and their closeness would last a lifetime.

Maynard with his younger brother Jack circa 1932

Even still, George and Bill expected a lot of my father. He was told that he was born to live two lives, his own and the life of his infant older brother who perished right before Maynard was born. They would make young Maynard read, memorize and recite Shakespeare at the age of five. As a result of that, my father wrote sonnets on every occasion (and even when there wasn't an occasion) for the remainder of his life, and he was Valedictorian of his high school class, graduating at fifteen years old.

Maynard's brother George was an excellent baseball pitcher with a strong arm. George was a tough guy, entering the United States Navy as a young man and serving in Guam from 1927-1931, when Maynard was just a boy. George intimidated Maynard and my father would spend a lifetime trying to impress his oldest brother.

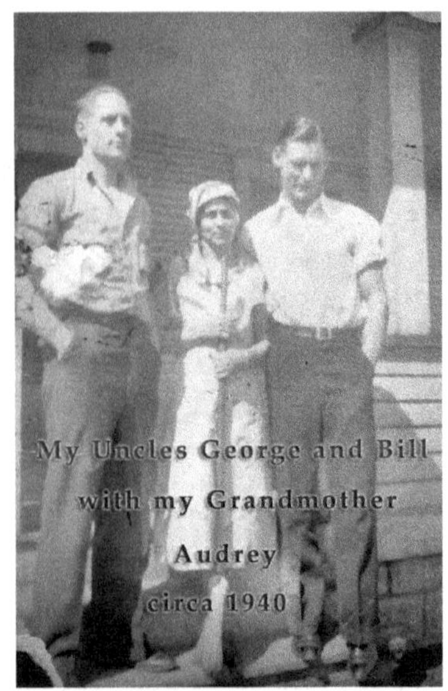
My Uncles George and Bill with my Grandmother Audrey circa 1940

Before all of that, though, when my dad was around six years old, his parents lost everything in the stock market crash of 1929. They had saved almost a hundred thousand dollars, the equivalent of about a half a million dollars today, and in an instant, it was all gone. His father could find no more work in Ohio, where my father had been born. The family moved back home to Shepherdstown, West Virginia, where my dad would spend the rest of his childhood. It was shortly after that that Bennett was killed, and my father recalled how his mother's lovely long hair changed color from dark brown to grey in just one summer.

•••••

As I mentioned, my grandmother Audrey's grandfather, James Athey, had served as a Sargent-Major in the Confederate Army, in Stonewall Jackson's First Virginia Brigade (as my grandfather George's father Abraham had fought for the Union in Cole's Cavalry). Emotions were still extremely painful and divided in the years following the American Civil War. Virtually everyone had lost loved ones and friends on both sides, and although the scourge of slavery had been finally wrested from the American consciousness, many people's consciences were still compromised on the issue.

Today, I believe that it amazes most of us that slavery could ever have existed in a "free" country, but, as they say, we must learn from our history or we are condemned to repeat it. In my grandparent's time, America was beginning to evolve towards the reality we know today, and I remember many times my grandparents talking about their families having been on opposite sides of the issue.

My Grandparents Audrey and George Sisler circa 1930

Yet, when my grandmother talked about it, it was without prejudice. Nobody in his or her right minds would have longed for slavery to come back at all. Audrey didn't have a racist bone in her body. She was the kindest, most giving person I knew, to anyone and everyone. Those tragic experiences were remembered with sadness for the lives of relatives lost on both sides, and a pride for heroism and sacrifice. My grandparents were the children of people who experienced the Civil War first-hand, on both sides.

During the genesis of these great United States, Benjamin Franklin abhorred the idea of slavery, but he and many others knew that they could not yet solve the problem of slavery and still get the Constitution and Bill of Rights passed within all of the Southern States, at that moment in time. The tragedy of slavery left unsolved created a perfect storm that brewed for eighty years before it exploded. In the Union Army, many Caucasian and African-American men sacrificed their own lives, side by side, to end slavery. And… Confederate soldiers were no less brave as they fought hard to retain an old order that should never have existed in the first place.

•••••

Following the stock market crash, my grandfather's alcoholism became a greater issue. Drunk, he would demand that my grandmother take my father and his brothers upstairs and beat them for any small infraction. My grandmother would dutifully take them up the stairs, and then she would beat the bedpost with my grandfather's belt and tell her sons to scream like hell as if they were getting hit. She wouldn't dream of hurting them. Today, a woman would just pack her things, grab her children and leave a man like that, but divorce was out of the question in those days.

These experiences would fashion in so many ways the way my father would later act towards his own family, unfortunately.

Maynard Lee Sisler 1937

Even still, when Maynard recalled his childhood many years later, he would emphatically say that it was a happy childhood. His parents were poor, but he never knew they were poor because he had everything he needed.

My dad recalled his first crush, a young lady named Agnes Calvin, who was a French teacher in High School, but close to his age. His friend Harrison Boyght introduced Maynard to Agnes. Maynard took her out on a date, but nothing happened between them.

Maynard tried once to ride a horse, but his crotch was so sore, he never mounted another. He did assist in milking cows, and he drank a lot of milk! His mother would make butter and homemade ice cream. Because Maynard admired his older brother Bill's muscles, he offered to churn the ice cream in order to build up his own muscles.

CHAPTER TWO
My Mother, Elaine, and her Family

My Mother, Elaine Age 16 1941

I've heard the saying, "Talent is God's gift to you. What you do with it is your gift to God." My mother, Albertine Elaine Witt (known as "Elaine"), was a supremely talented, outstanding classical pianist. At the age of three at a yard sale, she walked up and began to play a piano sitting on a lawn. Her mother promptly put her into piano lessons, and Elaine gave her first recital at age five.

By the time she was seventeen, Elaine was a soloist with the Chicago Symphony, a star performer who received roses after each performance and many accolades. She was a dedicated, hard-working professional who paid attention to every detail, and performed with passion. But, her life beyond that was far from rosy.

•••••

Elaine's parents had both emigrated to America from Europe. Elaine's mom, my grandmother Gizella Adorjan, came to America on the great ship *Carpathia* from a small town, Timisoara, in Hungary, now a part of Romania, at the age of eight. Gizella was born on July 3, 1906. She was a descendent of Austria-Hungarian royalty.

Gizella Adorjan Age 2

Gizella's great-grandmother was a Lady in Waiting for the Queen of Austria/Hungary. Gizi's grandfather was a career Colonel in the military. His family owned a big estate in Kormocz Banya in the Karpatian Mountains, one of the more important mining towns and monuments in the former Kingdom of Hungary, a bastion of civilization with a rich history dating back to the Inquisition. Gizi's grandmother was a very beautiful lady. Her grandfather was an accomplished pianist.

Gizella's parents, my great-grandparents on my mother's side were Albertine Von Horvath de Gement (from whom my mother was named), born November 11, 1871 in Kosice, Slovakia; and Martin Adler, born September 9, 1862, in Nagy Karoly, in the region of Carei, Romania. (Martin changed his last name to Adorjan as noted below). Gizella was the eighth of nine brothers and sisters born to Martin and Albertine: Geza (oldest son); Lillian (died at age two); Albert [Bela] (died in

World War I); Andrew [Bandi], born June 9, 1896; Priscella [Piroska], born December 20, 1898; Louis [Laci], born June 13, 1900; Elizabeth (died as a toddler of diphtheria); my grandmother Gizella [Gizi], born July 3, 1906; and William [Vimos], born October 26, 1909.

My Grandmother, Gizella
circa 1916

Martin became a pharmacist, as did Bandi. Louis and William became fur coat manufacturers. Albert was a Catholic priest, and a chaplain in the Army in World War One. He was killed in the war. Lilly and Bessie died young of diphtheria. Pricscella lived until the age of 72 and married Henry Kuester. Her two sons Edward and Bobby were in the meat packing business in Michigan, and Bobby eventually became a doctor.

My great-grandmother Albertine's parents were Joseph von Horvath and Illma Zaman. As I mentioned, Albertine's mother and grandmother were closely tied to the royal family of Austro-Hungary. Threatened by the political events surrounding the fall of the Austro-Hungarian empire, Albertine emigrated to the United States ahead of her husband and children in May 1914, sailing to America on the *Kaiser Wilhelm II.* Because of her family's status, Albertine and her family were able to bypass the rigorous, exhausting regimen of being processed through Ellis Island.

•••••

Martin Adorjan

Gizella's parents were lovely, genteel people. Her father, Martin was born to Esther and David Adler in the village of Nagykereki, Austria-Hungary, in the Northern Great Plain region of eastern Hungary. David was an Executive and owner of a bank. They were a very wealthy family.

Gizella's grandparents Esther and David had three children, Nathan, Martin and Justine. David's father also had an estate in Kiss Karoly-tanya with a very large vineyard. Every October they hosted a Vine Festival, inviting all of their relatives and friends for a week. It was a beautiful affair. Gypsies performed at the event. When David's father died, Martin, Nathan and Justine inherited all of the beautiful homes they owned, along with the estate and some money.

Albertine Horvath Adorjan

Martin was a pharmacist; Nathan became a Supreme Court Judge and an attorney, and Justine married a pharmacist.

•••••

Albertine and Martin met at a Military Ball, and it was love at first sight. Although Martin's parents were Jewish, when Martin and Albertine were married in 1890, Martin converted to Catholicism, as Albertine's mother, Anna, would not let them marry otherwise, for she was a strict Catholic. Martin even changed his name from Adler to Adorjan, a Christian name. Martin's mother lived until the age of 93. She also played the piano and sang beautifully. She was very educated and extremely intelligent.

When Albertine and Martin were married, their parents hosted a military wedding in Budapest. Martin soon left the service and opened a Pharmacy in Szerb Ittebe, Czechoslovakia where Geza, Elizabeth (Bessie) Albert (Bela) and Andrew (Bandi) were born. Elizabeth died of diphtheria. About fifteen years later, the family moved to Timisoara, Hungary, now a part of Romania, where Martin again opened a Pharmacy.

Gizella and Priscella 1919

Timisoara was a large, beautiful city known for Secessionist architecture. Baroque buildings and the Metropolitan Orthodox Cathedral surround the central square, Piata Victorei, with its mosaic-patterned roof tiles and icon gallery. It remains a thriving city and a regional center for arts and architecture today.

Martin and Albertine had a lovely home; Gela, Bandi, Louis (Lacy) and Priscella were educated there. Priscella went to a girl's school and the boys went to a boy's academy and college. Little Lillian died at the age of two of diphtheria. Louis and my grandmother Gizella were born in Timisoara.

Gizella, her brother Andrew and mother Albertine circa 1922

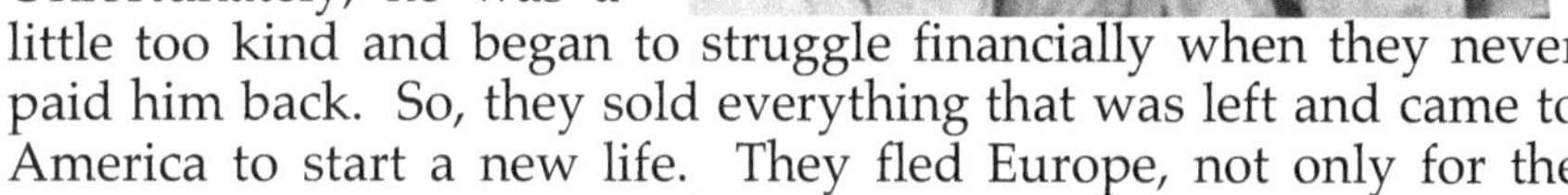

Gizella, her brother Bandi and mother Albertine, c. 1921

Martin had inherited a fortune when his father died. He was a very kind person, loaning large amounts to his friends. Unfortunately, he was a little too kind and began to struggle financially when they never paid him back. So, they sold everything that was left and came to America to start a new life. They fled Europe, not only for the greater opportunities to be found in America, but because of the increasing persecution unfolding in Europe at the time.

•••••

Gizella's parents moved to Chicago, Illinois, and with lots of hardship and work, everything turned around for the family. The family, together in America, had a few wonderful years until both parents perished too young. Martin died of liver cancer at the age of 56, and Albertine died of abdominal obstruction at the age of 57. They were very good looking, loving and educated people. They both spoke five languages fluently. Gizella recalled that they were the nicest parents anybody could ever have wished for and the family was always very happy together.

Albertine and Martin Adorjan

•••••

Each one of my ancestors whom I've listed in these pages most likely lived unique, meaningful lives, yet I know virtually nothing about them. Bela, my great Uncle, for instance, was a chaplain, and he died in World War I. That is literally everything I know about him. I have one photo of Bela. I can discern that Bela was probably a very good, religious man, full of morality and care for others. I have no idea what fear he must have felt or how he actually met his demise in that brutal war. He is a statistic, like the hundreds of thousands of other young men who perished

Albert "Bela" Adorjan

in that war. But, he must have been so much more than that to my grandmother, his younger sister Gizella.

This was primarily the impetus that caused me to write this book; to pass on my life story to my successors, to include as much important information about family and friends as I can remember, and to encapsulate my own struggles or revelations in a way that may enlighten others who may have endured similar struggles…. And my own story is fascinating, at times tragic and at times beautiful.

•••••

My Grandfather Ted Witt circa 1935

Elaine's father, my grandfather, Theodore (Ted) Claude Witt, was eighteen years older than my grandmother. Theodore was born on January 27, 1889, the same year as my father's mother, Audrey. Although he was also Hungarian, he emigrated from Europe in the first decade of the twentieth century.

Theodore's father, my mother's grandfather, was also pharmacist in Hungary in the late 1800's. He had changed their surname to Witt, having witnessed the persecution of Jews by the Greek Orthodox Church during that time period. I'm not sure what their last name was, before it was Witt.

Theodore had a brother, Bandi, and a sister Margaret. When Theodore and Bandi made the long journey to America, Margaret stayed behind in Budapest, and remained there for the rest of her days.

•••••

Theodore followed in his father's footsteps. He was already a successful pharmacist in Chicago, and Gizi's parents were his friends when Theodore and Gizella were introduced. They fell in love and married in 1924. Gizella gave birth to my mother Elaine at age eighteen on April 1, 1925, when my grandfather Ted was thirty-six. Ted owned a corner drug store and pharmacy with a soda fountain in Chicago, on a busy corner at 11012 Michigan Avenue, for twenty years. He died in July of 1951, at the age of sixty-two, from complications due to low blood pressure, long before I was born.

My mother, Elaine c. 1930

Ted and Elaine Witt c. 1930

My grandmother recalled that her husband was a kind and well-bred gentleman who loved children. He was generous and loved by his friends and family.

My grandmother Gizi was very much a part of my childhood, and I loved her dearly. She was always cooking and baking goodies for us, and she doted on me. She called me "my one and only grandson," which was true for many years until my Uncle Ted had his first son.

My Grandparents Gizella and Ted Witt 1945

My grandfather, Theodore (Ted), was a hard worker and a traditional European man who loved to smoke cigars, drink a little and gamble in his spare time. Apparently, he was quite proficient at craps. Although my mother's birth certificate states that he was born in New York, his brother Bandi told my aunt and uncle that Bandi and Theodore had actually jumped ship into America, having garnered passage from Europe sometime in the first decade of the twentieth century. They were able to secure papers and both became American citizens.

Ted had been educated as an engineer, and had some pharmacy training in Europe. He taught himself English, and then he learned enough to pass the American Pharmacist's Boards in San Francisco in order to become a pharmacist here in the United States. Theodore was apparently actually born in Buda (the "Buda" side of the city that eventually became Budapest).

My Great Uncle
Andrew "Bandi" Witt

My grandfather Ted's brother, Bandi, became a jeweler in San Francisco. Bandi was also a famous bachelor. He always said, "Why should I make one woman miserable when I can make two hundred women happy?" He did end up getting married in his late fifties, and lived to a ripe old age. Years later, Bandi instructed my sister Judith on jewelry making. She remembered him as a darling old man and a character.

•••••

Bob Kuester
Elaine's cousin

My grandmother Gizella's sister Priscella's two sons, Bob and Eddie, were very close to my mother growing up, particularly Bobby. I remember, as a child, hearing my grandmother and her sister talk on the phone in fluent Hungarian for hours. I learned a few curse words in Hungarian from the experience! I am told that there's nothing like the feeling you get when you unleash a little Hungarian profanity on your friends and family, every once in a while.

Gizella and Priscella
1923

•••••

When my mother, Elaine was eight, her parents were in a terrible auto accident with Elaine in the back seat. Another car hit them on the backside near where she was sitting. Ted and Gizi weren't terribly injured, but Elaine broke her back and endured a hot summer, unable to move, mostly alone in a full-body cast while she was healing. I believe this experience was the genesis of her unwavering stubbornness and of the need to speak her mind to be heard.

As she grew, an only child, she began to work in the pharmacy with her father, which also contained a small retail store and a soda fountain, as many did around that time. When Elaine was fourteen, Gizella had a son, Ted, and when my mother was seventeen, her other brother Gerald was born. Her brothers loved her, but because of the age difference she was truly more like an aunt to them than a sister.

My Mother, Elaine
1938

Elaine's father Ted was the light of her life. He admired her as a person and as a pianist. He encouraged her to play passionately. In a letter he wrote to her, he mentioned, "Take two musicians playing the same piece to perfection as to technique – the one who will bring home the bacon is the one who's music will sing. Sing with… what the French call nuance. Try to sing with your playing if only mentally, and all of a sudden you will cease to be an organ-grinder." My mother taught me to feel the music, not to just play the notes. Although I never met my grandfather, his words and wisdom, through her teaching, had a huge effect on me.

CHAPTER THREE
My Parents Meet

Maynard Lee Sisler
1942

World War II exploded in the early 1940's when my parents were teenagers. My father, Maynard was eighteen when he enlisted into the Navy in early 1942, shortly after Pearl Harbor. Following his enlistment and basic training, he was swabbing a deck on a hot summer day on a Navy ship when he looked into a porthole and saw a pharmacist's mate (the Navy equivalent of a medic) drinking coffee with his feet up on a desk, inside the ship. Maynard promptly signed up to be a pharmacist's mate, and so began his illustrious career in medicine, which lasted a lifetime.

Around his nineteenth birthday, Maynard was transferred to Chicago to outfit a ship that was being built. Upon completion, the newly built ships would be launched through the Chicago Portage, and travel down into the Mississippi River, through the delta into the Gulf of Mexico and through the Panama Canal to begin their service in the South Pacific. The sailors would remain in Chicago for as long as needed until the ship was built, outfitted and ready for battle.

•••••

My Grandfather's Drug Store
Chicago, IL circa 1945

While my father was briefly stationed in Chicago, he happened into my grandfather's drug store and saw my mother working behind the counter. In those days, you would pay to use a phone. Telephones either took a nickel, or you would ask the proprietor for a 'slug', which you could purchase. Maynard asked seventeen-year-old Elaine if the phones took a nickel or a slug; she gave him a slug and he made a phone call. She would tell me years later that he was a strikingly handsome and kind young man, dressed in his uniform, with straight, clean jet-black hair, a strong cheekbone and a compassionate spark of strength in his green eyes.

Elaine - 1940

My mother was only seventeen and a darling girl, with long, dark hair and brown eyes. She was talented and outgoing, had a good figure and she was well educated, so she presented herself well to everyone. She was also a teenage girl, wearing bright red lipstick as all the young women of the time did, but not much other makeup. She didn't need to wear much makeup due to her strong, European features, and she had a conservative father who watched over her carefully from the back of the pharmacy.

My Grandfather
Ted Witt

Elaine was very close to her father but she was also weary of working every available moment in his establishment, and longing for a life of her own. She had been sent to a boarding school for girls for a couple years, out of town, and she did cherish the quiet moments she had with her father at the drugstore after being sent away.

Elaine (2nd from left) with girlfriends
1942

She would later tell me that she had been sent away to boarding school because her mother had seen her talking to a young African-American man at school, and Gizi didn't want her to get caught up with him. In those days, people of certain ethnicities wanted their children to marry within their nationality to carry on the bloodline. My mother said that he was just a friend, and a very kind person too, but they sent her off to boarding school anyway.

While in boarding school, Elaine went through a "finishing school", in which young ladies would learn manners and how to carry themselves. My mother was a very classy woman throughout her life, as a result of that experience. But, now she was back with her father, and she loved her special moments with him at the drugstore.

With her toddler brother Ted and infant brother Gerald now at home, Elaine's mother's hands were full, and Elaine was expected to step up and work in-between her studies and performances. She was a disciplined girl.

Teddy, Elaine and Gerry

•••••

Maynard - 1942

On the day they met, my father, Maynard asked for the slug, as he was calling around to find a room to rent. He asked Elaine's opinion about the quality of the neighborhood of a certain address he wanted to pursue. She told him it was a little too far to walk, but it was located on her way home, and if he wanted to come back, she would take him there in the family car and show him, personally, at the end of the workday. He quickly agreed.

When he later returned to the drugstore, they began to talk. Maynard hadn't eaten and she offered to take him to her house for dinner, following the trip to the flat about which he would inquire. She called her mother and told Gizi she was bringing a sailor home for dinner. This was customary during the war. Everyone was very patriotic and it was an honor to help enlisted men in any way. However, my grandmother was exasperated.

Elaine 1942

As mentioned, she had a toddler and a newborn at home and was not prepared to feed anyone. Gizi told Elaine to drop by the store and pick up some pancake mix because she hadn't planned a dinner, and Elaine agreed. She couldn't find a place to park at the grocery store, so she sent Maynard in to the store to get the groceries. He came out with buckwheat pancake mix, which his mother Audrey had always made for him back in West Virginia. Gizi was aghast! She had never seen nor

Elaine and Maynard
early 1940's

cooked anything with buckwheat! So, began a long and complicated relationship between my father and his future mother-in-law.

•••••

Elaine and Maynard really only spent a handful of days together in early 1942 before my father was deployed to the South Pacific, but Maynard fell completely in love with Elaine, and he wrote to her each and every day during his long tour in the South Pacific. He wrote of his four bouts of malaria, and of how he was the only 'medical' person on the ship, so during battle he had to learn fast how to perform surgery in order to save lives.

Many of Maynard's shipmates died during battle as they made their way through the Philippines, Guadalcanal and Midway Islands. He told me once of a battle he endured. As Japanese aircraft were bombing his ship, he followed a shipmate up the stairs. His shipmate took the right stairs and he took the left stairs. His shipmate was blown up and Maynard would have died on the spot had he followed the young man. He went to his brother-in-arms and cradled him, as this very young man looked at him with pleading eyes, and said, "I'm going to be all right, Doc, aren't I?" Sobbing, my father held tightly to him as the man died in his arms.

Maynard also spoke of when his ship received the very first shipments of newly discovered penicillin. There wasn't enough of the antibiotic to go around, so they would give a dose to the sickest sailor, and then that sailor would urinate, and they would make another sailor drink his urine in order to get a 'second dose' of penicillin.

My father told me of the night before Christmas, 1942, a sticky but quiet night on a lonely ship in the middle of nowhere during an ugly war in the South Pacific. He and his shipmates were standing on an eerily quiet deck, and for the first time ever, over the loudspeaker they heard Bing Crosby's recording of *White Christmas.* Even though these were battle-hardened sailors, there wasn't a dry eye on the deck, dreaming of their homes so far away, and wondering if they'd ever see them again.

After three long years stationed in the South Pacific, Maynard's ship made it into Tokyo harbor and docked next to the *USS Missouri* on the day the Japanese signed their surrender. My father's brother, Bill, was fortunate enough to be standing at attention in a prominent position on the deck of the *USS Missouri* actually witnessing the surrender ceremony on that day in 1945.

Like my father, I buried many traumatic experiences from my youth. When I was a young adult, the trauma began to emerge in the form of a series of painful epiphanies. It was an emotional growing spurt. Had I not allowed the trauma from the experiences to be released, I would still be holding on to it today. It was the beginning of a healing process that unfolded over many years.

•••••

When I was a child, my father hardly ever spoke of the war. I believe strongly that he experienced post-traumatic stress disorder for many years because of that war, but PTSD wasn't something that had yet been diagnosed or treated. They just called these men "shell-shocked". But men were men back then, and he 'manned-up' and dealt with life, only to find it coming out in spades through his alcoholism and bad behavior later.

You really couldn't tell that anything was wrong, because he was extremely intelligent and very witty, and he knew how to charm anyone. But these disorders germinate like cancers within the hearts and souls of so many soldiers, only to come out years afterward in some unforeseen way.

I remember that my father had kept a small wicker basket containing his medals, a pack of cigarettes from the Philippines, and other memorabilia that he had saved from the war. As a young boy, I would get permission from him, and then go into the basket and marvel at the trinkets and medals, handling them all carefully. To me, as a child, my father was bigger than life.

CHAPTER FOUR
Maynard and Elaine Marry

Elaine

Following the war, when he finally returned stateside in 1945, Maynard made his way to Chicago as quickly as he could, and asked Elaine to marry him. Elaine's father, Ted, liked Maynard. Maynard was kind, helpful, extremely intelligent, and Ted liked my dad's sense of humor. In return, my father revered Elaine's father. Maynard still spoke to me fondly of Ted years later on his own deathbed.

My father's parents were too poor to travel to the wedding, so just my mother's family and some scattered friends were on hand for the ceremony. My grandfather, Ted, made sure that it was a grand affair for his beloved daughter. My father was upset that his family did not come, but he did not let on to it.

December 23, 1945

Bandi, Ted, Maynard
Gizella and Elaine

It was a Catholic wedding. My father had been raised as a Protestant. In fact, his parents later became Seventh-Day Adventists, but Maynard converted to Catholicism to marry my mother, and he took his conversion very seriously. His parents and especially his brothers had tutored him in bible study as a child, being forced to memorize long verses from the Good Book.

Maynard's studies in Catholicism brought him to a higher level, in a sense. As a child, when I would ask him questions about forgiveness, he could quote sacrament, instructing me that true forgiveness only comes when you are heartily sorry for your sins, vowing to do your best not to repeat them. His extensive knowledge of these lessons would later bring Maynard back from rock bottom, more than once.

Elaine - 1945

•••••

Elaine, Maynard, Teddy and Gerry
1945

Following the lovely wedding of my parents in the winter of 1945, they held a reception for the guests. After they cut the cake, my mother's seven-year-old brother, Ted, tugged at Elaine's wedding dress and pleaded with her to let him go with them, to

spend the night with her and my dad. My father said a resounding, "No!" He had been waiting for that night for years!

After my parents married, my grandfather Ted offered to pay to put his new son-in-law through college and medical school. My father had come from a proud family that, although poor, would not accept handouts from others. My father reluctantly agreed, but refused any other financial help from his in-laws.

CHAPTER FIVE
My Sisters Are Born

Elaine, Suzanne and Judith

Maynard remained in the Navy, and he was stationed at Great Lakes, a large facility overlooking Lake Michigan, in North Chicago. On November 28, 1946, Elaine gave birth to my oldest sister, Suzanne Elaine (Suzy). After Maynard was transferred to Long Beach, California, my sister Judith Barbara (Judy) was born on August 18, 1948.

Bob Kuester, Maynard, Eddie Kuester and Ted Witt

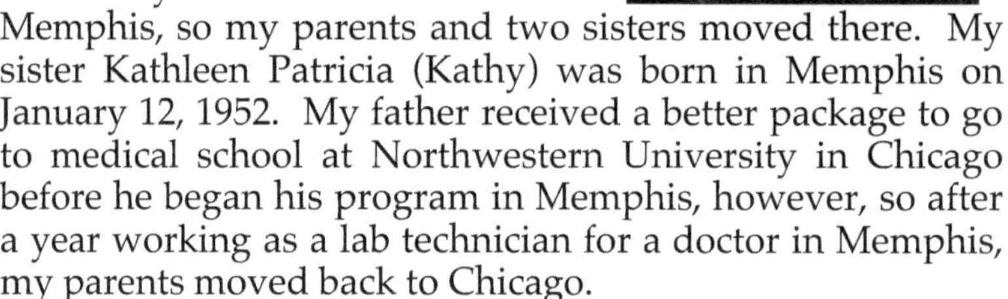

Maynard left the Navy (for a short while) and was accepted into the University of Tennessee in Memphis, so my parents and two sisters moved there. My sister Kathleen Patricia (Kathy) was born in Memphis on January 12, 1952. My father received a better package to go to medical school at Northwestern University in Chicago before he began his program in Memphis, however, so after a year working as a lab technician for a doctor in Memphis, my parents moved back to Chicago.

Although my mother missed her Chicago roots while in Memphis, my father was very happy because his parents and a couple of his brothers had moved from West Virginia to Memphis in 1948, and he enjoyed being close to them. Maynard's father George wanted to move to Memphis to be close to his ailing sister, Mary. She passed away shortly after they moved there.

My father recounted an experience he had with a priest, Father Schneider, at *St. Peter's Catholic Church* in Memphis. Father Schneider was close to my parents and a great confidant. Once, my dad went to confession and mentioned that he was struggling to put food on his children's plates and unsure if he would be able to pay all of his bills that month. Later that week when Maynard brought the family to Mass, Father Schneider came over to him after the service and quietly placed a fifty-dollar bill in my dad's palm. Maynard wept, and vowed to pay him back. Years later, he found Father Schneider, paid him back and gave a generous donation to the church.

Elaine with her Father 1935

When I was in my early twenties while I was performing in Reno, Nevada, I met a woman who knew my parents around this time in their lives. She mentioned that they were very much in love and that they were "the life of the party." My father was quick with wit and humor, my mother was vivacious and classy, they were both informed and intelligent, and their friends would marvel when my mother would play her outstanding classical pieces on piano at their get-togethers. It was great to hear that, because I grew up in the tail end of their marriage when there was anger and resentment, and I always wondered if they were *ever* in love.

It was while Elaine was pregnant with my sister Kathleen that she got the news that her beloved father, Ted, had died. Her parents had sold the drug store in Chicago a handful of years back and moved to Long Beach, California. Her father had low blood pressure and his heart just stopped, one night. He was only sixty-two. She was devastated, only twenty-seven years old, and all through her childhood and young adulthood he had been her mountain of strength.

Gerry, Ted and Gizi

My grandmother Gizi, just forty-five years old, was tasked with raising her two younger sons alone with just enough saved to invest a little. She learned investment, made a few good moves, investing in *General Motors* and *General Dynamics*, and was able to eventually put both boys through college. But, meanwhile, Maynard left the Navy to finish medical school at Northwestern and my family moved back to Chicago, where my sister Mary Elizabeth (Betsy) was born on September 28, 1953.

•••••

Maynard, Suzanne, Kathleen and Judith 1952

Maynard was working full-time as a lab technician, cleaning a morgue at night and going to medical school full-time, with a wife and four children. They lived in the projects in Chicago with virtually nothing. Elaine would be worried, because sometimes cockroaches would climb into the girls' mouths while they were sleeping. My sister Kathy's crib was near a wall heater, and one night she rolled over into the heater and experienced third-degree burns on her leg. As she screamed in excruciating pain, they rushed her to the hospital where she received multiple skin grafts. It took a long time for her to heal.

•••••

Life was very difficult for my mother, who had given up stardom and accolades, performing with symphonies, living a certain lifestyle, to be in this situation, and I believe she started to become somewhat bitter through this time. She was a rigid, controlling young mother, strict with her daughters and sometimes emotionally unavailable. She kept a clean house, however, and my sisters always were bathed with clean clothes and a hot meal, somehow.

Life slowly improved for my parents in Chicago. My father served his internship and residency at Cook County Hospital. He would make house calls in the slums with his black medical bag, delivering babies to poor African-American women, sewing up and treating stab wounds, doing triage after car accidents. He would work 24-hour emergency room shifts to make extra money for the family, and through it all, he became a very good physician. Maynard discovered that he was ambidextrous in surgery, using a scalpel with his left hand and stitching with his right hand.

My sisters, 1956
Suzanne
Judith, Betsy and Kathy

In other tasks, Maynard, my sister Judy and I were all left-handed. My mother, my sisters Suzanne, Kathy and Betsy were right-handed.

CHAPTER SIX
Born in Annapolis, Maryland, Moved to New York

My birth photo
June 28, 1958

My father, Maynard, re-entered the Navy and continued his schooling to become a specialist in Internal Medicine. At some point, he was transferred to Annapolis, where I was born on June 28, 1958. My grandmother, Audrey, had come to stay with the family for a few weeks to help with my birth.

Tad and Elaine
1958

On the night I was born, my mother had received a tranquilizer during my birth procedure. In the middle of the night, she woke up in a sweat and asked the nurse to open the window. The nurse asked, "Don't you want to see your baby?" The nurse brought me into the room. My mother said, "Isn't she beautiful," at which time the nurse just dropped my diaper and exposed my genitalia. My mother was in shock! She had four daughters, and just expected a fifth. What was she going to do with a boy? She confided later that she was worried that with the influence of so many females, I would naturally play with dolls, but I went instinctively for the trucks and army men, so I guess I was 'all boy'. I am grateful, however, for the heavy female influence of my sisters and mother. It shaped me into a more compassionate person, I believe.

Also, on the night I was born, following the birth, my father went home to tuck my sisters in to bed. He read them a book for bedtime. It was a children's book about Abraham Lincoln. When my father told my sisters that Abe Lincoln had a son named Tad, my sisters all exclaimed, "Let's call the baby 'Tad'!" My father was bent on naming me after him. So, my legal name became Maynard Lee Sisler, Jr., but from birth, my sisters called me Tad, and that became the name I would use for life, except on insurance cards and legal documents!

I was baptized in the chapel at the Naval Academy in Annapolis, next to the grave of John Paul Jones. My father was teaching interns as he was becoming an Internist, and one of his students would later become Senator John McCain of Arizona. My dad would later tell me that McCain, although the son and grandson of great Admirals, was a terrible student! McCain did go on to be a Prisoner of War to the North Vietnamese for five years, and an American hero, before his years as a maverick, controversial Senator.

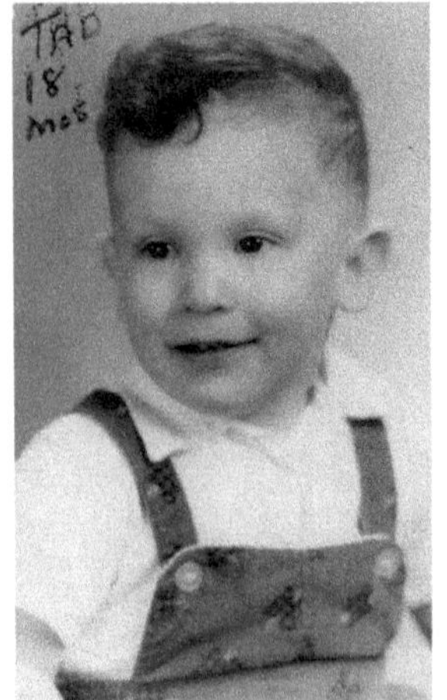

At one point in 1958, Maynard met the esteemed West Virginia Congressman (and later long-term Senator) Robert Byrd. He and a small group of other young officers were invited by the Congressman to enjoy a cup of Navy Bean soup with a group of legislators in the Senate Dining Room.

My mother would talk of those days in Annapolis fondly, and of the days that would last so briefly later in the three years they spent in New York. Finally practicing medicine, Maynard started actually making enough money for the family to buy enough food, clothes, school uniforms and tuition for the Catholic schools in which my sisters were enrolled, and to buy nice homes.

•••••

My parents bought a beautiful three-story home, which had been built in 1928 at 22 Cornwall Lane in Hempstead, on Long Island while Maynard was stationed at St. Albans, New York. My oldest sister, Suzanne, at the age of twelve was given the attic as her bedroom, and she loved it! It was there that I experienced my very first core memory, a vague recollection of the excitement of sledding down Cornwall Lane, one snowy day when I was just three. I was a curious child. I played with toys in a different way than other boys did; more as a builder or developer might do.

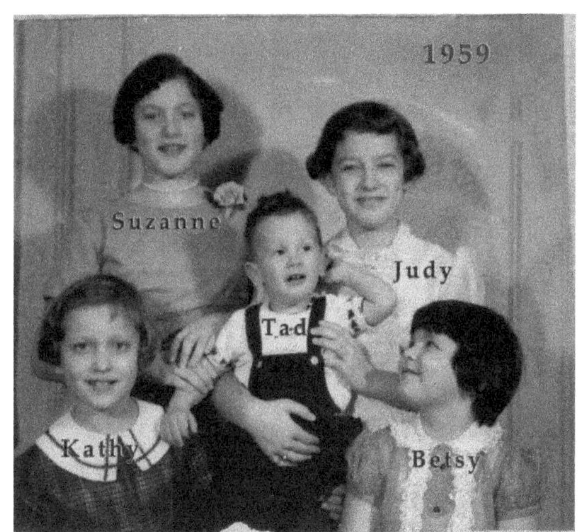

My sisters loved this time. My father was not drinking; it was an easy neighborhood for a young girl to navigate, with a candy store on the corner, a vacant lot down the street where they played, and a short walk to their parochial school. Children were treated in a freer manner during that time period, mostly allowed to go roaming out on their own without fear.

Other snapshots from this toddler's mind were of being warmed by the fire after being outside perhaps a little too long; being held at a carnival by my mother and crying when a scary looking man with a long, black beard talked to me; sitting on top of my father's shoulders, seeing the motorcade of newly-elected President John Fitzgerald Kennedy as my sisters swooned and swore that he waved to us from the back seat of the convertible he was riding in as they made their way down Northern Boulevard in Hempstead; seeing Niagara Falls for the very first time with my mom and dad; pulling the Christmas tree down (more than once) and being scolded for it, but mostly, the adoration I felt from my sisters, one always holding me when my mother wasn't.

I was told that I didn't necessarily throw fits when I didn't get my way as a toddler. I would just hold my breath until I turned blue and then I would pass out! Perhaps that's how I have had the lung capacity in later life to sing for four hours at a time without a break...

I had a recurring dream, a nightmare, which began with my earliest memories and continued until I was around ten years old. In the dream, I was being swept in circles within a huge wave in a tsunami and I couldn't breathe. It was the exact same dream each time. As I got older, the dream generally only occurred when I was ill. I would wake up in a cold sweat...it was real to me. I have to admit that it felt as if this was the way I died in a previous life, and I was carrying the memory into this life. I hated that dream. It scared me even to think about it.

•••••

When I was three, my parents took me on a trip to Niagara Falls. I briefly remember my father lifting me up to show me the majesty of the waterfalls. American life did have innocence to it then, before the turmoil of the late 1960's. Automobiles of the late 1950's were generally huge metal beasts, with no seat belts. My mother would instinctively throw her right arm across the front seat to hold me back when she braked, as I stood next to her in the car as a toddler.

The GI bill had allowed veterans to buy homes and get an education, and baby boomer children lived in manicured neighborhoods with cookie-cutter homes. Boys in crew cuts would tease girls in gingham dresses with ponytails. We were taught impeccable manners, and patriotism was essential.

CHAPTER SEVEN
Memphis, Tennessee

My parents had just bought two new cars for the first time in their lives. My father purchased a brown 1961 *Buick Skylark* for himself, and a white 1962 *Buick Special* station wagon for my mother. They loved their new cars.

Around my fourth birthday, my father was transferred to Memphis, Tennessee. My parents sold their house in New York and bought a huge, five-bedroom home in a nice neighborhood on 267 N. Rose Road in Memphis.

My mother did not want to leave Hempstead. She had been as content in Hempstead as she would ever be. She had friends there, my sisters were doing well in school, and my father was sober. I remember hearing my mother talk about how an African-American couple came to look at the house in Hempstead, and her neighbors begged her not to sell it to them, fearing that the neighborhood "would go downhill." The couple chose not to buy the house anyway, but my mother was insulted by the idea that anyone would care what color the people were who bought the house. Today, that neighborhood in Hempstead is an almost exclusively entirely African-American section of Long Island. So, I guess those white neighbors probably ended up moving out themselves at some point. Racism was rampant in this era.

•••••

My father was thrilled to move to Memphis, because his parents, George and Audrey, had relocated to Memphis, and two of his brothers, George and Jack lived there as well, with their families. For a time, Maynard's brothers were involved in a marble company, supplying headstones to graveyards, but the business failed at some point. My grandfather had just retired from his sheet metal business, having become too old to do the hard work, and my grandmother was very involved with her church.

Maynard and Audrey

At first, in Memphis, we had what seemed to me as a happy home. In the beginning, my mother was adjusting well. Elaine was involved with Maynard in a bridge club. She played piano for fashion shows and other events. She and the other Naval Officer's wives would get together on occasion.

At night, my family would eat dinners together at our dining room table, and one of my sisters (usually the one closest to the kitchen) was designated "the up-up-girl." She would be the one to get up and get anyone what he or she needed. We would do the chores together. One of my sisters would wash the dishes and another would dry while yet another would put them away. My mother would sometimes 'let' me vacuum, and later she gave me the very important job of ironing my father's white handkerchiefs. That was a hard one to mess up.

My parent's loved show tunes. They had taken my sisters to Broadway shows when we lived in New York, and they constantly played records. My father would sing at the top of his lungs to the songs of *My Fair Lady* or *Guys and Dolls.*

My mother would play our piano when she had time. Knowing my own experience, music has always been our saving grace. Whenever I was upset, or angry, I've turned to music, and in an instant, I felt better. In the same way, through her life, my mother's music became an outlet for all of her frustrations. As an adult, for the duration of my lifetime, I would always cry whenever I heard *Chopin's E Minor Concerto,* or any Hungarian Rhapsody, remembering her smooth, precise hands on the keyboard flawlessly performing those pieces.

Sometimes at night when I was supposed to be sleeping, I would sit at the top of the stairs listening to her passionately performing on our little *Gulbransen* upright piano. She deserved a baby grand, but she could make any piano sing.

•••••

When I was four years old, my mother took me shopping with her at *Sears* one day in Memphis. In the furniture department were several displays showing entire rooms of furniture, including a couple of bathroom displays. I went up to one of the toilets in the bathroom display, pulled down my pants and pooped in the toilet, right there in *Sears*! My mother was horrified! At least I was toilet trained!

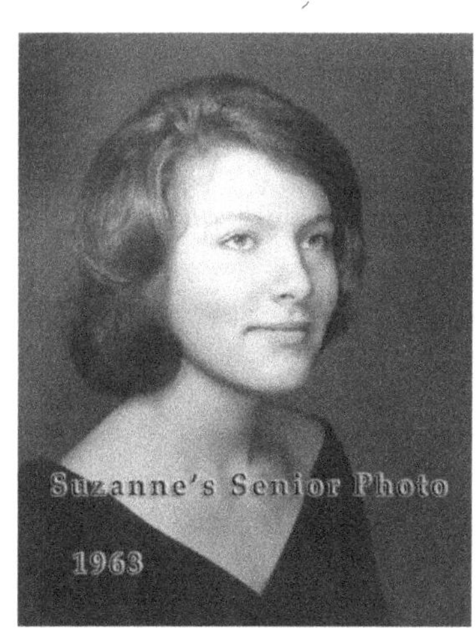
Suzanne's Senior Photo 1963

My sister, Suzanne, being almost twelve years older than me, was already in high school when we moved to Memphis. Suzy was extremely intelligent and truly the apple of my father's eye. She was his favorite and neither was afraid to show it. Suzy always had a vivacious personality. Truly, she has always been an exceptional person, always helpful, always doing something to improve the day or to help someone out.

Suzanne did very well in school, and she was a compassionate, caring older sister to all of us. Being the oldest, she had quite the burden of responsibility to watch over her four younger siblings.

My sister Judy was 'paired up' with Suzanne with only two years difference in their age, and Kathy and Betsy were sort-of paired up as well. Judy seemed to sometimes resent Suzanne's authority, but still they were very close and truly inseparable. My mother was rather strict with my sisters, buttoning them up tightly with perfectly manicured hair and brushed teeth before sending them off to their Catholic school, and through this period my mother was beginning to regularly experience depression, due to my father's increasingly bad behavior.

•••••

Elvis Presley's girlfriend, Priscilla, attended the same Catholic school as Suzanne. When Elvis came to get Priscilla, the nuns would keep all the other girls away from him. The 'word' around the school was that Elvis and Priscilla were getting to 'third base' a lot, but they hadn't yet had intercourse because he had promised her parents he wouldn't. The girls would giggle about it. The organizers of the school dance reached out to Elvis and asked if he would perform for the dance, but he turned them down, believing it might be too chaotic.

Being a teenager with so much responsibility, my sister Suzanne had a heavy heart, particularly after my father had his first big 'episode' of alcoholism. The Navy sent Maynard away for several months to a rehabilitation program. Through this event, Suzanne and my mother bonded. They would go to church every day and pray the novena, asking the Lord for my father to return before Christmas. He did make it back by Christmas.

•••••

My dad and I were very close. Up to this point, whenever he had spare time, he would spend it with his children. I was lost without him. I remember one day when he had been in treatment for a while, I was sad, missing him. I began to cry. Suzy took me over to the window and said, "Do you see that red bird over there?" I nodded yes, and she said, "Every time you see a red bird, it's a sign of hope, and it will always remind you that everything will be okay." She always seemed to know what to do when I needed her. From then on, every time I was down, someone in my family would say, "Remember the red bird?" ...and everything would be okay.

Through a symbol like the red bird, or through every other object of beauty we see within a day magnifying our own experience of God, we should all remain aware of every bit of visible evidence all around us reminding us that hope is eternal.

Memphis had a certain smell to it, especially after the rain, and it rained a lot. Sometimes the rain would come down in sheets, and sometimes it was so intense that it seemed like water was just being poured onto your windshield as you drove slowly through the thunderstorms. Greenery was everywhere; summers were hot and wet with humidity.

Memphis was a big, new world for me, and this very young boy would roam the expanse of our large yard, climbing trees and creating whole new worlds within my imagination. In the winter, we would sit on the tops of trashcans and slide down the snowy hills, squeaking with delight.

•••••

A young man named Bill Brannon was obsessed with my oldest sister Suzy. He was a couple years older than her. His parents owned a beautiful, big house on many acres with chickens and horses, and big tire swings on the huge poplar and oak trees that graced their property. Bill was persistent, and Suzanne was weary of the burden placed upon her as the oldest, even parenting her own parents so very much of the time. Eventually, Suzanne relented to Bill's persistence. She loved the attention, and her sixteen-year-old hormones were strong. She and Bill would spend every available second together, and Suzy became pregnant before her seventeenth birthday.

My parents were devastated, and they pretty much forced Suzanne and Bill to get married. My father blamed himself, because he had seen the responsibility Elaine piled upon Suzy. He had also applied pressure to her studies, always wanting Suzanne to become a doctor like he was, and he had also been absent much of the time in Memphis, dealing with his own alcoholism.

I believe that Suzy was just overwhelmed with responsibility and she felt for a time that my mother didn't like her. Elaine was a tough cookie! She was a 'Type A' personality, very controlling, and when she didn't get her way, somehow you would be reminded of all the nice things she had done for you until you gave in out of guilt; even so, my mother adored me, and I believe during this time she was doing her best to keep her family intact in an insane situation with my father.

On my fifth birthday, Suzy and Bill had the wedding ceremony elsewhere while I was having my birthday party. My parents had hired a portable merry-go-round, towed in on the back of a truck, which was in the front yard of our beautiful big house, and I had several friends enjoying the day with me. Although it was a great day, I remember sitting on a bench in the hallway of our house that evening in my new red pajamas, when Suzy and Bill arrived and told me that they were married. Suzy said she loved me but she wouldn't be living with me anymore, and I was just devastated. I was profoundly sad, and I missed her a lot following that day. I began to 'act out' a bit, following that.

•••••

There was a cute little five-year-old girl named Miriam Jacobs who lived down the street. We would play together quite a bit of the time. Her grandmother would bake tiny chocolate chip cookies and put them into *Luden's Cough Drops* boxes and give them to us to eat. One day, Miriam and I decided to run away together. We made it a couple miles, actually, all the way to the *Piggly Wiggly* where we were enjoying some candy together when the police showed up. My parents were panicked. It was the only time, ever, ever, that I got a spanking. I guess I was quite the Casanova.

I was the understudy for the kindergarten play. I knew everyone's lines perfectly. My parents were noticing that I was exceptionally bright, and a couple years later had my IQ tested, which scored very high, around 175. They never told me, however, thinking it would go to my head. I actually never knew this fact until I was in my fifties, believe it or not, and by then, I'm sure I had already wasted quite a few of those amazing brain cells on unnecessary partying… if I only knew!

One day, I wanted to please my father by filling his car up like they did at the gas stations. So, I got the hose and filled up his gas tank with water. He made it about a half block before the car needed to be towed…he was actually pretty forgiving about that one, though, considering my good intentions.

My father planted a tree next to our house on Rose Road in Memphis. It was my size, about four feet tall, and my parents proclaimed it, "Tad's Tree!" Years later, I went to see the house and the tree had grown to over one hundred feet tall.

•••••

The Hughes family lived next door to us in Memphis. Their teenage son was a patient young man, and I enjoyed afternoons with him in the back yard sometimes, as we would play 'catch' with a football. He was on the High School football team, and he told me I was helping him with his skills, although I believe he was bored and just being a nice kid. A mean lady lived down the street, and she would always yell at us if we got even slightly close to her garden while we were playing.

One afternoon, I was playing on a chaise lounge outside of our home. The lounge collapsed under me and my head hit the concrete. I was bleeding pretty heavily. My mother poured hydrogen peroxide on the wound and rushed me to the hospital, panicked. I needed stitches, and it took a month or so for me to fully recover. Shortly thereafter, I contracted the shingles, otherwise known as *Herpes Zoster.* My parents described it to me as a 'cousin' to the chicken pox, but it travels along the nerve, and it was on my face. Kids naturally scratch the sores, and as a result of my scratching, I grew up with several little scars on the left side of my forehead and face. Apparently, it came very close to the nerves in my left eye, and I could have lost the eye if it had travelled closer.

It was an agonizing illness, causing an incredible amount of pain to this young boy. For years, I proudly proclaimed to my friends that I had *Herpes Zoster* when I was four, until I became a teenager and I learned that *Herpes* in any form is not something you want to go around and tell people you've had!

At the age of five, I still wasn't ready to sleep alone at night. My parents had a large bed, which actually encompassed two twin beds pushed together with king-size sheets. I would sleep between my mom and dad at night, and slowly slip into the gap between the beds, with the bottom sheet cradling me like a hammock. It was warm and cuddly, and the memory lingers, reminding me that at one time in my life, it was pretty close to normal.

•••••

Maynard and George "Pop"

My grandparents, George and Audrey, lived in a very small, one-bedroom tenement apartment in Memphis. My mother would drop me off to stay with them on occasion, and my grandmother would dote on me, play with me and make food for me. Grandmother Audrey had a little clear glass candy jar on her hutch, to the right as you walked in the door. It was always filled with these large orange marshmallow candy 'peanuts', which were very good when I reached up as high as I could to take the top off of the apothecary cookie jar.

Right around the time I was born, my grandfather George had quit drinking and womanizing (after all, he was practically seventy years old at that point), and he became a religious zealot.

I remember "Pop" sat in a big chair in his study, with his religious books and binders full of his writings all around him. He would take my tiny hand into his huge hand, hard as a rock from years of working with sheet metal, and, crushing my little hand, he would look into my eyes with his fiery eyes and declare to me that Jesus was the first and last and everything, and that I would go to Hell if I didn't believe!

Memphis 1962

Audrey, George and Audrey's sister Rose

On good days, Pop would find a twinkle in his eye and ask me, "How's your hypercopperosity segatiating today?" I had no idea what that meant, but I would laugh along with him. When my sisters visited him, he would ask them, "Are you pretty?" And, he would persist in asking the question until they found an answer that satisfied him. I don't think we ever had a normal conversation in my entire life.

My grandmother Audrey, on the other hand, was friendly and normal and just loved to be with me. I had her dimples. She wore her grey hair up on her head in a bun. Her eyesight was bad and she wore 'coke bottle' glasses with very thick lenses, so when you looked directly at her, her eyeballs looked huge! But, she always had a sweet smile.

One night when I was about five, I was spending the night on their little couch. I got up to use the bathroom and I looked down the hallway into her room. She was sitting at her vanity and brushing her long, gray hair that went all the way to her knees. I had never seen her hair down! In fact, I had never seen so much hair! But, she was beautiful and she smiled at me and continued to brush her long hair while I dutifully went back to bed. It stays in my memory like the vision of an angel.

Gizella, Maynard and Audrey
Medical School Graduation
1958

•••••

My father's oldest brother George had been a war correspondent during World War II, and following that, he became a newspaper writer and reporter for the *Commercial Appeal* in Memphis. As a result of that, he was quite well known in all of the social circles in Memphis.

My Uncle George
and his wife
Maxine
1948

George was married to a conservative woman named Maxine, and they had a daughter, Janet, who was around the same age as my oldest sister, Suzanne. Janet was actually Maxine's sister's daughter. Maxine couldn't have children and she and George adopted Janet, but they never told her.

Years later, when my mother was angry at my dad for whatever antics he was pulling on her at the time, Elaine called Janet and told her she was adopted. That was a rather vindictive move, wouldn't you say? My mother was not afraid to speak her mind, ever, and quite often didn't use finesse when making a point. Janet had a darling little red-haired daughter named Jamie. Jamie was a couple years younger than me, and I loved it when she came over to play while I was visiting my grandparents.

Following his stint as a reporter, my dad's brother George became a *Southern Baptist* minister. He was a "fire and brimstone" preacher, pointing his long finger down at his congregations for their sins and promising Hell to anyone who didn't believe. My sister Suzanne recalled that she sat through some of his sermons, and the words he said were vitriolic, hate-filled and disturbing to her. He had bullied my father when they were young, and he had a hard edge, but nevertheless, George was very popular and a respected icon of the community. He was always gruff in my presence, but still nice to me, as I recall. Even after all of these years, my dad was still desperate to please his brother George.

Later, when I was in High School, I got to know uncle George a little better. He was kind to me, but not easy to make small talk with. I do remember a conversation with my uncle about his father. Even though he was my grandfather George's namesake, my uncle George hated my grandfather for all of the transgressions and bad behavior he had witnessed, as well as the way my grandfather had treated my grandmother. My uncle told me that on the day my grandfather would die, he would attend his funeral if it weren't raining on that day. My uncle did not outlive my grandfather after all. George died of cancer when I was a junior in High School.

Most of us have issues with our parents. My uncle George, in particular, had a lot of negative things to say about his father. I believe, though, that my grandfather Sisler couldn't have been all bad. He toiled very hard for many years, doing back-breaking work to support his family. Yes, he made mistakes; Pop didn't take care of himself until he had his epiphany at age seventy, and by that time he was diabetic and weak. I know that he had a good heart, underneath it all, and although we didn't really have much to say to each other apart from his preaching to me about Christ, I loved him. I was grateful to know him and to be able to help him to tend to his garden and putter around in his old age.

•••••

Jack and Ann Sisler

My dad's kid brother Jack was an excellent architect. He was responsible for the design of many buildings that still grace the skyline of Memphis, Tennessee, including the *Union Bank* building. Jack loved to have fun, and he and my dad would get together and drink. He was also a veteran with some emotional issues from his war experience, and the chosen remedy of the time was alcohol. Jack's wife, Ann, was gorgeous and sweet, and they had three children, Dylan, Dixie and Pamela. Dylan was a couple years older than me. Dixie was my age, and Pamela was a couple years younger.

Because Dylan had his umbilical cord wrapped around his neck at birth, he was deprived of oxygen. As a result, he had very slight brain damage, but he was a good boy. Dixie and I were very close. She was my first playmate, my darling cousin, and my favorite reason for living in Memphis. Dixie had short, cropped blonde hair and a sweet, innocent smile that you would expect from a five-year-old. I remember that we held hands a lot. My mother would load our tricycles into her station wagon and take us to the *Pink Palace* where we would enjoy the sites and ride around the parks. As I mentioned, Memphis was green and lovely most of the year, and my childhood mind remembers well the laughter and *camaraderie* she and I shared.

My Uncle Jack Sisler 1958

Such was our life… only a couple years later, immediately after we moved to San Diego from Memphis when I was almost six years old, a terrible tragedy occurred. After a night out partying, my uncle Jack had stumbled home drunk almost at daylight to their two-story home in Memphis. Not wanting to wake Ann and the kids, he decided to sleep on the couch downstairs. He fell asleep while smoking a cigarette and the couch caught on fire. They were in the midst of repainting the house, and paint cans exploded next to the couch. Soon, the entire house was in flames. Jack stumbled out the front door. Ann ran down the stairs to see what was happening, and miraculously little three-year-old Pamela made it outside, but Ann couldn't get back up the stairs to save her other children as they were screaming for her to help. Dylan and Dixie both died in the fire. Devastated, Ann left, taking Pamela with her, shortly after that. We were all overwhelmed with grief, and my dad's kid brother was inconsolable in his sorrow, guilt and shame.

My cousin Dixie 1961

We didn't hear from Ann again until forty years later when my sister Judy found Ann somewhere in Mississippi, and rekindled a friendship. It was shortly before my sixtieth birthday that I got a letter, all these years later, from my cousin Pamela. Her mother had shielded her from any knowledge of what happened for years. It was only when she discovered an old photo album in the attic that she knew she had an original family.

We began to correspond and to get to finally know each other, over fifty years later. I was able to tell her that she had a wonderful brother and sister that I loved with all my heart. If there was a silver lining to this darkest of clouds, it is that I found that my little surviving cousin was alive and well, somewhere, with her own happy family.

In those dark days, though, my uncle Jack was beyond grief; he was devastated, needless to say, and never recovered from that. Three or four years later, he took his own life. My dad was hit hard from this tragedy. He loved his brother Jack dearly.

We are never too young (or too old) to know the pain of sorrow, and to be reminded of life's fragility.

The tragedy of losing my dear little cousins was my first experience of personal loss, and to a small child, it is confusing and profound. The feeling was multiplied from watching my parents' and my sisters' own pain as we struggled to cope with this awful experience.

CHAPTER EIGHT
San Diego, California

Maynard and Tad
San Diego, 1963

Before I lost my little cousins, we drove from Memphis to San Diego, California to relocate. My dad had once again been transferred, this time to the *United States Naval Hospital* in Balboa Park, overlooking the Pacific Ocean in south San Diego. On our road trip to our new home, we stopped and marveled at the Grand Canyon, the Painted Desert and Carlsbad Caverns on the way. It was a fun trip for me.

Shortly after my father was transferred to San Diego from Memphis in my sixth year of life, President Kennedy was assassinated. Pallor hung over the entire country, like an unrelenting storm cloud, and even as a small child, I remember the deep emotion of it. My father made me watch the funeral procession on our little black and white television, and he told me that I would remember this for the rest of my life. Perhaps because he said that, I do remember every moment of it. President Kennedy's daughter Caroline was my age, and little John-John was only three when he stood forward and saluted his father's casket. Even if one disagreed with his policies, it was as if this brutal tragedy had left everyone believing that hope for a brighter future had faded away for us all, for a time. It was the day that innocence was lost.

•••••

Kirk Gentry
and Tad - 1963

In spite of those tragedies we endured, I loved San Diego. We lived in a cute little house at 5721 Breton Way in East County in a little neighborhood named Del Cerro. My best friend, Kirk Gentry, lived next door. His mom had a little Pomeranian dog named Susie. She barked all the time! I started kindergarten at *Hearst Elementary School* in Del Cerro, and halfway through the year, I was assessed for knowledge and IQ, and promoted to the second half of first grade, effectively 'skipping' a year of school. From that day forward, I was the youngest, smallest member of every grade until I made it to High School and grew taller.

I believe this is a reason why I developed my wit, perhaps to compensate for my size compared to my friends. Also, there is a family 'ecosystem'… a dynamic, which exists in families, particularly dysfunctional families. Everyone takes on a specific role, whether it is caretaker, black sheep, the silent one, or whatever helps us to cope and overcome our obstacles.

Suzanne and Charles

Suzanne was the caretaker, the vivacious one, and we had left her and her husband, Bill and new baby, Charles, born on January 24, 1964, back in Memphis.

•••••

As much as my sister Judy hadn't liked being under Suzy's thumb, she didn't like even more being now the oldest child left at home. All the burden of responsibility rested upon her now. Judy was quiet, introspective, yet she would speak her mind. She was a very calm person, in general, however. She was cerebral; very intelligent, a good student and in many ways, she kept to herself.

There was a culture shock in moving to California from Tennessee, and I believe that my sisters and I embraced the more laid-back atmosphere. We would go to the beach together, and although they were all older and more involved in their own lives, they still mostly found time here and there for me.

Betsy, Judy, Kathy and Tad 1964

Kathy was the meek, humble one. She gave me the most attention and care through this period. Kathy began to discover her talent, learning to play acoustic guitar and complementing it with her beautiful voice.

Betsy was starting to take on a tough edge, and I believe that she wore it like a badge. It was her way of making it through. Betsy had relied so much on her sister Suzy. Really all of us did, but mostly Betsy felt her absence heavily.

These were our roles in the family ecosystem. When I was in first grade, I remember seeing my sister Betsy over the fence and waving. Betsy was in sixth grade. It was the only time I would ever be in the same school as any of my sisters. Betsy quickly looked the other way. I felt she didn't want to be embarrassed by her little brother while she was with her friends. Today, I get it completely; this behavior is how children cope with their peers at times…but at that moment, as I recall, it was kind of painful for me.

•••••

Elaine at Officer's Club 1965

My mom and dad were doing pretty well in their relationship at first when we moved to San Diego. There was an event at the *Officer's Club* on the Naval base, and they dressed up. There was a piano at the Club. Elaine performed her classical pieces for everyone and was very well received, which made her happy. She started to give piano lessons, mostly to young children, which took a lot of patience but gave her an outlet for her creativity. At home, she would always play records for me, including *Herb Alpert and the Tijuana Brass, Sergio Mendes and Brazil 66, Frank Sinatra* or *Ferranti and Teischer.* We were a musical family.

Maynard and Elaine 1963

My father taught me how to ride a bike. He would run down the street holding on to the bike as I pedaled madly. At one point, I made a comment to him and I noticed that he was no longer beside me. I was riding all by myself! I was so excited; I rode all the way around the block and crashed the bike into the sidewalk back where I began! From that point forward, I would always fracture the popular quote by saying, "You never forget how to fall off a bike." That's actually more of a lifetime truism than forgetting how to ride one.

Dad was a coffee addict. In the mornings, he would make me "little boy's coffee," which consisted of mostly milk and sugar and a little coffee. It started me early on a lifetime obsession with coffee.

Once you learn how to ride a bike, you never forget how to fall off of it. It is the same in life.

Times were different back then. Every adult smoked cigarettes. I mean everybody. My parents would both smoke in the car while we were driving, with the windows up. We thought nothing of it.

People smoked on airplanes and in their homes. We had ashtrays everywhere. Sports figures and farmers chewed tobacco, and spit it out with ceremonious aplomb. A "real man" smoked a cigarette without a filter on it.

•••••

My parents gave me a lot of freedom for a six-year-old. I would walk a mile or so to school and back most days by myself. I would ride my bike to the convenience store and buy ten candy bars for the dollar my mother gave me, and eat them all! I would journey alone through the storm drains underneath the freeway…they were my fortresses, and the unique smell of the canyons I wandered would stay with me forever.

When I felt bold, I would cross under the freeway in the storm drain and climb the long set of a thousand stairs up to *San Diego State College*, wandering around the campus as if I belonged there. It was hot sometimes but never sweltering in San Diego. The climate was mostly perfect year-round.

•••••

I remember seeing a movie that deeply disturbed me. I can't remember the name of the film, but it opened with a boy in a field somewhere in South America playing with his dog, gleefully. All of a sudden, the dog was shot dead and the boy ran back to his compound. Soon, soldiers came into the compound and raped his sisters and killed his parents. I had to hide my eyes and eventually I left the theatre, crying. The memory of that carnage stayed with me for years. It was devastating to believe that people could do that to each other, and it chipped away at my innocence. Later, as an adult, I was fairly conservative with my children, carefully monitoring what they were watching until they were old enough to figure it all out for themselves.

•••••

My father was given much responsibility at the Naval Hospital in Balboa Park in San Diego. He was in charge of several buildings, and he trained the interns. He was proud of an award he received for being the best teacher of the interns, and he embraced his new position. Maynard was an outstanding doctor and teacher. He continued to write his sonnets and stories, and he won several *Freedom's Foundation* awards for his essays on freedom and the American way. He had penned a short story entitled *The Boy, The Fence and Indian Summer*, published in *Ohio Magazine.*

•••••

At first, life was good for us. My mother's mom, my grandmother Gizi, had remained in Long Beach, California since her husband's passing, and we visited her often. My mother was happy to be within driving distance of her mother.

Ted and Candace Witt 1966

My mom's brothers were finishing college. They both went to *Notre Dame* and then *University of Southern California.* My uncle Ted met Candace Rich in college and they were perfectly matched. In fact, they shared the same birthday. They married, and when he graduated from *USC* dental school, he set up a practice in a small farm town in Orange County, California called Mission Viejo. As it grew into a huge metropolis, his family grew as well. Ted and Candy had three children, Michelle, Ted and Warren.

Gerry and Kathy Witt's Wedding

My uncle Ted and my aunt Candy were a huge part of my childhood. As my parent's relationship deteriorated, I was dropped off to their home in Orange County many times, sometimes for a week at a time, and they treated me as one of theirs. I would help Ted with projects, and I learned about simple carpentry, masonry and how to fulfill a "honey-do" list. He also gave us all free dental care for many years, for which I remain forever grateful.

My mother's youngest brother, Gerry, became an attorney and moved to Encino, a suburb of Los Angeles. He married a woman named Kathy and they had three children, Gerald, Jr., Kelly, and Christopher.

•••••

Kathy and Gerry Witt 1969

I received my first communion in San Diego. After my second-grade year, we moved across the freeway to a house on Dorman Drive, in the area by *San Diego State College* (later *San Diego State University*), and I started in a new school, *Hardy Elementary School*. This would become a trend for me, which lasted throughout my childhood. We would move. I would start at a new school. I would meet new friends and learn to adjust. When I was finally adjusted, we would move again. Navy life was that way and we just learned to accept it, although some moves were very hard and it was always heartbreaking to leave close friends behind.

My mother enrolled me into swim lessons. I quickly went from beginner to advanced beginner, intermediate and then "swimmer." I wanted to go on to junior lifeguard but I was still too young. I loved to swim, which helped me later when I would go out into the ocean alone to body surf or 'boogie board'.

•••••

One day when I was six or seven years old, I was watching *Frankie Valli and the Four Seasons* performing on television. Frankie was singing, *Sherry, Sherry Baby* with his high falsetto voice, and I was singing along in perfect pitch to the song. My mother looked at me in amazement.

Seeing my musical talent for the first time, she began to immediately teach me how to play piano. Within a week, I was able to play *Yesterday*, the Beatles song and *Blue Moon*. From that point forward, in my spare time, I would play the piano. My mother continued to teach me throughout my childhood.

•••••

1965 Betsy, Judy, Kathy and Tad

One day, I was playing ball with my friend in our back yard on Dorman Drive. The ball went into the bushes and, retrieving it, I stepped on a rusty nail that was exposed from a board that had fallen from our fence. The nail went through my 'flip-flop' sandal and deep into my foot. I was rushed to the hospital, stitched and patched up. Two weeks later my foot was oozing from infection. Back at the hospital, the doctor discovered a piece of rubber from the sandal had lodged in my foot. It was removed.

Apparently, the infection traveled up my leg and caused an abscess in my bone. A year or so later, I started having pain in the bone of my upper left leg. It was misdiagnosed as an *Osteoid Osteoma*. I was given crutches and told that eventually it would go away.

From the age of nine, all through my childhood and into my adulthood, I experienced pain every day of my life from my leg.

The daily pain actually lasted until I was in an auto accident at age thirty. After a biopsy was done following the accident, the pain subsided and only came back about once a month, and then even less frequently for the rest of my life. The experience taught me about the value of mind over matter.

Dealing with pain is never easy, but our minds are powerful, and after a time, most of the time I could handle it. It helped me later whenever I dealt with extreme conditions in my life.

The most important thing is to figure out a way to deal with pain without narcotics, if at all possible. That's an awful, ugly road to go down. Fortunately, I never became addicted to anything except cigarettes for about five years when I was a teenager, and coffee always!

When you are feeling pain every day of your life, you have two choices: You can go insane, or learn how to overcome it with the power of your mind.

•••••

My father's alcoholism reared its ugly head after the move to Dorman Drive. He was a mean, vitriolic drunk. It was amazing, because his demeanor was so genuine, straightforward and almost righteous when he was sober. He had a temper, sober, but it would mostly only come out when he was disappointed at a nurse or if someone did not follow his orders properly. He really had a *Jekyll and Hyde* personality when he drank alcohol. Later, when I was in High School, I would describe him as an "instant asshole, just add alcohol."

My mother was tired of putting up with it. As I mentioned, he had such a bad episode when we lived in Memphis that the Navy had sent him away for several months, and she had to handle everything alone, and now it was coming back. My parents argued a lot, and the atmosphere in our house was becoming increasingly more toxic by the day.

Judy and Tad 1965

I had my own room in San Diego, but I still liked to crawl into bed with my parents and sleep between them, when I could. One night, they were out, so I went into their bed and fell asleep. I was awakened in a panic, witnessing my mother screaming as my drunken father pinned her against the wall of the bedroom and tried to strangle her. My sister Judy called the police. She calmly grabbed me and took me into her bedroom and locked the door.

That night, Judy held me in bed until I fell back asleep, traumatized. I was so embarrassed the next morning when I realized that I had wet Judy's bed. I had never wet a bed, ever, and she had saved me and cuddled me and I peed in her bed. Judy was always calm and loving, and she actually laughed about it. She laughed with me at everything I did. She was my special Judy.

Judy - High School Graduation - 1966

For a few days, my mother was in the hospital and my father was briefly jailed. She recovered and dropped the charges against him, he stopped drinking for a few months, and we moved on as a family, just a little more fractured.

•••••

Judy was about to graduate High School when my father had another episode with alcohol. He was drunk and belligerent. The commanding officer at the Naval Hospital in San Diego was Admiral "Red" Warden. Admiral Warden loved my dad. He knew how much the interns loved him; Maynard was one of his best doctors, and he was also a World War II veteran, having served in the South Pacific with the Admiral. Alcoholism was looked at differently then.

Warden suggested that my father see a psychiatrist. My father dutifully went to the psychiatrist. Maynard had taken psychology in college and he knew what to say and how to act. The psychiatrist told him that he was perfectly fine, cleared him and told him not to drink.

Some people are just allergic to alcohol. The problem with alcoholism is that it is a disease. It is a progressive disease, and it just keeps getting worse as long as you take another drink. If you just stop, you are 'cured' until you take another drink, but if you don't stop, you are in big trouble. My father did not stop drinking, and Admiral Warden did him the greatest of favors; instead of throwing him out of the Navy, the good Admiral transferred my father to the largest Army-Navy Hospital in the world, in Corpus Christi, Texas, and made sure he was given the top position, as *Chief of Medicine.*

I believe that the Admiral thought that if he gave Maynard a huge position elsewhere, the problem would no longer be his, and maybe the gravity of the position would keep Maynard from drinking.

My mother was exasperated and completely fed up with my father at this point. My sisters Kathleen and Betsy were in Junior High school and were both very happy living in San Diego. Judy graduated High School in 1966 and enrolled in *San Diego State College.*

We left Judy behind in a college dorm, and my remaining two sisters reluctantly moved with us to Corpus Christi.

CHAPTER NINE
Corpus Christi, Texas

We made the drive across country from California to Texas. When we arrived, we found that we were living for the first time on a military base. There were seven "Quarters"; actually, they were small mansions, lovely homes that the Commanding Officers lived in with their families.

Across the street were tenement apartments for the enlisted men and their families. We pulled up to our beautiful new home, "Quarters H-E", and excitedly, I ran barefoot across the long lawn to the front door. The grass was full of sticker burrs, which I had never experienced on a grassy lawn, and when I made it to the door, my feet were bloody and full of stickers, and I cried. That was my introduction to my new home.

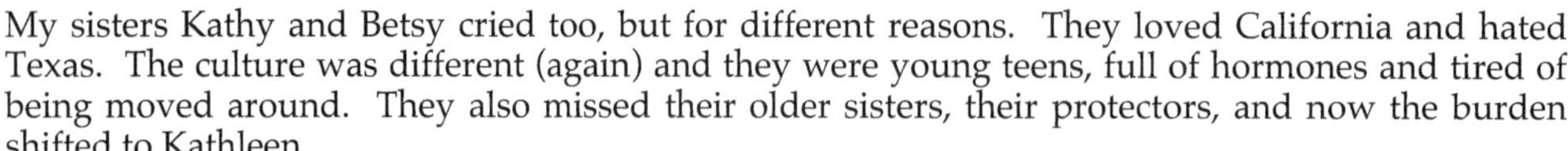

My sisters Kathy and Betsy cried too, but for different reasons. They loved California and hated Texas. The culture was different (again) and they were young teens, full of hormones and tired of being moved around. They also missed their older sisters, their protectors, and now the burden shifted to Kathleen.

Corpus Christi had a more tropical climate than San Diego. We were back in extreme humidity during the summer months. The beaches on the Gulf of Mexico seemed a bit dirtier than the pristine California beaches, and the waves were small or nonexistent. Padre Island on the Corpus Christi coast was the nicest of all of the beach areas, and we would occasionally go down and play on the beach. My family was a bit more fractured in general, however, and I missed my sister Judy.

•••••

We were in Corpus for about a year and a half. Slowly, Kathy adjusted. She became a "Candy Striper", a volunteer assistant helping at the hospital. Kathy continued to learn the guitar, and she was really becoming an excellent singer. She was still and always meek, gentle and kind, and constantly very protective over me. She was truly my 'little mother'.

Betsy started to come into her own in Corpus, although she might tell you otherwise. I know she hated the experience in general. Betsy was the forgotten child. She had been the youngest, the light of my parent's lives, until I was born when she was four. The double whammy of myself being the youngest, and the only boy, was a lot for Betsy to handle, and she slowly developed her dynamic into becoming the black sheep of the family ecosystem, as I had mentioned.

Betsy, Tad and Kathy 1966

Betsy would silently torment me under her breath when we were young, just to make me upset, and most of the time it worked. Years later, we laughed about it and turned our relationship entirely around, but at the time, it was her way of coping with the hand she was dealt. It didn't help at all when, later, my drunken father tried to crawl into bed with her. Betsy had it tough, but she became strong and knew how to endure; she learned the hard way to survive.

•••••

It was shortly after my eighth birthday that we moved to Corpus Christi. After an adjustment period, I started to love living on the base. It was during the height of the Viet Nam War, and soldiers were training on obstacle courses down the street from our house. I would watch them, and when they left, I would run and climb the obstacles on the course with my new friends. We would see how far we could make it, before collapsing from exhaustion into the mud.

In a field not far from the obstacle course existed a 'graveyard' of burnt out helicopters and planes that had been shot down in Viet Nam, recovered and returned to the states for parts and scrap metal. The graveyard became our playground. Some of the helicopters were laced with dried blood, and the putrid smell of burnt flesh still permeated the stale air inside the skeletons of many of these great fighting machines. We were oblivious to it all as we laughed and played in the rubble.

To a young boy, the remnants of a vicious battlefield can be an imaginary paradise.

Most of my friends lived in the enlisted men's apartments across from our house, and they LOVED to come over and play with me in our nice home. I would wake up on a Saturday morning, eat an entire bag of white powdered sugar donuts and watch cartoons. At night, I watched brand new episodes of *Star Trek, Lost in Space, Bonanza, Zorro, Gilligan's Island* and *The Twilight Zone.*

We had a 'maid's quarters' that was unoccupied behind our house. There were medical books with photos of naked people with whatever disease they were illustrating. My friends and I would giggle, looking at boobs and other body parts for the first time. It was an innocent time for me, but far from innocent for the world at war (with the constant reminder of the ravages of war all around me) or for my parents.

Kathy with "Prince" - 1966

•••••

In the early morning of January 27, 1967, a cabin fire killed three astronauts in the Apollo 1 spacecraft on the Launchpad in Florida. It was a terrible tragedy for this young boy to witness. We were all enamored with the space program. Boys wanted to grow up to be astronauts. They were our heroes. I was deeply affected by this tragedy.

•••••

My mom and dad bought a cocker spaniel dog. We named him "Prince". He was my first pet, and I loved him. Unfortunately, Prince had the terrible habit of running away from home and biting strangers. More than one person threatened to sue my parents. The wounds were real, but they hung in there with my little dog. He was a beautiful dog with a mean streak, and I loved him. When everyone in my family was lost in their own world all around me, I had my dog.

Hurricane Beulah formed in the ocean, gained strength to a Category 5 storm, and then hit the Texas coast within the Gulf of Mexico around Corpus Christi on September 19, 1967. The vicious storm ravaged through the area and did some damage and flooding to our house.

Do not mess with Mother Nature. She will always prevail.

After boarding up all of our windows, we were ushered to a huge secure building with all the other families, and it was an amazing experience. At one point, I stole away from everyone and opened a door, which led to an outdoor passage between the buildings. These passages were concrete on the bottom, and the top half of the walkways were screened in, in order to minimize mosquitos and flies. I fell on the ground within the protective concrete, and the storm raged above me. The screens had been ripped apart and debris was flying by at a furious pace. It was pure, unadulterated terror, and I wanted to experience it, not realizing how dangerous it truly was to be out there during a hurricane. Somehow, I made it back inside the building and I was scolded, but I will never forget those moments of witnessing Mother Nature at her worst.

It reminded me of the power of the Pacific Ocean when I wandered out a little too far, being pummeled like a feather into the surf by the crashing waves.

I was in fourth grade at *Flour Bluff Elementary School*, which was off of the Army-Navy base. We would take a school bus every morning, several miles into the town of Corpus Christi to the school. At first, I had a difficult time understanding the Southern drawl of the teachers. Oral spelling tests were particularly hard. The teacher would tell us to spell "tired", but I clearly heard "tarred" and that's what I wrote!

I liked my fourth-grade teacher. She was a patient younger woman. Each afternoon, she would read passages from Laura Ingalls Wilder's *Little House on The Prairie* series of books, and my mind would wander into another place. Life on the prairie was tough for the early settlers, but I loved the characters in the book, and she read each page in a vibrant and animated fashion.

One day, a food fight erupted in the cafeteria. Even though I had nothing to do with it, I was taken with all the other boys and whipped with a huge wooden paddle by the Principal. Later that evening, when my father saw the welts on my body from the paddle, he erupted in anger. The next morning, with his Commander's uniform on, my father marched me directly to the Principal's office. I remember hearing his loud voice screaming at the principal, in muffled tones through the wall for quite some time while I was sitting in the front room of the office.

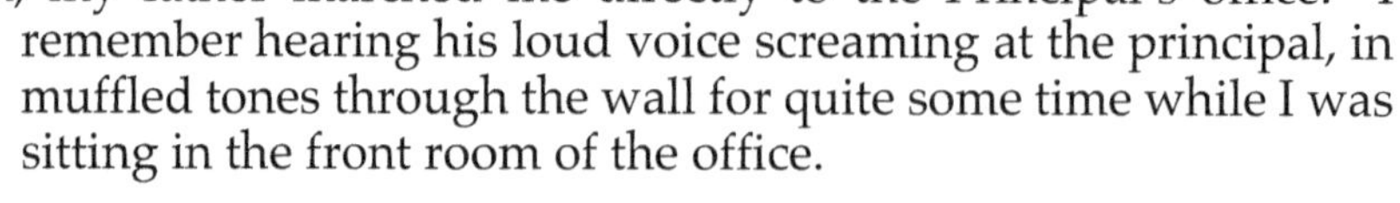

Me and My Dad
1963

I was never touched again by the Principal, or by anyone else at the school. In fact, with the exception of the spanking I had received in Memphis for running away with Miriam Jacobs, I was never afforded corporal punishment more than once.

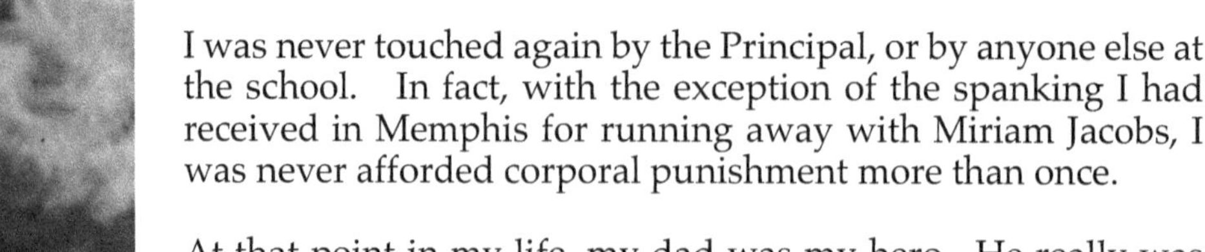

At that point in my life, my dad was my hero. He really was larger than life to me. In spite of the incident I had witnessed in San Diego, my parents had done their best to protect me and shield me from his alcoholic behavior to that point. As a sober man, he was compassionate and kind, at least to me. He was promoted to Lieutenant in Memphis, then Lieutenant Commander in San Diego, and then Commander while in Corpus Christi. Each time he was promoted, when I saw his new uniforms with the added stripes on them, I was as proud as he was.

Maynard was a war hero and an excellent doctor. He called me his good buddy. I felt an immense patriotism when I went on his 'rounds' at the hospital and met some of the young men who had been injured terribly in Viet Nam. Dad would help me with my homework, and he instilled in me a love of history, particularly American history. We would read stories of great American heroes and important moments in history, and he would embellish them with a sense of adventure. I would imagine myself in the Constitutional Convention or alone and cold with George Washington during a bitter Valley Forge winter.

•••••

I thrived in Corpus Christi. I was a cub scout, earning patches and rising through the ranks with my friends. My mother put me into little league. Although I was actually a pretty good sportsman, my father had no interest in sports and he never participated with me, so I became disinterested pretty quickly. I remember standing in left field hoping nobody hit the ball to me! I evolved into a much better sportsman on my own as I grew.

I always wondered, when I later saw my grandson Giorgio running faster than any other child in a track meet, scoring seven goals in soccer, hitting home runs in baseball, or scoring touchdowns on his own in a football game, if I would have been a star athlete with more direction in my childhood. After all, I had a great uncle in the *Major League Baseball* Hall of Fame! My life was destined in another direction.

I bought my first forty-five RPM single record in Texas. It was *Good Vibrations* by the Beach Boys. Everyone was listening to *Herman's Hermits* and *The Monkees.* Kathy and Betsy had *The Beatles-Rubber Soul* and *Simon & Garfunkel-Bookends* albums. I was beginning to love pop music.

•••••

Maynard worked to become a Diplomate in the *American College of Physicians.* He passed his boards, and was a revered and respected doctor. Unfortunately, he was also a drunk. He truly was the best and worst of people, all in one.

My mother was beginning to learn how to cope with my father's behavior by becoming more independent. She went back to college in Corpus Christi. She 'frosted' her hair blonde. When my father began to drink again, she was far more indifferent than she had previously been. She privately began to have an affair with her college professor, and she started to believe that she was falling in love with him. My father was emotionally unavailable to her, and she was cold to him in return.

One Sunday, I was playing with some toys in the front room of the house and my mother came in and told me to watch out the window for my father. He was drunk, and he hadn't come home the night before, and she was worried. I really didn't know yet what 'drunk' meant, and to me it was an exciting experience, watching and waiting for my father to come home in this condition. I wondered what he would be like. I had already buried the traumatic experience I had endured in San Diego. It remained buried within me until much later.

•••••

Before I knew it, right before I had started fifth grade, we were being transferred back to San Diego. Maynard had been discovered drunk in a closet having sex with a nurse, and his Commanding Officer in Corpus Christi wanted to give him a dishonorable discharge. My mother begged the C.O. to just give Maynard one more chance, and Admiral Warden agreed to accept him back to San Diego due to my mother's pleadings.

A new Chief of Medicine was brought in to Corpus Christi before we received Maynard's transfer papers, and we were relegated to live in a small trailer for a month during the transition. It was somewhat humiliating to me, but I was learning to adapt within a family in crisis. I had my sisters Kathy and Betsy still, and I could always turn to them, even though they were disinterested teenagers for the most part.

Suzanne's Children
Wendy, Michael, Lori and Charles
1972

My parents shipped me off to stay with my sister Suzanne and her family for a month. Suzy and Bill had moved to Greensboro, North Carolina. Bill had a job as an insurance agent. They had a nice home. Their son, Charles was three, and they had an infant daughter, my niece, Lori. Suzy was already pregnant with her third child, Michael.

My Sister Kathy
with Charles and Lori
1968

Suzanne and Bill were living on a very tight budget, and although she was glad to have me with her, I know it was probably even harder for her to have yet another mouth to feed. She never, ever let me feel anything but wanted and loved. She was truly great to me. Later, in 1970, Suzy gave birth to her fourth child, a darling daughter, Wendy.

CHAPTER TEN
Back to San Diego

The world had changed as much as our lives were changing again. The "summer of love" in 1967 had just happened, and when we returned to San Diego, the antiwar movement was going strong. My sister, Judy, was very much a part of the movement in college, briefly becoming a member of the communist group *Students for a Democratic Society.*

Judy had changed since we left. She was a hippie, and very much into social change. At one point in 1965, during the Watts riots when she was just seventeen, she went up to Los Angeles to see if she could somehow help or protest. When she arrived in that volatile section of Los Angeles to protest, an African-American man raped Judy in an alley.

Most people bitten by sharks are swimming in shark-infested waters wearing a black wetsuit, which resembles a seal, otherwise known as shark food. While you're caught up in the moment, be bold, but be careful not to put yourself in danger.

Although this experience was very traumatic for her, she kept it from me and I didn't learn of it until many years later. I believe this experience tempered her enthusiasm, although she held on to her liberal philosophy for life. To her, liberalism was compassion, and I understood where she was coming from.

My mother wanted to move back into our old neighborhood in Del Cerro, and she found a house for us at 6344 Rockhurst Drive. She believed that our original San Diego neighborhood was the safest option, as my father was generally under control when we lived there just a handful of years back. The house wouldn't be ready to rent for a few months, however. She enrolled me back into *Hearst Elementary School* where I had gone to kindergarten, first and second grade. Now in fifth grade, it was nice for me for once to be back with children I remembered.

•••••

While we were waiting for the house to be ready, my father had the great idea of finding a home in Mission Beach on the ocean to rent for a few months. Mission Beach was lovely, and we literally lived on "Ocean Front Walk." Our front window was a huge picture window overlooking the ocean, a mere twenty yards away from the surf and sand.

It was the optimal place to be for a nine-year-old. I would go, alone, into the waves. I learned to body surf by myself. In retrospect, I would never have let my nine-year-old go into the ocean alone!

But, I was always given too much freedom. My parents were pretty much done parenting by this time, and fortunately I had a fairly good head on my shoulders (and one amazing Guardian Angel!).

Most mornings, a coastal eddy would hug a narrow stretch of coastline until about noon; the weather was cool and somewhat gloomy. As if on cue, the sun would burst from the clouds in the early afternoon and the ocean glistened with a thousand jewels of light, mirrored by a suddenly cloudless sky. I was back in paradise.

On weekends, my mother would sometimes take me to the stately old pool at the *Naval Hospital.* Dark blue tiles accented the water, and I was usually the only person in the pool, playing while an ensign guarded the pool, never taking his eyes off of me. Other Saturdays, my mother would drop me off at *Balboa Park* to explore the *Natural History Museum* or the *Museum of Man* on my own.

On occasion, we would bring a group of friends to the *San Diego Zoo.* It was the world's largest zoo, and we would spend the entire day there, running gleefully through the different exhibits and marveling at the exotic animals. In the summer months, the pungent smell from the huge eucalyptus trees would permeate the trails, mixed with the scent of sweaty animals. It was a great experience for a nine-year-old!

•••••

It was a half hour drive back and forth from Mission Beach to my school every day in Del Cerro. My sister Kathy had just gotten her Driver's License. Sometimes she would take Betsy and me to our schools in the morning. We would stop by *Heavenly Donuts* and I would get a chocolate glazed donut. Then we would continue on to school with *The Beatles, The Doors, The Rolling Stones* or *The Guess Who* blaring on the A.M. Radio station.

Some Sundays, Kathy would offer to take Betsy and me to church when the parents didn't go. We would skip church and decide what we would tell our parents about the sermon if we were all asked so we could be on the same page with each other, and we would go to the beach! Weekends were fun on the beach, until my father started drinking again…

•••••

A dive bar named *The Cave* on Mission Boulevard was literally around the corner from our house, and Maynard would drop by the bar on the way home for a few drinks. He would stumble in the concrete entrance of the bar, which resembled a cave. After a few pops, belligerent and charged up with alcohol, he would barge into our tiny beach house and verbally attack my mother, my sisters and me. This was the first time I actually witnessed and understood the extent and ugliness of my father's drunkenness and addiction.

Maynard in 1969

One morning after a particularly nasty night, my father came into my room, hat in hand and he kneeled at my bedside. He held my hand and pleaded with me for my forgiveness.

I loved my dad. In life, you only get one father and one mother. Some people are fortunate to have a great stepparent and that can make all the difference in their lives. Some fathers are only sperm donors. My dad was bigger than life. He was the best of men and the worst of men, all in one.

I knew my father loved me, in spite of his disease. He was a renaissance man, extremely intelligent and a very hard worker. When he took me on his 'rounds' at the hospital, I could see in his patient's eyes that he was greatly respected and revered. Other physicians and nurses looked up to him as a great teacher and mentor. His opinion was respected as gospel. Also, I felt sorry for him. At this point in his life, he really couldn't beat this demon of alcoholism.

That morning, he looked at me as he was kneeling at my bedside and he humbly asked me to say a prayer for him. I told him, "I always do." From that day forward for the rest of our lives, whenever we parted or hung up the phone after talking to each other, my father would say, "Say a prayer for me." And I would dutifully answer, "I always do."

•••••

My mother was angry. She was becoming more and more miserable. She had just literally saved his Naval career and kept him from losing his medical license by getting him back to San Diego, and he was immediately back to his antics. I think she put her foot down at some point, because after we moved into the house in Del Cerro, for a short period of time, Maynard would just disappear for weekends and come back hung over, instead of hanging out and terrorizing us all. That bothered her equally as much, and I can understand that. Who would want to be with a husband who doesn't bother to come home for days at a time?

When he did stay home and drink, my sister Kathy would sit up with him until all hours of the night, trying to keep him calm and reason with him. Kathy had an even temper. She could truly soothe the savage beast. One night, Maynard was so drunk that he climbed into my sister Betsy's bed and started to fondle her. She got up and ran out, crying.

After that incident, he stayed sober for a few weeks, and life seemed almost normal for a minute. Elaine was giving piano lessons and she would give recitals with all the students together. I would hear kids downstairs playing wrong notes, and I would want to run down and tell them, "THIS IS HOW TO PLAY IT!" I realized quickly that I could never be a piano teacher.

I was never prouder of my mom than when she hosted recitals for her students. She had a knack to mold children into finding what talent they had, and maximizing it. She was as proud as they were, as they performed in front of a large group, one by one.

•••••

My parents bought me a ten-speed *Schwinn* bicycle. Although it was tough to learn how to shift the gears properly, soon I was riding my new bike all over Del Cerro to my friend's houses and to my favorite convenience store to buy candy.

My father had prescribed *Valium* and *Librium* for my mother. This was kind of a trend in the nineteen-sixties, particularly among married women, just like *Xanax* and *Prozac* became big in the eighties. Elaine was starting to take these depressants regularly in order to cope with her life. She would also drink wine with these pills sometimes. I would look at her and think she must be thinking, "If you can't beat 'em, join 'em." Or maybe she was just giving up on life.

One day my sister Betsy found my mother slumped over, in her own vomit. She had overdosed and Elaine was rushed to the hospital to have her stomach pumped. My father's behavior was driving my mother to the brink of suicide. My sisters believed that it was an intentional overdose. My mother recovered from it, and nobody told me about the incident in order to protect me.

•••••

One night, I was watching television on the living room floor with my cocker spaniel, Prince. I reached back to pet the dog, and he had a sticker burr in his fur, which pierced his skin when I petted him. Instinctively, Prince lunged at me and bit me behind my ear. I was bleeding profusely. Apparently, the bite missed my carotid artery by a millimeter, and I could have bled out. I needed stitches, and when I got back from the hospital, the dog was gone forever. My father had taken him to be euthanized. I was devastated and I blamed myself, but what could my parents do?

My dad went out and bought me a hamster, and my mother took me to *Sears* and bought me a couple small turtles, contained within a little plastic habitat. My parents were trying to compensate for the loss of my pet. I loved the hamster. One day I was playing with the hamster. I had a plastic clothes hamper turned upside down. I rocked the hamper back and forth as the hamster ran, then turned and ran the other way to try to escape the hamper. In an instant, I lost my balance and the hamper slipped. The edge of the hamper landed on the hamster. The hamster went into convulsions and died right before my eyes. Again, I was devastated. I killed my hamster!

It was an accident, but I was inconsolable. My father got a little shoebox, and we buried my hamster in a ceremony in our back yard, with a little cross, made of *Popsicle* sticks. I would visit my hamster's grave every day and say prayers asking for forgiveness.

Kathy and Betsy brought home two kittens, which they had named "Aquarius" and "Israel". The kittens disappeared after a couple weeks. I think my mother was a bit overwhelmed with them, and she probably took them to the animal shelter. I spent days scouring the neighborhood, looking for them.

Bill Sisler
1985

•••••

I was born with large, floppy ears that stuck out like *Dumbo.* My uncle Bill, my dad's brother, had the same ears, and my mother thought it detracted from his good looks. Right around my tenth birthday in 1968, my mother decided to have my ears cosmetically pinned back. I went into the *Naval Hospital* and had my first surgery. I remember waking up in the middle of the surgery, and hearing the doctor tell the anesthesiologist to give me more medication.

It was a good move. Although my ears were rigid for many years afterwards, and they would hurt if someone bent them forward, I was grateful for the way it changed my appearance. As an adult, I couldn't imagine living my life with ears that stuck out of my head!

CHAPTER ELEVEN
My Grandmother Gizella

My Grandmother
Gizella

When I went to visit my Grandma Gizi in Long Beach, she would implore me to never, ever talk to anyone about my father's alcoholism, or of any of my family's problems. It was nobody's business, she would say. She didn't want to be embarrassed in front of her friends. It was our dirty little family secret, and no one was to know.

I do understand her feelings, in retrospect, but this behavior shames a child. I felt that we were living a dark, ugly scandal and I had to protect that secret from getting out, at all costs. I thank God I always had one of my sisters to talk to, when I needed them. I can't imagine how one can cope with something so large and important when you're not even allowed to mention it and you have no one to turn to. Children without siblings have their own set of challenges. I was grateful once again for the love and support of my sisters.

Even so, I do remember many wonderful visits to Grandma Gizi's apartment on Carson Street in Long Beach. She had an old baby grand piano in her living room next to a big window. It was the piano my mother had played as a girl. The pedal was always breaking on it, and I would climb under and fix it so I could continue to play my pieces for her. Eventually, the piano ended up with my daughter, Regina, years later, and had yet another life.

When I stayed alone with Gizi, I would hear her whistling in a beautiful vibrato from the other room. She would even whistle when she was going to the bathroom! I would play with my uncle's old steel toy trucks she had saved from the 1940's. She would make me sponge cake and banana cake. Gizi had a Roman-styled marbled music box in her bedroom, which played *Lara's Theme from Dr. Zhivago.* Eventually, I inherited the music box and it remained a sweet reminder of her for the rest of my days.

Gizella had a parakeet in her kitchen. The bird kept her company, and I would try to teach it to say things like, "My, my you're getting fat!" My grandmother would just laugh. She was good to me. Gizi had a "party line" telephone in her house. Nobody was allowed to call her before nine in the morning or after nine at night. She instructed us to be careful in what we talked about on the phone, just in case the neighbors were listening. Again, she did not want to be embarrassed!

•••••

When the whole family was at Gizi's house, they would play penny poker with her until all hours of the night. Sometimes my uncles would show up. They called her silly names like "Minnesota Mom" because she was a shrewd poker player. She would put the leaf into her huge, old, dining room table, expanding it when the whole family came to play with her.

Gizi's sons Ted and Gerry had a friend from college named Guy Weismantel. Guy would come with them to visit Gizella. He adored my grandmother. Guy had the idea of starting yearly *Gizella Witt Picnic* events, where all the family and friends would gather in a park somewhere in her honor. This went on for years. My "uncle" Guy was a great guy!

Gizi had a huge, white 1966 *Chrysler Newport* 4-door automobile. She would 'warm it up' for fifteen minutes in the garage before she drove it. She loved driving eighty miles an hour or faster on the freeway, which would astound anyone who knew her to be a slow, plodding person. Her knee was bad and she was overweight, so she would walk slowly and carefully wherever she went.

CHAPTER TWELVE
Our Last Experiences as a Family Unit

At home in San Diego, my sisters, my parents and I played the popular card game *Bridge*. My parents were good *Bridge* players, and they taught my sisters and me how to play *Bridge* competently. Whenever four of us were together, we would play the game. Elaine and Maynard would argue about conventions and bidding, and we would always find a way to hint to our partner's what was in our *Bridge* hands, to my parent's disdain. We would ask questions like, "So, if I bid one short club, does that show that I have only six to eight points?' or "How many points do I have to have to open with two no trump, even though I have a LOT of hearts?" My mother, in particular, would get angry and then shrug her shoulders with a stern look, saying, "Honestly!"

My sisters played a lot of records. The sounds of *The Doors, The Beatles, Joni Mitchell, The Rolling Stones* or *Simon & Garfunkel* emanated from our living room. My father would sing *The 59th Street Bridge Song-Feeling Groovy* at the top of his lungs. He loved that song. For me, it was a nice departure from the show tunes he would belt…

I was glad to be back at my school in Del Cerro. My friends embraced me. They knew my given name was Maynard from my school records, and instead of insulting me they called me "Big Maine!" I enjoyed playing kickball, tetherball and foursquare with them. My fifth-grade teacher gave me a 'job' editing all of the papers for grammatical errors. The school had a program where they offered typing. I learned how to type sixty words a minute at the age of ten, and this skill was a great blessing, which I would utilize for my lifetime. When the typewriter evolved into a computer keyboard years later, I was prepared.

•••••

One of my dad's patients was the father of the astronaut David Scott. He hooked me up with the coolest things! Pretty soon, David Scott was mailing autographed pictures to me, models of spacecraft as well as future prototypes. I was always obsessed with the space program during the golden age of NASA. From my earliest childhood, there was nothing better for a boy than watching the *Mercury, Gemini* and then *Apollo* spacecraft blasting off and later reentering the atmosphere. These astronauts were our heroes.

Around this time, my father suffered a detached retina in his eye. He was rushed into surgery. During this time period, they would literally sew it all back together or clamp it. Then, they would cover both eyes for three or four days, so you were totally blind until they removed the bandages. My dad was horrified at the prospect of blindness, and it kept him sober for a short period of time following the operation. Later, his other retina detached and he had the surgery all over again.

•••••

Maynard had a terrible habit when he drank. He would get on the phone and call nurses or some of the Officers' wives in the middle of the night, making lewd comments and asking them if they wanted to have sex with him. More than once, we had angry men at our door wanting to beat him up or kill him, and my mother had to shoo them away.

The death of a relationship more often comes from a thousand small cuts than from one big gash.

Admiral Warden was hearing again of my father's behavior, and it was wearing even more on him because Maynard, at this point, was in charge of most of the hospital. It was insane to everyone who knew him. He had a flaw, a mechanism within him that forced him to fail when he was accomplishing such great things. Admiral Warden began to recommend to Maynard that he start thinking of retiring from the Navy. My dad's dream had always been to become an Admiral, and he would have become an Admiral had he not had the disease of alcoholism. He had been promoted to the rank of Captain while in San Diego, one rank short of Admiral.

One morning, the police came to our door, pulled my father out of bed and arrested him. He asked them what he was being arrested for, and they showed him. He had been driving home drunk the night before and he went up onto someone's lawn. The car knocked down a fence and destroyed much of their property. It was easy to find him. A huge rock he had driven over had been stuck underneath the car, and dragging it through the streets, the rock drew a straight line, like chalk, down the asphalt and into our garage! There the rock still was, underneath his car. Yeah, that one was pretty embarrassing.

One day, I woke up and my mother had disappeared. My father was beside himself. He didn't know what to do without her, or how to react. He stopped drinking completely, immediately. We had a *Missing Person* report out on her when Maynard received a call almost two weeks later from the professor in Texas with whom she had the affair. My father had not been aware of my mother's affair. Elaine had driven to Texas and she was staying with the professor. She was taking her *Librium* and drinking massive amounts of wine, and she was angry and suicidal.

The professor did not actually want her in his life. During the time we lived in Corpus Christi, he had just wanted sex with her, and she thought their relationship was more than that. When she arrived at his doorstep, he rejected her and it was more than she could handle. Without an ounce of compassion, the professor demanded that my father come to Corpus Christi immediately, take her out of his house and bring her back home to San Diego.

Maynard believed that, if he drove to Texas to get her, Elaine would not leave with him unless I came along with him and she actually would see me there with him.

So, my father and I took off on a road trip from San Diego to Texas. This began a chain of events catalyzing a bizarre few weeks of my life. My father was sober and determined, all of a sudden, and my mother was the one who was out of control.

My mom had always been my rock of stability through all the madness along with my sisters, but for a time in San Diego I had only been getting that feeling of comfort and security from my sister Kathy. Elaine was out of control; Kathy intuitively knew it and stepped in and protected me. But here I was with my determined, sober, worried and kind father, driving endlessly on a long highway back to Texas, to rescue my mother from death.

CHAPTER THIRTEEN
Insanity Begins

Five days from the call we had received from the college professor in Corpus Christi to 'rescue' my mother, and almost three days after we left San Diego on our road trip, my father and I arrived in Corpus Christi.

When we made our way to the professor's apartment, my mother was completely out of her mind. She was drunk and on pills. As soon as she saw us, she started screaming at my father and hitting him, even with me there. Somehow, my dad and the professor physically dragged her to our car, and she sat in the back seat screaming and yelling profanities at us, in a drugged-out state, as we drove away. The professor made some kind of "Good riddance" comment, which stuck with me for some time. I had never, ever seen my mother acting even close to being this much out of control. She was exactly the opposite of the Type A, control freak mom I knew.

She truly was suicidal and out of her mind. I remember at some point she passed out, and my father and I had our first moment of peace in a whole day.

•••••

My dad and I had bonded during this trip. We were on a mission to save my mom together. He decided that it would be best to drive from Corpus Christi north to Memphis, Tennessee to my grandparents' apartment. This would give us a chance to help Elaine through her despair, and wean her off of the depressants before we just brought her right back to San Diego. This was the plan, anyway.

As we drove up the humid Texas coast along the Gulf of Mexico, my mother would go in and out of consciousness, waking up, crying hysterically, and sometimes screaming. It was such a very profoundly sad experience for me. I remember at some point we made it to Galveston and she was sleeping. My dad and I were starving so we decided to go into a restaurant and eat, carefully parking the car right in front where we could see it. Our plan was to eat, get her some take-out food and hopefully convince her to eat. You can imagine our faces when we saw her climb out of the back seat, disheveled, and walk into the restaurant screaming at us.

We stopped for the night at a motel. Elaine bathed and got some sleep. When we started again towards Memphis the next morning, she sat in front with my dad. They spent the entire trip screaming at each other at the top of their lungs, and I curled a pillow around my head to muffle the sounds as I lay in a fetal position in the back seat, trying not to cry. We couldn't get to Memphis soon enough.

•••••

The day we arrived in Memphis, my grandmother Audrey was distraught. My cousin Billy, my Uncle Bill's son was in his twenties and he had been struggling with heroin addiction. Billy would show up at her doorstep, wet and freezing and drugged out, and she would nurse him back to health on her couch. When he started to feel better, Billy would slip out the back and disappear again for a few months. Later, in the mid nineteen-seventies Billy would be one of the first people to die of *AIDS* from using a dirty needle, even before it was diagnosed as a disease.

Billy had just left again, and my Grandmother was sad and worried about him. But, the very worst thing that could happen was yet to come on that day.

As day turned into night, my grandmother got a phone call from my dad's brother Jack's girlfriend in Arkansas. Jack had taken his life and his girlfriend had discovered his body. Jack just could not cope any more with another day of life knowing he had a part in his beloved children's death. Maynard and my grandmother Audrey were devastated. We were all in shock. My grandfather George was also very sad, but he began to preach the gospel to all of us, as if it was going to make everything all right, which seemed somehow extremely inappropriate to me. In retrospect, one had to admire his faith, but his timing was very bad.

Proclaiming faith is noble in times of need, but sometimes, silent compassion is more effective.

Again, they kept the fact that it was suicide from me. They told me he died of a heart attack, at the age of forty-four. I didn't find out until thirty years later that my Uncle Jack killed himself. I could have handled it. It might have even made more sense to me. The pain of my cousin's deaths was still strong in my heart.

We stayed for Jack's funeral, and somehow this experience snapped my mother out of her despondence. I now believe that she came back to life in viewing the actual effects of suicide on a family. It was almost as if my Uncle Jack's actions had released her from her own death wish. If something good can be gleaned from such a tragedy, I imagine it would be that his tragic death might have saved my mother's life, at least temporarily.

My poor grandmother Audrey had already lost two sons, and Jack was her youngest. She was long-suffering, yet she somehow woke up each day with positivity and thankfulness for what she did have. I promised myself that I would do my best to follow her example and always try to be kind and grateful.

When my parents and I returned to San Diego, the damage had been done. My father accepted a retirement package from the Navy. They retired him as a Navy Captain, one rank short of Admiral. A couple years later, Maynard got drunk, put on an Admiral's uniform and had photos taken. He told everyone for a short time that he was a retired Admiral. He called it a 'graveyard' rank that was bestowed upon him after retirement. When he sobered up, he corrected the record.

It was tragic to me that a man who had given more than twenty years to the Navy was not given the rank he coveted. I understood, however, that he did it to himself.

A thousand good deeds can easily be erased by a few mistakes.

CHAPTER FOURTEEN
My Parents Separate

Following the completion of his retirement papers, my father accepted a position at the *Baptist Hospital* in Memphis, and he moved back to Tennessee alone to be close to his parents, and to help his mother through her grief. My parents were now officially separated.

I remember as if it was yesterday, sitting at his desk in our house in San Diego, after he left. He had left behind a bottle of his cologne for me, and I would screw open the wooden top and smell his smell. I cried hysterically for days when he left. I felt betrayed and abandoned. We had bonded so heavily on that awful trip. On the other hand, for the first time in years, it was calm at my house in Del Cerro.

•••••

My mother was having a hard time with the separation. She had her brother Gerry draw up divorce papers, and my father signed them. She held on to the papers and didn't file them just yet. Elaine continued to give piano lessons and I went into sixth grade. One thing I was grateful for was that, for the moment, my mother seemed back in control of herself. She had been grieving the slow death of her marriage for years from all of my father's transgressions, and she had finally thrown her hands up, given up, and had transgressions of her own. I believe it had been more of a revenge move for her than any other influence. For the first time, I heard her say a phrase I would continue to hear from her for the rest of her life, "I gave Maynard all of the best years of my life." They had been together for twenty-five years. At least for now, she had the situation enough in perspective that she wasn't suicidal. But, she was searching.

•••••

My mother went to a priest for a consultation. She had been a devout Catholic for the entirety of her life. My sisters were all in Catholic schools until we moved to San Diego. She told the priest that she was filing for divorce, and he promptly excommunicated her from the church and instructed her to never step foot into a Catholic church again. She was devastated.

It took a few months, but my mother began searching for a new church, and for something new to believe in. She found the *Religious Science* church in San Diego, with Chet Castellaw as minister. It was a new-age kind of church, with a positive thinking kind of philosophy to it. Elaine was searching for something, anything to help her to cope with her life. *Science of Mind* helped her to figure it out, at least for a while. She would take me to the church to go to their youth group while she went into the sanctuary for the service. I would walk in one door and out another, and go down to the convenience store to get candy until the church service was almost over.

Elaine also became involved in Astrology. She met a young gay man named Robert St. Germain. He was a master Astrologer, spending hours at a time compiling charts on people, based upon the minute and location they were born. My mother would talk to me for hours about someone's chart, and I was actually impressed at how close some descriptions came to people's personalities. I was impressed at how certain astrological influences appeared to affect people's lives in real time. Later, my sisters and others would enlighten me to numerology, past life regression therapy and other metaphysical concepts. I was fascinated, but I also saw some people get so caught up into it that they lost touch with the reality of the life they are living right now.

Don't live in the past or the future. Live here now. Many great influences affect our lives. Some are fascinating; others can help us to have a greater understanding of ourselves, but we must also always remember that our own Free Will trumps all influences.

For God so loved our Free Will that in giving it to us, he gave us the choice to choose against Him.

•••••

My sisters were all now involved in the *Peace Trains* and the anti-war movement. Judy was still a little more political; she was into the social change aspect of the movement, but it was now tempered with realism, due to the tragic memory of her rape.

Kathy was a senior at *Crawford High School* and she loved being a flower child. To her, the movement was all about peace and love. Kathy took the basement room of the house and made it into a pretty cool bedroom. She had the "Desiderata" poem on her wall. Kathy, in her flowing, flowered dresses would play her acoustic guitar with her long, blonde hair falling over the guitar, singing *Joni Mitchell* or *James Taylor* tunes, or an original song entitled *Pandora's Box* that she had just written with her lovely, elfin voice.

Betsy was a little more edgy but she followed suit. Eventually, Betsy lived hard for a time, and was into the drug counterculture. Betsy had been an overweight, insecure child, but by this time she had developed into a stunningly beautiful young woman. She had dark hair, dark eyes and a great figure. Boys were very interested in her; boys were interested in all of my sisters.

Suzanne, even though she had four children, was lovely and somehow maintained her figure and her positivity through it all. Judy wore glasses and not much makeup, but she had a natural beauty that drew you to her. Kathy had a sweet, pixie smile and beautiful, flowing long hair. Betsy had a huge, dimpled smile and all of the dark features of our mother's Hungarian ancestors.

Kathy
High School Graduation
1969

•••••

Judy was still in college. She met a young man named Peter Keyser. He was friendly and hip, with long, frizzy red hair and a mischievous smile. They were very much in love. As a great example of how the morality we knew was degrading all around us, I remember Peter telling me that he and Judy had just heard the *Beatles* song, *Why Don't We Do It in The Road?* And so, they went out and "did it" in the road, and it was so cool to him! It was also inappropriate to say any of that to an eleven-year-old boy, but any vestige of innocence I had once enjoyed was now completely out the window.

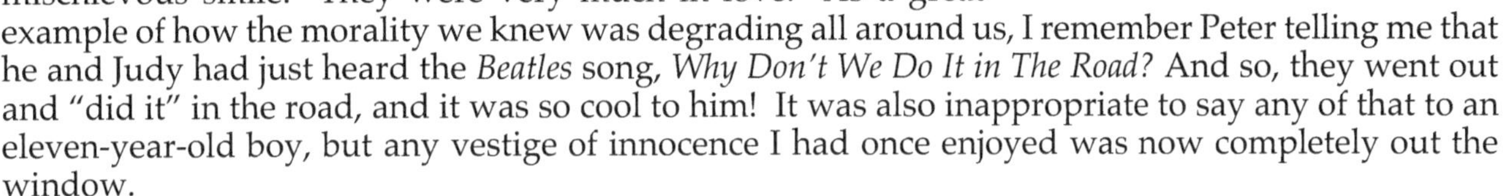

Judy and Peter
1969

I remember looking in the mirror one morning and thinking, "I used to always smile and be so outgoing. Will I ever smile again?" Not that my father had been much of a male influence through his alcoholism, but for now there was no male influence whatsoever in my household.

•••••

Drugs were becoming mainstream as part of the counter culture, and I'm sure my three sisters in San Diego were experimenting with drugs on different levels. We would go to festival concerts together to see *Jefferson Airplane*, *Canned Heat* or whatever other popular band was touring. They were mostly the same types of events, with thousands of people sitting with flowery clothes, or no clothes, on a grassy knoll below the stage with the scent of patchouli oil and marijuana emanating through the breeze coming from the ocean. It was cool.

I started to grow my curly hair out, like most boys were doing. My sisters would iron my long hair in the morning to get it to be straight and longer! It was a lost cause. My hair would crinkle back up and be curly within a couple of hours.

•••••

On my eleventh birthday, I had ten friends for a sleepover at my house. We stayed up all night, darkened our faces, and crawled across the street. We "Tee-peed" a house using toilet paper. My mother finally came out of her room at three in the morning and yelled at us to go to sleep.

One day I was at my friend's house and he decided that he wanted to smoke, so we rolled up some tree leaves in a cigarette paper he had stolen from his mother, and we lit them as if we were smoking.

I promptly told my sister Betsy the next day that I smoke now. She pulled out a cigarette from her purse and I lit it and took a puff. It was awful! But, I tried my best to act as if I liked it.

One day, I walked to the park by my house. Betsy was sitting in a circle with three other friends and they were smoking a joint of marijuana. Betsy asked me if I wanted some, and I said, "Sure, I smoke now," not knowing what it was. After I took a couple hits with them, I was feeling a little woozy. Betsy looked me straight in the eye and said; "Don't ever let this lead you into doing hard drugs!"

My mother was having a hard time parenting without my dad there. Even though he was more like a child to her than another parent, we all felt more independent without him, and it felt to me like our lives were a little out of control.

Many days I caught myself still looking in the mirror and feeling as if I had lost my ability to command any situation. My 'healthy ego' was gone. I felt that I would never be the same person again. In a heartbeat, I changed from healthy assertiveness to painful insecurity.

•••••

My mom tried to keep me busy. She put me into Judo classes. I took one class and came home. My mom asked me what I learned. I went up to my sister Betsy and grabbed her arm. Although she was much larger than me, I flipped her over and slammed her on her back onto the ground. I wasn't intentionally trying to hurt her. I was just trying to show them what I learned, but Betsy was very unhappy with me! So, that was the end of Judo lessons.

My mother put me into swim team at the *Jewish Community Center*. One day in the locker room, I stood on a chair to get my goggles out of the top locker, and the chair came out from under me. My head hit the side of a bench, and a big gash opened up next to my eye. I had stitches in my face, and by the time I healed, swim team was over.

I was cast as *Hamlet* in the sixth-grade play. I learned all of my lines quickly. In fact, for the rest of my life I could still recite the entire soliloquy word for word, beginning with, "To be, or not to be, that is the question…"

I enjoyed acting, so my mom put me into the *Little Theatre* in downtown San Diego. I acted in a few plays with other kids and enjoyed it. I remember we did a takeoff on *The Elves and the Shoemaker.*

•••••

Although my sisters were very much into their own lives and rejecting whatever authority my mother had left to give, I began to become very protective of her starting around this time. Elaine had bared her soul to me and I had seen her at her worst. I was worried about her always and in many ways, I parented my parent from this point forward. My dad had told me when he left, "You're the man of the house now. It's all up to you." I took his charge very seriously, and I was bound to watch over my mother. My sisters were in their own worlds and very resentful of my mother. I felt responsible for her.

I was going to go away to sixth grade camp for a week up at Palomar Mountain, north of San Diego. When we woke up on the morning of camp, we had overslept. My mother and I grabbed all of my things and we drove quickly to my school. The busses had already left. She got on the freeway and drove for miles and miles, down Route 80 (Now Interstate 8) to the 395 (Now Interstate 15) and continued several miles until we caught up with the busses. She flagged them down and I jumped out of the car with my bags and into the bus.

As I watched my mother drive away, I realized that I had forgotten to say goodbye to her. Parenting my own parent weighed heavily on my soul; it was a trend that would last too long and affect my relationships as I moved forward in life. At that moment that she drove away, I became profoundly sad that I didn't say goodbye and hug her. The days at camp were fun and full of activities, but at night when the lights went out, for an entire week, I silently cried myself to sleep, making sure nobody saw or heard me.

CHAPTER FIFTEEN
Caught Within the Shuffle

My Grandmother Audrey

When sixth grade ended, I went to Memphis for a couple of weeks to visit my father. It was really weird to me. He was already dating younger women. In fact, I found out when I was there that he had tried to date some my sister Suzanne's High School friends. I think he actually went out with one. He was greasy and stinky from his drinking and his apartment smelled like sweat and alcohol. I guess that he had figured out how to get away with it. Maynard was in private practice for the first time in his career.

I spent days at my grandparent's house while my dad was working. It was great to see my grandmother Audrey. Audrey's sister, my Great-Aunt Rose, lived down the street and she would visit. I would spend a few minutes each day in my grandfather's office with him in his big chair, and listen to him preaching the gospel to me. I loved him, but he was tough and didn't show much emotion, except when he cried about his love for Jesus.

Audrey would sit and pore through her huge, tattered scrapbook with me, her nimble fingers carefully turning the pages, pointing out old newspaper clippings, telegrams of birth announcements or reassurances that her sons at war in foreign ports were still alive and well, and photos that meant so much to her. So very many years after she lost her fifteen-year-old son Bennett, hit by a drunk driver, she still grieved, weeping silently as she read to me a letter she had written to him, ten years after his death. She recounted the heartbreak of losing another infant son, Norman, just a few years before Bennett died. She would never stop grieving their loss, yet she filled every day with optimism and pride for what she did have. My grandmother was an inspiration to me like no other person, and I vowed to retain her optimism through each of my own trials ahead.

Once or twice, my cousin Janet came over with her daughter Jamie. We would play outside my grandparent's apartment. Janet had just become one of the very first three policewomen in Memphis. She was very respected, and my grandmother Audrey was very proud of her.

•••••

Ivy engulfed the sides of the aged, dirty red brick buildings of my grandparents' neighborhood in Memphis. A drug store with a soda fountain, similar to the one my Grandfather Witt had so many years back in Chicago, sat directly across the street on the corner. My grandmother would give me some change, and I would go over and have a cherry coke or a milkshake, or buy some penny candy. I looked forward to that. I imagined my mother at my grandfather's drugstore in Chicago when she was young, working behind the soda counter, making milkshakes and cherry cokes for the neighborhood children fortunate enough to come in with a penny, nickel or a dime.

One day I was walking to the drugstore in Memphis, and as I approached the street corner, a station wagon with a large, African-American family drove to the corner. There was a little girl in the back and she looked at me and smiled. I waved to her. The station wagon pulled out into the intersection. It was hit hard on the side by a speeding car. The sound of metal against metal right in front of me was deafening.

Bodies were scattered all over the pavement in front of me. I ran up to the sobbing little girl and held her in my arms until the ambulances came. I was told that the man who hit them driving the other car had died, but I never found out what happened to the family in that station wagon. It shook me to the core, and I was literally afraid to ride in automobiles for a long while, following that experience.

My dad was really glad that I was there in Memphis. He couldn't wait to see me after work, and he tried his hardest to give me a good time. I was glad to see him, too, in spite of his condition, and I cried when I left him. He started a habit of writing me a letter to read on the airplane after he left me. The letters would always be a tearjerker about how hard it was to live without me, and of how he would hold me close to his heart until our next meeting. Usually his letters to me would end with a melodramatic statement like, "Godspeed, my son, until we meet again, Godspeed."

•••••

From Memphis, I went to stay with my sister, Suzanne, again in Greensboro, North Carolina. It was the summer of 1969. The Woodstock festival in Bethel, New York happened. The very first man walked on the moon. It was unreal. Suzy was pregnant with Wendy. My nephew Charles was only six years younger than me. Charles would throw temper tantrums regularly and he was difficult to control. Later, he was diagnosed as bipolar, and it all made sense, but we had many frustrating moments working through it. Nevertheless, Charles and I were very close. He clung to me much of the time. My niece Lori was a bubbly little three-year-old girl, and my nephew Michael was just a giggling little one-year-old baby.

Suzanne was happy I was there to help her with the kids, and they loved me. I always felt that they treated me like their 'hero' uncle. I did my best to mentor them all, including Charles, giving him lots of love and patience. I changed a lot of diapers. I would play piano for them quite a bit.

Suzanne and Bill had a huge pool table in their den. It was always covered with unfolded, clean clothes and other knick-knacks, like a HUGE junk drawer! Suzy was overwhelmed, but she handled it like a pro.

Suzanne's husband Bill, my brother-in-law was kind of odd. He was very quiet. He usually only spoke when spoken to, unless he had a couple of drinks late at night when my dad visited, and they would stay up and tell jokes, trying to outdo each other well into the night. He wasn't mean to me, but I think he wanted to impress me, or possibly help me to "man up" when we were together.

He would take me out to shoot quail out of the sky. On the way to the lake area, he would drive a hundred miles an hour. I would act as if I wasn't petrified as my hand was frozen to the handle on the door. I actually was a good shot, but I avoided hitting the quail because I didn't want to kill the cute little birds! It was the same way when we went fishing. I felt sorry for the worms! I dutifully fished, though and caught a few, here and there. Bill did try to give me a vibe, and his dry humor never eluded me. He worked hard for his family, selling insurance and rapidly moving up in the ranks of *General American Life.*

•••••

Suzy gave me the option to stay with her in Greensboro and go to seventh grade there. My life was topsy-turvy; Suzy's house was the closest thing to normalcy I had left in my life. I agreed, and she enrolled me into a new school. This school had just been built, and it was gorgeous, but here I was again, not knowing anybody.

I enrolled in band but they already had a piano player. I had to pick an instrument so I picked flute. I played that flute for a whole two weeks until Bill found out that I was not planning to go back to San Diego. He had never given his permission, and he wasn't about to have me actually live with them, so he put me on the next plane back to my mother in California.

•••••

When I got back to San Diego, I found that my mother had moved out of the house on Rockhurst drive in Del Cerro and over to a house on Lake Andrita Drive in La Mesa, another neighborhood a little further East in San Diego County. Kathy and Betsy were also living there.

Elaine enrolled me into yet another school, *Pershing Junior High School*, and I went there for almost three months. I was lost, already in my second school in seventh grade and somehow, I didn't 'click' at this school. I was becoming an awkward pre-teen, and I had no friends. I was miserable. Seventh grade was more complicated and I had virtually no help from home. My mother and my sisters were all caught up in their own lives.

CHAPTER SIXTEEN
Palm Springs, California

My parents decided to reconcile. Maynard came back from Memphis, and he took my mother, my sister Kathy and me on a little trip up to Lake Arrowhead. Kathy and I bonded all over again. She was my little mother at times. It was kind of weird but also really great to have my parents together again. They really had a passionate relationship, regardless of whether that passion manifested as love or hate.

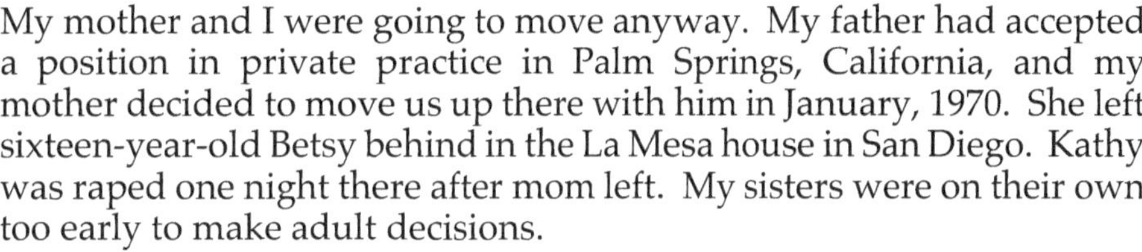
Kathy and Betsy 1969

The opposite of love is not hatred, but indifference. Love and hate are equally passionate emotions. Chances are... if you hate someone you once loved, you're not yet over them.

On January 12, 1970, my sister Kathy had her eighteenth birthday. On that day, my mother got into a shouting match with my sister and threw her out. Kathy would never forget, and she had a lot of trouble forgiving my mother for that day for the rest of her life. For a short while afterward, Kathy lived with her boyfriend, Andy Robinson.

My mother and I were going to move anyway. My father had accepted a position in private practice in Palm Springs, California, and my mother decided to move us up there with him in January, 1970. She left sixteen-year-old Betsy behind in the La Mesa house in San Diego. Kathy was raped one night there after mom left. My sisters were on their own too early to make adult decisions.

•••••

Life was difficult for my sisters in San Diego. Betsy was only fifteen, and she got involved with a guy named Jim Arnott. Jim eventually became a close brother-in-law to me, but my first impression of him was rough. He appeared to love methamphetamine, shooting guns, fast cars and basically anything that boosted the adrenaline. To me, my sisters seemed lost for a time, until my three sisters decided to move together into a huge old Victorian-style house on Washington Street near downtown San Diego.

For the first time, I didn't have a sister living with me to turn to. It was going to be just me with my mother and father in a fragile relationship, in a small apartment in Palm Springs.

•••••

A couple years before we moved to the desert, my parents and I had taken a trip to Palm Springs shortly before Maynard retired from the Navy and moved to Memphis for a year by himself. We had attended the groundbreaking of *Eisenhower Medical Center*. At that time, Maynard was trying to decide where to set up private practice when he was out of the Navy, and my parents liked the idea of Palm Springs before they separated.

I remember we stayed at the *Desi Arnaz Hotel* in Indian Wells, a suburb of Palm Springs. I thought the desert was cool, almost exotic. Golf courses were everywhere. Palm trees lined cloudless, sunny skies at the base of a huge mountain. One could ride the *Palm Springs Aerial Tramway*, the largest single-span tram in the world, and be lifted up thousands of feet to the mountaintop within minutes.

Just a two-hour drive from the beaches of San Diego or the huge metropolis of Los Angeles, it felt like it was nestled into its own little world behind the mountain. Desert life was different; it was slower, hotter, dustier and drier than other climates. The air was cleaner; the water was fresher. You needed to acclimate, but when you adjusted it was a magical place to be in so many ways.

The desert is ugly and beautiful at the same time.

During the winter, it would snow on the mountain and the views were breathtaking. It was different from my little beach home, but my parents both thought it would be a good idea to move away from San Diego and get a fresh start when they decided to reconcile. It felt clean. The roads were wide; elderly people dominated the desert, and as a result, life felt slower and easier.

I think quite possibly my parent's relationship had suffered too much collateral damage already. There was too much water under the bridge, too much resentment between them, but they were both clinging on to the dream they had created so many years ago. There always exists a forever bond between two people who have given birth to a child, or five.

•••••

In January of 1970, my father accepted a position in a practice with Dr. Fitzmorris in Palm Springs. We were back, this time attending the dedication of the newly built *Eisenhower Medical Center.*

My father was in the front of the audience as one of the attending doctors, and his photo was on the front page of the *Desert Sun* newspaper, right there in the middle of the audience. My mom and I were in attendance, but more towards the back.

Bob Hope and Frank Sinatra spoke at the event. California Governor Ronald Reagan spoke and finally President Richard Nixon made some comments. It was exciting for me to be in the presence of so many stars and dignitaries.

•••••

Palm Springs took a moment to get used to. As I mentioned, it was primarily a retirement community when we first arrived. In fact, one of Bob Hope's jokes that day was something about the hospital being in a perfect location, because the average age here is deceased! People would literally wear their pajamas and slippers to the grocery store, getting there in their golf carts. Movie stars were everywhere. It was not uncommon to run into Bob and Delores Hope window-shopping, Red Skelton signing autographs, William Holden drinking at a bar, or Liberace walking his dogs.

We were living in a two-bedroom apartment with an outside entrance on the second floor of a large building, in a complex called *The Springs Apartments*. It was the first time I hadn't lived in a house, and the first time I didn't have my sisters with me.

•••••

I was going into my third school in seventh grade alone! My mother enrolled me into *Nellie Coffman Junior High School* in Palm Springs. The school was already halfway through their year of studies and it was weird for me trying to integrate at first, picking up on lesson plans I wasn't familiar with, and meeting new kids.

My mother tried to get me into the school band, but they were full, so she enrolled me in choir. Lo and behold, I found out I really could sing! I loved choir; it was my saving grace. Mardale Nokes was a young teacher, very vivacious, and she picked up on my talent (and my shyness) immediately and decided to pull that right out of me. She took me under her wing, and it meant the world to me, as I was transitioning into yet another new life.

There was a girl in choir named Sheryl Otte. She was a year older than me but in the same grade, and of course she didn't know I existed. I was infatuated with her beauty! She had a darling face and long, flowing dark hair. She was sweet and kind, and really my first crush. I tried so hard not to let her see me staring at her, but I couldn't help it. She was like heaven to me.

One day, later when I was in eighth grade, I put a note into Sheryl's locker proclaiming my undying love for her, and then I spent the next four hours, horrified that I had done it, trying to get the note out of that locker! I couldn't get the note out. She never mentioned it to me, but we became friends, although I swear I went mute whenever I was around her.

•••••

Kurt Handshuh was also in choir. He had recently moved to Palm Springs from New Jersey. His parents had divorced, and his mother remarried a man named Stanley Gold. Kurt's mom Marlene was gorgeous and young and hip, and Stanley was a conservative, hard-working upholsterer. It was a mismatch and the marriage didn't last long, but when I met Kurt, he and his nine-year-old sister Cathy were living with Marlene and Stanley in a nice home in the *Deepwell* area of Palm Springs. Kurt was a cool kid and displaced like me, and we became inseparable friends throughout Junior High School. We would ride our bikes from one end of the city to the other.

After school, I would go over to the *Boys' Club* with Kurt. We would play pool or foosball, or swim in the big pool at the club. I liked it there for the most part. There was a lot to do in Palm Springs. Kurt and I would ride our bikes to *Smoke Tree Stables* and go horseback riding. We would hike up in the beautiful Indian Canyons, even in *Tahquitz Canyon*, which was off limits. Waterfalls, big rocks and the occasional big horn sheep truly transported us to paradise in a matter of minutes.

Kurt's cousin Jeff Gold was visiting with his sisters from Los Angeles. Jeff was our age, and the three of us went out into the desert looking for lizards. We came upon a man. We thought he was sleeping. I went to wake the man and touched him and his whole body moved. I saw a fly crawl out of his mouth, and I screamed, "He's dead!" We ran out of the desert and down the street to a telephone booth, and called the police. Apparently, the man had drank and wandered out into the desert the night before. He had a heart attack and died in the desert, alone. His family was notified and they were grateful to us that we found him.

The police drove us back to Kurt's house in the evening after their investigation, and Kurt's nine-year-old sister Cathy saw us getting out of the police car. She ran out and said, "What happened?" Kurt looked at her, brushing her off and said, "Official business," and we laughed through our tears. It was a bizarre day.

•••••

Not long after we settled into our new life in Palm Springs, my father started drinking heavily again. Alcoholism is a nasty disease. As it progressed, his behavior became more and more belligerent when he was drunk.

One day, Kurt and I were riding our bikes down Arenas Road in Palm Springs and we saw Maynard inside a pool hall. We went inside and my dad was playing pool with some other drunks. He saw us and took two hundred dollars bill out of his pocket and gave one to each of us, basically telling us to get lost in a very nice way. Kurt was thrilled! We took the money and left. My dad was a terrible, stinky drunk, but you couldn't say he wasn't a colorful person.

One night when I was sleeping, my mother woke me up, crying and screaming that my father had come home drunk and he was going to kill us! She made me get up and help her put the dresser against my bedroom door, and we huddled in my bedroom as he pounded on my locked door and yelled for us to let him in. This went on for an hour or two until he gave up and passed out.

The next morning, he was apologetic. Again, he kneeled at my bedside asking my forgiveness. Again, he said, "Say a prayer for me," and I said, "I always do."

That morning, I went out and downstairs to ride my bike to school, and someone had cut the chain lock and stolen my ten-speed bike. Life basically sucked for me that day.

•••••

A bright spot during this time was when I met the famous actress Elizabeth Taylor and her husband, one of my heroes, outstanding actor Richard Burton. They were Hollywood royalty, always splashed on the tabloids and bigger than life. Maynard had removed a hemorrhoid…or something to that effect…from Elizabeth Taylor, and they became friends during the experience. My father's charm and knowledge of Broadway shows, Shakespeare and the films they had starred in, won her over. When she was released from the hospital, we were invited to visit them for an afternoon at their home in Palm Springs.

My mother, father, sister Kathy and I spent most of a day with Richard Burton and Elizabeth Taylor. Richard couldn't have been more kind or accommodating. Hearing that I had played *Hamlet*, he allowed me to recite the soliloquy and gave me an acting lesson. He recalled how, when they were trying to adopt their daughter, he had to perform in front of some dignitaries who stood in the way of the adoption in order for it to go forward.

Richard Burton, being from the United Kingdom, hated these people who had oppressed his own people during the war, but he performed out of obligation and a desire to adopt this beautiful girl; as he performed the soliloquy, he acted as if he picked his nose and during the entire performance, he was trying to get the booger off of his hand and his clothes. It was hilarious to watch him replicate the performance, especially for twelve-year-old me! It was his way of fulfilling his obligation to these people he hated, while literally giving them the 'finger'!

Richard Burton also admitted that, since they were big drinkers, Elizabeth wanted alcohol against doctor's orders while she had been in the hospital previously. Richard told us how he injected oranges with vodka, and brought her a basket of fruit. She sat, smiling, sucking on the oranges all day! Yes, they were a fiery couple with a troubled relationship that didn't last, but on that day, they were so wonderful to us, and I will never forget their sincerity and generosity of spirit. Elizabeth gave my father a beautiful signed portrait of herself holding one of her big jewels, and he cherished that photo for several years until it incinerated in our house fire in 1975… but, that's another story yet to come.

•••••

As the months went by, it became increasingly apparent that my parent's reconciliation was a mistake. My mother and I endured many more incidents similar to the night we barricaded ourselves in the bedroom. It was a tragedy to me; I wanted so much for my parents to stay together, but it was also an extremely toxic environment living alone with them together.

Don't stay together for the sake of the kids if your life together is more toxic and abusive for them than it would be if you were apart.

In May of 1970, we were going to take a trip to San Diego to see my sisters and spend the weekend. My new best friend Kurt went with us on the trip, and we planned a day ice-skating at the rink. When Kurt and I got onto the rink, we started some horseplay. Kurt chased me and slapped me on the back, and then I went to chase him to slap him back. He took a sharp turn, and when I turned, I fell on my wrist and broke both bones in my arm at the wrist. It was the most excruciatingly painful experience I had ever endured. My parents rushed me to the Naval Hospital and they put a cast on my bent arm, all the way up to the shoulder.

We drove back to Palm Springs that night, and I was in terrible pain. My father knelt at my bedside and he told me that his belief was that for every bit of pain we feel in this life, we have that much more of a special place when we get to Heaven. He tried hard to comfort me, and I loved him for that. My father truly was two different personalities: A kind, sober man, generous of spirit, and an ugly, angry drunken man. But, the little boy in me cried out for the kind father I needed at this moment, and he showed up.

I was supposed to play piano for the spring concert for the choir, and I hadn't rehearsed, so I was relieved in a sense because my broken arm got me out of that gig. At the spring concert, Mrs. Nokes awarded me a scholarship to attend the summer session as a member of the International Youth Festival Choir at *ISOMATA*, The *Idyllwild School of Music and the Arts*. *ISOMATA* was then affiliated with the *University of Southern California*. It was located up in Idyllwild, CA in the mountains above Palm Springs. I was to go for three weeks in August, between seventh and eighth grade. This was a shock to me, and a huge honor for a seventh grader. It kind of validated that, yes, I could actually sing.

•••••

My mother found a house for us over on the North end of Palm Springs before school ended. It was a comfortable, three-bedroom house, and it was particularly nice to be out of the small apartment with all the bad memories.

Moving to this house put me into another school district, but my mother knew that I had already been shuffled through three different schools in seventh grade, and she promised to keep me at *Nellie Coffman Junior High*, even though it would be a drive for her every day. The North End of Palm Springs was in the wind tunnel, and as a result, we would get blinding sandstorms on a regular basis. It took a little getting used to. We would joke that the guy on the end of the block was the only one who paid for trash pickup!

CHAPTER SEVENTEEN
Crazy Summer of 1970

When I finished seventh grade, around my twelfth birthday in June of 1970, my cast was removed from my arm, and I began the process of physical therapy to bring my wrist back. Bending my arm was difficult after six weeks of a full arm cast, but I was young and I healed quickly.

•••••

My Uncle Ted and Aunt Candy invited me to fly in their single engine *Cessna 172* airplane with their daughter, my four-year-old niece, Michelle, down into Mexico. It was a relief to get away from my parents, who were arguing daily and becoming increasingly more toxic to each other.

It was also nice to be out of the double-digit heat in Palm Springs in June. The desert heat in the summer was a whole different animal. It was brutal.

Candace and Ted Witt
1971

We flew to Guymas in Mexico and then on to Mazatlán, Puerto Vallarta and Guadalajara. On our way back, we stopped in Alamos and then flew back into San Diego. It was amazing to me to experience all of these exotic locations, and so wonderful to be with even-tempered, loving family members who took very good care of me. I ate food I had never eaten.

I had never experienced another culture to this extent. My parents had brought me a handful of times to Tijuana, right across the border from San Diego, but it was nothing like this. The further south we went in Mexico, the more beautiful it seemed.

Mexico is a country steeped in a rich history, yet plagued with deep poverty. Children begged on the streets; people lived in cardboard shacks with no electricity and no running water, yet we stayed at exclusive resorts and ate the best food. The experience reminded me once again of how fortunate I was to be born free in America. It also gave me a clear understanding of our obligations, as humans, to do whatever we can to help those less fortunate than us.

I wrote a journal on the trip, and I kept it for many years following that experience. Puerto Vallarta was just a gorgeous, tropical place and it was the first time I saw a full bar that you could swim up to, in a pool at our resort. My Uncle Ted was really a steadying influence on my young life, a calm in the middle of my storm. My Aunt Candy made me feel like one of theirs, and it meant the world to me. They knew the turmoil of my life, and they wanted me to stay centered and good through it all.

•••••

When we returned from Mexico at the end of June, I got word that my sister Judy had experienced a terrible tragedy.

Judy had just graduated from *San Diego State* with a Bachelor's Degree in Psychology. A professor at the college was going to drive his *Volkswagen* van across country to see relatives, and he invited whoever wanted to go with him. He had one of those funky *VW* vans, painted in psychedelic colors, with peace signs on it. Everybody in that universe was a hippie.

Judy and her boyfriend Peter decided to go on the trip. Judy planned to see our grandparents in Memphis along the way. All in all, nine young people including the young professor packed into this van to take the trip. Three sat in front, three in the middle seat, and three took turns in the very back, usually sleeping.

Volkswagen vans in that day were very dangerous. The engine was in the back, so there was nothing between the driver and another car if it was hit in the front. Even the metal that encompassed the shell of the vehicle was thin. It was a cheap automobile, but it was a favorite of young people back then. Even in a van, nine people were excessive, but it was the era of free love, drugs and living life to abandon.

By the time this band of hippie travelers made it into New Mexico, it was nighttime. Somewhere outside of Albuquerque, Judy and Peter had rotated to the very back of the van and were going to try to get some sleep along with another guy, not completely able to stretch out in their closed quarters. They drifted off, and at some point, Peter was shocked awake by the swerve of the van. As he raised his body up to look at what was happening, he witnessed a logging truck coming towards them, swerving to avoid hitting an animal. As the truck swerved back into its own lane, the chains broke and the huge heavy logs fell onto the Volkswagen van. Instinctively as he saw it coming, Peter dived on top of Judy and the other guy sleeping in the back.

The logs crushed the van. All six people sitting in the front two seats were killed instantly. Peter's back was crushed. Judy's back was broken and the other guy's leg was crushed. The three survivors were airlifted to a hospital in Santa Fe.

Peter was in a coma, and his injuries were so severe, he was eventually flown to *Rancho Los Amigos Hospital* in Downey, California. He remained in a coma for almost a year, and doctors performed a *Harrington's Rod Procedure*, a surgery that basically fused his crushed back into a straight position with rods. When he finally came out of the coma, he was paraplegic for the rest of his life.

Judy's back was severely broken, and she healed slowly in Santa Fe. The doctors and nurses who helped her were mostly Native American. In the process of her healing, she became enamored by Native American culture. There was an elder of the Arapahoe tribe named John Pedro. He was a kind, wise old man and she enjoyed so much learning from him and from his family the sacred Indian customs and traditions that had been passed down for millennia. Judy was to stay until she was able to travel, which might take six months or more.

•••••

Santa Fe was tucked into the mountains of New Mexico, a quiet mecca for travelers who wanted to get away from it all. Red Clay ridges jutted like skyscrapers of red ice bulging vertically out of the arid soil. As winter approached, snow blanketed the mountain village, and Judy learned to walk again, gingerly up and down the steep hills with her Native American guides.

After several months, Judy was cleared to travel, and she flew to California. My grandmother Gizi was still living up in Long Beach, which was close to the hospital where Peter had been admitted. Judy lived with Gizi for several months, and they bonded heavily for really the first time.

During the day, Judy would go over to the hospital and visit Peter. Although he was in a coma, she would read to him and talk to him as if he was coherent. She would tell stories of the Native Americans and really anything that may jar him into consciousness. When I came to visit, I would play the piano for him. I remember I had learned this song in choir entitled *Io Ti Voria*, and I would play it and then sing it in Italian.

Eventually, when Peter came out of the coma, he recalled that he was aware of everything that was going on around him, he just couldn't respond. And... he recited every word of *Io Ti Voria* in Italian as I had sung it. It was almost eerie.

Peter would never be the same. He was so intelligent and so hip for so long, and then all of a sudden, he was a little bit insane from what had happened to him. He would ramble in his speech and go off onto tangents.

He was to spend the rest of his life in a wheelchair, and it was all too much really for Judy to handle. At some point, after he left the hospital, she went on with her life and he moved back to San Diego with his father. It was tragic for me to see this broken man who had been so full of life and energy. I did contact him several times, and I would listen on the phone while he rambled on insensibly, patiently trying to understand and to tell him I loved him and tried to stay in touch until he finally died about twenty-five years later.

•••••

Following Judy's accident, in July, 1970 while Judy was in the hospital in Santa Fe, my parents sent me off to summer camp, to the Boys' Club's *Pathfinder Ranch* up by Idyllwild. I spent a week up there...I didn't shower for the entire week. By the time I made it home, I was filthy and disgusting!

We rode horses during the day, and at night I heard disgusting, perverse jokes by the campfire told by some counselors (who shouldn't have been counselors) for the first time in my life.

I remember on several days we played a pick-up basketball game. There was a tall, African-American boy named James on my team. We would all yell, "James, throw it to me!" But, James was more than content to keep the ball, drive it up the court and make all of the baskets for us, all by himself, each and every time. It was a spectator sport for me and the other teammates, except, of course, for James. In spite of his lack of team consciousness or the ability to see beyond himself, James was a pretty good player.

Immediately when I returned to Palm Springs at the end of July of 1970, it was time to go to *ISOMATA*. I was the youngest person in the choir. I'm pretty sure I was the only twelve-year-old almost-eighth-grader there. I was used to being the most excellent vocalist in my choir. All of a sudden, I was one of fifty of the very best vocalists in my age group, from all walks of life.

I was surrounded by people who were so much more polished than I was. It was truly a humbling experience. I had a couple of friends from my school in Palm Springs with me. One of them was Sheryl Otte, the beautiful girl who was my crush. I was determined just to somehow get to know her, but I never got up the nerve to actually hang out with her.

Michael Schwartz was another kid at *ISOMATA*. He went to the other Junior High School in Palm Springs, *Raymond Cree*. We became fast friends. Michael was kind of bohemian. He was half black, half Jewish, and super cool. He loved marijuana, and we spent some time getting stoned together.

I had an acquaintance, a boy in his early teens; he stayed in the same dorm at *ISOMATA*. This boy was extremely religious. He loved to talk about Jesus. Zealous eyes punctuated a pale face with bad complexion. Most of the other kids avoided him, but I could tell he was a good boy, so I talked to him here and there to make him feel more at ease. The enlightened, almost fanatical look in his eyes made it easy for anyone to predict that he would grow up to become an evangelist or minister.

One night, he asked me if I knew how to pray. I thought it was an odd question, but I had an inquisitive mind, so I answered as best I knew how, from a teenager's perspective. I was raised Catholic and schooled well in the Catholic doctrine, but my mother's experience with *Religious Science* had opened me up to new thoughts regarding spirituality.

He told me that he had a system for prayer: First, he asked forgiveness for his sins. Then, he thanked God for all of the blessings bestowed upon him. Next, he asked God to please watch over all of his loved ones. Only then, would he ask the Lord for specific help or guidance for anything else. It's funny, because I don't even remember this kid's name, but from then on, for the rest of my life, I followed his "system" of prayer… and, strangely enough, the method gave me comfort in hard times.

•••••

I was going to try out for the coveted solo, singing *In Idyllwild*, the song written specifically for *ISOMATA* by Meredith Willson, the outstanding Broadway composer who had written all of the classic music from *The Music Man*, and other great shows. When I was waiting for my turn, I heard some of the other boys singing, and I was too embarrassed to even try out next to them.

The solo, that year, was given to a boy named Kevin Golden. Years later, I heard Kevin had died way too young, and I was glad he had his moment in the sun. He sang the hell out of it, with a strong, vibrato-filled voice.

The choir director was a stately old man named Robert Holmes. Mr. Holmes, I believe, had been the choir director for years at *Beverly Hills High School*, and he was an amazing teacher and mentor. We would branch off into smaller groups to learn our parts, and the staff always planned fun activities, mostly musical. It was the first time I really felt camaraderie among my peers. Following the final tearful show, which we performed with the full choir and orchestra in front of our parents and educators, I left *ISOMATA* determined to be a better vocalist and a better person. The experience left a huge impact on my life.

I arrived back in Palm Springs just in time to see my father say goodbye. Things had gotten even worse between my parents over the summer, and Maynard had decided to take a position in Kennett, Missouri, a little cotton town in the Bootheel of Southeast Missouri.

CHAPTER EIGHTEEN
Living Alone with my Mother

Partially out of guilt, and also to help me to have my own way to get around, my mother bought me a new ten-speed bike. It was a *Motobecane Namade*, a very nice bike. To my surprise, Kurt's mom had gone out and bought him the very same bike as mine, that very same day. Since my mom and Kurt's mom didn't communicate much, and we went separately, we were amazed at the coincidence. It was great to be mobile again. Kurt and I rode our bikes everywhere.

Kurt Handshuh
and Me
Palm Springs
1970

•••••

Although I was devastated to see my father leave, my life with both of my parents alone in Palm Springs had been far from acceptable. I truly lived a tormented life throughout that entire six months, always worried about my mother's safety, and even more worried that my father would finally do something so stupid, it would do irreparable harm to him, or someone else, or even worse.

I was surprised to see Maynard choose such an obscure place to go. At one point, he was being courted by the finest medical centers in the world. He had actually been in charge of the largest Army-Navy hospital in the world. But, in his heart, he harkened back to his childhood in a small town and he always had the dream of being a country doctor.

Tad in 1971

At first, that was easier said than done. His years away from the backwoods of West Virginia had produced a sophisticated scholar and an excellent doctor. He had run huge hospitals in the Navy, and he was used to giving commands. He was a reader of classics and a writer of sonnets and prose. Maynard's knowledge base had become huge, and it took some time for him to learn to accept and embrace the 'simple' people around him.

Sometimes, these people were so poor that they would 'pay' him with a chicken, or watermelons. At some point, he actually was amazed to learn that keeping it simple made life easier for the people he served, and there was certain wisdom in the simplicity of their lifestyles.

Maynard's brother, George, by this time, led a *Southern Baptist* church, preaching his gospel in Hornersville, Missouri, just about twenty miles south of Kennett. George had found an opening for Maynard in the office of Drs. Dunmire and Cash in Kennett, and convinced my dad to come back to be close to him. A large hospital, located in the heart of Kennett, which was the county seat, was essential as a force for jobs and healthcare. The hospital serviced most of that area from the Mississippi River in Hayti and Caruthersville, over into Rector and Piggott, Arkansas.

My Uncle Bill Sisler

Kennett was a typical Midwestern town, with a large Town Square. An old stately courthouse loomed in the middle of the Town Square; aging buildings, some empty and boarded up, some with thriving businesses, surrounded it. The population always seemed to stay the same. Some people left, some died, some stayed. There wasn't much to do in Kennett if you weren't a farmer or storeowner. It had the feeling of *Brigadoon,* the mythical town that appears every hundred years and never changes.

Bill and Doris

•••••

My Uncle Bill with Ann and Billy
Circa 1948

Maynard's other surviving brother, my uncle Bill, lived only a four-hour drive north in a suburb of St. Louis, with his wife Marlin and their young girls, Julie and Amy. Bill's first wife, Doris, had died young and left him to raise his son Billy and his oldest daughter, Ann. Ann lived in St. Louis as well. It wasn't long after Maynard moved to Kennett that Bill's son, Billy, died of immune deficiency syndrome in Memphis. Bill was an engineer for Monsanto, and he was in politics as an Alderman in Crestwood, close to St. Louis. Maynard relied on Bill's evenness even still, and he was happy to be close to his brothers.

After Maynard was settled into an apartment in Kennett, he sent for my sister Betsy and me to visit. We spent a week with him around Thanksgiving. He was already dating a woman named Sandy Venters. Sandy had a daughter named Leandra who was about eight-years-old. Leann was a sweet, outgoing child but her mother was kind of weird to Betsy and me.

Amy, Bill, Marlin and Julie Sisler 1990s

Sandy was a nurse, and we had the distinct impression that she was trying to 'snag' a doctor to marry her and be a father to her daughter. Maynard hadn't slowed down on his drinking, and I remembered again that smell of sweat and alcohol lingering in his apartment. When we left, I got another letter to read on the plane from him, and again I cried, reading his lines of longing until the next time he would see his son again.

•••••

Although my mom and I lived in a nice house now in Palm Springs, life was not okay. Elaine had suffered yet another nervous breakdown, and she was taking her *Valium* again and drinking a bottle or two of wine some nights. I was alone with her, and again, I parented my parent. I worried about her night and day.

At the age of twelve, I would take her car keys after she passed out crying, take money out of her purse and drive the back streets to the grocery store to get us food.

In August, our air conditioner went out for almost four days. The temperatures exceeded 118 degrees that week, and it was almost unbearable inside the house. I learned a way to stay cool while I was sleeping. I would get a bowl of water and dip my feet in the water several times during the night. An oscillating fan set to high blasted on me and when it hit my feet, my whole body cooled off. It was an even greater lesson in mind over matter.

We can overcome so much with the power of our own minds.

Elaine was getting a small check every month from my father and she was too emotionally unstable just yet to go back to giving piano lessons or to perform in a restaurant, so I went out and got a couple of jobs bussing tables on weekends. I worked weekend mornings at *Sherman's Deli.* Years later, Sherman Harris, the owner, remained my close friend until his death. Also, Joe Hanna, who managed *Sherman's Steak House* at the same location, ended up being a huge influence on my life, as I'll outline later.

At night, I would bus tables at *Giorgio's Italian Ristorante.* Giorgio was this tiny, chubby Italian man who would scream, "Thatsa Nice" all night as he greeted his customers. His crusty old wife Luisa was the chef, and you could always hear her yelling or barking orders from the kitchen. Luisa was a tyrant, but she liked me and she left me mostly alone. I would soak the labels off of wine bottles for them to pour their generic house wine back into; I would carefully remove the labels from the water and put them all up on the wall, wet and gooey, to dry. Luisa loved that, and she told me years later before she died that those labels stayed up in that room for many years until they sold the place.

My Eighth Grade Photo 1970-1971

•••••

I was in choir again in eighth grade, and Mrs. Nokes put me into Madrigals. Sheryl Otte was also in Madrigals, along with another girl, Linda Janes, who had also been to *ISOMATA.* Linda was a sweet, vivacious, tall red-haired girl. Very outgoing, she had a huge singing voice. We became fast friends.

We would practice next door at the *Palm Springs High School* auditorium in the evenings. One night after choir practice, I was waiting outside of the school for my mother to pick me up. She had some wine and she had fallen asleep. I sat outside of the school until almost midnight, shivering, until she drove up, apologizing. I wasn't even angry; I was actually relieved to see her.

I really, really worried about my mother all the time, and it was "You and me against the world," with her. She was grieving the death of her marriage. She was not okay, and this desire, this need I had inside me to 'fix' her or to help her overcome her problems, to help her to stay alive, never left me; as I've mentioned and I later found out, it reared its ugly head later as an almost neurotic protectionism over my companions, which literally permeated every relationship I had moving forward for as long as she was on the planet.

•••••

My sister Kathy came up to visit a few times, and she started to think it might be a good idea to move up to the desert just to be close to me. Kathy was worried about the burden on my shoulders with our mother, and she had always been my protector. At first, Kathy would drive out from San Diego in her big, white panel truck and spend the weekend. She would take me out to the back roads and let me drive for hours at a time, so that I could become a better driver when I had to drive mom's car, alone.

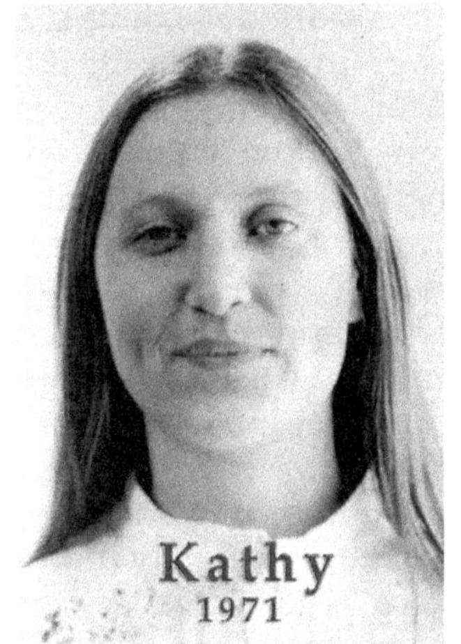
Kathy
1971

Soon, she decided to move up to the desert. Kathy got a job as a lab technician at *Desert Hospital*, and she and her new boyfriend Jack Wexler moved into a trailer up at this huge tangerine ranch in Thousand Palms, about twenty miles from where I lived with our mom in Palm Springs.

There was a sign outside the tangerine ranch, "Dr. C.C. Carlson". Dr. Carlson (we called him Doctor Kuh-Kuh-Carlson) was a crusty old man who owned the property but never showed up there. It was an investment for him, and he had someone manage the property. He had allowed about twenty trailers onto his property, which were mostly occupied by hippies. Kurt and I would go to the ranch to visit. In the middle of the ranch, surrounded by hundreds of tangerine trees, was a swimming hole.

All of these hippies, including my sister and her boyfriend, would just walk around naked all day. Kathy had a few gorgeous girlfriends, and to a couple thirteen-year-olds, it was pretty much heaven to hang out with a lot of beautiful naked young women. And… in retrospect …having had children of my own later, it was totally inappropriate. But this was the evolution of our life after the crazy 1960's. All of the young people I knew were rebels. And we had all the tangerines we could eat, fresh and free.

Kathy was a free spirit. Her songwriting and musical talent amazed me. She mostly wrote songs about peace and love. Kathy and I would spend hours playing and singing together, with her on guitar and me on piano, mostly. We were invited to perform together on the *Red Baron Radio Show.* We went on to the show and sang a couple original songs together. We sounded great together. In retrospect, I'm not sure how the audience of mostly elderly people might have reacted to our songs of peace and love. They were probably hoping for Sinatra.

One key to happiness: Be grateful for what you have, instead of longing for something you can't.

Later, when I was in ninth grade, I had a little girlfriend for a couple months named Julie Lentz. She was in seventh grade, only a year younger but two grades below me. She was beautiful, with long, flowing dark hair and a pixie smile, but she wasn't Sheryl Otte. And I was crazy about Sheryl. Julie was enamored with me, though, and it felt good for the first time in life to be with someone who actually wanted me.

Once, I took Julie out to the tangerine ranch and we kissed heavily and petted each other a little out by the swimming hole (with our bathing suits ON). We got to about second base, but I was filled with a conscience that wanted to love and protect her, and also just a little too young to let my hormones entirely take over. It was pretty exciting, though, for both of us. We became friends once again many years later, but never made it past second, not even to third base.

•••••

But, back in my eighth-grade year, after a few months, my mom started improving. She was in counseling and group therapy. In the beginning of her therapy sessions, though, it was kind of rocky. I remember her coming home from group therapy one day and telling me that she learned that you have to "stay in your own back yard", to learn to let go and go with the flow… while in the same breath slapping my hand for fidgeting and saying "Stop that!" I'm guessing I learned to develop eternal patience by being with Elaine. But, I loved my mother unconditionally.

My Mother, Elaine 1973

Elaine started back to teaching piano, and went back to college, enrolling into the *College of the Desert*. Eventually, she got her *Associate in Arts* degree, and she began to finally perform as a classical piano soloist again with the *Desert Symphony*. Elaine was finding her way back from the darkness.

With no real parenting, Kurt and I started stealing stuff from grocery stores. We would go in and shoplift little things like candy. It was a thrill for two bored teenagers. Once, I was at *Vons* with my mom and I went around the store to another aisle without her. I put a candy bar in my pocket, and just at that moment, I saw the store manager out of the corner of my eye. He had seen me steal the candy. I quickly walked around the corner, took the candy bar out of my pocket and ran back to where my mom was shopping. The store manager marched up and demanded that I empty my pockets. My mother was appalled. I emptied my pockets and nothing was there. He told her that he SAW me steal a candy bar. My mother told him, "My son would NEVER do that! How dare you!" The manager walked away in disgust. After that experience, I gave up shoplifting. I didn't want to be a bad boy. I was just doing stupid teenage pranks.

•••••

Joanna Hodges was a famous concert pianist, and a winner of the esteemed *Van Cliburn International Piano Competition*. My mother had met her in Long Beach. Joanna's mom lived around the corner from my grandmother Gizi. Joanna started a competition out in Palm Desert called the *Joanna Hodges International Piano Competition*. Many of the world's finest pianists arrived to compete, and a spark was lit again within my mother. It was great to see her come around more and more, although she still suffered from bouts of depression through it all.

I was letting my hair grow really long. It was nearly 1971 and most of the boys had long hair. I could tell that my mother was starting to feel better when she started chasing me around the house with a pair of scissors, trying to pin me down to cut my hair. I was faster than her…

•••••

My best friend Kurt Handshuh was involved in the Jewish Youth Group at the *Temple Isaiah* in Palm Springs, and he would drag me to their events. It consisted of a group of Jewish kids our age who got together and had fun. Sometimes we would go on field trips or overnight camping in the mountains above Palm Springs. It became like a second family to me, and I was always grateful for their kindness and acceptance.

I also learned about the Jewish faith, of which, up to that point I knew nothing about, having been raised Catholic. It was cool!

Once or twice we would go over to a friend's house with a small group of girls and kiss or play spin the bottle. It felt exciting and daring, but it was mostly innocent. These kids took me in as one of their own, and it meant the world to me.

From that day on, I had a much greater understanding and affinity to Jewish people in general. Years later, I would find out that I had a good amount of Jewish blood in my DNA, but at that point, I was a displaced Catholic boy who was grateful to have friends who embraced me wholeheartedly.

•••••

My mom started getting into taking all kinds of vitamins and supplements. I have to admit that I eventually inherited that trait from her, becoming a huge vitamin freak in my later life.

She would give me vitamins to take, as well as some new supplements she had discovered. Usually, Elaine would give me vitamins to take in the morning before school. Once, she gave me niacin, and when I walked into school, I started flushing and hot flashing. Another time, she gave me a garlic pill. I remember burping in class, and this awful, ugly smell came out of my mouth. Another time, she gave me a cayenne pepper pill. By the time I got to school, I was snorting fire out of my nose! It was starting to become difficult to trust what she was giving me, although I knew her intentions were good!

•••••

Elaine was no longer able to teach me piano as she had done for so many years. I was becoming a teenager, and I wasn't responding to her the way I used to. She convinced Joanna Hodges to give me private classical instruction in piano. I would go to the practice rooms at the College and Joanna would sit with me and "beat me up," pointing out every small mistake I would make, and forcing me to 'feel' the music through the crescendos and pianoforte moments.

I was playing difficult classical pieces. At some point, I entered the competition for classical students on my level, and I won superior ratings in piano performance, due to her strict instruction. It was a great foundation for everything I would do later. Although I quit playing classical music a couple years later, the discipline and technique I learned would prove to be essential for my eventual success as a pianist.

Being in choir and madrigals really helped me to regain my self-esteem. When I got home, I would pound out all of my frustrations onto the piano, playing for hours at a time. It was a great outlet for attitude adjustment.

•••••

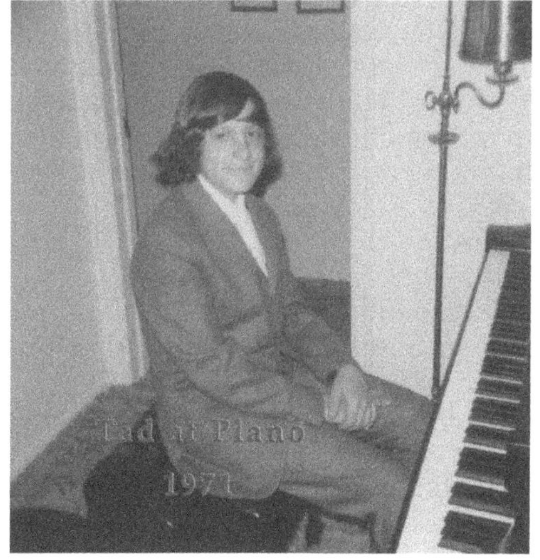

I was still hanging out with Kurt every day. We were inseparable best friends. Kurt would say that I was the one with the brains and he had the common sense. He affectionately called me "Dippy," which I think is short for dipshit. This was not the greatest nickname I ever had.

I spent so many nights at Kurt's house that I had a toothbrush in his bathroom. One night, I was brushing my teeth and from the hallway Kurt and his sister Cathy were laughing hysterically at me. I asked what they were laughing about, and Kurt told me that Cathy had brushed their dog's teeth with my toothbrush. I spit out the water in my mouth and gave them both a dirty look! I was angry for a minute, but we all got along well and played a lot of pranks on each other all the time. It was my solace from the heaviness of life with my mother at home, although life with my mother was starting to improve. I was lost without my dad, and my friendship with Kurt was a good fill-in for my loneliness.

Kurt and I joined a youth Bowling league. We spent a lot of time at the bowling alley, playing pinball or bowling. I became a pretty good bowler during that time. We would go around the back and smoke cigarettes and pot with the other boys. Sometimes, we would buy a "four-finger lid" of weed from someone. Generally, the marijuana was low to mid-grade, with plenty of seeds and stems. I would hide the grass in my bathroom above the ceiling by the fluorescent lights. We spent a lot of time 'stoned'. I bought a "roller" and always seemed to have a plethora of joints to smoke on demand. This habit was part of the culture that we lived in during the late 1960's and early 1970's in California. It was mostly harmless, I believe, but again, in retrospect, I wish I had never done any of that. But, I was a teenager with too much freedom and very little oversight.

•••••

One weekend, my "Uncle" Guy Weismantel came out to visit. His sole purpose was to give me a 'vibe' and be a kind of big brother to me. We talked, went to lunch, and then we searched for a block of wood to carve a saying onto it. I'm pretty sure we carved these words: *The ornaments of a house are the friends who frequent it.* Uncle Guy was a good friend to me when I needed a big brother influence.

When Monday arrived, he took me to school before driving back to Los Angeles, and he saw my pretty, twenty-seven-year-old *World Problems* teacher, Roxanne Ploss. He tried to get me to go to Miss Ploss and ask her if he could take her out, which was gross! We laughed. I couldn't do it. I always remembered that visit, though, and I was grateful that he took time out from his busy life to hang out with me. A year or two later, Guy got married and asked me to be an altar boy at his wedding. Of course, I was honored to participate.

CHAPTER NINETEEN
Coming Into my Teenage Years

From this point forward in my life, I was forced to grow up too soon. I lost my compass when my parents divorced. I had always excelled in school, and suddenly I was struggling on my own, being in charge of myself and of my homework with no real direction. God bless my mother, she was so wrapped up in the sorrow of her divorce, she just needed me to be self-sufficient, and so I did what I knew how to step up to the plate for her. I skated by in school, not working to my potential but still scraping out acceptable grades.

In the middle of my eighth-grade year, around January of 1971, my sister Betsy came out to stay with us for a few weeks. She brought her beautiful dog. He was half German shepherd, half collie, and his name was Oso. He was a beautiful dog, and I really loved having Betsy and her dog at the house. Betsy was mellowing out with me and becoming more of a friend. She had been through so much in her young life, and she understood the hell that I had lived recently. She started to let go of those childhood resentments of me, at least for the time being.

•••••

My sister Judy came out to visit, since she was able to walk a little better. Her back was slowly healing. She was always a calming influence on me, and she laughed at all of my jokes!

Kathy bought a little 150cc *Yamaha* motorcycle and left it for me at the house. I rode the motorcycle all over with reckless abandon, without a helmet. Finally, I got a helmet. One day, Kurt and I took the motorcycle out. Kurt was on the back and I was on front. We thought it would be best for me to wear the helmet, since I was driving and I looked really young. I didn't have a driver's license yet; I wasn't quite thirteen! We were going to drive about forty miles down to Indio to eat at McDonalds. At the time, it was the only fast food place in the desert!

On the way down to Indio, a policeman stopped us. He told me that he probably wouldn't have stopped us if Kurt were wearing the helmet, because at the time California law stated that passengers, not drivers, were required to wear helmets. He gave me a ticket and told us to go straight home. Kurt had to drive. He looked older than me, and the policeman didn't question that he was only thirteen. I had to go to court with my mother for driving without a license. We had to pay a fine. I was devastated! I was a good boy and I didn't want my mother to be disappointed in me. I had gotten in trouble.

In school, I was awarded a second scholarship to *ISOMATA* by Mrs. Nokes. I was to go again in August.

•••••

My Dad, Maynard with his second wife Sandy

At the end of my eighth-grade year, in June of 1971, my mother put me on a plane and I spent a month with my father in Kennett, Missouri. He had already gotten married to Sandy, and he had a three-bedroom house on Michael Street in Kennett with Sandy and Leandra.

The third bedroom was converted into a library/office. It had a hide-a-bed couch that unfolded to a thin mattress. That was to be my bedroom while I was there. The metal bars below the mattress made for an uncomfortable bed, but I was thirteen and I made the best of it. I spent a lot of time that summer reading many of the books in his library. He had all of these books on sex by *Masters & Johnson*, and other books on the art of making love. I read them all, and I was totally ready to please a woman at the age of thirteen! He did have other good books on other subjects, which I also read. I virtually spent that entire summer reading many classics of literature, and some trash as well.

•••••

It was weird to me that my dad was married to another woman so quickly. It was obviously a rebound relationship… she was twenty years younger than him. Sandy had big breasts. She curled her hair and wore a lot of makeup when they met. By the time they were married, her hair was usually stringy and she walked around in t-shirts with no makeup on. She was sort of nice to me but mostly arrogant. There was nothing you could tell her that she didn't already know, and she always had another fact to add on to yours, which, to her, was much more interesting than your own idea.

Sandy's daughter Leann was around nine when I met her. She craved attention and she loved being with me. We became friends in this bizarre environment. Pretty quickly, Maynard legally adopted Leandra, which I thought was weird… as if Sandy was just snagging him in every way she could. At least, it seemed that way to me.

Summer in Kennett, Missouri was extremely hot and much more humid than in Palm Springs. When we were outside, we generally walked around feeling pretty miserable. It was a cotton town, and when the cotton was full, the blankets of silky white fields had a certain beauty to them. Farmers would pull their tractors directly out onto the highways without looking, forcing cars to slam on their brakes. The watermelon fields were stocked with ripe, huge melons ready for market. People were really outwardly nice, but I was told that gossip was the driving force in a town where there was not a lot to do.

My dad took me to my Uncle George's church in Hornersville a few times. After his fiery sermons, we would go into George's office in his rectory. Maynard was intimidated in his brother's presence. He had a subconscious need to impress and please him. One Sunday, Maynard asked George to explain to me about the "Peckerwoods." George looked at him sideways, and then figured it out. He said, "You mean the rednecks?" My father agreed, and George proceeded to tell me that a lot of prejudice still existed in this area, and there were white people with little knowledge who were as trashy as the black people they hated.

I got it. California was different. Everybody got along out there. In Missouri, there were still divisions, but still I seemed to get along with everyone there, including the 'rednecks'. Most of them were simply people with less opportunity and education who were decent folks. Many of them made up the heartbeat of the nation, working and sweating under the hot sun to eke out a better life for their family. I learned to have a great respect for the 'common man' through this experience.

•••••

I met a boy named Randy, who lived down the street in Kennett. His father was a policeman in Kennett. Randy and I would sneak over behind the trees, sitting on a *John Deere* tractor, smoking cigarettes and acting bored. Once, he took me over to his house and showed me his dad's secret stash of dirty magazines. Some of these magazines were really filthy, with pictures of naked women and horses together. It was disgusting! That revelation took away yet another a piece of my innocence. Like most boys my age, I loved *Playboy* magazine, but these magazines were just disgusting!

Sandy didn't cook much. One night she barbecued some chicken and we ate it along with barbecue potato chips. The chicken had salmonella and I became deathly ill for a couple of days. After that experience, I never touched a barbecued potato chip for as long as I lived.

Sandy's parents lived in a small town just north of Kennett named Holcomb. When we went up to visit them, Leann and I would sit around, bored, all day while they made small talk. Sandy's mother was a kind old lady. Her father was very ill, and he would spend all day sitting and coughing in a kind of weird way. "Ahump, hum. Ahump, hum." My dad would mimic his coughing and mock him when we left. They never had anything to say to each other. Her father died soon after.

Sandy's brother had just gotten back from Viet Nam, and he was a pretty heavy dude. He was definitely affected by the war. He would come by in his big pick-up truck and raise hell. He made fun of their Chihuahua, mentioning that Vietnamese rats were larger than that dog.

One night in Kennett in August, just before I flew back to Palm Springs, I was sitting in the study reading, next to dad and Sandy's bedroom. Soon, I drifted off to sleep. I woke up an hour or two later in a panic. Sandy was screaming bloody murder in the next room! I was disoriented and in a fog. I think I may have flashed back to the time I saw Maynard try to strangle Elaine. I thought, if my father wasn't attacking her, maybe a burglar had burst in to the house and attacked them. I rushed out of bed, ran to their room, opened their bedroom door and turned on the light, and there they both were, having rough sex, completely naked, and they both simultaneously looked over at me.

I was shocked and embarrassed, and I shut off the light and slammed the door and ran back to my room. A moment later, my father came out angrily and yelled at me, "Why did you do that?" I was like, uh, really? How do I tell him I thought she was being skinned alive? It was just an awkward summer all around for me, and at the end of it all, I was glad to finally go back to Palm Springs.

•••••

Before I was to go into ninth grade, I went back to *ISOMATA* in Idyllwild for another summer session. The festival choir was amazing, and my sister Judy and my mother came up for our final performance. Sheryl Otte was up there again, along with Linda Janes. I was starting to be able to talk to Sheryl a little bit more, but she was interested in other boys, although she was very kind to me always. I wrote my first couple songs at *ISOMATA*. One was a rock-style piano piece and another had lyrics. It was my first stab at what would become a lifetime of songwriting.

In Palm Springs, ninth grade was still located within the Junior High School, so we were the 'seniors' there. I was glad to be back with my friends. My grades were stabilizing after tanking in seventh grade, and beginning to recover in eighth. I was back singing in madrigals with Mrs. Nokes.

My mother was handling life better. She began dating, and she got a gig, playing piano at the *Riviera Hotel*. After her gig, she would go around to the other clubs and see George Momb performing at *Banducci's*, and then Sonny Evaro at *The Amigo Room*. She was learning jazz music. She would bring her cassette player into these other places and learn the other performer's arrangements note for note. They would be amazed when she sat down and played their songs exactly as they had! Elaine had a real talent.

•••••

Elaine met a Chiropractor named Bart Palazzolo. He was living in Yucca Valley, a small town in the high desert above Palm Springs. It was kind of bizarre because my dad had always called Chiropractors "quacks" because they weren't 'real' doctors. I wondered if she picked this guy just to spite my dad, but he was a pretty kind, studious Italian man. My mother was beautiful. She could be difficult, but he was patient with her, at least at first.

My mother and I went up to Yucca Valley to visit Bart. He lived behind his Chiropractic office. Yucca Valley was a remote town in the middle of nowhere. Surrounding his office in a sparse neighborhood were miles of desert punctuated with Joshua Trees, Ocotillo and tumbleweeds. I guess you could say that it had its own natural beauty but I absolutely hated it there.

Bart took me back in his examination room and showed me how he would x-ray people, measure and mark how the bones were out of alignment, and then use this machine which 'knocked' the bones behind the ear back into perfect alignment. It was interesting and he took it very seriously, but his office was dank and uninviting.

•••••

My sister Betsy, at this point, had moved into a beach house with her boyfriend, Jim Arnott, in Ocean Beach, a little beach town in San Diego. It was a funky little one-bedroom cottage his parents owned about two blocks from the beach. They had an old rusty trailer in their back yard, fetid with the smell of mildew, where their guests would stay. At some point, Betsy and Jim married.

Betsy and Jim
1975

A bowl of marijuana with rolling papers rested prominently on their coffee table. Jim had turned Betsy on to all kinds of drugs, and she later told me that his influence kept her on them as long as she and Jim were together. It took her a long time to overcome that, but later she cleaned up her life amazingly. Ocean Beach was, and remains, a hippie town. There is a food cooperative where most of the people shop, and it was an extremely laid-back environment.

When I went to visit them, Jim would be working, restoring classic automobiles. He would take me in his big truck, driving through the streets of O.B. and catcalling at girls walking by. He took me out to the county to shoot guns at cans, and in the morning, they would slip 'crank', a form of methamphetamine into my coffee. I was literally flying when I was there, and it was a hard-core place to visit. In January of 1972, Betsy became pregnant, and their child Lucas would be born in October.

•••••

One weekend, around the spring of 1972, my sister Judy came to Palm Springs to pick me up and take me down to the *Sports Arena* in San Diego, to see this new artist named Elton John. His *11-17-71* album with the hit *Your Song* had just been released. The arena was full. The smell of marijuana floated in the air. Elton gave a flamboyant performance, changing costumes, marching around the stage, singing and playing excellent rock piano. I enjoyed it immensely and I was grateful that Judy picked me to go with her.

Not much later, Judy would move to Santa Fe, New Mexico to be closer to the Native Americans with whom she had recently bonded. She was fascinated by their culture, and she was drawn back to them, now that her back had healed enough.

I was given another scholarship to *ISOMATA* by my teacher, Mardale Nokes. My time being mentored by her was coming to an end. The vocal technique she taught me, as well as the opportunities she gave me to experience the programs at the *Idyllwild School of Music and the Arts*, were essential in shaping my future, and I was forever grateful. She was a pretty cool person, too.

•••••

After ninth grade ended in the summer of 1972, my mother sent me back to Kennett for a month again, before *ISOMATA*. My father had stopped drinking and he was in the process of buying a larger house down the street on Michael Street in Kennett.

This was a stately old home that actually had an elevator in it, and there was a bedroom for me. Throughout the summer, my father tried everything he could to convince me to come out and live with him. A year before this, I wouldn't have dreamed of leaving my mother in her unstable condition, but she was healing and she finally seemed happy again. So, I began to contemplate what it would be like to live with him, and I wanted to always be close to my grandmother Audrey.

My dad was in the process of moving his parents from Memphis, Tennessee up to Kennett. They hadn't lived in an actual house for many years, and my grandfather had dreamed of having a garden with a compost hole. Maynard had found a tiny house for them across from the High School in Kennett.

My grandmother was actually not happy to move. She had friends at their church, and she didn't want to leave her little community of support that she had nurtured for all these years. She was happy in Memphis, but they were getting a little too old to be living alone so far from one of their sons.

•••••

Maynard announced that we were going to go on a road trip. Maynard, Sandy, Leann and I made the trip down Interstate 55 to Memphis. From Memphis, we drove to Nashville. We stayed in a nice hotel and went to Opryland. Up until this point in my life, I hated Country & Western music. Experiencing this unique art form, watching the eyes and reactions of the people who loved it, moving to the beat and listening to the stories interwoven within the lyrics changed me and led to a lifetime love of Country. I began to understand the allure of the artists and the community of fans that unashamedly love them. It was an eye-opener and a very cool revelation!

From Nashville, we drove to Washington, D.C. Every monument came with a fascinating history lesson from Maynard. My dad knew some amazing, obscure stories about all of the Founding Fathers, and he made it a fascinating experience. We went to the Smithsonian, the Washington, Jefferson and Lincoln memorials and soaked in the malls and parks full of cherry trees. The District of Columbia was fashioned from swampland, offered up to the Union by the state of Virginia. The Potomac River was dark and lovely, flowing by the estate of General Washington. The weather was extremely hot and sticky, but the adventure was captivating to me, and continued to fuel a lifetime of patriotism.

•••••

From Washington, dad drove us through the Shenandoah Valley to his childhood home in Shepherdstown, West Virginia. He showed us the small schoolhouse he had attended. We went to a drugstore with a soda fountain in the small downtown area. Old photos hung on the wall, one of a group of people including my grandmother when she was a girl. I was delighted to see a piece of my family's history. Maynard showed me a tin roof, still standing, that he had helped his father construct when he was a teenager. We went to the Shenandoah River in which he swam with his brothers as a child and saw the looming granite Confederate Monument he played underneath all those years ago, a quiet sentry to another time and place.

I don't think the trip to Shepherdstown had much of an impact on Sandy or Leann, because they had no history with him or our family. To me, it was an unbelievable experience. It was a healing time for my father and me. He had not had any alcohol for almost a year at this point, and his love and kindness were genuine.

As we were driving back to Kennett, I looked into his eyes and asked him to make me a promise. I told him that one day I would have a fourteen-year-old son, and I wanted him to promise to take this same trip, to Washington and to Shepherdstown, with my child and me in my own son's fifteenth year. Maynard solemnly promised me that we would do just that, some day. But for now, I was going back to Palm Springs.

•••••

The 1972 summer session of *ISOMATA* was my third year at the lovely music school in the mountains of Southern California above Palm Springs, and I was elevated to a more important role in the International Youth Festival Choir.

I assisted in running some of the breakdown sessions with the other tenor vocalists. My voice was beginning to change, and I was able to sing lower than before. After an amazing three weeks and a tearful farewell concert combining the choir with the orchestra, I went back to Palm Springs.

•••••

My mother had moved out of our house on the north end of Palm Springs, and we were now living month-to-month in a rental house on the south end up against the mountain. We lived next to Giorgio and Luisa, the owners of *Giorgio's*, and they would come out and wave to me in the mornings as I rode my bike to school.

Elaine found a *Religious Science* church to attend. A new minister, Tom Costa, was doing services at the *Camelot Theatre* in Palm Springs. He was in his early fifties, about five feet two inches tall. Tom was a feisty, gay Italian Catholic man who had been a bartender for thirty years and in his mid-life, he embarked on a new career as a minister. He had a large nose and a *Prince Valiant*-style haircut. My mom would take me to his Sunday services and I actually enjoyed hearing his sermons. They were full of great stories, of positivity, and everyone who attended was very kind. He would jump and prance around the stage, animated, telling great stories and reminding us that we are all very valuable, worthwhile people. Tom was working hard, going from his services in Palm Springs to another theatre in Palm Desert every Sunday to do another service.

Kurt started to blow off our friendship when we entered tenth grade. We were at *Palm Springs High School* now, and he decided to 'run' with a group of the 'cool kids'. It was painful for me, but I had other friends. Mr. Reed was the choir director at the High School and he liked me. He put me right into Madrigals. He was young, but very friendly and a good teacher.

My Mother, Elaine with her second husband Bart Palazzolo

CHAPTER TWENTY
Kennett, Missouri

Bart Palazzolo proposed marriage to my mother, Elaine, and she accepted. In November of 1972, my mother informed me that we were going to move up to Yucca Valley to live in the back of Bart's Chiropractic office. She took me up there to see it again, and I cried hysterically all night long at the prospect of having to leave Palm Springs and live in a dark back room, in this hellhole of a place. I was going to have to leave my friends in Palm Springs and go to yet another High School up in Yucca Valley. I was depressed for weeks, crying just about every day. My father called me and asked me again if I wanted to move to Kennett to be with him.

Kennett was literally the lesser of two evils for me, at that moment. The thought of living for one minute in this remote place in an ugly desert town was too much for me to handle. As desolate as it seemed to move to the Bootheel of Missouri, I made the decision to move to Kennett, Missouri, to be with my dad.

•••••

In January of 1973, in the middle of my tenth-grade year, I started all over again in Kennett. Dad had fixed up my bedroom and put cork on all four walls, so I turned it into a huge bulletin board with thousands of photos and posters. It was my refuge as I learned to adjust to a whole new life.

Sandy immediately acted different towards me when I actually moved to live with them. I've seen this phenomenon many times since. There is a 'nesting' issue with many women, and when another's child comes into their nest, they subconsciously reject them. She became the epitome of the mean and cruel stepmother much of the time, excluding me from her 'inner circle'.

I was pretty much lost anyway, and for the most part I mostly didn't let it affect me. Every once in a while, she would be nice to me. I had ingrown toenails which hurt me and she cut them for me. But, in general, she wasn't great to live with. Eleven-year-old Leann and I bonded some more. She was a very kind little girl and she loved being around her new 'big brother'.

We would ask Sandy what was for dinner, and she would say, "Scrounge. There's food in the kitchen." So, we would make a peanut butter sandwich or have a bowl of cereal most of the time. She went around the house with no makeup, kind of looking like a tomboy with big, baggy shirts and shorts. Dad worked a lot and wasn't home very much.

•••••

I enrolled in *Kennett High School.* The kids in Kennett were mostly very kind to me. All of a sudden, instead of being just another kid in Palm Springs, I was the funny, cool kid from California with long hair. I made fast friends.

I enrolled in choir. James Finch was the choir teacher. I think he was intimidated by my knowledge, training and experience not only in vocal music, but also in piano. This was kind of a backwoods place, and I might have known more than he did about what he was teaching. At least, I thought I did, and I felt that he resented me. As time went on, our relationship grew and eventually we became lifelong friends, but at first, we were like oil and water.

My father had purchased an old upright piano, which was in the living room close to my bedroom. That piano was my saving grace. After school, I would play the piano for hours. My ear training was good, so I picked up popular songs and taught myself. I wrote songs and played them. It was like emotional salve for me. The piano was and remained my coping mechanism throughout life.

Joe Newman taught English to the juniors and seniors, and he was also the director of the plays. He would have an enormous impact on my life. I played bit parts in the first couple plays he did when I first arrived in Kennett. Later, I tried out and got a role as the elderly judge in Heaven, in the play *"Liliom."* I brought the house down with my performance, and I loved acting. After that, I was in several other of his plays throughout the rest of High School, including *"Lil' Abner"* and *"Paint Your Wagon."* I had a solo on the song *"Another Autumn"* in that musical, and for years afterwards when he came to see me perform, my father would make me sing that, and *"They Call the Wind Mariah"*. Dad loved that I was in these plays. It was right up his alley. Years later, another teacher at KHS, Dennis Nail (the father of the famous Country singer David Nail) would remind me of how touched he and everyone else were by my performance of *Another Autumn.* I was grateful that he noticed and remembered.

•••••

Betsy and Lucas 1973

For an hour each day, I was in Study Hall. Carol George was a senior while I was a sophomore, and she sat next to me in Study Hall. She was beautiful and friendly, kind of cynical and judgmental and I thought she was cool. We would talk about *"The Glass Menagerie"* or whatever books we were reading. At night, when I was done with my homework, I would call her and we talked for hours. I knew she liked me and I liked her a lot, but she already was engaged to an older guy, Mike Day. He was just four or five years older than her, and they were going to move to Jacksonville, Florida as soon as she graduated.

Carol's father was a farmer. He hardly ever bathed, and he spent most of his time farming. At the end of a long day, he would usually hang out in his barn drinking cheap beer with his helpers. Carol's mother, Barbara, was an obese woman who always cooked, mostly fried food but it was always excellent. They lived on a tight budget, and Barbara couldn't have been kinder when I went to their little farm to visit Carol. Her father would look me up and down and try to intimidate me.

Carol's friendship meant a lot to me. It soothed the scars I had from being removed from my previous life. I was still enamored with my childhood crush, Sheryl, in California, even though we had never even kissed once. Sheryl wrote me a few letters. They always smelled like perfume, and her perfect, tiny handwriting melted my heart. I imagined that she loved me and only me, and I was so happy to hear from her when she wrote to me, so far away from this bizarre place where I was now living. She cared enough to do that much.

But, I had a real connection with Carol, as if we were meant to meet each other. Nevertheless, at the end of my sophomore year, in June of 1973, Carol got married and moved away.

•••••

Towards the end of June in 1973, my sisters Betsy and Kathy drove to Kennett from California in Kathy's white panel truck. Betsy had her eight-month-old baby boy, Lucas, with her. They spent a few days at my dad and Sandy's house in Kennett, and then they 'kidnapped' me to drive to North Carolina with them to see my sister Suzanne and her family. It was a wonderful trip. I was so grateful to be back with my sisters again.

We listened to cassette tapes of music on the way, including *Carole King's Tapestry* album, *James Taylor's Sweet Baby James* album, and *Joni Mitchell's Blue* album. We laughed and talked, and it was great to be back with my sisters again after so much time apart. We stayed at Suzy's house for a week or two and then drove back. While we were in North Carolina, we would all stay up late, smoking cigarettes and playing cards.

Suzy's children were growing; Charles was nine, Lori was seven, Michael was five and Wendy was three. We would play with them and tickle them, and help Suzanne be a little less overwhelmed by giving her some quiet time. We had deep talks about our childhood and our parent's divorce, and it was a healing time for all of us.

Top: Sandy, Maynard, Uncle George & Maxine
Bottom: Grandparents Audrey & George
My Grandparent's 65th Anniversary
Kennett, Missouri 1973

After we returned to Kennett, I stayed for a couple weeks and then flew to California to see my mother briefly before my junior year of High School started. It was good to see Elaine again, and she clung to me the whole time I was there. She didn't make me stay in Yucca Valley. She took me to see my Uncle Ted and Aunt Candy and their family, and then to stay with my grandma Gizi for a few days.

•••••

Coming back to Kennett, I was delighted to have my grandmother Audrey so close to me. I believe that I was her saving grace, being in a place so far away from her friends. I would go over for lunch once or twice a week, and on weekends. My grandparents literally lived across the street from my High School.

I would help Pop in his garden. I dug his compost hole and mowed their lawn. Sandy went over to hang wallpaper (crooked!) and I helped clean up afterwards. Grandma and Pop were around eighty-five years old, and we celebrated their sixty-fifth (they lived to see their seventieth) anniversary with a cake and a party. At the party, I played her favorite song, *"O Shenandoah"*, and my father sang the song in his booming voice with tears in his eyes.

GEORGE & AUDREY SISLER

I would help my grandfather walk two blocks on his artificial leg to the grocery store. He was on a tight budget and he had a little handwritten list of groceries for me to fetch. Whenever I found an item, he would check it off the list. We would pick up what he wanted, and I would carry it home, holding firmly to his arm with my other hand. It was a slow, arduous process but I had plenty of patience for him. It was the one time we actually bonded in our lives. Later, I took a job as a stocker and wrapper at that grocery store for a short period of time.

•••••

Maynard published a book of his poems and sonnets. He called it *"A Large Slice of Life (Carved into Pieces, More or Less)"*. It contained a lot of gushy love sonnets to Sandy, which I thought was a bit overboard, considering they had not been together all that long. His mawkish, undying love would not last that much longer anyway.

•••••

My uncle George took on a new position as minister of the *Southern Baptist Church* in Parma, Missouri, about an hour's drive north of Kennett. Parma was a small farm town with one stoplight on their main street. On the corner were a "greasy spoon" diner and a general store and not much else. We drove up some Sundays to listen to George preach the gospel, and then we would go to George and Maxine's house for dessert. She made a great chocolate cream pie, and I looked forward to that. They had an organ in their parlor, and I would play it for them on occasion.

Parma's only physician had been an old country doctor who had died about ten years before. George had convinced Maynard that he should drive up to Parma every Saturday and treat patients, as the locals were in dire need of a doctor. The old doctor's office was still there, shades drawn, dark and full of cobwebs, with instruments dating back to the turn of the century. It was like going back in time when you walked in the office. Apothecary jars full of spoiled liquid lined the cabinets. Huge forceps used for delivering babies lay on dusty shelves next to ancient examining tables.

We drove up to Parma every Saturday, and over the course of two or three weeks, we went through everything, kept what could be used, cleaned it up and ordered new medical equipment and examining tables. We created a little pharmacy, and my dad trained me to dispense medicines. Some of the medicine required prescriptions in triplicate, because the FDA closely regulated these drugs. I also learned how to process urinalyses and blood draws.

When the office finally opened, it was filled every Saturday with grateful patients. One Saturday, a farmer came in and proclaimed that he had been deaf for ten years. Maynard looked in his ears, and then began to irrigate them while I held a bowl underneath each ear. Chunks and chunks of filthy earwax flew out of each ear, and the farmer could hear again! He screamed, "It's a miracle! I'm healed!" That farmer left happier than I had seen anyone in years. Another Saturday, a drunken African-American man stumbled in with a stab wound in his back and passed out. Maynard looked at me and said, "Son, I'm going to let you sew this one up. You've been watching me enough." My eyes got wide and I started to feel anxiety, but I followed his directions and when I was done, he took a smaller needle and plastic surgeon's thread. He finished the job I had started, to perfection. The man woke up grateful, I think more for the painkillers than for the patching of the wound.

Maynard wanted me to follow in his footsteps and become a doctor, and I loved medicine. My dad would tell me, "I don't care if you're a plumber, as long as you're the best damn plumber in the business!" But he did care. He wanted me to be a doctor.

My uncle George suddenly developed lung cancer. He died very quickly. My dad was again beside himself with grief, and out of all of his brothers, now only he and his brother Bill remained. George was buried on a hill out in the middle of nowhere in Missouri. In life, George had been a famous war correspondent, newspaperman and then a preacher with large congregations. In the end, he was buried alone in an obscure location. Shortly after George died, Maynard closed the satellite office in Parma, and eventually they found another physician.

•••••

At this point, I had some close friends in Kennett. Tracy and Timmy Sturch were identical twin boys who lived by the High School. Tracy had diabetes and he had to give shots to himself every day. Mike Rogers was a transplanted Army brat. His father had been stationed in Germany, and Mike was somewhat worldly and cool. Mike and I had a lot in common, having been raised by parents in the service. Dale Fender was the son of my biology teacher, and he was a really fun guy to hang out with. I took his sister, Rosie, to the prom. She had braces and I looked dorky in our photos, but she was a sweet girl and we had a good time. We didn't even kiss, and I think her father might have flunked me in biology if we had done so.

Harold Donovan was fun to be around. His father was a chiropractor who later became a Pentecostal Preacher, which was totally weird. At some point, his dad insisted that if I wanted to stay Harold's friend, I had to attend his church. It was a bizarre experience. Everyone would be speaking in tongues and pushing each other down by their foreheads. Surrounded by a babbling congregation, Harold's dad would put his hand on my face. With fire in his eyes, he would scream at me at the top of his voice, pushing on my forehead and making me swear to be a Soldier of Christ. It was kind of scary to me. Of course, I did what I was told and swore my allegiance, hoping this would be enough for Harold's dad to now leave me alone. Later, Harold and I would go out and smoke pot and cigarettes, and basically be bad boys.

I was raised Christian. Instilled within me was a deep love for Jesus. I understood that these people at the Pentecostal Church were worshipping in the way they wanted, and that was fine. It just wasn't the way I was comfortable worshipping. On many Sundays in Kennett, I would go to the Catholic Church and experience Mass by myself. I would then walk through the cemetery, saying prayers by many headstones for faceless people I didn't know, wondering what their lives were like. I would then meet my father and Sandy at the Presbyterian Church and go to that service. It was more out of a lack of anything else to do than a profound religiosity on my part. My father later told me that he felt strongly that if you have a communion with God, and you live life as close to the example of Jesus as you know how, that church is really only an extension of that and not particularly necessary. That made sense to me.

•••••

A carload of my friends and I would drive out to the levees by Jim Green's property outside of Kennett. An overgrown little forest existed there, which led to a small pond. We proclaimed it "Chunchville." We would smoke pot and bring machetes to get through the forest to the little pond.

All of the boys smoked in the boys' restroom at school. We would pass around cigarettes to each other, and when you took a hit off of one, it was hot and putrid. You could hardly breathe in there and it was always stinky.

My dad would go to the Air Force Base in Blytheville, Arkansas and buy cigarettes. He would buy me a couple cartons of Marlboro Reds and buy himself three or four cartons for a two-week period. I guess he was trying to be a cool dad to me. That kind of thing, buying cigarettes for your kid, would probably be frowned upon in this day and age.

Harold Donovan had a sister, Pam, who was a year younger than him. She was pretty and she had a crush on me. I would go over to their house and play piano, and she would sit on the bench with me, swooning. I liked her.

Lee Ann Holt and Elaine Nugent 1974

Lee Ann Holt was a darling girl with large breasts. She was thin and sweet, with long, dark hair and big, expressive eyes. She was a year behind me in school. She had a friend, Elaine Nugent, who became my girlfriend. Elaine was another sweet, innocent girl, tall with lovely long, blonde hair and a pretty smile. We hung out a lot on weekends and kissed. Her father didn't like me at all, and he was very strict, but I was respectful to her and I think we were kind of in love. She was pretty straight-laced, but we had a lot of fun together and she was very good to me. She was shy and didn't talk a lot, but she loved to kiss and so did I.

•••••

I took the bus to school, and it was during that winter President Nixon cancelled the change from Daylight Savings Time to Standard Time; in the mornings, it was pitch black as I stood, shivering in the freezing night waiting for the bus to come. The sunrise would hit our eyes like a bullet as we approached the High School. Nixon was a powerful man (until he wasn't). He changed time by Executive Order!

•••••

I had a buddy in school. He asked me if I wanted to go over to Jonesboro, Arkansas, which was about an hour's drive from Kennett, to *Arkansas State University* to see this new artist named Billy Joel performing at the college gymnasium. The *Piano Man* album had just been released, and Billy was touring colleges mostly, trying to generate interest. We went to Jonesboro and I sat, cross-legged on the gymnasium floor about twenty feet from the stage, watching Billy perform. I was blown away. I said to my friend, "That's what I want to do!" Shortly after that concert, Billy Joel became a huge rock star. It was cool to see him in the beginning of his storied career, before he was somebody.

Another grocery store hired me as a checker. It was closer to home and I would work after school and weekends. I held this job during the time before groceries with barcodes were scanned. It was a laborious task, looking for prices on each item, and punching them in to the old cash register, one by one. Although I became rather proficient at the task, people were always looking at me impatiently and it was a high-stress job. When I finally made it home, I would play piano for hours and then mostly hide in my room, doing homework.

(Left to Right) Kathy, Suzanne, Leandra, Maynard, Tad Judy and Betsy 1974

•••••

Maynard became a city councilman in Kennett. He was appointed Police Commissioner. He started his own private practice in an office building that was close to the town square, across from the police department in Kennett. He was sharing the building with a kind, old pharmacist named Ernie Simer. Ernie had two daughters who went to *Kennett High School* with me, Cindy and Linda. Linda became a famous photographer, and Cindy remained my friend for life. Down the street from Maynard's office in the town square was a music store. I would go in and play the very first models of the *Fender Rhodes* electric pianos, and wish I owned one.

•••••

In April of 1974, dad, Sandy, Leann and I took a trip to New York where I witnessed my father become a Fellow in the *American College of Physicians*. This was a big deal to him. He had worked for years towards this honor, and shortly afterwards he was inducted into the *Royal Society of Medicine* in London, and into *Who's Who of American Physicians*. I was very proud of my father, for the moment.

Maynard was a member of the *Kiwanis* club, and they met for lunch every Wednesday at *McCormick's* restaurant in Kennett. I would meet him at the restaurant sometimes and have lunch with all of the businessmen. They usually invited a speaker. Once, a man came from the phone company in St. Louis, and he talked about this amazing, new invention called fiber-optic cable that was going to transform the world. He said that the old cables were huge and could handle 50,000 calls, but the new fiber-optic cables would be able to handle millions of calls at a time and would change the way we communicate. It was exciting to dream of the future. The world of telephone communication had just evolved from the usage of old rotary dial phones to the new push button phones. Cell phones didn't exist yet, but life was changing.

When we returned from New York, *Kennett High School* was giving out their awards, and all the students selected me as "Wittiest Boy"! I was delighted, although, in retrospect, I think that means "Class Clown." I've spent my life cultivating and storing bad jokes into my memory, ever since.

CHAPTER TWENTY-ONE
My Father Divorces... Again

I was doing my best to be happy, but I missed my mother and my sisters, and it was really weird to live with Sandy. Being in Kennett, for me, felt like being banished to Siberia, after living in California. Towards the end of my junior year in High School, Maynard started drinking and raising hell again.

In June of 1974, I turned sixteen years old. On my birthday, the Department of Motor Vehicles in Kennett was closed, so I drove a half hour to Malden, Missouri on that day to get my license. I was determined to have my license on my birthday!

•••••

Having my driver's license opened up a new world to me. My father bought me a dark brown Pontiac Firebird, a little kick-around car, and I went everywhere with my friends. About the only thing to do in Kennett was to drive from one side of town to the other and back, all night. There was a drive-in burger joint on one side of town; we would hang out there a little and then drive down to the bowling alley and hang out in the parking lot on the other side of town, smoking cigarettes.

Sometimes, we would drive like crazy down the hundreds of dirt roads that enveloped Kennett, and occasionally we drag-raced on an old asphalt road, getting to speeds of over a hundred miles per hour. My guardian angels again were working overtime.

I drove my friends to Memphis to see concerts. We saw *Crosby, Stills, Nash and Young*, and then David Bowie came to town with his *Ziggy Stardust and the Spiders from Mars* tour. David Bowie had been a favorite of Carol's. I had learned some Bowie songs to sing to her when we were hanging out before she married and moved away.

It was a bizarre dynamic, because Maynard was drinking again and causing trouble, but he was also the Police Commissioner, so he could pretty much get away with anything. Sandy was getting increasingly tired of his antics.

•••••

In July of 1974, my mother Elaine and her husband Bart went to Kansas City, Missouri for a *Clinic Masters* Chiropractic convention and I joined them. We stayed at the *Hall's Crown Center* hotel, a majestic hotel with a huge lobby, with waterfalls, close to downtown. I sat in on a few of the *Clinic Masters* sessions. It appeared to me that it was basically a scam to get Chiropractors to upsell people full packages of adjustments that they probably didn't need, and to charge more for their services.

Elaine and Bart were starting to have problems in their relationship, and at the end of the conference, she decided to drive with me alone back to California to spend the rest of the summer with her. Bart flew home and went back to work.

It was great to be with my mom again, one on one. We drove to Colorado. She showed me the *University of Colorado* college campus in Boulder and I fell in love with it. We took our time driving back, and bonded.

By the time we got to California, everything had changed. Elaine was beginning to realize that this had been a rebound relationship with Bart. She was contemplating divorce. I spent some time with my Uncle Ted and Candy at their house. I went to visit my Grandma Gizi in Long Beach for a week.

I went to Ocean Beach in San Diego to visit Betsy and Jim. It was fun playing with Lucas when I got there. Even though he was small, he had thick glasses and looked a little dorky, but he was the sweetest boy and he soaked up my affection.

Once when I went to San Diego, Betsy told me to open my mouth and close my eyes. I have no idea why I trusted her. She put a small tablet on a piece of paper in my mouth. It was a tab of blotter acid, LSD. I asked what she had done, and she said, "You'll see. Let's walk to the beach."

By the time we got to the beach, I was totally tripping on acid. The entire world was a maze of psychedelic colors. I was holding the sand, watching it go through my hands, and it was breathing and flowing as if it was a life form of its own. The ocean waves were pure energy, flowing with light and rainbow color like I had never experienced. My mind was opened up to a world I had never seen, and it was amazing. I couldn't believe the experience. I thought I was going out of my mind and Betsy just told me to go with it. Betsy, the sister who gave me my first drag of a joint of pot and made me promise not to let it lead to hard drugs, had just turned me on to acid.

After a couple hours, we went back to her house and the effects of this dangerous drug started to ebb. I went into the stinky, dark trailer in her back yard and had the worst ten hours of my life. Coming down from this drug was painful. It was agonizing. My skin crawled and my brain felt like it was bursting out of my head. I couldn't stay still and I writhed around on a smelly blanket for what seemed like an eternity. I couldn't believe that my sister did this to me. Finally, mercifully, I fell asleep. I must have slept for twelve hours.

When I awoke the next morning, I was angry, woozy, depressed and confused. In retrospect, I'm glad I had the experience because it did open my mind to a whole new world and new thinking. Also, I'm glad because it was so painful ultimately that I never, ever again wanted or tried acid. I did a handful of other awful drugs later, but never LSD after that experience. My sister told me that she loved the drug at that period in her life, and I honestly believed that she thought she was doing me a favor, and that I wouldn't have such an awful reaction. I forgave her, and, again, in retrospect, I'm grateful that it gave me a new perspective on life. I highly wouldn't recommend it, however.

•••••

My sister Kathy had broken up with her boyfriend Jack, moved away from the tangerine ranch, relinquished all of her possessions including that cool, white panel van that I had learned to drive in, and joined an *Ashram* in Los Angeles. She had become a follower of Guru Maharaj Ji, and she embraced it completely. Guru Maharaj Ji was a thirteen-year-old boy who came over from India to enlighten Westerners. He was considered a Messiah to his followers. The *Hindu* brand of Eastern religion had been made a mainstream phenomenon by *The Beatles.*

Kathy did 'service' with other devotees, and they meditated and had 'satsang', discussing the amazing experiences they were having since they 'received knowledge' from a Mahatma of the Guru.

Whenever the Guru came to town, he spoke at huge arenas filled with people. It was a new trend and Kathy gave herself completely to it.

I went to visit Kathy at the *Ashram*, and they put me into a room to receive knowledge. Mahatma Ji was there and it was apparently an honor for people to receive knowledge from him, which I understood was a technique of meditation that would bring you to a blissful state. Halfway through the session, my mother came and picked me up. I never received knowledge, but Kathy stayed faithfully devoted to the Guru from then on. At the time I wrote this book, he had begun to call himself Prem Rawat, and he still had many followers.

•••••

So, all of a sudden, my world consisted of a divorcing mother, an alcoholic father who was drinking again, a conservative Catholic sister in North Carolina with four children, a sister who embraced Native American ways and went to live with the Indians, another sister who embraced the Far Eastern *Hindu* culture of India, and another sister who was part of the hard-living, drug-laced, motorcycle and guns culture of Ocean Beach, California.

Tad High School Senior Photo

In Santa Fe, New Mexico, my sister Judy met John Pedro's son, David, a full-blooded Arapahoe Native American and married him. Shortly thereafter, they had a son, Abraham, and moved to Oklahoma.

On the way back to Missouri in the late summer of 1974, I went to visit Judy in Oklahoma for a couple weeks. Judy and David were on their way to Wyoming to the *Sun Dance*, a kind of ceremonial gathering of many tribes that had been happening for generations. No white people were allowed, but since Judy was married to David and I was her brother, I was considered a Native American. I went with them and I witnessed amazing rituals. It was like going back in time two thousand years. They danced in ceremonial headdresses, held peyote meetings, hunted venison with spears, skinned and cooked their prey over open fires, smoked their pipes and slept in teepees. I was a part of it all, and it opened my mind up to yet another world.

This was a really turbulent time period for America. On August 8, 1974, Richard Nixon became the first President of the United States to ever resign from office. The cloud of Watergate and the political turmoil in our country set a tone in our lives, and it was distressing.

•••••

Returning to Kennett, I was ready to go into my senior year of High School. I had my senior pictures done. I went to check out my classes and I noticed that I had been placed in typing class. I went to the counselor and told her that I already type sixty to seventy words per minute! She told me that I needed the credits to graduate, so when I got into typing class, my instructor allowed me to type my way through the whole course in two weeks, and the rest of the year I slept, or studied in class.

Shortly after I started my senior year, Sandy left Maynard and filed for divorce. Later, one of the nurses that had worked with her at the hospital when she met my dad told me that she was determined to "snag a rich doctor" and take him for all he had. I think she was just waiting for an excuse to leave him, and he probably wouldn't have continued drinking if she had stayed, but who knows?

My dad did admit to me that he had gone to a convention in Chicago and somehow gotten a venereal disease from a toilet seat, and he couldn't understand how she was so bent out of shape about it! I don't think VD from a toilet seat is listed in the medical journals as something that could actually happen, and neither did Sandy.

It was actually great to have her out of the house in one sense. She had been really negative towards me for a long time. Dad would meet me at home for lunch. He would tell me to make him a crazy, bizarre sandwich and he would eat it. I would put anything and everything on these sandwiches…salami, sardines, pimento bologna, Muenster cheese, and he would eat them!

On Wednesdays, I would walk over to my grandma Audrey's house across from the High School and she would make me a sandwich. Her eyesight had gotten so bad that she would sometimes put mayonnaise on toast instead of butter, or mix the wrong ingredients. I didn't want to embarrass her, so I would just eat them and smile. She sat with me at her little kitchen table while I ate and we would chitchat. I knew how much this meant to her, and it meant the same to me! It was our special time. Pop would be sitting in his study, and every once in a while, he would yell, "Mama! Mama! Come here!" She would roll her eyes and go to dote on him as she had always done.

They had a little pug dog that they named "Black Boy" because he was black and he was a boy. This was one weird dog. He would hump my leg when I came over. It was disgusting. One day he got out and ran away and my grandma asked me to help find him…so I went through the neighborhood yelling, "Black Boy! Black Boy!" I thought I was going to be killed by some of the African-American neighbors she had! But, I would do anything for my grandma.

•••••

Maynard continued to drink heavily. He was again and always a belligerent drunk, and to this point I had never lived alone with him while he was drinking. He was truly possessed by the devil when he was drunk. I found "inappropriate" Polaroid photos in the drawers of his bedroom. One night I came home and a bunch of my high school friends were sitting in the living room drinking with him. These boys were more acquaintances than friends to me, and they were the troublemakers in the school. One night, he gave the car keys to Sandy's car to a boy to get more beer, and the boy took it joyriding down the dirt roads and wrecked the car. He staggered back to the house and gave my dad back his keys.

Life was totally out of control, all of a sudden. The County Sheriff would come over to visit. He was a good man, but he had suffered through a series of back surgeries due to an injury on the job, and he was in constant pain. Maynard had a safe in the house full of prescription medication. He would give the sheriff injections of morphine. This became a daily task, and in return, the sheriff protected my dad from himself. It didn't hurt that dad was also Police Commissioner.

When dad began to drink, he would play old show tunes on his record player and sing out loud with his booming voice, *"A little tin box that a little tin key unlocks"* or *"A law was made a distant moon ago here"* or *"Anything you can do, I can do better."* It was practically like an education in old Broadway music, led by a madman! But, as the night went on and he drank more, he would get angry and lash out at me. He would yell, "I DEMAND respect" for no real reason at all, since I wasn't being disrespectful.

You must never demand respect unless you earn it first.

I was smoking a lot of pot with my friends. I had virtually no supervision. I was on my own. Marijuana was not only illegal in Missouri; it was dangerous to even have a joint in your possession. You could serve prison time for the smallest amount. I have no idea what I was thinking, but a buddy and I decided to buy a quarter pound of pot and sell three ounces of it to get one ounce free. My buddy scored the pot and he went to break it into ounces in the back of my car in the school parking lot one night when I was at play practice.

I was off-stage and I looked outside, and there were two policemen escorting him into the back of a police cruiser with flashing lights on. I panicked. I just knew I was going to be arrested and sent to jail. The policemen took my buddy out into the country, confiscated his marijuana and told him to get out of the car and never do it again.

I have no idea if they knew my dad and let my friend off the hook because of me, or if they just wanted pot for their own use. Either way, I was grateful and I never said a word about it. When I met up with my friend, he said, "Look, I stashed an ounce in my socks when they were pulling up! So, we're not completely dry!" I couldn't believe it! But, Kennett was like that for a lot of people. There was not much to do but to get into trouble.

One night, at play practice, I was acting up. I'm sure I was being too silly and probably being a little bit of a jerk to Mr. Newman, the play director. He wasn't one to take much from anyone. When he completed working on a particular scene, he took me aside, grabbed me by the shirt and with deep, piercing eyes, he told me, "You sicken me! You have all of this amazing talent, and you're squandering it. You have a responsibility, not only to yourself and God, but to others to be an example to them and you're failing!" I was devastated. I listened to those words, and they helped to shape the way I would carry myself from then on. I began to take my talent seriously again, and worked hard on bringing the best performances I had in me, from then on.

All talent comes with responsibility.

Mr. Finch was taking a busload of students up to Cape Girardeau to audition for All-District Choir at *Southeast Missouri State University*. In the past, Mr. Finch had little success with getting too many students into All-District Choir. The competition was tough. It was a two-hour drive, and when we got there, we went into rooms individually and sang for a panel of judges.

A week later, I was informed that I made All-State choir! I was the only kid in the whole southeastern quarter of Missouri who was sent to Jefferson City to sing with the *Missouri All-State Choir*. It was really a big deal to the people of Kennett. I "lettered" in choir. I know it wasn't quite as manly as lettering in football!

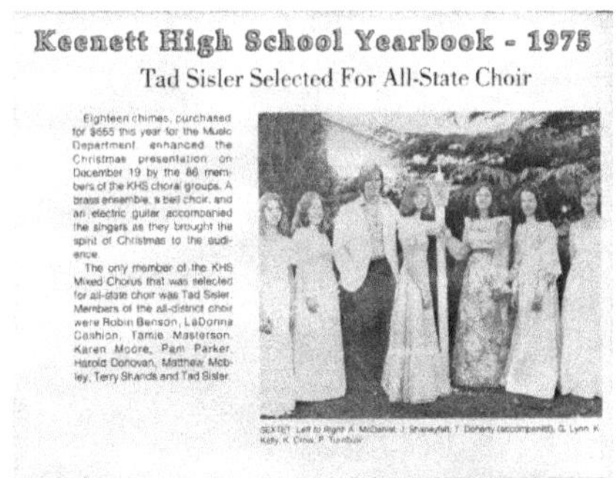

Keenett High School Yearbook - 1975

Tad Sisler Selected For All-State Choir

Eighteen chimes, purchased for $655 this year for the Music Department enhanced the Christmas presentation on December 19 by the 86 members of the KHS choral groups. A brass ensemble, a bell choir, and an electric guitar accompanied the singers as they brought the spirit of Christmas to the audience.

The only member of the KHS Mixed Chorus that was selected for all-state choir was Tad Sisler. Members of the all-district choir were Robin Benson, LaDonna Cashion, Tamie Masterson, Karen Moore, Pam Parker, Harold Donovan, Matthew Mobley, Terry Shands and Tad Sisler.

I drove to Jefferson City and Columbia, Missouri for rehearsals and performances throughout the year. I would play *Elton John* or *David Bowie* albums on my quadraphonic eight-track stereo in the car on the way there and back. It was kind of like being back at *ISOMATA*. We sang for the governor and some other dignitaries throughout the season.

•••••

At this point, my mother was officially divorcing Bart. She moved into a condo at 186-C Via Escuela in Palm Springs. She was back in Palm Springs, and I wondered how life would have been for me if I had stayed and she had never married him. I think she was doing okay. She wrote me once a week or more. I missed her.

Maynard hired a secretary named Sandra Wilburn. She was in her twenties, recently divorced, with a cute little daughter named Kimberley. Sandra was handling all of Maynard's paperwork and dictation, and she was becoming increasingly concerned about his alcoholic behavior. He would drink, and then, just like when I was a child, the next morning he would be kneeling at my bedside begging my forgiveness for his 'flaw'. I loved him and I always forgave him. And then he would repeat the process.

It didn't help that I was in my senior year of High School. I wasn't concentrating enough on my grades, or getting scholarships, or really doing much of anything more than parenting my dad, avoiding him, or dealing directly with a belligerent drunk at midnight when I should have been sleeping. It also didn't help that my house was usually full of people he invited to party with him, quite a few of them my age, until all hours of the night. I would walk in the house sometimes, and someone would say, "Who the hell are you?" And, I would tell them that I actually lived there. Again, in my life, insanity prevailed all around me.

•••••

One night, I came home, a little stoned. Dad was drunk and sitting on the leather couch with a young woman. The living room stank of sweat and alcohol, a smell that rarely subsided even during the day with the windows open. This woman had a little too much makeup on and she was wearing a skimpy dress, smelling of very strong, cheap perfume. Maynard told me that she was a friend of my sister Kathy's and she was here to visit us. She didn't look like somebody who would be Kathy's friend, but all of a sudden, she became very friendly to me.

She walked me to my room and started to undress herself. She literally physically attacked me, and it was totally weird. I completely understand how teenage boys can say that a woman raped them because that's exactly what happened to me. I was completely turned on and off at the same time. Before I knew it, I was finished in about ten seconds. I got up and went directly to the bathroom and threw up. It was actually a very traumatic experience for me, my first sexual encounter with a woman. Through the years, I've smelled that same perfume on a handful of women and I still gag whenever I smell it. My father had procured a prostitute for me, and I didn't have a clue what was happening until it already happened. I hated myself for months after that event.

The next day, I met him at his office and he gave me a shot of antibiotics and a condom to put into my wallet. I had no idea how to use it, but I held on to that condom. It made a little ring indentation in my wallet. I thought, well, this is about a day late.

I couldn't figure out how Maynard could get so falling-down drunk at night, and then arrive at his office in the morning, looking chipper, until one morning, when I saw him reaching into his safe. He didn't know I was watching as he injected methamphetamine sulfate into his veins. This was a triple prescription drug, and I knew he could get into big trouble if he ever got caught doing this.

The weirdest thing to me, and it remains that way to this day, was the fact that my father, an outstanding, compassionate, kind physician who was revered by his patients and respected by his peers, had this terrible alter ego. With just one ounce of alcohol, he became an angry, perverted, belligerent, ugly man who was tortured inside. He would drink and cry out that he used to be able to drink and have fun and be light-hearted.

Somewhere in that terrible man lived beautiful, innocent, loving Maynard. He only had to figure out how to suppress this demon, or else he was going to die. I honestly felt that he blacked out and didn't even know half of what he did when he woke up the next day. My mother used to quote the old saying, "What's on the sober man's mind is on the drunken man's tongue." I questioned if that was the case when it came to Maynard. He was maintaining the separate personalities of two truly completely different people when he was sober and drunk.

Carol George
1975

CHAPTER TWENTY-TWO
Carol

In January of 1975, Carol George moved back to Kennett. Her marriage had ended quickly, and she was back living with her parents.

Carol started coming over to the house a lot. We were hanging out and smoking a lot of pot with my friend Mike Rogers. Carol's friend Cathy Story started dating Mike Rogers.

One night, Carol and I made love. I had never done this before, with the exception of that awful night with the prostitute. I felt guilty because I was dating Elaine and she was such a sweetheart, but I was becoming infatuated with Carol. Elaine was innocent and kind, and although we had made it to second base a couple times, I always respectfully held back and didn't force her into anything she wasn't ready to do yet.

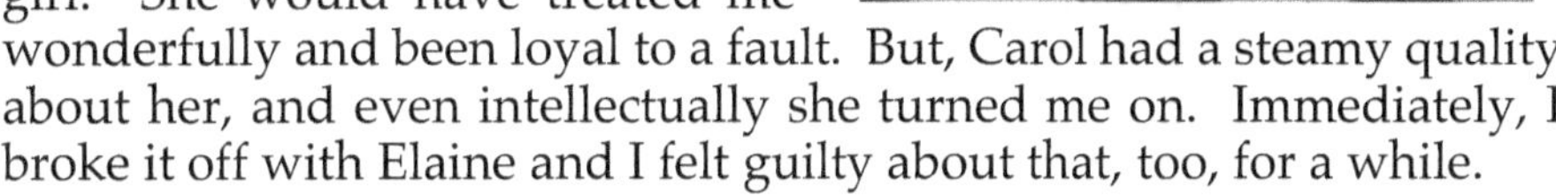

In retrospect, Elaine was the perfect girl. She would have treated me wonderfully and been loyal to a fault. But, Carol had a steamy quality about her, and even intellectually she turned me on. Immediately, I broke it off with Elaine and I felt guilty about that, too, for a while.

From that point on, Carol and I were virtually inseparable. She practically moved in to my dad's house, sleeping over many nights when Maynard was delirious in the other room. High School boys were still out there drinking with dad, and I was lost in the madness.

•••••

Somehow, through it all, I was doing the best to maintain my grades, and I received a Congressional nomination to attend the *United States Naval Academy* in Annapolis, where I was born and baptized. I went to the Air Force Base in Blytheville, Arkansas for a physical, and although I was still in daily pain from the abscess in my leg, I lied about it and told them I was in perfect physical shape.

I passed the physical, and about a month later, I got a letter from the Navy. The letter informed me that my grade point average, although admirable, was one tenth of a point too low to qualify for the *United States Naval Academy* based upon the other applicants. I then applied to the *University of Missouri* in Kansas City for their accelerated medical school program, and I was accepted immediately, providing, of course, that I could make it through the next five months and actually graduate High School under these extreme conditions.

•••••

I think that Mr. Finch was proud that one of his students made All-State Choir, but I think he probably was hoping that it wouldn't be me. He just tolerated me. He wasn't ever mean; he was a very religious man. Whenever one of the kids pulled a prank, he assumed it was I, and it wasn't! But, I did pull one thing on him that almost got me expelled…

Mr. Finch was planning the spring talent show for *Kennett High School*. He was holding auditions, and I came in, wearing a bowtie and nice shirt. I auditioned with *"Does Anybody Know What Time It Is?"* It was a fine little song by the group *Chicago.* Mr. Finch was delighted and he gave me a slot in the talent show.

I had been rehearsing with a little garage band with my friends Chuck Long and Joe McDaniel. On the day of the talent show, we dressed up as *David Bowie- Ziggy Stardust and the Spiders from Mars.* We all painted our faces and wore bizarre outfits with leotards, and we sang *"Suffragette City".* Towards the end of the song, we all yelled out, "Wham, bam, thank you ma'am!" just like *Bowie* did in the song. That was a little too much for the conservative staff of the High School.

Maynard had to go down to the principal's office and beg them to forgive us and keep me in school. We stayed in school, and we were heroes. All the kids thought it was SO COOL! We had to act humble and contrite, though, because we were on the edge.

•••••

During spring break, we only had nine days off from school. I decided to invite Carol, Mike Rogers and Cathy Story to drive with me to California and back. I took Sandy's car, which had been poorly rebuilt after the accident that night my dad had given the random kid the keys to the car to get alcohol. It was a *Chevrolet Monte Carlo*. It was a nice car; it was badly out of alignment because the frame had been bent in the accident, so the steering wheel pulled to the left, but we drove day and night and made it there in less than three days.

We stayed with my mother, who was overwhelmed with us the whole time. I saw Sheryl Otte while I was there, just briefly. She was extremely happy to see me and my heart melted for a moment. The trip was a long run for a short slide. We were only in California for three days and traveled six, but it was an adventure. My uncles Ted & Gerry and their families and my grandma Gizi were in Palm Springs and it was great to see them all. We took photos…I had long, curly hair and I wanted to try to get it as straight as possible, so I wore this stupid red bandana around my head while my hair was drying. I have no idea what I was thinking, but my bandana got into some of those photos.

Carol and I could talk about anything. We made love constantly. She couldn't believe that she was my first one (the stinky prostitute who raped me didn't count!) … She told me that I was way too experienced and good for that. I told her I had been training for years, ever since I read all of those books in my dad's study when I was thirteen.

These three friends of mine were terrible influences on me. We were always searching for drugs. In California, someone gave us a joint laced with PCP. We were in another universe; it was like I was looking through a long tunnel into the world. Another time, we did mescaline and laughed all night. Thankfully, I had a good enough head on my shoulders that I refused to ever put a needle in my arm and I would never take LSD after my bad experience. Mostly, though, we just smoked pot, but we were in a culture of drug use then and most of our friends were participating.

•••••

My dad didn't like Carol. He thought she was a distraction to me and she had no ambition. He was absolutely right. The larger problem was that I didn't respect him or what he had to say because of the terrible example he was setting in my life at that time.

About a month before graduation, things had gotten so bad at the house with my father that I had fallen way behind on preparing for my senior English final essay. After a particularly rough night with my father, when he had begun to try to hit me in his drunken anger and I had to hold him down for a minute until he calmed down, he showed up again at my bedside the next morning.

He asked for my forgiveness, and I asked him for help on my essay. He and my uncle Bill basically wrote my senior essay on President Monroe and the effects of Manifest Destiny on the Western Hemisphere.

Mr. Newman knew what I was going through at my house. It was a small town, and everyone got wind of what was happening. He called me into the classroom alone after I turned in my final essay, and with a wink he told me, "I'm going to give your father an 'A' for this excellent paper, but I'm giving you a 'B Minus'. Don't worry, you'll still pass the class and graduate, but don't pull this shit again." Mr. Newman had become a friend and confidante, and through all of the plays and musicals of which he directed and I performed, we had bonded, after I finally started following his direction, of course. I admired him.

•••••

My sister Betsy and her husband Jim came to visit us for a few days, a couple weeks before my graduation. They plotted with my father to help him to get me to break up with Carol. Their plan was to get us to California after graduation. They had a friend named Bill Atherton in Ocean Beach.

He was a suave, good-looking man in his early thirties, and he was big with the ladies. They would get him to seduce Carol and then tell me about it so I would get angry and leave her. They were serious about this! When we finally got to California after my graduation, Bill Atherton actually turned out to be a cool guy who took us aside and told us what they were plotting. He thought it was hilarious but unacceptable, and we thanked him for his candor. In retrospect, my relationship with Carol was a train wreck, and I'm glad they cared enough to try something to show me the light. I just wouldn't have done it that way.

•••••

My sister Judy and her new husband David came to Kennett before my graduation as well. Maynard was floored by David's looks. David was full-blooded Arapahoe Indian, and he had almost the stereotypical look of a Native American: A long ponytail of black hair that went to his waist, dark skin and high cheekbones, big buck teeth.

Maynard's demeanor probably intimidated David, so David just giggled a lot and stayed quiet. Compared to Judy's previous boyfriend Peter, it was like night and day, but if you took the time to get to know David, he was a loving, compassionate soul. I could tell why Judy liked him.

•••••

My High School graduation was a total fiasco. My mother flew out from California, and my parents were together for the first time since their divorce. I think they both maybe had an inkling of an idea that they might get back together through this, but in fact the opposite happened. Dad was drinking through the whole week, and totally out of control, and mom was sick of it and glad to not be a part of it anymore. Suzanne came out with her darling four-year-old daughter, Wendy. My grandparents were there. Grandma Audrey still and always gave me unconditional love.

When I arrived in this remote little town in the middle of nowhere, I had practically come to Kennett kicking and screaming. I wanted to live in Palm Springs with my mother, but it didn't work out. Now, after living for two and a half years in Kennett, I had secured many lifetime friendships; I had grown and become accepted in a new environment; I was able to understand better and to embrace the culture of the Midwestern United States, and I also became stronger, learning to deal alone with my father during the lowest, darkest days of his life. Even so, emotionally, I felt lost.

My sister Suzanne had just suffered her own detached retina in her eye, and endured the same surgery my father had gone through, six or seven years before. Later, her other retina would detach, and they would use the new laser surgery to fix her other eye. She became a textbook case of surgeries from two different eras.

•••••

My plan following graduation was to go to California for a month or two with Carol, and then prepare to move to Kansas City. I was to get an apartment up there and enroll in *UMKC*.

I wasn't yet seventeen when I graduated. A few days after everyone left in mid-June, I made the drive out to California in my *Pontiac* with Carol. It took us three or four days to get there. We went to Ocean Beach and dealt with the Bill Atherton fiasco, and just a day or two later, I got a call from my dad's secretary, Sandra. He had gotten drunk and set our house on fire. He almost died in the fire, but they got him out with minor burns and heavy smoke inhalation. He was in the hospital, and the house was practically burnt to the ground.

We left California immediately to drive back to Kennett on my seventeenth birthday. When we got there three days later, I went to the hospital to visit Maynard. He had suffered a minor heart attack along with his other injuries, and he would be in the hospital for a few weeks.

After our visit, I went to survey what was left of the house. I had locked all of my childhood memories into my closet in my bedroom when I left just a week before; in the closet, I stored hundreds of record albums, photos, mementos, and a little jewelry. Looters had come in and stolen everything that would move. It was all gone. Later, a friend of mine from High School called me and told me that he and another guy had taken most of my stuff. He wanted to give it back, but the other guy had taken it all and moved out of state. He told me he was sorry and asked my forgiveness. What was I supposed to do? It was a tragedy. The whole thing was a tragedy.

•••••

All of a sudden, I had no money, only the possessions I had carried with me to California in my car, and nowhere to live. When he got out of the hospital, my dad promised me that he would provide the money I needed to start college and get an apartment in Kansas City, because I had not applied for scholarships due to the insanity in my house.

Meanwhile, I lived with Carol at her parent's farm on the outskirts of Kennett for the summer and Maynard lived with some friends. His secretary, Sandra, was fed up with him and also scared for him. I think, despite the twenty-seven-year age difference, that she was genuinely falling in love with him.

Sandra told Maynard that if he didn't stop drinking and doing any substance at all, immediately, that she would petition the State of Missouri to take away his medical license. That threat, and the fact that he had actually burned his house down and lost everything, stopped him from drinking. She also stayed with him and compassionately helped him back from the abyss.

Carol's mother was so nice to me. I stayed with Carol in her bedroom at night, and during the day I did what I could to help around the farm. I pitched watermelons all day during season, which lasted a month.

It was backbreaking work. Four men would pick watermelons and throw them to each other and then up to a man on the wagon. We would work for an hour and then take a ten-minute break. It was extremely hot and humid. We would kick open the watermelons and scoop them out, stuffing the ripe melons into our mouths for hydration. The following day, we would walk by the same melons, now rotting with flies all over them. I swear, after that experience, I never touched a watermelon again as long as I lived.

Carol's father would look at me with stern eyes, drinking his cheap beer, and tell me, "I know what y'all is doin' in 'ere. Y'all is sexin' it up, isn't ya?" I didn't know how to answer him, so I would just smile. He was an unhappy old man who worked his ass off from dawn to dusk.

CHAPTER TWENTY-THREE
Kansas City, Missouri

At the end of the summer of 1975 it was time for me to enroll in the *University of Missouri* at Kansas City. I didn't have much to take with me; I took only the clothes and scattered possessions I had with me when the house burned down. Carol wanted to move there with me, and we were pretty much inseparable at this point anyway. Having basically lost everything else, I was clinging to her, as wild as she was! So, we boarded a Greyhound bus for an eighteen-hour trip. The bus stopped in every little town all the way north to St. Louis, and then repeated the same process all the way to Kansas City.

Maynard was still in pretty bad shape when we left Kennett. He was still living with friends and drinking again, on and off. Although we didn't communicate much that summer after I turned 17 years old, I met him before I left and he gave me two checks. One was for tuition at the University, and the other was to get an apartment and for living expenses.

When I arrived in Kansas City, I opened a bank account and deposited the two checks. Carol and I found a cute, one-bedroom apartment at the *Village Green* apartments, fairly close to the college, and I enrolled and paid my tuition. Although I no longer had a car or bicycle, Kansas City had a pretty good bus system, and I figured out the bus routes to and from school.

•••••

A few days after we settled in, I got a call from the bank. Both of the checks my dad had given me had bounced. In a panic, I tried to reach him, and his secretary, Sandra, answered the phone. She told me that dad's second wife, Sandy, had won a divorce judgment in court and wiped out all of his bank accounts over the weekend. Apparently, she had put a lien on his money, and the courts had taken $27,000.00 out of one account alone on her behalf. He was penniless, and even more, Sandra had threatened again that she would have his medical license revoked because of his drinking, so he had agreed to go into a three-month treatment facility, and he was unavailable.

My father had sold the *Pontiac* he had given to me in High School, along with Sandy's *Monte Carlo*, and left me with no transportation. He left me high and dry on every level.

So, there we were, in an apartment with rent paid for one month and a security deposit, and my bank account was minus several thousand dollars. I was on my own, and I was not going to be able to go to college after all. It was metaphoric. What little that was left of the innocence as well as all of the physical mementos of my childhood had gone up in a huge blaze. I was barely seventeen and on my own, already in debt.

I wasn't even an adult yet. I couldn't vote or get a credit card on my own. My childhood dream of college had been ripped away from my grasp.

This little boy who had grown up surrounded by the love of his sisters and parents was now on his own, without any of them to support him. One by one, they had all abandoned me, and now I was alone in a strange place where I knew nobody, with a dysfunctional girl, who wouldn't get a job, in deep debt, watching what little dreams I had left to hold on to, slip away.

I wrote to my Uncles' Ted and Gerry asking for help. I needed $500.00 to keep going, even though it wouldn't even bring my bank account back to zero. Gerry just ignored me, and Ted wrote me back a stinging letter. Obviously, he had been misinformed. He told me that I should have gone to the *Naval Academy* instead of dropping out of *UMKC* and to not bother him again. I was devastated. I was turned down from the Academy, and I didn't drop out of *UMKC*, I was thrown out because my father's check bounced!

It was the first time I realized that I was going to have to dig myself out. From that day forward, I never received any help from anybody. I did it all on my own. The only one who ever would step up in any way later would be my mother. But, now, she was broke too, and couldn't help me. It was scarier than shit!

•••••

In a panic, I combed the want ads of *The Kansas City Star* newspaper, and I applied for a job in the delivery department of a ladies' department store named *Harzfeld's* on the Country Club Plaza in Kansas City. I was given the job, a full-time, forty hour per week job at two dollars and sixty-five cents per hour.

Harzfeld's was a huge department store for women, similar to *Macy's*. It was a four-story building with everything from designer dresses to furs to perfumes to shoes and everything in-between. My job was to accept everything that came in to the loading dock, organize it and deliver it to all of the different departments quickly, as well as to accept and process all of the merchandise that was to be mailed or shipped out to customers.

It was backbreaking work; I spent most of the day pushing huge carts and carrying heavy boxes, running as fast as I could through the huge, four-story building.

Many of the ladies who managed the specific departments at *Harzfeld's* were beautiful, and very kind to me. They were always stressed, though. It broke up their day to see me bringing them new items, and their smiles brightened my day when I was dragging huge boxes or racks of clothes into their departments. An old perverted gay salesman lurked in the shoe department. When I brought boxes of shoes up to that floor, he would look me over like a predator, and make lascivious comments to me, usually about how he wanted to get me back to his apartment. He was creepy and I avoided that section of the store as much as possible.

•••••

Tad in 1976

Carol didn't want to work. Initially, she was happy to stay in our apartment and wait for me every day. She had brought her orange tabby cat, Angie, with her and we had acquired a couple of kittens, which we named Tess and Eater (all Eater did was to eat, so that was a no-brainer). Carol had issues. She had been adopted, and although Barbara adored her, I think she felt a little lost in life when we got together. She was gorgeous to me. Her long, dark hair and green eyes accentuated her thin, shapely body, and she always seemed to have a look of mischief on her face. She hardly ever wore makeup, but she had a natural beauty that melted my heart. She was bored a lot, and didn't do much about it.

Carol had bouts of depression here and there, and it fit perfectly into my need to fix her, just like I had tried to fix my mother. I was becoming codependent upon her, and she was bored and usually looking around the apartment complex for people who might give us or sell us cheaply some marijuana or other drugs.

I was making barely enough to feed us and pay rent, and still trying to pay off the debt to the bank that my father had created, in my name. I was scared. Occasionally, I would call my sister Suzanne and she would stay on the phone for hours reassuring me that I could make it on my own.

•••••

There were two African-American janitors at *Harzfeld's.* One was an elderly man named John who had been there for forty years, another was a middle-aged man named Gilbert who had been there for twenty years. I would see them every day and say, "Hello, how are you?" They would smile a tired, resigned smile, and Gilbert would say, "Tryin' to make a livin'." Boy, could I relate to that. In fact, I realized for the very first time the struggle that most people have to keep food on the table, the struggle that I would endure for most of my adult life from then on.

A couple weeks after I started at *Harzfeld's*, they hired a man to work with me. His name was Bill Dunphy. He was in his fifties, and he was extremely kind and helpful. I would do most of the physical labor and the running of merchandise, and he would mostly stay in the delivery department working. We became fast friends, and he acted almost as a mentor to me. We would have deep conversations while we were organizing merchandise. Sometimes I would tell silly or dirty jokes, and Bill would smile, almost with a look of kind pity on his face…not the reaction I expected! Once, I asked him what he did on his day off. He told me that he had gone downtown and helped a homeless man, finding him food and clothing. I thought, wow, this guy is cool!

I believe that sometimes God sends you Spiritual Guides in the form of people.

•••••

Carol had a penchant for winning contests. She would listen to the radio and always be that tenth caller who won the prize! Twice, she won record album giveaways; one was *Abandoned Luncheonette* by Hall & Oates, another was a Paul McCartney and Wings album, *Wings at The Speed of Sound.* She

won tickets for us to see Gary Wright. He had just come out with his hit, *Dreamweaver.* I was super interested to see Gary Wright, because he was one of the first to heavily use synthesizers in his recordings. The concert was a total letdown. He did about seven songs, and it lasted about forty-five minutes. But, we did get the tickets free!

Carol won tickets to see the group *Chicago* at the *University of Kansas* in Lawrence, Kansas. It was about a two-hour drive from Kansas City, and we didn't have any way to get there. I mentioned it to Bill Dunphy, and he let us borrow his old *Volkswagen* van to get there. It was a great concert, but I remember on the way back he had no heater in the van. There was some kind of hole in the floorboard, and freezing air came up through and kept me wide-awake for the drive back. Even still, I was sincerely grateful for Bill's friendship.

We went to a Billy Joel concert. At this point, only two years after I had first seen him, he was performing in a huge arena in Kansas City. My creative juices boiled up and again I remembered what I wanted to do with my life… for a minute, anyway.

•••••

I continued my program of backbreaking work. I woke up at five o'clock each morning, took the bus from our apartment complex to the *Country Club Plaza*, to *Harzfeld's*, worked from 8AM until 5PM and then made the trek home. I was getting paid around $20.00 per day for all of that, before taxes, and as hard as it was, I was still grateful that I even had a job. In retrospect, it was such a waste of time for someone like me who had so much potential to do more to help the world. I'm sure there are millions of other very talented people out there just like I had been, just "tryin' to make a living." I had a work ethic, and I took it seriously.

If you're going to do a job, do it right or don't do it at all.

At the end of a year of working with me at *Harzfeld's*, Bill Dunphy told me that he was actually a Catholic priest who had taken a year's sabbatical away from the priesthood to find himself. In that moment, everything made sense to me about him. I was ashamed for the dirty jokes I had told him! But, he had a good point. He told me that if he had told me originally when we met that he was a priest, I would have thought of him differently and treated him differently. Because he didn't, we were able to bond much more as friends. I believe that God sometimes sends you Spiritual Guides in the form of people.

He told me that my struggle in life and the way I handled it, like a man, had actually helped him! Eventually, Bill left the priesthood, got married to a wonderful woman, and lived out his years in Kansas running big nursing homes and senior care facilities. His friendship was crucial to me in a time that was so scary in my life.

Kansas City winters can be brutal. Sometimes the blizzards would prevent the buses from running, and I would walk to work many miles in snow made filthy by plows clearing the way, chilled to the bone. I didn't have much money to buy warm clothes, so I had to improvise.

I worked with a girl who owned a *Chevrolet Corvair* automobile, and she offered to trade the car for my quadraphonic eight-track stereo that I had extracted from my *Pontiac* car before my dad sold it. I had a car! Unfortunately, the car lasted only a week before it completely broke down, and I couldn't afford the repairs. I had basically been ripped off. I cried as I made the fifteen-mile walk back to my apartment in the snow from where the car had broken down. Life was difficult, and at times it felt like I couldn't get a break.

•••••

Carol was getting more and more bored, not working, waiting for me to come home exhausted after working hard all day. Once, I had only a ten-dollar bill left to my name, and I went to the store to get groceries. Somehow, I lost the money. Somebody must have picked my pocket, because I was always so careful never to lose anything. I was devastated. We had no food. I went back to the store and stole a steak, slipping it underneath my shirt just so we could eat. I felt guilty for that for a long time. I had not stolen anything since Junior High School.

Carol met this young couple. They were very good looking. I could tell that she liked the guy. Somehow, around my eighteenth birthday in 1976, Carol told me she wanted us to 'swing' with them, to swap partners. I would have sex with the girl, and she and the guy would have sex with each other. I didn't want any part of it. She went ahead with her part of it all anyway, and they tried to push the other girl on me. I couldn't go near the girl when we got together. I was a one-woman man. I was codependent and obsessed with Carol, and I couldn't imagine touching anyone else. Carol obviously didn't feel the same way.

This girl that they wanted me to screw was gorgeous and voluptuous, but I was miserable and angry and sad, and I learned a valuable lesson. If you want a real relationship with someone, one based upon trust and love, you must never poison it by allowing shit like that! My relationship with Carol never felt the same. One more slice of innocence was lost.

Our life in Kansas City was deteriorating. I wanted to get away from these people. *Harzfeld's* offered me a position downtown in their accounting department after a year and three months of dedicated service. They were going to raise my pay to a whopping two dollars and ninety cents per hour. I was disillusioned. I wanted to get out of Kansas City.

•••••

I constantly felt desperation during the entire time I lived in Kansas City. I was basically still a child who had been dumped into the world in a way I had never imagined, while assuming the responsibility of supporting a dysfunctional young woman. Looking back, I remember feeling that Carol was the last and only person I had left who hadn't dumped me, and I was terrified of being abandoned completely. The albatross I carried didn't just drag me down; it also perpetuated the illusion that it was protecting me from my greatest fears.

But, on the outside, I was a man so I did what men do. I stepped up to the plate. "Manning up" was my antidote to self-pity. It gave me what little self-esteem I did have, under these circumstances.

Everyone who has truly lived has a tragic story to tell, but one must never use pity as a crutch.

We made the decision to go back to Kennett in October of 1976. After another eighteen-hour bus trip, we arrived, exhausted at Carol's parent's farm. The next day, I went to visit my father.

Maynard was not drinking at that point, but he was very cold and he didn't want to have much to do with me. I tried to talk to him about what had happened with me in Kansas City, and how hard life was when he basically just dumped me. He didn't want to hear it. In fact, he was so detached from reality that he asked me how my studies were going up there. I just shook my head in disgust. Was he so out of it that he didn't have a clue what he had done to me? I became angry, but held my feelings within.

Sandra, Kimberley and Maynard 1977

His secretary, Sandra, was now his girlfriend, and she was very possessive over him. She wasn't about to let anything compromise his sobriety. Although I believe she had compassion for me, I believe that she worried that I would be a threat to his sobriety. He was going to *Alcoholics*

Anonymous meetings, and they had moved together into a house in Kennett with her daughter, Kimberley, who was now around seven years old.

I went to a factory in Kennett and applied for a job as an assembly line worker. We drove Carol's dad's beat-up old *Chevy* around, and I was lost and unhappy. My mother called me one day and asked me if I would help her to file a lawsuit in Missouri against my dad. He was years behind in alimony and back child-support and she was struggling.

I found an attorney over in another town and gave her the information on him. I hated to be put into the middle of my parent's ongoing battles. It was a tragedy that my own mother and father hated each other so much that they wouldn't speak to each other or even have civility.

CHAPTER TWENTY-FOUR
Starting Over Again in Palm Springs

My mother, Elaine knew I was miserable in Kennett, and she asked me if I would like to move back to Palm Springs. I said I would if I could bring Carol with me. Elaine scrounged up the money to purchase two airline tickets for Carol and me, and a week later we flew to Palm Springs to start a new life.

Looking back on my life later, I realized that my mother was the only person who consistently tried to come through for me. I would get angry sometimes when I was younger, because I felt that her gifts were conditional. Yes, she could be manipulative and she had the tendency to remind you of all the nice things she did, in order to get her way. The older I got, I started to realize that it's really not unreasonable to expect loyalty when you are generous and giving. Elaine didn't have much to give, either. She lived frugally, so I realized later that it was even more special that she gave to me, and denied herself in the process.

I didn't make it easy on her sometimes either. Carol and I arrived with three cats, and we moved into her two-bedroom Palm Springs condo. Elaine had a roommate in one bedroom, so we stayed on the hide-away bed couch in the living room with cats everywhere and it was untenable for Elaine.

She had our old upright *Gulbransen* piano in the condo. I hadn't touched a piano since my house in Kennett burned down. I remember fingering my way through the song *Georgia On My Mind*. Elaine came down the stairs and frowned. She said, "That's terrible!" She was one to speak her mind. She remembered me playing difficult classical pieces, and she was disappointed.

•••••

Steven and Kathy

My sister Kathy called from Brooklyn, New York one day. She had met a young man named Steven Soffer at a festival of devotees of Guru Maharaj Ji. He invited her to New York for a few weeks to stay with him. After a few months together, she was pregnant, and she was going to stay. In September of 1977, Kathy gave birth to a son, Michael. He was a beautiful baby.

I went out looking for work. I got a job on a construction site, digging ditches in the hot sun. I came home and dropped from exhaustion. It was backbreaking work, and it lasted about a week. I applied as a busboy at *Marie Callendar's* and got the job. After a couple weeks, my mother and Carol were arguing regularly and I decided that we needed to move out and give Elaine a break. I used my first little paycheck to pay the rent on a filthy, disgusting little studio apartment in the drug-infested area of Vista Chino in North Palm Springs. The pool was green from disrepair and cockroaches ran from room to room.

There was a young man named Mark who was staying in the studio next to us. He gave Carol some pot. One day, I came home from work early and I walked in to catch the two of them having sex. I was furious and I confronted them. Mark beat the hell out of me and left. I suppose I had forgotten the one judo lesson I had. What can I say? I'm a lover, not a fighter.

Again, I was devastated. I have no idea why I didn't leave Carol. She apologized and said it would never happen again. I was young and foolish. I was allowing this person to manipulate me, and I was just miserable. I had a black eye and bruised ribs, and a destroyed ego. I never saw Mark again, thankfully.

•••••

After a month at *Marie Callendar's*, I applied for a job at *Sunshine Meat, Fish & Liquor Company* in Palm Springs as a waiter, and got the job. At first, I was working mostly days, but I was finally starting to make enough money to survive. Carol and I moved out of the slum apartment and got a nice, two-bedroom apartment at the *Palm Canyon Apartments* on the South end of Palm Springs. We scrounged some furniture together. I bought a little motorcycle and made it back and forth to work on it.

Sunshine was a large, hip restaurant with wooden walls, separating one huge restaurant into seven comfortable dining rooms; Mexican red tile floors accentuated lush green plants hanging from huge planters everywhere in the restaurant. We did incredible business.

Lyman Martin - Mid 1970s

The owner of *Sunshine* was Lyman Martin. He was a bearded, strong-willed, intimidating sort of person who ran a tight ship. After a couple months, his manager quit. I was working with a waiter named David Webb. I thought he was a good guy, and we worked well together. Lyman made David manager and asked me if I would like to be an Assistant Manager. I agreed, and started to learn the restaurant business from the ground up. David's personality changed as soon as he got a little power. He became a total asshole to everyone, and within a month, Lyman fired him and made me interim manager.

Bob "Andy" Andersen 1979

One day, I was outside, changing light bulbs in the parking lot, and this little bearded guy drove up in a Volkswagen bug. His name was Bob Andersen. He asked me if they were hiring, and I told him to come in and fill out an application. I hired him as a waiter. Bob wanted me to call him "Andy." Andy had traveled to Palm Springs from Tacoma, Washington with his girlfriend, Pam, and he moved in to the same apartment complex where Carol and I were living. Andy and Pam were both around five feet four, and the kindest people you will ever meet. After work, we would meet in the hot tub of our apartment complex, and talk for hours about anything and everything. At some point, Lyman made Andy and me co-managers of *Sunshine*, and I got a little raise.

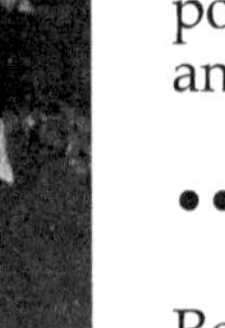
Andy, Friend, Joan, Pam and Tad -1977

•••••

Restaurant management is a lot of work. I would work eighteen-hour days, arriving early for inventory and scheduling. We would set up for lunch and run the floor, supervising the hostesses and waiters, making sure the bartenders had what they needed, and checking quality in the kitchen. We would repeat the process during the long dinner hours. Sometimes we would plate as many as 700 dinners in one night. Lyman was extremely influential in my young life. He taught me concepts, which stayed with me forever. He had five basic tenets: Be firm, fair, consistent, use common sense, and kick ass!

Be firm, fair and consistent, use common sense, and kick ass!

I think he would have liked it if Andy and I were stronger in a sense, but we both felt that we could earn the respect of our employees by hard work, persistence and kindness, rather than demanding respect because of our position. And, it worked. I made lifetime friends out of the experience.

Tad with Bob Andersen 2018

In fact, forty years later, in 2018, Andy (Bob) and I met and had lunch one day. He looked at me, and he told me that, back during this time, he knew I was only eighteen but, in his eyes, I might as well have been thirty years old. He knew that I had been forced to grow up too soon, and he saw the weight of the world on my shoulders.

Andy told me that he had never seen anyone that age with such a work ethic as me, with so much direction or strength of character. I laughed, and said that I certainly didn't see myself that way at that time. For most of my adult life I was just freaked out, desperate to make a living and determined to work my ass off for my family and to make something out of myself, on my own, with no help, against all odds. Since the college option of an expensive medical school had been pulled out from under me, I rolled my sleeves up and did what I had to do to survive.

And, Andy had an almost carefree reckless abandon to his personality. When we were driving, he would put rock music on the radio really loud and flail his arm back and forth as if he were conducting the song to the entire world! I didn't know how to be that way. I was always so scared to act out in the real world on my own, so I 'toed the mark,' never wanting to upset the apple cart, always working hard and keeping my nose to the grindstone. Andy's attitudes and emotions began the long process of showing me that it was okay to be myself and to be a little less stressed out.

•••••

Tim McFall - Mid 1970s

Tim McFall was a cook in the kitchen at *Sunshine.* He was also a drummer. He had just come off of a tour with Merilee Rush, who had a hit, *Angel of The Morning.* Tim had a magnetic personality. He was always upbeat, telling jokes and stories that captivated you. It's funny… we integrate pieces of people's personalities into our own as we evolve. Tim's outward, funny outlook helped me out of my shell; it helped me to remember the confident person I once was before everything came crashing around me. And, he did it without even knowing he did it!

Willie Lynch was the chef at *Sunshine.* He was a tall African-American man from Mississippi. Willie was mean to the waiters, but always with a gleam in his eye. He was a great chef, and he could pump out a thousand dinners a night if it was called for. After it was all done at the end of the night, he would stay and talk with us for a few minutes, delighting us with his Southern wisdom.

1978
Willie Lynch and Joan Clark

Joan Clark was the bookkeeper/office manager at *Sunshine.* She was like the gel that kept the restaurant humming, and we remained friends for many years afterwards.

Lyman had live music upstairs at *Sunshine.* Bands would come in and I became friends with musicians I would later work with. At some point, he decided to transform the upstairs into a disco. Disco was the craze. *Saturday Night Fever* was the top movie, Donna Summer and the Bee Gees were hot, and all the top hits were disco. Lyman called the disco *The Chrome Parrot* and we were just packed every night until two in the morning, extending my hours even further.

•••••

A new disco opened down the street named *Zelda's*. Nobody thought it would make it because *The Chrome Parrot* was so busy. Andy left to go work as a waiter at *Zelda's*. It's funny to think back, because *The Chrome Parrot* only lasted a couple years after that, and *Zelda's* celebrated its fortieth anniversary in 2017.

Across the street from *Sunshine* was a bar called *Josephina's*. The bartender, Michael Lecari, was a friend of mine. He came over to *Sunshine* on occasion and we would buy him a drink. Another friend of mine, Mark Picaar, played an acoustic guitar and sang mellow songs at *Josephina's*. One night I went into *Josephina's* with friends. I was only nineteen, and I ordered a beer. The bartender asked me for my ID and I turned red. One of my buddies said, "Don't you know Tad? He's the manager across the street at *Sunshine*." The bartender apologized profusely, shook my hand and gave me my drink. I felt empowered but also embarrassed because I should have not been at a bar drinking underage. I didn't drink often anyway. I had a really bad taste in my mouth for alcohol because of all of the tragic experiences I had with Maynard. Thank God, I never inherited the scourge of alcoholism.

I was finally able to scrounge enough money together to purchase a used car. I bought a Maroon 1975 *Dodge Charger*.

•••••

Carol became pregnant with my child. She didn't want to have the baby, but I did. Reluctantly, upon her insistence, I agreed to let her have an abortion. I regretted that for years, and always wondered what gender my child would have been, and how they would have turned out. I felt I would have been a good father, even so young, and in my youthful mind I thought that maybe having a baby would have settled her down. We drove to Riverside for the abortion.

Carol was bored. She didn't like that I was working so much, and she finally decided to actually get a job. She went to *Melvyn's* Restaurant and became a cashier. It was perfect for her, because she sat in the back, handling all the checks, and she didn't have to interact with the customers. After a few weeks, though, one of my buddies told me that she was staying late with some of the better-looking waiters and customers, and he just wanted to warn me that she was probably cheating on me.

Carol came home one night and told me that Elvis Presley's bodyguard approached her and her girlfriend at *Zelda's*. Elvis was in town and according to the bodyguard, he wanted two sexy girls to go to his house and have lesbian sex in front of him. In return, the bodyguard said that Elvis would pay six months' rent for them. Carol and her friend declined. I was glad because I thought it was sleazy, but I have to admit there was a part of me that thought, "Really? You've done it with at least two other guys I know since we've been together, and we could have had six months' rent paid!" Sadly, Elvis died just a few months later in Memphis. I think he was just so consumed with drugs that he wasn't thinking correctly anymore.

•••••

I got a roommate for our second bedroom. His name was Richard Apodaca. He was quiet and kept to himself, and at the moment I thought that the best part about him was that Carol was not attracted to him! It helped to have the extra money for rent.

Carol went to Las Vegas for a few days. When she got back, she told me that she was unhappy with our relationship. She had 'hooked up' with someone in Vegas and she thought there was more to life than just living in some apartment with me. She told me, "Variety is the spice of life." I was devastated, and yet I still let her hold me and I made love to her. I begged her to stay, and she agreed, for the time being. I was a pushover, and ashamed that I hadn't yet found my backbone when it came to her. She was my weak link.

Elaine and Tad - 1979

•••••

My mother was becoming strong and whole again. She had a boyfriend named Dick Kane. He was a local jazz pianist. Dick had a trio at the *La Quinta Resort* for years. He was a little older than her, but they got along well. He would come over and teach her jazz progressions. They were 'together' for a couple years when she found out that he was still married and had a wife back East somewhere. She wondered why he would leave for months at a time... poor Elaine.

•••••

Karen Rhodes was a bartender at *Sunshine.* She had a cute little ten-year-old daughter named Amber. Karen was dating my friend Gary Kindlund, another bartender. After a few weeks, they broke up. Karen was about twelve years older than me, but she was so kind and sweet. I would go and visit her and her daughter in Desert Hot Springs, and help her around her house doing little fix-it things. I think we might have been perfect for each other, but we couldn't get over the age difference.

•••••

An African-American waiter named Desi worked lunches at *Sunshine.* He was from the Bahamas and his girlfriend, Judy Williams, was head waitress at *Pal Joey's* in Palm Springs. Everyone knew that *Joey's* was the best place in town to work. The owners were Joe Hanna and Sam Bianco. Joe was a long-time restaurateur in the desert. I had worked with him at *Sherman's* when I was just thirteen. Sam was a quiet, Italian man from Chicago.

Judy Williams 1986

Sam's father was apparently 'connected' in Chicago. Sam was quietly gay, and it was a poorly kept secret. Judy, the head waitress, was the ex-wife of a local entertainer named Jesse Davis. Jesse was a kind African-American man who was very popular in Palm Springs, Los Angeles and San Diego. I had met Jesse briefly when I was twelve, riding my bike past the *Howard Manor* in Palm Springs one evening when he was singing there. Judy was now with Desi, and I was Desi's boss at *Sunshine.*

One late morning, it was Desi's day off and he called me at *Sunshine.* Desi said that he wanted to order some lunch to go. He was going to bring it back to his apartment to eat with Judy. I told him I would deliver the food because I had to run some errands for the restaurant. He thanked me. I didn't have to run any errands, but I did want to impress Judy in case I ever needed another job! I brought tablecloths, napkins, and wine glasses, the whole works. I knocked on their door and there they were in their pajamas. I went in and served them a formal lunch on their coffee table, putting napkins on their laps and pouring their wine. They loved it! Judy told me that if I ever, ever wanted a job at *Joey's* she would make sure to get me in.

We started doing Sunday Brunch at *Sunshine.* Some of my buddies who liked to give me a hard time would come in for brunch. Danny Moffett came in one day with Chris Cardi and Mark Piccone. I thought I would impress them by bringing over three flaming snifters with *Bacardi 151* in them. As I approached the table, one of the snifters fell over and started the tablecloth on fire. I guess I impressed them! I had to live that one down for a while.

•••••

My roommate Richard's brother came to visit and ended up staying for a couple weeks. He was a hard-driving druggie. I came home one night after an exhausting eighteen-hour day and walked in to my apartment. Carol was gone, and she had taken everything. She took the cats, all of her stuff and all of our furniture. She took the stereo system that I had bought piece by piece over a period of a year and a half. She had run away with my roommate's brother.

I went out onto my dark, quiet back patio, curled up into a fetal position and just sobbed for hours. I had been abandoned again. I knew in my heart that Carol wasn't good for me; she wasn't right for me, but my heart was broken. She was my first real love, and I had picked a wild one. I cried for what seemed like forever.

After a couple of weeks, my roommate told me that Carol and his brother had gone down to Del Mar, by the ocean in North County San Diego, and that he was going to move down there as well. He wanted half a month's rent back and he wasn't giving me notice. I told him I didn't have it, because I needed to figure out how to buy a household full of furniture that had just been stolen from me by his brother and my girlfriend.

A couple weeks later, I was able to recover the stereo and a couple of other personal items she had taken. I got a little kitten and named him Julian. I slowly started all over again.

•••••

I wasn't talking much to my father through this whole period. He had basically dumped me and forgotten to check to see if I was still alive. I understand that he needed to find himself again and become whole in his sobriety, but I still felt abandoned by him. Maynard could be narcissistic, yet also an extremely compassionate doctor. At this point, he wasn't a father at all to me.

I heard that Maynard had married Sandra. She was younger than my sisters Suzanne and Judy. Sandra did try to dress and look older than she was. I was appreciative that she had basically saved Maynard's life, but she was very protective still over every move he made. I heard later that my dad owed a huge amount of back taxes, and Sandra's family loaned him the money to overcome the debt. He was indebted to them, and paid them back slowly over a few years.

Betsy, David, James, Jim and Lucas

I heard that my dad and Sandra had made a trip to San Diego to see Betsy and Jim, Lucas and their new baby, David. Sandra almost fainted when she saw the bowl of marijuana on the coffee table. She was very conservative. I thought that they didn't bother to drive the two hours north to see me, and I was insulted.

I was told later that Maynard owed Elaine money from back alimony, and he had to sneak into the State of California to visit Betsy, so he wouldn't be arrested. Although he was bound to pay alimony and child support until I was eighteen, he had cancelled all payments to Elaine when Sandy wiped out his accounts in 1975, and had never resumed them. Elaine was struggling to live on her own. She eventually was able to secure half of his Navy retirement, which helped her to eke out a living, along with giving piano lessons and performing on the piano in lounges here and there.

•••••

Judy with Abraham 1983

My sister Judy called from Oklahoma and told me that she had given birth to a little boy named Abraham. He was half Native-American. He had amazing features; Abraham was a beautiful baby. My sister's lives all seemed so full and I was alone. I was happy for them but I felt so unfulfilled. *Sunshine* became a job instead of a profession that I had thought I wanted to pursue to create a life with Carol.

•••••

Shortly after Carol left, I reconnected with my childhood friend Kurt. He was living in a little one-bedroom apartment on *Calle Abronia* in Palm Springs with his girlfriend, Janet. They had been together since High School. Janet was cool! She was intelligent and kind and a little sarcastic. At least at this point in time, she had learned to put up with Kurt's antics. Let's just say that Kurt was a free spirit, and he had the preclusion to partake in whatever stimulus was around him at the time.

Tad, Janet and Kurt
1978

I found myself at their apartment a lot. They had a little upright piano in their tiny living room, and whenever friends came over, I would play and sing *Tiny Dancer* by Elton John, or some Billy Joel songs. Janet had a couple girlfriends.

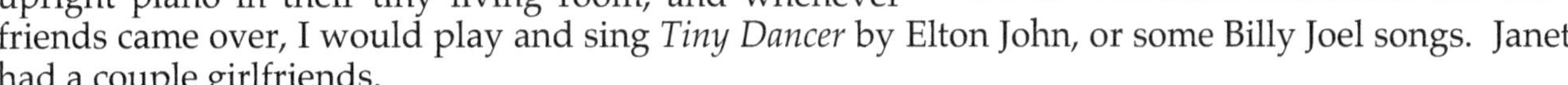

Beverly had a little harelip and she was self-conscious about her looks, but she was a sweet girl. We fooled around a little, but mostly we had good conversations, and later she told me that I really helped her to figure out her life. I thought, "Me, really?" At that point in my life I believed that I was probably the worst person to ever give advice, but I had been through a lot already, so I guess I had something to say. Janet had another girlfriend who was ten years older than me. We hooked up a few times, but I felt so much younger than her and I thought I could never have a relationship with her. It's funny, she was beautiful, sweet and sexy, but I can't even remember her name…

•••••

At some point, I ran into Ken Dobbins. He was a kid I went to Junior High School with. Ken had become Sheryl Otte's boyfriend for a short time in High School. He somehow knew I had been madly in love with her as a young teenager. She had probably told him about my feelings for her in some intimate conversation they had while they were together.

I have no idea why, but Ken apparently felt the need to tell me about how wonderful his relationship had been with Sheryl and exactly how intimate they had gotten. It was a total ego trip on his part. I asked him if they were still together, and he said, no, she had gone off to college. I was kind of bothered by that, mostly because I found it hard to see how Sheryl could hang out with somebody like him.

Later, I heard that Sheryl had found a great guy in college named Mike Coughlin and they had gotten married. It meant a lot to me that she found a good guy. She was just a dream to me, really, but on a soul level, I really wanted her to have a great life.

•••••

One of my buddies was going to Chicago and he wanted to score some Quaaludes to bring back with him. These powerful depressant pills were the rage at the time. I had a friend, an African-American chef (not Willie Lynch from *Sunshine!*), who was also a drug dealer. I contacted him and acted as the middleman, delivering some pills to my buddy.

I felt really guilty about that later, even though I had rationalized that I was just doing a friend a favor. As I was transporting the pills through Palm Springs, a police cruiser came up next to me and I almost panicked. Why would I ever put my life and freedom on the line? I had been through so much that for a time I lost my compass here and there. Yet I was so consistent in my work ethic at the same time. It was weird.

Once or twice, I had tried a Quaalude, and I didn't like the downer feeling. I wanted to be in control always. I was always grateful that I didn't inherit my father's addictive personality. Yes, I had experimented with many drugs during my crazy teenage years, but mostly in moderation as I was navigating my way through an insane young life. I regret allowing so many outside influences to affect me, but I also believe that I had excellent Guardian Angels through it all, and they kept me alive. Through it all, I never, ever had gotten 'lost' into any drug, or any addiction.

•••••

A pretty, kind of flaky girl would flirt with me at work, and I heard she was going to be at a friend's party. One of my buddies told me that she really liked to do cocaine. I thought I would be cool, so I scrounged a hundred bucks together and bought a gram of coke. It was wrapped in a little piece of aluminum foil. I went to the party and saw the girl. Trying to be sophisticated and suave, I said, "Hey, I have a little coke! Do you want to go into the bathroom and do a hit with me?" She said, "Sure!"

We went into the bathroom and I carefully unwrapped the aluminum foil. Just then, she sneezed and the cocaine went all over the room! She said, "Oops, sorry," as she giggled and stumbled out of the bathroom. I was devastated, standing there and feeling really, really stupid! Another lesson well learned. I hated cocaine anyway. But I liked the smell of it (That's an old bad joke).

•••••

(Left to Right) Kenard Riding, "Grandpa Harry" Lyman Martin and Jeff Boardman

Lyman Martin hired a new General Manager named Kenard Riding to oversee his two restaurants. Kenard was a bearded, imposing figure and from the moment he started, he was on my ass for every little thing. I had the restaurant running like a well-oiled ship, but I think he needed to exert his new authority over everyone, so he would nit-pick every little thing he found, and my job became a living hell.

My uncles Ted and Gerry had decided to move my aging Grandma Gizi down to Mission Viejo in Orange County, California, closer to my uncle Ted, from her longtime apartment in Long Beach. My mother was going out to see her for a couple days, and I had a day off, so I met them at Gizi's condo in Mission Viejo. It was perfect for her, and she was delighted to see me. I spent the night in my grandmother's guest room. That night, I had a bizarre dream.

Gizi, Elaine, Ted and Gerry

In my dream, I walked into *Sunshine* but I went into a room I had never seen before. I looked over and there was a picture on the wall. In the room, Kenard was sitting at a desk. He gestured for me to sit down. Kenard began to speak, and he told me that he felt I wasn't strong enough for his liking towards the employees and that I wasn't cut out for restaurant management. He fired me in my dream. When I woke up, I had an unsettled feeling but I shrugged it off. Lyman loved me and he was a loyal man, I thought.

That morning, I drove back to Palm Springs and walked into *Sunshine*. A waiter told me that Kenard was looking for me. I asked where he was and I was told that he was setting up a new office in a room upstairs that had been a storeroom. I walked into this room and it was exactly like it had been in my dream. It was eerie. My hair stood on end as Kenard said, word for word, what I already knew he was going to say from my dream. I had experienced a full-on premonition.

It was a week before my twentieth birthday and I was fired from *Sunshine* for no good reason at all. A day later, Lyman called me and told me that I had been an excellent manager and if I wanted to come in and talk about it, he would go to bat for me to keep my job. In my heart, I knew I was done, so I declined.

•••••

On my twentieth birthday, June 28, 1978, I went water-skiing in Lake Havasu with some friends. It was a wonderful trip, and when I got back to Palm Springs I found myself right in the middle of a huge identity crisis.

I was unemployed and my girlfriend had left me. I had asked my mother to watch my cat Julian for a couple days while I was gone, and she decided on her own that I didn't need a cat with everything that was happening, and she had the cat euthanized! I went out of my mind in anger towards her and sorrow from my cat being killed. I was beside myself. I called my sister Kathy in New York and asked her if I could come and visit her. She was delighted and she told me to come as soon as I wanted to.

So, I put my possessions in storage and I took off in my 1975 *Dodge Charger* on a road trip to find myself.

CHAPTER TWENTY-FIVE
Brooklyn, New York

Betsy, Kathy, Tad, Elaine, Judy and Suzy
1978

My car had a flaw in its carburetor. It wasn't until I sold it years afterwards that I got a letter from Chrysler recalling the part. I took it in to several mechanics and they couldn't find anything wrong. On my road trip back East, the car would sputter and stop on occasion, usually in the worst places to be alone. I would wait a half hour and then start it up again, continuing until the process repeated itself. It was frustrating and scary.

My plan was to first drive to Oklahoma to visit Judy and David and see their new baby boy, and then to Missouri to see Maynard, Sandra and Kimberley, and my grandparents. I was told that Carol had moved home to Kennett with her new boyfriend and she was back on her parent's farm. After Missouri I would drive to Greensboro, North Carolina to visit Suzanne, Bill and my nephews and nieces, and then up to New York.

As I drove the endless miles, first through Phoenix and Flagstaff, Arizona, and then through New Mexico and Texas into Oklahoma, I reflected on my time with Carol. I had healed just a little bit since she left me, so I began to put it all into perspective. Carol had been my bridge from childhood to adulthood. She stayed with me through the darkest period of my life. We were young teenagers in love.

She never made it any easier on me, or on our situation, by working to contribute towards our lives, and when she finally did, she took a part-time, minimum-wage job and probably fooled around with everyone there behind my back, but she was content for a while with what little I could scrounge and bring home to her. Through all of the madness, I believed that she genuinely loved me.

Really, she was her own worst enemy. I feel that she had an inability to be happy and content at that time in her life. Like so many people of our generation, she was caught up in looking for the next high or the next rush. That wildness was exciting to me at first, but although I loved the highs and the rushes here and there, it didn't consume me. I had a built-in work ethic and a strong desire to succeed in the face of unbelievable odds and the worst of circumstances. She was content to hang out and not work much, and it worked for a while.

Naturally, we grew apart because ultimately, we weren't meant for each other. But, that last and final security blanket had been pulled out from under me, and it was unnerving. Subconsciously, it added to my abandonment issues, but I decided to move on and be functional until I was emotionally whole enough to look for love again.

•••••

Judy and David 1978

When I arrived in Oklahoma in July of 1978, it was dusty and sweltering hot. Judy and David lived on an Arapahoe reservation in Calumet, Oklahoma. A cluster of government-built houses sat on dirt lots, and old dilapidated automobiles and trucks were parked everywhere. David welcomed me with an open heart. Abraham was a beautiful baby, and Judy was thrilled to see me. I remember talking to a couple of old Indian men, and they were telling jokes. One of the jokes had to do with the astronaut who landed on the moon, and as he got out of the spaceship, the Indians behind the moon rocks said, "Oh, no, not again!" They all laughed heartily, and I was introduced to my first Native American humor.

After a day or two, I continued on to Kennett. It was great to see my grandmother Audrey again. Pop was sick and unable to tend to his garden, so it was in disrepair. I spent an afternoon cleaning it up for him, and sat watching baseball with my grandma for a while.

Sandra was accommodating to me, and I could tell that she felt compassion for me, but we really had never spoken about anything. We stayed up all night one night, my father, Sandra and I, talking until almost dawn. Sandra explained why she did what she did and how it saved my father, and Maynard dutifully agreed. He didn't speak much, but I was able to pour out my sorrow about how the last couple of years had turned out. I started to 'get it' about my dad. He had to give his life to a higher power in order to stay alive, as he was being taught in *Alcoholics Anonymous*. His higher power was Sandra.

Sandra, Kimberley and Tad 1978

Maynard was not quite himself yet, still experiencing bouts of drinking here and there, but Sandra had the reins pulled tight. I would never get from him what I wanted, not financially or emotionally, so I had to learn to reset the bar of my expectations so I would never be disappointed again.

Little Kimberley was now nine years old, and she was a darling girl. She loved the idea of having an older brother, and she sat on my lap a lot and we laughed and talked. We bonded during that brief time.

I had made the decision to go and see Carol at her parents' farm while I was there in Kennett. She greeted me with open arms, and hinted that she would do anything to run away with me then and there and be together again, but at that point, I knew better and I was truly over the major part of the pain she had caused me. Still, I was loving and kind to her, and I admitted to her that she would always be my first love, and she would remain in my heart, but she had made the decision to move on with her life, and I needed to do the same.

I learned to believe that everything happens for a reason. We may not understand why, when it's happening. God always answers our prayers. Sometimes, however, the answer is "no."

A couple months later, I found out that she was pregnant with this guy's baby and she was keeping the baby. Also, I heard that he beat her up regularly. I thought, how weird it was that I was so kind to her always and she aborted my baby, but she was having the baby of an abuser. Anyway, I was determined to go on with my life.

I traveled on to Greensboro, North Carolina to see my sister Suzanne, stopping briefly in Memphis to visit my Aunt Rose and some cousins. Suzanne's kids had gotten older. Charles was now fourteen, Lori was twelve, Michael was ten and Wendy was eight. They were so happy to see me. They had all moved into a huge house in Brown's Summit, North Carolina.

Bill had planted an enormous garden, and I spent a day or two picking peas with him. I had learned to play (sloppily!) Billy Joel's *Root Beer Rag* on the piano, and the kids asked me to play it over and over again. Billy Joel was coming to Greensboro, and somehow, we got tickets to see him again. I went with Suzanne to the concert, and he was now in the prime of his career. His album *The Stranger* was a huge critical success in 1976, and he had just released *52nd Street*, with a number of hits.

Again, I felt my calling to try to become a star as a singer, pianist and songwriter. I felt that I was not doing what the Lord intended for me to do, and I needed somehow to make it happen NOW!

After a week at Suzanne's, I made the road trip up the East coast of America to Brooklyn, New York. Kathy and Steven were living in the attic of an old Victorian-Style house in the West Midwood section of Brooklyn. It was actually a charming area in the middle of a chaotic city. These homes had been built around a hundred years before. The floors were creaky and the electricity was antiquated, but they were really cool.

Youth is impatience. We all want revolution. What we get instead, if we are persistent, is evolution mixed with heavy doses of reality on the way.

Kathy and Steven's son Michael was just nine months old, and he took to me very quickly. I held him a lot and helped Kathy with him. My sister and I talked a lot. Kathy and Steven meditated and went to "satsang" to talk to the other devotees, quite a lot.

They were completely into health foods. In fact, Steven and another man had invested into *Swan Foods*, a tofu factory in Miami, which distributed soy products and teas to health food stores throughout the East coast.

I would take off and ride the subways all over New York, exploring and not having a clue that I was walking through terrible neighborhoods without the slightest fear. I met a few people, but mostly I stayed with Kathy in her attic house and we reconnected.

Kathy, Steven and Michael 1978

Steven had great pot and an excellent stereo system. He had just purchased a four-track reel-to-reel tape recorder, and we made a cassette of Kathy singing and playing guitar on about ten original songs she wrote. The cassette ended up sounding great, and I kept it and played it for years afterwards. We went to *New York Yankee* baseball games, including the 1978 *ALCS*, watching the legendary team with Thurman Munson, Reggie Jackson, Ron Guidry, Goose Gossage, Bucky Dent, Graig Nettles, Lou Pinella and Willie Randolph. I became a lifetime *Yankee's* fan.

•••••

I hadn't really thought past what I was going to do after I made it to New York. I was kind of lost in a way, and after a couple weeks, Steven started to ask Kathy how long I was planning to stay. After a couple more weeks, we had a little confrontation, and I cried because I really didn't know what I wanted to do with my life, or where I was going to go from here.

All these guys in New York were into this huge ring, transporting large amounts of super high-quality marijuana from coast to coast. I needed money and I offered to get involved as a 'mule', moving it. I wasn't greedy and I wasn't in it for the rush. I was desperate for money and I stupidly got involved. Fortunately, my Guardian Angels were again working overtime.

They would stuff two huge *American Tourister* suitcases full of pot, lining the insides with *Noxzema Lotion*. The lotion would kill the smell so that the suitcases would make it past the drug-sniffing dogs.

I would be dropped off at JFK airport and take a *Boeing 747* jet from New York to San Francisco under an assumed name.

I would be picked up at the airport in San Francisco and brought to a safe house. I would spend a couple days tripping around San Francisco and then fly back and do it all over again. I did this about four or five times and the last time I did it, I rented a car, drove down to Palm Springs to visit my friends, and then drove back across country, stopping in Missouri, on my way back to New York. I was paid about $500.00 per trip. I remember on this last road trip from Palm Springs to New York in September, I rolled seventy-five joints and stayed high throughout the entire trip in my car. I was a lost puppy, living on the edge.

•••••

On September 10, 1978, I ate my last piece of red meat ever. At *Sunshine* I had been instructed by the owner to try new items on the menu each night for quality control. I had eaten so much meat that I was turned off by it. At Kathy and Steven's, I pored through books on health foods and the brutality of the meatpacking industry. On this road trip back to New York, stopping over in Kennett, Dad and Sandra took me to *McCormick's Steak House* in Kennett, and I had my last steak.

Quitting eating red meat wasn't ever really a religious or political thing for me. Later, when I had kids, I let them eat whatever they wanted. I didn't want them to go on a baseball trip to *McDonald's* and not have a hamburger with everyone else if they wanted to. It was just a personal decision, and I never looked back. I did feel healthier in general without consuming red meat.

When I arrived back in New York, Steven asked me if I would consider going down to Miami to manage *Swan Foods.* He and his partner were concerned that the company still wasn't making profits, and they thought that my management experience might help the operating owner down in Miami to streamline the business. I gladly agreed. I needed to open a new chapter in my life, and this sounded like an excellent opportunity.

CHAPTER TWENTY-SIX
Miami, Florida

I arrived in Miami in late September of 1978, and met the operating owner of *Swan Foods.* His name was Richard. He was a quiet kind of hippie guy with a girlfriend who was a fruitarian. All she ate was fruit. As a result of her diet, she had these lesions on her body and she was pretty unhealthy, but beautiful, with big brown eyes and long dark hair. She went braless with loose-fitting flowery dresses.

Miami was amazing. The Atlantic Ocean was greener and a bit murkier than the blue Pacific water. White sand on Miami Beach poured into the high-rise hotels dominating the skyline. Cubans cooked and served ethnic delicacies at roadside stands. Floridians were laid-back, somewhat like Californians. It was hot and humid, but avocado trees were everywhere, and, at first, I loved working at the tofu factory, although I was a little lonely with no friends anywhere around.

I learned the process of making tofu from soybeans. *Swan Foods* sold baked tofu, caraway seed tofu, eggless egg salad; soymilk, soy yogurt and a myriad of really cool items. I quit eating dairy products while I was there, and just ate soy products, mainly because they were free!

I needed to find a place to live, so I looked in the want ads of the *Miami Herald* newspaper. An elderly lady was renting out her back house in Miami Springs. It was pretty reasonable, so I went by to meet her. She told me that her husband had died about five years back, and the little back house had been empty since he died. It was a charming little furnished one-bedroom cottage, and I gave her a deposit immediately. She had cleaned it up as best as she could at her age, so I moved my stuff in and decided to deep clean the little house the next day.

After my long day at the tofu factory, I drove back to the cottage to get some sleep. I sat in bed for a few minutes reading, and then reached over and turned off the light to sleep. I drifted off, but I woke up about an hour later. I thought I felt something crawling on me, so I reached over to turn on the light, and the moment the light went on, a thousand huge cockroaches scattered in every direction! These enormous, ugly roaches were literally all over me, all over the bed, the lamp, the walls, the ceilings, the floorboards, everywhere! It was like a scene from a horror movie. I screamed! Needless to say, I couldn't sleep at all that night, or really any night afterwards for as long as I stayed there. I bug-bombed the place every day before I left for work, and I never got rid of all of the cockroaches. Nor did I ever get one good night's sleep.

•••••

At the tofu factory, I was hard at work every day. The co-owner Richard didn't keep good books, so I set up an accounting system and started trying to make sense of receipts, shipping invoices, inventory control, and all the other things a manager does. I had the experience from *Sunshine* to manage every facet of the business, although I learned a lot about manufacturing and distribution of products in this job. I thought that Richard would be grateful for my help and organization, but he almost seemed to resent me for 'cleaning up' his operation.

Richard had big ideas. He wanted to manufacture and freeze tofu pizza with whole-wheat crust, and he needed new equipment to expand. He called Steven and asked for ten thousand dollars to buy a new *Hobart* machine. One night, I left Miami after work and flew to New York. After sleeping a couple hours at Kathy and Steven's house, I was given a bag with ten thousand dollars cash and I got back on a plane to Miami. On the way down, I witnessed the most amazing sunrise on the Atlantic Ocean! I felt like a jet setter.

•••••

In October of 1978, the devotees of Guru Maharaj Ji organized this massive worldwide festival in Orlando, Florida. Many of the people I knew and worked with at the tofu factory were going to the event. Kathy and Steven rented a motor home, and they drove to the festival from New York with their young son, Michael.

Steven offered to purchase a tent for me to sleep in, if I wanted to make the trip from Miami. I agreed and planned to take a few days off for the event. I wasn't really into the whole thing from a religious perspective, but more as an observer. I've always kept an open mind, feeling that there is something to learn in every experience, as long as it's not harmful to you. I also wanted to see my sister!

Orlando is only about an hour North of Miami up the Florida Expressway. A British girl I had met offered to make the drive with me. She was about ten years older than me, and she was in to the Guru. Her name was Penny. She was sweet and kind and pretty. I loved her accent!

We stopped halfway and went swimming in a little pond next to the *Florida Turnpike*, oblivious to the fact that alligators are everywhere in Florida. Thank you again for watching over me, my Guardian Angels!

Continuing on, we made it to Orlando around dusk. I asked Penny if she wanted to stay in the tent with me, and she agreed. When morning came, we cuddled together in the tent. She came on kind of hot and heavy to me and I asked her if she wanted to make love. She said that she was very attracted to me, and she really wanted to, but she felt that she was married to the Guru, so she didn't think it would be appropriate. At that point, I started to think that maybe this was a cult or something that I was in the middle of. It was bizarre.

More than twenty thousand people were at the festival from all over the world. The best way to describe these people would be to say that they were experiencing bliss and would sometimes chant loud slogans, like "Bolie Shri Satgurudev Maharaj Ji Keeee Jayyyyy!" Mahatmas walked through the masses, and music was on the main stage, leading up to the last day when Guru Maharaj Ji talked. It was really cool and people of all walks of life were very kind and helpful to each other.

I realized that people were experiencing this on many levels. Just like a church can be cult-like to some and just a really cool experience to others, I got it. For me, I enjoyed the experience and I got a lot of philosophical meaning from the speeches, but I never got to the point in it where I was meditating, or "receiving knowledge," which, I'm told, was a big step in the process of knowing what it was all about.

When I went back to Miami, I went to a couple meditation events with Penny, but I just sat there with my eyes closed and my mind very active. They tell you to clear your mind and not to think of anything, so I would think about not thinking about anything, and then I would think about that. Meditation, in that form, wasn't for me either, although in later life, I learned to meditate in my own way during my long walks on the beach, or late at night in my stillness before sleep.

•••••

A month or so after the festival, I started to complete the process of pulling all of the accounting books together at *Swan Foods* from the previous year, and in the process, I discovered that Richard was stealing huge amounts of profits from Steven and his partner. I was in a huge quandary. I knew that the moment I let Steve know, the business would probably fall completely apart, and it was a promising upstart, making a lot of money. It's just that none of that money was actually making it back to the investors, one of whom happened to be my brother-in-law.

The key to the success of *Swan Foods* up to this point had been Richard and his knowledge of soy products. For a moment I thought about confronting Richard before I told anyone else, and making some kind of a deal with him that if he cleaned up his act and started sharing profits with the other owners, I would be cool, as long as he let me take control of the finances on behalf of Steve. Richard was a loose cannon, though, and I felt that I would literally fear for my life if I even mentioned it to him. I was right. I couldn't stay silent, though, and I stayed up all night that night at my little cottage, spraying roaches and praying on what to do.

The next day, I called Steven and told him what I had found out, offering proof.

As spiritual as he was, Steven was also a tough Brooklyn boy and he was not about to be ripped off. He flipped out and called Richard immediately.

The last memory I have of *Swan Foods* was of being chased out by Richard brandishing a huge knife, trying to kill me. He almost succeeded as I slipped and he lunged at me. I barely made it to my car and locked the doors as he banged on my windows and I drove away. I went right to my little cottage, grabbed everything I owned and left Miami that afternoon, knowing that he would come after me and finish the job if he had the chance.

It was just before Christmas, 1978, and I drove to Suzanne's in North Carolina without stopping. I arrived, exhausted, late the next day at Suzanne's house.

•••••

Suzy welcomed me with open arms. She and Bill were having marital problems, and it was nice for her to have a sibling and an ally there around Christmas. When I was finally out of danger, I sighed and reflected upon what had just happened. I realized that during all the time I had been in Miami, a huge part of me longed to be back in California again, as if my destiny were waiting for me there and I was in the wrong place, missing out on it.

I remembered what Judy, the head waitress at *Pal Joey's* had said to me, that if I ever needed a job, to come to her, so I called her and she hired me immediately as a waiter. She told me I could start right after the first of the year, in January of 1979. I called Kurt and Janet, and they offered to let me stay with them until I found a place of my own. This was going to work out great, because their apartment was only a few blocks away from *Joey's*, and I could walk to work until I figured how to get my car back out to California.

In Miami, I was supposed to be paid for the month, but Richard decided to try to kill me instead of paying me, so I was completely broke. My brother-in-law Bill paid for a one-way ticket for me to fly back to California, and I left my *Dodge Charger* parked on their property in North Carolina.

CHAPTER TWENTY-SEVEN
Meeting Stephanie

I flew into San Diego on the 29th of December 1978, and Betsy picked me up at the airport, giving me a huge hug. It was nice to see little Lucas again. He followed me around and clung to me, with his glasses on and his huge smile. Betsy's other son David was around two years old, and he would furiously ride his tricycle all over the neighborhood with a determined look on his face. He was a strong-willed little guy.

Betsy drove me to Palm Springs. Janet, in particular, was really happy to see me again. We got along great. She and Kurt opened their little home to me, set me up on their little couch and I started working at *Pal Joey's* shortly after the New Year. Kurt had an old 1954 *Buick Roadmaster* that was his prize. He let me drive the car whenever I wanted. It was so huge it felt like I was driving a tank, literally, from a different era. But, it was a really cool car and people would stare and wave at you when you were behind the wheel.

•••••

On the very first day I worked at *Joey's*, I met two people who would be linked with my destiny from that day forward. Stephanie Haddock Burge was the head cocktail waitress. She was twenty-one years old and she had a five-year-old daughter, Regina, and a twenty-one-month-old son, Kevin. I met her little ones for the first time at an employee meeting, a couple weeks after I started.

Stephanie was of Irish and Eastern European descent, very much like I was. Her fair skin was tanned. Sparkling green eyes and reddish, shoulder-length brown hair gave way to a somewhat pear-shaped figure formed from giving birth to two children. She hid her smile with a closed mouth much of the time because of teeth that needed braces and never got them, but she was a darling, sweet, hard-working young woman with a strong outward persona. Although I worked back in the restaurant, I would see her when I was in the bar ordering drinks, and she was always kind and helpful. We became friends quickly.

Stephanie was Joe Hanna's 'go-to' girl. Joe was a bubbly, friendly light-brown skinned Lebanese-American man with little to no hair on his head, so he wore a toupee´. He had started out with the *Rim Rocks* restaurant in the late 1950's in Palm Springs, and had owned several other establishments as well. But *Pal Joey's* was his prize. It was always packed with socialites, millionaires, movie stars and yuppies. People would come in the front door and Joe would yell out their names in a loud voice, "LOOK WHO IT IS! LOOK WHO'S HERE! IT'S JOHN ROTHSCHILD! JOHN, HOW ARE YA? STEPHANIE, GET MR. ROTHSCHILD A DRINK!" Joe had the knack of making people feel like they were important.

Stephanie was the best cocktail waitress I had ever seen. She could handle a whole room on her own, running circles around the other waitresses. Underneath her friendly façade, I sensed a troubled girl who had grown up too fast.

Eddie Balderama was another waiter at *Pal Joey's* working with me. Sometimes we were assigned a certain section to wait on as partners. Eddie was Pilipino-American, born and raised in Los Angeles. He wasn't short but wasn't tall either. Eddie had long, dark hair, dark skin, piercing, inquisitive eyes and a dry sense of humor. Most of the time he wore glasses. Eddie was observant, taking in everything around him as if he was creating a snapshot in his mind for later. His kindness made me feel right at home from the first day I walked in the place. We also became fast friends.

Eddie had a small apartment down the street from the *California Angels* spring-training camp in the heart of Palm Springs. He had a record collection that spanned an entire wall of his apartment, and Eddie turned me on to R&B music. We would listen for hours, and later he made me cassettes of his favorite music, which helped to expand my musical awareness. Eddie was cool.

Eddie and Tad
1979

•••••

Although I had to work my way up in the chain of seniority at *Joey's*, I was still making better money than I ever had, and working fewer hours than I had as a manager at *Sunshine* by far. Judy was a hard-core head waitress to work for, but she was great to me and I worked hard to make her proud.

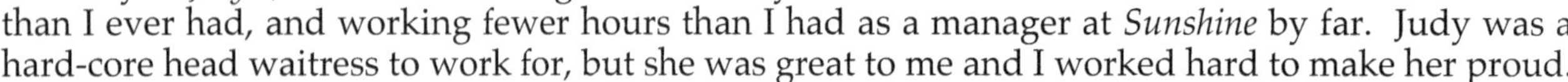

One night, Eddie and I were waiting tables as a team. A famous mobster, Frank Bucceri, was having dinner in the restaurant. The other owner of *Pal Joey's,* Sam Bianco was from Chicago, and Frank Bucceri was connected with Sam's father back in the windy city. Judy told us to take very, very good care of Mr. Bucceri.

Frank Bucceri was a big smoker, and Eddie was paranoid about making sure that Frank's ashtray stayed clean. Eddie would go to the table and replace the ashtray every five minutes or so. At one point, Eddie went to change the ashtray once again, and Mr. Bucceri slammed his hand down on Eddie's hand, looked at him with piercing, angry eyes, and said, "If you touch my ashtray one more time, I'll kill you!" Eddie was shaking so hard he couldn't go back to that table, so I finished waiting on Mr. Bucceri for the rest of the evening.

In my career, I've worked for many Italian restaurateurs. Many, many guys from the "syndicate" hung out in these places. Men who were connected didn't bother me or scare me. But, I never would have dreamed of crossing any one of them. I was very, very respectful to them, and I stayed aloof to their activities. I didn't even want to know what was going on.

Also, I think, later when I performed for "connected" Italian men and their entourages; they admired my talent, although I could have learned a few more songs in Italian if I really wanted to schmooze them. I just never was that guy who did that. I always just tried to be myself and hoped that would be enough. Respect was the key. Looking them in the eye with respect and acknowledgement… and treating them with kindness while not being intimidated… worked for me. On any given night, "Jerry the Crusher", "Big Tuna" or "Fat Philly" would be holding court in *Pal Joey's* with their *Paisans;* their *Goombahs.*

•••••

Greg Jacobs - 1979

Greg Jacobs was one of the food preparers in the kitchen at *Pal Joey's.* He was an amazing artist and the son of George Jacobs, whom had been Frank Sinatra's valet of many years. Later, Greg changed his name to "Snake Jagger," and today, many people prize his artwork.

Greg decided to live outside in the elements, up by the *Palm Springs Aerial Tramway*, out in the desert. He literally 'built' a home out of rocks and dirt, and lived out there for months. My friend Andy, at this point still working at *Zelda's*, would go up there with Eddie and me, and we would spend whole days out in the wilderness getting high with Greg. He learned to deal with snakes out there, so we called him Snake Man, which led to Snake Jagger… Greg's dad George would later become a very close friend of mine.

Snake Jagger's Desert Compound 1979

George Jacobs

Sam Bianco, the other owner of *Pal Joey's*, usually stayed in the shadows, working in the office during the day and then coming in for dinner most nights. He was a quiet man, and very observant.

Sam had a jewelry business and he was training a young, Italian man to be a jeweler. Sam was putting this "Italian Stallion" through jewelry school. This kid didn't look or act gay at all, but it was generally expected that Sam was probably doing all this stuff for the young man in exchange for something. Aside from that, Sam was a great guy. In times of need, I was able to go to him and he would figure out some way to help me, without ever expecting anything in return (thankfully). I appreciated Sam.

•••••

Living with Kurt and Janet was good for a month or two, but we really were in closed quarters. They were so kind to me, but I started to feel as if I was outlasting my stay. The ten-year-older-than-me girl I had dated before would come over and we would hook up. Once, Kurt and Janet went out with us on a double date to *Joey's*, and Stephanie waited on us in the bar before dinner.

Kurt, Janet and Tad 1979

Janet and I had a wonderful connection. She would ask me to play my original songs, and I would pull out my fragmented lyrics and ask her opinion on them. She was very supportive of me, and our closeness meant a lot to me.

•••••

My friend Michael Schwartz from *ISOMATA* would come over to Kurt's apartment, looking to get high. Half the time, we would pull out a bag of mostly seeds and stems and smoke it anyway. We wrote a couple of songs together…one song, *San Francisco, I Owe It All to You* was actually a pretty good song and I ended up recording it years later. Mike was positive and fun and cool to hang out with.

One weekend, he offered to come with me to visit Betsy and Jim down in San Diego. I wanted to hang with Betsy, and to see her kids, Lucas and David, so Mike went along for the ride. On the way down to San Diego, he confessed to me that he was bisexual. In a weird way, I felt like maybe he was hitting on me, or exploring to see if I felt the same.

Throughout my life, I've had many gay friends and I have absolutely no problem with it, if that is your preference, but it's not mine and never was. I felt uncomfortable for the rest of that weekend, but Mike and I stayed good friends anyway afterwards. Mike went on to become a great ballroom dancer, winning national competitions, and we did write a couple more songs together, later in life.

•••••

Kurt was involved in some business dealings with Walter, an older man who was dating Kurt's mother Marlene, for a time. Kurt would go around to businesses and homes and try to sell this stuff called *Perma Rock.* In the desert, people would put rocks outside their homes or businesses for landscaping. I always thought it was ugly, but it's environmentally efficient. *Perma Rock* was a glue-like substance that would basically freeze all the rocks in place. Some people would actually spray the glued-down rocks green to resemble grass.

Kurt and I installed this stuff on Portola Avenue in Palm Desert, outside a mobile home park, and for years and years, I would drive by and marvel that it lasted so long. It was hard work, though, and the rock was more hideous than you could imagine!

•••••

Janet was working for a law firm in Palm Desert, *Hirschi, Healey and Healey*. One of the partners, Jean Hirschi, was in a wheelchair. She was a kind elderly lady, and she was having a house party in June of 1979. Janet suggested to Mrs. Hirschi that she hire me to perform for the party. Janet got me my first paid gig!

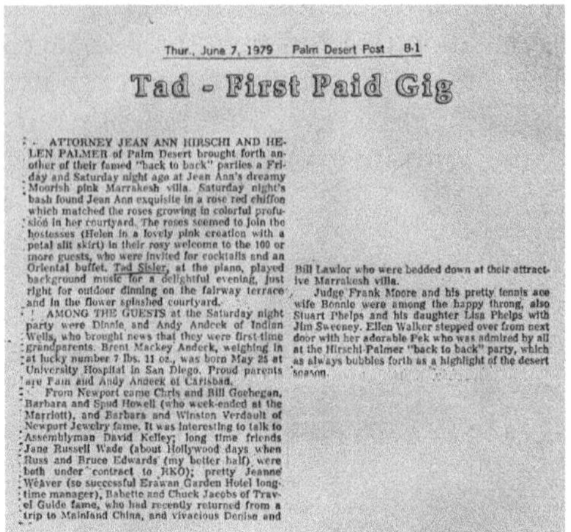

Thur., June 7, 1979 Palm Desert Post B-1

Tad - First Paid Gig

ATTORNEY JEAN ANN HIRSCHI AND HELEN PALMER of Palm Desert brought forth another of their famed "back to back" parties a Friday and Saturday night ago at Jean Ann's dreamy Moorish pink Marrakesh villa. Saturday night's bash found Jean Ann exquisite in a rose red chiffon which matched the roses growing in colorful profusion in her courtyard. The roses seemed to join the hostesses (Helen in a lovely pink creation with a petal slit skirt) in their rosy welcome to the 100 or more guests, who were invited for cocktails and an Oriental buffet. Tad Sisler, at the piano, played background music for a delightful evening, just right for outdoor dinning on the fairway terrace and in the flower splashed courtyard.

AMONG THE GUESTS at the Saturday night party were Dinnie and Andy Andeck of Indian Wells, who brought news that they were first-time grandparents. Brent Mackey Andeck, weighing in at lucky number 7 lbs. 11 oz., was born May 25 at University Hospital in San Diego. Proud parents are Pam and Andy Andeck of Carlsbad.

From Newport came Chris and Bill Geehegan, Barbara and Spud Howell (who week-ended at the Marriott), and Barbara and Winston Verdault of Newport Jewelry fame. It was interesting to talk to Assemblyman David Kelley; long time friends Jane Russell Wade (about Hollywood days when Russ and Bruce Edwards (my better half) were both under contract to RKO); pretty Jeanne Weaver (so successful Erawan Garden Hotel long-time manager), Babette and Chuck Jacobs of Travel Guide fame, who had recently returned from a trip to Mainland China, and vivacious Denise and Bill Lawlor who were bedded down at their attractive Marrakesh villa.

Judge Frank Moore and his pretty tennis ace wife Bonnie were among the happy throng, also Stuart Phelps and his daughter Lisa Phelps with Jim Sweeney. Ellen Walker stepped over from next door with her adorable Pek who was admired by all at the Hirschi-Palmer "back to back" party, which as always bubbles forth as a highlight of the desert season.

When Janet told me that Jean Hirschi wanted me to perform for her party, I almost fainted from fear! I had never done a paid gig! In the two weeks I had to prepare for the party, I put together a book of about fifty popular songs and standards that I felt comfortable enough performing. On the night of the event, I was jittery but well received. Jean wanted me to play the song *You'll Never Walk Alone* which I thought was kind of an interesting choice since she was unable to walk, but I knew it well from the years of hearing my dad belt it out in his booming drunken voice, with all his other favorite show tunes. I was on cloud nine after the party. I had done my first gig!

•••••

Late at night, *Pal Joey's* turned into a disco. It was a classic setting with a mirrored disco ball rotating, and mirrored walls on the dance floor. Celebrities would come out to the desert from all over the world and go into *Joey's*. On any given night, you could see David Bowie, Denny Terio, Nick Nolte, Bernie Taupin and many others. Frank Sinatra would bring big groups in, always with his friend, comedian Pat Henry. People would go back and forth between *Zelda's, The Chrome Parrot* and *Pal Joey's*. There was a waitress named Danielle at *Joey's*. I wanted to ask her out but I didn't know how. She was kind of a party girl, but she was gorgeous.

One night in April, I heard that everyone, including Danielle, was going to go over to *Zelda's* to party after work. Toni Prenesti, a big Italian guy had just moved to Palm Springs from Alaska. He looked, acted and talked like he should have been from Philadelphia or Chicago, but he was a good guy. Tony had a big table at *Zelda's* that night, and he had invited everyone to come over and drink with him. Eddie and I decided to go over after we finished.

When we arrived at *Zelda's*, Danielle wasn't there but Stephanie was sitting at Tony's table. Eddie and I sat with Stephanie, and we danced through the night. Eddie and Stephanie were both good dancers and I was a dork. They would laugh at me, but at some point, I did some John Travolta disco move that almost looked like break dancing, and everyone in the disco went crazy, surrounded me and cheered. I guess Andy's influence of learning to let go was starting to rub off on me, as long as I had a drink or two!

Stephanie was pretty drunk when it was time to go, and I offered to drive her home. I had Kurt's old tank of a *Buick* sitting outside the disco. After we said our goodbyes, we walked down the steps from *Zelda's*, hand in hand, and in the moonlight, we looked into each other's eyes. We walked through the courtyard, holding on to each other. A white butterfly hovered around us, out of nowhere, and we laughed. It was a surreal experience for me; like lightning struck my brain; as if I finally recognized a very important soul I had known in another place or time. We kissed. For a few minutes, we window-shopped outside the businesses around *Zelda's*, and then I helped her into Kurt's *Buick* and drove her home.

Stephanie was renting a huge, three-bedroom house on a golf course. When we arrived at her house, we walked into the sparsely furnished living room, talked for a few minutes, started to kiss and then we went into her bedroom and made love.

I fell asleep in her bed, and a handful of hours later I awoke to two children bouncing on top of me on the bed! The first thing that came to mind was that childhood book I read, entitled *Are You My Mother?* At that moment, I hoped that I wasn't just one of many other men who woke up to these darling little children.

Kevin, Tad and Regina
1979

Wiping her eyes, Stephanie reintroduced me to Regina and Kevin, and they welcomed me into their home. Dragging me around with a huge smile and disheveled, long blond hair, Regina showed me every room and the pool outside, which had turned green from algae. Looking around, I noticed that the lovely large house, although nicely furnished in certain rooms, was in total disarray. Stephanie was obviously overwhelmed with her life, although her children were happy and very nice to me.

Stephanie had a live-in nanny named Jeannie. She was a heavyset, kind Mexican girl and the kids were comfortable with her. Stephanie told me that she had a new toothbrush in the bathroom drawer that I was welcome to use, and when I went in to brush my teeth, every drawer I opened in the bathroom was stuffed with cash. Stephanie would come home late at night, exhausted from hard work, and just stuff her tips in all of her drawers.

Jeannie told me that most of the time Stephanie would forget to pay the electric bill. When the man from the power company came to the door to turn off the electricity, Jeannie would just go to a drawer, count out the cash she owed and hand it to him to keep the power on.

Stephanie was making huge money for a cocktail waitress, bringing home sometimes a thousand dollars a night in tips. All the high rollers came into *Joey's*, and she was their main girl. She was also surprisingly not sleazy, considering the way her profession was perceived during those turbulent times of the late 1970's. Reading the stories about the insane drug culture of *Studio 54* in New York City, one would imagine that everyone in this business was a whore or con artist. Although there were elements of that (as I'm sure there are in every business), most people in the service industry were far from that stereotype, working hard to support families or build dreams in the only way they knew how. Stephanie had a certain morality to her outlook, and she tried her hardest to be classy, even when filthy old men pinched her on the ass.

After a nice morning with Stephanie and her children, I drove back to Kurt's house. I was off for a couple days before I went back to work, and I remember seeing her again for the first time as we were driving up to work. About a block away, we stopped our cars, got out and hugged each other. We were both kind of embarrassed but there was an enormous spark between us, as if we were meant to find each other.

•••••

Over the course of the next couple months, I stayed with Stephanie most nights. Regina and Kevin accepted me completely and loved me as their own from day one. One day, I took little Kevin in the car with me back to Kurt's. Kevin called me "Taddy" and Janet thought he said, "Daddy." She was upset and she asked me what I was getting into. Was I ready to have a family? I told her not to worry and that I was following my heart. I knew I was supposed to be with Stephanie like I knew I was breathing. It was that simple. Little did I know how complicated this relationship would eventually become.

CHAPTER TWENTY-EIGHT
Stephanie's Family

As I got to know Stephanie better, she told me her story, and it may have been even more bizarre and heartbreaking than my own.

Stephanie's grandfather, Ambrose Haddock, had been a powerful judge in New York City in the early to mid-twentieth century, working with Mayor LaGuardia on many issues. He was the first policeman in New York to become an attorney, and then a judge. He was so well respected that he was given the task to counteract the gangsters' monopoly on gambling in New York City. There were gambling machines in bars all over the city, and in the middle of the night, New York's finest confiscated all the machines. Knowing that some officials were being paid off, at Mayor LaGuardia's direction, Judge Haddock ordered all the machines to be dumped immediately into the New York Harbor so they couldn't be used again.

For several months following his decision, gunshots broke the windows of his house in the Bronx, and the family had to be guarded. Ambrose and his wife Ruth had four sons and two daughters. Their youngest son, Russ, was Stephanie's father.

As a young adult, Russ Haddock became a jazz pianist, touring all over the country with his trio and recording on *Decca Records.* Stephanie's mom, Alice was a troubled but pretty young girl from a Jewish family in New York. Stephanie was told that her mother's family pushed her to marry Russ because of the influence his father had in New York, hoping he could help them with their business.

RUSS HADDOCK

The marriage of Alice and Russ didn't last long. They had a son, Russ, Jr., born on March 2, 1956 and a daughter, Stephanie, born on April 9, 1958. Stephanie's dad Russ was absent most of the time touring with his trio. Alice became tired of it and left him. According to Stephanie, Alice and a few of her relatives had some mental health issues.

Alice wanted custody of the children, and at the hearing, the attending Judge put the children on the stand and asked them whom they wanted to live with. Stephanie's brother Russell said that he wanted to be with his grandfather, the only constant person in his life, and Stephanie just wanted to be with her brother, wherever he was.

Judge Haddock took control of custody of Russell and Stephanie. The Judge raised them for most of their childhood. At one point, Alice came to pick up the kids for one day and kidnapped them. She was working at an orphanage out of town, and she put the kids into the orphanage. At some point, she quit the orphanage and left them there. Stephanie was very sick, anemic and thin. Although she and Russell were separated at the orphanage, she saw him on occasion and she told me that it literally kept her alive to see him. They remained at the orphanage for almost a year.

Eventually, the Judge found them and brought them home. Alice was not allowed to see her children again. When they were young adults, they went back to see her. Initially, Russell was going to live with his mother, but Alice freaked out, yelling at Russell; she put all of his clothes in the incinerator in an angry tirade, and he left. As a result of their traumatic childhood, Russ, Jr. had anger issues. He was an extremely negative person. He was cocky and arrogant, and with a little empathy I could tell that it was a front for painful insecurity and self-loathing.

Ambrose's wife, Stephanie's grandmother Ruth had debilitating Parkinson's disease. She spent Stephanie's entire childhood upstairs in bed. Steph would go to her room and rub her hands, which had been cramped into deformity. She would brush her grandmother's hair and try to comfort her. This had a huge impact on Stephanie. She was compassionate to a fault.

Judge Haddock loved his grandchildren, and although he was a tough man, he provided well for them. They were strong Catholics, and he instilled into Stephanie a need to insist upon justice whenever she saw anything wrong.

After years of living with the Judge and going to a Catholic school in the Bronx, when Stephanie and Russ, Jr. were young teenagers, the Judge had a stroke. Their grandmother had died a couple years before. At that point, their father Russ was performing in California, and the two young teenagers were sent to live with him.

•••••

Russ, Sr. was living in an apartment that was unfurnished and empty. Russ, Jr. and Stephanie would take his tips down to the second-hand store and pick up a dining room table and chairs, or a sofa, and literally carry them a couple of blocks up a hill to his apartment. They actually bonded with their dad for the first time and things were going well until Russ' girlfriend Barbara showed up with their infant son, Craig. Russ had impregnated Barbara and she moved in with them and the baby. Barbara didn't like Russ, Jr. or Stephanie, and Stephanie recalled that Barbara was a filthy, unkempt person. The Judge, in spite of his condition, missed his grandchildren.

Russ finally purchased a house in Corona, California, in the Inland Empire just east of Los Angeles, and the Judge moved out from New York to live with them. For a while, Stephanie was delighted to have her grandfather with them, although he had trouble speaking legible words because of his stroke. Stephanie could tell that Ambrose didn't approve of Barbara and her toddler Craig. Although her grandfather couldn't talk, snickering, he would still put his cane out and trip little Craig as he ran by, with a half-smile on his wrinkled, distorted face.

Barbara was tasked with taking care of Ambrose in exchange for a generous sum of money contributed by his other children, and soon the judge developed an infection and died. Stephanie was just fifteen and devastated. Ambrose had been the guiding light in her life. Stephanie blamed Barbara's neglect for Ambrose's death. It was a hard time for her.

According to Stephanie, Russ and Barbara lived a swinger's life. She recalled that they had orgies out at the pool at their house, and Stephanie was a straight-laced girl, raised by a judge in the Bronx. She would hide in her room and deal with it.

•••••

A boy from school named Bucky started coming over to visit Stephanie all the time. She had no sane parent watching over her in her most vulnerable time, at the age of fifteen. Only a handful of weeks after her Grandfather died, Bucky took advantage of a confused Stephanie and impregnated her with Regina, just a month before her sixteenth birthday.

When Stephanie revealed her pregnancy to Bucky and his mother, he quickly dumped her. Stephanie was alone and she decided to keep the baby. Bucky's family shunned Stephanie. His mother called her a slut and a whore, and they wanted nothing to do with the baby. Stephanie was devastated. This experience profoundly affected her ability to trust. She had no one to count on but herself.

She got a job at *Del Taco*, working well into her eighth month of pregnancy, pulling together enough supplies and furniture to create a darling room for the baby. Regina was born on December 27, 1973. Russ, Jr. was present at the birth. Bucky was nowhere in sight and he would take no role whatsoever in Regina's life. When I met Stephanie, Regina described her absent father as a kind of mysterious knight in shining armor that one day would come and be her wonderful daddy. He never showed up. God sent me instead! But first, he sent Dennis Burge.

Stephanie was forced to quit High School. She began to work full-time as a waitress. She got a job at *Norm's Cafe in* Los Angeles, and it was while working there that she met Dennis. He was a cook. Dennis was very kind to Stephanie, and he fell in love with her quickly. Stephanie was overwhelmed and so glad to be with a man who exuded goodness.

They were married around her eighteenth birthday. Following the marriage, she became pregnant pretty quickly. In her fifth month of pregnancy, she became deathly ill. Her body was in septic shock. The baby had died inside of her almost a month before, and she was deteriorating fast. She was rushed to the hospital and the baby was removed. Stephanie remained ill for many months afterward.

Stephanie and Dennis were devastated. It was a dark time for her, losing that baby. Only a few months later she became pregnant once again and gave birth to a healthy son, Kevin.

Stephanie told me later that she had ceased being attracted to Dennis after the baby died. She didn't know if it was about that or the kitchen grease smell that he came home with, but whatever it was, she stopped being intimate with him most of the time.

According to Stephanie, and as many young men deprived of intimacy by their mates will do, Dennis strayed and apparently, she found out about it on the day Kevin was born. She told me that she saw Dennis' new girlfriend driving Stephanie's little Toyota car while she was waiting to go to the hospital. I'm sure there are two sides to every story, and Dennis was always a compassionate and very religious man, in my opinion.

Regardless, Stephanie broke up with Dennis shortly after Kevin was born. I came into the picture right around Kevin's second birthday. Stephanie and Dennis had long since separated, and when I met Dennis I think he was relieved that Stephanie had found someone who was cool and who loved his Regina and Kevin as much as he did. As Stephanie and I evolved in our relationship, I always made a big deal to Regina and Kevin about the fact that they were lucky because they had two daddies, Dennis and me. I think he appreciated that, and we got along well from the moment we met.

CHAPTER TWENTY-NINE
My First Experience Performing Professionally

Stephanie and I were together for about a month when I told her that I was a pianist and singer. She laughed and rolled her eyes. She didn't believe me! Her father, Russ, was living in Palm Springs and performing at *Lucifer's* with his trio. Stephanie's brother, Russ, Jr. was also an entertainer. I didn't push the issue.

Russ Haddock had a popular jam session on Sunday afternoons, going well into the evenings, at *Lucifer's*. Russ had asked Stephanie to moonlight and serve cocktails on just Sunday afternoons at *Lucifer's*. She agreed. She loved her dad and wanted to be close to him. Also, Russ had just experienced a series of minor strokes and she was afraid for his health. A year or two before, Russ had gone through surgery on his carotid arteries, and he wasn't taking care of himself any better than he had been, before the surgery.

At *Lucifer's*, all of the local musicians would bring their instruments, and some vocalists would also show up to sit in. One Sunday I came in and told Stephanie I wanted to sit in and perform. Stephanie was a little embarrassed that I showed up, and she reluctantly asked her dad to work me in to perform at some point. She didn't want me to be awful and then upset.

I sat on a chair at *Lucifer's* from four o'clock until after eight o'clock at night, nursing a drink, and finally everyone else on the list had performed. Russ finally called my name over the microphone and asked me if I wanted to sing or play piano. I told him, "Both, please" so he got up from the piano, helped me to adjust the piano bench and set up a microphone for me to sing. Stephanie was ordering a tray of drinks and she had her back to me at the bar. She was oblivious that I had finally made my way to the stage.

As I began to sing *Misty*, she turned around to see who was singing and when she saw it was me singing and playing, her mouth dropped wide open. She almost dropped her tray of drinks. Stephanie was transfixed. After I was done and we left the club, she asked me over and over again why the hell I wasn't doing this for a living instead of waiting tables? I told her I had done one gig a couple months back for Janet's attorney friend.

From that day forward, it became Stephanie's mission to make me a full-time performer and help me to become a star. She couldn't believe I wasn't a full-time musician. How could I tell her how it had always been my dream to make it big in the music business, but of how lost I had become in the insanity of my life up until this point?

•••••

I went to *Tony Roma's*, which, incidentally was in the same building as *Sunshine*. Lyman had sold *Sunshine* by this point, and now it was called *El Papagayo*. *Roma's* hired me to play piano and sing on an off night, so now I was working one night a week performing. It was bittersweet to pull up to that building, remembering all the effort I had put into *Sunshine* as a manager, but now at least it appeared as if I was beginning to fulfill my dream.

Tony Roma's was a bizarre gig. I had my little book of songs, and whenever anyone asked me for a request, I generally didn't know it, but I would promise that if they came in next week, I would know it. On my spare time, during the one day I had off before I waited tables during the rest of the week, I would search for sheet music, or get lyrics painstakingly off of a cassette, listening over and over to try to figure out what the hell the singers were saying half the time! Fortunately, I had a good ear and I could pick up music and lyrics quickly.

My buddies caught wind of my one-night a week performing, and they would come in and harass me. Danny Moffett, Chris Cardi and Mark Piccone would bring their friends in and throw bread at me or mock my singing as obese people sat directly in front of me devouring ribs, red sauce dripping from their chins. It was all in fun and it was a learning experience for me. A kind older manager named Barbara would ask me for Frank Sinatra songs. I learned the popular song *Come Fly with Me* for her and as many others as I could find. It helped me later to have that as part of my repertoire.

Stephanie convinced Joe and Sam at *Pal Joey's* to hire my band to play one night a week there. I needed a band quick! I called my friend Tim McFall and he offered to play drums. Bill Saitta played bass and sang some backgrounds, and Brian Sward played guitar. Brian was a kind-of cerebral guy, an excellent guitarist with not a lot of personality. I had never worked with a band, so he somehow found the patience to work past my wrong chords and overplaying.

Tad's Band at Pal Joey's - 1980
Tim McFall, Bill Saitta, Tad & Brian Sward

It took a long time to learn finesse, but on my first band gig, we were well received. Bill Saitta played well and added a lot with his vocals. We all had long hair and I hope we didn't sound too much like a garage band, looking back.

I learned another valuable lesson with my *Pal Joey's* band gig. Women would come in and swoon over my singing and playing.

Beautiful young women with lovely smiles and perfect bodies would be practically all over me as I sang love songs and looked into their eyes. I thought, "This is great!"

But then, on another night, those same women would come in and I would be their waiter. They didn't realize I was the same guy who sang to them, and they would treat me like dirt. That's when I realized that this club scene is really an illusion, and the reality is your life outside that scene.

Another time, a woman would come in and catch my eye, and I would think, "Wow, she's classy and gorgeous." I would look over a couple hours later, and she was drunk and sticking her tongue down some rich, fat old guy's throat, and again the illusion was shattered!

•••••

At one point, Stephanie asked her brother, Russ, Jr., to give me pointers on how to be a performing musician. One day, Russ, Jr. met me at Kurt's apartment and showed me the 'correct' way to play certain songs. I realized in that meeting that I had vastly more experience and training than he did, and I struggled to find guidance through his ego and brashness.

Russ, Jr. had an obsession for all the new keyboards and equipment. During this era of analog keyboards, some of the new sounds were exciting and interesting. I found a common ground with him there, poring over new patches and sounds on whatever new keyboard he purchased. He had a *Rhodes Chroma*, a *Prophet,* and later a *Korg Trident* and a *Roland Juno.* I wondered how he could afford to buy all of this stuff. Stephanie told me that his girlfriend Denise actually subsidized most of it. Russ, Jr. was in and out of bands, usually quitting or being abandoned on the road by his band mates because of his anger issues. But, he was very serious about it, preparing and practicing for most of the day, every day. One had to admire his persistence.

•••••

Stephanie would also sit at the piano with me and look through songbooks, suggesting songs I needed to learn to broaden my repertoire. She didn't know how to describe what I should do, but she had an opinion about it! My singing was really carrying my piano playing up to this point on these gigs. Stephanie thought I needed to use the whole keyboard, low notes and high notes, rather than playing so much in the middle! It was cute, and I got it.

I started becoming a little bit more of a showman on the piano. My classical training was still there, even though I had forgotten all of the music. I still had the foundation of having learned to play classically when I was younger. Every time I performed, I would find a new chord structure or inversion that made my playing a little better or more interesting. I learned that I could play in any key, which is very helpful. As I mentioned, my ear training was strong, thankfully.

My mother used tell me a line that, back in the 1940's, male musicians would use to pick up on women: "I'll play in your flat if you give me the key…"

CHAPTER THIRTY
Evolving Towards a Family Life

I wanted to make a life with Stephanie and the kids. She decided to move out of her big house and get an apartment with me over in a complex of low-income apartments where her dad Russ and his wife Barbara lived, on the east side of Palm Springs. Stephanie and I moved in together in August of 1979.

Regina and Kevin accepted my love unconditionally. In return, I felt completeness within myself that I hadn't felt since my own childhood. In my heart, I believed they were the keys to my own soul's progression. It was also great to relate to them one on one. Children speak innocence within their truth; they provide an unfiltered view of life that is healthy for us all to remember.

In September of 1979, I took Regina to her first day of kindergarten! She was so darling with her little backpack, and so proud to be off to school. Regina was quick to adapt to new situations, and she always approached each day with optimism and pride. She was a little inspiration to me!

Eventually, my children grew me up.

During that same month, I finally flew back East to North Carolina to retrieve my *Dodge Charger* and make the 3,000-mile drive back to California. It was great to see Suzanne again, although her marriage was truly on the rocks at this point.

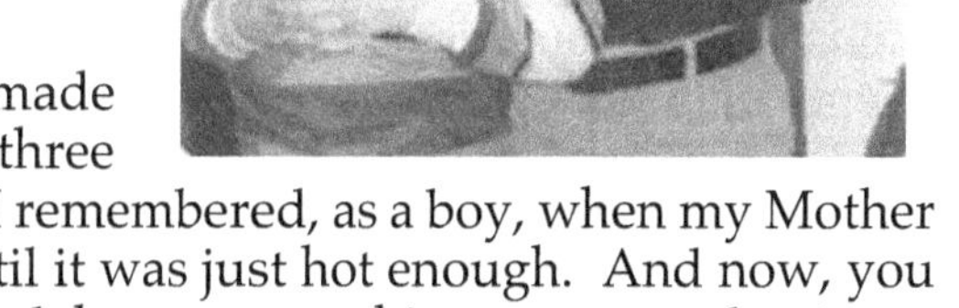
Michael and Charles Brannon 1979

My nephew Charles was a kind of savant. Later, as I mentioned briefly earlier, we found out that he was bipolar, but at that point, Bill had bought him one of the very first personal computers ever made. This was at that period in the late 1970's before the advent of the first mass-produced personal computers.

It was a huge contraption, and Charles learned everything about it. By the time Charles was eighteen, about three years later, he was writing articles for *Compute! Magazine*, and later he wrote the definitive book for *Microsoft's Windows '95* platform. I had never seen a personal computer before this moment in 1979, and I was fascinated!

Bill and Suzanne also had one of the first microwave ovens made for home use. It was enormous, about four feet wide and three feet tall, and I couldn't believe how fast it heated up food! I remembered, as a boy, when my Mother made hot chocolate on the stove, stirring and stirring it until it was just hot enough. And now, you could do it in thirty seconds. Amazing! At least in my mind, however, nothing ever tasted quite as good as when mom made it from scratch.

After a few days, I said my goodbyes and started the drive back to California. My *Dodge Charger* had been sitting for eight months, and the carburetor acted up a few times on the way to Missouri to visit my dad on the way back. I would stop on the side of the road, frustrated, waiting until it magically worked again.

When I got to Missouri, Maynard and Sandra were actually very kind and loving to me. They offered to loan me one of their vehicles to complete the drive to California, and to leave my car in Kennett to be repaired. When it was completed, they would drive out and meet me halfway at some point in the near future.

Sandra in 1980

While I was in Kennett, Maynard and Sandra drove me over to a fancy restaurant by the Mississippi River in Caruthersville, and we had dinner. I noticed that Sandra had an alcoholic beverage but Maynard did not. I was afraid that her drinking would set him off, but for the very first time, he seemed content not to drink and he said it didn't bother him at all.

I showed them a Polaroid photo I had in my wallet of Stephanie, wearing a blue dress and relaxing on the grass on a sunny day, with Regina and Kevin in her lap. It wasn't a great quality photo, and it appeared as if Stephanie had too much makeup on. She did wear a lot of makeup at night, and this photo of her holding her children outside of her home was taken right before she went to work. Sandra made a comment about her heavy makeup, and they both asked me if I was ready to take on another woman's children. They were skeptical of her, but I assured them that she was a great girl and I was very happy.

I drove back to Palm Springs in their *Toyota* station wagon to resume work, and a few weeks later, we made plans to meet in Albuquerque, New Mexico to switch cars.

I asked my friend Eddie Balderama if he wanted to make the trip with me, and he agreed. First, we went to Los Angeles to see *The Cars* in concert. They were a cool punk band with huge current *Billboard #1* hits and we enjoyed the concert immensely. Then, Eddie and I made the road trip to Albuquerque, making sure to stop and "stand on a corner in Winslow, Arizona," just as the lyrics to the *Eagles* song *Take It Easy* dictated.

•••••

Returning to Palm Springs, I enrolled into the *College of the Desert*, but I dropped my classes after a couple weeks. I had realized as I was growing that I couldn't let what happened to me in Kansas City prevent me from pursuing my dreams, be it through getting a degree on my own or from other means.

The curriculum at *College of The Desert* did not fit my vision of moving forward at that point in life. The music classes were all classically based. Joanna Hodges was a professor and she had been a huge part of my young development, but I hadn't played classical piano in almost a decade, and the prospect of 'catching up' didn't appeal to me. I vowed to continue my education at some point.

Little did I know then, that my education would evolve through years and years of hard knocks and hard experience from the ground up; performing for countless days and nights in a myriad of diverse musical situations, learning recording techniques from masters in the industry, composing thousands of complicated pieces, teaching myself computer programming, producing live concert events from the ground up and producing endless engineering sessions in major studios.

Also, I had picked up a morning job at the *Canyon Hotel* doing room service to pick up some extra money, and the class schedule would have prevented me from making a living. Or, at least that was the excuse I gave to myself at that moment.

Shortly after I started the room service job at the Canyon Hotel, I was delivering food to a room at six o'clock in the morning and as I walked by the pool, I saw the dark silhouette of the body of a man floating in the water. Immediately I called for help, but it was too late to save this man who made the mistake of swimming alone late at night. Apparently, he had a heart attack. It was an eerie feeling walking by that pool later, seeing children swimming and playing right where I had discovered this gruesome sight.

•••••

One night after work, Stephanie and I had our first argument. Strangely enough, it was about the fact that I had quit eating meat a year earlier. We had invited some friends over to our small apartment and Stephanie cooked omelets for everyone. She put ham in the omelets. I wouldn't eat it. I was gracious and told her not to worry, that it was fine and I would find something else to eat. She told me to pick the ham out of the omelet, and I told her, "But there will still be ham juice!" I think that offended her, because later after everyone left, she stayed angry until the morning.

It was early on in our relationship that I started seeing the depth of the emotional trauma that Stephanie was carrying within her. For one, she had body-shaming issues. When we met, Stephanie was very thin, just a little over a hundred pounds.

She and many other people in the service industry were turning to methamphetamine to perform at high levels with a good attitude. I didn't realize the extent she had been partaking in the substance until she confessed it to me one night. She also admitted that she couldn't make it through a night serving cocktails without drinking alcohol. She would try to keep it to a minimum, asking the bartender for white wine spritzers, but some nights the amount of alcohol she consumed would be way more pronounced than that. Also, she carried her weight around her waist and buttocks, which gave her a pear-shaped figure. I didn't care about any of that; I thought she was beautiful.

Stephanie was also carrying an enormous burden of posttraumatic stress disorder from her childhood, and from the fear of having been thrust out into the world at sixteen alone with a child. She had endured a stillbirth and then had another child, seeing her brief marriage fail and instantly becoming a single mother following Kevin's birth, until I came along.

More and more, Stephanie was becoming reliant on my strength and consistency, and that worked well for me. Having a young family grounded me, and I wanted to build upon this foundation to make a life. Regina and Kevin were very happy to have a father figure in their lives.

On the other hand, as the old adage says, "You marry your parents." Stephanie was very much like my mother; she was strong-willed and she liked to control the situation. She was an Aries, Type-A personality. She needed to be 'fixed' in my mind in the same sense that my mother had been.

Stephanie was also very much like my father in the sense that she had an addictive personality and her personality changed when she added alcohol. This became more pronounced over time. Alcoholism is a progressive disease. When Stephanie drank alcohol, she would become belligerent. Her behavior reminded me so much of my father's own behavior when he drank.

I don't know if it was because she was raised in a tough section of the Bronx, but Stephanie would become extremely condescending after a few drinks, calling me an idiot and starting sentences with, "Did it ever occur to you…" as if I was an imbecile. It hurt me to the core, and yet I stayed and took it.

Again, I felt like I could fix her like I needed to try and fix my mother and father, through love and compassion in spite of the way I was treated along the way. From the experience of my father's endless apologies on his knees at my bedside, I had become quick to forgive. On the other hand, I was too young and not strong enough yet to not allow myself to take anything personally. It was her 'movie', her circus and her monkeys. Increasingly, I was allowing myself to be drawn into that very circus.

•••••

One late night at our apartment on our day off, Stephanie was drinking and she began to cry. She told me that she was haunted about what her mother had put her through. The last time Stephanie ever saw Alice was when Alice had incinerated Russ, Jr.'s clothes on their trip to New York when Stephanie was seventeen. She didn't even know if her mother was still alive.

Even though it was late night, we called all over New York looking for an Alice Miller, or Isadora Miller (her father) to no avail. Stephanie's demons were pronounced, and she was carrying a huge emotional burden within herself. Later, Stephanie's Aunts Faith and Adrienne would tell me that Stephanie's mother and her family had issues with mental health, and that a few of Alice's siblings and cousins had committed suicide. But, at that moment, for the first of many, many times, I wondered how and why she could be so depressed when she had two beautiful children and a man who adored her. My 'fixer' would kick in; my philosophical side would remind her of the power of prayer, and forgiveness of self.

Sometimes we can't see beyond ourselves to appreciate the beauty that surrounds us. It is during those moments that faith is essential.

I was working a lot. Most mornings I was doing room service at the *Canyon Hotel*. I was still waiting tables four or five nights a week at *Pal Joey's*, and performing with the band on one off night. I was performing at *Tony Roma's* on an off night. Sam Bianco had opened a *Chicago Pizza* joint and I would work over there when they needed me, making pizzas and serving, if I was available. I had a new little family, and I wanted to provide for them. It made me feel worthwhile and secure, and it gave me the foundation to become more grounded, with a compass.

•••••

Stephanie wanted to get her breasts enhanced. She had tiny boobs and she thought she would be shapelier with her large bottom. I wanted to save money to pay for it. I came up with this idea to open up several bank accounts, and write checks back and forth to the accounts so I could float money for a few days here and there to keep the bills paid on time.

At some point, I got a call from a bank manager at *Barclay's Bank* and I went in to speak with him. He was a kind, elderly gentleman and he informed me that he had discovered my transactions. He explained that I was 'kiting' checks, which was a federal offense. I had no idea that anyone else had ever done this but me, and I was devastated that it was illegal.

He saw the genuine fear and earnest guilt in my face, and he not only offered to stop any action against me, but he lectured me for an hour and ended up helping me get a loan for Stephanie's boob job! I remain forever grateful for this man's kindness and compassion, and I vowed to never again pull anything like that!

Stephanie 1980

Stephanie was thrilled, and we made the appointment for her surgery. When she came out of surgery, she was pleased. Her breasts were large, but not huge, and it did help her body shaming to subside, for the moment. It was like a gift for both of us!

•••••

She and I were very much in love. Even so, Stephanie was very opinionated about my career and the direction I should take. Stephanie thought that her brother Russ could help to make me a more rounded entertainer, and he needed help getting work, so she talked me into performing as a duo with him. We worked a couple nights a week at *Delmonico's* for a month or two. It was a disaster for me. I hated every moment of it.

Russ, Jr., was very rigid in his approach. He wanted to perform the same songs and the same arrangements. Since we were both keyboard players, he had these arrangements worked out where we would literally play the same notes in certain phrases, and it wasn't a very musical experience for me. I felt as if his performance was rigid and did not allow nuance. In fact, I was miserable working with him. I missed my fun band mates from the original *Pal Joey's* gig.

•••••

Finally, Russ, Jr. decided that he needed to move to Reno, Nevada to further his career. He had proposed marriage to Denise, and she secured a job in Reno as a respiratory therapist. Denise had a daughter, Tiffany, who was around ten or eleven. Tiffany was not happy with her new stepfather and he was very strict with her. I got along very well with Tiffany, and later she would use me as a shoulder when she needed a kind confidant.

Stephanie with her brother Russ Haddock, Jr. 1980

Stephanie wanted to fly up to Reno for the wedding. I offered to stay with Regina and Kevin while she was gone for the weekend. On the morning of the flight, we dropped Regina off at preschool. Russ, Sr.'s wife Barbara wanted to ride with us. So, I drove Stephanie and Barbara the almost two-hour drive to the airport in Ontario, California, with Kevin sitting in the back in his little car seat.

At that time, the airplanes at the Ontario airport were all accessed from outside the plane, with stairs pushed up to the plane. Stephanie went to board the plane, and Kevin wanted to wave goodbye to his mother. I put Kevin on my shoulders so he could see, and when the plane engines started up, Kevin became nervous from the noise and peed all over me, through his diaper, all the way from my shoulders down my shirt and into my pants. I was drenched with urine. We had brought a nice change of clothes and fresh diaper for Kevin, but not for me! I was miserable all the way to Palm Springs, stinking and wet, with Barbara (who also kind of stank by nature herself) in the car…and happy, dry, sleeping Kevin in the back.

In late 1979, I was asked to wait tables for a private event at the *Canyon Hotel*. Frank Sinatra was having one of his "Love-In" concerts to raise money for charity. John Denver was going to perform. Even though I was serving people their food and drinks during the event, it was exciting to be just twenty feet from the stage watching John Denver first, and then witnessing Frank Sinatra, performing and joking with the audience of a thousand people in the ballroom of the *Canyon Hotel*. To witness his fantastic orchestra playing iconic arrangements by Nelson Riddle, Gordon Jenkins, Billy May and Don Costa was just the coolest thing ever for this young wide-eyed musician. At the end of the night, Jilly Rizzo, Frank Sinatra's best friend, handed out hundred-dollar bills to all of the servers, and shook our hands.

•••••

Around this time, I got a call from my sister Kathy in New York. Steven's mother had recently died, and they had been driving in pouring rain to the cemetery to put flowers on her grave when they were cut off by another car on the expressway.

Their *Volvo* was crushed and they both were in intensive care. It was an awful accident. A part of Steven's ear was severed and was sewn back on. Kathy had a terrible concussion. It took months for them to recover, but they eventually got a settlement and it helped them to buy a house in Brooklyn. I always worried about Kathy. She was a fragile soul. Steven was her protector, as brash as those New Yorkers can be!

•••••

I really didn't like the apartment we were living in. Stephanie's father Russ and his wife Barbara lived in the same complex, and their place was really filthy. When we went to visit, it smelled really bad, but Russ didn't really care. Russ had been an athlete as a young man. The son of a judge, he had a certain status in the community, and he was a good-looking young pianist back then.

On the road, he had many women chasing him, and he became complacent. He would stay in bed all day until work, and he got into the habit of drinking regularly. He was a kind drunk, not a mean one at all, but over time his lifestyle affected his health greatly. Because of his series of minor strokes, he was on blood thinning medication. He didn't change any of his habits, however, and he just continued to stay ill much of the time. Russ and I were very close, however. I admired his jazz style on the piano, and he assured me that eventually I would become a much better jazz pianist than he ever was. He was very kind to me always.

Tad and Kevin - 1979

•••••

In January of 1980, I rented a nice house with a pool on *Calle Conajera* in Palm Springs for my new little family. My mother had recently moved in with my grandmother in Orange County, and she gave us some furniture she had in storage, including the old *Gulbransen* upright piano, for which I was very grateful.

Elaine in 1980

After a week in the house, though, my mother came to visit us with her friend. Elaine walked through the house and pointed out all of her stuff to her friend, saying, "This is the painting Maynard and I got back when he was in Medical School, and this is the vase I got for my birthday…" Stephanie was angry and felt like she wasn't even living in her own house. I didn't quite understand why Stephanie got so angry with my mom about that. I think it was a territorial thing. But, also, I noticed that Stephanie was isolating herself more from the world in general.

My sister Betsy showed up, unannounced, and Stephanie stayed in her bedroom for two days while Betsy was there, without even coming out to greet her. Stephanie had a meltdown. I thought she was upset that Betsy just showed up without calling, and that was a valid point; I was guessing that Stephanie wanted to take a stand or something, but her reaction was extreme.

I would understand later that Stephanie was increasingly becoming agoraphobic. Soon after that weekend, Stephanie told me she was overwhelmed and she needed to stop working. She told me that she hadn't had a break from life or responsibility since Regina was born, and she was losing it. I felt that maybe she was finally feeling comfortable enough with my presence as a father figure and protector to her kids, that she could finally just discorporate.

Later, looking back on this time, I was able to realize that I was witnessing the beginning of her bipolar condition emerging. I just had no clue at the time what was going on. I attributed much of her behavior to her "Irish temper" or the fact that she was a hardened, Aries Type-A controlling personality who was raised in the Bronx.... Or, perhaps it was hormones, I thought. After all, five women raised me and I had endured five menstrual cycles going on all at once, in my youth.

•••••

Now that we were in a newer house, Stephanie wanted to put an ad in the paper and offer to babysit to make money, instead of doing cocktails, so she wouldn't have to leave the home. This was a huge step for us to take, because she had been making a lot of money up to this point. I could tell that she was unstable and, of course, I agreed. But now, the bulk of the moneymaking was up to me. Not that I wasn't used to that arrangement after the years I spent with Carol, but now I had taken on a woman with two children and I felt responsible to make it work.

The first people to answer Stephanie's babysitting ad were Greg and Sherry McDonald. Greg was a protégé of Elvis Presley's manager Colonel Parker, and the Colonel had helped him get a job managing Ricky Nelson, a former child star turned rocker. Greg was constantly on the road with Ricky and they needed someone to take their three children for days at a time. Gregory was their oldest. He was around seven years old, a couple years older than Regina. Their twins, Tommy and Susie were three or four years old.

When they first came into the picture, little Gregory was a bit of a problem child. When Greg & Sherry dropped their kids off for the first time, Gregory ran away shortly after they left, and I had to run down the street and drag him back, kicking and screaming. He told me that he was upset because my toddler Kevin had taken a potato chip out of his bag, licked it and put it back in the bag. I knew he was really upset because his parents had abandoned him (temporarily) and placed him with strangers. I got it, and I was compassionate towards him, in spite of his behavior.

Even so, it was a handful to have five children at a time. How did my mother do it? No wonder she went crazy there for a time! More so, a few years down the line, it would become bizarre to me that these people, Greg and Sherry McDonald, who randomly came into our lives through a babysitting ad, would have such a huge impact on us later.

•••••

One day in January of 1980, Stephanie saw an ad in the newspaper. A new restaurant named *Rockefeller's* was opening up on the north end of Palm Springs, where the old *Ranch Club* had been. Rosemary Cinque was the owner, along with her boyfriend, Lenny Epstein.

Rosemary had placed an ad seeking musicians or waiters who had a talent to juggle, or bartenders who could do magic tricks. They were putting in a piano bar. Stephanie made an appointment for me to audition, and I nervously went down to the restaurant one afternoon.

My mother had a saying, "If you don't toot your own horn, who else will?" I repeated that saying as I nervously made my way into the restaurant that day.

When I walked in, Jilly Rizzo was sitting with Rosemary. I couldn't believe it! Frank Sinatra's best friend was there for my audition. I was scared, but I took a deep breath, relaxed into it, played a couple songs, and finally Jilly said to Rosemary, "Are you going to wear him out or hire him?" I got the job! It was to be my first full-time job performing, five nights a week, for seventy-five dollars a night, and Jilly Rizzo told her to hire me!

Stephanie went to a little music store in Indio and bought me a rudimentary drum machine, a microphone with a cord, and a *Polytone* Amplifier. It was the first equipment I ever had!

I remember pulling up to *Rockefeller's* each night before work, and praying in my car before I went inside, "Please, Lord, give me the strength to face all of these people, and make me likeable. Help me to do my best!" I was scared! This was an older crowd. When I walked in, ninety-year-old people would sit around the piano bar, smiling and shaking maracas or a tambourine while I was playing. That was kind of annoying, but they loved to participate and the owners liked me. I was so green! I worked hard to expand my repertoire and to fit in. Jilly came in once or twice to see me, and we started to become friends. I was grateful for his support and encouragement!

Rosemary Cinque was a darling lady to work with, but the restaurant wasn't in a great location, and they were struggling to stay open after only three months. Rosemary finally came to me and told me that they couldn't afford to pay me. Nevertheless, Rosemary and I remained friends for many, many years.

•••••

At the same time, I got a call from Alan Mald at *Melvyn's*. Alan was the manager of *Melvyn's* at Ingleside Inn. Mel Haber was the owner and it was the prime place to perform in Palm Springs. My mother was giving Alan Mald's daughter piano lessons, and she suggested me for the job. I went down to *Melvyn's* and auditioned, and they hired me in May of 1980. I was thrilled! *Melvyn's* had a high-class clientele; movie stars came in all the time. It was truly the most prestigious place to perform in Palm Springs, and somehow, I had gotten the gig.

A very wealthy man and his wife decided that I was the greatest thing since sliced bread. They started hiring me to perform at their house for private parties whenever I was available. At one of their parties, I met the famous actor Patrick Macnee, who starred in one of my favorite childhood television shows, *The Avengers*. It was exciting for me and I thought I was really in with the right people until they tired of me at some point and stopped calling. I was just the flavor of the month for them. It was yet another lesson learned. It was fun while it lasted, and it was only the first of many similar experiences.

In the great scheme of things, it makes no difference if you're hot, or cool, or 'in' with the right crowd. It only matters to be special and important to the people who love you and rely upon you.

In spite of my good gig at *Melvyn's*, we were having problems paying for the big house we were in. We moved into a condo in South Palm Springs in June of 1980. We were in there for a month or two when Stephanie got a call from her brother, Russ. He was in Reno performing at the *Gold Dust* Casino and he told her they were looking for other entertainers to perform around the clock at the *Gold Dust*. He was working with an agent, Terry, who told him to have me come up and audition, but that the audition was just a formality. They offered a room with the gig, and Russ had a hotel room we could stay in for the audition.

Russ convinced Stephanie that I was going to rot in Palm Springs in my career, and Reno was the place to be. He told her this was a sure thing and I needed to come up immediately. I was very happy at *Melvyn's*. I was only about a year into my career as an entertainer, and already I was performing at the very best venue in Palm Springs.

I didn't like the idea of uprooting after we had just moved, again, and starting all over in a new city. Stephanie was a very strong-willed woman, and she insisted that this was the right move for me and for my career. She wouldn't take 'no' for an answer. Russ convinced her that I should just quit my job at *Melvyn's* and come right up to Reno immediately.

So, I gave my two-week's notice at Melvyn's and made an appointment to audition two weeks later at the *Gold Dust*. Stephanie wanted to come with me, so she and the children flew up to Reno along with me. When we arrived in Reno, I found out that the agent was a flake, and he had no audition for me.

•••••

We were staying in Russ, Jr.'s hotel room and I was broke and unemployed. I couldn't believe that Stephanie had allowed Russ to talk us into this. Worse, that night, Stephanie went down to the bar 'for a minute' leaving me in the room with Regina and Kevin, and she didn't come back for hours. She stumbled in, drunk, six hours later and her clothes were disheveled.

She was so out of her mind drunk that she had been picked up by another man and taken to his hotel room where he had his way with her. I was disgusted and angry. I was sad and frustrated. I didn't want this life for me or for Regina or Kevin.

The next morning, Stephanie woke up hung over and crying about the reality of what she did. She had gotten too drunk to know what was happening to her until it was too late. She begged my forgiveness. I felt sorry for her. Although I didn't want to talk in front of the kids, I had a quiet but strong conversation with her and I told her I was not going to put up with this bullshit and she was going to either get her act together or I was gone. Still, I was just devastated about everything. I was pissed that I had taken her and Russ Jr.'s word for it and quit the best job in Palm Springs, and at the same time I was just beside myself with sadness to find myself with yet another dysfunctional woman.

Stephanie promised me that she would come around, but she said that she still felt that it was the right move for us to move to Reno. She got on the phone and started calling around to every place within a hundred-mile radius that provided entertainment.

After a day or two of calling, Stephanie found me a weekend gig on the outskirts of Reno at the *Donner Trail Dinner House.* This place was so far out of the beaten path that people had actually cannibalized themselves at some point in time somewhere around there, just to stay alive. I could relate.

We also found a condo to rent in Sparks, Nevada, a suburb of Reno, and Stephanie promised me that she would do everything she could to work with me to make it as a family. That was the thing about Stephanie. Underneath the illness and in spite of the occasional bad behavior that resulted from it, dwelled a moral girl brimming with goodness to her core.

Through all of this upheaval, Regina and Kevin seemed to take it all with a grain of salt. They were darling little children with an endless of supply of love to give, when I needed it the most.

CHAPTER THIRTY-ONE
Reno, Nevada

Stephanie flew back to Palm Springs with the kids, to begin the process of packing up the condo. I flew back with them and drove my car back up to Reno so I could get back and forth to work. In Reno, I applied at *Harrah's* for a bartending position and they gave me a job as a bar back. It was literally backbreaking work. I was carrying huge trashcans full of ice up flights of stairs. I was dragging cases and cases of beer to bars all over the hotel and casino. This went on for three or four months while I was working weekends at *Donner Trail Dinner House.*

It was bizarre to me, having managed a huge restaurant and also having had the experience of waiting tables at a fine dining establishment, now relegated to being a bar back in Reno. But, I handled it like a man, and worked my ass off.

•••••

A week or two after I drove my car back, Stephanie was ready for the move. We were literally broke, and I didn't have enough money to rent a U-Haul truck for a one way, out of state trip. I had the idea of going to a cheap rental place and renting a truck locally with no mileage charges, and then driving it down to Palm Springs and back with Steph, Regina, Kevin and all of our possessions.

So, I rented the truck and embarked on the trip down to Palm Springs. It was August of 1980. On the day we moved from the condo in Palm Springs, Eddie came over to help me. The temperature was over one hundred and fifteen degrees in the desert, and it was pretty intense loading the truck. We suffered a bit of heat exhaustion that day. Eddie was an amazing friend; he was always there for me if I needed him.

The following day, after cleaning the condo, Stephanie, six-year-old Regina, three-year-old Kevin and I took off to make the ten-hour journey back to Reno, all tucked into the front cab of the rental truck. By the time we made it into the mountains south of Reno, it was nighttime. The truck began to overheat and broke down on a dark, desolate mountain highway.

About a mile before the truck broke down, we had seen a bearded man hitchhiking with a wild look in his eyes. Regina and Kevin were scared. It was freezing, pitch black outside and we were stuck in the mountains with a rental truck we weren't supposed to bring out of Reno, with everything we owned in the back of the truck. We huddled in the locked cab of the truck, calming the children and waiting for help. Again, I felt the familiar feeling of desperation and fear that had so permeated my young adulthood.

In the early morning, a ranger found us and called for a tow truck. We were towed into a small town in the Sierra Mountains, the truck was repaired, and we finished the trip to our little condo in Sparks. Exhausted, I emptied the truck anyway and returned it with a bill for the repairs. The rental company refused to pay for the repairs, and now I was really broke. But, we had officially relocated to Sparks, Nevada, and we were safe.

•••••

Over the next few months, I worked my ass off. One afternoon, Stephanie came in to *Harrah's* to surprise me and she saw how hard I was working. She told me that day that she wanted me to quit that job and we would figure something else out. I gave my notice and went out on my own to audition at some of the other casinos.

Within a week, I got two jobs performing. I was at *Mapes* hotel, one of the oldest casino hotels in Reno, performing in their piano bar six nights a week, from five o'clock to seven o'clock at night, and then from eight-thirty PM until twelve-thirty in the morning. It was a six-hour gig. Then, I would rush across the street to the *Gold Dust* and perform from one o'clock until five o'clock in the morning, five nights a week. I had finally gotten the job at the *Gold Dust* that I had initially moved to Reno to do.

Four days a week, I bussed tables at *Victoria Station* during their lunch shift, from eleven o'clock in the morning until three o'clock in the afternoon, training for a waiter position, and on Saturdays I waited tables during lunch at a little boutique restaurant off the beaten path in Reno. I was literally working around the clock, and running home to take naps between it all whenever I could.

Even still, I would get phone calls from my dad and he would ask me, condescendingly, "Are you working?" After all, stereotypically, musicians don't work very much. Little did he know; I was working around the clock. I told him that, not only was I working, but also people were comparing me to Billy Joel and I could play piano like Jerry Lee Lewis. Still, by his demeanor on the phone I could tell he was unimpressed.

•••••

Stephanie found a nice three-bedroom house down the street from the condo in Sparks, and we moved yet again after only a couple of months. Moving was an exhausting chore for me that happened way too often in my life.

Regina
First Grade Photo

In September of 1980, Regina started first grade. She was adorable in her little dress with her backpack and lunch pail in tow.

Kevin was home alone with us during the day for the first time in his life. He would watch cartoons. He loved *Scooby Doo*! He would become lost in his own world playing with his *Star Wars* figurines. Sometimes, when I had a moment in my crazy schedule, we would play ball. He was a good boy. We all hugged a lot.

Stephanie was becoming a little better, more even-tempered and relaxed. She was happy living closer to her brother. Russ, Jr.'s wife Denise was pregnant, and several months later, Denise gave birth to Adrienne, so the kids had a little cousin to fawn over.

One night at *Mapes*, a young girl who appeared to be homeless came in and sat at the piano bar. I ran home during my hour and a half break to have a quick bite and to kiss my young family, and when I came back the girl was gone and she had stolen all of my tips. I guess she needed the money more than I did, although I would have argued that point at that moment in my life.

Mapes was a run-down old hotel, and after a few months, a new company bought them and the new owners decided to tear it down and build a larger property. So, I was in on the tail end of a historic hotel, and it felt that way to work there. Almost like a looming time-stamp was inevitable, I would look around at the dingy, old-fashioned fixtures and I was transported into another era while I performed there. Customers had obviously been coming there for years and years, as all of the regulars were very old.

Even though I had a bad experience with the flaky agent when I first arrived in Reno, I was able to get into the *Gold Dust* on my own. They were literally remodeling as I was working there. They would move the gaming tables every night and some nights they were very close to the room I was performing. I would have to adjust my volume accordingly. Casino work was weird. I was told to play my ass off for a half hour, get them in and get them drunk, and then take a half hour break so they would all go out and gamble and blow all of their money. It was impersonal and it felt sleazy to me.

•••••

After *Mapes* closed, I got a job performing at the *Vasser-Wells Music Hall*, not coincidentally on the corner of Vasser and Wells in Reno. This was a bizarre place. It was an old Catholic church that had been purchased by a Jewish couple and turned into a bar. The altar was turned into a stage where Rock & Roll bands performed in the same place that priests had given communion. It had a feeling of decadence just being in there. For someone who was raised Catholic like me, it was just wrong, but to many others, it was cool.

Downstairs in the old rectory, they put in a restaurant called *The Spaghetti Joint*. It was packed every night, serving cheap pasta and wine.

At *Vasser-Wells Music Hall*, my name was prominent on their marquee outside in lights, "TAD SISLER PIANO MAN." Most nights, I was the sole entertainment. On other nights, I would perform as a solo before a band came in.

One of the bands was particularly good, and wild too. The lead performer, Angel South, was a classic Rock & Roll guitarist. He had performed with Edgar Winter, Janis Joplin and B.J. Thomas. At this point in his life, Angel was literally out of his mind, but he was one of the best rock guitarists I had ever heard. He would literally drink an entire bottle of Jack Daniels on stage while he was performing. His guitar would scream with amazing distortion and he was all over the place. By the end of the night, he would grab the microphone and scream, "Fuck! Oh shit, I said fuck! Oh fuck, I said shit!" ... and his fans would quiver with delight. It was hilarious but again, it all felt so very sacrilegious to me.

Stephanie felt as if she was ready to work again, finally. I got her a job doing cocktails at *Vasser-Wells Music Hall*. On Halloween 1980 she dressed up as *Wonder Woman*. She looked just lovely to me that night, and her sweet smile was back. Stephanie worked hard when she worked, and everyone loved her. She always ran circles around all of the other waitresses.

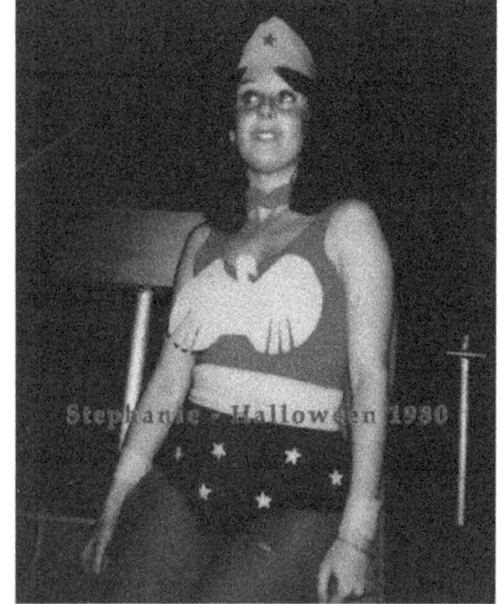
Stephanie - Halloween 1980

•••••

Stephanie and I were very close during this period in our lives. We were finally working on a life. We were both on the same page. Just a few weeks after Halloween, Stephanie became pregnant with my child.

When I met Stephanie, she told me that she did not want any more children. She was very happy with her two beautiful kids. This was a huge issue to me. I told her that I needed to have the life experience of having at least one natural child of my own, as much as I loved Regina and Kevin.

I had made her children my own, and their love meant everything to me, but I wanted to experience the joy of parenthood from the very beginning. Stephanie reluctantly agreed to have one more baby. In fact, we were both very excited about the future and what it might hold. I wanted a son, but I also wanted a daughter. I had Regina and Kevin already, so I resigned that whatever child Stephanie had, boy or girl, I would love the baby with all my heart and these three children would be enough for me moving forward.

My sister Kathy was also pregnant, and in February of 1981, she gave birth to her second son, Yash. My sister Betsy also gave birth to her third son, James, later, in November of 1981. We were all having babies!

In December of 1980 I was on my way to my late-night job at the *Gold Dust* in Reno when I heard the news that John Lennon had been shot and killed in New York. John and *The Beatles* were such a huge part of my childhood. I mourned his death as if he were a family member.

•••••

Craig Evans was a forty-something pianist and singer in Reno. He was an excellent performer and he was sought after in the more exclusive piano bars. His claim to fame was that he had apparently written the hit song *You've Made Me So Very Happy*, and then sold it to *Blood, Sweat and Tears* for a few hundred dollars. He felt ripped off and believed that he could have been much more famous if he would have gotten the credit he deserved. In spite of that, he was a really good guy and a great performer.

Craig was dabbling in booking entertainment, and he came to see me. Craig had this idea that if he secured two or three piano bars as an agent, he could put entertainers in all of them along with himself, and we would all switch to one of the other venues every three months, kind of like a rotating schedule of entertainers. That way, no club owner or crowd would get tired of us. It was a great concept for a casino town, with so many transients. It would not be a good concept for a place like Palm Springs or San Diego, where people actually appreciate the consistency of the same good entertainment at a venue for years at a time.

Craig was working at the *Continental Lodge* on Virginia Street in Reno. It was considered the best piano lounge in Reno. Right next door was *Vario's*, a cute little Italian place with a piano and dance floor, and I was already performing there on an off night. Craig asked me if I wanted to work full-time at the *Continental Lodge* for three months, three months at *Vario's* and then to work three months at *The Timbers* in Carson City. I jumped at the prospect.

Continental Lodge 1980

The *Continental Lodge* was great for me. It was always packed, and my name was in lights again on a huge marquee that lined Virginia Street, one of the busiest thoroughfares in Reno. The tips were great, and I finally quit my day job at *Victoria Station.* From that day on, every amount of work I did would be done within the entertainment business. I never went back to waiting tables or restaurant management. Somehow, I raised my children doing it. It was definitely the road less traveled, and as life went on, I paid my dues hugely.

Bob Allen 1985

A nice young man named Bob Allen performed on drums behind me at *Vario's* and at *The Continental Lodge,* on occasion. He played a little piano and sang too, and I convinced him that he should become a piano player full-time, instead of a drummer. That way, he wouldn't have to rely on others for work. Bob took my advice, and he became very successful at it. We remained friends for life.

•••••

Although (as I've noted) I had dabbled in drugs many times as a teenager, I had no desire to do drugs or drink alcohol moving forward. I thrived in my family situation, as hard as I worked, and I had no desire to lose myself into drugs or alcohol, with a few exceptions. I maybe smoked pot three or four times in the next ten years, and I might have had a drink here or there, once every couple of months. This was a pretty amazing feat for a person who worked full time performing in bars and lounges with drunks all around me.

I had grown up during a period of time where a new drug culture among young people was prevalent. Peer pressure had been huge. Literally, everyone I knew was doing drugs when I was a teenager, with very few exceptions. Tragically, many of the people with whom I grew up succumbed from their substance abuse, and it would continue to affect society adversely for generations. I was not going to become a statistic. I found my joy in being a consistent, hard-working companion and father.

Just because everybody is doing something wrong does not mean you should do it. Instead, do the right thing. It sounds simple because it's supposed to be. Just say no.

Tad Promo Pic 1980

My uncle Ted once told me that he was a troublemaker for a short period when he was a teenager. He found that being that way made his life more difficult. His advice to teenagers was simple: Do the right thing, because it actually makes your life easier.

I remember a story about identical twin sons of a murderer on death row. One of the sons became an icon of his community. He was a minister and volunteer, and he lived a stellar life. The other twin murdered someone and he, too, was on death row. A journalist interviewed both, and got the same response: "Given the example of what my father did, how could I have turned out any other way?" One took the example and learned the lesson, the other repeated the mistake. Tragedies and mistakes can teach us. It's up to us to learn the correct lesson from the experience.

•••••

Stephanie was a binge drinker. She would be great for a month or two, and then have a weekend where she completely drank herself into oblivion. She also suffered from strong bouts of deep depression. This behavior continued for the rest of her life.

I was always grateful for the months at a time that she was just fine, loving and a great mother and companion. Her episodes became more pronounced through the years, and it eventually became pure hell. But, in these first years of our relationship, when she did go on a binge or sink into depression, I had no clue that I was witnessing early signs of bipolar disorder.

I knew nothing about bipolar disorder. I don't think I had ever heard the term. I still wonder if that's exactly what Stephanie suffered from. She certainly had symptoms of imbalance, but by the time they started treating it with drugs years later, I'm a firm believer that the drugs made it worse. At this point in time, I did see elements of both of my parents in her, and at the same time I was viewing a new, unfamiliar, more complicated face on that old familiar disease.

It's hard to explain how wonderful Stephanie was when she was okay. She was a strong-willed, protective woman who would do anything for the people she loved. I was deeply in love with the "good' Stephanie. She worked harder than anyone else when she worked, and she was efficient and kind. Everyone loved her. Her grandfather had instilled in her a deep moral code and a need for justice in any situation she viewed that she felt was unfair or unjust. She was a great mother and friend. And now she was pregnant with my child.

•••••

At the end of my three-month stint at the *Continental Lodge*, it was my turn to perform at *The Timbers* in Carson City. *The Timbers* was an authentic, stinky old dive bar across the street from the historical *Ormsby House*, about an hour's drive south of Reno in downtown Carson City, Nevada, completely different from my gig in Reno. Out of control, unkempt drunks would throw silver dollars at me for tips and I would have to dodge them, hoping not to chip a tooth, and yelling, "Thank you" so as not to upset them for their 'generosity'. It was like a scene out of an old Western movie.

People drank heavily and they wanted to dance! The owner was a very kind older man who adored me. He told me that unless Frank Sinatra came in and wanted the gig, it could be mine forever!

I would jokingly tell people at the end of the night, "I'm going to take a short, twenty-hour break, and I'll be right back tomorrow night." The next night, many of the same people were still there! They had slept in their barstools and still hadn't showered, but they were raring to go again! It was hilarious!

I actually had a wonderful time at *The Timbers*. An elderly lady frequented *The Timbers*, holding court at the bar, many nights. She looked like an old, wrinkly, used-up biker chick with her blue jean jacket on, but she was very kind and fun loving. She would buy everyone in the bar a drink, and then buy them all another drink. She was absolutely the most popular person in that bar full of degenerates. She would tip me a hundred dollars every time she came in. Somebody told me that her last name was Busch, and she was heir to the *Anheuser Busch* beer fortune.

Driving home from Carson City back to our house in Sparks every night, I made my way down the roads carefully, making sure to stay alert after a long, arduous gig.

One night, a congenial, well-dressed elderly man came in to *The Timbers*. A week later he brought back a group of well-dressed people. His name was Harvey Gross. He was one of the richest men in Nevada, and he owned *Harvey's Resort Casino* and *Harvey's Inn* in South Lake Tahoe.

Harvey wanted to put a piano bar into *Harvey's Inn*, and he brought his associates in to see me. I got a call the next day from the casino manager asking if I wanted to meet with them and look at the room they were transforming into a piano bar lounge. I jumped at the prospect, and soon we were designing the room at *Harvey's Inn*.

•••••

When I first saw the room I was to perform in at *Harvey's Inn* on the south shore of Lake Tahoe, I noticed a huge fountain with a waterfall built into one side of the lounge. They removed the fountain and put a piano bar in for me. In May of 1980, I started performing in South Lake Tahoe, and *Harvey's* put my photo on the front page of the *Tahoe Daily Tribune* in a huge ad, right next to photos of Dean Martin and Jimmy Buffett. Dean was performing across the street at *Harrah's* and Jimmy was at *Caesar's.* It was pretty cool to see my photo on the front page of the newspaper, right next to iconic entertainer Dean Martin!

Harvey's Inn was a lodge with an adjacent casino, located next to *Harvey's* on the main drag in South Lake Tahoe. Driving over the mountain from Sparks, the view of the lake was breathtaking every day. It was a difficult gig for me. I drove almost two hours each way, six days a week. I had to set up and break down all of my equipment each day, and it was a five-hour gig. So, I would leave home shortly after noon, and I wouldn't be back sometimes until three or four in the morning.

Some nights as I was driving home after a long day of setup, performance and breakdown, I was so tired I would open the window of my car and stick my head out into the freezing night as I drove down the hill from Tahoe, slapping my face to stay awake. I listened faithfully to the *Larry King Radio Show* on the radio, doing whatever I could to keep my mind active.

Then, when I finally made it home, my pregnant wife would say, "Thank God you're home! I've been so bored. Let's stay up and play cards for an hour or two." I loved her so much. She looked so beautiful to me, pregnant with my child. So, I would sneak into the kitchen and eat spoonfuls of instant coffee just to stay awake for yet another hour or two.

Waking up early the next day, I would take Regina to school, come home and try to sleep for another hour or two, pick Regina up from school and then repeat the process of the drive to Lake Tahoe.

At first, I liked *Harvey's Inn.* Freddy Powers performed in the showroom. He was Willie Nelson's good friend, and when Willie was in town, he came in to perform with Freddy. Willie was nice to me, but very quiet. Freddy and I became fast friends.

I was being paid well, and the top brass respected me. I had yet to learn the nuances of what makes a lounge work or not work. In retrospect, I know now that the lounge was doomed to not work for a number of reasons: It was too bright; the atmosphere was sterile and not welcoming; the noise of the casino permeated the room and didn't give the listener a warm feeling from the music; concentration and relaxation were broken by a chaotic environment beyond the room, with an open entrance.

Most notably, what I didn't know was that the lounge they created for me had been a lounge that people with free drink tickets would frequent before they changed the lounge format to accommodate my performance. The management had cancelled the free drink tickets when I began the gig in the lounge, hoping to actually build up a clientele of heavy drinkers and gamblers like I had at *The Timbers.* This lounge had been packed with people who drank for free and tipped the bartenders very well before I began performing there.

Also, the bartenders had some sort of racket going on where they were making a fortune off of these free tickets. I didn't quite know how it worked, but from the first day I started at *Harvey's Inn,* after Mr. Gross and his associates' left and went on with their business, the bartenders despised me and treated me like dirt. I couldn't even get a glass of water from them. I would have to go to the main casino bar. The culture of the room had changed when they inserted me into the equation, and it was affecting their bottom line.

I started getting death threats. When I came in to work, I would find a different note every night telling me that if I didn't quit, I would be killed, and if I told the management, they would find me and kill me. It was really scary for me. I had a pregnant companion at home and two small children. I had quit a lucrative job to take this one.

After about six weeks of this, I contacted Craig Evans and asked him if I could get back into his circuit of working piano bars in Reno and Carson City. He agreed, so I went to the *Harvey's* management and gave my two-week's notice. I guessed that the bartenders won their battle, because after I left they replaced me with a fountain again. It's the only time in my career when a fountain has replaced me! As sad as I was about losing the big gig, I was relieved to be back at the *Continental Lodge* in Reno, just a month before Stephanie was supposed to give birth to my baby. The *Continental Lodge* was just blocks from *Washoe Medical Center* where Stephanie was to give birth.

CHAPTER THIRTY-TWO
New Additions to our Family

In the process of my *Harvey's* job, Stephanie and I had been able to put together a darling room for the baby. Although we didn't yet know if we were having a boy or a girl, we had already purchased a crib, a bassinet, high chair, car seat and many other items for the baby. I paid the estimated fifteen-hundred-dollar hospital bill in advance.

Stephanie was very uncomfortable in her pregnancy. She was larger than she remembered from other pregnancies, and the summer heat saturated our home with no air conditioning in Sparks. I set up fans and swamp coolers in our bedroom. Regina and Kevin would come in to sleep with us, and I would inevitably end up sleeping on the floor next to the bed just to find enough room to move around.

I bought a little aboveground pool for our back yard. I would help Steph over the little stairs into the pool, and she would soak for hours, displacing some of the water as she climbed in. Our next-door neighbor, John Driscoll, was in his early twenties. He was a congenial young man, living with his mother, and he would come over and keep Stephanie distracted from her discomfort with his conversation sometimes during my crazy work schedule. His kindness meant a lot to us.

In mid-July of 1980, Stephanie was about eight months pregnant and we went in for her prenatal doctor's appointment. She told the doctor that she was worried. This was an entirely different pregnancy than her others had been.

She had lost a baby once and she didn't know if she was just paranoid, but she had morning sickness well into her second trimester and she was becoming huge, much larger than during any of her other pregnancies. She asked the doctor if perhaps she was having twins. He laughed, and said, "That's nonsense! It's ridiculous!" He took out his stethoscope and heard a healthy heartbeat. He put Stephanie at ease. But, did he hear a second heartbeat too? Just to make sure she was progressing well, the doctor sent Stephanie for an ultrasound.

We went to her ultrasound appointment, and I waited in the waiting room as she had her procedure. A few minutes later, a staffer brought me into the room. The ultrasound technician moved the wand around Stephanie's belly and showed me the pictures coming from the womb.

The technician said to me, "Here's the baby's head, and here's the torso; here's the legs and the little feet, and here's the other head." I screamed out in horror, "My baby has two heads?" She said, "No, silly! You're having twins!" I couldn't believe it! One baby was nestled behind the other, so she couldn't tell the sex of the babies. She thought one might be a boy, but she couldn't be sure. 3-D color ultrasounds didn't exist in those days.

I was excited and scared! I couldn't believe we were having twins! But, we only had purchased one of everything. What were we going to do? We were already broke paying for everything in advance. I was just going to have to wing it and do what I could to prepare. Again, I found myself in a situation where I was coming from behind financially, even though I had done my best to work it all out in advance.

I took Stephanie to the library and she found every book on the subject of twins. As she read, she would inform me. I knew a lot already about twins from growing up in a medical family, but I would listen intently to her information anyway.

Most twins are same-sex. Identical twins are from one egg splitting and fraternal twins are from two eggs. Stephanie decided that we were probably going to have two boys. I asked her if I could name one of the boys Maynard Lee Sisler, III after my father and me, and she agreed. She wanted to name the other boy Matthew. I thought that was fine.

We talked about baby names in case we had a girl or two. I would mention a name, and she would say, "I knew a girl in school by that name and she was mean to me!" She would pick a name and I would say, "Oh, that was the name of a girl I liked." So, after a bit, we narrowed our two girl baby names down to Rachel and Rebecca.

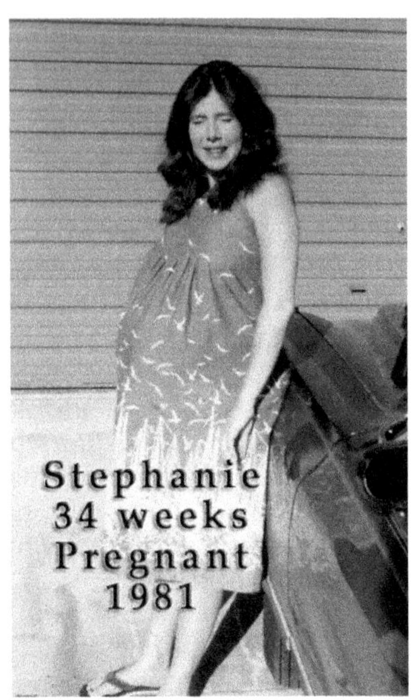
Stephanie
34 weeks
Pregnant
1981

•••••

From their comfortable womb, whenever the babies heard me singing, even if it was just from a cassette recording I had made of myself on the gig, they would kick and kick. They liked my voice! Either that, or they were kicking for me to stop! I hoped for the former conclusion.

Stephanie was going to need a Caesarean Section instead of natural childbirth due to the position of the babies. We went back to *Washoe County Medical Center*, and they told us that the procedure was going to require two teams of doctors and nurses and it was going to cost us close to ten thousand dollars. We didn't have insurance, so I made payment arrangements with the hospital.

The initial appointment for the birth procedure was going to be August 12, 1981, which was cool because it was my dad's birthday. But, after doing an amniocentesis, they discovered that the babies weren't quite ready yet, so they postponed it for August 18, 1981, which was my sister Judy's birthday!

As I mentioned, I was performing at the *Continental Lodge*, which was only a mile or so from the hospital. On the night before the procedure, Stephanie was admitted into the hospital. After I finished performing, I went to visit her on my way home. Our friend, Michelle Haldeman offered to watch Regina and Kevin on the morning of the Caesarean Section, and I went home to get a short amount of sleep. I set four alarms to make sure I woke up on time!

Michelle Haldeman
1981

The next morning, August 18, 1981, I followed Stephanie as an orderly pushed her on her gurney into the operating room, and I witnessed the most miraculous, amazing experience ever. The doctors had given Stephanie an epidural, so she was awake for the birth. A vertical blanket kept her from seeing the surgery.

I was standing right over her head, peering over the blanket, watching everything while stroking her beautiful, wet hair and wiping the perspiration off of her forehead.

As the doctors cut into her, I was amazed. I would say, "Oh, my God!" She would say, "What's happening?" and I would say, "Oh, my God!" She would say, "What's wrong?" I was entranced, watching them open her belly up.

Moments later, they removed what first looked like an organ to me. It changed colors, from a greyish brown to red to pink in front of my eyes as they carefully removed it and cut the umbilical cord, and I realized it was a baby! In a moment, the first team of doctors tapped the baby's foot and it began to cry. They exclaimed, "It's a girl!"

I started crying and telling Stephanie, "We have a daughter and she's beautiful!" Stephanie said, "We're going to have two girls then." Moments later, the second team of doctors repeated the process and pulled out another baby, tapping its little foot until it cried, and exclaiming again, "It's a boy!" We had a girl and a boy! Stephanie and I both cried and gazed into each other's eyes with excitement and a little apprehension.

The doctors told me that it was time for me to leave the room. They were going to give Stephanie more anesthetic to knock her out, and sew her up. Stephanie looked up at me with concerned eyes, pleading with me to watch over the babies. I reassured her and ran over to the prenatal unit to see my babies.

In the nursery of the hospital, my darling girl was snug in her little hospital bassinet, but I couldn't find my boy. Panicking, I asked the nurse and she ushered me over to a little incubator where my boy was sleeping soundly. The nurse informed me that my son's lungs weren't quite as advanced as my daughters, and he would need to be in an incubator for a few days. She told me not to worry, that he would be just fine. Other babies in the nursery were yellow with jaundice, and they looked like little people in tanning booths with tiny sunglasses and a huge light shining on their delicate skin.

Both babies were over five pounds each and around twenty-one inches long, which is considered premature, but very healthy and not unusual with twins. Other than my son's lungs needing a little more development, they were both completely healthy and just beautiful. They both had an abundance of dark hair, and their beauty transfixed me.

I camped out in the hospital nursery, going back and forth between my daughter and son all day until Stephanie started to awaken from her surgery. Although groggy, she immediately asked me about the babies. I told her about our son being in an incubator, and that I was reassured that it was temporary. She started crying, and I held her head in my hands. I said, "Don't worry, my love. I'm here and I'm not leaving you or our babies." She began to calm down, and she drifted back off to sleep.

At some point, when I knew she was okay, I ran back to the house to check on Regina and Kevin. Our friend, Michelle, was having a great time with them and they were just fine, so I went back to the hospital.

•••••

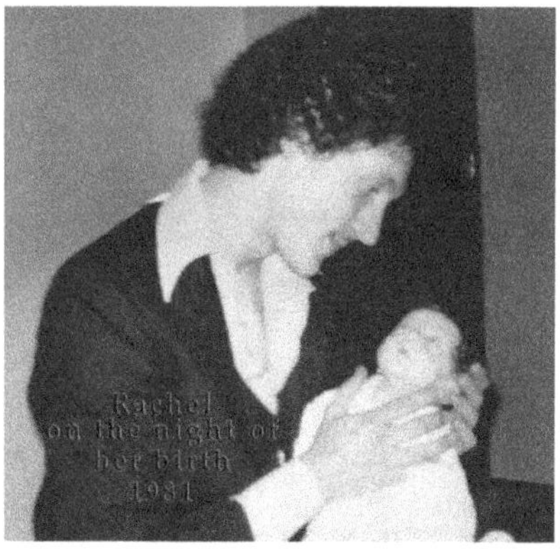

On the evening of my babies' birth, the nurse brought my daughter into Stephanie's hospital room and placed her into my arms. I had just finished my gig, and I was dressed in a suit. Stephanie was groggy and she wanted to hold the baby, but only for a minute, so they gave my darling little girl to me first.

Rachel
on the night of
her birth
1981

I looked into my daughter's wide, amazingly perceptive and aware eyes, and I instantly recognized her. I already knew her, and she knew me! It was as if we were old friends or soul mates that finally were back together again. It was truly the most amazing experience I've ever had. We named her Rachel Anne Sisler.

Later that evening after they brought Rachel back to her bassinet, I went to check on my son and I was shocked to see them holding his tiny body up for an x-ray. He had a panicked look on his little face and they were holding his arms and legs out to get a good picture. I was overwhelmingly sad and scared for him. When they were done, they put him back into his incubator and I reached my hands through the holes, stroking him carefully with my finger and speaking to him in a calm voice. "I'm your daddy, and I'm here. I love you so much and I'll never leave you." His little eyes focused on me as his lips pursed into a little 'ooh' and I smiled. I knew him too!

After a day or two, they brought our son into Stephanie, and she held him for hours. He was going to be a mama's boy. We named him Maynard Lee Sisler, III, and we decided to call him Taddy. My Taddy boy was a beautiful baby.

•••••

Bringing the babies back home was an exciting experience. Stephanie was just starting to walk slowly again following her surgery, and the burden was on me to take care of as much as I could when I wasn't working. We each took a baby into a separate bedroom and slept alone with that baby. The babies would wake up every two hours, and sometimes they alternated to every hour on the hour! They were allergic to the formula *Enfamil* so we put them on *Isomil*. Stephanie had initially tried to breast feed them but it was too uncomfortable. Her breast enhancement was beginning to bother her. Back in those days, they used silicone implants and they sometimes became painful.

•••••

Regina was a good little helper! She took her role as oldest very seriously, and she was determined to be the second mama. Stephanie needed help, and she put a huge onus on her little seven-year-old daughter.

Kevin began to act out as many middle children do. He had been the youngest and the focus of so much attention. I had read that it was important when you're actually holding a baby, to look at the older child and say, "I love you" to them, so they understand that even though you're giving attention to another child, you haven't forgotten how special they are. Kevin was never, ever a bad boy, but he started to do things to get attention.

One morning, I woke up to find his little hamster sopping wet and dead lying on the kitchen floor. Kevin looked up at me, crying, and said, "I was just giving him a bath." I wasn't angry; in fact, I remembered the day I had accidentally killed my own hamster at the age of ten. I held him and comforted him, but we decided that he was just a little too young to have a hamster. As time went by, Kevin and his little brother would become inseparable.

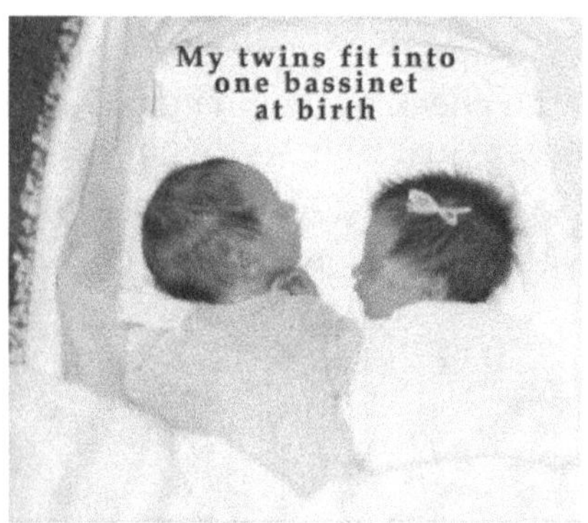
My twins fit into one bassinet at birth

In my little bit of quiet time that I found late at night, I started to read the writings of the great philosophers. I studied Socrates and Plato, Jung and Freud. I delved into the common denominator between all of the great religions, reading about Hinduism, Buddhism, and Judaism and refreshing my memory about Christianity. I had heard about Edgar Cayce, and I read the books that chronicled his trances and revelations. It was all like soul food for me, unlocking the secrets of why we're here and why shit happens. It kept my attitudes and emotions in check through it all. I was blessed with a positive outlook, and now with four children, I needed to be centered more than ever.

My mother came to visit for a week shortly after the twins were born. She marveled over my babies, and I was so very proud! It was great to see their grandmother holding them, and Elaine was also conscious of the two older children, bringing them gifts and playing with them. Stephanie was healing a little more each day, and she was a devoted mother. At first the babies could both fit into one bassinet, but as they grew, Stephanie always made sure they were clean, fed and happy.

Regina started second grade, and we began to look around for a preschool for Kevin.

•••••

I was so grateful to be performing at the *Continental Lodge* through all of this period. It was close to the hospital and only about a thirty-minute drive to our house.

One night, a man came in and sat at the piano bar. He introduced himself as Rader Rollins, and proceeded to get really drunk. As he was drinking, he told me that he owned *Statewide Lighting Company* in Nevada. This was the company that put most of the lighting into the casinos. He was very wealthy.

Rader lived in Incline Village, on the North Shore of Lake Tahoe. Just a few months back when I was performing at *Harvey's Inn*, Rader had seen the front-page ads about me in the *Tahoe Daily Tribune*. Rader was buying the huge old *Boise Cascade* A-Frame building in Incline and converting it into a restaurant with an oyster bar and a lounge. He was going to name it *The Conservatory.*

He wanted to put piano music upstairs, and he came in to *The Continental Lodge* that night specifically to hire me. He gave me his business card. Rader told me he would give me a year's contract and he asked me how much I would charge to perform for a six-night week. I told him I would do it for $450.00 per week, which was about what I was making at the *Continental Lodge.*

A few minutes later, he looked at me and said, "I'm opening up a bar in Incline Village and I want to give you a year's contract. How much will you charge?" I thought he was kidding, so I said, "$500.00 per week." He agreed, and then about a half hour later he repeated himself all over again.

Never sell yourself short. Be bold and ask for what you're worth.

I realized that he was so drunk he had forgotten our conversation, so, just to have a little fun, I said "$550.00 per week," and he agreed! Again, a little while later he asked the same question, and I said "$600.00 per week," and he agreed! It was like a bizarre game we were playing.

When it happened again and I mentioned $650.00, he said, "Oh, no, that's too much, I only want to pay $600.00." Soon, he stumbled out drunk. The next morning, I called the number on his card, and his son-in-law hired me for $600.00 per week for a year, which was more than I had ever made in my life. I learned a valuable lesson from that experience.

The drive, up *Mount Rose Highway* to Incline Village on the North Shore of Tahoe, was too precarious for me to drive every night from Sparks, Nevada, so we made the decision to move to Lake Tahoe at the end of September of 1980.

CHAPTER THIRTY-THREE
Incline Village, Lake Tahoe, Nevada

Taddy and Rachel
1981

Stephanie and I rented a lovely, three-story house on *Winding Way* in Incline Village, overlooking the lake. The house sat on a hill with pine trees everywhere. Pristine mountain air hovered over the huge, magnificent glassy lake; the view was breathtaking, and it was only about six blocks to my new gig at *The Conservatory*. Our twins were not even two months old yet, and our family had been immediately placed into a mountain paradise, at 6,350 feet above sea level. The majestic summits surrounding the lake jutted past 11,000 feet.

Moving once again out of our house in Sparks, we loaded up a U-Haul truck with all of our possessions, and I drove it up the mountain highway while Stephanie followed me in the car with all of the kids. When we arrived, it was late afternoon. I backed the truck up the long driveway to the front of the house and we unloaded all of our furniture and boxes. By the time we were done, night had fallen and it was becoming very cold, so I locked up the truck and we pulled enough together in the house to secure the children get a good night's sleep. We were again in a new universe, and it felt scary but wonderful to snuggle with our babies.

In the morning, we pulled open the shades and couldn't believe what we saw! Overnight, six feet of snow had fallen. Our truck needed to be returned that day, and thirty yards of six-foot snow sat on the driveway between the truck and the street. I got out a shovel and began to shovel the snow. After six hours of shoveling, I was able to get the truck out to return it.

•••••

Very quickly I learned how to deal with mountain life. I learned the ugly, dirty job of placing chains on my tires and taking them off, which I sometimes had to do twice a day, depending upon road conditions. I ordered a couple cords of firewood and spent an entire day carefully stacking the huge piles of chopped wood against the side of the house, because I was told that the power would go out during snowstorms and we had to be prepared.

That winter in Lake Tahoe was magical, but also very harrowing. The power did go out for two weeks right before Christmas! We had to pile everyone into our living room, and I would keep the fire going all night long in order to keep my family warm. We lived like pioneers. Half the time, I would walk to work and back in the snow, because I couldn't get the car out of the driveway. More often than not we would have blizzard conditions, with high winds and twelve to fifteen feet of snow.

Our twins would grow from infants to toddlers in Lake Tahoe. Still all-consuming of our time, they were starting to become more aware of their surroundings, and the joy I felt from watching them grow was immeasurable. Regina was happy with her new first-grade class; she chatted away every day when she got home from school about everything and everybody as she plunged right into helping me and her mother take care of the babies. Kevin was a great little helper and a happy boy. He loved to play with the twins, handing them his toys or balls and marveling, as they looked them over. I felt that we were now, finally all related by blood through the babies, and I loved my family. Regina and Kevin were my own now, and I knew my lifetime task would be to mentor and watch over them from now on. Although Stephanie could become overwhelmed (what mother wouldn't with four kids including two infants?) she was a master at mothering and she seemed content.

Rachel and Taddy

•••••

I met a young man named Steve Cantore one night while performing at *The Conservatory*. He was an aspiring songwriter, and he was working for the power company. We became fast friends, and wrote a couple songs together. When I got my power bill, I was floored! Heating the huge house was costing over $1,000.00 per month, and that was when the power was even on! Steve offered to put our power bill into his name, because he got his power for half price. It was literally a lifesaver, and I was indebted to him from his kindness.

Steve Cantore and Tad - 1985

The floor plan of *The Conservatory* was set up in a really weird way. The bar was downstairs, and the piano bar was way upstairs, detached completely from the rest of the place. An enormous picture window towered behind me as I performed. I was surrounded by glass, and it was impossible to heat this huge building adequately, so during the winter months, I wore a parka, sometimes with the head piece on, because it was so cold in there! In retrospect, I should have learned some Eskimo music.

Sometimes through the huge window, particularly in the summer months, my audience could see an image of the full moon reflecting on the lake behind me, and it was lovely. During blizzards, the panoramic windows made you feel as if you were in the snowstorm!

People still came in and danced. Rader Rollins, the owner, and his wife were very kind to my family, and I appreciated the money I was making. I started to figure out that Rader had opened the club so he could have a place to drink that was closer to his home. He was in there most nights drinking heavily and requesting his favorite song, which, ironically was, *Try to Remember.*

I was able to buy a better drum machine and, although the added programmed drums were rudimentary and tinny at that point in the development of drum machines, the beat helped to get the crowd going. The metronome-style rigidity of the early machines and the video-game-style drum sounds were very tacky, but it really helped me with my inner time. After years of working with a drum machine, I would never let a drummer rush the timing. It was just built-in time. You know what they say, "So many drummers. So little time." Later in my career, I was fortunate to work with great drummers with great timing, and it was easy.

•••••

Experience is the best teacher. You can speed up the process while gathering your own experience by borrowing from others generous enough to share theirs with you.

A crusty old African-American singer named Bill Hawkins came in to *The Conservatory* on many nights to see me. He would sing with me. He introduced me to a ton of old standards, and he would 'beat me up' with my arrangements, giving me suggestions in a stern manner on how to improve my performance. I appreciated his insight. I was young and hungry to learn.

Bill had a huge record collection. He turned me on to Lou Rawls, Ahmad Jamal, Bobby Short, the Ella Fitzgerald- Joe Pass duets albums, and so many more great artists. His influence really helped to broaden my knowledge and technique as a performer. He was a good old guy with a ton of experience who cared enough to mentor this young performer.

•••••

I proposed marriage to Stephanie. After all, we had children together. I knew she had a ton of issues, but I loved her dearly and she was a good woman. There was a problem, though. She had never been divorced from Dennis Burge. We called Dennis and he was glad to participate in the divorce. He had been thinking about it for a while, and had not known how to approach the issue.

They decided to file the papers in Nevada where we were living, because it only took six weeks for the divorce to be final in Nevada. Dennis flew up, and we found "Do It Yourself" legal papers to type up. Neither Dennis nor Stephanie could type very well, so they asked me if I would type up their divorce papers. It was pretty weird for me to have them both looking over my shoulder and offering suggestions while I typed up their divorce papers! But, I guess it's a testament to how well we all got along with each other.

Yes, I had a pretty unconventional life experience going on here. Dennis could never afford to contribute much towards child support for Regina and Kevin, but he consistently gave a little amount each month to help us, and on holidays he was very generous with the kids. He would even buy Christmas presents for the twins. When the school year started, he would contribute to their clothing expenses as well. Dennis was living in San Francisco at this point, going to culinary school. So, they filed the papers, and by late January, the divorce was final.

•••••

Stephanie's dad, Russ Haddock, came up to visit us, and he sat in on the piano at *The Conservatory* with Bill Hawkins singing. It was a special time, that first winter in Lake Tahoe.

During that year in Tahoe, I witnessed my twins as they learned to sit, then crawl and eventually to walk. Before they could walk, they would have races up the long flight of carpeted stairs from the front door to the living room, sliding back down and racing up again, giggling the entire time. They were truly best friends. Rachel's hair was wild like mine! Taddy was the most darling boy, and they were both so intelligent and insightful. Regina finished second grade, and after the summer, she went into third grade as Kevin shyly walked in to his first day of Kindergarten.

•••••

Gary and Glenna with Tad & Stephanie 1982

In late March of 1982, Stephanie and I drove with the children down to Reno. Her brother Russ, Jr. and his wife Denise met us at a little wedding chapel along with our friends, a performing duo, Gary and Glenna.

I had scraped together enough money for a wedding ring for Stephanie, but she couldn't afford one for me yet. Russ, Jr. brought a plastic ring from a dime candy machine for me to use for the ceremony. It didn't go all the way around my finger!

Kevin, Tad and Regina 1982

This Elvis-style minister came out and married Stephanie and me while the twins were playing nearby in their playpen, and Regina and Kevin looked on. I remember that he kept saying that the ring is a symbol that your love will be unbroken, because it goes all the way around in an unbroken circle. I kept looking at my plastic ring that didn't go all the way around my finger, and I thought, geez, this is bad.

The heart is the infinite multiplier of love; we are liberated when we cease to divide our affections.

It was kind of a sleazy little wedding chapel, but at that moment my little family all loved each other so much we didn't care. I was married to Stephanie. I told myself: now that we were all related by blood through the twins, we would always be one family from now on.

Rachel, Tad, Taddy and Maynard - 1982

Until the twins were born, I didn't completely feel like a father to Regina and Kevin, although they always unconditionally accepted me. Of course, I loved them so much, but I was still so young when we met. From that day forward, I vowed to myself to always watch over all four of my children, and to help them in every way to become the best people they could be, until my last breath.

In April of 1982, my father, his wife Sandra and her daughter Kimberley came to visit us in Lake Tahoe. This was the first time they had met Stephanie or the children. They brought a video camera. It was a special week, watching Maynard, who had now been sober for a couple years, bouncing my babies on his knee. Stephanie and Sandra bonded as beaming pre-teen Kimberley played with all the children while they visited.

Charles and Taddy 1982

Around that same time, my nephew Charles, Suzanne's son, came to visit us in Lake Tahoe. Charles truly was a computer genius, and he had gotten a high-profile job at *Epix*, an early video gaming company in the Silicon Valley of Northern California. He was still a teenager, and he was great with the kids, but we noticed something was a little 'off' with him. Shortly thereafter, he had a full-on manic episode, and he was hospitalized in

North Carolina. Diagnosed as bipolar, he was given Lithium, and his condition generally improved. So many geniuses are diagnosed as bipolar. Processing knowledge on a grand scale can be overwhelming to a brain.

•••••

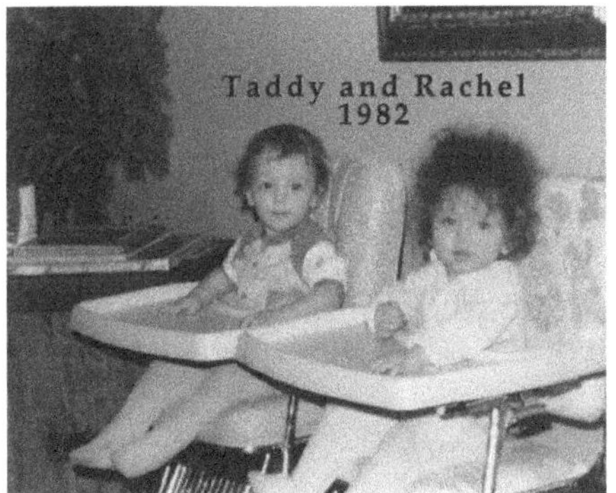

Eddie called from Palm Springs and wanted to come to Tahoe for a visit. We told him that he was welcome to stay for the whole summer if he wanted to. He took us up on the offer! We had a downstairs bedroom that was not being used, so Eddie set up shop there. He was very helpful to Stephanie, and the kids called him Uncle Eddie. They would sneak down to his room many early mornings and wake him up at the crack of dawn! This was something he was absolutely not used to, but he embraced his role with the kids. They would continue to rely on their Uncle Eddie for love and advice for a lifetime.

One day, in May of 1982, Stephanie and I were driving down the hill towards the lake with the twins in their car seats. Steph was talking to me about something negative that somebody had told her, and I said, "How rude!" All of a sudden from the back seat, we heard a tiny voice say, "How wude!" These were Rachel's first words! The next day, we were watching television and a commercial came on. The man said, "For just nine ninety-nine, you can get the full set of knives!" Rachel said, "Nine ninety-nine!" Very quickly thereafter, Taddy started talking too. His first word appropriately was, "Daddy!"

To me, the most amazing thing about parenting is watching a child develop their own unique personality from scratch right before your eyes.

Eddie wanted to work while he was up in Tahoe. I had a friend named Parviz Pedersani. He was an Iranian man who had worked for the recently deposed Shah of Iran, while the Shah had been in power in Iran. Parviz had access to a lot of money, probably offshore accounts. He would just make a phone call, and $50,000.00 would magically appear in his bank account. Parviz bought me a sound system for *The Conservatory,* including a top-of-the-line Yamaha mixing board, and I was grateful. I used that mixer on gigs for many years following. Parviz wanted to open up a nightclub with a disco. He found this downstairs location and called it *The Cellar.* Parviz hired Eddie to wait tables and to manage for him during the summer.

Eddie also spun records at night in the disco. He had an amazing knowledge of music, and through Eddie's direction, Parviz purchased a great collection of record albums for *The Cellar.* Eddie really enjoyed his little stint as a DJ, but *The Cellar* was a short-lived venture. Businesses were hard to maintain in Lake Tahoe, particularly during winters when blizzards would happen sometimes right before the weekends, and tourists couldn't get up the mountain to enjoy the ski resorts and casinos. And, the establishment actually kind of looked and felt like a cellar! It wasn't the warmest of places.

On his off-nights while I was working, Eddie would have long talks with Stephanie at our house. They were close friends, and it meant the world to me that Eddie loved us like he did. I knew he had a special feeling in his heart for Stephanie. Later, he told me that Stephanie was one of the only people who truly understood Eddie. He relied upon her friendship and advice.

•••••

When the summer came to Tahoe, it was breathtakingly beautiful. Incline Village had a private beach for residents, and we took the children down most days to play in the sand. I would swim in the freezing, pristine water, about a hundred yards to a buoy and back every day, sending ripples through the glassy water. I wore a silly looking little blue Speedo bathing suit, which was the rage in those days. It was hard work getting four children, chairs, food and everything else down to the beach, but once we were there, we had a great time.

With children, vacations are hard work!

I met new friends at *The Conservatory*. Ed Hartsink owned the only high-rise condo complex on the North Shore of Lake Tahoe. He was an elderly man, a character with a large venous nose, swollen from alcohol consumption. Always smiling, he would march into the lounge singing fractured lyrics at the top of his voice, like, "Hello, young lovers, you're under arrest!" At any given moment in the evening, he would break out in song. Whenever he sang a tune that I didn't know, I quickly learned it and I was ready for his outburst, next time.

Tad with Ed Hartsink 1985

Once, Ed invited Stephanie and me over to his residence for cocktails. It was on the ground floor of his huge condo complex at lakeshore, and the patio opened up to a private dock where his boats sat on the lake. It was a breathtaking view. We sat, enjoying the sunset on the mountains above the lake, with his friend Sid Kaufman. Sid married a younger woman named Cheryl, and they remained my friends for many years. Even after Sid died, I would see Cheryl down in Del Mar, twenty years later, still partying like she did then. Even though I was light-years younger than these men, they treated me with kindness and respect, and it meant the world to me.

•••••

A little recording studio buzzed with music up on the hill at *Sierra Nevada College* in Incline Village. I had written some original songs and I wanted desperately to record them.

I scraped together a few hundred dollars and hired a drummer, Ed Pias and a bass player friend of his to come up from Reno. Ed and I had worked together on a couple private parties while I was in Reno. We recorded ten songs that day, and it was rudimentary, but very cool.

•••••

Stephanie and Eddie decided to throw a surprise birthday party for me in June of 1982. They invited a hundred of our new friends and acquaintances up to our house. On the evening of the party, I was genuinely surprised. Eddie had found some excuse to drag me away from the house for a few minutes. As we drove up the street, I mentioned that somebody must be having a party, because of all the cars parked up the street! I actually saw Bill Hawkins walking in my door, and I said to Eddie, "Look, there's Bill! I guess he came over to wish me a happy birthday!" I was so naïve.

When I walked in to a cheering throng of friends, Steve Cantore handed me a note to read, as if I had prepared a note to say how surprised I was. It was funny. Ed Hartsink and Sid Kaufman were there, along with many other wonderful friends.

Connie Griffo was a local real estate agent. She was a wonderful woman. Connie's daughter Rosalie was in her early twenties. Rosalie was stunningly beautiful and I believe that she had a crush on me. I was flattered and I liked her a lot, but very devoted to my family. We all became good friends.

•••••

In July, Stephanie's brother Russ, Jr. announced that his wife Denise had given birth to another daughter, Hillary. Denise's oldest daughter Tiffany helped them with the two baby girls, Adrienne and Hillary. Russ, Jr. and Denise had bought a house in Reno. Her parents had given them a down payment.

Russ, Jr. would call his sister Stephanie and brag about the house. He would say, "Why don't you and Tad buy a house up here?" We didn't have a parent to give us a down payment. Stephanie would tell him that, and he would say, "Well, then, why don't you go back to work? You're just a baby maker. You don't have any skills." Stephanie would cry after she hung up the phone. Her brother was holding a lot of anger inside, and I worried for his mental health at times.

Russ, Jr. was performing with different bands and traveling a lot to remote parts of Nevada. He would play in casinos in Elko and Winnemucca. Although I really did admire that Russ, Jr. kept up on all of the new equipment and did whatever he could to continue to perform and bring money in to his family, I was also grateful to have a gig so close to home, which prevented me from having to travel too far.

We spent a lovely Fourth of July in 1982 on the lake with the babies and Eddie, watching the fireworks. My mother came up to visit us. Elaine watched the children one night, and Stephanie and I had our first date in over a year since the babies were born. We went to a French restaurant and ate *escargot*.

Stephanie was getting a little bit of cabin fever, and she wanted to go back to work doing something. She decided to become a waitress at *Denny's*, which was close to our house. At first, I tried to talk her out of it. After all, most of her other jobs serving had been at much nicer venues, and I was also afraid that she may feel the need to drink again, but she insisted. She worked at *Denny's* for several months while we were up in Tahoe. Although in so many ways it was beneath her to work there compared to other jobs she had worked, she handled it with grace and actually enjoyed it. Years before, she had worked at *Norm's* in Los Angeles, which was another chain of coffee shops, so she knew the drill.

On the babies' first birthday in August, we started the tradition of having two cakes, one for each of them, so they would always feel like a special individual and not half of a whole. They spread the cake and frosting all over their little happy faces and it went everywhere!

I did my first corporate gig ever. Some friends who owned a garage door company needed to hire entertainment for a garage door-maker's convention in Reno. They paid me $1,000.00 for the night. I performed for more than 1,000 people in a ballroom, and it went very well.

I had some business cards printed up. Stephanie and I thought it would be fun to call our business "Twin Productions" as we knew we were good at producing twins!

•••••

After the summer, Eddie went back to Palm Springs, and the first snow came early, in September. Rader Rollins was still consuming large amounts of alcohol. He was losing money on his gamble of a restaurant in Lake Tahoe and he was becoming argumentative about little things. One night, Stephanie came in to see me and he didn't like that. Another time, someone made a comment that the bartender was only three years younger than Rader, but the bartender looked twenty years younger, and he flew off the handle. Business wasn't great because of the way the bar was set up, so far away from the piano bar on a different floor. After a year and a month, Rader decided to start taking steps to sell *The Conservatory*.

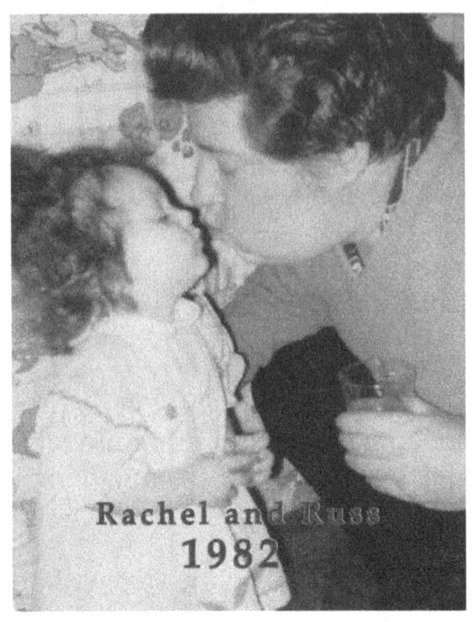
Rachel and Russ
1982

Stephanie had the idea of having her father Russ come up to Lake Tahoe and start a band with me. I thought it was a totally weird and ridiculous proposition, but she became hell-bent on the idea.

Russ and his drunken bass player Scotty came up to stay with us. Scotty was a darling man who could not stay sober to save his life. But, he was a happy drunk. Russ was still drinking a lot himself, and still not taking care of himself.

I called Ed Pias to play drums and he brought a female vocalist with him. We did one night at a dive bar called the *Jaegermeister*. We auditioned at the *Crystal Bay Club* and got the gig. It was ironic, because Russ and Scotty had performed with Russ' trio at the Crystal Bay Club twenty years before then.

Tad and Scotty
1982

Before we could do the gig, Russ had a minor stroke. We had to call it all off. After Russ got out of the hospital, he and Scotty went back to Palm Springs. I was relieved. Out of that experience came the absolute worst, most embarrassing promotional photos I've ever had… of this bizarre band that never was!

Tad's Band
with Russ Haddock
1982

After Russ and Scotty went home, I performed one more night at the *Jaegermeister*. I had purchased a keyboard bass, to start learning to play bass with my left hand, for a bigger sound. The *Jaegermeister* had an old upright piano which was tuned exactly a half step lower than it should have been tuned. In those days, keyboards did not have transposers built in, so I was forced to play in one key with my left hand, and in another key with my right hand all night long! It was agonizing and I doubt seriously if many people could pull it off. I'm sure I sounded awful. It was too difficult to play in a coordinated fashion in two different keys at once.

•••••

I called Craig Evans and he put me back into the *Continental Lodge* in Reno. It was tough, though, making it back and forth to Reno from Lake Tahoe during the winter. Sometimes *Mount Rose Highway* would close from the blizzards, and I would have to go around Truckee to *Interstate 80* and down into Reno.

A normally forty-five-minute drive in clear weather would turn into a six-hour ordeal in a blinding snowstorm; I would drive three hours each way, stopping to put my chains on and take them off twice each way. After performing all night, I would find myself shivering in a blizzard, sopping wet under my car in a pile of dirty slush, hooking up chains, and then praying I would make it home safe through the snow as other cars veered off the highway into the ravines below.

After an exhausting day and night, stressed from driving, soaking wet, I would make it home. Immediately I would have to go out and get stacks of firewood to replenish our supply inside, at three o'clock in the morning. Then, Stephanie would hand me both babies so she could try to get some sleep before her *Denny's* job in the morning.

Exhausted, I would hold my darling babies, one in each arm, and walk them back and forth in the living room by the fire until they eventually passed out. Then, we would all cuddle together until morning. When morning came all too quickly, we would dress Regina and Kevin, and I would walk them down the hill to their school, getting back just in time for Stephanie to go to work so that I could stay with the twins while she was gone.

•••••

Sometimes, on a windless, misty mountain morning as snowflakes delicately landed on your cheeks like perfect, stinging communion wafers, the atmosphere was so very quiet. Boots broke the silence, crunching through frozen twigs as we carefully made our way down the snowy hill to the road below, holding hands. I could feel the excitement building in my Regina and Kevin as we approached the school.

My babies were very well behaved from the beginning. They were kind and helpful, and they always worked together, even in mischief. Whatever it was that they wanted (when I wasn't looking), he would help her up onto the counter…she would grab it and hand it to him…he would help her down off the counter, and then they would spread it all over! Of course, the house was baby-proofed but they still found a way to grab cereal or cookies!

The winter of 1982 in Lake Tahoe was brutal. It is listed as one of the top ten snowiest winters ever recorded in that region of the Sierras. My trips back and forth to Reno became more and more precarious, and our power went out again for two weeks in December. Again, my guardian angels were working overtime.

One night, after a particularly scary trip home from Reno, I came in almost delirious from exhaustion and told Stephanie that I had seen a bad accident in Truckee on the freeway. She suggested that we consider moving back to Southern California.

Stephanie thought that perhaps we should move to Los Angeles to further my career, but she believed that I might get lost in the shuffle in L.A., as one of many entertainers trying to make it. Also, the gigs didn't pay very well in L.A. compared to Palm Springs.

Stephanie knew that many producers came to Palm Springs on a regular basis, and I would probably have a greater shot of being seen by an important person in the industry if we went back to Palm Springs instead of moving to L.A.

So, in February of 1983, we packed up the children and all of our belongings, moved back and found a rental house on Del Lago Road, only two doors down from where I had lived with my mother years before, on the North end of Palm Springs.

The Reno-Tahoe experience had been life changing. In Lake Tahoe, I had experienced some of the very best and also most precarious moments of my young life to this point. Driving through many raging snowstorms with a rear-wheel-drive *Dodge Charger* with chains on my tires; carrying stacks of firewood into my home to keep my family warm; these experiences toughened me and made me into a more rugged individual. Coming home to my sweet babies softened me; fatherhood grew me into a man, even more so than my adventures through blizzards had done. I had risen to the challenge and survived.

CHAPTER THIRTY-FOUR
Returning to Palm Springs

After settling into our rental home in Palm Springs, I performed for a couple weekends at the *Iron Gate*, a restaurant in Palm Desert that had originally been built by Lyman Martin, the owner of *Sunshine.*

Following that, I found a couple off-nights at *Delmonico's Restaurant*, on the North end of Palm Springs. *Delmonico's* had originally been *Jack London's* in the 1950's and 1960's. During that period, Dominick Zangari was the bartender. He was a congenial character; a kindly young Italian man with a bow-tie, pressed white shirt and vest; Dominick was known for his penchant to perform magic tricks for his clientele, and for his outstanding memory. He could remember people's names he hadn't seen for years at a time.

Eventually, Dominick bought out Jack London and in time he sold *Delmonico's* to Jojo Comi and his brother. Dominick then went on to open the famous *Dominick's Restaurant* in Rancho Mirage, right down the street from Frank Sinatra's house. *Dominick's* was a staple in the Palm Springs area for twenty-three years. It was Mr. Sinatra's favorite place to dine when he was back in the desert. I had met Dominick several times and he was always very good to me. Through the years, I performed a few times at *Dominick's*, always to a packed room.

Jojo Comi and I got along really well at *Delmonico's*. He remembered me from *Pal* Joey's, and he was always kind to me. His brother had just sold out his half of the business to Tony Prenesti, and Jojo was livid about it. He didn't like Tony and he didn't want to be his partner. Jojo could smell trouble with Tony, and shortly after I started performing off-nights at *Delmonico's*, Jojo sold out his half of the business to Tony. Eventually, Jojo and I would work together again at *Patti Z.*

Tony Prenesti and I got along well. He was a big guy; opinionated and at times obnoxious and intimidating, but always very respectful to me, as I was to him; it had been at Tony Prenesti's table at *Zelda's* that I had first hooked up with Stephanie.

Tony was one of those restaurateurs who didn't pay a lot for entertainment, so he didn't keep his entertainers for long, but if you were ever down and out and you needed a gig, you could always count on Tony to come through for you. I appreciated that. I was back in the desert and I had a family to feed.

•••••

Stephanie reached out to the Livreri family to get a waitressing gig at *Livreri's*. She was still a little large from having given birth to twins, and she didn't feel that she could do cocktails again just yet, so she asked Alan and Jane Livreri for a job as a food waitress. They remembered her from *Pal* Joey's; they knew her work ethic and they jumped at the prospect of hiring her. Stephanie and I had been ordering take-out food from *Livreri's* for years. She loved their *Clams Oreganata.*

Alan Livreri was a character. He was a true Italian. Family meant everything, and if you worked for him, you were family. Alan and Jane had three teenage children, Peter, John and Kim. He was known for his Italian food, and his bar was usually empty.

He offered to have me come and perform for $50.00 per night on Friday and Saturday night. That was really low money. In fact, I had never performed for money that low but I wasn't working on weekends so I accepted the gig gratefully. The Livreri family was very involved with us when we were there. Little Kim would sit next to me at the piano. The boys would sit in the bar close to me and ask me to play songs they liked. I was closer in age to the children than I was to Alan and Jane. There wasn't a lot of business in the bar, though.

My voice could sound a lot like Neil Diamond, especially when I sang his music. One night, Neil Diamond came into *Livreri's* to eat dinner with his family and Stephanie waited on him. After a few minutes, Neil asked Stephanie to check and see what recording that was of him singing in the other room. He told her, "I know that's me, but I can't remember when I recorded that." Stephanie told him that it was not his singing, but it was actually her husband, Tad, performing live. He couldn't believe it! He thought I was actually a recording of him singing! He came around the corner and just stared at me in amazement, shaking his head. So, I went in and introduced myself to him on a break.

Stephanie wanted to give him some of my original music, but he couldn't accept it for legal reasons. He gave me the name of his publisher, David Rosner with *Bicycle Music Company* in Los Angeles. I contacted David and he worked with me for a while attempting to place some music. He was a very nice man. Eventually my friendship with David Rosner would pay off, in the early 2000's while I was working for *Yamaha* and we needed to secure clearance of Neil Diamond songs.

Kevin with his Mom
Stephanie
1983

•••••

We had a lot of problems with our rental home on Del Lago Road. The owner was a physician who lived out of town, and he didn't want to fix anything. There was no pool at the house either. After a couple months, Stephanie begged me to break the lease and move. She found a rental house on Riverside Drive in South Palm Springs. It was an old home from the 1920's. The back yard was full of mature fruit trees and the pool was in front of the house, behind a big concrete wall. The owner of the Del Lago house kindly let us out of the lease, and we moved again over to Riverside Drive, right after we had a little birthday party for Kevin, who was now six years old!

The Riverside Drive house was a nice place to be for a while. We rented from an agent and she was happy and quick to get us in there. We didn't understand why she was so delighted to rent the place to us until one day a bearded, beatnik-looking man was sitting at our pool with his feet in the water, watching my pre-teen Regina swimming. Regina saw him and immediately got out of the pool and ran into the house.

I came out and asked him what the hell he was doing in my pool, and he informed me that he was the owner of the house and it was his right to be there. We got into a shouting match and I threw him off the property, threatening to call the police. I called the agent and she apologized. When he came back a month later, I threw him out again. I thought that maybe he was slightly insane.

Regina - 1983

As a general rule, when your hands are full, your life is full.

I spent my twenty-fifth birthday in June of 1983 at the Riverside Drive house with my wife and children. I remember floating in the pool on that hot summer day, reflecting on my young life to that point. Yes, I had bitten off more than I could chew. I had my hands full in my life, but my life was full and I was generally happy.

My father called me and marveled at how his son was a quarter-century old. Maynard was doing well. He was in his sixtieth year. He had no desire to drink and hadn't for some time.

I began to learn a valuable lesson that I would appreciate later. My father was incapable of crossing a line to be the person I wanted him to be. I knew that he loved me, in spite of that. When I stopped trying to get him to cross the line, when I lowered my expectations and hopes of the kind of person I wanted him to be, I was able to let go and I could get along with him much better. It was a tough lesson, but it brought serenity to me.

It's a waste of time to attempt to get someone to cross a line they are incapable of or unwilling to cross. Don't allow frustration to build; instead, let go of your hopes or expectations that this person will change. It won't cure the situation but it will allow you some peace.

•••••

In midsummer, our air conditioning went out in the Riverside Drive house and the owner refused to pay to have it fixed. After arguing with the agent for a few days while doing everything we could to keep our children cool with oscillating fans, bugs began to overrun the house. We realized that we were going to have to move yet again. Somehow, through all of this, we had a little birthday party for the twins second birthday. They were my little loves! Fortunately, they were too young to

Taddy and Rachel - 1983

experience the anxiety their mother and I were experiencing, doing our best to keep our children cool and fighting off bugs everywhere. Taddy would say, "Ooh, that's yucky," in his cute little voice, fascinated as he watched a bug crawl across the floor.

In September of 1983, we found a rental house on San Martin Circle in Palm Springs. It was a fairly new home, and although the owner of the Riverside Drive house threatened to sue us for moving, the agent couldn't be kinder and she was relieved that we got out of the house without any more incidents with her crazy owner. The San Martin Circle house was literally the fourth house we were living in, within only 8 months. It was a tough year for us, but we had finally found a home we loved, on San Martin Circle. The house had a very nice pool. It was in a newer neighborhood on a cul de sac. We enrolled Regina into third grade, and Kevin went into kindergarten.

•••••

Tad and Grandmother Audrey 1978

At some point, around this time, I got the news that my beloved grandmother, Audrey, had died. She was one of my loves of my life. After my grandfather George died in 1980, she lived alone for a year or so, and then my dad made the decision to put her into a nursing home.

My grandmother wanted to stay at Maynard's house and he had room, but Sandra didn't want to be her nursemaid, and she convinced my dad that Audrey would be more comfortable in a home. I cherished the few letters she had written to me in her last couple years of life. She had never met my twins, but she knew they existed and that made me happy. She was ninety-four years old when she died, and I was grateful that she had a long life, although it was beset with so much tragedy. God bless my wonderful grandmother! I would have gladly taken her in and taken care of her if circumstance had allowed it. She was certainly one of my best friends ever in this world. I grieved.

•••••

The death of a relationship typically comes from a thousand small cuts, rather than one large stab.

My sister Betsy had broken up with her husband, Jim. I had seen with my own eyes the chaos of their relationship. Jim had started working at *General Dynamics Space Systems*. Even as he pulled his life together, they both still lived on the edge. He wanted an open relationship, which, as I had learned, never works in the long term. Jim was talented at auto restoration and he was super-intelligent, as was Betsy, but their relationship had become toxic.

Betsy and Mark Moura
Mid 1980's

Betsy met a kind bearded man named Mark Moura. I thought he was a little trippy when I met him. He liked to talk about the energy that permeates from certain rocks and gems, and he spoke of wizards and other planes. I wondered if he had just done too many drugs or if he really saw stuff that I didn't see! But, as time went on, I began to really like Mark, and I especially liked the way he treated my sister, with love and dignity.

My mother would sometimes single out a grandchild and shower them with gifts and attention. This usually made the other grandchildren feel left out, but her intentions were good. Because Betsy's son Lucas wore glasses with thick lenses as a child, he had the look of a dorky kid, but actually he was very gifted and always so sweet and kind.

Lucas and David Arnott
1978

Elaine would take her grandson Lucas on long trips and buy him new shoes or clothes or whatever he needed. Sometimes she would drop Lucas off with us for a week or so. Later, Lucas would tell me how special those times were. It reminded me of how much my Uncle Ted had meant to me in my childhood, so maybe I paid it forward a bit by loving Lucas along the way.

My sister Judy had also broken up with her husband, David. She had decided to go into the *United States Air Force* and become a Registered Nurse. The *Air Force* put her through college and she eventually got her Master's Degree in Nursing. Around this time, Judy met a man named George Kane and they dated for a year or two before they married. My oldest sister Suzanne had divorced her husband Bill as well, all around the same time. When it rains, it pours.

Suzanne met a man named Irwin, and they married quickly. It was a rebound relationship. The marriage lasted until she caught him in bed with another man. My poor sisters!

Paul Schaeffer
1984

•••••

An entertainer named Paul Schaeffer was performing at the *Trinidad Hotel* in Palm Springs at a restaurant and nightclub called *Patti Z.* Patti Zangari had recently divorced Dominick Zangari. He had a choice of giving her his second restaurant, *Mister D's*, or their home in Rancho Mirage, so he kept the home and gave her the restaurant in the divorce. She changed the name of the restaurant promptly. Patti was a beautiful but hard-core, driven, strong woman with big dark hair and a big ego. She ran a tight ship. *Patti Z* was packed every night. It was the most popular piano lounge in town next to *Melvyn's.*

Paul Schaeffer came to me and told me that he was going to move on from the gig. He had another gig out of state that started in a week, and he was going to be gone for at least a year. He asked me if I wanted to take the job at *Patti Z.* I jumped on it. *Patti Z* was a five-night a week gig. It paid $90.00 per night and the tips were phenomenal. It was close to the money I had been making at *The Conservatory* in Lake Tahoe. The hours were tough. The gig went from 8:30PM to 1:30AM every night, but I was young and my voice was strong enough to handle it.

I could still do the two off-nights at *Delmonico's*, but I was going to have to go to Alan Livreri and give him a week's notice, which I didn't like. Alan was paying me so very low, and for only two nights a week, and he knew I had a family to feed. Surely, he would understand, I thought. He didn't.

Alan told me that family is family, and family doesn't do this to family. I wasn't allowed to quit his restaurant at all, at least not without plenty of time for him to find someone else (even though he had nobody performing at *Livreri's* before I had started there and his bar was generally empty even with me there… oh, and he didn't replace me with anyone anyway after I left).

I told Alan I absolutely meant no disrespect, but I had no choice. Low money, two nights a week was not going to feed my children. Of course, I was so grateful that he had created a gig for me, but I still had to keep a roof over my children's heads. We were barely scraping by with Stephanie's tips and my two little gigs. I said, "Come on, man! What do you expect me to do here? If I don't take the gig now, I won't get it at all."

Alan threw me out and fired Stephanie on the spot. He told me that I was never allowed to step foot into his restaurant again. I was floored. I thought that his behavior was ridiculous; he was paying me only $50.00 per night for two nights, and his lounge was always slow so there were hardly any tips. This was insane. But, I learned another valuable lesson.

Some people are rigid and will not bend. To me, that is a prescription for unhappiness.

Still, I was living my life with a certain fear that I would not be able to support my family, and when a great opportunity arose, I responded to that fear sometimes by compromising my integrity just slightly. If I could have given him two-week's notice instead of one, even, he probably still would have thrown me out, but that would have been the right thing to do.

I promised myself that I would never let that happen again. But mostly, I was sad because Alan took his rage out on Stephanie, too, and she didn't deserve to be treated that way. She was a very dedicated, hard worker.

Alan and I didn't talk for many years after that. Years later, he called me out of the blue and said that he had a special event at *Livreri's* and he wanted me to perform for it. He said that if I would perform for the event, that he would forgive me for what I did to him and let it go. I was still angry about what he had done to Stephanie, but I swallowed my pride and used the event as a chance to heal a rift that should have never existed.

Letting go and swallowing some pride is sometimes more important than allowing old wounds to fester.

•••••

Patti Z was everything I hoped it would be. My friend Jojo Comi, who had sold *Delmonico's* to Tony Prenesti, was now bartending at Patti's. He was delighted to see me! My friend Mark Piccone was parking cars some nights, and Mark's wife Cathy was waitressing. She was beautiful and sweet, and very kind to me.

Years later, Cathy Piccone would become the General Manager of *Gibson's Steakhouse* in Chicago. It's almost impossible to get a reservation there, and I would call her at *Gibson's* occasionally to get a friend in who was in Chicago trying to do a business deal. She always came through. Even back then at *Patti Z*, Cathy was a doll and we worked well together.

People were sometimes three-deep at the bar, and I was finally making enough money again to support my family. At the end of two weeks, Patti came up to me and thanked me for performing. She said that Paul had told her he would be back after two weeks, but that she loved my performance and she hoped I would work for her again soon. Paul hadn't told her he wasn't coming back! I told her that Paul told me the gig was mine and he was not returning, ever, and that I quit another job to take this one. Patti was incensed. I thought she knew! After throwing a huge fit and yelling at me, she asked me if I wanted the job, and I told her again that Paul had told me I was going to take over for him and I had quit another job to do this.

After that, we got along very well, Patti and I. She was hard-core, though. One night, she was standing at the bar with a customer, and they called me over to ask a question. We were talking and I called her by her name, Patti. She looked at me, thrust her nose up into the air and said, "From now on, you will address me as "Miss Patti" when speaking to me. I looked at her like she was crazy and said, okay. From that night on, I never uttered her name again when we spoke, and I surely was not going to call her "Miss Patti!"

A kind, European Maître 'D named Eddie Dolenz ran the front desk at *Patti Z*. Eddie was a very proper, balding man with a thick European accent; he was fifty-five years old. The Maître 'D lived in a small apartment, close to the restaurant, with his wife.

One night at work when I took a break, Eddie pulled me aside and told me that he had experienced a nightmare, the night before. In the dream, he said, he was sitting at his kitchen table and he couldn't breathe. He tried to call out for his wife, but he couldn't speak. He said it was really unnerving, and he was having trouble shaking the feeling that came from the nightmare. I comforted him, we spoke for a few more minutes about it and we went on with our work.

That night after work he said his goodbyes and went home, and the next morning they found him slumped over his kitchen table, dead. I couldn't believe it. He had a premonition of his own demise and he told me about it, literally on the night that it happened. I was haunted by that revelation for years.

•••••

Right around this time, I performed at a charity event and I shared the stage with the great screen actor Robert Wagner. He had been married to one of my favorite childhood actresses, Natalie Wood, and she had died in a terrible boating accident only a couple years before. I always thought she was beautiful inside and out, and there was some doubt about whether or not he may have had something to do with her death. When I met him, though, he was a complete gentleman, and I found it hard to believe that he might even be capable of anything like that.

CHAPTER THIRTY-FIVE
Frank Sinatra

One night, Patti came up to me and told me that Frank Sinatra was coming in to have dinner and drinks with a large group of his friends. She told me, "Whatever you do, do NOT play any Frank Sinatra songs. He'll make me fire you if you do!" I was beside myself. I was confused. I didn't know exactly what he did or didn't do. Frank had recorded literally thousands of songs in his career!

I had heard that Mr. Sinatra would go into nightclubs and a singer would be up on stage, trying to sound like him and sing his songs. They would try to do Frank better than he did; they wanted to "Out-Frank" Frank, and it bothered him to the core. He would get angry and tell club owners to get rid of this bum.

I decided that I was going to sing what I always sing, but I was going to do it the way I always do it and with a gentle tone vocally while they were dining. I wasn't going to go out of my way to impress anyone; I was just going to be myself. I still couldn't believe that he was going to come in and hear me perform!

Mr. Sinatra came in with his wife, Barbara and a large entourage of friends. They sat at a large table across the restaurant from the bar, with Mr. Sinatra directly facing me with his back to the wall. He always sat with his back to the wall wherever he went, and the smart club owners knew that and prepared for it in advance. Jilly Rizzo was with the group. I waved at Jilly when they walked in, and he nodded back at me with a big smile.

About halfway into their meal, I was playing *What Are You Doing the Rest of Your Life?* Mr. Sinatra got up out of his chair and started walking directly to me. I kept singing but I was panicking. I knew this was one of his songs! He walked right up to me and said, "Tough bridge on that tune, huh? Good job, kid." And then, he continued on to the bathroom. I couldn't believe it. He had spoken to me!

A week or so later, Mr. Sinatra came in alone with his wife Barbara and had dinner. After dinner, they met a couple friends at the bar. Frank and the bartender Jojo Comi were old friends, and Jojo joked with Frank about the time he ordered warm gin.

Patti Z had an "Island-Style" bar that went all around the room in a circle. Frank and Barbara sat on my side of the bar, close to the piano. At some point, Barbara came up to me and asked me if I wrote music. I played my original song, *You're My World*, for them.

She loved it and asked me if I could get her a recording of the song for Frank. I was broke and didn't have access to a recording studio. I made a cassette recording of the song but I was too ashamed of the quality of the recording to get it to her. This is one of my great regrets in life. If he had recorded my song, it would have been a career changer.

•••••

Eddie King was a crusty old man with a crew cut and a huge nose; his face was always red from too much booze. He was an old friend of Mr. Sinatra. Eddie King was almost a legend in his own right in Palm Springs. He had managed *don The* Beachcomber in its prime, and Sinatra hired him for a time to run the restaurant at his *Cal Neva* Lodge in Lake Tahoe. Eddie would come to the bar at *Patti Z* to hang out while Jojo was bartending.

One night, Mr. King called me over to the bar. He asked me if I would like to perform for a private party for Mr. Sinatra. I said, "Of course! I would LOVE to!" With a twinkle in his eye, he told me, "Okay, I can get you in, but first you have to buy me a case of *Acushnet* golf balls." I quickly agreed. I went home and told Stephanie that Frank Sinatra wanted me to perform for a private party! She was delighted!

The next morning, I went out to find these golf balls. I went to virtually every golf store in the desert. Nobody had even heard of this *Acushnet* golf ball. Finally, in a last act of desperation, I went to this tiny old golf store in Cathedral City. An elderly man behind the counter laughed and he said, "What you want is these *Top Flite* golf balls. They're in every store! See here, they're manufactured by the *Acushnet Golf Company*." Eddie King had intentionally sent me on a wild goose chase to see if I could figure out his request. I got him a case of his golf balls, and he got me the gig. I probably would have gotten the gig anyway, but a promise is a promise.

•••••

This first party I was to play for Mr. Sinatra was going to be held at the home of Danny and Natalie Schwartz, good friends of the Sinatra's who lived in the same general area in Rancho Mirage. Ambassador and Mrs. Walter Annenberg were going to attend.

I ran into Sam Bianco, my old friend who had co-owned *Pal Joey's.* Sam told me to come by *Madison & Company,* his jewelry store. He loaned me a *Rolex* watch to wear that night. Sam told me that he had just sold one to Mr. Sinatra, and the one he was loaning me was actually a nicer watch than the one he had sold to Frank. I was grateful, and extremely paranoid not to lose or damage that watch!

On the night of the event, I showed up at the Schwartz' house, and Mrs. Schwartz informed me that I was not to bring in any equipment whatsoever. I was just to play background piano. I said, okay, whatever you want, and I sat and played piano for a roomful of celebrities.

I was playing *The Girl from Ipanema* and Ambassador Annenberg came up to me and said, "Oh, *Meditation*, I love that song!" I wasn't playing *Meditation*, but I immediately began to play it instead of *Ipanema*. And, I made a mental note of his favorite song, so from that night on, whenever I saw the Ambassador, I played his song and he loved it.

Mr. Sinatra was kind to me. At some point, he came and stood by the piano and talked to me for a moment.

I was called several more times after that night to perform for more events for the Sinatra's. It was cool, because I knew the chef, Johnny Costa and some other of his staff from just hanging out with them at my gigs. Many of his friends were also my customers at *Patti Z*, so they were all very accommodating. Sometimes, Mr. Sinatra would stand by the piano and sing a bar or two of whatever I was playing, in the middle of a conversation with his buddies about that song and the people involved in it. Other times, he would make a point of coming up and making small talk with me for a moment or two. I believe that he appreciated my talent on piano and vocals, but even more so, the fact that I would show up, do my job, be kind and not ask for anything, not try to get any extra attention than I should, and be respectful; these things were as important to the flow of the event as was my talent.

In the meantime, I had learned a ton of Jimmy Van Heusen songs. Mr. Van Heusen was a great lyricist for Sinatra, and he lived in the desert.

One night, I was doing an event at *Don the Beachcomber* for Mr. Sinatra, and Jimmy Van Heusen walked in. At that point, he was a very old man, and he walked right by me without acknowledging me. Still, I played his music in the background while he dined, and he winked at me. I felt like the proverbial fly on the wall at these events. At that point in time, there was no bigger star in the universe than Frank Sinatra.

Jimmy Van Heusen

•••••

Out of what became many encounters with Mr. Sinatra, first at *Patti Z* and then performing for him later at different events over the next few years, I was constantly amazed at how very much he treated me with respect and kindness. The best way for me to describe it is to say that he appreciated my talent as if I was the special person in the room! Being such a young man in the presence of greatness, it blew me away, but I had heard many stories about how he openly expressed appreciation for musicians and songwriters with whom he worked. It was a magical experience for this young

performer, to be accepted and to see my talent recognized by the legend himself. I also believe that my calm demeanor and the fact that I didn't belt out songs to try to make some big impression; that I would never 'take the spotlight' or 'over-perform' during these performances meant a lot to him.

As the years went by, I realized more and more how fortunate I had been to have known and had a friendship with Frank Sinatra. Hundreds of years from now, he will be remembered as an icon of the twentieth century, and I played a bit part in his story.

You are never too big or too important to remember to appreciate or compliment the talent and the unique spark of magic in others.

CHAPTER THIRTY-SIX
The 1980's Palm Springs Experience

The great *Chicago Cubs* (and before that, *St. Louis Cardinals*) sports broadcaster Harry Caray frequented *Patti Z* during the off-season of baseball. He was a delightful man, and usually pretty drunk when I saw him.

Harry and his wife Dutchie hosted lavish parties at their Palm Springs home when he wasn't broadcasting. They hired me to perform a few times, which I enjoyed immensely. Harry was hilarious, always joking and laughing with his guests.

Harry walked with a limp from being hit by a car in the late 1960's, but he never complained. My grandmother Audrey was a huge *St. Louis Cardinals* fan, and she had listened to his sports broadcasting for many years, even before I was born. I was honored to be in his presence. Somehow, he had kept a good attitude and found bright spots through all of the *Cub's* losing years.

Tad with Jan Hasman
Patti Z - 1983

My new friend, Jan Hasman was a good man. He was a great saxophonist who also played piano and sang. Jan was performing next door at the *International Hotel* in Palm Springs. We would go back and forth on our breaks and sit in with each other. Later, Jan played saxophone on New Year's Eve at *Patti Z* with me, and even later, we did quite a few corporate gigs together.

Irving Mills, the great publisher, musician and lyricist came in very often to listen to me at *Patti Z.* He was approaching ninety and in very ill health. Irving invited me to his house to perform on his piano. He boasted that the cabinetry of the piano was made entirely of plexiglass, so it was entirely see-through. I planned to perform for him at his house, but he became very ill before I could make it over there. Nevertheless, I would go and sit with him on my breaks, and he loved to recall great memories of the early days of American jazz, when he worked with the Dorsey brothers, Duke Ellington, Hoagy Carmichael and many others. He was a delightful old man, and it was amazing for me to get to know him.

Irving Mills

•••••

Stephanie had not graduated from High School. She dropped out and went to work to feed Regina when Steph was just sixteen years old. Still, she wanted to go to college. Her brother and her father were musicians, and she had always wanted to learn music herself. She had a great business mind when it came to music, but she knew nothing about the creative element.

Stephanie enrolled into *Music Theory & Harmony* and a couple other classes at the *College of The Desert.* She got Straight "A's" until it came to sight-reading and ear training. It turned out that her talents were much stronger on the technical side than the musical side.

Although she didn't continue after the school year, it emboldened her to be more involved and to start to look for another way to make an impact in the music business. Through this time period, Stephanie was a compassionate mom and a wonderful, involved wife. She was not drinking; Stephanie was motivated.

Meanwhile, we were raising four young children. My focus was always on being a good father and husband. My children's goodness made it easy on me. They were all very close, working and playing together and not arguing too much.

Taddy and Rachel
1983

Of course, it was always overwhelming, with mounds of dirty dishes and clothes to fold, homework to do and bedrooms to clean, but there was so much love in our home at this time. Stephanie was trying to get healthy and lose weight. She started to take walks every day and tried every diet on the market. She wasn't working a job at this point, so it helped her to have less stress and to work on herself.

•••••

Kevin was a good son. Now in first grade, he was friendly and kind to everyone. Whenever we had a teacher meeting, though, his teacher would tell us that Kevin wasn't slow, he was very intelligent, but he was kind of a spaced-out kid. His goodness propelled him.

Kevin and Stephanie
1983

At the end of first grade, they created a special award for Kevin for his kindness and uniqueness. Kevin would turn out to be a bit of a late bloomer, but eventually he prevailed in a big way and grew up to become a strong, intelligent, completely aware and successful person. I was always grateful to be his dad, and although he was my stepson, in so many ways he took on my personality and habits.

Genetics is only responsible for half of development; the environment you create for your child is equally as important.

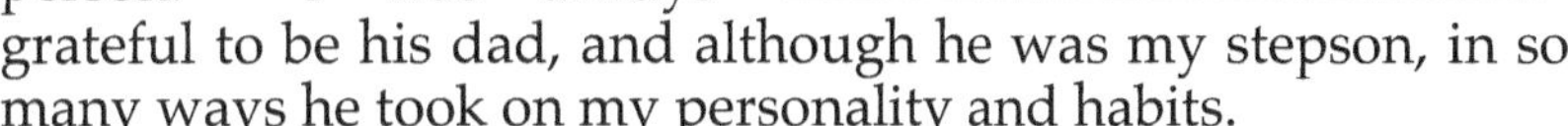

I always hoped that the environment I created for my children would help them to succeed. Parents naturally make mistakes and you can't do much about it except to keep trying to be the best.

I picked up a couple off-nights performing at the *Canyon Hotel* in the Greenhouse lobby lounge. I continued to work on my skill of using my left hand to play keyboard bass. The little bass unit was a rudimentary, twenty-note keyboard that I placed to my left playing bass with my left hand as I played piano and sang, and used the drum machine. *Yamaha* made a newer drum machine that was better than the ones I had before, and I was able to squeeze enough money to buy it. So, my sound was getting fuller and I was becoming a more skilled performer.

It was nice performing in the hotel in which I had been a Room Service waiter just four years before. The *Greenhouse* lounge was kind of impersonal. It was very well lit so the atmosphere was more like a lobby than a lounge, but we had some regular customers, and many conventioneers too.

One evening, at the *Greenhouse* I was performing in a particularly impassioned manner. The room was full and people were smiling, but nobody was reacting at all to me. It was eerily weird for a few minutes. Finally, a young lady walked up to the piano and put her hands on the piano. Soon, the piano was full of people smiling and nodding their heads in approval with their hands on the piano, feeling the energy coming up from my performance. I realized that they were all deaf. It was a convention for the hearing impaired! They were enjoying me anyway in their own way, and it moved me deeply.

Another night, the band *Jefferson Starship* was staying at the hotel. Paul Kantner and Marty Balin came down from their rooms. Joey Covington, their drummer, was in town and he joined them as they partied with us. I played *Hearts*, one of Balin's huge hits, and he came and harmonized with me on the song. It was really cool!

On another night, when I walked into the hotel, the General Manager called me over and spoke in hushed tones. He told me that there was a big meeting of Mafioso's from all over the country, in the hotel, and the FBI was also there watching them.

He didn't want any trouble, and he wanted me to be aware of what was going on. He told me that if anybody asked me any questions about anything, I was not to answer, but just refer them to the Hotel Management.

I told him not to worry, that I actually knew a lot of these guys from *Pal Joey's*, and I would handle it. I did see a few of the guys in the lounge, said "hello," played a few of the songs I knew they liked, and we kept it all low-key. It was surreal. As long as I was playing *Vic Damone, Jerry Vale, Sinatra* or *Dean Martin* songs everybody was happy. And, I stayed out of the way.

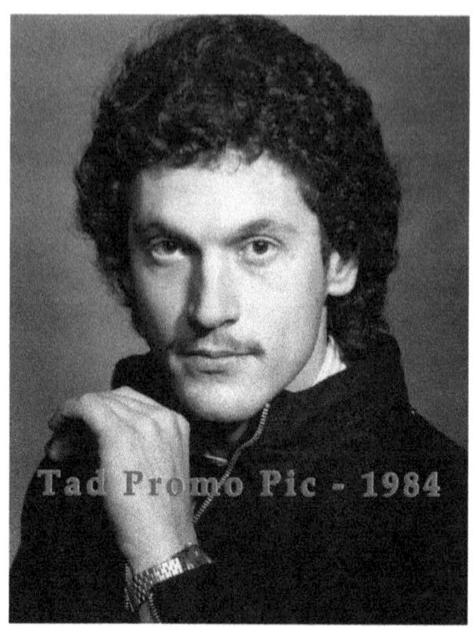

Don Adams, the actor who played Maxwell Smart in one of my favorite childhood television shows, *Get Smart*, came in a lot to the Greenhouse lounge. He was rude and obnoxious, and at first, I was devastated that one of my childhood heroes was such an asshole! But, one night, he asked me to play Neil Sedaka's *The Hungry Years*. I played the song, and he almost started crying. He called me up to the bar and we had a long conversation. Underneath his brash exterior, he was actually a nice guy after all.

The great actor Cameron Mitchell was doing his *Red Baron Radio Show* from the *Greenhouse* lounge, and he hired me to be his assistant on the show. He was a fascinating character and he had many celebrity guests like Jane Wyman and William Holden. I had remembered seeing him on an episode of *Bonanza* when I was a kid, and I was enamored.

•••••

I worked with a pretty young waitress at the *Canyon Hotel* for several months. She was always sweet and kind to me. On slower nights, I would try out some of my original songs. I had written a melody that the waitress liked. I hadn't found lyrics to it yet, but she would always ask me to play this melody for her when I came in to perform.

This waitress had a friend who was a bartender down at *Banducci's*. He wanted her to come down and work nights with him. She really didn't want to do that. She liked her little afternoon-evening job at the *Canyon Hotel*. One evening, he called the *Greenhouse* lounge in a panic and begged her to work that night at *Banducci's*. Apparently, they were packed and the waitress had not shown up. Flustered, she reluctantly agreed to do it, and flashed me a smile as she rushed out.

When she arrived at *Banducci's*, she was hit by a car and killed as she attempted to run across the street to the restaurant. I was in shock. What a lovely, kind girl she was. That night, I went to sleep and when I woke up, in my mind I had every lyric to the song she liked. I named it *Song For A Friend* and I've performed that song at countless memorial services since. I often think of that sweet girl who became one of God's Angels, way too young.

•••••

I was working at *Patti Z* five nights and at the *Canyon Hotel* two nights. *Billy Reed's* was opening up their huge new restaurant on the North end of Palm Springs, and Billy wanted to run piano bar music from ten in the morning until ten at night. I was hired to do the early shift, four days a week, from ten o'clock in the morning until two o'clock in the afternoon. On Thursday, Friday and Saturday I went across to *The Riviera Hotel* and performed for their happy hour from five in the afternoon until seven-thirty at night, and then I would run to *Patti Z* and perform from eight-thirty until one-thirty in the morning.

In 1984, I worked 176 days and nights in a row without a day off, most days performing on multiple shifts, and then after my one day off, I worked another 79 days and nights before I had another day off.

Still, my father would call about once a month and ask if I was working at all, being that I was a musician and everything. It always felt like an insult. He just didn't get me, and he was living in another Universe. But, I was thriving on my routine of hard work and nurturing my family.

Routine is a sign of good character. It shows structure and discipline in your life. The trick is to find something new, and to find joy within that routine. Each day is a special gem that must be treated individually with the greatest of care. Embrace your routine, but take care not to make it mechanical or joyless.

I learned a valuable lesson when I was young; people stereotype musicians. Many musicians deserve the stereotype of being lazy, sleeping until noon, doing drugs, showing up late, eating all the free food, screwing all the women, and basically being the flaky dregs of society. I fought that stereotype for my entire life, even with my own father.

I always made a point of dressing well; showing up early, being consistent and respectful, and I believe it mattered. Later, I would introduce myself as anything but a musician. I would tell people that I was a music producer, or composer, entertainer or anything but musician. It's sad but I get it, because I've known many stereotypical musicians.

•••••

The great Las Vegas entertainer and pianist Liberace lived in the desert. As a kid I would see him walking his dog in downtown Palm Springs, and I thought it was cool. Liberace was homosexual, and in the early 1980's, I would sometimes see him in the grocery stores or at an occasional event. His eyes would fixate on me from afar, and it was a bit unnerving to me. I had gay friends, but I was one hundred percent attracted to women only. Many times, I caught him staring at me with a huge smile and inviting eyes, even when I had my small children with me at the store! Poor Liberace died of HIV in 1985. He was a great entertainer and an excellent pianist.

•••••

One morning around eleven, I was performing at *Billy Reed's* and this drunken, loud guy came in with a huge laugh. He got right into my face and started asking for Billy Joel and the Rolling Stones. I was in a room full of elderly people waiting to have a late breakfast or early lunch! But, I played some Billy Joel and Stones for him as he spoke loudly and laughed heartily right in my face the whole time. His name was Jimmy McShane. He was a bartender next door at *The Big Yellow House*, and he was drunk and obnoxious, but we became lifetime friends. Years later, we worked together a few times. He was one crazy guy!

Pat Rizzo, Jimmy McShane and George Jacobs

In November of 1984, I was working one night up at the *Canyon Hotel*. On a break, I was walking by the front desk, and the clerk held up a tiny black kitten. He said, "Somebody found this kitten out by the pool area. Do you want it?" I said, "No, thanks." He said, "Okay, then, I'm just going to take it around the corner and wring it's neck and kill it." I said, "Give me the cat!" I took this little four-week old kitten home and we bottle-fed it. She turned out to be the greatest cat ever, and she lived with me for almost twenty-two years before she died.

You never know where life's blessings will come from. Sometimes you just have to go with it.

•••••

In December of 1984, my dad's wife Sandra called me from Missouri. She wanted to surprise Maynard by flying us all out to Kennett for Christmas. I was touched, and we agreed to go. December 27th was to be Regina's eleventh birthday and we wanted to celebrate both. Stephanie wanted the children to have a "normal" Christmas, so we shipped a couple huge boxes of wrapped gifts to Kennett, and Sandra hid them for us.

A few days before Christmas, we flew into Memphis. It was my children's first flight and they loved it. It was cold when we got out of the airport, and my little three-year-old Rachel looked up at me and asked, "Daddy, will you please yip up my jacket?" So, I 'yipped' it up for her. She was the cutest!

We rented a car, and by the time we made the two-hour drive to Kennett it was after midnight. I knocked on the front door of my father's house. He answered the door, bitching loudly, thinking it was a patient bothering him in the middle of the night about some minor ailment, as many often did. When he saw my face, he broke down crying and held me. Then, he embraced Stephanie and each of the children. He was so very happy. We had a wonderful Christmas in Kennett. Sandra couldn't have been nicer or more accommodating to us, and I appreciated her generosity, something I had never seen before.

Taddy, Regina, Kevin and Rachel with Buffy Christmas 1984

Kimberley was fifteen. She was a 'Straight-A' student and very helpful and kind with the children. Kimberley was in her first year at Kennett High School and she had some of the same teachers that I had, years before. She was in drama with Mr. Newman. It was nice to see her blossoming, and she was truly the apple of Maynard's eye. They were extremely close, and I was glad that my father had that kind of love around him.

Until that time, it had been really weird to me that he had first adopted Leandra, and then taken Kimberley into his heart, while pretty much disowning my sisters. But, I realized that Maynard needed to create a world of sobriety that was safe and full of boundaries that removed all of the triggers that put him there in the first place. And, if that meant letting go of his past, even his own children, he was willing to do so. In his heart, he still loved all of us, but he was going to do what Sandra told him to do. She was his higher power, and she protected him from anything and anybody that could compromise his sobriety. In a sense, she saved his life and in return, he lived in a new world that worked just fine for him. Whenever we were in his presence, any of us, he would be kind and generous, but otherwise, you could forget about it.

Earlier that year, Maynard and Sandra had taken Kimberley to New York for a week. At the end of the week, he finally called my sister Kathy and told her he was there and asked her if she wanted to go to lunch before he left. Kathy was insulted. He had never even met her children. He was there for a week and he didn't call until the last day when her kids were in school? Kathy and Steven pretty much disowned Maynard after that experience, and he didn't do much of anything to reach out to them afterwards. As a result, he never knew her children until they were adults, and even then, Maynard only met them briefly.

But, anyway, that Christmas of 1984 was a very special one for my family. My little twins were very happy to be at their Grandpa's house and he got to know us all a little better. Maynard had a large riding lawnmower; he gave the kids rides all over his property. Their dogs and cats got a lot of attention that Christmas. Regina had a nice eleventh birthday and we flew back home just in time for me to perform for New Year's Eve at *Patti Z*.

•••••

Sam Kaufman 1985

After the first of the year in 1985, a small kitchen fire closed *Patti Z* for a few days. Sam and Cheryl Kaufman from Lake Tahoe happened to be in the lounge that evening. They were watching me perform when the kitchen caught fire. They helped me remove my equipment, just in case the whole place went up. We laughed about that night later, but it was a bit scary when it was happening. Although she reopened quickly, everyone was noticing a change in Patti's behavior. She started dating one of her busboys, a nice Mexican man named Miguel. He was cool, but it was a total mismatch, considering her personality. She was drinking a lot more and there was a question about her books, as if someone was skimming off the top of the business. It was clear that she was having financial problems. Business was still really good there, though, in early 1985.

The *Canyon Hotel* management had decided to bring in *The Coasters*, the famous 1950's group, into their main showroom. For years, Bobby Craig and his trio had performed to a packed house in the showroom.

Previously, I would watch Bobby's performance style and I began to emulate it. He didn't take a break between songs. He just went right from one song into another, so there was no 'dead air'. He would perform several fast songs, do a slow dance song, and then bring the energy right back up. This realization really helped me as I matured. Using that technique, I was able to pack rooms and keep them busy. But, at that point Bobby Craig had moved his trio to a new club in Palm Desert called *The 40's Again*, and I eventually performed there too, on some of his off-nights with my trio.

Bobby was very good at what he did. He told me once that you can learn 5,000 songs, but you'll find that people only want to hear the same fifty songs, the iconic melodies they are used to that make them feel good. I learned through the years that there is much truth in that statement, and it helped me in my choices of music when reading specific crowds. There have been many magical nights, however, with smaller groups of people, that I've been able to 'stretch out' musically and break that mold, too.

•••••

The Coasters were going to be performing at the *Canyon Hotel* on a long-term contract for the entire 1985 season. At that time, several groups were touring using *The Coasters* name, and this was likely an offshoot group of the originals. The tenor singer was Tony Cook. He and I became fast friends. Tony would come into my lounge after their performance, and sing with me for another hour. He was a sweet African-American man with a baby face. When *The Coasters* had been in Vegas for two months, Tony would change clothes, run across town and become an *Ink Spot*. Then, he would change clothes and run to another casino and be a *Drifter*. He was a character, and he died only a couple years later, way too young.

Wendell Perry was the bass singer. He was a large, outgoing African-American man with a huge deep voice. Wendell was cool.

The Coasters backup group included Jeff Edwards and Kenny Ray, both guitarists/vocalists. Jeff and Kenny Ray were young, white rock & rollers with an air of living on the edge. Jeff had an intense look in his piercing blue eyes. His long, straight blonde hair would move around as he gyrated on stage, eyes on Kenny Ray with a wild look as he played a slamming rock solo. The young girls would swoon at his magnetism. Kenny Ray had a different approach. He was fun loving and very kind, always smiling and engaging, smooth with the ladies on stage and after the gigs. Kenny Ray played guitar too, and every once in a while, he would pick up an alto saxophone and play a few riffs.

They started to hang out a lot with me when we were off of work, and they would come in and listen to me when I performed at the *Greenhouse*. These guys were only a couple years younger than me, but they had a freedom and carefree attitude that I had lost somewhere along the line. I was a conservative family man. There was a part of me that emulated their wild rock & roll life (until later when I actually found out how they toured through one horse towns and performed in lonely dives for low money). Later, I would find that all they wanted was to have my life!

Jeff was laying down some tracks in Wayne Boyer's little 8-track reel-to-reel studio in his garage in Palm Desert. I did some background vocals on a track. Wayne was cool. He was a flugelhorn player who doubled on drums and played a little piano. He had pretty good skills as a recording engineer, and he was patient teaching me about splicing tape and how to get a good sound using the technology of the day. A few weeks later, I went in to Wayne's studio and recorded a few originals. Jeff did background vocals and guitars, and Kenny Ray played saxophone on the tracks. They came out sounding pretty good and I was happy. It was a large step in my learning process when it came to recording techniques of the day.

•••••

My son Kevin joined the AYSO soccer team. He played for a couple seasons at age eight and nine. On Sundays, I would rush over to see his games when they were early enough, before I had to work. He was a good little player, his long blond hair flying back from the wind, always smiling and doing his best.

My father hadn't been a good influence on my childhood when it came to sports, so I wasn't programmed to encourage sports with my own children. I'm grateful that they were all good at what they did, and I supported whatever they wanted to do. I tried to be as involved as I could, but I was just working so very much that it was touch and go sometimes.

My darling twins had their own language, and they figured out how to do mischief when they could. They knew not to speak any curse words…but, they would sit in their little car seats in the back of our automobile and Taddy would say, "Shh.." and Rachel would say, "…it!" So, together they were saying, "Shit!" They would laugh hysterically, and we would laugh too. They were always best friends and all my children were just good people always.

Stephanie had suggested that I grow a mustache to look 'older'. I had attempted a mustache years before and given up. It took me several months before I had a 'stache' that looked like more than a dirty upper lip. I started to grow my hair out again, which heavily resembled a mullet. Mullet cuts were very popular then! We bought hip suits in different colors for me to wear to perform, including pastels and pinks. It was the eighties and the *Miami Vice* look was in for a minute. It was not my mid-life, but it felt to me like a mid-life crisis! I know everybody at some point will look back at old photos and wonder what they were thinking back then…

•••••

The great boxer Marvin Hagler was training at the *Canyon Hotel* for his upcoming fight in April of 1985 against Thomas Hearns. The National Media was covering his training, and many celebrities came down to watch him train during the 1985 season in Palm Springs.

One evening, I was performing at the *Greenhouse* lounge and a well-dressed African-American man was sitting at the bar. He came up and introduced himself as Hillery Johnson. Hillery asked me if I wrote music, and I told him, "Yes!" He asked me to play my best song. I told him that my originals were almost like children to me. I couldn't pick a favorite. But, I would play three of my original songs that other people seemed to like a lot. One of the songs I performed was my original, *You'd Be So Good To Come Home To*. Hillery loved it.

He gave me his card and we met for lunch the next day. Hillery told me that he had been a Vice President of *Atlantic Records* and he had just left and started his own label, *Valley Vue Records*. He told me that he wanted to record my song. I was delighted!

Hillery Johnson had made his way up the ladder of the music business in Chicago. His best friend was Donny Hathaway. They grew up together in Chicago. When they were very young, Hillery became Donny's manager and got him his first record deal. Donny became a huge star, eventually scoring many Platinum hit recordings.

Eventually, Hillery rose up in the ranks at *Atlantic Records* to become a Vice President. He told me that he knew he would never be President of the company, so he left to start his own label. He had already signed Craig T. Cooper, Jerry Butler, The Manhattans and Johnny (Guitar) Watson.

I sent Hillery a cassette of *You'd Be So Good to Come Home To*, and he hired producer Lonnie Reeves to do an R&B version of the song.

•••••

Judy and George Kane with son Brian 1986

In early June of 1985, my sister Judy gave birth to another son, Brian. He was a beautiful baby! She was delighted, as was her husband, George. Judy continued to work hard as an *Air Force* nurse.

At the end of the 1985 season in June, *The Coasters* finished their stint at the *Canyon Hotel*. *Patti Z* was going to close for a month in August. Summertime in Palm Springs was hell. What little financial progress I might have made during the season was usually wiped out during the summer. On top of all of that, the owner of our rental house on San Martin Circle had allowed the home to go into foreclosure and we were going to have to move, yet again.

My friend Connie Griffo reached out to me from Lake Tahoe. She had opened a restaurant, *Griffo's*, in Incline Village and she asked me if I would like to come and perform for her there for the month of August. I jumped at the prospect!

•••••

Tony Prenesti

Around this time, I picked up a couple nights again at *Delmonico's* for Tony Prenesti. Tony had a lot of heavyweight Italian guys always hanging out at the bar at *Delmonico's*. Jojo Comi called them "The Powder Puff Mafia." These men were always amped on something, running back and forth to the Men's room.

Bobby Milano would come in to *Delmonico's* and sing with me. Tony Marsh also sat in with me. Tony had a huge voice. He didn't even need a microphone and his voice would boom through the restaurant as he sang Old Italian songs.

My best friend Eddie Balderama was waiting tables there. Pat Rizzo, my friend, the great singer-saxophonist who had worked with Frank Sinatra and Sly & The Family Stone, was hanging out at *Delmonico's* a lot with his new girlfriend.

I had no clue of what was going on in front of me. They were running a huge cocaine ring out of the restaurant. Someone would call with a 'reservation' for a 'table of eight' (which meant an 'eight-ball' of cocaine) and they would come in to have the order fulfilled in the Men's room.

Pat Rizzo's girlfriend found out about it, and she didn't like what was going on, so she called the DEA. An undercover agent came in and 'infiltrated' the place, dining with the big boss and befriending everyone. He even did a little cocaine. One day, *Palm Springs Life* Magazine photographers came in to take a cover photo for their *Entertainment Guide*. On the cover of the *Guide* magazine was a photo of a table at *Delmonico's* with Tony Prenesti, Pat Rizzo, his girlfriend, the DEA agent, and another Italian guy. It was bizarre that they were all living it up, not knowing that their lives were about to come crashing around them.

On a night I wasn't performing there, they raided *Delmonico's* and another nightclub Tony owned, *Delmonico's Fish* Market, where my friend Paula Stapleton was performing. All of the men in the cocaine ring were arrested and *Delmonico's* was shut down. That was the end of that.

Pat Rizzo's girlfriend had done a deal in advance where he would not be in trouble, so Pat did no time. He wasn't involved in it anyway. I'm pretty sure Pat was pissed, though, and he and the girl broke up. Tony Prenesti was Pat's friend and Pat wouldn't have dreamed of getting Tony in trouble. He was just a party guy. Tony went off for a year or so to prison.

CHAPTER THIRTY-SEVEN
Summer in Lake Tahoe

Taddy – Lake Tahoe 1985

In August of 1985, Stephanie and I moved out of the San Martin Circle house in Palm Springs, put everything in storage, found a rental condo in Incline Village up at Lake Tahoe for one month, and we packed the children up into the car to make the trip. My old Dodge Charger still had its carburetor issues, and we stopped twice on the way up to Tahoe to let the car catch up.

Lake Tahoe is heavenly in August! We spent our days at the beach on the lake. Connie Griffo couldn't have been more accommodating. Our old friends from Tahoe poured into the nightclub at *Griffo's* and it was an outstanding month.

Connie Griffo 1985

One night, Stephanie and I hired a babysitter and slipped off to the *Hyatt* casino. We played the draw poker machines, and I won a $2,500.00 jackpot! I had been hoping to buy a new keyboard for work. *Yamaha* had recently released the DX7, the first major digital keyboard. Jeff Edwards had purchased one while they were at the *Canyon Hotel* with *The Coasters*, and I fell in love with all the sounds.

The price was around $2,000.00 for the keyboard, and Stephanie told me to go out and buy it while I could. I was so happy with the DX7. I started using it on my gigs primarily to play left-hand bass. Later, in the studio, I would use all of the digital sounds on the DX7 to layer and create multi tracks of sounds for my original songs.

But, while we were up at *Griffo's* that August of 1985, the world seemed beautiful in every way. My darling twins turned four years old on that trip, and we had a big birthday party for them with two cakes! Regina was eleven and Kevin was eight. All of my children had their own unique personalities, wants and needs. Although I worked six nights a week while I was up there, the entire month felt like a vacation.

There is nothing like the feeling you get, standing lakeside at Tahoe. Pine trees hug the lake on all sides, jutting up to the high mountains above on all sides, in all their glory. The lake water is so clear; it looks like God's huge mirror, revealing the beauty of the puffy clouds in the dark blue sky above.

One night, a doctor came in to *Griffo's* and told me that he had worked his entire life to be able to spend summers in Lake Tahoe and winters in Palm Springs, and here I was doing it at the ripe age of twenty-seven!

The difference between me and that kindly retired doctor was simple; he had money in the bank, he was relaxing and enjoying life, and I was always struggling to feed my family and to keep the bills paid. As a result of that, I was always stressed and freaked out about my life, and it was hard but important to remind myself to stop and appreciate the moment.

Rachel and Tad - 1984

It reminds me of the joke about the guy who constantly complained about the job he was given, following the horses around in the circus with a broom and dustpan, picking up the horseshit all day. His friend said, "Why don't you quit?" The man said, "What, and give up show business?"

I guess that show business was just in my blood and it was the path I was destined to take with my life, no matter how rocky the road became. And somehow, I was getting away with raising my children by doing music. We always seemed to live beyond our means, and it was rare when I wasn't stressed out about how I was going to pay all the bills and do all of this. My children were always my saving grace. No matter hard the moment was, looking into their eyes made it all okay. And, I did love Stephanie dearly, although I seemed to be always on guard with her through all of her mood swings.

•••••

Angelo Serio
1986

Angelo Serio was a waiter at *Griffo's.* He was a strong-willed, muscular Italian man, about my age, and very protective over Connie and her daughter Rosalie. He admitted to me that he was jealous of me before we ever even met, because of the way they all raved about me. But, as soon as we met, we became fast friends. A month or two after we returned to Palm Springs, Angelo called and said he wanted to move down to the desert. We offered to have him stay with us and he agreed.

Rosalie Griffo
1985

At the end of August, we needed to rent a house. Stephanie flew down to Palm Springs in advance of us driving, in order to get a move on finding a rental house. I drove the children down, and we moved into one hotel room while we were finding our rental.

We had four children and a cat in one hotel room in September in Palm Springs! It was crazy. After a couple weeks, we found a nice rental house on Eagle Way in South East Palm Springs.

While we were waiting to move in, we took our clothes to a Laundromat in Cathedral City. We walked next door for a minute to get something for the children to drink, and when we came back, all of our clothes had been stolen. The babies' blankets that they had cherished since birth were gone.

We were crushed, and even sadder, I saw little Mexican children riding bikes in Cathedral City for a year after that, wearing my children's clothes, and I couldn't do anything about it. You could say that they must have needed it more than we did, but that was probably wrong at that moment in time. We were broke, homeless for a couple weeks, and school was about to start for all of our children.

CHAPTER THIRTY-EIGHT
A New Start Back in the Desert

When we did move into the house on Eagle Way, it took a couple weeks to settle in, but the house was very comfortable.

Gloria Becker was an agent in Palm Desert. She had booked my mother for many years on solo piano events, and once or twice Gloria had booked me on private events. Gloria was booking *The Biltmore Hotel* in Palm Springs. The owners of *The Biltmore,* Richard and Robert Levine, were looking for a piano player for their lounge, and they offered a sizeable amount of money more than *Patti Z* was paying me.

I felt that Patti was not going to be in business much longer, and my suspicions were right. Her restaurant only lasted a few months after I left. I was grateful for my two-year run at *Patti Z.* I had met Frank Sinatra there, and I continued to do private events with the Sinatra's here and there, for a few years following.

The problem with *The Biltmore* was that it was past its heyday. This hotel was a very important piece of Palm Springs history. The hotel's original bungalows were built in the 1940's, and the lounge had been packed for many years with headliner acts and celebrities. Experiencing the mid-century architecture of the pool area at the hotel was like taking a step backwards in time, to another era. It was moving into disrepair, although the owners did their best to keep it up. The pristine *Biltmore* golf course, which had been adjacent to the hotel for many years, had been scrapped and replaced with tacky condominiums; the only remaining vestige of the golf course was an untended, ugly driving range.

Business was not great when I started performing there. The piano bar lounge was dank and dated, but overlooked a lovely restaurant, which was generally empty. Many nights would be slow. I wasn't used to this, because we had always been packed at *Patti Z.* There was a huge *Biltmore Hotel* sign out front, which lit up on Palm Canyon Drive at night for everyone driving by to see. My name was on the marquee, in big letters, although it was a bit confusing. For a while, the sign read TAD SISLER DANCING LOBSTER. Many people came in to see the dancing lobster named Tad!

Kenny Brown and his wife Jeannie came down on weekends to relax. They liked the old-style bungalows at *The Biltmore*. They would come in for dinner and stay at the piano bar until I was done. Jeannie was a singer and she would sit in with me. Kenny and I became friends.

One night, we were kind of busy in the lounge and a huge, 300-pound biker dude came in. He was obviously on drugs. We thought he was maybe on PCP because of his behavior. This guy was all over the place. At some point, he looked at me with wild eyes and lunged over the piano at my throat. Kenny Brown calmly got up from his seat at the piano, calmly went over to the guy even though he was about half his size, pulled him off of me and put a stranglehold on him, writhing around on the floor for almost twenty minutes until the police came in. I couldn't believe it! Kenny was ex-military, and I was forever grateful that he jumped up and probably saved my life. I always said after that, "I want that guy on my side!" We stayed friends for the rest of our lives. Later, Jeannie sang with my band a little before they divorced.

One of the owners of *The Biltmore,* Richard Levine, was dating my eighth grade World Problems teacher, Roxanne Ploss. She was now in her mid-thirties and still very beautiful. One night, I swore that she was trying to pick up on me. I thought, "Wow, Miss Ploss, my teacher, wants me?" It was bizarre but I was flattered. I mean… we were only about ten years apart in age. She was a sweet lady anyway.

•••••

The twins were going in to Kindergarten. Stephanie and I both volunteered to assist at the school. I was so happy to learn that my twins were so intelligent and so ahead of all the other kids!

They assessed the children into four groups. Rachel and Taddy were far and above the smartest children in the class. Still, Taddy was a shy boy. Rachel would march into the class holding his hand, and he would kind-of hide behind her, smiling sheepishly. Every week they got a "Tommy Turtle" award for being so good, and Stephanie and I really enjoyed working with them at the school.

One day when we weren't there, a substitute was teaching the class. Somehow, a bully child had cornered Rachel, and she tried to calm him down. The substitute grabbed both children and threw them into the corner for punishment. When I got to the school, Rachel was sobbing. I was incensed! I got right into that teachers face, yelling, "My daughter is not a corner child! She is exceptional, and you will never, ever do this to her again, do you hear me?" The substitute never came back to teach there again. And, my daughter was very proud of her daddy. My father had done the same for me, once.

•••••

Stephanie and I had a handful of quiet, wonderful days together during this period. She liked to play *Yahtzee.* We would play *Triple Yahtzee* and double it to sextuple, sitting out by our pool for hours on my rare days off while the children swam.

As my children were my source of strength through all the years I worked day and night, Stephanie was there with them more than I was, loving, mentoring, disciplining them and giving them strength. She imparted the good parts of her heart and soul into them and her influence made an indelible mark on their character. Yes, she had emotional and mental issues, which flared up at times, and then progressed into full-blown illness, but the Stephanie I knew and loved was an amazing mother and friend, and I was grateful for her in so many ways. I was also always worried about when the next shoe would drop. That's the nature of the illness she had. She would be great for months, and then a family member would come and see her as a mess, thinking she was always like that. She wasn't.

Angelo Serio lived with us on Eagle Way for a few months until he found a job and a place to live. Shortly after he left, our friend John Driscoll from Sparks called and he wanted to move down, so he stayed with us for a few months. John was cordial and fun to be around, for the most part, but we had such a full house already. John started bartending, first at *Melvyn's* on off-nights, and then at *Hank's Café,* at the *Sheraton Oasis Hotel.*

Stephanie wanted to go back to work. She reached out to Joe Hanna, our old friend who had owned *Pal Joey's* when we met. Joe was partly running *The Ocotillo* lounge with Fat Philly. Fat Philly told Joe not to hire Stephanie because she was "Too fat." That really hurt Stephanie's feelings to the core. Eventually, she went to work there, anyway, for a short while.

Stephanie was hired at *Melvyn's* and started her downward cycle again of drinking. She was making really good money, but she immediately saw a racket going on between one of the bartenders and another waitress. They were stealing literally thousands of dollars per week, right in front of her eyes. Her sense of justice tortured her, but she also feared for our safety, so she kept her mouth shut.

One night, after work, I went into *Melvyn's* to hang out with Steph until she was done working. She asked me if I would run downstairs to the liquor room and grab a bottle of vodka. I went downstairs and turned on the light, and a thousand cockroaches scattered in every direction! I was spooked! It was my Miami experience coming back to haunt me. I thought, this is the swankest place in Palm Springs and nobody knows cockroaches overrun it!

•••••

On January 28, 1986, I woke up early to watch the space shuttle *Challenger* launch. I was still a huge fan of the space program going all the way back to my childhood. The world watched in horror as the *Challenger* exploded quickly after launch. It was a terrible tragedy, killing the seven astronauts aboard, including a young schoolteacher and mother, Christa McAuliffe. The nation mourned and we prayed for their souls.

I met a meeting planner named Shari Kelley. In February of 1986 she hired me to perform for a wedding at *The Marquis* hotel in downtown Palm Springs. She was amazing, planning huge events down to the finest detail, always plush and elegant with thousands of flowers everywhere. She liked me and began to book me on many events.

My *Dodge Charger* was on its last leg. I needed a new car but my credit wasn't good enough. In March of 1986, my mother cosigned for a new *Dodge Caravan* for us. It was our first new car, and it was a very popular van in the 1980's. I was grateful again for my mother's help. She knew she didn't have much to offer in her financial condition, but she was truly the only person who ever came through in my life when I needed it the most.

Kevin, Regina
Taddy and Rachel
1985

We hosted parties at our house. Stephanie's dad and brother would come over with their families. Her brother Russ, Jr. and Denise had moved back to the desert from Reno with their girls and bought another house in Palm Desert. Scotty would bring his bass. Sometimes, Bob Allen would come over to play drums and we would do little jam sessions. The Eagle Way house had a beautiful grand piano that the owner left behind. It also had a full bar that we stocked with alcohol. It was an older house. Mature vegetation lined the pool area, and we enjoyed living there.

I found a 1973 White *Mercedes 450 SEL*. It was old, but beautiful! I bought it cheap for Stephanie and got her a customized license plate. The name STEPH was not available, so her license read STPH S. She loved it! Some guy with a wife named Stephanie kept trying to buy it from me. I declined. It was an amazing car, although the leather was old and damaged. When it broke down, though, it was ridiculously expensive to fix.

Regina with Buffy
1986

Stephanie wanted a dog. She decided that she liked little dogs, so we bought a little black Pekingese dog and named her "Buffy". This puppy quickly became Regina's dog. She slept with Regina and ate with her.

Regina was a vibrant teenager. She was used to taking a lot of the burden of watching her brothers and sister, and helping her mother and I to clean and cook. This dog was her salvation in so many ways, and Buffy was a very sweet dog.

In July of 1986, we were awakened in the middle of the night by a huge rumbling. It sounded like someone was banging heavily on our sliding glass doors. I woke up in a cold sweat and realized we were having an earthquake. Instinctively, I ran to the twins and scooped them up out of their beds to protect them.

Regina and Kevin ran out of their rooms and we huddled together for about a minute until the earthquake subsided. It was surreal. This was a 6.0 earthquake, which was pretty substantial. Although it was scary, earthquakes of smaller magnitude had become a way of life in California. A few dishes broke but thankfully we had no real damage.

•••••

In August of 1986, Stephanie and I went on our first official vacation alone together. We asked my mother to come and stay with the children for a week. Stephanie's uncle Don had just passed away. She had flown back alone to see Don right before he died and she longed to go to Westchester County in New York to visit her Aunts and cousins. I hadn't seen my sister Kathy in over eight years.

Tad and Stephanie 1986

We flew into New York City and took a cab to Kathy and Steven's house. When we walked in the door, my sister Kathy and I held each other for about ten minutes. It had been so long since we had connected. She had been my little mother when I was growing up, and we cried. It was so great to see Kathy again, and to experience her Steven, Michael and Yash.

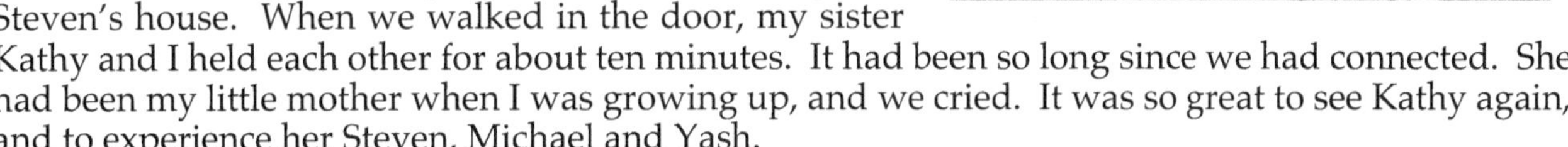

Kathy with her sons Mike and Yash - 1988

After staying in Brooklyn with Kathy and her family, we followed them in our rental car up to Westchester County with their sons. We met Stephanie's cousin Donald Bleasdale at *Rye Playland*, an amusement park, and played all day. Afterwards, Kathy and Steven drove back to New York, and Stephanie and I went on to Mount Kisco in Westchester County, New York.

We stayed at the *Kittle Inn*, a revolutionary war hotel, preserved to appear as it looked more than two hundred years ago. It was a very much-needed vacation for us, and Stephanie was able to bond with her Aunt Faith, and her cousins Lisa and Don. After the trip, our children were relieved to see us when we made it back to Palm Springs. One week without us and with their grandma was a lot! Elaine had done a great job taking care of them, and we shared some laughs about the time they had with her.

Shortly after my mother went back home to Orange County, my grandma Gizi had a minor car accident. It was totally her fault. She had driven into an intersection when she had a red light, and she was hit by another car. My uncles didn't want her to drive anymore, but she told them she was not going to stop driving. So, they bought her a bright red *Buick*, so at least other people could see her coming!

•••••

In September of 1986, my Regina went into seventh grade. She went to *Nellie Coffman*, the same Junior High School that I had gone to, and she had my same choir teacher. Mrs. Nokes had divorced and remarried since, and she was now Mrs. Mardale McCoy. I was amazed that she was still teaching, and Mardy took Regina under her wing as she had done with me, all those years ago. In fact, she gave Regina a scholarship to ISOMATA, and Regina was later able to experience that amazing place just as I had done years earlier. Still, Regina was having a hard time in school.

The school had relocated from the original campus that I had attended in Palm Springs to a tough section of Cathedral City. Gangs of girls beat her up a couple times, and she had to overcome all of that. We would complain but the school was overwhelmed and did very little about it. She was a strong girl, always, and Regina would not let anything hold her down for long.

•••••

Towards the end of 1986, Hillery Johnson called me and said that Lonnie Reeves was almost done producing my song. He invited me up to a studio in Los Angeles to see Don Myrick, the great saxophone player from *Earth, Wind and Fire* play saxophone on my track! I was so excited!

On the morning of the session, I left Palm Springs in a huge rainstorm and crawled on the freeway all the way into Santa Monica. When I reached the recording studio, Don Myrick was already in the booth laying down his track. At first, I didn't recognize my own song! Lonnie had completely transformed it into a classic R&B feel, even changing the beat from 4/4 to 6/8, with complicated synth horn parts with a driving drum and bass track.

The studio was beautiful, with a state-of-the-art 2-inch 24-track tape machine and a huge SSL analog mixer. They were recording to SMPTE time code and it was all very fascinating to me! Within a few weeks, Hillery also brought Donny Hathaway's daughter Lalah in to do the vocal on my track.

Eventually, Lalah used the track as part of a demo to get her deal with *Virgin Records*, but my song didn't end up on her first album, which was a great disappointment to me. Still, I had the reel, and later in the 1990's I transferred the tracks from 2-inch to ADAT digital tape. Later, I transferred the ADAT version to my hard drive and I reissued the song, rerecording and remixing some of the parts within Pro Tools on my Mac, after the turn of the 21st century.

Lonnie Reeves was an amazing young black producer, and he had an enormous effect upon my life. His style of keyboard bass was complicated and funky; I emulated his bass style and his hip chord progressions, integrating his ideas into my own performance, and my playing improved vastly throughout this period.

I bought a little *Tascam PortaStudio*. It was a 4-track studio based upon the small cassettes that were popular in the day. Although rudimentary, I had to get creative and learn to "bounce" the tracks down, so I could record more than four tracks. I learned how to mix multiple tracks together by trial and error, and my ear training came in handy.

I would work all week, usually multiple shifts performing each day, and at the end of a long week, exhausted, in the middle of the night, I would set up my equipment on the dining room table of our house and record until I couldn't keep my eyes open any longer. I looked so forward to those late nights, alone in the house on Eagle Way while the children were sleeping, creating new content and feeling somehow like I was moving forward in the business because of it. But, I was becoming increasingly more frustrated; in general, about the direction I had taken in my career.

CHAPTER THIRTY-NINE
The Band Experience

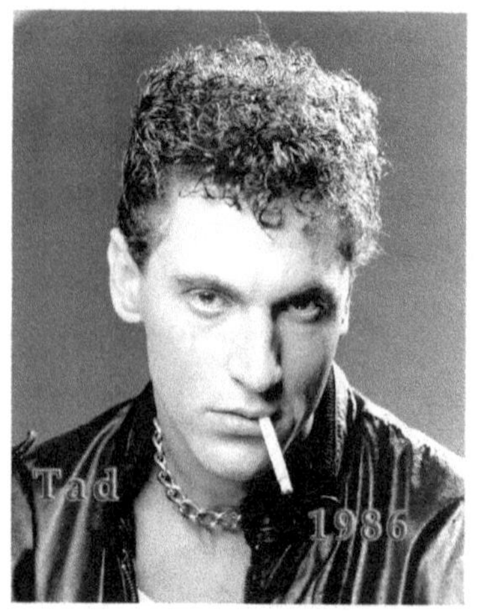

I had been a solo performer, for the most part, for the entire first seven years of my career. I started to feel like I wasn't developing fast enough as a performer. The few experiences I had working with other musicians and studio engineers were opening up my mind to a new world, and I craved the interaction of other musicians. The problem was simple: I could make money and raise my family doing a solo in a nightclub. Doing band work was a gamble, and I would have to rely on other musicians, on their quirks or attitudes or reliability issues. Still, I really wanted to try. I went out on a limb.

Danny, the drummer that worked with Jeff Edwards and Kenny Ray in *The Coasters* back-up band, started dating Billie Jo, one of the waitresses at *The Canyon Hotel.* Billie Jo's sister Vickie, who lived in Washington State, had an African-American boyfriend named Carl Joiner. Carl was an amazing singer. He also played bass. Carl wanted to move to the desert, so he came down and sat in with me on vocals. I called Tim McFall and he was available to play the drums. Carl, Tim and I auditioned for a trio gig at the *Erawan Gardens Hotel* in Indian Wells, a suburb of Palm Springs. We got the gig.

Carl was a wonderful man and a great soul singer. His bass playing was acceptable, but at this point I was playing very strong keyboard bass and I knew about a thousand more songs than he did. So, we were locked into a set list of about thirty songs per night. Still, the public responded well. It was not really what I had imagined, working with this particular trio.

Taddy and Carl - 1990

As time went by I began to love Carl as a brother, but he was like a bull in a china shop. When we moved our equipment, he was such a great helper but he would drop and break keyboards, or forget to pull the wire out of the speaker and rip out the plug completely from the back of the speaker as he rushed to move it.

Tim got another gig with a country band so we replaced him with a guy named Warren Wood. Warren was a good drummer, but he didn't have the energy of a younger performer. He was in his late fifties; Warren played everything well, but he preferred to play jazz and Bossa nova music. I enjoyed working with him, but he was not a good fit for what we were trying to do. When I wanted to play a fast rock song to get the crowd going, he would instead strongly suggest that he sing a very slow version of "Unforgettable" by Nat "King" Cole instead. I started to wonder what the hell I was thinking, to leave the consistency of my solo gig to work with all of these personalities!

•••••

Tad Promo Pic - 1986

Jeff Edwards called me from Wyoming. His band had left *The Coasters*, and they had left to tour the country as a rock & roll band. That sounded so cool to me until he started to describe filthy venues in the middle of nowhere that they would drive all day to get to, and then find out their accommodations were one smelly hotel room for all four of them.

He told me that they had a young girl traveling with them; she announced that she was pregnant; immediately she got an abortion and then was put on the next *Greyhound* bus home. One of his band members quit or was fired in Montana somewhere, and they had to find another band member immediately. The band was always fighting. At some point, Jeff left the band, found a girl singer and did some duo gigs with her in hotel lobbies, but he wasn't happy.

Jeff Edwards with Rachel 1986

He wanted so much to come back to Palm Springs, and in a moment, I said, "Why don't you come back and work with me at the *Erawan Gardens*?" Jeff pretty much dropped everything and showed up at my doorstep a week later. John Driscoll had just moved out, and Jeff moved in to our revolving guest room at my house.

Jeff had a new *Yamaha QX1* Sequencer. It was a machine that used sounds from your keyboards in layers like multi-track recordings, through a midi interface to produce full versions of songs that you programmed into it. First, you would ordinarily program the drum part exactly like it was on the record. Then, you would add bass, guitar, keyboards and anything else you heard.

The *QX1* was one of the first good rudimentary midi sequencers in the early era of computer music programming, but processing each track took forever. Whenever you went to 'save' a part that you had programmed, the sequencer would do its work and you would just sit and stare at it for a few minutes until it stopped, and then you could do another part. The entire process was frustrating and extremely time-consuming, but it opened up a whole new world for me. The final product was stored on large, flimsy floppy discs and, even when you were done programming, songs took a few minutes to load in.

The sequencer was cool in the sense that it gave a full sound to a small group of musicians in the form of a background track, which sounded almost like the original recording; some current music was full of electronics and hard to emulate otherwise. In these early days, the downside was that it tended to sound more mechanical and less free, as you would quantize the beat on a grid. Jeff and I would stay up late at night and sequence new songs. One night, we worked so hard that Jeff puked.

I gave Warren his notice and he gracefully didn't hold me to it. He found another gig that fit him perfectly. So, Jeff and Carl and I were to be the trio. We were three completely different personalities, with three different styles. I was kind of a rounded, Billy Joel / Elton John-style keyboard player. Jeff was a full-on heavy metal rocker, and Carl was a soul man. We all had excellent vocals and our harmonies were great. It was sort of musical, although the sequencer took some humanity out of it all.

Jeff Edwards with Stephanie
1986

Even so, people loved our sound, and we ended up being hired a few months later at *Marriott's Rancho Las Palmas Resort.* Ricky Smith, a strong but friendly woman, was the Director of Restaurants at the *Marriott*: Ricky's husband John was my friend. John was a bartender at the *40's Again* club and we had already worked together. He highly recommended me for the job.

•••••

The *Marriott* was a high-profile gig. The band was advertised everywhere in the desert. Eddie Balderama had bought me a really nice Canon AE-1 camera for my birthday, and we decided to use the camera to do a photo shoot at home. Jeff had brought some lights and a light sequencer off the road that he had purchased for his band. We were using the lights on the gig with different programmed settings. It was cool. We dragged the lights to my house and set them up for a photo shoot. By then, my hair was extremely long and my mustache was thick. Carl had a big Afro, and Jeff had huge long blonde hair, all pulled out like a lion's mane. We looked just like a 1980's hair band! The stage lights didn't really work well for a photo shoot, but through the advertising and because of the high-profile venue, we became a popular trio.

The gigs were fun at first, but as time went by, Jeff and Carl started to clash. I started to wonder if Jeff was bipolar, because he would fly off the handle about the smallest things. He was also super paranoid about his equipment. He needed his wires to be wrapped a certain way and put into the containers in a certain way. I understood conceptually that he wanted to preserve the life of his wires, and the concept actually helped me as I went on with my own career, to keep my own equipment in great shape for as long as I could.

Carl couldn't help himself. He was just clumsy when it came to equipment. His bass was always humming and he would sit in the corner and 'calibrate' it during the breaks. Jeff had this really current looking portable keyboard that we strung on to our backs like a guitar and played synth parts on stage with it.

One night as we were breaking down all of our equipment after a long night of work, Carl was grabbing equipment to run it out to the waiting van outside. Carl strapped the portable keyboard around him as he was carrying a big speaker, and when he got out to the parking lot, the strap broke and the synth crashed to the concrete, breaking into pieces. Jeff just completely lost it.

I ended up paying for a new keyboard because Carl was broke and Jeff insisted that I replace it. That same night, when we finally got everything into the van and started driving away, we heard this loud "whack, whack, whack!" sound on the side of the van. We screeched the van to a stop and looked around outside the van. Carl had 'hung' his bass onto the side view mirror and forgotten about it! The bass was crashing against the side of the van! The funny thing was, the next time Carl went to play, his bass finally sounded good for a few minutes after the bashing!

Jeff and Carl continued to be at each other's throats, and it was becoming impossible for us all to work together. At this point, Jeff was kind of 'controlling' the situation. After all, the sequencer was his. The lights were his. Half of the keyboards and equipment belonged to him.

I bought myself a *QX1* sequencer, which was a great move for me anyway, although I really was having trouble affording all of this and still feeding my family! Eventually, I bought the lights and light sequencer from Jeff. He just kept demanding more and more from me as we went along. The funny thing was, when we were on stage together it was powerful. Jeff and I were as good as the popular duo *Hall & Oates*. If he had a different mindset, we could have gone all the way to stardom.

Finally, it got to a boiling point and Carl quit the band. I hired my friend Mike Capitanelli for a few weeks. Mike was a drummer and disc jockey, and he had a stand-up drum set which was hip and fit our Top-40 show. At some point, the *Marriott* wanted to reduce our budget, so Jeff and I just did a duo for a few more months.

•••••

At the same time, I got a job doing a solo at *Hank's Café* in Palm Springs. The new owner of *Hank's* was spending lots of money on music. He had Bobby Craig's band on one stage, and when they were done with a set, Craig Eaton's band would perform on another stage. He wanted me to do a solo from four to eight o'clock at night, to cover happy hour and until the bands began. The idea was to have continuous music all night. My band was also to perform there on off-nights on stage. The acoustics were bad at *Hank's*. It had high ceilings and tile floors, but people packed in to see the excitement.

At *Hank's* I met and developed a lifetime friendship with Trini Lopez. Trini had several *Billboard #1* Hits in the 1960's, and he was a legend in the desert. Trini would come in and sit in with me, singing *A Day in The Life of a Fool*, or another Latin favorite.

On weekends, my *Hank's* early solo gig overlapped with the *Marriott* gig, so Jeff agreed to do a solo for the first half-hour until I could get to the *Marriott* and set up. We had two different drum machines, so he would set his up until I got there, and we would then replace it with my better one. On New Years Eve, Jeff threw his drum machine to the floor. He got drunk over the course of the night, and stomped on his drum machine. It broke into pieces. The next day, Jeff insisted that I pay for it because he wouldn't have brought it to the gig if I hadn't been doing a solo elsewhere. I couldn't believe it! But, I gave him the money. I was a pushover. I also felt like I was stuck in this situation with him. I needed the gig money to feed my family. But, he was one intense dude.

Sometimes, due to the obligation of feeding your family, you may need to temporarily swallow your pride. Try not to put yourself in that situation in the first place. It's a terrible place to be.

Jeff had a girlfriend named Sally Jo. He had met her when he was in the desert with *The Coasters* a year before. They had a pretty volatile relationship. One night, he borrowed the Mercedes to take her out. A week or so later, Stephanie found panties in the back seat and asked me, "Where the hell did these come from?" That relationship ran its course, and then Jeff started dating Lolita Falk.

Stephanie was starting to go downhill quickly. She was drinking a lot, working at *Melvyn's*, and I guessed that she was maybe doing cocaine too. I would come home from work, and she would be drunk and angry about life. Like my dad, she was a belligerent drunk. Then, she would go into a huge depression and talk about ending her life. Sometimes, she blamed me for her unhappiness and acted like she was just tolerating me. It was frustrating, because in my heart I felt that I had always been an extremely loving, loyal husband.

At times, I could also be pretty codependent; I didn't know how to handle it; I would tell her I was sorry and buy into her drunken bullshit, and beg her forgiveness for whatever it was that she perceived that I had done wrong. I just wanted to somehow keep an even keel… to make everything okay for her and our kids. But, I was really frustrated.

I was approaching twenty-nine years old, and I started to feel that I had given up my twenties for a dysfunctional relationship with an addict who experienced depression on a regular basis. As wonderful as Stephanie was so much of the time, I have to admit that sometimes it was hard to see through all of the garbage to the beauty of her soul. I was starting to experience my own identity crisis as I was almost in my thirties.

We did get some good news though. My sister Judy had given birth to her daughter, Jenny. Jenny would grow up as Judy's mini-me. Jenny and her brother Brian would become extremely intelligent children, and I was grateful that Judy was doing so well with her family.

•••••

A girl named Monica started coming into the *Marriott* every night. She was around twenty-two years old, and very pretty and sexy. She was infatuated with me. Almost like a stalker, she would come in every night and just stare at me all night with hungry eyes. She also showed up at *Hank's* sometimes. It was kind of bizarre: she even had hair like Glenn Close in the film *Fatal Attraction*, but she was really, really nice to me and I knew she just wanted me.

I had always resisted temptation, believing strongly that life performing in the bars was all an illusion and my reality was my family. The problem was, my wife was going off the rails, I was dealing with a hard-core rock & roller at the gig, and my life had become very difficult to manage.

I hope you never find yourself in a situation where you allow yourself to be beaten down so much that you would even consider compromising your integrity.

Hank's Café hired Jeff and I to work as a duo on The Craig Eaton Band's off-nights. We were on Craig's stage. Craig was a good guy and a great performer, but he admitted to me that he had a drug problem. It wasn't a secret anyway. One night, he didn't show up to perform with his band. When it happened once again, the owner decided to fire the band. The other band members begged the owner to let them perform there and just replace their leader, Craig. He agreed. This was the first 'band mutiny' I had ever experienced! These guys decided to rename the band, calling themselves *The Palm Springs Rockets* and ended up performing in big venues in the desert for a couple decades after Craig was fired from the band, including at *Cecil's on Sunrise*, a huge disco and bar in Palm Springs owned by Mel Haber.

One night, while I was performing at *Hank's* with Jeff, Stephanie was at home from work. She was sleeping in her bedroom and the children were playing in the front room. Somehow, our little dog Buffy wandered out of the house and onto the street. Buffy was hit by a car and killed. This just devastated all of us but mostly Regina. She was beside herself with grief. When I got home, Stephanie was holding Regina and she blamed me for not being there to keep Buffy safe.

I didn't know how to react. I held Regina tightly, giving her all my love. I went out and found the dog, wrapped her in a towel and brought her back to the house. We buried her in the back yard the next morning. It was a dark time for my family. Stephanie just kept saying that all of this was my fault, and why couldn't I have been strong enough or protective enough to save her? I wasn't even home when it happened! I was working. But, it was more than all of that. I started to realize that Stephanie had a real problem with depression. I didn't even know what being bipolar meant at the time, but looking back, her behavior mirrored bipolar disorder. She was miserable and I was miserable.

One night, I had a few drinks at the *Marriott* and I took Monica out to the parking lot and kissed her. She invited me to her place and I declined. Within a week, though, I was meeting her at her apartment and we were making love. Now I was out of control. This went on for a month or two.

Jeff suspected that something was going between Monica and me, and he chastised me. He wanted to know what the hell I was doing with my life. I was surprised, because in so many ways, I felt that he was an out-of-control rock & roller with no real moral compass at this point. I realized that Jeff, along with so many others, saw my family life as a shining example of what he wanted for himself. He looked up to me, as if I had achieved a much greater goal than success as a musician, simply because I had chosen the path of a family man. And, he was right.

One night, I was driving to work and I saw Monica following me in her car. She was actually stalking me! It was creepy. Soon after that, she disappeared. One night, I was performing my solo at *Hank's* and a young man approached me. He asked me if we could talk. I said, "Of course!" He took me aside and told me that he was Monica's husband. They had been separated for about a year, and in the interim, she had been caught embezzling money from a local card store where she worked. She had just been convicted and she was sent off to serve time in prison, but she left a journal behind and it was all about me.

In the journal, she described in intimate detail every time we touched, every time we made love, everything, including the fact that I was married and having an affair. She was truly obsessed with me. And, I was shocked that I knew absolutely nothing about her. I didn't know she was in trouble with the law. I didn't know she was married and separated from her husband.

This young man was obviously disturbed and angry. I told him that I really didn't know much about her, that she just came in to see me a lot. He told me that I'd better look out, that she was pregnant with my child, and she had a really bad disease that I had probably been exposed to. I never heard from her again, and I know he was just trying to freak me out with the pregnancy and disease comments. I felt sad and sorry for her, but also relieved, in a sense. I was also ashamed of myself. No matter how bad life had become with Stephanie, I had always held my head up and followed the example of Christ, putting my vows and my family ahead of anything else as much as I knew how, until this point in my life.

After work that night, I came home to my out-of-control wife and stayed with her. Stephanie had been binge drinking again, and I calmed her down and held her until she fell asleep. Then, I got dressed, left my house and walked all the way to downtown Palm Springs at three o'clock in the morning.

I walked for more than three hours, probably a total of about fifteen miles, and when I got home, I decided that I was going to just suck it up and stay in this relationship. I was going to try to make the best of my marriage, to try to heal my life and become a better man. No matter what, I wasn't going to ever, ever abandon my children and they needed me to help them to hold their mother up until she could stand on her own again.

It was a decision I made to sacrifice my own well-being in order to do whatever it would take to at least try to make my family whole again. And, from that day forward I started to have a different outlook.

The grass is not greener on the other side. The grass is greener where you water it.

I started to run every morning. I changed my diet. I picked up a couple of books by Tony Robbins and read them religiously. I went back to my philosophy books.

Out of my tragic experience of the death of my own parent's marriage, I had made a solemn vow to myself that I would never ever do to my children what was done to me by my parents. Although in so many ways my life with Stephanie had become untenable to the point where I had compromised my own values and the sanctity of my vows, I still could not bear the thought of my children growing up in a broken home. I was going to make this work somehow, some way.

•••••

Shortly after Buffy died, we went out and bought a Shih Tzu puppy. She was black and white, and very sweet. We named her Sushi. She didn't take the place of Buffy but she filled a void and that made all the difference. Sushi loved Kevin. As Buffy had been Regina's dog, Sushi was all Kevin's. It helped to have another dog, although the burden was on us to train her. In retrospect, I can honestly say that I've spent much of my life wiping shit off of babies, dogs, and floors, and off of my pride.

Taddy and Sushi - 1987

Shortly thereafter, Jeff moved out of our house and got a place with Lolita. Scotty, Stephanie's dad's bass player, was homeless and Stephanie offered to take him in. Scotty was a trip. He was an old guy and he couldn't make it through even a few hours without a drink. He would set an alarm and wake up in the middle of the night to have a beer. He called his beers "cold sandwiches."

Scotty was actually very helpful around the house. He was a bit of a handyman, and he painted and refinished some of our old furniture. He would change a light bulb, or fix the sink. There was one big problem, though. He had been living with us for a couple of months, and one night, we invited some friends over after work. I went to pour some vodka from a bottle behind the bar, and it was watered down. I started to check some of the other bottles. Scotty had been taking shots from all the bottles, and replacing the alcohol with equal shots of water so we couldn't tell the alcohol was empty. I had a talk with him, and he knocked that one out right away.

Russ and Scotty - 1985

•••••

In September of 1987, the owner of our house on Eagle Way came back from New Zealand, and she wanted to move back into her home. We had to move again. I was sad because I loved the house on Eagle Way, but it did hold some pretty bad memories.

We found a house on Miraleste Court in Palm Springs. It was by *Desert Hospital* on the north side of Palm Springs closer to the mountain. It was a nice neighborhood, but we were also on the edge of the slums. Our street was nice, but tenement apartments towered over our back fence. Once or twice we heard gunshots or screams, but we made the best of it.

There was an old shed in the back yard, and Scotty moved into it. He wired it for electricity, and put a little twin bed in there. One day, I went into his little shed and he had a tennis ball hanging from a string. I said, "What's this?" He told me it was his "earthquake detector." If he woke up in the middle of the night and the ball was moving, it was an earthquake. If the ball wasn't moving, it was Scotty just being drunk. He was a sweet old man, but boy, could he drink!

We enrolled the twins and Kevin into a new elementary school. Regina was still going to *Nellie Coffman Junior High*, but we were out of the bus route so we had to drive her every morning.

Stephanie had quit *Melvyn's*, and Joe Hanna had hired her at *The Ocotillo Lodge*. I guess Joe had won the 'fat' battle over Fat Philly, and Stephanie was glad to be back working for Joe. My old friend, saxophonist/vocalist Pat Rizzo was performing at *The Ocotillo* with Dennis Michaels on piano and Steve Neilen on drums.

On her off-nights, Steph picked up a job cocktailing at *Bobby Milano's Supper Club.* Bobby was a semi-famous Italian singer who had a brush with fame in the 1950's. He was a classic crooner, and it was rumored that his family was connected with the Mafia. I knew him from my days at *Delmonico's.*

Bobby had served time in the 1960's for armed robbery. Bobby's brother, Jimmy Caci, was in and out of jail for most of his life. Bobby's nephew, Joey Caci was a good friend of mine. Joey bartended at a few places I performed, and he would get up and sing *This Moment In Time* with me. He had a good voice and he was a good guy. Bobby's very kind other brother Al Caci owned a great Italian restaurant, *Alfredo's*, in Palm Springs. The family was from Buffalo, New York, and Al had the best wings I have ever tasted, not to mention his pastas and pizzas.

Bobby Milano had a big ego, but he backed it up with a powerful voice and a huge following. Bobby was living with Keely Smith, the famous torch singer who performed with (and was married to) Louis Prima in the 1950's.

Dennis Michaels was an excellent pianist and singer, and he played keyboard bass better than anyone I had ever seen. He taught me a lot about technique on key bass, and he was a character. Dennis was married to Tony Prima, Louis Prima's daughter. Dennis was loyal to Bobby Milano, performing with him for years and arranging for Bobby's girlfriend, Keely Smith. When Bobby wasn't working, Dennis was available to perform for Pat Rizzo and a select group of other performers.

Keely's brother, Piggy Smith, was a talent manager, and he approached me to be my manager. I declined, because Hillery Johnson seemed to have strong plans for me. Piggy was also into providing vending machines for the various venues. It was a racket, and there was strong competition to provide these machines, especially the vending machines that provided cigarettes in those days. They were big moneymakers.

Rumor had it that Piggy Smith called Fat Philly at *The Ocotillo* and told him that he wanted to put his vending machines into the lobby of the hotel and the lounge. Apparently, Fat Philly was already being paid a kickback from another company, so he declined the offer.

Bobby Milano was so angry that he called Fat Philly and demanded that he put Piggy's machines into the lobby. If Fat Philly didn't comply, Bobby would yank Dennis Michaels from Pat's trio at *The Ocotillo.* Philly told Bobby to go to hell, and Bobby pulled Dennis from *The Ocotillo.* Pat Rizzo was in a bind, so he called his old Brooklyn friend Andy Fraga, who was in Ohio, to come out and take the gig. Andy was only going to stay for a couple of weeks until Pat could find someone else. He ended up staying in Palm Springs for the rest of his life. So, began a long friendship between Andy Fraga and me.

•••••

The City of Palm Springs was hosting a song contest. The song that won the contest would forever be the "official" song of Palm Springs. Stephanie wanted me to enter the contest, so I wrote, *I've Learned Just What It Means (To Love Palm Springs).* It was actually a pretty cool swing tune in the style of Sinatra, and we made it to the top three choices in the contest.

In the end, we came in second behind a ninety-five-year-old guy who wrote a forgettable song, but they gave it to him because of his age and his ties to the city founding fathers. It was cool. I was happy for him. Nobody ever heard his song again…I think they buried it because it didn't work in advertising. Years later, I re-recorded the Palm Springs song and included it on a CD for the *Well Of The Desert* charities. My buddy Jimi (Fitz) Fitzgerald would spin it quite a bit on his radio show.

My old friend Jan Hasman called me. He was marrying a lovely lady named Sara, and he asked me if I would perform for the ceremony at the *Palm Springs Botanical Gardens.* Not only did I agree, but also, I refused to allow him to pay me.

When I arrived at the gardens, the minister was Tom Costa (later Dr. Tom Costa, *Doctor of Divinity*). Tom was the minister at the *Religious Science Church* that my mother had attended since I was a teenager. It was a beautiful ceremony, and afterwards, Tom and I talked.

He told me that, after ten years of running back and forth, doing services in theatres in Palm Springs and Palm Desert, he had found a location for his church. It was the location in Palm Desert where President Eisenhower worshiped in the 1950's. He had built up a big congregation at this point in his new home.

Tom asked if I would like to come and perform at his church on Sunday. He said they had a budget and would like to hire me to do Sunday's if it felt right. I jokingly said, "I always said they'd have to pay me to get me to go back to church!" I agreed to try it, and I continued to perform every Sunday at the church for almost fifteen years after that Sunday.

The congregants became a family to me. Dr. Tom and I joked and bantered with each other through the services like Johnny Carson and Ed McMahon...I was his sideman on the pulpit. People loved the music, and they loved the combination of my silly humor and Tom's light-hearted wisdom. I was able to make people laugh and cry with my music.

It was tough, sometimes, working until two in the morning on Saturday nights, and then sleeping a little bit and showing up with red eyes at the church. During each of three services, four hundred people had their eyes fixed upon me. I had their undivided attention, which was entirely different than performing at a nightclub. *Religious Science*, or *Science of Mind*, to me, is more of a philosophy than a religion. I was raised Catholic and I know the difference. It became a way of life for me. It was like going to this huge, really cool positive thinking class every Sunday. You would leave charged up!

CHAPTER FORTY
Moving On... To Corporate Gigs

Greg McDonald had come back to Palm Springs. Stephanie and I had not seen Greg, Sherry or their children since Stephanie was watching their children for them for weekends at a time back in 1980. The great performer Ricky Nelson had been killed in a plane crash, and somehow, his manager Greg became the beneficiary of his Will. Although the Nelson family was suing Greg, he had some money and he decided to buy out Bill Renner's talent agency and book corporate entertainment in Palm Springs. Greg also bought control of Elvis Presley's honeymoon hideaway in Palm Springs, and he wanted to turn it into a destination for tourists.

Greg had a friend named Paul Rose. Paul had been a big boss at *Capitol Records* in the 1970's, The Payola scandal rocked the industry; the record companies were caught paying off radio stations with money and cocaine in exchange for promoting recording artists, and Paul became a fall guy for the label. He was one of only a few men who took the rap for the wrongdoing in order to save the label.

Through the years, Paul had been a collector of 1950's memorabilia. He had a storage vault with juke boxes, signed guitars and photos, and many more items that Greg thought would be perfect to put into the Elvis house.

Also, Paul Rose was broke and he owed more than $250,000.00 to the IRS because of the scandal. He basically couldn't earn a large salary because the IRS would confiscate it. Greg made a deal with Paul to come to Palm Springs, loan Greg his memorabilia for the Elvis House, and work for Greg as an agent, securing all of the corporate music in all the big hotels in the desert. Greg would give Paul a stipend, but he would pay for his Mercedes and a nice condo. Paul agreed. He really had no choice. It was his best option.

Paul came into the *Marriott* and saw Jeff and me performing. He started working on me, telling me that I could make a fortune just doing corporate band work for him. They had created a company called *Sun Presentations*. Bill Renner actually bragged around town that he had basically sold them his Rolodex for $40,000.00 and a non-compete clause.

Paul told me that if I came to work for him, he would guarantee me a certain amount of money each week, no matter how much work they had. The guaranteed money wasn't great, but the potential to make better money was huge. I discussed it with Jeff. Jeff jumped on the idea, but he thought we could make even more money if we just used our sequencer, and hired young guys off the street for $25.00 per night. We would put these guys on stage and tell them just to pretend to play their instruments. Then, we could keep our money and most of theirs. I thought it was the sleaziest idea I had ever heard, and it certainly didn't fit into my idea of wanting to better myself by working with other musicians. Jeff had a guitar student who could play a few chords, and that guy had a friend who was a garage-band drummer. They both jumped at the chance to do gigs, and I agreed to at least try it. After the handful of gigs we did with these guys and the experiment predictably became a dismal failure from my point of view, I never heard from the guitar kid again, but the little drummer kid kept learning and eventually would become a pretty good drummer. So, I guess it was productive in the sense that we gave a young drummer the confidence to continue to improve and grow.

Jeff was an entrepreneur, and later in his career he would make a tremendous amount of money. Jeff also had a penchant for flair. He thought that when we did gigs that required a tuxedo (and most of them did), he and I should wear "tails", the long tuxedos that were popular back in the 1920's with movie stars like Fred Astaire, and also worn by most orchestra conductors. It was a cool look, two dudes with super long hair and tuxedos with tails fronting a band.

•••••

In January of 1988, Jeff and I started to work for *Sun Presentations* doing corporate gigs. For a couple months, it was working pretty well. Most of the people we worked for loved the group, but there was the occasional person who could see through what we were doing with the 'fake' musicians on stage. Jeff liked the money we were making. He went out and bought a brand-new Amp and huge speaker. He bought a new guitar. One night, he was rolling the new amp up to a corporate gig, and it fell and got scratched. He became really angry, and threatened to quit because of it.

We were still doing off-nights at *Hank's.* One night, Jeff's girlfriend Lolita came in to see us, and she was sitting in the audience. I could tell that Jeff was really bothered by everything; I thought he was almost manic. I had bought a couple of shiny jackets and I decided we should wear them for a hip, classy look. Jeff refused to wear his jacket and gave me dirty looks through the whole set, just going through the motions. At the end of the set he said, "You know what? Fuck you, man. I'm out of here!" He walked out and I finished the night off as a solo.

So, I went to Paul Rose and told him what happened. I asked him to give me a week or so and I would figure it out. He told me he didn't like Jeff anyway, and I could pull it off by myself. I called Carl Joiner and he jumped at the proposition of working with me again. I also started to reach out to other musicians.

Jay Lewis was an excellent drummer. He was about ten years older than me; very hip looking, and he had a nice singing voice. Kenny Ray was back in town, and he played guitar and saxophone on many of our gigs. Kenny was always friendly and kind. He was kind of a rocker, Carl was an R&B guy, and Jay could play really any style well. As time went by, I met and started working with other great performers.

The wonderful thing about doing corporate gigs was diversity of engagements. One night we would be a jazz trio. Another night we were an eight-piece Motown Revue. Another night, we would be a beach band, with Hawaiian shirts playing the Beach Boys and Jimmy Buffett's music. Some nights, we were an Awards Banquet band in tuxedos. I did background piano-only solos.

I began to reach out to other musicians, depending upon the vibe of the gig we were going to do. And, as time went by, I learned to weed through the musicians that were maybe great performers but were unreliable or had a bad attitude. Finally, I had my core group of amazing musicians, and when they weren't available, I could turn to others who were equally as great. I was becoming a more proficient performer working with amazing musicians.

Glen Myerscough 1998

Glen Myerscough was a world-class saxophonist who had recently come off the road with Andrae Crouch. Andrae's band, with Glen, had won a *Grammy Award*. Glen was a strong, Christian man with a darling wife, Lena, two older daughters and two children at home. When we started working together, he was so much better than me in so many ways. He was well rounded, and I began to learn from his nuances. Over the years, we worked more than a thousand gigs together and recorded an enormous amount of material.

Gary Bias 2009

In those early days of corporate work, I was fortunate to work with *Grammy Award* winning saxophonist Gary Bias, who performed with us when he wasn't on the road with *Earth, Wind and Fire*. Michael (Patches) Stewart was an amazing trumpeter who worked with Whitney Houston and Al Jarreau. Patches performed and recorded a good amount of music with me. So many other good players, including saxophonists Pat Rizzo, Steve Tavaglione and Steve Alaniz; legendary Steve Madaio or Stan Watkins on trumpet; Michael Higgins, Bill Ferguson or Michel Monsalve on guitar; and female vocalists like Paula Stapleton and Jeri Lyne rounded out my bands; we became a cohesive unit through time.

Pat Rizzo 1978

Michael (Patches) Stewart 2018

Steve Tavaglione - 2008

Steve Madaio - 2018

•••••

Paul Rose had secured the vast majority of the corporate events at *Marriott's Desert Springs Resort*. It was the huge new property in the desert with tons of convention space. The general manager, John Cirieli, wanted music at the pool. He wanted a duo to do island music with no vocals. Paul asked me if I wanted the gig. It was a six-day a week, five hour a day gig that would pay me $100.00 per day and my sideman $75.00 per day. I jumped at the gig, because I knew the extra $600.00 per week would help me to pay my bills and feed my family.

Steve Neilen, the drummer who worked with Pat Rizzo and Andy Fraga at *The Ocotillo*, had been talking to me a lot about hiring him to work with me. I was happy with Jay Lewis, but Steve had a ton of percussion equipment, so I hired Steve to play congas and percussion with me at the *Marriott*, and I kept Jay on the corporate gigs at night.

Steve Neilen 2008

Steve and I became fast friends. Poolside was a tough gig. Each day I would arrive at the *Marriott*, park in the garage, walk a mile to the golf course, grab a golf cart, go back to the garage and load up all of my equipment, drive it to poolside through all of the little paths and bridges, set up my equipment, drive the cart back to the garage and meet Steve, load up all of his equipment, bring it back to poolside and set it up, and then return the cart. Then, I would walk another mile to poolside and we would perform for five hours, before repeating the process to break down and remove our equipment.

Nature had its way of eating away at our strength and stamina. The elements were difficult. Sometimes, we would play in windstorms or sandstorms. Other days, bugs would be all over us as we performed.

Through the summer, the temperature sometimes reached as high as 127 degrees and stayed painfully hot for months.

We had oscillating fans pointed at us, but we couldn't use mist because we had electronic equipment. In the winter, it would be freezing out there. If it rained, we would have to break down our equipment in a matter of minutes and get it out of there so it wouldn't get ruined. We would laugh and wonder what the "element of the day" was going to be, tomorrow. Then, after an entire day dealing with all of that and working our asses off, we would repeat the process to get out of there and go to our night gigs.

If I was lucky, my corporate gig would be at the same hotel, but many times I would have to bring a change of clothes. I would change in a restroom or the back of the van, and set up all the equipment in a ballroom or on a stage in an outdoor venue to do the next gig. By the time I finally got home, I was just exhausted, but I would wake up and do it all over again the next day. I missed my wife and children a lot, but when I was home I gave them all of me!

Working poolside with Steve Neilen helped me to become a much more rounded player. Steve had a strong knowledge of Latin and Cuban rhythms, of jazz nuances and Caribbean or Reggae beats. We had long conversations on our breaks and became best friends from all the time we spent together on the gig.

•••••

Everyone has something important to teach you if you're open to learn. Even a drummer! (A little joke there...)

I moved on from my gig at *Marriott's Rancho Las Palmas Resort* and committed to Paul Rose to do corporate gigs full-time.

Wayne Boyer 2010

My friend Wayne Boyer was doing a lot of work with guitarist Chuck Buffamonte. In 1986 they hooked up with a really good local singer named Jimmy Hopper. Jimmy went on to gain some fame as a finalist on *Star Search* on CBS, and later as a Las Vegas Headline entertainer. At this point, however, Jimmy's band had been at the *Marriott's Desert Springs Resort* in Palm Desert, CA, at *Costa's* lounge. One of the band-members had apparently been caught in the Men's Room of the lounge with some drugs, and the band was fired from the gig. After a short period of time, Wayne asked Jimmy if he would like to front the band he was putting together with Mike and Chuck. Jimmy jumped at the prospect, and they booked themselves into *Marriott's Rancho Las Palmas Resort* after I left the gig.

Paul didn't like Jimmy Hopper, and he had a little power, so he called the powers that be and told them that the same guy whose band got caught with drugs was going into the other *Marriott.* Instantly, they called Wayne Boyer and told him that he was not allowed to use Jimmy Hopper. (In retrospect, for Jimmy, this was probably one of the best things that could have happened to him, because it propelled him to go for the *Star Search* experience, and then on to minor stardom.).

Jimmy Hopper 2017

Wayne was in a pinch, so he called Mike Costley, the great vocalist who was a good friend of Chuck's from Buffalo, New York. Mike had been in Los Angeles for a few years, and he moved out to the desert. Mike did the gig for a while, and then he recommended Paula Stapleton to replace him. Paula was a female vocalist from Toronto, Canada.

Mike Costley

Paula was cute and she had a great voice. She came down and did the gig with Wayne and Chuck. While working together, Wayne fell in love with Paula and left his wife, Chris. Wayne and Paula ended up getting married and had two sons following that experience. All of these people would play major roles in my life, as we interconnected over the years.

•••••

Shortly after my family moved into the house on Miraleste Court, Stephanie had a meltdown. She was working four nights at *The Ocotillo* and two nights at *Bobby Milano's Supper Club.* Waitressing had taken its toll on her, and although I hadn't identified it yet, her alcoholism was progressing. She was extremely depressed.

One night, I came home from work. I had done a long poolside shift and a corporate event following, and I was exhausted. When I walked in, I found her in her room. She had been drinking. Stephanie had slashed one of her wrists, and she was crying and bleeding. I freaked out. It had just happened, and I bandaged it immediately. It wasn't a deep cut, but she was obviously crying out. I wanted to call an ambulance, but she begged me not to, crying even harder. I held her and rocked her in my arms until she finally fell asleep. What was I going to do? I kept a close watch on her even though she seemed to wake up the next morning with a different frame of mind.

I suggested that she talk to a psychiatrist and she got mad at me and told me she wasn't crazy. She was off for the next couple days. She went back to work that Thursday. On Friday late afternoon, I came home quickly from my poolside job to shower and change for an evening gig, and I found her in a fetal position in our bedroom, sobbing. She was having a full-blown panic attack.

Stephanie asked me to call Joe at *The Ocotillo* and tell her she couldn't come in to work. It was going to be a huge Friday night there, and he was extremely upset that I called him only fifteen minutes before she was supposed to be there. I made up some stupid excuse about how she hurt herself and wasn't able to make it.

I had to leave to go to work, and I didn't know what to do. I got a cold washcloth and helped her on to the bed. I wanted to take her to the emergency room but she refused to go. She couldn't move. I brought Regina in and she stayed with Stephanie until I was back from my gig.

After that night, Stephanie quit all of her jobs. I got her to the doctor on Monday morning, and he prescribed *Xanax* for her anxiety. This was a short-term blessing and a long-term curse. To this day, I curse the day Stephanie took her first *Xanax*. Yes, it did help her to become calm, but it was extremely addictive, and after a certain point, it actually *created* anxiety within her when she was coming down from it.

She continued to increase her dosage, and when she ran out, she went to another doctor and got another prescription for it. She went up the chain from white to yellow to blue *Xanax*, and she absolutely needed it, in order to feel okay. On the other hand, she did become extremely even-tempered here and there, and it helped immensely that she didn't have to face the public as a waitress.

It's always great to get accolades or to be recognized for a great performance. An aware person realizes that accolades are not intended as an ego-boost, but rather an acknowledgement of hard work mixed with talent. Humility is essential always.

Even through it all, she was a devoted mother. I just didn't 'get' the depression. I couldn't understand why a woman who had beautiful, intelligent loving children and a devoted husband, could be so sad, so much of the time. As much as I knew she loved me, she would tell me that she was jealous of me and envious of the accolades I got when I performed. She felt like I had all the glory and she was unfulfilled.

So much of the time, I felt like Stephanie was just tolerating me, but again, my codependence probably fed into it. I was consumed with fixing her, or helping her to overcome all of this and finally be okay. In many ways, this became the main focus of our life together, but at the same time, life went on every day and we had work to do and children to care for.

•••••

We bought a nice new television and stereo system for the living room, and our first personal computer, an *Atari 8-bit* computer. It was amazing to us! We used the computer primarily for word processing. My kids would type homework on it, and print it out through a clunky little dot matrix printer. We also played video games on it, like *Missile Command*. My children loved it! It's hilarious now to look back on how rudimentary it was, but at the time, it was really something.

One day, I was maneuvering a golf cart through the small paths at the *Marriott* with Steve Neilen. We came around the corner and startled a man who was walking. He started screaming and yelling at us. He got right in my face and I apologized. As we were driving away, I mumbled something to Steve. The man started to chase us and said, "What did you just say?" I calmly and respectfully told him, "I was telling my drummer that you must be having a bad day, and I hoped I hadn't made it worse." He shrugged his shoulders, told us to be more careful and walked away.

That evening, I was doing a band gig at *The Grove*, an outdoor amphitheater at the *Marriott.* The master of ceremonies got up and introduced the speaker. He said, "Ladies and gentlemen, please welcome the General Manager of the *Marriott's Desert Springs Resort,* Mr. John Cirieli!" Everyone clapped, and the man who had harassed us got up to speak. I realized that the GM had tested us on that day to see if we were going to be jerks or nice people. He winked at me as he walked up on to the stage. I was grateful at that moment for my even temper, even in the face of an asshole!

As I worked more and more with different musicians doing corporate events, I began to understand the nuances of finding the right people. One night as a jazz band I had a choice of the finest jazz performers to choose from. If we were a Motown revue, I would hire musicians accordingly.

Through trial and error, I realized that so many great musicians also have great attitudes, and so many other great musicians are negative sons of bitches! Other musicians are good but unreliable. Weeding my way through many performers over the years, I came up with a core group of the best of the best. For the most part, I was fortunate, yet I learned many lessons along the way.

In the world of employment, do not let attitudes and emotions hold you back or thwart your progress. There are many others available in this world with great attitudes, doing comparable work with a great work ethic.

I got a call in May of 1988 from my sister Judy. Her three-year-old son Brian had a huge tumor in his abdomen and it was cancerous. I was scared for her and I prayed daily. After they removed the tumor, he went through chemotherapy and radiation. It was a lot to endure for a three-year-old boy. Brian was brave and went through the whole experience with a smile on his face most of the time. He was a good boy, and we were so grateful later when he was given a clean bill of health.

Judy's husband, George was clashing with her Native American son, Abraham, though. Abraham was an angry child and George didn't seem to like him, which didn't help. Judy felt enormous guilt and without knowing it, she fed into Abraham's anger by appeasing him. At some point, George sent Abraham away to an Indian School in New Mexico. Judy had a hard time being away from Abraham, and it eventually wore on her marriage. She also held on to guilt for a long time after these events. But, at that time, she was a Registered Nurse and an Officer in the Air Force, first stationed in

Ventura, California, and then in San Antonio, Texas, so she was obligated to fulfill her duties. My mother visited her on occasion. She and my sisters remained close.

•••••

In June of 1988, the corporate gigs were dwindling as the heat index rose in the desert. During the summer, the hotels would sell the venues cheap, so there was little call for entertainment. I got a job with my band at *Reuben's* in Palm Desert for the summer. I played keyboards and sang. Carl Joiner played bass and sang. Kenny Ray played saxophone and guitar, and sang. Jay Lewis played drums and sang.

We did a lot of sequenced material with my QX1, interspersed with live music. *Reuben's* was packed, even in the summertime, and we had a good run there. I was still doing my six days of poolside through the summer at the *Marriott* with Steve Neilen. On my thirtieth birthday, I worked all day and all night, and then came home to my smiling wife and children with a cake with thirty candles for my exhausted lungs to blow out. I had survived my own emotional crisis of becoming thirty years old, and I was kicking ass.

In August of 1988, after a long week, Saturday came. I still had an entire day at poolside and a night at *Reuben's* ahead. Sunday, I would be back at poolside and I would finally have Sunday night off. At the end of the long day and night, Carl helped me break down all the equipment at *Reuben's* and get it into my van. Carl normally rode back home with me, but on that night he decided to ride with someone else.

On my way home, I was driving down Monterey Avenue in Palm Desert. It was a two-lane highway back in those days. As I approached an intersection near the freeway, a car with no headlights going about 100 miles an hour blasted in front of me from a side street, and my van hit it head-on. I spun around but the van didn't roll. The car that hit me rolled over on the side of the road.

I jumped out of the van, dazed and injured, and I noticed that my engine was crushed and on fire. All of my equipment was in the back of the van. Just then, a man in a truck stopped and brought out a fire extinguisher. He put out the fire in my engine, which saved my equipment, although some was destroyed by the impact.

I hobbled over to the car that had hit my van, hoping that no children were in it. Just then, two drunken Mexican men crawled out from a broken window of the upside-down vehicle, took one look at me and ran off into the dark desert.

An ambulance came and I was put onto a stretcher and taken to *Eisenhower Medical Center.* I was wearing my seatbelt and it saved my life. I was really glad that Carl was not with me, because he tended to not wear his seat belt. My knees were pretty banged up.

Stephanie came immediately to the hospital. My van was towed away with all of my equipment in it. We found where the tow yard was. I was released at around four in the morning and we went to the tow yard to move my equipment into Stephanie's car. By the time we made it home, it was six o'clock in the morning and I was in pain. I called my boss at *The Marriott* and told her what happened. She told me that if I didn't show up, I was going to be fired. I couldn't believe it!

For once, Steve Neilen went to the *Marriott* early, got the cart, found me, helped me with my equipment and we got through the day that Sunday. A week later, I went in for a biopsy on my leg. The osteoid osteoma that I had been diagnosed with at the age of ten was inflamed. The surgeon thought it was a Brody's Abscess instead, and he was afraid it might even be cancerous. He did the biopsy.

Strangely enough, somehow the biopsy relieved some pressure from my leg, and the daily pain I had felt for twenty years started to ease. After a time, I only felt it about once every month or so, and it continued that way throughout my life. That was the blessing that came out of the accident. Later, I found that my leg problem was actually an abscess and not an osteoma. I could have gone through a painful surgery to hollow out the bone, but I chose instead to just endure the temporary pain, which continued to flare up on occasion for the remainder of my life.

The police had me look at some photos, and I correctly identified the driver of the vehicle. He didn't have insurance but I had uninsured motorist coverage along with my insurance. I got a little settlement from my own insurance company, which was enough to put a down payment on a new car.

•••••

My mother offered again to co-sign on a vehicle. The *Dodge Caravan* had been a reliable minivan. We decided to buy a larger version of that vehicle. It was a *Plymouth Voyager*. It would be the last Chrysler product I would ever buy. It was a nightmare.

The *Voyager* immediately had a number of recalls, including a transmission problem that they couldn't figure out. The transmission kept going out. The engine would race, and I'd have to drive it back again into the dealership. But the worst thing about it all was what transpired with my mother and us after she co-signed.

I was grateful for my mother. Even though she was a difficult woman at times, her heart was in the right place and she somehow came through for me again and again when I needed her the most. But, she had a very strong personality and so did Stephanie. And… my mother was still suffering from post-traumatic stress disorder from the abuse she experienced during her marriage.

Stephanie and Elaine were like oil and water. They were so much alike, really…both stubborn and jealous of my love for the other. When Elaine came to stay with us, she would be demanding of the children. I was working so much that I wasn't there a lot when she was staying with us.

One night, a day or two after she co-signed on the new car, my mother was at my house. She wanted to watch *Wheel Of Fortune* on the television in the living room. Regina wanted to watch another show, and Elaine told Regina to go into her bedroom and watch it. Elaine shushed the other kids so she could hear the television. It really wasn't a big deal, but Stephanie felt that Elaine was trying to rule the roost.

Stephanie became angrier and angrier about it as the night went on, and when I came home from work around eleven at night, Stephanie burst out of the bedroom and started screaming at my mother. Elaine wasn't one to back down, so she started screaming back at Stephanie. I was standing between them both screaming even louder for them to please stop!

Stephanie had Elaine cornered in the kitchen and I was standing between them. My mother felt threatened and she grabbed a knife from the dishwasher and held it up to me. I got the knife out of her hand. I knew that the level of anger was so severe that I told Elaine to just go and get a hotel room for the night. She left the house and she didn't talk to me for almost two years after that night. I felt so badly about it. Yes, my mother was a pain in the ass but I knew that Stephanie had overreacted. She was not okay sometimes.

•••••

Maynard and Kimberley
1987

In September of 1988, my father called me and informed me of how proud he was that Sandra's daughter, his stepdaughter Kimberley had been accepted to the medical program at the *University of Missouri*, in Kansas City. She was starting classes that month.

I was happy for her. She was a good girl and she deserved it. I have to admit, though, that I was taken aback for a moment that he was eagerly calling and telling me how proud he was to be paying for her tuition, enrolling her into the program I was supposed to do and would have done in 1975, if he hadn't completely screwed up his life and mine.

I mean… it was the exact program I had been enrolled in, at the exact college; it was what I had thought I was going to do with my life, until his bullshit had pulled the rug out from under me as he abandoned me.

Looking back at that moment in time, though, I knew that, even though I had taken the hard road and suffered heavily since that fateful year, at this moment in time I was doing what I was supposed to be doing with my life. After all, I could have figured out a way to go back to college on my own by now, if it had meant that much to me. I was making leaps and bounds learning and growing in the business I was intended to thrive within.

I decided to be happy for Kimberley and to wish her success. My father's karma was another story, however…I mean, wow, how oblivious to another's feelings can you get?

Everything happens for a reason, and we must not hold on to negative thoughts or feelings; jealousy and envy are acids that eat their own containers.

•••••

Right around this time, MGM/UA producer Anthea Sylbert was putting together a film starring Goldie Hawn entitled *Criss Cross*. The film was about a single mother who had become impregnated by a Vietnam Vet who had PTSD. In the film, she turns to stripping to make a living. Her edgy, strong but disturbed pre-teen son had a huge role in the screenplay.

The producers of the film went to San Diego and did a search through the school systems for the right kid for the part. Out of 10,000 boys they screened, they auditioned 1,000. Narrowing it down to 100 and then 10, they ended up selecting my sister Betsy's son David Arnott for the part.

David Arnott in Criss Cross

They shot the film in Florida, and Betsy brought her son David for his filming dates. It was a great experience for them, and David was an excellent actor. The film wasn't released for almost three years following. When it did finally come out, the critics loved David's performance. Some even wrote that he was by far the best part of the film.

Agents started calling him like mad. The problem was, though, that he was no longer a pre-teen. He was a full-blown teenager, a foot taller and out of control at this point. His film career never went further than this, but it was a big moment of pride for my sister and our family. David's life spiraled out of control for a while. He was in and out of trouble for a few years but eventually he ended up pulling his life together.

•••••

New corporate events started to kick in again for me in October of 1988. Although I loved working with Jay Lewis on drums, it started to make more sense for Steve and I to just move equipment together to the gigs. Steve was a world-class drummer, and he worked every day with me at poolside, so we were already together most of the time. Logistically, it just made more sense to me.

I started to phase out Jay as my full-time drummer over a period of weeks. Fortunately, I knew that Jay was a good enough drummer to keep working anyway, and I was so grateful for the time we worked together. Jay and I ended up doing gigs here and there for many years afterwards. I actually missed working with him, although I enjoyed Steve's playing immensely. Jay was a good hang; he was a really good guy and he taught me some subtleties, refining my performance.

Carl Joiner, Steve Neilen and Tad

1989

With Steve as my drummer and Glen Myerscough as my saxophonist, I became a more nuanced player. They taught me how to work the keyboard bass to make it feel more like an authentic bass, when I was using an upright bass patch for jazz. I learned about multi-rhythms and became a better performer on waltzes and tunes with unusual tempo maps, like 5/4 or 7/4. My jazz repertoire grew greatly when we did the jazz trio gigs. Glen would bring Fake Books and put songs in front of me like *Windows*, *'Round Midnight*, *Invitation* and *I'll Remember April.*

CHAPTER FORTY-ONE
Stephanie Becomes an Agent

Paul Rose was giving my band all of the premiere gigs. *Sun Presentations* was growing. Someone told me that Greg McDonald and Paul Rose had bought a swimming pool for the General Manager of the *Marriott,* and now *Sun Presentations* was the exclusive agent for the *Marriott Hotels* in the desert. I guess Paul was back to his payola again.

Whatever they were doing, it was working. They became so busy in their office that Henny, their secretary (who had been an assistant to Greg during the Ricky Nelson days, and really wasn't a secretary) was too overwhelmed to handle it all. Paul mentioned to me that he was looking for a new secretary, and asked me if I knew somebody. I told him I would look around.

Stephanie hadn't worked for a few months since her meltdown. When I told her about what Paul said, she begged me to tell him to hire her. She had always wanted to be in the music business, and she had her heart set on this job.

I was really apprehensive about it. Stephanie was my wife. I loved her but I didn't trust her emotional state; in the past, I had seen her be the best at whatever she put her mind to, but we had been through so much together in the last few months. In my gut, I didn't feel that she was mentally stable enough. Stephanie was really persistent with me. I began to think that maybe this would help her after all, so I suggested that Paul hire her part time to help Henny.

From the moment Stephanie stepped foot into *Sun Presentations*, she was determined to prove herself. As she had been the very best cocktail waitress I had ever seen, she was intent on becoming the very best secretary.

Henny was easy-going. She had a ton of stories about drug-induced sexual escapades she witnessed with the Ricky Nelson band while they were on the road. All of the experiences she had would make a great book, but it's probably better for Ricky's memory that it never came out. I've heard that Ricky Nelson was a genuinely good man underneath (and in spite of) all of the dysfunction around him.

Henny was delighted to have Stephanie helping her. They got along very well, and before too long Stephanie was working full-time at *Sun Presentations.* At that point, it really did seem to be a good move for Stephanie. She was more confident and seemed happier in general.

•••••

Greg McDonald was branching out into new ventures. He decided to promote some Headliner events in the desert. Stephanie volunteered to help him, and, in a heartbeat, she was producing sold-out events with Greg, including *Chuck Berry*, *Jerry Lee Lewis* and *The Judds.*

Initially, she was thriving in this environment. I was so grateful that she was doing so well. In fact, there was a kind of tug-of-war between Paul and Greg for Stephanie. Paul was almost jealous when Stephanie worked with Greg. He wanted her exclusively to help him book all of the corporate events.

My band was the top band for *Sun Presentations*, and we were working virtually every night of the week through the season, doing huge events for *Fortune 500* companies. Through this period, my band opened for Gladys Knight, Marilyn McCoo and Billy Davis, Jr., Shecky Greene, Peter Marshall and Jay Leno.

We made the five-hour road trip by van to Phoenix, Arizona several times, performing at *The Phoenecian* and *Hyatt Gainey Ranch*. In Scottsdale, Arizona we opened for Rita Coolidge. We traveled to Las Vegas, Nevada and performed at most of the major hotels on the Las Vegas Strip, doing corporate events.

Around this time, Steve Neilen found out that he had degenerative disc disease in his back. It was a bad prognosis. I sent his X-Rays to my dad, and he confirmed it. He told me that it didn't look good for Steve. He was going to need a series of back surgeries.

•••••

Chuck Buffamonte was a guitarist-vocalist from Buffalo, New York. He was a great player with an acceptable singing voice and good stage presence. As I mentioned earlier, Chuck performed a lot in Los Angeles with Mike Costley. Mike was a strong, dark-haired Italian male vocalist. He had an amazing voice that he used as if it was an instrument. Mike moved out to the desert around this time.

Chuck wanted to work with me. We did a few gigs together, and we clicked on stage. He was high-strung but he worked hard, and he wanted to work. He had a wife and children to feed. It was rumored that Chuck had a problem with cocaine. I didn't see it when we met. Chuck would party late with Steve Neilen. Steve was reeling from the diagnosis of his disease. Apparently, they would do cocaine together and Steve would get so whacked that he couldn't show up at poolside, so Chuck would offer to come in his place.

Chuck really wanted the poolside job. One day, Chuck showed up in Steve's place at poolside with an *8-ball* of cocaine. I have no idea why, but I tried some cocaine with him that day, and on some other days when he worked. One night, the band was at the *Ritz-Carlton* doing an event, and Chuck brought some coke. We all went into the Men's room, and lined up huge white lines on the green granite in the stalls. It was exciting and we felt like we were living life in the fast lane. It was also very stupid.

Fortunately, I didn't really like how I felt when I did the drug. I was just 'off'. I wasn't myself. For years, I had witnessed people who ingested cocaine in the nightclubs; they would have to drink alcohol to even themselves out, and then they would do more coke, and then drink some more alcohol. When the gig ended, they would stay up all night expounding upon the wonders of the universe, as if all was revealed to them and they had to talk in depth, right now, about everything. And then, they would feel like shit the next day, not remembering a word they even said. There's a joke that goes something like this, "I don't like cocaine. I just like the way it smells." Although I really never was stupid enough to do cocaine on any regular basis, at some point, I just stopped doing it altogether forever, and I felt a lot better about myself.

CHAPTER FORTY-TWO
Recording my First Album

When you're young, you might think you're invincible, but, I assure you, you are not. So, take care of your body. Don't be stupid.

Hillery Johnson called me in July of 1989. He had moved to Van Nuys, California, in the San Fernando Valley just north of Los Angeles. Hillery had installed a beautiful recording studio with a 2-inch, 24-track tape machine and a huge *Soundcraft* mixing board into his compound. He wanted me to come out and start recording my album. He lined up Lonnie Reeves to produce the album with me.

Chuck came over to my house on many nights. I had written some songs, and we would play around with chord arrangements. When we went into Van Nuys, we would stay up for two days at a time recording. Sometimes, someone would bring methamphetamine and we would be all amped out through the sessions. My voice was strong and the album was coming along great.

It wasn't always that way. Many times, I drove out alone and calmly worked out horn parts and arrangements, completely straight. It just seemed that every time I was around Chuck, drugs were in the picture.

Hillery had a staff of people that worked all day, promoting *Valley Vue Records'* R&B and Jazz music. One night, after I had been in Van Nuys alone for a couple of days working in the studio with Lonnie the engineer looked at me and asked, "Aren't you a little uncomfortable here?" I said, "Why? What do you mean?" He said, "Well, you're the only white person here." I looked around, and about twenty African-American people surrounded me. They were all my friends, and it hadn't even dawned on me that I was the only white person there! I asked him, "Should I be feeling uncomfortable? Because I'm not!"

I never 'got' the whole racist thing. I mean, we all share around 99% of the same DNA. Just a small part of our DNA differentiates ourselves from others. I read somewhere that we have 80% of the same DNA as a banana; so, on a broader scale of life itself, all life is interconnected. I think the foundation of racism is more about not understanding a culture, which leads to fear, which leads to hatred. It should never be an issue to begin with. No baby is born racist. That shit is baked in. Yes, racism is real where it exists. However, an entire industry exists to call out contrived racism in order to advance a political agenda, but that's a whole other story. Anyway, these people I worked with in Van Nuys were kind, encouraging, professional and cool; they also happened to be black.

The more we work to understand and appreciate each other; the better off we will be as a society.

The Van Nuys experience was musical and amazing; it was a great growth-period for me. I gained so much soul. I learned how to become funkier. I learned a depth musically that only working with great African-American producers and artists can do for you. Also, we brought in musical greats to perform on the album like Gerald Albright, Brenda Lee Eager, Teri Lynne Carrington, Michael (Patches) Stewart, and, of course Glen Myerscough and Carl Joiner. The CD came out great, although it took a long while for it to be mixed and mastered. In fact, I had no idea when we were recording the music just how long it would take to complete the process.

•••••

One Sunday night in May of 1989, I was at the end of a six-day, six-night workweek, performing poolside all week during the day in 100% weather and doing long, involved big band corporate gigs at night. Stephanie and Scotty had organized a yard sale at the house that weekend, and they dragged everything into the garage after the sale.

When I arrived home after midnight that night, I was beside myself with exhaustion after working in the heat all those days at poolside, and completing an especially hard engagement with my band that night. I needed to park my van in the garage because it was full of equipment. When I opened the garage, I saw a huge glass table in front and I realized that I needed to move it in order to get the van in.

As I lifted the table ever so slightly and started pulling it, the one-inch pane of glass came undone from the frame and crashed through, breaking and slicing completely through my socks into the tops of my ankles, cutting my feet all the way to the bone. I wrested the glass off of me, bleeding profusely, and crawled towards the entry door to the house. When I got to the door, I began to scream out for help. Everyone was sleeping.

After a few minutes, Stephanie came to the door and saw me in a pool of blood. I had already lost so much blood I was passing out. She ran and woke Scotty and they lifted me into the car and drove me the three blocks to the Emergency Room at *Desert Hospital*. I was given blood. My left foot required about a hundred stitches. My right foot needed only about twenty stitches.

I was in massive pain, and I only had one day off before I had to work another six-day, six-night week. Hobbling, I made it through the following week and the week after that before I could actually walk properly again, all the time moving heavy equipment and standing up to perform all day long. I just couldn't afford to take any time off. I had a family to feed, and I was taught to be a man and suck it up. I had become extremely tough when I needed to be.

It's amazing what your body and mind can endure when you have no choice.

We had sent my daughter Regina out to spend the summer with my dad and Sandra in Kennett, Missouri. She was almost sixteen and going into tenth grade. Regina worked at Maynard's medical office all summer, and in August, Stephanie and I brought Kevin, Rachel and Taddy back to Missouri to spend a few days and then bring Regina back home with us.

Maynard, Tad and Bill Sisler
1989

We had a nice visit, going to *Liberty Land* in Memphis with my dad. Kimberley had dropped out of the medical program at *UMKC* after only a year, and while she was up there, she married a young Middle Eastern man named Osama.

You can imagine how Sandra and all of the people back in small-town Kennett, Missouri received that. We met Osama, and actually went bowling with him while we were there. It was a total mismatch. He was a nice kid, but the relationship only lasted a few months. In Kansas City, Kimberley was trying to find herself, reaching beyond her cocoon of protection in Kennett.

Eventually, Kimberley decided to become a nurse and she enrolled into a nursing program down in Memphis. Meanwhile, my sister Suzanne's children were having babies of their own. On October 5, 1989, Wendy gave birth to Logan (my parent's first great-grandchild). On October 9, 1990, Lori had a son named Jim…shortly afterwards on July 22, 1991, Wendy had a lovely daughter named Brynn. Not to be outdone, Lori had another son named Sam on March 27, 1992.

Kevin, Regina, Maynard, Rachel and Taddy
1989

•••••

Stephanie was not happy living with Scotty in our house any more. He had been with us for two years, and his alcoholic behavior wasn't helping the situation. She was dealing with some depression again anyway and our house on Miraleste Court was feeling more and more dangerous with gunshots over our back fence.

We found a rental house near our old San Martin Circle house, on the next block over. In September of 1989, we moved into a house on Loma Vista Circle in Palm Springs, and Scotty found a place to stay with an old drummer friend of his.

We were back in a nice area, and for a moment in time, it seemed to help Stephanie. She was working hard for Greg and Paul; her stress level was always high, but during this period I was very proud of her accomplishments. I was constantly worried about her, even though, at this point, she was thriving in her work and respected and loved by all.

In October of 1989, Paul Rose called me and asked me if I would do a favor and perform with my band for a Halloween event for a group of the most influential meeting planners in the desert. I was happy to do it, knowing that it would help our band to maintain our profile as the most sought-after corporate band in the Palm Springs area through *Sun Presentations.* A very popular commercial on television at the time was the *California Raisins* promotion, which featured animated raisins dancing to *I Heard It Through the Grapevine*, a huge Motown hit. Paul had the idea of dressing my band up as raisins, with me as the *Fruit of the Loom* grapes. I thought it was a novel enough idea, so I agreed. We performed for the event in costume, doing an entire set of *Motown* music, including marching in to *I Heard it Through the Grapevine.* The meeting planners loved it so much that they ended up booking us as the *California Raisins* for about fifty other events! My band members HATED it, but we made money doing it, and it was all in fun.

Carl Joiner, Steve Neilen, Michel Monsalve and Tad - California Raisins 1989

In November of 1989, Shari Kelley called me and asked me if my band would do an event on Thanksgiving for the Nationwide *Toyota* Dealers convention at the *La Quinta* Resort. I accepted the job, and they liked us so much that they hired us for the next ten years on Thanksgiving. It was really good money, but looking back; I missed ten Thanksgivings with my family. You never get that back. All you can do is vow from this moment forward to make it right. I did what I had to do to feed my family, but I never worked on Thanksgiving again after that.

•••••

I became friends with the famous singer/songwriter/television star Sonny Bono and his lovely wife, Mary. Sonny had *Bono's* restaurant in Palm Springs, and when my friend Joe Jaggi wasn't performing there, I would sit in for him on many occasions. When Sonny Bono founded the *Palm Springs Film Festival* in 1989, my band performed for the very first gala event. Later when he became the Mayor of Palm Springs and then a U.S. Congressman, we performed for him at many events.

We did an event honoring television's *Jeopardy* host Alex Trebec. He thanked us for "playing the *Jeopardy* theme correctly" as he walked to the stage!

Greg McDonald had done some questionable deal buying a music store in the mall in Palm Springs. I heard from the ex-owner later that he had been totally conned out of his store and he was owed a ton of money.

Greg was investing in the *Field of Dreams* sports memorabilia stores and somehow that went sideways, too, at some point. He also got involved in the *Palm Springs Vintage Auto Race*, and the promoter, Keith came to me a year later swearing he was going to sue Greg for stealing a couple hundred thousand dollars from him.

Stephanie was becoming concerned about all of these people making accusations against Greg, and she started to look a little closer at what they were doing at *Sun Presentations.* Paul Rose told me to go into the music store and pick out whatever I needed for the corporate band gigs, so I did. I grabbed some new equipment for which I was grateful. I offered to pay for it, but they insisted that it was a business write-off.

•••••

One night in early 1990, I was doing a private party for Governor Deukmejian and Senator Pete Wilson at the *Marriott.* I was playing an early solo in the foyer of the ballroom before my band was scheduled in the main room.

A kind, old man came and sat down on the piano bench next to me. As I was performing, we talked and joked for almost forty-five minutes. He told me that he had been a jazz singer way back when, and he had recorded a few albums way before I was born. He was delightful! I was touched by this man's kindness and willingness to sit with me and reminisce. When the man got up and left, an event organizer rushed over to me and said, "Do you know who that was?" I said that I didn't have a clue. She told me that it was Buddy Rogers, the silent film star who won the very first *Academy Award* for Best Actor in 1927 for the movie *Wings.* I had actually met and talked with Buddy Rogers! To me, that was like meeting royalty.

Shortly after that gig, I did an engagement at a country club in the desert, and the great Broadway actress Carol Channing was in attendance. She was bright and bubbly and cheerful, and I saw her many more times at other events over the years. Once again, I saw actress Jane Wyman and got a photo with her at an event. She was Ronald Reagans first wife, and could have been First Lady if fate hadn't worked out differently for her. Nevertheless, she was kind and classy as always.

In April of 1990, I got a call from an African-American promoter who wanted me to open for B.B. King in an event he was promoting. His next-door neighbor was a large, elderly female jazz vocalist and he wanted us to back her up on a few songs, and then play the rest of the set to open for Mr. King.

I had never heard of this promoter, and something felt wrong with it, but it was a thrill to open for B.B. King, so I accepted the gig. When the event came, we had not yet been paid. He promised to pay us from the proceeds at the door, so we went ahead and played. After we finished, B.B. King didn't come out to perform for at least an hour. People were screaming for him. Finally, he came out and performed.

The promoter didn't have the funds to pay B.B. King, and he had to go and borrow money from someone to get Mr. King to go on stage. We never got paid for the event. I was livid about it, and his next-door neighbor, the female vocalist, said afterwards that she thought he was a drug dealer, because he skipped town after the event.

I did get a nice write-up from Bruce Fessier in *The Desert Sun*, however…except for the comment that Bruce made about the fact that I played Billy Joel's song *My Baby Grand* on a keyboard. Bruce had written kindly about me over the years, but he always had to find something wrong to point out! Also, I had a chance to visit with B.B. King for a few minutes before the show. He was gracious and kind, and boy, could that man play the guitar!

I've been fortunate; only a handful of times in my career was I not paid for my services. I tried to make the best of this, having met and spent time with the legend B.B. King, although I needed the money; it stung that I actually lost money paying my musicians for working with me. I wasn't going to let them get ripped off too.

•••••

In mid-1990, my friend Michael Schwartz reappeared in Palm Springs. He was living in Florida and winning national ballroom dance competitions. Michael had a Mac computer and he was hip to this brand-new thing called the Internet. Nobody had heard of it before, but he showed me that we could hook our computers up to a phone line and use a network called *Z-Net* to communicate in real time by text. When he returned to Florida, we communicated by Internet many times, several years before it became mainstream. We were really on the cutting edge!

Stephanie and I had decided to keep our twins in the same classroom throughout elementary school. Educators frown on this with twins (particularly same-sex twins), generally because one is prettier or smarter or more outgoing than the other. Our twins were best friends and they always worked together. Besides, it was more practical for us to do one set of homework together with them, and as a result, they were always at the head of their class.

In third grade, Rachel was so very helpful with all the other children that she was the only child in the class who received a plaque for excellence instead of just an award at the end of the school year.

Regina, Taddy, Rachel and Kevin

Taddy was so proud of his sister and not the slightest bit jealous. Taddy was a very special boy, too.
He was always motivated to do the right thing. In fact, he was mortified if it was ever even perceived that he didn't do the right thing. He had a strong moral compass and it served him well.

It was around this time that I started running again to stay fit. I would continue to run just about every day for a few years, and then slow it down to a speed walk for many more years. On average, I made a point of walking or running about three or four miles minimum, four or five days per week. It helped to keep my lung capacity up for all the singing I was doing on a regular basis.

I also started taking naps whenever I could when I was working that night. I woke up so early with the children, and even years later it was built into my biological time clock to wake up soon after sunrise. I didn't want to give that up, working so late at night, so I took naps! I would tell people, "I sleep in shifts." I always tried to be the early bird, although most of the time I felt like the worm, dodging danger wherever I looked!

Be the early bird; don't be the worm.
But, don't be too early; remember,
the second mouse gets the cheese.

Stephanie's father Russ was devastated because his wife Barbara had left him. We went to clean out his apartment and help him move into a nicer place. The apartment was filthy. Bags of potatoes had turned into grotesque plants in their kitchen cupboards. Their bed sheets had black rings around where they slept. They hadn't been washed or changed in years.

We helped Russ clean up his life. He got a new car and some new furniture. He got a solo gig, working at a really nice restaurant close to the *Biltmore* in Palm Springs. Russ was still drinking, but not as heavily as he had, and his health seemed to be improving somewhat. After a few months, he couldn't have been happier, and Stephanie was thrilled because she HATED Barbara with a passion.

•••••

My daughter Regina and I were very close. Her mother was sometimes hard on her, because she was the oldest. Many times, during her formative years, Regina came to me for reassurance, and I just loved this girl. She always worked so hard to help.

Regina and Taddy - 1988

Regina loved to watch cartoons. She loved to play the role of teacher in the game of "school" with her younger siblings. She was kind of a slob, but whenever her room became dirty, I would just pile everything on the bed and she would have to put it away before she slept. And... she made up for it by cleaning the house sometimes. Her mother would instruct her to "clean the front three rooms" and it would be done quickly with the smell of *Pine Sol* pungent in the air.

My mother had a mantra when I was growing up: When the beds are made and the dishes are done, the house is halfway clean. There's some wisdom in that.

At the Loma Vista Circle house, my girls shared a bedroom and my boys shared another. All the kids were helpful when we asked them to be. Kevin was always kind and gracious and caring to everyone, but he was going through a rough patch towards the end of Junior High School.

He and his buddy got caught shoplifting at *Wal-Mart*, and then they got caught again. The security people at *Wal-Mart* were great to us, but Kevin was banned forever from *Wal-Mart*...or at least until he was old enough to not look like the photo they put up in the office! That was about the worst Kevin ever got. Even through that experience, he was never defiant. He was ashamed and devastated, but he bounced back quickly and never did that again. He was like me in so many ways, especially in his personality. I had made the same mistake in Junior High School, and I almost got caught! I always felt a very strong affinity to my first son.

•••••

In May of 1990, I got a call from a promoter. Tito Puente was going to perform with his twenty-piece band at the *Riviera Hotel* in Palm Springs. They needed someone to open for the Latin legend, and to provide the sound equipment for the group. I offered to do it. Of course, I got paid in advance this time!

When I got there, I couldn't believe that all twenty pieces in his band were acoustic instruments. I had to put separate microphones on each one and it was scary, but the sound turned out great and the band was phenomenal.

I was never a huge Barry Manilow fan, but when I heard Tito Puente's group do their version of *Copacabana*, I loved the song from that moment on. Pat Rizzo had performed with Tito's group when he was younger, and he came over and sat in on flute. It was a great experience to meet the legend himself, Tito Puente, and to work with that group for one night.

CHAPTER FORTY-THREE
Stephanie Discovers Wrongdoing

Life tends to change in an instant. One day, Stephanie discovered that *Sun Presentations* was taking much more money for their bands than she thought. They were paying the bands only about half of what *Sun Presentations* was being paid for their services.

Stephanie realized that Paul Rose and Greg McDonald were ripping me off hugely, and apparently, they had been doing it for as long as I had been working for them. I was getting about half to split between my band members and myself, and they were keeping the other half as their fee.

Stephanie called the *State of California, Labor Board* and she found out that agents are only allowed by law to take a maximum of twenty-five percent for an engagement, and most take between ten and fifteen percent. Also, she found out that *Sun Presentations* was not licensed as a talent agency.

Looking back on that moment, I realize that Stephanie was in the process of experiencing a manic event. It was like a perfect storm for her. Her grandfather had taught her about truth and justice, about doing the right thing, and in her mind, she believed that she had been aiding Greg and Paul in basically stealing from musicians on a huge level for more than two years. She couldn't take enough Xanax to be okay. She had a complete meltdown. She refused to go back to work and stayed in bed crying for an entire weekend.

At this point in time, my band was the top band for *Sun Presentations.* We were working all the time, doing huge corporate events, and between the gigs and the poolside gig I was making good money. I didn't want to rock the boat. I was respected everywhere I went, and I was paralyzed with fear at losing the ability to feed my family. I was doing very well. Admittedly, I was working ridiculously hard for the money, and in retrospect, it would have been great to get what I deserved, but I never looked at it as being as terrible as she thought it was at that moment. Many musicians work for union scale, and I was making more than that. It was true, however, that Paul and Greg were acting outside of the confines of the law, and Stephanie's sense of justice, in her manic condition, became frenzied and all consuming.

Stephanie wouldn't...she couldn't...allow this to happen anymore. I suggested that she take a couple weeks off and then we would have a little perspective. She screamed at me in a zealous tone that I just didn't get it. She wasn't going to let this go on for another minute.

Not only was she going to quit, but also, she was going to sue them for the money they had 'stolen' from us. I knew that if she did this, I obviously could not continue to work for them, or to work the poolside job. She didn't think I would be fired from the poolside gig, but I knew better.

Stephanie told me that summer was coming on anyway, and the corporate jobs were going away for the summer. By the end of the summer, we would have it all figured out. I knew better, but I could not talk her out of it.

Shortly after she quit *Sun Presentations*, we found a crusty, cranky old attorney out in Bermuda Dunes who agreed to file a case with the *Labor Board* in my name against *Sun Presentations,* Greg McDonald and Paul Rose. Suddenly and unwittingly, I was the face of Stephanie's rage and of her need to seek justice at any cost.

As I predicted, I was fired from the poolside job at the *Marriott* within a week. Steve Neilen had just bought a house in Desert Hot Springs, and he was counting on that income. Summer was coming on strong, so I started performing at *Nonchalance*, a dive bar with a piano bar and dance floor in Palm Desert. I did a duo with Steve. The club was packed at night, and the money they were paying us was decent enough income to tide us over while we were figuring out what was ahead.

Carl Joiner and Vickie Sprague 1992

Greg McDonald came after us with both barrels. He filed a defamation and slander suit against me. He filed a separate suit claiming I had 'stolen' the equipment they had given to me from the music store. Paul started talking to all of my band members, trying to get them to jump ship from me and offering them lucrative packages if they would stay with *Sun.* Although I understood that everyone needs to take care of his or her own situations, I was forever grateful for the loyalty and kindness that Steve Neilen and Carl Joiner showed me throughout this period.

On the other hand, Chuck Buffamonte saw greener pastures with Paul, and that would have been fine with me, but Paul convinced Chuck to file a small claims lawsuit against me claiming that we had written songs together and I had not put his name on them. That was devastating to me.

First of all, I had copyrights on all of the material in question proving I had written the songs a couple years at least before I even met Chuck. But, even more, if he would have just come to me and said, "Hey, man, will you consider making me a co-writer on this song that we played around with?" ...I would have gladly put his name on it. I've co-written songs with many people before and since, giving them fifty percent where ninety-nine percent of the song is actually mine and one percent is theirs, but I always felt an obligation to give credit where credit was due. But, Chuck crossed the line in so many ways. First, he showed his true colors by aligning with them. Second, it was beyond ridiculous for him to hit me below the belt with a lawsuit just to please Paul and Greg and to get into their good graces.

It was extremely uncomfortable to show up in court against Chuck. Mike Costley showed up with Chuck to give him support for whatever reason that day, which was also painful for me. These guys were my friends, and it was completely wrong for him to act in this way towards me. For what it's worth, that lawsuit was thrown out of court. The judge wouldn't even consider it after a brief hearing.

In general, I am a nice person. I have found that many people equate being nice with being weak. They will put you into a position where you are compelled to show your backbone. It's uncomfortable, but necessary. Eventually, they will get the message. Even still, we must never allow other people's attitudes, emotions or behavior to stop ourselves from being optimistic and kind.

I knew that Greg was trying to intimidate us into dropping the lawsuit. Since he had absolutely no evidence that I stole anything from the music store, that suit was eventually dropped, and the baseless slander suit lingered on without a hearing as we went to the labor board over the wrongdoing of *Sun Presentations.* It was a deep and emotional time for us. Paul made sure that I was blackballed from all of the hotels that I had proudly walked into as the top band for those years.

It was during these days that I was particularly grateful for the church gig I was working. Every Sunday, people I loved, who loved me back and appreciated my contribution, surrounded me. Dr. Tom's messages were spiritually uplifting every time, and it helped me to stay on track throughout it all.

Through this period, I also got to meet and work with celebrities and heavy-hitters of the movement, including Dr. Wayne Dyer, Teri Cole Whittaker, Deepak Chopra, Anthony Robbins and Mark Victor Hansen. I was able to stay spiritually strong, and, in fact, to contribute a certain ministry through my music and positive thoughts on the pulpit with Dr. Tom.

Sometimes, Stephanie and the kids would come to church to see me, and whenever my mother was in town, she was there also on Sundays. Although this was also a great influence on Stephanie, I could see the burden on her soul as she fought her way through our lawsuit and her depression at the same time. She was so strong and so weak, all at the same time.

At the church, I met and befriended the great actor-singer Herb Jeffries. Herb was already an old man when we met and he performed with me. He ended up living to be 100 years old. Herb was best known for his hit song *Flamingo* with the Duke Ellington Orchestra, but he was also the first African-American cowboy movie star back in the 1930's. Mostly, he was a kind, unassuming man with a big deep voice.

Tad with Herb Jeffries 1996

Another man who had an impact on me was Billy Farrell. He was also an elderly man when we met. Billy had a huge hit back in the 1940's with a song entitled *You've Changed.* I learned it and played it for him to sing at many events.

Billy Farrell showed me a photo of himself with Frank Sinatra and Sammy Davis, Jr. in the 1940's, and he told me "At the time this photo was taken, they were both unknown and I was the big star!"

He had somehow been a one-hit wonder as they went on to become legends, and I understood the bitter taste of regret in his voice. I would cheer him up by telling him, "Bill, you had one more hit than I ever did!"

A few years later, another acquaintance of mine, Frankie Laine, passed away. Frankie had a HUGE career, selling something like ninety million records. He was a household name in the 1940's and 1950's. When I told my kids he died, they said, "Frankie who?"

Be careful what you chase. Fame is fleeting, even for the very famous. The love you give and receive will endure long after life is done. Chase love, not fame. Do what you do for the love of the craft, and if fame comes, it's just a bonus.

Around this time, I did a corporate event with my band, backing up the *DeCastro Sisters.* These three ladies had a huge hit with the song *Teach Me Tonight* in 1954, but at this point, they were in their seventies, and not at all very healthy for their age. Although they were sweet and put on the best show they could, the client was unhappy because the performance was below par. I was always so grateful, because, more often than not, I could control the quality of the music as the band leader. There were a few exceptions, here and there, but we made the best of it and made sure that the quality of our musicianship backing other acts was superb.

My band and I also backed up *The Diamonds* for a few

corporate events. This group had sixteen billboard hits back in the 1950's including *Little Darlin'* and *The Stroll.* They were energetic and the audiences loved them. They did a killer version of *Unchained Melody*. I borrowed their version with my band, and for many years it was a big closing number for us, usually bringing down the house with huge applause.

Riff Markowitz was an aging television producer. He settled in Palm Springs and created the *Palm Springs Follies*, an exceptional show exclusively featuring performers who were over fifty years old, including some stars from past years like *The Mills Brothers.* He called me to play piano for their rehearsals, and I ended up doing the gig for many years. It was cool and my sight-reading "chops" got better. I also gained some experience in coordination of choreography, which helped me later in similar experiences. I once jokingly complained to Riff that I was only in my early thirties, so I couldn't be in the show, and I was going to sue him for age discrimination! The *Palm Springs Follies* were a staple of entertainment in downtown Palm Springs for quite some time, and Riff made a ton of money producing these shows.

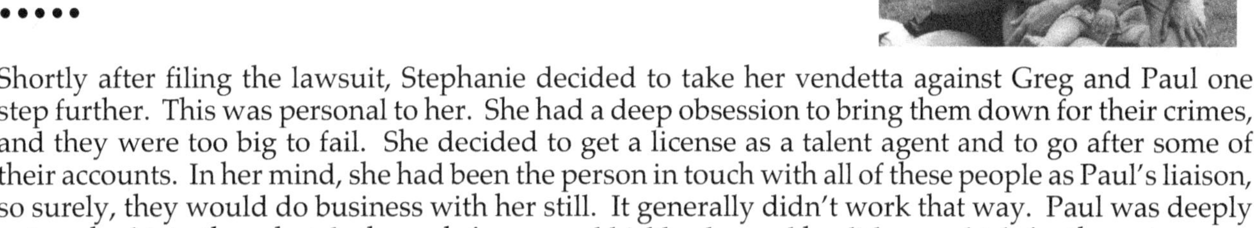
Betsy, Elaine and Shana 1991

•••••

On June 15, 1990, my sister Betsy gave birth to a daughter, Shana. This was a welcome lift to an otherwise excruciating month.

•••••

Shortly after filing the lawsuit, Stephanie decided to take her vendetta against Greg and Paul one step further. This was personal to her. She had a deep obsession to bring them down for their crimes, and they were too big to fail. She decided to get a license as a talent agent and to go after some of their accounts. In her mind, she had been the person in touch with all of these people as Paul's liaison, so surely, they would do business with her still. It generally didn't work that way. Paul was deeply entrenched into these hotels through favors and kickbacks, and he did a good job for them, too.

Sara Melendez and Hillery Johnson 1990

Hillery Johnson stepped in. He saw what was going on, as I was recording my album even still throughout this period with him. On my trips into Los Angeles, I would record in his studio, and in the time in-between sessions, I would go into his offices and talk with his associates including his daughter Lajuana, who was also his secretary. Hillery's girlfriend, Sara Melendez was big in the industry, and she was helping me with my image, so we would all talk about everything.

In addition to *Valley Vue Records,* Hillery had another corporation that he had done nothing with up to this point. It was called *Valley Vue Entertainment.* He knew that Stephanie had promoted concerts, and he wanted to promote some concerts as well, so he offered for us to go into partnership with him and use the *Valley Vue Entertainment* Corporation as our name. We accepted and went to work trying to build this company as we were fighting the labor board lawsuit.

Stephanie met a kind elderly man who owned some business property in an office park on Highway 111 in Palm Desert. He offered to allow her to move into an office for free. She accepted, and after a month or two in the office building, the owner announced that he was going to start charging her rent, after she had moved desks, phone systems and she was pretty much entrenched. It was a sly move by the man, offering her free office space and then insisting on rent. So, now, she had to figure out how to keep the rent paid on the office with little work coming in. It was a scary period for us.

We needed a computer for the office. We went to the computer store and bought our first *Apple* computer. It was a *Macintosh SE30,* with a whopping four megabytes of internal memory. We bought a state-of-the-art laser printer with it. We got a fax machine, which was essential for business at the time. I loved that computer, and became a lifetime *Apple* fan. I only wish I had invested in *Apple* stock back then…

Stephanie worked very hard trying to get new accounts. One of the country club managers she worked with told her not to worry. She said that *Sun Presentations* didn't control ALL the business, and there should always be enough overflow to keep the bills paid while you're building your company.

I created a promotional packet for our new company. In it, I mistakenly wrote that *Valley Vue Records* was a subsidiary of *Capitol Records.* In fact, *Valley Vue* wasn't a subsidiary, but *Valley Vue* instead had a distribution deal with *Capitol,* and I misunderstood when I was told about it.

Paul Rose pounced on my mistake. He still had friends at *Capitol* from his payola days, and he had them do him a favor and write a cease and desist letter to us, telling us to retract our statement. Paul went a step further and persuaded *Capitol* to drop *Valley Vue* from their distribution arm. It was a dirty deed, and I was devastated.

Hillery wasn't too upset about it. He just found another distributor that actually paid him more per unit. I was grateful for his kindness and steady hand. But, it was literally like being at war with a powerful adversary, and I was scared.

•••••

A gruff, cantankerous man named "Mac" ran the *Musicians Union* in the desert. He had long been angry with Paul Rose and Greg McDonald, because they ignored the union in so many instances and refused to file union contracts unless it was absolutely required. As I mentioned, even the half of what they were paying the musicians was still more, at times, than union scale. But, the union controlled two hotels in the desert, the *Riviera Hotel* and the *Marquis Hotel,* both in Palm Springs.

Mac offered to help Stephanie to secure both hotels as long as she would file union contracts. She agreed; because of that favor from Mac we finally started to have enough business to pay the rent on the office space. We were still struggling to keep all of our bills paid, and the managers of *Nonchalance* were never happy when I had to send in another performer, usually on a weekend night, so I could work some of these gigs that Stephanie was getting. In a sense, I was her ace in the hole. She was able to boast that she was the exclusive booking agent of the Tad Sisler Band, which was very popular among corporate clients.

Mac helped Steve Neilen and me to get a weekend poolside gig at the *Desert Princess Hotel.* It was on the north end of Palm Springs in the windy area, and we only lasted about a month out there. The wind was so bad that umbrellas would fly across the pool and practically impale sunbathers. One Saturday we had such a bad sandstorm that it ruined most of my equipment. It was depressing, after having worked at the *Marriott, which* was a much nicer resort. After that, Steve and I moved over to the *Riviera Hotel* in Palm Springs and did a weekend poolside gig there for about a year.

•••••

In August of 1990, the great Broadway dancer Jacque D'Amboise embarked upon a huge undertaking. He was going to organize a children's dance recital at the *McCallum Theatre* featuring hundreds of children from all over the Palm Springs area.

His management came to us and wanted to hire several pianists to rehearse the children at the local elementary schools, and one pianist to work with Jacque throughout the main rehearsals following all of the teaching sessions with the kids.

I coordinated all of the pianists, and I also went around to local elementary schools as a pianist working with dance instructors who taught the children their dance moves. It was fascinating and fun to learn music in choreography from such a great performer.

One of the dance instructors was Elyssa Guardino, the wife of my friend, the great screen actor Harry Guardino. Elyssa was young and pretty; she had a newborn baby, so I would rock the baby with one foot, as I played piano and pedaled with the other foot! The children at the schools were delightful, and some remembered me later in life when I would happen upon them. They would come up to me as teenagers' years after this and say, "Hi, Mr. Sisler!" It was weird being called that by anybody, in my early thirties!

When we finally finished the process of all the separate rehearsals at all of the different elementary schools all over the desert, buses of children arrived at the *McCallum Theatre.* The performances with all of the children together were amazing. The concert was sold-out and Mr. D'Amboise raised money and awareness with the project. He was always kind and professional.

•••••

Our labor suit against *Sun Presentations* dragged on and on. We drove to Riverside to the Labor Board and went before a moderator on numerous occasions. I had to sit across from Greg and Paul at a table. Greg did everything he could to charm the moderator. He was a friendly man with a big personality. Greg had a knack to make people like him.

They brought in many of my musician friends to testify on their behalf, which was painful to us. I was grilled over and over again by Greg's attorneys, and all I could do was to answer truthfully exactly what my experience had been.

They did everything they could to intimidate us. Our attorney was past retirement and he had only taken on our case to have something to do. He was generally brusque, irascible and disinterested, but he plodded through on our behalf.

•••••

With her talent agency, Stephanie was doing everything by the books. She honestly thought that musicians would flock to her, because she only took the legal amount of commission and paid more in general than Paul and Greg ever had.

She also thought that they would band against these people who abused their power and ripped them all off. She was wrong. Most musicians, unfortunately, are just happy to be working at all and many have no business sense. They are artists, and they have no backbone when it comes to going up against the people who control all the work. In fact, too many musicians are happy to work in the nightclubs for practically no money, just to perform. The fact that Paul and Greg were paying them more than they would make in the clubs kept them coming back for more. This broke Stephanie's heart. Admittedly, sucking it up and staying with Paul and Greg to keep stability in our lives had been my first instinct, but as we got deeper into the lawsuit, I became a cheerleader for Stephanie and for her desire for justice.

•••••

In late September of 1990, Stephanie decided that she needed to go back East to visit her aunts and cousins, once again. She had been back twice since her Uncle Don Bleasdale passed away; I had gone with her one of those times, but I could not afford to miss work this time. Don had been an attorney; Don and his wife, Stephanie's aunt Faith, had stepped up and allowed Stephanie and Russ, Jr. to live with them and their children for a short while after Stephanie's grandfather's stroke. Stephanie was slowly spiraling out of control. Her mood swings were all over the place at this point. She carried an enormous amount of stress and had way too much on her plate.

When she flew back to New York and made her way to Westchester County, Stephanie later admitted that she hoped to see a boy she had a crush on when she was there as a teenager. When she got to

Faith's house, Stephanie began to drink and cry about the fact that she was estranged from her mother, Alice. Stephanie didn't even know if her mother was still alive.

She asked pointed questions about what her mother was like, and Faith honestly told her that she recalled that Stephanie's mother's family had a history of mental illness. According to Faith, Alice was always a bit unstable. A few of Stephanie's aunts and cousins had committed suicide on her mother's side of the family, and Faith was worried for Stephanie.

When the man showed up whom Stephanie was enamored with, when she was younger, he didn't apparently react to her in the way she hoped, and she drank more. Everything came crashing down on her soul during that trip. Stephanie drank so much and lost so much control that her aunt Faith ended up putting her on a plane early to come home. Stephanie came home a tortured soul, with more questions than answers about herself.

As she continued to spiral, Stephanie's huge mood swings continued. One night, as I was getting ready to leave for work, she began to drink and I told her to please stop drinking. The children didn't like her drinking and I wasn't going to be there to help them deal with it. She became very angry and stormed out the door.

Stephanie drove to the Trinidad Hotel that evening; she went to the lounge that had been *Patti Z* and was now *Bobby A's*. Antheny Shane was performing on that night. He was a cheesy but popular Italian singer in the desert, with a good voice and a pretty good following.

Stephanie had told me once that she had a crush on Antheny. It was kind of weird to me because he was much older and not someone I would consider sexy if I were a woman, but even so, as a young man, I was naturally jealous of her feelings for him. She went there specifically to 'show me' that she didn't need me to tell her what to do and she could do whatever she wanted.

She continued to drink heavily at the nightclub, and some friends told me later that it was embarrassing and they were worried for her. At some point, she stumbled out and got into her car. As she was driving away, a policeman pulled her over and gave her a sobriety test. Her blood alcohol content was 2.7, which was way above the legal limit. He arrested her for driving under the influence of alcohol, impounded our car and took her to jail.

When I got home from work that night, I got a call from the jail telling me she was there and they were going to keep her overnight. The following morning, I went to bail her out and she was still drunk. It was a miserable time. She was in a deep depression, and the legal fees and higher insurance rates didn't help. We were already struggling to keep the bills paid.

•••••

For a short while, the DUI shocked Stephanie into sobriety. She was forced by the court to go to Alcoholics Anonymous meetings, and that seemed to help. My sister Suzanne came out for Christmas of 1990 with three of her four children, Charles, Lori and Wendy.

Lori, Michael & Wendy 1989

We had a warm Christmas and made the best of the situation. Lori baked sweets, and we all laughed and played games with my children. Christmas sometimes worked against us, as it would bring up old memories for Stephanie and add to her depression, but for this year, it was helpful to remind her of the love she had all around her.

Charles and Margaret

Suzanne drove back to North Carolina with three of her children. Soon after, Charles would meet a girl named Margaret and marry her. She was a patient, kind woman who stayed with him through his manic episodes. On July 30, 1999, they had a son, Gregory, and later their daughter Elizabeth was born on January 24, 2003.

Vicki Diestlekamp called me from the *Esmeralda* Resort and asked a favor…the *Angel View* foundation was hosting a Christmas party for their children with muscular dystrophy. The resort was funding the event and they asked us to donate a Santa Claus and a couple elves for the children. Vicki was sending a lot of entertainment our way, which was wonderful. I wanted to do whatever I could to keep her happy. She was a good friend to me aside from the work we got.

I volunteered to be Santa. I dressed up in the red suit and my twins were my elves! It was an amazing experience. When I walked in, I was like a God to these lovely children with wide eyes. I danced throughout the room, saying, "Ho, ho, ho!" When I sat in Santa's chair, so many children who were physically bent from dystrophy and unable to control their reflexes were placed into my arms. They were all delighted to see Santa!

I gave each child as much incredible love and care as I could, looking into their eyes and reminding them that they were a very good boy or girl and Santa loved them very much. It truly was one of the holiest experiences of my life; Rachel and Taddy looked on with care, giving each child the same amount of love in their own special ways. I volunteered for three more years afterwards to do this party as Santa with the twins as elves, and each time it was a sacred event.

Rachel and Taddy as Elves
Tad as Santa - 1990

•••••

Slowly, my mother came back into my life. At first, it was through a request from her for me to help her. She was struggling and my father owed her so much back alimony and child support. She had finally found an attorney in Missouri, and he was suing my father for those funds. She knew that I had lived there, and she needed my advice about the attorney he had, and the judge. I felt sorry for my mother and I missed her in my life, so I tried to help her.

Parents should be able to reconcile their differences without bringing their children into the middle. It's already painful enough for them.

My father's attorney was Wendell Crow. Wendell is the father of the famous recording artist Sheryl Crow. Sheryl grew up in Kennett, and she was younger than me, but I remember meeting her when I was a teenager. Wendell was a good and powerful attorney; the continuing litigation was painful for my mother and my father, and for me too. I always felt like I was unwittingly in the middle of it all, and I loved them both. But, again, I felt sorry for my mother. She was living with my grandmother and taking care of her.

Elaine was longing for a companion. Her on-again, off-again boyfriend Dick Kane, who had a wife but swore he wasn't with her anymore, wasn't fulfilling her needs. And, Elaine never did and never would get over the loss of her relationship with my father. My mother would say, "The world is made for two." That statement is true to some extent, if you think about it. Even still, when she spoke of Maynard, she would refer to him as "my husband."

•••••

In early 1991, I had completed my album and we needed to begin the process of mixing the tracks. By chance, I ran into Jeff Edwards and we began to talk again. At this point, Jeff had married Lolita Falk and they had two small children. Jeff was beginning to make some ground working in the studios in Los Angeles, and he offered to mix my record with me.

Although I was still apprehensive because of my negative past experience with Jeff, I knew he was very good at what he did, and I was eager to learn about the mixing process from someone willing to teach me. I also thought that possibly the experience of having children of his own had mellowed him somewhat. I contacted Hillery Johnson, and they worked out the details.

Soon after, Jeff and I went into Hillery's studio to begin the mixing process. It was fascinating to me.

We would spend an hour equalizing a kick drum, and then move on to the next sound. When we had all the sounds right, with the proper effects attached to each, we would start to build on the mix, first with the drums, then to add bass and all of the other instruments, ending with the vocals or lead instrument.

The mixes came out great, and I learned so much from that experience. It was amazing to work in a full-on 2-inch reel-to-reel 24-track studio with a huge mixing board. I vowed from that experience to eventually own and manage my own recording facility.

•••••

I found a renowned photographer and we did a photo shoot for the album. Following the mix, Hillery booked a mastering session for me at *Bernie Grundman*, the premier mastering studio in Los Angeles. The mastering process brought out frequencies I had never dreamed of, from the overall mix of each song. We decided to name the album *So Good to Come Home To*, and the title cut would be the first song I ever played for Hillery at the Canyon Hotel, *You'd Be So Good to Come Home To.*

In May of 1991 Sara and Hillery organized a CD release party for me with Stephanie. It would be held at *Hank's Café* in Palm Springs, where I was still performing. My sister Kathy and brother-in-law Steven flew out with their boys. We rented a limousine for the event. The release party was a huge success with hundreds of people, but we didn't have any CD's to sell or give away yet.

Hillery was reorganizing. He was planning to move to Palm Springs. He had sold his house in Van Nuys and found a house in Palm Springs. He found a separate facility in Palm Springs for the recording studio and offices. Over the next few months, we worked with my friend Bruce Feagle, building out the studio with a control room, tracking room and vocal booth. Hillery hired a couple of marketing people. It would be more than a year before I would get my CD's. I learned a valuable lesson: Don't have an album release party until you have an album.

•••••

It's probably not a good idea to have a party to celebrate something that hasn't happened yet.

In late May of 1991 we went out one night and Stephanie got really drunk. Somebody gave us some cocaine. I did a little and she did a lot, and I stayed up with her until she took some Xanax and passed completely out right before dawn. I hadn't been ridiculous with my partying. As an adult and a father, I never lost control. Never. I was up with the children the next morning taking them to school, not feeling great but being functional.

Around noon, I got a phone call from our attorney and he told me that we won the lawsuit against Greg and Paul. The *Labor Board* had ruled that we should be awarded $80,000.00 going back one year, which was the limit for Labor suits. If we wanted, we could sue them in civil court for an additional $250,000.00 that they had taken above and beyond what they paid me for previous years, but the attorney told us that Greg would probably hide his assets before we came close to winning anything.

The attorney also mentioned that our case would be used as precedent in future Labor cases involving private contractors as a deterrent for anyone else, should they decide to do something similar. In other words, our case would be enshrined in the law books. Collecting from Greg would probably be close to impossible, though, the attorney mentioned, because there are no teeth in the Labor code to insure compensation. This was huge. This was as close to getting justice as Stephanie could ever get. It was what she had prayed for.

I tried to wake Stephanie to tell her the good news, but I couldn't. She was completely out of it. So, I waited for hours for her to come around to consciousness. It was surreal to me. I had learned that she had at least won a moral victory, if not a financial one, and I couldn't even tell her yet.

When she finally came to, it took some time for us to feel the actual feeling that we won. It was a bittersweet victory. We had lost so much in order to win. Later, we would settle with Greg for $35,000.00, and he paid us slowly in increments of $500-5,000 dollars over two years. The money we got from the settlement was nothing compared to the income we had lost from being blackballed by Greg. He knew that he had won in the long run anyway.

Sometimes, winning entails losing more than you eventually gain. Moral currency doesn't pay the bills. Choose your battles wisely.

Stephanie was sober after this for the next month or two of 1991. She wasn't drinking, and she was working on her health and well-being. She was still taking too many Xanax, but I was just grateful for her even-temperedness whenever it happened. Since we were paying so much rent at this point on the Palm Desert office location, she decided to move our offices to a nice complex in downtown Palm Springs. We completed the move in May of 1991.

CHAPTER FORTY-FOUR
Concert Promotion

Hillery wanted to utilize Stephanie's talents to promote a concert. He had the idea of putting together a *Power Jam* with four Top-40 artists. We had a mutual friend, Judy Gilliard, who was the general manager of the top FM radio station in the desert, *KPSI 100.5 Power Radio*. At this point in time, FM radio was a powerhouse in media and advertising. Partnering with *KPSI* would give us a huge amount of exposure in the Palm Springs area. We met and decided to produce a concert in June of 1991 at the *California Angel's* Spring Training Stadium in Palm Springs. We would call it *POWER JAM '91*.

This was my first experience with building a concert from the ground up. Fortunately, Stephanie already had some experience producing headliner events. It was fascinating to me, and I jumped into learning about every facet of promotion and production. We had to work with agents to book the acts. We organized staging, lighting and contracting with the venue. We had to deal with ticketing through Ticketmaster. Judy Gilliard helped us organize radio advertising in different formats. We printed posters and manufactured T-Shirts. When the artist's Riders came in, we had to put together a green room, and get mobile-home-style trailers for each artist. It was deep. We had to hire security, and also coordinate additional police with the Palm Springs Police Department. We needed permits, and additional permits to sell concessions.

We procured the artists Timmy T, Will to Power, Candyman and Tara Kemp. Each of these artists had a major hit on the *Billboard Top 40* in 1991. With the exception of Candyman, they all sang to tracks. Candyman had a DJ-style band, pretty much also rapping to tracks with some instrumentation. The concert was a sell-out, but we still lost about $5,000.00 after expenses.

Power Jam loads stadium with Top-40 bands

By PAMELA LITTLE
The Desert Sun

Who can draw the young crowds on a late June afternoon?

The Candyman can, predict local concert promoters.

The rap star will be featured at a youth music festival, Power Jam '91, being promoted by KPSI Radio and Valley Vue Entertainment at Angels Stadium June 29 at 6 p.m. Also slated to perform: Tara Kemp, The Cover Girls, Timmy T, Will To Power, Brandon, and local performer J.T. Nice. A portion of proceeds will benefit the D.A.R.E. program to fight drugs.

Valley Vue spokesman Tad Sisler said there's an audience for youth-oriented, contemporary music.

"In the past, it seemed we always brought in a '50s act . . . I don't want to say 'has been' . . . But we do feel there is a definite need to bring in this kind of entertainment," he says.

These acts might be unfamiliar to the over age 35 group, but three of them currently have a total of five songs on Billboard's top 100, including Timmy T with his tune "One More Try," which has sold over a million copies. He's opened for groups including New Kids on the Block, Expose, Tiffany and Stevie B.

Kemp, whose second single "Piece of My Heart," is inching toward the top 10, is already in the Top 40 after only five weeks.

Brandon's "Kisses in the Night" is approaching Top 40 after five weeks on the chart. "It's a surprise to us that as a brand new artist, he's doing so well," Sisler says.

Candyman, whose "Knockin' Boots" hit the top 10 last November, has completed a tour of Europe and is making a special appearance for the Power Jam '91 because of its tie-in to D.A.R.E., Sisler says. "He's popular with all ages. He does a lot of work with charities."

The Cover Girls, whose "Show Me" album had five hits in the top 100, have been on tour with Stevie B and New Kids on the Block. And Will To Power is best known to many contemporary music lovers for their songs "Freebird/Baby, I Love Your Way" and "I'm Not in Love."

A local musician, J.T. Nice of Palm Springs, has been added to the bill. He's familiar to the students who've seen him perform at high schools or other youth-oriented shows in the valley.

Power Jam '91 tickets: $15 advance; $18 day of concert. Available through KPSI Radio, Ticketmaster, Record Alley, Record Shop, 99¢ Video and Valley Vue Entertainment. Information: 778-5711.

Outwardly, though, it was a huge success, with the exception that Candyman dropped his pants during his performance, and he was almost arrested. The concert was almost shut down as a result of his antics. We had to beg the powers that be to allow us to continue. My friend, Ronnie King was part of Candyman's entourage, and he was there and apologetic. Ronnie went on to become a huge producer of hip-hop music, but in these early days he was still learning to rein-in his acts. But, the stadium was filled with young people. The sound was good and the artists were vibrant…and it helped to give *Valley Vue Entertainment* a name in Palm Springs. We started to get more calls for entertainment because of the success of the concert. Hillery was happy in spite of losing a little money. Stephanie was relieved that it all came together.

In August of 1991, Hillery brought Judy Gilliard, Stephanie and me to see Al Jarreau perform in Orange County. It was a 'concert in the round' with a round stage surrounded by the audience. Lalah Hathaway opened for Al Jarreau; it was a great experience. We met Al after the concert. He couldn't have been more gracious to us. He signed our programs.

•••••

My twins turned ten years old on August 18, 1991. They were both exemplary children; helpful and kind, intelligent and giving of themselves. They were best friends and going into fifth grade. To me, they were the most beautiful people in the entire world!

They were still in the same classroom together. This would be the last year they were in the same class, and they had a very good teacher named Mr. Smith. Shortly after they started fifth grade, I purchased my first cell phone. It was an enormous contraption that looked like a huge walkie-talkie. My mobile phone must have weighed about ten pounds. This was brand-new technology (mobile phones had been around for several years, but were expensive and not in the mainstream or mass-produced until this point in time, as cell-tower networks began to appear around the world). I remember calling Stephanie from the twin's school after I dropped them off and thinking how bizarre it was to be able to actually talk on the phone from my car! It was phenomenal witnessing and experiencing the advent of technology we now take for granted.

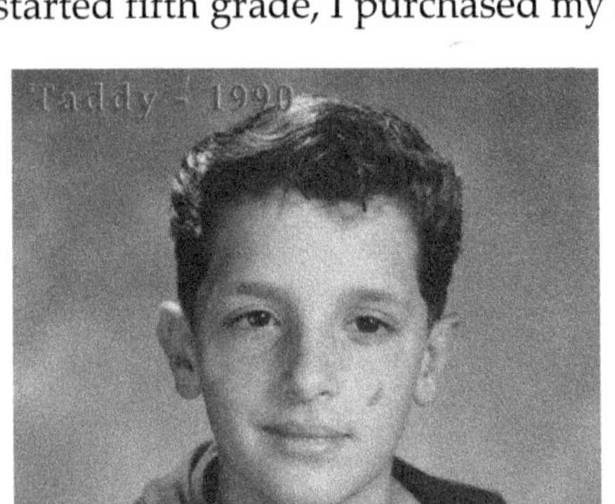

•••••

In September of 1991 a young man named Joe Elkins approached us. Joe had seen the *Power Jam* event and he wanted to promote his own concert with a headliner artist. He had this idea of taking out a personal loan to secure the artist, and then to pay the other half of all the expenses through ticket sales. Stephanie went to work on suggesting artists and venues.

At some point, Joe chose to promote a Kenny Rogers concert. We booked Kenny Rogers, who was a huge headliner at the time with plenty of *Billboard #1 Hits*, and we secured the *Hyatt Grand Champions Resort* stadium for the event, which was to be held in April of 1992. The stadium seated a little more than 10,000 people. This was going to be our biggest event yet.

September of 1991 would be the beginning of Regina's senior year of High School. She would be eighteen in December. At this point, Stephanie had established a pattern of months of good behavior and being mostly even-tempered, with a few exceptions.

Stephanie was an intense person. She was brilliant and she pulled together all of these amazing things in life…the agency, concerts, helping me with my career…she was delightful at times, sweet and kind, charming people, working hard and doing good business. Other times, her fears would overcome her and she couldn't leave the house.

For months at a time, she would be a caring, involved mother and wife, sometimes exploding with anger or mood swings; becoming depressed, out of the blue, but mostly wanting the best for her family and working her hardest towards that goal. Her life was sometimes a smooth ride for a month or two and then a roller coaster for another month or two. As the holidays approached, Stephanie started to drink again and began a terrible spiral. I was beginning to witness full-blown bipolar disorder, although I had no clue yet what it was. Her alcoholism was progressing just as my father's had; more and more, she was a belligerent drunk.

CHAPTER FORTY-FIVE
Insanity Tears my Family Apart

Regina had a boyfriend. I didn't like him. He was cocky and very inappropriate with her in front of me. He would come over to the house and take his shirt off and sit around like a stud with his arm draped around her, and it upset me. He would look at me with this "I own her" look on his face, and he had no respect. Regina was in love, and I was tolerating this guy because I loved her.

She was not as helpful around the house as she had always been and her grades were going downhill. One night, Stephanie was drunk at home. At one point, Stephanie fell out of the bedroom, half-naked in front of Regina and her friends. Regina was embarrassed and it traumatized her. I didn't realize how much this affected her until years later when we finally talked about it. I was at work that night and I didn't see it.

About a month later, Regina started to rebel. Looking back on it now, I don't blame Regina at all. She was dealing with the situation in her own way, but it all came to a head one night when I asked Regina to do some chores and she ignored me. As I was leaving for work, we got into a screaming match, which we really never, ever had done before. I grabbed her and told her to knock it off and that she was grounded.

The next morning, Regina went to her school counselor and told the counselor all about it. The school counselor called the police, and a policeman came up to our office in Palm Springs and arrested me for child abuse. I was locked in a cell for a couple hours until I could post bail. I couldn't believe it!

It was one of the most awful experiences I've ever been through, having my freedom taken away. I had never been arrested for anything, and this was surreal. I had spent my entire adult life doing everything in my power to be a good, caring, loving father, and this was insane. After a hearing and some quick research, they dropped all charges against me, but Regina was taken away from us and handed over to *Child Protective Services*, one month short of her eighteenth birthday.

When the young policeman arrested me, he was eager to right a perceived wrong, and he was inexperienced. A more experienced cop would have been able to see through the situation without jumping so quickly to a conclusion of guilt without any real evidence.

Although I've always been a huge defender and proponent of public safety and the police in general, I did get a glimpse into how it feels to be unfairly persecuted and judged on the spot. It's a terrible feeling. Alfred Hitchcock, the great producer of thriller films and television shows, once was asked what one thing he was most afraid of, and he quickly answered, "The Police." He knew the blind power that comes with the badge, if you choose to use it that way. Unfortunately, as it is with all stereotypes, only a few bad apples make the vast majority of great people look bad.

I don't think this young officer was a bad apple, although there is no question in my mind that he overreacted. The larger point was that underneath it all absolutely was an underlying problem in our household, in our marriage, with our Regina and with Stephanie's illness spiraling. It all exploded that day into a tragic chaos.

Be careful how you wield your power. Get a little experience behind you before you jump to conclusions. There is no substitute for experience. A sword used without thought and surety leaves lasting blood on its victim AND its perpetrator.

All of a sudden, Stephanie and I were caught up in court, trying to get our daughter back. Stephanie was now completely, full on, losing it. She was a basket case on all levels. At any given time, she would feel angry, depressed, sad, violated, dejected, and spiritless…

Regina told us later that, as Stephanie and I were down in this shitty courtroom in Indio fighting to get her back, *CPS* was telling her that we didn't want her anymore and she should prepare to be emancipated on her eighteenth birthday. Even though we kept fighting, we didn't get her back. On her eighteenth birthday, Regina contacted her natural father, Bucky, and told him she needed to move in with him.

•••••

Bucky had never, ever been in Regina's life. She had always fantasized about this knight in shining armor she would meet some day. Now was her time to meet him. He was living in a junky old trailer up in the high desert. He made her get a job and pay for his beer and food. He made her clean up after him. She had dropped out of school and she dealt with this for a few months while we were going through our own hell…

I never wanted Regina to experience the hell she was going through. But, out of her estrangement from our family and her negative experience with Bucky, I hoped that Regina would remember and know that I had always been there unconditionally for her, loving her with all my heart since the day I met her at the age of five… and that, ultimately, she didn't need to worry about what kind of man Bucky was. I couldn't keep her from experiencing her own pain, but maybe I could make it a little better with my love. This was a hard time for me, loving Regina as I did, yet feeling estranged from her. I prayed a lot that we would all come back together again as a family. I was the type of parent who would cry at every little school function my children were a part of, sitting in the front row, probably embarrassing them but believing with all my heart that they were the cutest kids ever. The hardest thing a parent can do is to let go and let their kids live their own lives. I knew in my heart that Regina would come back to me eventually. We had always been solid until all of this happened. We would somehow figure out a way for it to all be okay again.

Before any of this had happened with Regina, in addition to beginning to plan the Kenny Rogers concert for the following April, Stephanie had already made plans to promote and produce her own New Year's Eve show at the *Riviera Hotel* ballroom, to ring in 1992. She was going to sell tickets. The main act would be the artist Fabian, who had a few hits on the *Billboard Top 40* in the early 1960's. He was popular among the older people. Our friend Paul Casey was one of the top Elvis Presley impersonators in the corporate circuit. We had booked him several times, and in fact, I had backed him up with my band for a few shows. He agreed to perform on New Year's Eve as well. My band would open the show, and then play the dance set ringing in the New Year after the Elvis impersonator and Fabian performed.

So, we were back to selling tickets and advertising, working on show prep and ballroom seating, and everything else a big show would entail. And, through it all, Stephanie was mourning the fact that her Regina was lost to the world. She was drinking and taking way too many Xanax. Her mood swings were all over the place. She was overwhelmed, trying to pull together two huge events while attempting to keep the agency afloat. In addition to all of this, New Year's Eve was a huge day for the agency, with a dozen other acts needing coordination at other venues.

As New Year's Eve approached, my sister Kathy and my brother-in-law Steven announced that they were coming from New York for the event with their sons, Michael and Yash. My mother was going to bring my grandmother to the event. Hillery Johnson would be there with his girlfriend Sara. My children Kevin, Rachel and Taddy would be there. And, we were working hard to sell out so we could actually make money on the event.

I was going to have a full band for New Year's Eve with Carl Joiner on bass, Steve Neilen on drums, Glen Myerscough on sax, Gary Hartman on trumpet and Michel Monsalve on guitar. We got rooms for my relatives at the *Riviera Hotel*. Stephanie had hired Sheri Brown to be her assistant at *Valley Vue Entertainment*. Sheri had worked with Stephanie at *Sun Presentations*, and she was a hard worker and a calming influence on Stephanie. With Sheri's help, we pulled the event together. I was so grateful for Sheri, and we had a closeness that helped me through the ups and downs of these turbulent times.

•••••

On New Year's Eve, Stephanie began to drink early in the day. She was nervous, running in and out of the ballroom, doing seating and preparing the green room for *Fabian.* I was there meeting the artists, sound checking and helping in any other way I could. Stephanie went home to change and came back early for the event.

When the night began, my band played an early set of standards and light dance music. It was an elegant setting and it was so great to see my family in the audience. Even my grandmother was having fun.

As the night progressed, Stephanie became so drunk that she was stumbling around and being inappropriate on the dance floor. My brother-in-law Steven saw what was going on, so he took her out of the venue and took care of her for the rest of the night while we completed the event.

The audience loved the Elvis impersonator, and Fabian did an excellent job in his performance. My band completed the long night with a dance set to ring in the New Year.

After the show was over, I arranged to get my children back to the house and broke down all of my equipment. Sheri Brown handled the rest of the details at the venue, making sure that our responsibilities were complete. At that point, Stephanie was passed out in a hotel room. We found her, helped her to the car and I brought her home. I was angry, sad, embarrassed from what I had seen, and I had finally had enough. We had lost Regina and Stephanie was literally going insane before my very eyes.

The next morning, New Year's Day 1992, I woke Stephanie up around eight in the morning and I finally gave her an ultimatum. I told her that if she didn't check herself in immediately to a rehabilitation hospital, that I was going to leave her. She began to sob uncontrollably. I held her in my arms and gently told her that I couldn't do this anymore. I couldn't watch her slowly dying before my very eyes. She was not okay. In spite of all of the wonderful things she was accomplishing, none of it meant anything without her health and well-being, and she had neither. As I rocked her back and forth, she agreed to go into treatment.

Hope is elusive, but sometimes it can keep you alive.

CHAPTER FORTY-SIX
Learning about Stephanie's Illness

On the morning of January 1, 1992, I got on the phone and first called the *Betty Ford Center*. We didn't have insurance and they wanted to charge an enormous amount of money to check Stephanie in for treatment. They also wanted all of the money up front. I called *Canyon Springs Hospital*. They charged $27,000.00 for a month of inpatient treatment, and they would take a $5,000.00 deposit.

That was exactly how much I had in the bank from the New Year's Eve event at the *Riviera*. I gave them the money and after a short conversation with her to make sure that she wanted to do this, they checked Stephanie in to treatment in the afternoon of the first day of the year. I stayed with her through the evening until it was time for me to go. We held hands and I reassured her. She smiled, but she was scared and beginning to detoxify, so I held her until I had to leave.

I had asked Kevin to keep an eye on Rachel and Taddy while I was gone. Kevin had a friend with him at the house and they were all horsing around. Somebody threw Rachel up in the air and when she landed, she broke her ankle. As soon as I got home, I took Rachel to the emergency room. The X-ray showed that it was a hairline fracture on Rachel's growth plate. It was a small but dangerous break. She was put into a cast and given painkillers, and I brought her home to rest. January 1, 1992 was an exhausting and emotional day. When it rains, it pours.

•••••

On the very next day, I was in the office of *Valley Vue Entertainment* working with Shari Brown to try to fill Stephanie's shoes. I didn't want anyone to know she was in treatment, so we told everyone she was on vacation. There had been an incident at one of the hotels we were to provide entertainment for on New Year's Eve. The hotel had cancelled the band they booked at the last minute.

The musicians were naturally upset, and I was obligated to make up for it. I paid the musicians out of my own pocket, even though it was clearly the hotel's fault. The bandleader, Stan Watkins, was naturally upset but totally cool with me. He accepted a smaller amount from me than the hotel had promised. Under the circumstances, that meant the world to me. We were getting corporate business from the hotel, so I couldn't make a big deal out of it. It was upsetting to me, though, because the mistake cost me several thousand dollars in addition to the money I had just paid to the hospital, and put more of a squeeze on us financially.

•••••

Joe Elkins was up at our office throughout the month that Stephanie was away, helping me plan the Kenny Rogers Concert, which was coming up in April. This was a huge undertaking, and I wanted to bear the brunt of it without having to ask Stephanie too many questions while she was going through her rehabilitation. I was crazily busy trying to run the office, working corporate events while still holding down the gig at *Nonchalance* with Steve Neilen, and also visiting Stephanie every night with the children in tow.

Valley Hi-Life

By Collette Wood

It all depends on what your druthers are, what musical state you are in or what you're in the mood for. If you would like to hear some nice soulful rock and roll or dance to the wee hours of the morning, then go to the Nonchalance Club and catch the Tad Sisler Band featuring Tad Sisler on keyboard and vocals and Steve Neilen on drums.

If, however, you would like to lay poolside on a lounge chair, sip tropical drinks and listen to some soothing, laid-back jazz, occasionaly spiced with a salsa beat, then go to the Marriott Springs Resort in Palm Desert and catch the Tad Sisler Band, featuring the aforementioned musicians.

By day — specifically, Thursday through Sunday from noon 'til 5 p.m. — Tad and Steve give the hotel guests and anyone else who would like to drop by, some excellent classic jazz selections such as "Stella By Starlight" and "Nature Boy," blended with nice contemporary sounds such as "After The Love Is Gone."

Mind you, the music is played with light overtones of Latin/Caribbean rhythms (thanks in part to the steel drums set in Sisler's keyboard) which we're sure give the guests a tropical feeling. It certainly gave us a tropical feeling.

Meanwhile, evenings (Monday through Saturdays), Steve and Tad serve up some pretty hot fare for the dance crowd (which ranges in age from 30 to 70 from what we discerned) at the Nonchalance Club in Palm Desert.

Last Saturday evening, when we dropped by, the room was chock full of people who seemingly couldn't stop dancing.

As for their musical talents, Steve and Tad are terrific and hopefully, the new album they are working on (for Valley Vue Records) with several other musicians, will reflect just how talented they are.

In the meantime, it's just Tad Sisler and Steve Neilen making as much music as any band we've ever heard. Well, let's just say for two guys, they make an awful lot of good music whatever the genre of music they're playing.

In addition to pulling together a whole new look at the Desert Inn with a major rehab overhaul, the new owners have also given the hotel a new name. Officially, the hotel is now called the Palm Mountain Resort. We will get back to you later with any grand opening plans they may have.

Do look out for the upcoming album release by the group War. Palm Spring's own Pat Rizzo, who we know will be doing his usual dynamite job on reeds, tells us that there will be several numbers on the album which deal with social commentary (homelessness, etc.). Meanwhile, we are also looking forward to the release of the album Pat and Andy Fraga have been working on with special guest artist, Tito Puente.

Til we meet again. We're on the road.

Stephanie was taking her treatment very seriously. She knew she had hit rock bottom, and she had done it in front of almost everyone we loved. After the first week of detoxification, it became somewhat easier for her. She was going through a psychiatric evaluation, and the doctors initially diagnosed her with depression and alcoholism. They also mentioned that she was most likely bipolar.

I wasn't really familiar at the time with the depth of bipolar condition, but upon researching it, so many questions about her past erratic behavior were answered for me. You can only rationalize your way out of the truth for a certain amount of time. Until this moment, at first, I would blame her behavior sometimes on her "Irish" temper...or tell myself that she just drinks like her Irish ancestors... or many other excuses.

As her illness had revealed itself to me over time, it mimicked my father's alcoholism at times, and at other times, Stephanie's illness had an entirely different face than Maynard's had. There was no question that Stephanie's full-on disease had progressed before my very eyes into an unmanageable situation. And I was watching it slowly kill her. Going into treatment was a *Hail Mary*, and I prayed that it would work. What I didn't know at the time was that this battle with Stephanie's demons was just beginning, and they were powerful.

According to the dictionary, a demon is a supernatural being. Although our own inner demons haunt us, and demons can be powerful influences within our minds and souls, they do not actually exist in the real world. That fact may not make them feel any less real to us, but we should know that we can overcome our demons by living in the here and now, in the real world, and never giving in or giving up.

Don't ever believe that you are not more powerful than your demons. Demons exist solely for the purpose for you to overcome them in order to learn life lessons.

In the 1980's and early 1990's, only a few classes of antidepressant medications were being used for bipolar condition. It was really a crapshoot to try and find the one that worked. Stephanie's doctors put her on a huge dosage of Desaryl otherwise known as *Trazodone*; 300 mg. per dosage. They also kept her on her *Xanax*, but tempered the dosage down.

When she walked into *Canyon Springs* she was eating Xanax like candy. The drugs seemed to even her out at first, although she was kind of spacy, slurring her words at times. I was pleased to see that she was wholeheartedly into the hard work of discovering what it was that made her want to drink, and all of the tools she could use to better herself. The kids and I got to come and visit for a short while each day. Regina was gone at this point, living with her father. She didn't even know what was going on until a few months later.

While Stephanie was still in treatment, the kids and I went in for some counseling that was tied to Stephanie's healing plan. Much of what happens with some addicts and alcoholics can be magnified by a dysfunctional life at home. We were pleased to find out that, in general, we were not contributing to Stephanie's illness. If anything, we were all trying to help her in our own way. But, we also had become enablers at times, and I know I personally had major issues with codependency.

Yes, the situation with Regina had put Stephanie over the edge, but her plunge over the edge had been building for a long, long time. And, we were finally starting to get some clarity on her prognosis. Bipolar condition brings on the highest of highs and the lowest of lows. Her manic episodes, her bouts of deep depression and propensity to binge with alcohol were seemingly all part of the package.

•••••

Regina's departure had also been a very traumatic event for my other children. They were all always-best friends. We were a close-knit family, with loads of love and care always for each other. Rachel and Taddy had just turned ten years old in August of 1991, and Regina had been a huge part of their security and safety throughout their childhood. Kevin had been the middle child, and all of a sudden, he was forced to take on the role of the oldest. He stepped up to the plate at fourteen years old with a calm consistency that helped. Rachel was healing from her broken ankle. Kevin and Taddy were both good with her, even helping her clean her room, in which she now was sleeping alone since Regina left.

On Stephanie's last day in treatment, the people in her group did an exercise in trust. They walked up a ladder to a tall platform with a rope attached to them, and they had to fall backwards to establish that they completely understood trusting your higher power. Stephanie was exhilarated when we came to pick her up. She brought home her *Alcoholics Anonymous* book, filled with notations throughout, and she really wanted to be sober and to stay sober.

•••••

As soon as Stephanie left treatment, Hillery Johnson came to us and said he wanted to sell us his half of the business for $1.00 and take the *Valley Vue Entertainment* Corporation back. I believed that he was also embarrassed from the New Year's Eve fiasco, and he decided that maybe Stephanie was too much of a liability, but he was gracious, and we accepted. He assured me that he still wanted me to work with him in the recording studio.

We started a Corporation of our own, naming it *Valley Wide Artists & Events, Inc.* To me, it was kind of a bummer because we had just started building up the *Valley Vue* name and then we changed it, but we did get a chance to bring out the new corporate name for the Kenny Rogers event, which was going to be huge.

•••••

Stephanie eased her way back into work, which wasn't easy because we were less than two months away from producing the Kenny Rogers concert. Kenny's management insisted on 85% of the gross ticket sales, which gave Joe Elkins a very small window for profit. I didn't like the deal. I felt that Joe deserved more and Kenny's people were greedy, but I guess when you're the star you hold all of the cards. We started working on selling corporate sponsorships just to help Joe to make a profit. It was going to be tough for him.

We had done a deal with Joe for a flat fee of $10,000.00 so that we would have no liability. It really wasn't even close to enough money for all the work we did, but Stephanie had decided that she wanted me as a performer to open the concert for Kenny Rogers, in order to give my career a boost. Instead of opening as I would perform with my corporate band, doing popular music, she wanted a rehearsed show of my original songs from my CD which was only about three or four months away from distribution.

Rose Winters

Again, we turned to Jeff Edwards to be my musical director. He was familiar with the music from our mixing session. I brought in Rose Winters to sing the male-female duets I had written. Rose and her husband Joe were performing as a duo at the *Hyatt Grand Champions* in the main lounge. The concert was at the stadium at that venue. Rose and Joe had four children as we did, and Stephanie had booked them into the main lounge. Rose was also a beautiful woman, with long, flowing dark hair, and very sweet; she was perfect for the gig.

I also had Glen Myerscough on sax and flute, Michael (Patches) Stewart on trumpet, Carl Joiner on vocals, Gilbert Hansen on bass, Steve Neilen on drums and Jeff was going to play guitar. Jeff handled all of the rehearsals and the band sounded great. I was going to play the grand piano on a song or two, and stand-up to sing the rest of my original tracks.

•••••

As part of the advertising, Joe Elkins bought a huge billboard on Highway 111 in Rancho Mirage with the concert information on Kenny Rogers, including my name as opening act. It was kind of cool.

As exciting as this upcoming concert was, I was concerned that it would be too much for Stephanie. She was newly sober and the *Trazodone* was doing a huge number on her. The doctors never lowered the dose from 300 mg, which, when I looked it up later, was supposed to be a starter dosage for no longer than six weeks. They kept her on that dosage for a year and a half after she got out of treatment, which is a crime. Later, she would literally be tearing her hair out because of what this drug was doing to her.

On the night of the event, my mother was at the stadium, along with my children, Hillery and Sara, most of my friends including Kurt and Janet and Eddie, and ten thousand other people. It was a gorgeous, cool but dry April evening with a beautiful moon in a cloudless sky. The concert sold out; it was the first time I had ever performed in front of so many people. I had done corporate band events with two or three thousand people, but never a concert with mostly everyone's undivided attention. And…I hadn't stood up and sang without a keyboard in front of me for years.

Kenny Rogers with my family, 1992

Stephanie and I got a hotel room across the street from the *Hyatt* so we could stay and sleep afterwards. The children would be at the concert, and then they would go with their friends and spend the night. Rachel's foot had healed enough that I wasn't concerned about letting her go with her brothers and friends. Kevin was a doting, responsible brother at this point and I trusted him.

We met Kenny Rogers and took photos with him before the event. He was gracious and kind. A sea of people awaited me as I took the stage. My band sounded great and it was exciting to perform, actually easier for me in front of thousands of people than it is in a piano bar with only a handful of people. When you're in an intimate setting, it can be intimidating. Performing to a stadium full of people is wonderful and exhilarating! I wished I could have done it every time like that.

Tad on-stage
Kenny Rogers Concert
1992

In the middle of my set, a spider came down from the rafters and landed on my head! I casually brushed it out of my hair in one fell swoop. I was unfazed. I thought, I could do this every night! It was fun playing my original songs with a great band and we were well received.

Behind the scenes, Stephanie was dealing with Kenny Roger's management. They were demanding all of our books and receipts, and she was prepared.

We hired a videographer who had done a lot of work with Paul Rose. He had a camera in front and one on the side. I was excited to see the footage, and later he told me that the front camera was never working for some unknown reason. I thought, how shitty of Paul to pay him off to give me only footage from the side and still get paid full price from us. Paul was still after us, doing underhanded stuff behind the scenes. But, we were gaining ground and this night was a triumph for us. Kenny Rogers was excellent and the crowd roared in a standing ovation after he sang all of his hits.

At the end of the night, Stephanie had just completed a harrowing accounting process with Kenny's management and they were satisfied. She came out and heard what happened with the videographer, which upset her more. Just then, my mother came up and started complaining to me about my performance.

My mom thought I should have included more popular music that people had actually heard along with my originals, and she thought that it was too loud where she and her friends were sitting. Stephanie and Elaine really didn't get along too well at this point still (or ever), and that conversation put Stephanie over the edge. She was quiet as my mother talked and went on to other things, but after we completed our last task, leaving the equipment manager to finish breaking down, Stephanie exploded with rage at me.

She was upset about many things, none of them really of great importance compared to what we had just accomplished; how could my mother say that on such a perfect night, and why didn't I yell at my mother? How could the videographer do that to us on such a perfect night? We would never be able to get that footage back. And…Joe Elkins had actually ended up losing about $10,000.00 on the event after all of that effort, because Kenny Rogers and his management had walked away with more than $225,000.00 due to their normal contract provisions negotiated by the *William Morris Agency.* I wanted to sit and reflect upon the major thing we had just accomplished; to tell her about how it felt to perform in front of such a huge crowd, and of what a major success and an incredible experience the night really was, but Stephanie was incapable of hearing or feeling anything except the rage she was experiencing.

•••••

After we completed our tasks at the stadium, we drove quietly to our hotel without speaking. When we arrived and she made it in to the room, Stephanie again repeated why she was disgusted with me and angrily told me not to say a word to her. It was hard, but I knew any argument would just escalate the situation, so I kept my mouth shut.

Stephanie put her pajamas on, got into bed and fell asleep immediately with her back turned away from me. I lay there in bed in disbelief. I had just stood in front of a sea of people and flawlessly sang my best original songs in front of an incredible backup band; it was unquestionably the greatest performing experience of my life up to that point; I was next to the one person who should have been sharing in that joy, including her amazing accomplishment of flawlessly executing a huge event, but instead she was angry and miserable about petty little things compared to what we had just done, and she wouldn't even talk to me.

Of course, I was proud of her accomplishments, and I knew the stress she must have endured on that evening. She was an amazing person when it came to these things, but it was becoming typical to me that Stephanie couldn't see beyond her own anger or depression or whatever else she might be feeling at any given moment. She never gave a thought to my feelings or my experience that night, expecting that I would accept her behavior as I had done so many times. Tonight, there was absolutely zero compassion from her, or reflection on what had just happened, or talking it out, or anything.

I had taken the ball while she was in treatment, and carefully worked to plan this concert for months, without question as she came back around. I didn't expect anything from it; I wanted no accolades or thanks; I was very protective over her recovery, but I did at least keep my hopes up for decency and respect and kindness from her. At this point in my evolution, I just didn't understand that Stephanie was incapable of this, at any given moment. Her illness did not eliminate her kindness or decency by any means, but she was a person who experienced anxiety, anger and depression on a regular basis; it was a narcissistic disease, rearing its ugly head at the worst times. Her actions and reactions were sometimes slaves to wherever her imbalanced brain was at any given time, and the medication she was taking was not a magic pill by any means. In fact, it was beginning to work against her.

After Stephanie passed out in exhaustion in the hotel room with her back to me, I started to cry. I was trying so hard to help her to be okay. I wanted her to be okay, but I was always swallowing my own feelings to accomplish that.

According to her, my feelings didn't matter because I was the 'star' and I got all of the applause on stage. I had just experienced the greatest night of my life as a performer. I was grateful for the gift I had and the love I got in return from my audiences, for sure. But, for some reason in my relationship with Stephanie, that trumped anything I might be feeling, and so my feelings didn't matter.

This had been going on for years as I dealt with her split personality, and for the first time, I just wanted my feelings to matter once. I always felt just tolerated more than wanted by her, and I would beg her forgiveness sometimes when she was angry about something, when deep inside I knew I had done nothing wrong. And yet, I knew underneath it all somehow that I was her guiding light; I was the foundation around her, which kept her stable enough to get through each day.

I was a father and a husband and a hard-working man; I knew I had to be the consistent, strong one always, in order to keep my family together. I would continue to be outwardly strong and to sacrifice my own feelings for the good of the family. Growing up in the Navy, I knew, very simply, that is what men do. And, I loved my family dearly. Even so, on that night of nights, I quietly cried myself to sleep.

I was raised to be a man. Men were men. We sucked it up and moved on.

CHAPTER FORTY-SEVEN
Stephanie's Father has a Stroke

On the morning following the Kenny Rogers concert in April of 1992, Stephanie and I got an early phone call, waking us up at the hotel room. Stephanie's father, Russ, had been in a terrible auto accident while the concert was occurring, the night before.

He had experienced a mini-stroke while he was driving home from his gig; Russ lost control of the automobile he was driving; he and his car had been extracted from underneath a semi-truck. He was admitted to *Desert Hospital* in Palm Springs with a severe concussion. He had no broken bones, but Russ had experienced lacerations and bruising all over his body. The hospital staff had tried all night to reach us at our home, and had finally tracked us down at the hotel.

Stephanie and I jumped up and drove quickly to the hospital. For fear of internal bleeding, the hospital had discontinued his *Coumadin* blood thinner. A couple hours after Stephanie made it to his hotel room, she watched in horror as Russ had a massive stroke in front of her eyes.

The next few days were touch and go. Russ was in ICU, and then they moved him back to a private room. After a week or so, they moved him to a rehabilitation facility for a month. His speech was impaired and he had no movement on one side of his body. Stephanie and I were there to be with him, every day.

She made sure her father had physical therapy daily and everything else he needed, in order to improve his condition as quickly as possible. After a month of inpatient treatment, in late May of 1992, we moved him in to our house, because he couldn't live alone. Russ moved into Rachel's room and she moved into our family room to sleep on the couch for a while. Our house was really too small for all of us with Russ, so we decided to start looking for a bigger place to live.

•••••

Through all of this, I continued to work full-time as a performer.

Around the first of May in 1992, my friend Jilly Rizzo came in to *Nonchalance* with Gus Pantele to sit at my piano bar. It was a mellow night, so I had a chance to talk with them in-between songs.

Jilly requested some of his favorites. Gus Pantele was a restaurateur in the desert, at one point owning *Panteles* and then *The Greek*; Gus and I had been longtime friends. He was a character, always smiling, and I was glad to tell Gus the story of how Jilly had been so instrumental in helping me get a full-time gig in the beginning of my career as a performer. I thanked Jilly for his kindness and support. Jilly laughed, and told me "I don't know if I did you a favor or not!" He was beaming. He made mention of a couple experiences he had with Frank Sinatra during their many years of hanging out together. *Jilly's Saloon* in New York City and *Jilly's* Palm Springs had been packed venues, always full of action and fun.

It was cool to me that Jilly and I had become good friends, and I was glad that he knew just how grateful I was to him for the boost he gave me when I was a young performer. We talked a bit about how I ended up working for Frank Sinatra, and how we all naturally had evolved into new roles in each other's lives.

I mentioned the first night I ever met Jilly at the *Canyon Hotel* when he was handing out hundred-dollar bills to all of the servers as a 'thank you' tip from Frank. I said, "You looked so familiar to me, and then it hit me: You were the guy who did those one-liners on one of my favorite television shows when I was a kid, *Rowan and Martin's Laugh-In!*" Jilly had been a very important man; famous in his own right from his restaurants in New York and Palm Springs, and from his close relationship with Mr. Sinatra. But, for that night, he was just a good buddy hanging out at my piano bar with me, and with Steve on drums.

Gus Pantele had a huge grin on his face. He was an easy-going man, and he had always welcomed me with open arms into his establishments. Steve Neilen and I had a great evening playing music and reminiscing with Jilly and Gus.

Jilly Rizzo told me that he was working to organize his seventy-fifth birthday party in just three days. It was going to be a huge event with Frank Sinatra attending. He asked me if I wanted to go, and I told him I couldn't; I was going to be working that night, so we got him a little cake with a candle and sang to him at the piano bar.

Three days later, in the midnight hour preceding his birthday, a drunk driver hit Jilly's *Jaguar* and it exploded in flames. Jilly died in the wreck. I was devastated. The pain of his loss stayed with me for many months. Even still, I felt blessed to have been able to thank him just days before, for everything he had done for me. God bless Jilly Rizzo.

•••••

Motorola was hosting the communications for the *America's Cup* Yacht races in San Diego in mid-May of 1992. They hired my duo to perform on the enormous *Motorola* Executive's Yacht during the races from May 9-16. Through that week, I worked with a couple different saxophone players. Glen Myerscough came onto the boat for a few dates, and I also used George Wilkerson, an African-American sax player who was becoming a friend of mine.

It was an amazing experience. We would perform for an hour as the yacht went out on to the open ocean, and then we would witness these amazing, sleek yachts racing for the coveted *America's Cup* from sometimes only forty or fifty yards away. We would basically party with the *Motorola* executives for four hours and then perform for another hour as the yacht went back to port. You can see photos or videos of the yachts racing, with entire teams using all of their strength to fight the winds and keep the yachts on course, but nothing compares to seeing it with your very eyes from only yards away.

George Wilkerson recorded a few times with me at Hillery's studio, and we did a few more gigs together. Several months later, out of the blue, he died a bizarre death, shot through the head by an arrow up in Tahquitz Canyon in Palm Springs. George had been a policeman on the vice squad in Los Angeles for a while, and some people thought that maybe it was a weird gang killing or something. It was sad. He was a good guy and the father of a young girl, but whenever we talked, he would confide in me that he was tormented by his recent divorce.

•••••

Tad, Rachel, Stephanie and Gene Barry 1992

In mid-May of 1992 Stephanie organized a benefit for her father, Russ. It would be held at the restaurant where he had been performing at the time of his accident. The benefit was a huge success and she raised several thousand dollars for his care. Most of the local entertainers were there, along with famous screen actor Gene Barry and actress Jane Wyman.

Stephanie got it into her head to do yet another benefit for Russ in June. This one would be a jam session with all the local musicians. She rented out the Pavilion in Palm Springs and got a one-day liquor license. This whole idea was a huge mistake, and she would end up losing money on it. Although she was still sober while she was planning this event, the antidepressants were beginning to take a toll on her psyche. She was also consumed with her father's illness and she wanted to do whatever she could to help him to want to continue to live and improve the quality of his life. Russ was mellow; he was going with the flow and very happy to be living with us. It didn't bother me that Russ was there at all. He was a very kind man and my children loved their grandfather.

•••••

In the meantime, the District Attorney wanted to look further into Greg McDonald's alleged wrongdoing. They were interested in the kickbacks *Sun Presentations* was allegedly giving to the hotels. Stephanie thought that this might be Greg's undoing, and so she enthusiastically encouraged them to pursue this. She was still angry with Greg, and how they had worked to blackball us long after the Labor lawsuit was settled. None of this was helping her sobriety or mental health, though. It was like she was back in the lion's den too soon.

The District Attorney wanted me to call Greg and try to entrap him in a recorded phone call. They were also extremely interested in anything we might know about Bobby Milano or any of his family and their actions. Bobby Milano was a great local singer; as I mentioned, I knew him from my *Delmonico's* days, Stephanie worked for him at one point at *Bobby Milano's Supper Club* and he also performed with a lot of my friends. It was generally known that Bobby was apparently connected to the Mafia in some way, but he had never done anything to hurt my family or me and I wasn't a snitch.

I was also aware of the gossip that Bobby's brother Jimmy was connected to the syndicate in some way, and he was working some business out of an office above his son Joey's restaurant, but it was none of my business, so I didn't offer anything to the D.A.

Stephanie insisted that I do what the District Attorney wanted, so I went ahead with the phone call with Greg. I asked the questions they told me to ask, but I didn't pry and I didn't really want to entrap him. It wasn't "who I am." It all seemed so surreal to me, like I was involved in spying or something.

Meanwhile, I was getting calls from some of Greg's previous associates, telling me that they had been ripped off by Greg. Greg was also building a huge complex in the heart of Palm Springs called *Sun Studios,* which would have a television studio and recording studio as well as the offices of *Sun Presentations.* This upset Stephanie even more, as she believed that he was using money he had basically stolen from others to build this little empire in Palm Springs.

Eventually, the District Attorney let Greg off with a slap on the wrist, and told the hotels to change their paperwork and not to deceive their clients, and that was the end of that. Stephanie was devastated that nothing more came of it. She began to think that there is no justice in the world and it weighed even more heavily on her soul.

Gregory McDonald and Regina

To top it off, Stephanie found out that our daughter Regina had left her father's trailer up in the high desert. It had become an unmanageable situation for her. Regina's natural father had been emotionally abusive to Regina, and she found her way back to Palm Springs. Stephanie also found out that Regina was dating Greg's son, Gregory McDonald, which threw her for a loop, to say the least.

Stephanie and Regina were still not communicating, and to Stephanie, this was the ultimate slap in the face anyone could do to her, let alone her own daughter. She sobbed one night, and we had a long conversation about it. I told her that sometimes people are drawn together as if they are supposed to be together, whether it's to learn a lesson or maybe fulfill some karmic responsibility to each other. Regina and Gregory had known each other since they were kids, and I felt that maybe it was just that kind of an attraction, more than some *Romeo and Juliet* story that was meant to hurt us. But, admittedly, it did feel that way for some time until we learned to accept it.

It might have helped if Stephanie and Regina were communicating, and as they eventually began to talk to each other, Stephanie and Regina did resolve most of these issues and became close again. In fact, later Regina told Stephanie that *Child Protective Services* had told her that we didn't want her, which was a total lie. We had been begging to get her back through the whole court process. It was a tragic part of our lives, losing our Regina in the way we did. It's also ugly whenever anyone gets caught up in the court system.

Avoid the court system if you can. It's a terrible, intrusive, negative place to air out your dirty laundry.

•••••

Canyon Springs Hospital wanted the rest of the money we owed them. They were sending us late notices. Stephanie contacted my brother-in-law, Steve Soffer, and made a deal, with my approval, to sell ten percent of my publishing company, *Tadco Music,* to Steve and my sister Kathy for $5,000.00 to help pay Stephanie's hospital bills from treatment. A couple months later she sold another ten percent to Steve for another $5,000.00, and we still owed $17,000.00 even after all of that. Those actions held the hospital off for a while, and I was grateful that Steve came through for us during such a tough time. However, I knew better than to get involved in monetary issues or transactions with family, but I did so anyway because we were desperate, and I later regretted that decision for a long time.

On the night of the second benefit jam session for Russ at the Pavilion in June, Stephanie announced to me that she was going to have a beer that night. I said, "Are you crazy? We just spent a fortune putting you through treatment and you mustn't drink!"

She said that she was going to prove that she could have just one beer and be fine. I was angry and sad and I begged her to just go one day at a time here, and make it through this night without drinking. She refused and had one beer. The next morning, she woke up proud of herself that she had been able to drink just one beer, but it was like the floodgates opened again. Within a week she was falling-down drunk. A little part of my heart died when that happened. We had all worked so hard as a family to help her to stop, and we were about to go bankrupt because of it. We had swallowed our pride, begging relatives for money for help. Again, I implored her to stop, pick herself up again and go back to meetings and sobriety.

When you know someone who has endured a long-term relationship with an addict, your first instinct is to question why… why would you stay with someone who constantly abused you and disappointed you? Why would you stay with someone who continued to pull the rug out from underneath you? Why would you allow yourself or your other loved ones to continue to endure bad behavior? Then, it would be normal to ask why you "enabled" the person to continue in their behavior, as if it was because of you allowing them to be out of control that they were out of control.

I never turned a blind eye to Stephanie's illness. Time after time after time I hoped… against hope… that this would be the last outburst or the last binge or the last time she needed to go and get help. And I held her hand, guiding her through treatment, AA Meetings, counseling, weight loss, depression, medical issues and other crises many, many times.

Then, you may go through months at a time where everything is seemingly fine and you feel a sense of normalcy. You love this person. In this case, she was my wife and the mother of my children. Before Stephanie, I had endured the alcoholism of my father. I hated his behavior and his illness but I loved him.

You constantly want to get away from the illness, but you ask yourself, how do you abandon someone like that; someone who obviously needs you, who relies on you sometimes for their very existence? So, you give away a big piece of yourself. Of course you're an enabler at times, usually when you've thrown your hands up in desperation or frustration… and when you're finally disappointed or disgusted or heartbroken one too many times and you find the strength to get out of this unhealthy situation, your mind tells you that you did everything you could have, but your heart stays broken and still believes there must have been one more thing you could have done, or one more chance you could have given, or one more glimmer of hope.

Without hope we have nothing.

In so many ways, I had come to the rescue in Stephanie's life when she needed someone the most. That had become part of my identity. We made a home together; we raised children together; and so, in those moments I lived for those times, here and there, when life seemed normal.

On my thirty-fourth birthday, June 28, 1992, in the early morning, a massive 7.3 earthquake hit the high desert around the town of Joshua Tree, in the high desert above Palm Springs.

Our house was shaking violently. Instinctively, I jumped out of bed and found the twins. Taddy had been sleeping next to Rachel out in the family room on the hide-a-bed couch that had become Rachel's makeshift 'bedroom', and I held them both in my arms, huddling with them on the floor by the back sliding-glass door. We looked outside the violently shaking glass doors and noticed that the water from our swimming pool was splashing out of the pool in big waves. The shaking was intense and it lasted for what seemed to be an eternity. I was calm and I helped my twins to feel secure as Stephanie had already run to make sure Kevin and Russ were okay.

•••••

Jeff Edwards got a gig producing Karaoke tracks for a Japanese company. He asked me if I wanted to help, and I agreed. I bought *Vision* and *Performer*, two new software bundles that allowed you to sequence music from your Mac computer. I was familiar with midi music production from working with the Yamaha QX1, but this was a totally new format. Music programming software would evolve into the standardized recording platform when digital audio recording became prevalent later, but that was still years away.

It was like learning a new language, and it was deep. But, it was a skill I would utilize for the rest of my life, and it was essential for my growth to come in to this, learning these software programs on the ground level. It was frustrating, though, because computers during this time period were slow and full of glitches. Sometimes I would work for hours on a part and the computer would freeze, and I would lose all of my work! I learned quickly to save, save, save, save after every phrase or edit.

With the karaoke project, I also had to use my entire ear training to hear a recording and try to duplicate every note that had been played exactly in the way it was played on the record. It was awful, and quite a struggle, but I eventually turned in some music for Jeff's project. Later, the small amount of experience I had gained from that would be essential when I began to work with Jeff again in the late 1990's and then for *Yamaha* in the early 2000's.

•••••

We had met a psychic lady named Geraldine Stringer. She was spot-on with so many of her predictions. She could look at photographs and 'pick up' amazing characteristics of anybody. She held jewelry and was able to tell more about a person in that manner. She saw "auras" around people, which, according to her, could tell even more about you.

Geraldine came over in early July of 1992 to do a psychic reading, which we taped. Stephanie was drunk when Geraldine came over. Geraldine looked deeply into Stephanie's eyes and held both of her hands. She told Stephanie point-blank, "You alone can change your destiny, but if you continue on this path, I promise you, you will be dead within three years."

Stephanie cried and promised to work on herself to be better. This experience shocked Stephanie back into sobriety for the time being. She also found the courage to reach out to Regina, and they began to talk again. Regina came over and we had a beautiful day full of long hugs and many tears. We all vowed not to ever let anything split us up again.

We had made plans before the summer to meet my sister Kathy and Steven, Michael and Yash in Florida and to spend a week at *Disney World* in Orlando. Back in December of 1991, before Stephanie went into treatment and after we had been paid the deposit on the Kenny Rogers money, we had bought our tickets and secured a condo for a week. At the time I made the arrangements, we were grieving the loss of Regina from our home; Stephanie was out of control and I organized the trip thinking it would be a magic fix to our problems. I had no idea of all of the events that would transpire after I made those reservations.

Kathy, Mike, Rachel, Kevin & Stephanie
Disney World 1992

As a gesture of her love for us, Regina offered to work the office phones at *Valley Wide Artists & Events, Inc.*, and to take care of Russ for the week we were gone. I was grateful, and Regina took it very seriously. She had grown up a lot in a short period of time. My heart had hurt for Regina for almost a year; I loved my daughter with all my heart, and I knew the pain firsthand of having to grow up too fast.

So, Stephanie and I took Kevin, Rachel and Taddy to *Disney World* and we had a wonderful week with my sister and her family. We arrived in Florida only a couple days after Hurricane Andrew had ravaged Miami. We flew over the damage as we changed planes in Miami to end up in Orlando. Witnessing the ravages of nature was amazing and terrifying to me.

These people were suffering. Some had lost everything. I fought back the guilt, knowing that we were going to have such a wonderful adventure in the midst of all of this suffering. But, I also vowed to give my family a great experience. We all needed it, big time.

Stephanie was sober throughout the experience. She looked great and she was very upbeat. Kevin and the twins bonded with their cousins and we went to most of the amusement parks, including a day at *River Country* where we played water volleyball and went down the waterslides. It was great for me to spend time with my sister, too. I was grateful for the trip even though I wouldn't have made the plans in the first place had I known how poorly we would be doing financially at this point.

•••••

We were beginning to lose it, money-wise. We were having trouble paying our rent and the office rent, trying to pay back the hospital, and coping with a big tax bill we received. The money we had received from Steve and Kathy was only a Band-Aid for our problems. It was the middle of the summer and the agency had no corporate work. I was still performing at *Nonchalance.*

Steve Neilen decided to take a job as a casino manager in Las Vegas at the *Riviera Hotel.* His girlfriend Debbie's father was a casino boss there and he got Steve a job. Steve's back was beginning to go out on him and it was painful for him to play drums. Debbie and Steve had just had a son, Cory, and he needed a real job. So, I replaced Steve with Bobby Dominguez, an amazing drummer. *Nonchalance* wasn't enough to completely support everything Stephanie and I were trying to accomplish, though. We were now supporting Stephanie's father, Russ and all of his medical needs. On top of it all, we now needed a larger house to accommodate Russ and our growing children.

•••••

Stephanie found a huge old 5-bedroom, 5,000 square foot house on the North end of Palm Springs, with a pool, close to the mountain on Via Escuela. The owner of the house had been the superintendent of schools in Palm Springs, and he had been fired. He sued the school district and had received a big settlement, and he moved up North to run another district somewhere else.

The rent payment on the house was more money than I had ever paid for a house, but it was a couple hundred dollars a month less than our current rent on our office and home combined. Although it was painful to move out of the nice location our agency had in downtown Palm Springs, Stephanie decided to move our offices into this house.

We moved into the house in late August of 1992. In my opinion, we weren't really saving enough to justify this move. We could have found something slightly smaller for less and accomplished the same thing, but she had her heart set on this house. So, we moved out of our office on Palm Canyon Drive and put it into the side room of this monstrosity we had just moved into.

The nice part of it was that everyone had his or her own room, including Stephanie's father. Our son Kevin's room was over on the side of the house with the office, and away from all the other bedrooms, so he felt a little bit of independence, being the oldest child still at home. He got a job at a hip clothing store downtown, and he was maintaining his grades. Kevin was very popular at the High School, and he was always dressed in a cool way, buying most of his clothing at a discount from the store where he was working.

Kevin took care of his stuff. His dressers and closet were impeccable. The twins would sneak in to his room after he left for school and grab clothes from his closet to wear to school. Now that they were in sixth grade, they were Middle School kids and being hip meant something, all of a sudden. After school, they would get home before Kevin and hang the clothes they had worn back in his closet, so he didn't know they wore them all day! This went on for a few months until he caught on. Kevin couldn't figure out why his clothes smelled so bad!

•••••

Finally, in October of 1992, we received my long-awaited CD's of my album *So Good to Come Home To*, from Hillery Johnson's *Valley Vue Records*. It was amazing to play my album in this fairly new format on CD, and Hillery's team was working hard to market the album, finally.

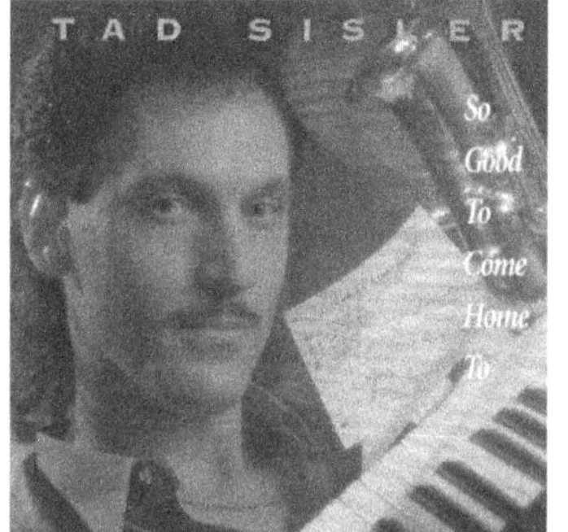

Within a couple months, my music was being played on over 100 radio stations, coast to coast throughout America. I received some really good reviews in the journals. The CD was listed as *Chart bound* in *R&R Magazine* and I got a great write-up in the *Gavin Report.* DJ's were digging it, and it was cool.

In December of 1992, my twins had a Holiday Concert with their sixth-grade choir at *Raymond Cree Middle School.* Sitting above them, crashing a cymbal in the band was Andy Fraga, Jr. My friend Andy Fraga, the piano player who worked with Pat Rizzo, had moved his son to California to live with him. Andy, Jr. was in eighth grade. This little guy would eventually become my business partner!

•••••

Hillery Johnson had completed building the recording studio in Palm Springs, and I was over at the facility recording new material. He bought a new set of ADAT machines, chaining three of them together to enable us to track 24-tracks digitally.

ADATS were digital tape machines, and it was an amazing new development in recording. It was also a new learning curve for me, and in an instant, it made the cumbersome 2-inch 24-track analog reel-to-reel machines obsolete. I took the time, though, to transfer some of the early recordings I had done from the 2-inch machines onto the ADATS. Years later, I would be able to transfer them onto Pro Tools; to salvage and remake some pretty amazing recordings I had done in the late 1980's.

But, for now, the ADAT machines were pretty cool. It was the first time you could 'copy and paste' audio in a multitrack situation, and it opened up a whole new world. It was also great to have access to a full-on recording facility again, and to not to have to pay for recording time. We created some amazing music throughout that period, in spite of my tumultuous life outside the studio.

•••••

Out of the blue in January of 1993, I got a call from Chuck Buffamonte. I guessed that he was no longer useful to *Sun Presentations* as they had lost their lawsuit against us and dropped all of the others. He asked me if I wanted to work a poolside gig with him at *Stouffers*, which later became the *Renaissance Esmeralda* Resort. I had opened that hotel with my trio at 6AM on their first day of business on September 13, 1989. It is a beautiful resort. He told me the pay was low but he would split it with me.

Against my better judgment, I took the gig, because my family desperately needed the money. It was a day gig so it helped to supplement my income. Our company was booking events at the *Esmeralda*. As I mentioned, Vicki Diestelkamp was one of the Directors of Food & Beverage, and we had become good friends.

I think Vicki liked me. She would meet me as I was loading in for poolside every morning and give me a big hug. Vicki was tall and thin with short, dark hair. She was a sweet lady, very attentive to me, and I was grateful for her friendship and the corporate gigs she was giving to us.

•••••

The effects of the antidepressants were taking a huge toll on Stephanie. In the early months of 1993, she spent many days crawling out of her skin. Several times she vowed to just quit taking them, but the doctors warned her against stopping without weaning off of them.

Stephanie's doctors were trying other drugs in addition to the *Trazodone* and *Xanax*. They were prescribing *Prozac* in the morning and *Trazodone* at night. *Klonopin* replaced the *Xanax*, and none of it was really helping more than it was hurting. So, she turned to drinking again, which, of course, magnified the insanity.

She would go through terrible binge days where she ranted and raved, raging in a drunken stupor. At the end of it all, she would wake up from it, finally sober, and look up at me with angelic innocence, with pimples all over her greasy face, almost as if she had come out of a trance and back to herself. I would help her to the bathtub, and, within a day or two, she was back to her version of normal for a couple weeks or more. My heart would break for her, even though she had just put me through hell for days at a time.

I had truly "married my parents." Stephanie was so much the woman that was my mother. She was an Aries, type-A personality, aggressive in getting her point across, intense at times, creative in her approach, stubborn. She was also so very much my father; a belligerent alcoholic, driven and intelligent with a propensity to be kind and win people over, but her own worst enemy.

Through it all, she loved her children dearly and I know she loved me, but when you marry your parents at a young age, more often than not you begin to grow out of the need to exist in that universe. You start to realize that you cannot fix your parents or yourself through this person, and you cannot fix the person you married any more than you can fix yourself.

I was becoming consumed by the burden I had taken on. I was so unhappy, and yet all I had to do was to look into my children's eyes and I would be okay again. My daughter Rachel and I were very close. I was careful not to let her 'parent' me, but she was wise beyond her years and we could talk about anything. Taddy was just as aware as Rachel was, and he was always concerned about his mother. He was a mama's boy, and he was fiercely protective over her, even at her worst. I admired him for that.

Of course, the children loved their mother with all their hearts, but things were so out of control at times, it was impossible for me to justify, rationalize or explain to them exactly what was going on. And, most of the time, I really didn't know what to do beyond what I was already doing.

Some things are out of your control, no matter how hard you try to make it otherwise. Some nights when she was drunk and belligerent, I would lock myself into the bedroom with her and just allow her to berate me so that the children would not have to endure it. Eventually, she would fall asleep.

When you live with insanity, you begin to wonder if you are crazy too.

One day in early 1993, we were driving to the bank and I looked over at Stephanie. Her hand was shaking uncontrollably. I wondered if it was because of the antidepressants or possibly if it could be early onset Parkinson's disease. Her grandmother Ruth had debilitating Parkinson's throughout Stephanie's entire childhood. I worried about her so much. I really, really loved Stephanie. So many times, I was just blown away by the things she accomplished. We were best friends, and we got along very well when her illness wasn't consuming her. But, I was losing all faith in the possibility that she would ever be okay.

•••••

Stephanie had a big corporate client coming into the *Marriott's Desert Springs Resort* in March of 1993. This was her first big event at the *Marriott* since she had stopped working for *Sun Presentations*. The client chose Johnny Mathis as their headliner, so she booked Johnny Mathis and we were tasked with putting together his orchestra. We called my friend Tommy Shepard. He was the very best.

Tommy was a great trombonist and orchestra leader. He had been on the staff orchestras at NBC, ABC and CBS, and he had done a lot of the *Disney* orchestral stuff in the 1960's. Tommy's orchestra had also backed up Johnny Mathis several times so we knew we were going to hit a home run with him.

Only a week after we sent Tommy his deposit, he died. I was so sad. Tommy's wife, while grieving, still pulled together the orchestra for us, and Johnny was very happy with the orchestra. He remembered Tommy Shepard, and he had always respected his work.

Mr. Mathis was a perfectionist, so Stephanie was relieved that the event went so well. I was able to hang out with Johnny Mathis, as I was managing the orchestra during the rehearsals. He was kind to me but very dramatic about every little thing. He was also very gay.

•••••

My gig at *Nonchalance* finally came to an end, and I got a gig with Chuck Buffamonte and Bobby Dominguez at the *Embassy Suites* in Palm Desert. My trio worked through the summer there, supplemented by my poolside gig with Chuck. It was usually busy at *Embassy Suites*, and the staff was kind and receptive.

Tad with Steve Neilen
1992

I was also still performing every Sunday at the *Religious Science Church* with Dr. Tom Costa as minister, and the congregation was becoming like a family to me. I was performing for weddings and funerals, and the positive message helped me through these difficult times.

I had built up a following in Palm Desert at that point. Steve Neilen came back from Vegas after only eleven months. His girlfriend's father had been fired from the *Riviera* and he saw the writing on the wall. Plus, he needed back surgery, so he came back and stayed with us while he was recovering.

Steve asked me if he could work with me again, and so I gave Bobby Dominguez his notice. Bobby was upset about it, which made me sad. He was a great drummer. I was grateful and lucky to work with Bobby. It wasn't personal. I was just a loyal friend, and Steve needed me. Steve went back to work at *Embassy Suites* with Chuck and me. He wore a neck brace for the first month. Steve even went into the studio with me with his neck brace, and he played his ass off on some amazing tracks.

CHAPTER FORTY-EIGHT
It Never Happens to You

Kimberley Wilburn

Right after my 35th birthday in June of 1993, my heart was broken with devastating news. My father called me one morning in early July and told me that my little twenty-three-year-old stepsister, Sandra's daughter Kimberley had been raped and murdered.

Apparently, after a long day working as a student intern at Baptist Hospital in Memphis, Tennessee, she drove home to her apartment at *The Pyramid* to quickly change clothes so she could go out and meet a girlfriend. When she made it back to her apartment, as she was walking towards her front door, she was held at gunpoint by three young African-American men and forced into the trunk of her car. They drove around with her in the trunk for a while, and stopped to get gas at a gas station. Even though she was banging on the trunk, nobody at the gas station came to help her.

Two more young African-American men got into the car and the five of them drove her for many miles out into the dark countryside on the outskirts of Memphis. She came out of the trunk fighting, but they gang-raped her, beat her almost to death and then ran over her with her own car. They dumped her body into a ravine. It was a brutal, nightmarish way to die. She was only twenty-three years old.

Kimberley was my darling little sister who sat on my knee when she was eight. She was always sweet and kind and full of life. Her future had held so much promise, and she was just coming into her own when this terrible act took her from us. I was beyond consolation. We were all grieving heavily at the loss and from the violence in which she was taken from us.

The next morning, by chance, workers from the *Tennessee Valley Authority* were out in the area of the ravine where Kimberley's lifeless body had been dumped, cutting grass with their huge tractor-motors and they came upon her body in the early morning following the murder. They called it in to the Memphis police, and coincidentally, my cousin Janet Gault was working dispatch that morning. My father and Sandra had already called Janet to tell her that Kimberley was missing.

klin County Press

Wednesday, July 14, 1993 — 30 cents

Former Kennett woman murdered

Kimberly Wilburn

Violent crime continues rise

On the very next day after the murder, the men who murdered Kimberley attempted to set her car on fire. Then, two of them wrote a check to themselves from her checkbook and went into a bank to try to cash it. In the 'comments' portion of the check, they had written "Gardening." The teller recognized the address; by chance, she knew that it was a condo complex and they didn't hire private gardeners, so she called the police on a hunch and they arrested the men.

Eventually, all five men were tried and convicted to life sentences without the possibility of parole. Only one was over eighteen and he had just been released early from prison on an earlier conviction. The other four were under eighteen, but they were all tried as adults.

Needless to say, Sandra was beside herself with grief. We all were in shock. Kimberley was Sandra's only child, and she was her everything. My father had raised her for the most part with Sandra, and he was very close to Kimberley. We were all just devastated.

Stephanie and I flew back to Kennett for the funeral. This is one of those things that you read about that happens to someone else but it never happens to you. It happened to our family, and it was just awful. She was a darling, young woman with so much potential, just beginning her life. Her mother never got over it. How could anyone? Her heart was broken. Our hearts were broken.

This added to the insanity in our life. Stephanie was fighting her illness with antidepressants and anxiety medication. She was overmedicated and it was difficult to watch her as she struggled through despair and emotional trauma. Antidepressants are supposed to help. These drugs were not helping her in the way they were supposed to. Maybe they were the wrong drugs. Maybe they were making it worse. Maybe she was beyond help, I don't know. But, we were trying very hard to find a solution, and grieving through this brutal tragedy was very hard for all of us.

•••••

My mother had been fighting my dad in court for many years, attempting to recover back alimony and child support. She struggled through life, barely making it with the little bit of his retirement pay she had garnished from the Navy, giving piano lessons and performing on piano at local restaurants.

Elaine was on the verge of a victory in her long-running lawsuit against Maynard when Kimberley was murdered. Even my mom's heart broke from this news. Just a week after the killing, the alimony back-payment case finally went before a judge in Kennett. He was a friend of my father's and everyone there felt so much compassion towards Maynard and Sandra. The judge dropped the case, and my mother never pursued it again. It was sad, in a sense, because my mother struggled for the rest of her life to make ends meet.

Elaine had always had this vision of being a doctor's wife and retiring with money and prestige, and although I believe she deserved much more from my dad than she ever got, everyone could understand why the judge dropped the case. My mother just decided to move on after that, and she and Maynard hardly ever had any contact from then on.

Years later, after both of my parents died, I received a box with all of the court papers and correspondence from those ugly lawsuits between the two of them and I had to shred them. The vitriol and anger that they had piled on each other for all those years was there for me to read and cry about. And yet, as I shredded each paper that had been so important and earth shaking at the time, it no longer meant anything to anybody. It was a sad memory, though, and at this moment in time, in 1993, it compounded the grief we all felt for Kimberley's death.

What good does animosity do? Why is it so hard to rise above vitriol? A great first step towards healing is to allow the past to remain in the past, and move on, keeping your eyes on the present and the future.

When Stephanie and I returned home from the funeral, she began to spiral out of control again. She was so wrapped up in the emotion of the tragedy, she couldn't handle it, and so she resorted to drinking again. It was late summer, and we had really old air conditioners that weren't energy efficient, so the enormous, aging house on Via Escuela was always hot. When we got our electric bills, they were ridiculous. We were paying $1,200-1,500.00 per month all summer long, and the owner wouldn't pay for the air conditioners to be overhauled. We paid to fix them constantly, and along with all of our other bills, including the hospital bill and the remaining court costs from Stephanie's DUI, we just couldn't keep up with our mounting bills any longer, so we filed for bankruptcy. It was difficult for me, because I had worked so very hard for so long, and I felt like I had failed.

Stephanie's alcoholism was progressing quickly. She was completely out of control. One morning, at six o'clock she woke me up. She had been drinking all night and she had run out of liquor and passed out. She begged me to go to the convenience store and get her some beer. I told her, "Absolutely not! It's six in the morning! Are you crazy?" She started to plead with me and then she started to scream at me, threatening to rip up all of my clothes in the closet if I wouldn't get her more booze, now. Stephanie would not relent. She was brutal and very serious about exacting some kind of revenge upon me if I didn't go and get her beer RIGHT NOW. I finally threw up my hands and drove to the nearest convenience store. I was disgusted and tormented.

When I came back into the house holding the six-pack of beer at six-thirty in the morning, I was walking through the hallway and my almost twelve-year-old son Taddy came out of his bedroom. First, he looked at me, and then he looked down at the beer. He looked back up into my eyes with anger, sadness and disgust and asked me why I was giving her more alcohol. I was just devastated. I slammed the beer down on her bed and walked out of the bedroom. I helped the kids get ready and then drove them to school. We were silent in the car. I felt just terrible. I didn't know what to do about her. I didn't know what to tell my son.

What made it even worse was that Chuck was back to doing cocaine, and when I showed up at the poolside gig at *The Esmeralda* to work with him, he was drugged out and out of control most of the time. So, I was basically enabling him by keeping our shit together at poolside, and then I was going home and enabling Stephanie to continue to get worse. I started to question myself. What kind of person was I, to allow this? How had MY life gotten so out of control? I needed to make some big decisions. I just didn't know what to do.

•••••

The church and my children kept me from going out of my own mind through all of this. Because, when you are around people who are acting crazy, naturally, you question if you're even sane yourself. You wonder if you're as crazy as they are.

In order to raise extra money, I did two concerts at the church. I performed to sold-out audiences, doing originals, spiritual music and even reciting the soliloquy from *Hamlet* word for word as I had memorized it in sixth grade. I would make a couple thousand dollars on each event, and still donate a couple thousand more to the church. These were really the most fulfilling performances of all, because you had a captive audience of people who generally loved what you do, so they were there to have fun and to be inspired. Doing whatever I knew how to stay optimistic throughout this period was difficult, but necessary for my well-being and for the well-being of my children. Dr. Tom would remind us all that we are very valuable, worthwhile people. His wisdom was a lifeline for me when I needed it the most.

•••••

Stephanie's dad, Russ, was slowly improving. His speech was mostly back, and he was very helpful, doing dishes as therapy sometimes, and being there in his own quiet way for the children. He drank orange sodas all day, and he liked to read a lot since his eyesight had improved. The author Allen Drury had been a good friend to Russ, and he had given Russ most of his works, so reading Drury's books kept Russ busy. Somehow, he always had a smile on his face, and he was grateful that I was helping to support him with my hard work.

As fall of 1993 came around, we started to get calls for corporate work again, and Stephanie was busy in the home office most days. At the same time, she was crawling out of her skin still from the antidepressants, and she was back to binge drinking again. She would not drink for a month or so, yet still she would experience mood swings and problems with her medication, and then she would tie one on and destroy it all.

It was a bizarre time for me. *Palm Springs Life* magazine released a gushy article on me, taking a cool photo of me in front of the big *Soundcraft* mixing board at Hillery Johnson's studio and outlining all of the wonderful success I was having in production and performance. Outwardly, everything looked great, but inside my little family circle I was tormented and scared for my wife's health and my children's safety.

CHAPTER FORTY-NINE
Stephanie's Illness Intensifies

One night in early 1994, I was getting off of work doing a corporate gig at the *Marriott* and Stephanie called me sobbing. She was delusional and hysterical, and she told me that someone had come into the house and raped her. I said, "What the hell are you talking about?" In her mind it was real, and by the time I got home, everyone was awake and trying to console her.

I talked to the kids privately, and they said that everything was calm in the house until she woke up screaming. Later, I read about the long-term effects of large doses of *Trazodone,* and I honestly feel that this medication was doing way more harm than good.

Stephanie went to a psychologist the next day. She told him what happened, and he told her that he was required by law to call *Child Protective Services.* In his mind, if it was true, the children were in an unsafe environment, and if it was false, she was unfit to be a mother. Shocked, she told the psychologist she made the thing up, and left sobbing.

He never called *CPS,* and she never got a resolution or any psychological help for something that was all too real to her. After having already lost Regina to *CPS,* this was the straw that broke the camel's back to Stephanie. She went off the deep end. She had tried to go and get help, and it backfired in her face. She holed herself up in the bedroom for days at a time.

•••••

Following that experience, things got too weird for my son Kevin at the house, and he went to stay with his sister Regina for a month or so, with my blessing. This did shock Stephanie into sobriety again for a short period of time.

Even still, Stephanie's mind was full of conspiracy theories and fear. She had read somewhere that California was going to have a huge earthquake on a certain day, and everyone would be without food and power. She had a big map on the wall in the bedroom. On the map it showed the west coast of America in Kansas.

In order to keep her calm, before the day the earthquake was predicted to occur according to this insane theory, I actually rented a generator for the weekend and it stayed out in the backyard, unused, until we returned it.

Earlier in our marriage, Stephanie had gone through this period where she wanted us to consult an *Ouija* board to get answers from beyond. She found books at the library about psychic experiences. I had experienced a couple of psychic events in my life, so I didn't just discount all of this, but I wasn't at all as enthusiastic about it as she was.

We read books by Ruth Montgomery and Shirley MacLaine on the 'beyond' and about psychic experiences. As a youth, I was particularly interested in the books about Edgar Cayce's readings. All of this was fascinating to me until I realized that, by supporting or encouraging it, I was feeding in to Stephanie's illness. This was the dichotomy of Stephanie; at times she was delightful, kind, insightful, deep, caring, loving and pure; other times she was engulfed with a need for justice, fairness and truth; she was a very hard worker and devoted wife and mother; she was also haunted with real demons that contributed to her despair.

I loved her dearly, and her spirit and goodness were driving forces in my life, but most of the time I was afraid of how she might become in any given moment. And, as alcoholism is a progressive disease, compounded by her depression and bipolar disorder, her demons were beginning to win more often than not. The medications were not helping, obviously, because she was crawling out of her skin. Inserting alcohol into the equation was like adding fuel to the fire. Yet, even still, our day-to-day life would go on, and there would be moments when everything seemed almost normal.

•••••

Tad with Larry King 1992

In April of 1994, Vicki Diestelkamp invited us to be her guests at the *Indian Wells Town Hall* festivities at the *Esmeralda*. The great radio and television host Larry King spoke at the first one we were invited to. I told Vicki the story of how Larry King kept me awake and probably alive with his radio show back in 1981 when I was driving so late at night to Sparks, Nevada from my gig in South Lake Tahoe at *Harvey's Inn*. She related the story to Mr. King and he shook my hand and smiled. We spoke for a few minutes and I got a photo with him.

Tad with President and Mrs. George H.W. Bush 1992

Tad with President Gerald R. Ford 1992

During that evening, I sat briefly with President Gerald Ford. I was photographed with him. I had performed previously for a few events featuring President Ford at the Ritz-Carlton, so he was familiar with me. We laughed at the fact that I was always told to play the Michigan Fight Song whenever he went to the stage.

A couple weeks later, we were able to meet and be photographed with President and Mrs. George H.W. Bush, prior to watching the President speak. The President was gracious and kind. We spoke briefly about my father's Navy career, and about the President's service in the South Pacific in World War II. President Bush was the youngest Navy pilot to be shot down in World War II. His eyes lit up as he reminisced about his youth. As I spoke with him, Stephanie had a few moments with Barbara Bush.

One evening, Stephanie and I took the twins and Kevin to see the movie *Forrest Gump* with Tom Hanks. We really enjoyed the film, and it was wonderful to see Stephanie happy and straight. We all hugged a lot and it was a welcome respite from all the craziness that had been going on. I thought, why couldn't every night be like tonight?

•••••

Stephanie wanted to get Liposuction. She had felt haunted by her pear-shaped body for so long, and she felt that it would help. We had booked a headliner event for October of 1994, and we had received a deposit of $5,000.00 in early May. Even though we were still struggling financially and I would have been much happier putting it in the bank to pay bills, she wanted this so badly that we gave the $5,000.00 to a liposuction doctor as a deposit for surgery, which was to happen in August. The doctor told her two things: Stephanie must lose some weight first, and she must remain entirely without alcohol or drugs, particularly in the month before the procedure.

We couldn't bear the idea of extreme power bills through another summer in the Via Escuela house and the owner was not responding to our calls to pay for the repairs we had done on his air conditioners. We decided to move again to a smaller house. We found a house directly across the street from the house we had lived in on Loma Vista Circle in Palm Springs.

Stephanie made a pact with me that if we did the liposuction, she would not drink a drop of alcohol and she would exercise and lose some weight for her own health. Shortly after we gave the deposit to the doctor and put a deposit on the new rental house, we began to pack to move yet again to a new location in Palm Springs.

Two weeks later, around the first of June in 1994, on the weekend that we moved, Stephanie got so plastered drunk that she couldn't help to do anything with the move. I handled it all myself, with a U-Haul and the help of my children. She was completely out of control. She stayed in bed literally until we had to move the bed. I was disheartened and disgusted again, and so sad.

We had withheld the cost of the air conditioning repairs from our last month's rent at the Via Escuela house, and the owner sued us. He had already won a big lawsuit against the Palm Springs Unified School District for being fired, even though he had done underhanded deeds while he was there. He was not a good guy.

He had an attorney and we didn't. All we had were receipts and more receipts for power bills that were out of control. The judge ruled in his favor, and now I owed him $5,000.00. We had already gone bankrupt and this went into collection. I started to make payments on that debt. It was sad and wrong, but I learned another valuable lesson. Never go to court without an attorney (especially when your adversary has one)! And…never enter into an agreement with a dishonorable person, if you can avoid it. Also…I should have paid the rent and gone after him for the bills, instead of deducting them. I would have had a case.

Being right and righteous isn't always enough, especially when you're dealing with people who aren't.

After we moved into the Loma Vista house, even though it was a tight fit for all of us again with Stephanie's dad in one bedroom, Stephanie did go through June and July of 1994 without drinking. The liposuction doctor had implored her to exercise for a couple of months before she was to undergo the procedure, but she was ill and having trouble getting out of bed in general.

Taddy would go in to our bedroom when I was at work, and he would watch television and cuddle with his mother. Rachel would help around the house, and Russ was even helpful with dishes and minor cleaning. Kevin was back in the house, living with us; that made his mother happy.

Things felt okay again for a minute, but I was always hypersensitive, losing faith, thinking that the ball might drop once again. I was also very concerned for Stephanie's health. She had no energy and she didn't look or feel good.

We were back into the sweltering summer month in the desert. I was without a gig again, so I went to Tony Prenesti. I had been working off-nights at his *Club 340* in Palm Springs. I could always count on Tony, even though he didn't pay much. Tony gave me the full-time gig at *340* through the summer of 1994.

•••••

On June 13, 1994, O.J. Simpson's wife Nicole and her friend Ron Goldman were murdered. During this period, news coverage was wall-to-wall O.J. The world was consumed by O.J.

In mid-June, Rex Meredith and his wife Tracy Tracton Meredith came in to *Club 340* to meet me. Coincidentally, Tracy had been doing the same job that Stephanie had done for Greg McDonald at *Sun Presentations* and Rex had briefly worked for Greg and Paul as a comedian and television show host. They had recently had a bad experience with Greg and were no longer working for them.

They wanted to meet me because they knew that Stephanie and I had gone through a lawsuit against Greg and Paul. Tracy thought I would be much older than I was because of everything they had heard about us. Tracy was then waitressing at *Paul D'Amico's* restaurant with my old friend John Smith bartending there. Shortly after I met them, *Paul D'Amico's* burned to the ground, and Tracy started working with me at *Club 340.* Tracy had three children. Mason was seven, Spencer was almost three and Blaire was eight months old. We became friends.

Tracy had long, dark hair and olive skin. She was very pretty, but also worn from living life hard and having three children. She seemed to have a little chip on her shoulder, but she was nice to me.

•••••

Chuck and I were still working poolside at the *Esmeralda* Resort during the day. Chuck's addiction was out of control again. One day as we were performing at poolside, he collapsed; face first, holding his guitar, right into the pavement. I heard from friends that Chuck's wife was on the verge of leaving him.

The General Manager of the *Esmeralda* was Tim Tata. Tim had a brother who had a drug problem and had gone to treatment, and Tim told Chuck that if he went through treatment and came back sober, he could have his job back. Meanwhile, I would keep the poolside job and use other musicians until Chuck was able to return. Chuck went in to treatment, and I got Glen Myerscough to play flute and Steve Neilen to play percussion in Chuck's place. Tim Tata was a good guy; he went out of his way for us when he could have just dumped us because of Chuck. I appreciated his even temper, and I knew Mr. Tata appreciated the professionalism I always had, as our agency was handling the bulk of the corporate events for the resort.

When I got the first paycheck in my name from the *Esmeralda* for poolside, I was incensed. Chuck had been making much more than me for the entire time we had been working poolside together, for over two years. He had lied and told me he was splitting a little amount of money with me, and through the whole gig, he was completely ripping me off. When Chuck came back out of treatment, I told him that we would be splitting the pay properly as he had promised me two years before.

Chuck came out of treatment with a bizarre attitude. He got a haircut and he was going to do everything by the book. He was angry with me because I had found out about the pay and he was no longer making as much money as he had made before. He was not grateful that I had held down the gig and stood by him while he was in treatment. We didn't speak to each other half the time. We just played the music and left. It was totally weird.

Chuck was sober, but his addictive personality had taken him over, and he was having trouble coping with life at that point. Even still, I tried to be cool and kept showing up and being professional through it all. My problem was that I would look beyond the garbage and addiction and try to see into the person's beautiful soul and forgive them and help them, and while I was doing that, they would screw me over again and again. It took a few more years for me to let go of that pattern and to not allow toxic people into my life in the first place.

•••••

Stephanie was bored and restless. The antidepressants were making her feel out of sorts. She didn't really feel good enough to get out too much, and she was getting cabin fever. I was making $125.00 per night at Tony's club, and at the end of each week, I would put $625.00 into an envelope in the dresser towards the rent and bills. We bought groceries with my tips.

One night, towards the end of July, I came home and the envelope was gone. Stephanie told me that she had taken the money and gone to the casino and lost it. She had been drinking again. I couldn't believe it! I was literally working my ass off to try to keep the bills paid, and I could have stayed home and not even bothered. I was so upset with her. I asked her how she was going to be able to do liposuction in August if she was going to be drinking.

She promised not to drink and we rescheduled the liposuction for September. But, here I was again…dealing with addictive personalities at home and at work. And…Stephanie was always too tired to exercise. I was worried about her, and deeply disturbed about everything. My heart was breaking into pieces.

Towards the end of August, we made plans to go into Orange County and to see my Uncle Ted and Aunt Candy. We all needed our teeth cleaned and checked, so I called Ted and got appointments at his dental office; we planned to go into Mission Viejo on the night before the dental procedures to spend the night at their house; this would give us a chance to spend some quality time with my Uncle and Aunt, who had always been so good to me, and now good to my family too. We were only two weeks out from Stephanie's liposuction, so we thought it would be a good idea to get the dental work out of the way.

We drove into Mission Viejo and had a nice dinner with Ted and Candy. Ted offered us some wine, and Stephanie happily obliged to my dismay. I took her aside and reminded her of her upcoming surgery. She got angry and told me to mind my own business. She then proceeded to get smashed. She stayed up most of the night drinking. She was slurring her words and acting weird. It was embarrassing to me.

The next morning, she was too sick to go to the dentist. I took the twins over and Ted took care of their teeth. His assistant cleaned my teeth, and we went back to their house to get Stephanie to bring her home.

When we got to Ted's house, Stephanie was still drunk and she refused to leave. I begged her, then I insisted, and then we virtually dragged her into the car. As the twins sat in the back, she screamed at all of us, and cried, and finally passed out. My hair stood on end remembering the trip my father and I had taken in the car from Corpus Christi to Memphis with my mother, out of it, screaming at us from the back seat. I was losing all faith in what was left of my marriage. I couldn't take it anymore, watching my children agonizing about their mother, and not knowing what more I could do.

Halfway home, I had promised Taddy that we would stop for dinner at his favorite restaurant, *Red Lobster*. We went in to get some food to go, and Stephanie woke up and followed us in. She was out of it, and I was just beside myself with anger and sadness.

After we got home, Stephanie spent most of the next two weeks in bed until her liposuction surgery. After her surgery she was very ill. An image of her that haunts me forever was that of seeing Stephanie sitting in a bathtub full of bloody water, crying from the pain, and watching my Rachel console her as she patiently brushed out her matted hair.

After I went to work, when Stephanie finally was back in bed, Taddy would bring her food or whatever she needed. Stephanie was taking painkillers. She was out of it, and I was watching my children parent her. After a couple weeks, I expected that she should be getting better but she stayed in bed. I wanted to take her to the doctor for a follow-up, but she didn't want to go in that condition.

I had suggested several times that she go back to Alcoholics Anonymous meetings. I went to a few Al Anon meetings. Stephanie had decided about a year before this that Alcoholics Anonymous makes you give up your power to a higher power, and she felt that she would be better if she took her power back. That obviously wasn't working at all.

•••••

I was working during the day and dealing with Chuck's bad behavior. Then, I was going home and taking care of Stephanie. I was at my wit's end. One night, my friend Lou Tockman was sitting in *Club 340* and he could tell that I wasn't my usual self.

He asked me if I wanted to talk about it, and I sat with him on my break, telling him about how I couldn't look myself in the mirror anymore because I was enabling addictive behavior and propping up people who needed to learn how to stand on their own two feet.

Lou listened, and then he said, "For what it's worth, if you need a break from it all, I have an extra bedroom in my house and you're welcome to stay there for a month or two while you sort it all out." I thanked him. I thought the idea was ridiculous at first, but I started thinking that maybe, just maybe, if I left, Stephanie would 'get it' and finally get back on track again. But, how could I leave my children? I thought about it for days, and I finally decided that I needed to do something drastic to get Stephanie back into treatment. So, I made the decision to move in to Lou's house for one month.

More often than not, difficult decisions are not a choice between the right and wrong thing to do, but instead a choice between two bad options. You hope you're choosing the "least worst" one.

This was an extremely difficult decision for me. As a child, after everything I had gone through with my parent's divorce, I swore that I would never get divorced. No matter what happened, I would figure out a way to stay married and hold on to my family. When we are children, few of us understand the complexities of relationships, of addictive behavior, of dealing with a self-destructive companion. I cried as I packed my bag to stay at Lou's house, and I prayed that I was making the right decision. I just couldn't take it anymore. I had learned to have enormous compassion for the tough decisions my mother had made when she was faced with similar insanity, all those years ago.

Our office was in the house, so, even though I was sleeping at Lou's, I was back at my house every morning helping my kids get ready for school and then working in the office with Stephanie. I hoped that what I was doing would shock her into getting the right kind of help, but it had the opposite effect.

She was angry and depressed, and she railed against me every day. A week went by, and then two weeks. Even though I was there every morning, I was out of sorts, being away from my family, but I felt that I was finally standing on my own, and making a stand. I remember hearing Stephanie on the phone with a client one day, and she was slurring her words.

I didn't think she was drinking that day, but she was taking a mixture of antidepressants, anxiety medication and painkillers. I wondered how much business we were losing from clients who could tell something was wrong.

•••••

After another week, Stephanie told me that she wanted to move out of the house and have me move back in. She didn't like the fact that I had 'my freedom' and she wanted to have hers instead. I began to realize that there was probably nothing I could do that would stop her from succumbing to her illness, at least for now. I agreed to move back in. Stephanie found an apartment over by the *Biltmore* and moved out with her father.

I felt like I had always been the consistent one in our family. It was natural and good for me to be back at home with the kids, but they were also unhappy and worried about their mother. We all were. Stephanie went through wild mood swings. One day, she came over to the house and ripped the computer out of the wall, taking it with her. She told me that she was going to sabotage our business and ruin my reputation. After I talked her down, she brought the computer back a day or two later.

Tad with Taddy and Rachel

•••••

On the nights I worked, Kevin would stay with the twins at home, so they weren't alone. Rachel and Taddy were just thirteen years old, and although they were very mature, I still felt they were too young to be alone. In October of 1994, we found out that Regina was pregnant with Gregory McDonald's baby. The baby was due in May of 1995 and they decided to get married in Las Vegas in January of 1995.

Stephanie began to try to reach out to Greg and Sherry McDonald and establish some sort of relationship with them. After all of the lawsuits and anger, she didn't get very far with them. She was agonized about all of it; she still felt conflicted about the damage they had done to our lives, and yet, now, she was going to share a grandchild with them. This did not contribute at all to her well-being.

I did spend many days with Stephanie working in the office through this period, and we had some long talks, reflecting on our lives. I wanted to continue to counsel her; I just could not live with the madness any longer. I still and always loved her. I was just watching her fall apart; it was devastating to my soul, but I had run out of options on how to combat her illness, and it had robbed me of my own sanity for years. I prayed that she would once again accept treatment, or go back to AA meetings, or something. I knew she was searching for an answer, but her demons were strong.

•••••

Tracy Tracton Meredith was getting a divorce from Rex. We worked together and found ourselves together at closing time, a few nights per week, so we would sit and talk about anything and everything. I thought she was a little bit stuffy but she could appear more sophisticated than you might expect. Her long, dark hair complimented her skin. She was thin and pretty, but a little worn from a life possibly lived too hard. Tracy was about a year older than me.

After a month or so, we started dating. This was really weird for me, because I had never actually dated anyone. I had fallen head over heels with Stephanie from the first night we stayed together, and I had generally been a loyal and devoted husband, with the exception of the Monica experience. My life was my wife and children, and my children were still most important to me, but it was fun feeling the spark again, and Tracy was a fun person to party with. Tracy was a party girl with three children. I should have seen it coming.

One night, Tracy's estranged husband Rex came in to *Club 340* and waited until I was done. He asked me if we could talk and I agreed. I stepped outside and he assaulted me. I didn't want to fight him, so I got away from him, but not before he damaged my ribcage. I was having trouble breathing when I went back inside, and the police came and arrested Rex. I didn't want any of this! I was in pain for weeks after that. I took a couple days of bed rest before I could get up and function.

I understood that Rex was in pain and jealous and I felt sorry for him. I also felt bad that his marriage had crumbled as mine had. He was remorseful for what he had done to me, afterwards. It took a while to heal after that experience, but Rex and I became pretty good friends years later.

A week or so after that experience, Stephanie came in to *Club 340* wearing a very revealing sparkling low-cut blouse. She stayed at the bar drinking all night. I wanted to tell her I loved her, and this was not the way to get at me...and to please go home, but she had a mind of her own and I knew she was there to flaunt herself and upset me. I took deep breaths and got through the night.

•••••

After we dated for about a month, Tracy revealed to me that her father was a famous restaurateur. He had a restaurant in Los Angeles for many years and he had moved it down to Del Mar in the 1980's. His name was Red Tracton. In November of 1994, we took a trip to Del Mar to meet Red. Tracy and I stayed at the *Winner's Circle*, a timeshare next to the restaurant. We had dinner at *Red Tracton's* and sat with Red for a while. I was told that Red was a hard-core person. He was like a character from a *Damon* Runyan story, brash at times and somewhat arrogant, with street sense. He could be brutal to his employees, but Red was very kind to me. I got the impression from some things he said that he didn't like Rex all that much, and he was glad Tracy was happy.

The General Manager of the *Esmeralda* resort decided to cancel the poolside gig for the coldest part of the winter. As sad as I was to lose that income, it was such a relief to not have to deal with Chuck and his bizarre behavior every day.

CHAPTER FIFTY
More Unbearable Tragedy Strikes

Christmas of 1994 was difficult. I invited Stephanie over to help us decorate the tree. When she arrived, she was slurring her words. I couldn't tell if it was the antidepressants or something else until Taddy found some booze in her purse and poured it out. He loved his mother so much and he wanted her to be okay. He tried in his own way to guide her and to let her know his true feelings.

Stephanie was condescending to me, but still I handled her with kid gloves and we got through it. For Christmas, Stephanie bought Taddy the *Star Wars Trilogy* on VHS, and he was happy to get it. He hugged her for a long time after he chastised her for drinking.

On New Year's Eve, my band was performing at the *Indian Wells Country Club*. Stephanie came to the event and danced through the night with different men in front of me. She wanted me to be jealous and take her back. I wasn't angry. I felt bad for her because I still loved her with all my heart. But, I had decided, and then she had decided, and neither one of us could see beyond the pain at that point. I still held out hope that she would get the help she needed.

•••••

In January of 1995, Regina got married in Las Vegas. Stephanie went to the event, and she again tried to make nice with Greg and Sherry McDonald, although I knew that in her heart she was hurting so much inside.

I wasn't invited, which I understood. I didn't want to rock the boat. Stephanie had just found out that I was dating Tracy. Regina decided to disown me for the time being, and I got it...I knew that it was good for Stephanie to have an ally in her oldest daughter. I wanted her to have support and encouragement from wherever she could get it. Regina and I loved each other, but her mother needed her way more than I did at that time. I wanted to be at the wedding, but I knew better. I was told that Stephanie drank through it all, and didn't seem to be getting any better.

•••••

When she came back from Las Vegas, Stephanie made a conscious decision to try to get me to reconcile with her. She was hanging out with a guy living in the apartment underneath her. I thought he might be a drug dealer, and later I found out that she was getting amphetamines from him.

Whenever we were together, Stephanie and I would talk about things. She was really disturbed that I was dating Tracy already. I just kept telling her that I wanted her to be okay, and if she would just get back on track and give me some kind of a track record that, of course, there was a chance we could get back together. I wasn't leading her on. I meant it. I just couldn't live with the madness anymore. I treated her with kid gloves. I wasn't "all in" with Tracy. I just kept praying that Stephanie would find a way to her own redemption.

Stephanie wanted Rachel and Taddy to stay with her during the first weekend of February of 1995. The twins knew she was out of control and they didn't want to deal with it. They were thirteen and starting to express their thoughts and feelings more. They loved their mother, but they didn't want to babysit her. Stephanie was upset, but I really felt like it was part of this group effort by all of us to tell her to please get it together and be okay again.

When a train is speeding towards a brick wall, no one else can stop it except for the conductor.

On the night of Saturday, February 4, 1995, I was over at Tracy's house after a gig. Stephanie called Tracy and they talked for about an hour. Stephanie was really high on something; the way she was talking, I thought she might have multiple drugs in her system. After all the years we had been together, I could easily tell what was going on with her just by listening to her voice.

Tracy told Stephanie that, if there were a chance that Stephanie and I could reconcile, Tracy would step out of the picture. Stephanie told Tracy that she was pregnant with my child and that Tracy needed to back off. Of course, that wasn't true, but Tracy was pretty bothered and upset after the conversation. I felt like Stephanie was lashing out and trying anything to convince Tracy to back off. I was profoundly sad.

I had to perform at the Sunday church services early the next morning, so I left and went home to get some sleep. Tracy agreed to go with me to church the following morning. As drugged out as Stephanie appeared to be, I figured that she was going to sleep late the next morning, so I didn't expect a conflict.

The next day, I was surprised to see Stephanie at the eleven o'clock service. She waited for me to finish performing and saying goodbye to the congregation after the service. Stephanie went into the church bookstore and bought a *Louise Hay Calendar* for 1995.

After I was finally done, Stephanie asked me to go to lunch with her. I was going to perform at the *Sons of Italy* function at the *Palm Springs Pavilion* that afternoon, so I told her I couldn't. She was angry and told me that I promised that I would back off from Tracy if there were a chance we could get back together. She wanted to talk about it. I promised her we would talk about it later. As she went to drive away, I looked at her beautiful face. It was contorted with pain. I guessed that she must have had amphetamines in her system. Her demeanor reminded me of my father, all those years ago, shooting himself up with speed after drinking all night just to be able to function the next day. I didn't know what was going on with her and I was very concerned.

•••••

Back in those days, we had pagers, which were actually a much more popular way for people to reach each other than through cell phones. Cell phones were extremely expensive to use, as the providers charged by the minute. Instead, a person would call a pager and put your phone number in, and expect a call back.

For weeks, Stephanie had been paging me incessantly for whatever was on her mind. At first, I would call her back breathlessly, thinking she was in trouble. Then, as time went by, I realized that she was reaching out to me at all hours for no reason other than just to connect and make small talk with me. She was lonely and confused. I had been her rock for so many years. Even through all of the anguish I had been through with Stephanie, I wanted to be there for her, yet I had made the decision to use tough love and it wasn't easy.

While I was at the *Sons of Italy* function, Stephanie paged me about five times with her number and then "911." Stephanie had done this so many times; it was like the boy who cried wolf.

I waited to call her back until after the function, and then she didn't answer her phone. I knew her dad was there with her. I told myself I would call her again in a while, and then I went home to pick up the kids. I had promised them I would take them to a movie, and we went and saw *Dumb and Dumber* with Jim Carrey. I wouldn't have chosen that movie to see, but the kids really wanted to see it.

•••••

The next day, Monday, February 6, 1995, I was supposed to work a solo gig for Shari Kelley that evening. I got up and worked in the office for a while. I didn't hear from Stephanie all day. I thought, maybe she's finally sleeping it all off. Around three o'clock that afternoon, her father called. Russ said that he had gone in to check on her and she wasn't breathing. I told him to call 911.

My son Kevin took off in his car to go right over to her apartment. He told me he would call me immediately when he got there. The twins followed a few minutes later on their bikes. I got on the phone and called Andy Fraga, asking him to cover my gig. He wasn't available, but he got on the phone and called Gino Antonacci to cover for me.

When Kevin got to her house, he found his mother dead in her bedroom. In a moment, our lives were all shattered forever. The twins had just arrived when Kevin called me, sobbing. I rushed over to Stephanie's apartment. Kevin wouldn't let me see her in that condition. He had placed a blanket over her so the twins couldn't see her either. In a moment, our lives all came crashing around us in hysterical sorrow.

Stephanie had apparently asked her father for a Vicodin, the night before. She had taken more than one, and drank red wine. She also had antidepressants, anxiety medication and amphetamines in her system. The mixture of the drugs was toxic and led to an accidental suicide.

•••••

This moment of horror was truly the worst moment of our lives. It was surreal watching the medical examiner come and take her body away. We cried uncontrollably together for hours, holding on tightly to each other in disbelief. Regina came right over, already six months pregnant, and stayed with us. We were all inconsolable. It was truly the worst day of my life, feeling the pain and sorrow, and even worse, seeing it on the faces of my devastated children.

Eventually that evening, we brought Stephanie's dad Russ back to our house, and I helped the kids to their beds in a profound state of grief and exhaustion.

Life-changing moments are the milestones that mark our lives. Never forgetting, we look back to these moments in the sense that everything that occurred before this moment happened in a different universe; following this moment our world irrevocably changed and would never be the same again.

I was never a big drinker, but someone had given me a bottle of *Goldshlager* and I poured myself a shot that night; I sat up crying until I couldn't keep my eyes open any longer. I had lived within this madness for years and years, and the madness was over in an instant. It was too quiet.

In all the years I've lived since that terrible night, I've soul-searched on every level. What I could've, would've, should've done... The mother of my children was gone. I would never again be able to look into her eyes whenever my children accomplished something amazing, and say to that one special person, "Look what we created together?" I would never be able to hold her hand or dry her tears.

I blamed myself to the core for her death. If I hadn't left her, I thought… in reality, I was the scaffolding around her foundation, and when I left, it crumbled. The Stephanie I knew and adored was a complicated person with demons and conflicts all over the place, and our lives had evolved into an insane, unlivable situation. But, underneath it all, the girl I fell in love with was a sweet and kind person with a heart of gold. Underneath all of her 'garbage' was a little girl who was thrust into the real world too soon, and did what she knew to do to cope with it until she couldn't. She was scared…we were scared…but we kept pushing on.

Even as her disease had become unmanageable, she had continued to do amazing things, and all I could feel was such a profound emptiness in my soul. It was almost as if she cared almost too much… so much that her passion and sense of moral obligation consumed her. But the reality of the situation was much simpler than that. She put too many substances in her body at once, and her body finally couldn't take it anymore.

•••••

Stephanie and Tad in better days

One night shortly after her death, I had my first and only panic attack thinking of what had just happened. For a moment, I finally understood the terror of anxiety, and how hard that must have been for her to try to overcome on a daily basis. And, even through all of her pain and depression and sorrow, we had experienced so many moments of love and joy with our children. I had felt pride for her accomplishments. I needed to somehow focus on these, to preserve the memory of this complicated, beautiful soul. And, I needed to somehow try to be there for my lost children whose mother had left us all too soon.

The weeks and months that followed were a blur to me. I spent the next year in a state of confusion and despair, trying to put on a strong face through it all for my children, but making bad decisions at times and always, always regretting her death.

Circumstance trumps even the most elaborate of plans. We are the ones who will choose to either be victims of circumstance, or to pick ourselves up and move on to other plans. Even in the darkest depths of sorrow, we must not allow circumstance to kill our ability to find the courage to continue to plan for a better future.

Years later, when looking back on the events that led to Stephanie's death, even after I had gone through intense therapy to understand and alleviate the guilt… of course I understood that Stephanie was ill, and ultimately her illness took her from us, but it was in those moments when she looked at me with pleading eyes and the greatest humility while surfacing from one of her lengthy binges, needing me, begging me to help her… to do something, anything… this is what will always haunt me. And I know I tried everything, until I couldn't any more. But, what I would give to have succeeded in making her okay! I've cried a million tears since she left us.

My father, Sandra, my mother and all of my sisters except for Kathy came out for the funeral. Kathy came a couple weeks later, which was great because everyone had left by that time, and I really needed her love at that point.

Dad and Sandra paid for half of the funeral expenses, for which I was grateful. It was the first and only time he had stepped up financially to help me since I left him at the age of sixteen. My boys decided to view their mother with me at the funeral home. My daughters didn't want to go and I honored their wishes. They wanted to remember her, as she had been when she was alive. I cannot describe in words the depth of sorrow and anguish I felt as I stood there, holding my sons in that mortuary.

I had a Valentine's Day gig with my band on Saturday, February 11, 1995 at PGA West, with my band. It was the hardest gig of my life. I had to play love songs for hundreds of couples while I was devastated with sorrow. I was professional and I got through it.

•••••

We had a memorial service for Stephanie on the following Sunday at the church. More than six hundred people were there. It was standing room only. I prepared a statement, and my best friend Eddie read it for me at the lectern. Mike Costley came and sang *Wind Beneath My Wings* and *Always on My Mind.* The children and I sat in the front row sobbing through the entire service. What happened to us was a true nightmare, but the outpouring of love from so many people was something we all would never forget.

My sisters and friends put together a reception following the memorial service, at a ballroom at the *Hyatt Grand Champions Resort* where we had done the Kenny Rogers concert just three years before.

At the reception, my friend Pat McCaffrey came in wearing a Hawaiian shirt and gave me his condolences. He told me that he was on break from working the poolside job with Chuck over at the *Esmeralda Resort.* I said, "What?" Chuck had 'replaced' me without even telling me after the worst experience of my life.

I was overwhelmed with anger. I had saved the poolside job for him while he was in treatment just six months before, and he did this to me on the week Stephanie died. In that moment, all of my pent-up sorrow and frustration exploded in anger. I marched over to the *Esmeralda* resort next door and confronted him. I told him that he should have died, not Stephanie. At least she was a good person and he was just an evil son of a bitch.

When you look past the garbage into a dysfunctional person's soul, don't be surprised when they throw you out with the garbage.

I was grieving and out of line, but it felt good for a minute to finally tell him off. He had already screwed me once before, and I allowed him back into my life. Fool me once, shame on you. Fool me twice, shame on me. This was a lesson I learned the hard way. And…it was virtually the last time I would ever let this man anywhere near my life.

It was so very painful for me to go back and recall all of the tragedy I experienced in my years with Stephanie, and how it ended. I feel guilty for writing down my own version of what happened, knowing that she left the planet without being able to tell her own story. She would have explained her illness in different terms, and possibly that might have helped others who cope with mental illness, bipolar condition or depression.

I can't even imagine the depths of despair she struggled with on a regular basis. I believe that if she were here to tell her own story, Stephanie would explain that she loved all of us with every bit of her heart… and, although she was unable to overcome her demons, she never meant to harm the people she loved the most.

Stephanie would not want to be defined by her illness. She should rather be defined by everything she worked so hard to do to make our lives better; to somehow reach through the fog of illness and do great things in spite of the battle she was fighting every day. She would want us all to remember that she embraced motherhood with passion; from the moment she became pregnant with Regina at such a tender age.

For years, we had lived for the months at a time when she was a functional, great mother, a strong influence, a beacon of goodness and justice and someone who accomplished many things in her short lifespan. In spite of bad behavior that generally originated from her illness and addiction, she was an exceptional woman to the core; a good person who lost the battle, but left a legacy of beautiful children who would go on to do great things, as much because of Stephanie's influence as my own. We would never stop grieving; only time and years of personal inner work would make it manageable.

CHAPTER FIFTY-ONE
The Aftermath

Bob Brown and Donna Dougherty worked a lot for Stephanie as performers. Bob was a trumpet player and singer, and Donna was a really good female vocalist and keyboard player. She was really kind to me always.

I felt that Bob had an agenda with everything he did, to make himself look better, but I passed it off as insecurity. I still believed he was a good man. They had recently married, and they offered to help for a few days in the office to keep things going after Stephanie died, while I began to pick up the pieces. I was grateful for their help, and I somehow made it through the next few months with the agency, booking what was left on the calendar and keeping the few accounts we had on line.

As I began to look at the books, I realized that we owed much more to musicians than we had in Accounts Receivable. I began to panic when I saw the financially devastating results of the last few months of maintaining two households. I had not paid much attention to the books of *Valley Wide Artists & Events, Inc.* until this point. It was always mostly Stephanie's responsibility, and we had both dropped the ball.

•••••

Regina was moving into a new place with Gregory, and she couldn't have animals there. She dropped off her two cats. We already had two cats and two dogs at the Loma Vista house. What she didn't tell me…or maybe she didn't know…was that both of her cats were pregnant. Soon, we had more than a dozen animals everywhere in the house, and it was out of control.

Kevin was dating a very beautiful girl who was also a total bitch. In my despair, I wasn't thinking clearly. It was hard to make it through a day; grieving and watching my children grieve. I allowed Kevin to let his girlfriend move in with us, thinking it might help Kevin to cope; our house became chaotic with animals and roomies and Grandpa Russ.

Russ' ex-wife Barbara came back into the picture and decided to reconcile with Russ. We all thought it was only because he was now getting a check from the government that she wanted for herself. Either way, he agreed to go with her, and he left the house. I knew that Russ, although he rarely showed emotion, was feeling an enormous amount of grief and guilt as well for not being able to help his daughter to cope with her illness.

Russ, Craig and Barbara Haddock 1984

Russ would live for about another year until his heart fell apart on the operating table. The children were so sad to lose their Grandpa, but they were also grateful that they had gotten to know him so well in the three years he had lived with us. In his own way, he had a quiet wisdom, and the children liked to hang out with him. We missed him when he left.

•••••

Tracy suggested that the children and I take a few sessions with a psychologist. I went a couple of times alone, and the twins came with me to a few more sessions. It was particularly uncomfortable and painful for Taddy, because he had withdrawn into himself after losing his mother. My thirteen-year-old loves had experienced way too much tragedy in their young lives, and they were forced to grow up too fast.

I was consumed with guilt, not only for any role I might have played in Stephanie's fall off the precipice, but also for the pain I saw in all of my children's eyes. We all make mistakes in life, but I had an albatross around my neck, and I wondered if I would ever be okay again.

As I mentioned previously, when you are dealing with someone who is ill, you begin to wonder if you're ill yourself. I knew in my heart that her suicide was accidental, but at the same time it was the ultimate "fuck you." How would I ever get over this?

The psychologist helped me with many ideas, but there were three ideas in particular that stayed with me. First, she told me that, although it was tragic that Stephanie took her own life, it could have been worse. What if she had been under the influence, and gotten into a terrible accident with other loved ones in the car? Or, any one of many other scenarios could have happened…

Next, she told me that it was perfectly sane for me to make the decision to not allow insanity to continue to pervade my life. And, she told me that many people latch on to another person (as I had done with Tracy) in order to get away from an untenable situation with a mate. Having another companion gives you a certain type of strength to make a difficult decision to save yourself.

Third, she focused in on my fear of abandonment that had caused me to make so many decisions up to this point in my life. I was born into a big family, and one by one, all of my sisters had left me. Having been left alone with my mother as a young teenager, I tried to help her through her pain, all the while motivated by a fear that she would abandon me too. Eventually circumstance forced me apart from her, and then again with my father, Carol and now Stephanie. Now, I was basically clinging to Tracy for support and encouragement.

The psychologist gave me one basic thought: I was afraid of being abandoned again, but I had survived through all of the other times I had been abandoned, and I would continue to survive. She gave me a lesson; I was told to go back and find the child inside me, hug him and tell him that the adult 'me' would protect him and he would be okay. As weird as that sounds, it worked very well and I learned over a period of time to overcome many of the fears and self-doubts that had plagued me. Eventually, we all have to grow up. But, I had yet to let go of the need to 'fix' the women I chose as companions, and that need would stay with me until years later when my mother left the planet.

Cerebrally, I understood and appreciated everything I was being told. But, in my heart, I was consumed with guilt, and that guilt really never left me. Years and years later, I still felt that emptiness in my heart and the lump in my throat.

It is said that time heals all wounds. In my case, time and perspective did help immensely. After a certain time, the horror of what happened didn't just appear on its own and consume me all over again. I was able to take it out when I could handle it, and feel the feelings, and then tuck it back again until another time.

In grief, you must allow yourself to feel all of the feelings that can surface, including guilt, anger and depression…and to let yourself feel them over and over again, for as long as it takes, in order to truly heal.

•••••

Somehow, during this entire period, I was able to go into Hillery Johnson's recording studio here and there, and do some amazing music. Music is a great healer and my grief brought out some of the best music I had ever written to that point.

I was able to bring in Grammy winners and legendary performers to record with me, including Glen Myerscough, Steve Madaio, Pat Rizzo, Michael (Patches) Stewart, Gary Bias, and so many more. Hillery asked me to produce an album for Loretta Holloway, a famous Las Vegas singer, and the tracks were coming out really well. It helped to keep me directed through this difficult period.

Hillery had worked so hard to build his label, but he switched distributors again at some point; the new distributor went out of business and kept Hillery's inventory…so that was the end of the record label.

I retained dozens of completed songs, and they were the genesis of the album I released many years later entitled *For Stephanie*. All of this music came out of our mutual love, pain and struggles. And, it should rightly be named for her.

During the course of my relationship with Stephanie, I wrote so many songs; I would play them for her and she would come up with just one additional line that would be so profound and pull the entire song together for me…so, even though she never became a musician as she hoped, she did co-write many of my best songs. I had lost my life partner. Yes, she was flawed and yes, it had become too unbearable for me to live in that situation with her, but I was lost; half of a whole, searching to become whole again.

When you are in a relationship, don't lose sight of the fact that you are a complete, whole person. If you're in a healthy relationship, your "other half" is actually another whole.

After Stephanie died, my relationship with Tracy was never the same. It was really almost out of obligation that we stayed together for so many years after Stephanie died. I felt, "I made my bed, now I have to lie in it." And I believe that Tracy felt that she had an obligation to my children, mainly, to see them through the pain…that, in retrospect is almost funny to me, because she could be cruel to them (or about them to me mostly) at times. But, I did appreciate what she did give towards their healing in the years to come. She did take on a tremendous burden, and I am grateful to her for that sacrifice. It's not that we weren't attracted to each other at first, but at that point in my life, any real chance for love, in my heart, died with Stephanie. And… it was ironic that, here I was again, emotionally counting on a woman who was emotionally unavailable.

•••••

Tad with General Colin Powell 1995

On March 28, 1995, General Colin Powell was speaking at the latest Town Hall reception at the *Esmeralda* Resort. Vicki Diestelkamp invited me to go with her. It was the first event I went to (where I wasn't performing) after Stephanie's death, and although it was difficult for me, I did enjoy meeting and talking with General Powell for a few minutes at the reception. He was gracious and brilliant. We took a photo together.

•••••

On May 15, 1995, Regina's daughter Whitney was born. Stephanie had a granddaughter and she was not here to experience the joy of it all. Worse, Regina stayed at arm's length with me through this period, mostly because she and Tracy weren't getting along, and the pain was too much to bear. Whitney was a darling girl, and her birth brought needed joy into our lives in spite of the circumstances we found ourselves in.

Gregory, Regina and Whitney 1995

In order to forgive, you must also learn how to let go. If you cannot let go, you have not truly forgiven.

Regina actually did reach out to Tracy several times to make peace, but Tracy did not extend an olive branch. Tracy would say, "I can forgive, but I won't forget," (the equivalent of not forgiving) as if Regina had done something wrong by supporting her mother. I felt that it was small for Tracy to be that way, but I was weak in my grief and confusion, and I didn't push the issue like I should have.

I didn't participate in Whitney's early life as much as I wanted to, but eventually I was able to begin to make up for it as she grew. They never were able to just come and hang out with us. I always had to go to them in order to see my first little granddaughter. I regretted that. Whitney was a darling baby and I was so happy for my oldest girl. My twins and Kevin stayed close to Regina always, and I was grateful that my little fractured family had banded together in unity.

Regina and Whitney 1996

Towards the summer of 1995, my household was out of control. Kevin was even getting tired of his girlfriend's antics and he wanted her out of our house but didn't know how to do it. We had dozens of dogs, cats and kittens roaming everywhere. I was doing everything I could to keep *Valley Wide Artists and Events, Inc.* afloat, in spite of our growing debt.

Summer was approaching, and Red Tracton wanted Tracy and her kids to come down for the summer. He had always had the thought of having Tracy work for him, but he never felt that she was stable enough in her life with Rex to give her the opportunity. He decided to give her the chance to start learning the business as a hostess at *Red Tracton's* during the lucrative summer season when the *Del Mar Racetrack* was open, directly across the street from the restaurant.

Red offered to give me the two off-nights performing at *Red Tracton's* throughout the racing season. David T. Smith was the regular performer at *Red's*, and Red loved him. I contacted the *San Diego Marriott*, located in downtown San Diego, and they hired me to work in their lounge on the main nights throughout the summer.

I decided to move out of our house on Loma Vista Circle and move to San Diego with the twins for the summer. Kevin was graduating from High School, and he decided to live with Regina for a short time before going to college. Regina took many of the animals, and we just brought our black kitty with us to San Diego.

•••••

I found a lovely little cottage in south San Diego, at Mission Beach for the twins and I. It was a healing place, very quiet. After living in the desert for so many years, I could feel the moistness on my skin. The smell of the eucalyptus trees within the canyons and the ocean breeze brought back memories of my childhood. Mission Beach was familiar to me from the short time I lived there after we moved back from Texas when I was a kid.

We had a nice couple of weeks until Tracy came down with her children to stay with us. Tracy's sons, Mason and Spencer were wild children. They would run around in circles screaming at each other, raising hell, and didn't have much direction when we all came into the picture. Blaire was just a toddler, and taking them all on was like allowing a new brand of insanity into our lives, when quietude would have been much more healing. It certainly took our minds off of everything, though, to have them around.

Tracy had an *Au Pair* nanny for her children in Palm Springs named Kiki. She was a lovely Swedish girl with a constant smile who just knew how to handle children. She couldn't come down to San Diego but she recommended her friend, Violetta. So, Violetta also came with the children and our little quiet house turned into a wild place to be.

Spencer, Bla[illegible]nd Mason - 1996

•••••

Although he was only seven years old, Mason had a huge emotional wall up against me... and he had a difficult personality. He had a big crop of straight dark hair. Mason was an inquisitive and slow talking boy, not afraid to let his feelings be known, even in the form of a tantrum. He was a daddy's boy and he was very upset about his parent's divorce.

I completely understood how he must have been feeling and so I handled him with kid gloves. I probably should have tried a little harder to be a stronger influence on him, but his mother allowed him to be selfish and cruel at times, and she coddled him. If another person took a drink out of Mason's glass, he would throw a fit and insist on a new glass of whatever he was drinking. If you went to wake him up and he wasn't ready, even if it was time for him to wake up, he would scream at you to leave him alone.

He was really a problem child who grew into a problem teenager later. At the same time, he was a darling boy and I knew that in many ways, he was just a boy trying to cope with life as it came his way. But, he had also brought a strong personality into this world with him; he was standoffish and rude so often, and he never let me in.

Mason did like to do certain things like fishing, playing *Pokémon*, and collecting dinosaurs. His dad was good to him when they got together, and Mason was his happiest when he was with Rex.

•••••

Spencer, on the other hand, was just turning four years old when we came into the picture, and although he was a wild child at first, over time he mellowed and accepted the love and hugs he got constantly from me, Rachel and Taddy. Spencer's mind was always going. He also was super-inquisitive about everything, and he didn't let anything get by him. He was an in-your-face kid with a gravelly speaking voice, but extremely cute! Like most kids of his time, he was into the *Power Rangers*, and little action figures, and he LOVED Michael Jackson.

Spencer would spend hours in front of the television carefully studying videos of Michael Jackson dancing and singing, and he would emulate every pose and dance. By the age of five, Spencer was a very good dancer, and he was hilarious, like a mini Michael Jackson!

•••••

Blaire was a darling little quiet girl. She became another one of my sweethearts through the years. She was fun and loved to play dress-up. She loved *Disney* princesses and fancy gowns. She had a little problem with a connection between her brain and her eyes; until it was corrected later, it presented itself as a learning disability, although it was not that at all. She was actually a very intelligent, happy little girl.

All the kids looked up to Taddy and Rachel. I think Rachel naturally evolved into being their big sister. Taddy was good to them but he was struggling with life in general, and although he never gave me a hard time and he was always gentle and kind, I was constantly worried about him. I just loved my boy and I couldn't bring his mother back. I prayed and prayed that he wouldn't blame me forever for what happened.

So, as chaos engulfed our little beach cottage, one night, Tracy came home from work inebriated and got into a loud argument with Violetta. The fight moved from inside to outside our little house, and they were screaming at each other at the top of their voices at three in the morning.

On the very next day, I got an eviction notice from the owner of the house. I was devastated. My life was still in chaos, and as time went by, I realized that Tracy had almost the very same disease that Stephanie had, except Tracy's disease had a different face on it than Stephanie's had. We found another place to live...I worked through the summer and we decided to go back to the desert.

•••••

At the end of the summer, I made a really bad decision for us all to move in with Tracy in Palm

Springs to her condo. At the time I thought it was a good idea, because I was working so much, the twins would have a home with a family to live in rather than being alone in a place waiting for me to come home every night, and being unsupervised. In doing so, I perpetuated the chaos in our lives.

Red had bought the condo in Palm Springs in the 1960's. He had actually put two condos together into one, so it was very large, but it had two kitchens! We needed to renovate one of the kitchens and turn it into a bedroom for Taddy.

I was seriously in debt and musicians were calling me to pay them for gigs they had done before Stephanie died. I owed a lot of money to my friends. I was scared. Red made a deal with me to pay a little rent. He was totally cool. I wanted to pay him something, even though Tracy had been living there rent-free because it was her dad's place.

I needed to pay for the renovation and repairs, so I became a couple months late on his rent, but I gave him all the receipts and he was totally cool. He knew what I was going through, and he was truly good to me. Tracy, on the other hand, was very upset that I didn't pay him rent AND pay for all the renovations.

•••••

I had musicians calling me and every extra dime I was making would go to paying them all back. It took me two years to pay back all of the musicians I owed, but I paid each and every one of them back. It was a huge blow to my reputation, but what could I do? And, the worst part was that I had no savings and no money to fall back on. All I could do was to stay focused, and rebuild my integrity by making sure that eventually they all got paid. Every time I had an extra $100.00 here and there, I would pay it to one of my friends, and check another $100.00 off of the list of the thousands of dollars I owed. It was a painful process, but most of them stood by me through it all. And, through it all, I was grieving and dealing with a 'new' family dynamic.

As we were finishing completing the remodel on Taddy's room, it started to rain. The roof had multiple leaks, and Taddy literally had a waterfall next to his bed. He was forlorn and I was so sad about it! Worse, one of the children had gotten into Taddy's room and torn up the *Star Wars* DVD set that his mother had given to him. He was crying when he showed me what had happened. I didn't know what to say.

I was angry and sad that Stephanie had left me with so much debt and responsibility. Still, I was determined to try to be the best daddy ever. I held my son for an hour until he went to sleep. Eventually, we got the roof fixed.

CHAPTER FIFTY-TWO
Picking Up the Pieces

The twins were now in ninth grade and I was working with my band at the place that had once been *Patti Z.* It was now called *Bobby A's,* and Bob Arrazano was the owner. He had been a friend of mine for years, and he was good to me.

I was still answering the phones for Valley Wide Artists & Events, Inc., mostly in honor of Stephanie, trying to keep the business going in her memory, although I couldn't carry Accounts Receivable as I had done in the past.

Fortunately, I had a group of loyal musicians who worked with me for the most part, understanding what I was going through and that I was committed to making sure they all got paid, no matter what. I had a couple of awful moments, though.

One night, I had hired a guitarist, Mark Linford, to work with me at the *Ritz-Carlton*. Mark arrived and set up, and then he refused to perform with me unless I paid him in advance, on the spot. I didn't have my checkbook with me, and I begged him to understand. I told him I would go home after the gig, write the check and hand deliver it to him but he refused and left. I was super embarrassed in front of my client, and very sad that my life had come to this.

I had always been super-reliable and consistent. I had always paid good money to my musicians, and always on time until this point in my life. And, it was due to circumstances beyond my control that I had found myself in this sad place.

The clincher to my embarrassment was when I hired Donna Dougherty and Bob Brown to do some Christmas Caroling with me at the mall for the Holidays. Donna was six or seven months pregnant at the time, and they did the gigs. I went to pick up the check at the mall so I could pay them, and the mall management office had moved. They sent me a letter stating that they had changed hands and accounting procedures, and it would be a month before I would get the check. I couldn't pay my carolers immediately!

I called Bob and told him what had happened. I offered to show him a copy of the letter from the mall management, but he exploded in rage at me. A day or two later, tragically, Donna lost their baby. Bob called me ranting and raving about how it was because of me that they lost their baby. He believed that it was the stress about not getting paid that caused her to miscarry. I was devastated. There was nothing I could have done to remedy the situation. I loved Donna and I grieved for them; I even understood how he needed to point his rage at losing a child at me, and it added to the enormous guilt and burden I was carrying in my life.

I did everything I could to try to make it up to him, but he wouldn't hear it. As soon as I got the check, I paid them immediately a month later, but it was too late to repair that friendship. He went on a crusade against me. Although I had no proof of it, I guessed that he was the one who wrote anonymous letters to all of my clients saying that I didn't pay my musicians.

It was awful and it was all happening in this year of confusion and despair following Stephanie's death. Soon afterwards, I gave up on trying to maintain her agency. I still got calls from good clients, but I picked and chose what I knew I could do faithfully.

Somehow, I picked up the pieces from those dark days and maintained most of my friendships. I was forever grateful to the musicians who stayed by my side through all of that, and I made sure later to pay more, by far, than any other bandleader did to his musicians, to somehow try to make up for everything bad that had happened. But, it did take me over two years of scraping cash together to pay back all of my friends. These were dark days. I paid each and every one of these musicians all of the money I owed them, though.

I continued to witness the effects of Stephanie's accidental suicide on my children and on my life. For God's sake, it seemed like only yesterday that Kimberley had been murdered, and the one-two punch of these tragedies hung heavily over our lives. Never once, even through the darkest moments, did I ever even consider the thought of ending it all. That's a fool's errand. I had too much to live for.

No matter how hard life gets at any given moment, God may just grant you the blessing of a new, better tomorrow. If you have loved ones for whom you are responsible, get your shit together and press on.

After that experience, I never looked back and I was never late paying anyone for his or her services. Red Tracton always said, "Fast pay makes fast friends." Boy, did I learn that lesson the hard way.

•••••

Meanwhile, I got the tax bill for 1995 and it was an even greater debt than the money I owed to musicians. I worked with an accountant to get an *Offer in Compromise* with the *IRS*, and in three more years, I had that completely paid off as well. So, slowly the phoenix rose from the ashes... One of my favorite quotes is by Albert Camus: *In the depths of winter, I finally learned that within me there lay an invincible summer.*

CHAPTER FIFTY-THREE
Family and Friends as a Healing Source

When the summer of 1996 came, I called my father and asked if he was ready to take me and my twins on the vacation he had promised to take me on when I was fourteen. He agreed to meet us in Washington, DC and to take us through the Shenandoah Valley to see his childhood home, as he had done for me when I was a young teenager. Knowing how I was struggling financially, he went a step further and paid for our round-trip airfare. I thought Sandra would join us, but she was ill and stayed home. Although it had been more than a year since Stephanie died, we all still felt lost in a sense.

In becoming whole again, every little step towards that goal is progress in your healing.

So, Rachel and Taddy and I flew first to North Carolina to visit my sister Suzanne. Suzy was now remarried to a man named Carey Ramsey, who was very religious and southern, and always kind to my children and me. Carey was a Vietnam War veteran with PTSD and back problems, and through his gruff exterior existed a man who was devoted to his wife and family.

It was great to see Suzanne again and to reconnect with her children. We spent a few days in Greensboro and then took the *Amtrak* train to Washington, DC. The twins enjoyed taking the train; the views through the woods of North Carolina and Virginia were breathtaking. When we got to Washington, D.C., my dad was waiting for us. We spent a couple days with Maynard in D.C., toured the *Smithsonian* and the great monuments. It just so happened that when we went to see the Capitol, a runner was carrying the Olympic torch to the *U.S. Capitol Building* and we witnessed the Speaker of the House, Newt Gingrich, do a ceremony honoring the Olympics.

At one point, we rented a car and drove with Maynard to West Virginia. We saw the sites of some Civil War battles, including *Manassas* (or *Bull Run*, depending upon what side you were on) and *Boteler's Ford* at Shepherdstown, which was the bloodiest battle site of what would eventually become West Virginia, during the Civil War.

At Shepherdstown, dad showed us *The Rumsey Monument*, a tribute to the inventor of the steam engine, in an obscure park by the Potomac River. It was the same monument he had showed me as a boy. My dad recounted to my twins that he and his brothers would swim near the monument in the river as they were growing up.

Maynard showed us his tiny High School where he had graduated as Valedictorian. We went to a general store that was filled with memorabilia, and on the wall was a turn-of-the-century photo hanging on the wall, which still included my beloved grandmother Audrey in a group of people as a young woman.

Maynard showed us a tin roof, still standing, that he had built with my grandfather who worked in sheet metal at the time, when my father was a boy. It was a healing experience for all of us, being together on that trip, and I was grateful that Rachel and Taddy got to see a glimpse into their heritage. After a wonderful day, we drove back to Washington.

From Washington, Maynard flew home and the twins and I continued on the train to New York. We were met at the train station by my sister Kathy and my brother-in-law Steven. We spent a few days at Kathy's; after our visit alone with my sister and her family, Tracy flew in to New York to see the sites with us. Tracy's big gift to us was tickets to see *Phantom of The Opera* on Broadway. Taddy and Rachel were delighted, and we spent a day seeing the *Statue of Liberty* and riding in horse-drawn carriages in *Central Park.* We stayed at Kathy and Steven's huge house in Brooklyn. Rachel and Taddy enjoyed being with their cousins Michael and Yash once again.

Walk in the path of your forebears and you just might find your own compass again.

It was during this trip that I really began to feel the seeds of discontent with Tracy. As generous as she was on this trip, she had a pessimism that was pervasive, and more than once she made a point of telling me how unhappy she was with me. I think she was unhappy in general, and she was going through the motions in life. We stayed together after the trip, but it always seemed like a struggle to maintain a relationship, as hard as I tried with her.

Tad with Tracy 1996

Tracy's children were another story. The twins and me were becoming really close to Spencer and Blaire, and we continued to try to show Mason love and kindness through it all.

•••••

Following our trip back East, we all went back to San Diego for the remainder of the summer. I worked at *Red Tracton's* again on off-nights and drove back to Palm Springs to work the main nights at *Club 340.* Taddy got a job in the kitchen at *Tracton's*.

Blaire - 1996

Brett Nicholson, the chef, was a pretty hard guy to work for but he liked Taddy and he treated him really well. Taddy worked hard for him too, and he ended up working two other summers in the kitchen with Brett. They became lifetime friends as a result of that experience. I was grateful that Brett took Taddy under his wing, and Taddy stepped up.

Other people who were working at *Tracton's* embraced me and my family. The waitresses were all so kind to us. The growing theme behind the scenes with all of them was… what the hell is Tad doing with Tracy? Everybody told me much later that they couldn't believe the way she treated me in general, and that she was as snobby as I was nice. It hadn't started out that way, but Tracy was beginning to change her behavior towards me, and it would become even more ridiculous as time went on.

•••••

I remember when Stephanie would come in to my gig in the early 1980's and get drunk. I would be so embarrassed and angry. I worked so hard to have a stellar reputation and to fight the stereotype, always showing up on time, being classy and kind and avoiding controversy. I felt like people were judging me, as if my life was out of control. She was the mother of my children, and I wanted people to love her and know who she really was; she was not this drunken idiot. It was different with Tracy. I didn't care as much how she behaved. Tracy was Tracy and everyone kind of knew that she was generally out of control. She was a party girl.

As time went by, Tracy would exhibit more and more narcissism. Many children raised alone without siblings become narcissistic naturally. Everything is always about them. They become almost detached as a way of self-preservation. Red Tracton would make a joke about Tracy, "She goes to a football game; they're in a huddle and she thinks they're talking about her."

Interestingly enough, most narcissistic people I've known also experienced painful self-loathing. It's almost like they actually hated themselves underneath the façade of narcissism. Tracy was a perfect example. Dr. Tom Costa used to say, "If I tell you that you're a very valuable, worthwhile person, you'll think I must be talking about someone else, but if I tell you that you're worthless and you're going to hell, you'll think to yourself, 'he knows me like a book.'" This is why we need to constantly remind ourselves how worthwhile we are, not from ego but to overcome self-doubt. Positivity can be like Chinese food... it goes right through you, and you have to fill up again with it quickly afterwards.

•••••

Jimmy the bartender was the 'character' at *Tracton's.* He was gruff and sarcastic towards everyone, and all of the old men who drank at the bar just loved him. I knew that Tracy was attracted to him as well in a kind of bizarre way; later, she would spend way too much time with him after work while I was at home with her children. But, Jimmy was always kind and respectful to me.

Jimmy Fulara

Some of the waitresses had been with Red for many years, back to when his restaurant had been located in Los Angeles. Anita, Linda and Randy were part of the 'old guard'. Pam was the head waitress. Robin Watters, Tammy Neeley, Barbie Hoover and Robin Dougan were the younger waitresses.

Robin & Danielle Dougan

Robin Dougan generally did cocktails in the lounge with me, and she could run circles around anyone else. She was the best waitress I had ever seen, at least since I had witnessed Stephanie at work all those years ago. Robin had gorgeous, thick, long reddish-brown hair and lovely green eyes, filled with compassion. She was a tiny girl with a darling face and a pixie smile.

Robin was married to a bipolar man... when we began to talk, we realized that we had a lot in common, and she became a wonderful, compassionate friend. She was a Midwestern girl, having spent much of her childhood in Akron, Ohio, so she was down-to-earth. Robin also happened to be a nurse, and she worked at Scripps Hospital in Encinitas.

•••••

As time went by, I began to finally realize that my early vision of being a 'star' in the traditional sense was probably not going to happen the way I imagined it all those years ago. I always felt like I was born to be a star, but little things began to chip away at my dream and they became big things, as I took on more responsibility and made different choices. But, I realized at some point that it's okay.

I was contributing to people's lives through my performances and recordings. People were always genuinely touched by my music and the messages that came out of it. When they came to watch me perform, they might come in for one drink and then stay for hours and hours. Many, many people would come up to me and tell me how their attitudes and emotions were turned around, or how miserable they were when they walked in, but now they were happy.

Through adversity, I learned that I was actually a lot stronger than I thought I was.

I never, ever lost my persistence, though, or belief in my talent. I began to realize as time went by that I was put on this planet to create meaningful content, whether it be a musical composition, or a book, or later, films (and even creating and/or raising children too!)

One of my favorite quotes about persistence is by President Calvin Coolidge: "Nothing in this world can take the place of persistence. Talent will not; nothing is more common than unsuccessful men with talent. Genius will not; unrewarded genius is almost a proverb. Education will not; the world is full of educated derelicts. Persistence and determination alone are omnipotent. The slogan Press On! has solved and always will solve the problems of the human race."

•••••

Red Tracton had been dealing with a slow-growing cancer for several years, and his health was beginning to fail. Later, in early 1998, Red was in the hospital at Scripps for a period of time with a really bad infection in his heart. Robin Dougan was five or six months pregnant at that point, working through her pregnancy at Scripps, and she was buzzing in and out of his hospital room when we came to visit. Red was grateful to have 'one of his own' helping to keep an eye on him in the hospital.

Red hinted that Tracy should possibly move to San Diego within the year. My twins were not going to graduate from High School until 1999, and I was determined to keep them in the same school with the same friends until they graduated.

•••••

Back in Palm Springs after the summer, the twins were now in tenth grade and I was still struggling hard to make ends meet and continue to pay back all of the taxes, musicians and creditors that arose from the incidents around Stephanie's death. Although it was a dark time for me emotionally, I was grateful to be with my children. Their calm love in return kept me going through this period.

Tracy was all over the map. She admitted to me that she was struggling with addiction to pills, mostly, and smoking a lot of cigarettes. I started smoking pot again with Tracy. I had not smoked any marijuana for years while I was with Stephanie, but Tracy liked to smoke pot and I followed suit.

One day, the twins found a bong water pipe in our closet and confronted me about it. I didn't deny it. I just said I was using it a little bit in order to cope with life, and I would be careful not to ever turn into an addict or to ever be out of control…and I never was. I was always the consistent one in their lives, and I wasn't about to stop now. I understood their fears. They had already lost one parent to addiction. I was going to do everything in my power not to let them down.

•••••

Mason, Tracy, Tad, Blaire, Rachel, Taddy and Spencer
1996

Christmas of 1996 was kind of weird. Tracy and I pulled together many gifts for the children. Through this period, I was consumed with guilt even still…guilt about losing Stephanie, guilt about putting my children into a new environment so quickly with other children. On Christmas day, as they all opened presents; I looked at my beautiful twins and thanked God once again for their grace and kindness towards others. It wasn't the perfect situation for them, but they were handling it like pros, like everything else they always did. They had been forced to grow up before their time, for sure. During this period, Taddy grew almost twelve inches in a year. He started out the year with a high voice, shorter than Rachel, and ended up the year towering over her with a new deep voice. My babies were growing up.

Taddy and Rachel were also very patient with Tracy's children. Mason, Spencer and Blaire looked up to them, and the twin's calmness made a huge impact, especially on the younger two children as they grew. Spencer's nervous, heady behavior began to wane and he became a calm, loving boy.

Even still, Tracy broke my heart one night when she told me that she couldn't wait until my twins grew up and left the house, so she could have her 'normal' life back with her children. That was such an absurd comment to me. My twins couldn't have been more gracious or kind or helpful. The truth is that we just really shouldn't have ever merged our households together, but I was 'in it to win it' at this point, and I continued to try against all odds to give my heart entirely to this new dysfunctional family unit. Looking back, the quality of my life would have been so much better with just the twins and me living together alone elsewhere, but I also believe that the Lord wasn't done working with me, putting me in a situation to raise new stepchildren and mold them into good people. No matter what, we all learned a myriad of new life lessons from this experience.

•••••

In early 1997, the great designer Blackwell, known for his *Worst Dressed* list, was coming to the *Ritz-Carlton* and he needed a musician-choreographer for his fashion show. I had experience in this from the work I had done in the early 1990's with Jacque D'Amboise so I volunteered.

Blackwell was a cranky old gay guy, full of himself, who took to me a little too quickly and enthusiastically. I fought him off the entire time, but I was competent, he was happy, and the fashion show went off well.

Also, in early 1997, I did an event with Glen Campbell. He was extremely kind and accommodating to me, and we performed many songs together. It was a highlight of my career in a sense. Years back, when I was ten years old, my mother and I were walking through the Memphis airport, and we came across Glen Campbell. He was in the height of his career at the time, with hits like *Galveston, Wichita Lineman,* and *By the Time I Get to Phoenix.* Of course, my mother dragged me over to meet him, and I was in awe of this superstar. So, on this night in 1997, I jokingly introduced myself, saying, "Hi Glen! Remember me from the Memphis airport in 1968?" He laughed. Glen Campbell's voice and musicianship were always amazing to me.

CHAPTER FIFTY-FOUR
Somehow Getting Back on Track

I put together a group of musicians to perform my original songs live for the first time since the Kenny Rogers concert in 1992. My friend Jeri Lynne wrote charts of my original music and I brought in Gary Bias and Glen Myerscough on sax, Michael (Patches) Stewart on Trumpet, Steve Neilen on drums and Gilbert Hansen on bass.

Gilbert Hansen was cool! We already went way back… he had been part of the Craig Eaton band and then the *PS Rockets*. Gilbert had been on the road with the *Pointer Sisters*. He was one funky bass player and a great guy. We recorded about a thousand tracks together over the years. Gilbert was my first-call for electric bass always. He was a bluesy singer and a good songwriter too.

We got a job at *Peabody's* in downtown Palm Springs on Wednesday nights for a while. The job actually cost me money, because they couldn't afford all of the musicians I had with me. It was a labor of love, but it was cool to play original songs and we were very well received.

One night, Jeff Edwards came in and invited me over to his house in Palm Springs. I hadn't seen Jeff in a year or two, and he showed me his recording studio that he had built into his house. He was using three *Tascam DA-88* digital tape recorders in sync, and *Studio Vision* music software on his computer with a ton of outboard equipment. I thought it was so cool and I made a vow to myself that I would build my own studio once I finished paying off all of my debt.

Later, Jeff moved his studio out of his home into a little house in North Palm Springs, which he dubbed the *Karaoke Casa*. He had just secured a huge contract to produce sound-alike versions of hit songs for karaoke. I had a little bit of experience with this from the last time I had worked with Jeff on Karaoke. I worked over there with him when my schedule permitted. My twins came in and sang some of the children's songs for karaoke, which was cool. I learned a lot about duplicating sounds and elements of production from different eras, through that experience. This would be essential in my future endeavors, particularly for the *Yamaha* gig I would get eventually.

•••••

In June of 1997, Tracy and I took Mason, Spencer and Blaire to Hawaii. It was my first time in Hawaii. We went to Maui and Oahu, and I fell in love with Hawaii. It was truly the most beautiful place I had ever seen on earth. The ocean water was like bathwater; the skies were dark blue and the tropical breeze engulfed you with a mellowing influence. Mangoes, papayas and pineapple were in great supply, and the fish was fresh and tasty. The local people were friendly and tanned.

Even still, I was unhappy on the trip because my twins couldn't go, and I really wanted to share Hawaii with them. I also had always had this dream of a romantic trip with a girl I loved, but it wasn't going to happen this time with Tracy and three kids. Tracy had a short fuse with her children, and sometimes she would scream at them when talking firmly would have worked much better.

But, I made the most of it, and it was breathtaking. Snorkeling and swimming in the ocean was amazing there. I thought I could bodysurf on the windward shore of Oahu, and I almost broke my neck when a wave crashed me in to the hard sand underwater with ferocity. Even with all my experience bodysurfing in San Diego growing up, I had no idea of the brutality and strength of the Hawaiian Pacific coast.

•••••

When we returned to the desert, I was struggling to stay working full-time. I got a call from a club owner in Palm Springs, wanting me to perform full-time for a month. I had never heard of the club, but the money was good, and I was delighted to take the gig.

When I showed up, I looked up at the sign and the place was called the *Rainbow Cactus*. It was a gay club! I thought, "Oh, no! I just signed a month contract to perform at a gay club!" As I was setting up, I didn't notice anything different than any club I had ever worked, but by the time I walked in on the first night, I knew right away that this was a full-on gay club.

Quite a few old monogamous gay couples were very kind and generous tippers, and there were a lot of young aggressive gay men who thought I must be gay if I was performing there. I began to understand how women feel when they say they feel like a "piece of meat" when men look at them. I handled it well, although at times I have to admit that it was uncomfortable. One time, a guy went to say goodbye to me and he tried to literally bite me on the neck. But, for the most part, the clientele was generous and kind, and it was an enjoyable gig.

When I was finally done with the contract, as I was breaking down my equipment, the cocktail waiter came up to me and said, "You know, I don't hold it against you that you're straight." That was his way of saying that he thought I was cool. It was a little backwards way of thinking for me, but I got it. I have had many friends throughout the years who were gay, but not a lot of social interaction with large groups of gay people until this experience.

Through that experience, I was able to understand and appreciate the fact that homosexual people are generally just wired that way, and if a heterosexual person can get around the naturally uncomfortable feeling, you will find that they are just people too… some good, some bad, with hopes and dreams, love and loss, just with a bit of a different perspective.

It might be that someone who reads this, a hundred years from now, will wonder why being gay or not gay was even an issue, as I'm sure society will progress as it already has done since this experience happened to me. But, many people in my generation frowned upon homosexuality, and there was huge pressure, particularly on boys, to denounce it. The Supreme Court had yet to rule on the legality of gay marriage, and acceptance of homosexuality wasn't mainstream in society. Just 3 or 4 percent of the population of the United States were homosexual, but they were a vocal group and made many strides towards acceptance by society as a whole as time progressed.

I remember when I was in seventh grade; my mother had bought me a pair of *Farrah* blue jeans. They weren't *Levi's*, and a young Mexican bully kid called me a "fag" one day when I wore them. I never wore those pants again, although they were a nice pair of jeans. It was just a part of living in those times.

I never considered myself 'homophobic'. That label was bandied about in order to make people aware of how they were treating gay people. To me, a phobia denotes that you are afraid of someone or something. I never had a fear of gay people. As I mentioned, I have had a lot of gay friends in my life and we get along great! I just never had any of those tendencies myself.

Later, though, in 2006, I performed for an *Equality California* convention. These people were fighting for equality for lesbians, gays, and transgender individuals. Hearing some of the speeches, I did get a greater understanding that people really are just wired a certain way, and it's fine. Frankly, I feel that everyone should have equal rights, but I'm not one who enjoys people shoving their beliefs in my face, whatever they are.

Live your life in peace and harmony, and let others live their own lives without repression. Speak freely but don't force your beliefs, religion or sexuality on others.

•••••

Around the middle of July, 1997, I was sitting with Red Tracton at *Tracton's*, having lunch. Sid Craig, the husband of Jenny Craig and mastermind of her huge weight-loss company, was quietly eating lunch alone, reading a newspaper across the restaurant. Red went to Sid and said, "I noticed your stock went down several points today. You lost ninety million dollars today, Sid, and you're sitting here, reading a newspaper and eating your lunch as if nothing happened! What gives?" Sid looked up from his newspaper and calmly said, "It will go up again at some point. It always does." He was unfazed! His reaction was a great lesson to me: What goes down, must come up again (at some point!) … in a nutshell, that was the story of my life.

•••••

In August of 1997, Shari Kelley wanted me to bring my band to Lake Tahoe to the *Hills Brothers* estate on the North shore, which had been purchased by a billionaire named Tim Blixseth. He was having a fourth of July party with fireworks on the lake, and Shari wanted my band to headline the event.

Tim Blixseth

Right before I was to leave for Montana, my ten-year-old *Plymouth Voyager* minivan exploded in our carport, setting the building on fire. The van was totaled, so I borrowed a *Ford Ranger* pickup truck from my friend Kenny Brown. Tracy rode up to Lake Tahoe with me, and we followed *Route 1* up the California coast to Big Sur and then to Monterey, before we went East towards Lake Tahoe.

Tracy was bent on going to see the scenic seventeen-mile drive in Monterey, California, so we left early morning from Big Sur on the second day. By the time we made it to Monterey, the fog was so deep that we couldn't see three feet in front of us. We were told that it is so beautiful, but we couldn't tell! After we arrived in Tahoe, Tracy flew home and Rachel flew up to spend the rest of the week with me before we drove back home together.

The event at Tim Blixseth's estate was amazing. He had a number of celebrities on hand, including Jack Kemp. Mr. Kemp had just unsuccessfully run as the Vice-Presidential candidate on Bob Dole's ticket against Bill Clinton in 1996. He was the architect of the concept of trickle-down economics, a former *National Football League* championship-winning quarterback, former congressman and *Secretary of Housing & Urban Development*. Jack and his wife JoAnne were very kind to me and we became fast friends.

Tad with Jack Kemp 1997

Tim's wife Edra was a great hostess and on the night of the fourth of July, the main event was amazing. My band was on a stage outside at the water's edge with our backs to the lake, only two miles from the house I had rented so many years before, when my twins were babies.

When the fireworks went off, all of the lights in the party were turned off for the spectacle; we had our backs to the lake, so, in the darkness we couldn't see the audience or the fireworks behind us. Tim had told me to play patriotic music throughout the entire spectacle. I started to play Neil Diamond's song *America,* and the fireworks continued on and on, so I kept the beat going and morphed into *America The Beautiful, The Star-Spangled Banner* and every other patriotic song I could think of, all while keeping the beat.

At the end of the twenty-minute fireworks display, the lights went up, we finished our patriotic medley with a great crescendo and we could finally see the crowd in front of us. Most of the people were crying from the emotional impact of the experience. Jack Kemp ran on to the stage, wiping the tears from his eyes and hugged me. He told me that it was the most powerful patriotism he had experienced in years! That was a great moment.

It was so very special to spend the week with my Rachel, although we found out during that weekend that Princess Diana of the United Kingdom had died in an automobile accident, and the world was mourning. Diana was an amazing, sympathetic, beloved figure, engrained into the imaginations of millions of adoring fans.

I took Rachel to Incline Village to see the house we lived in when she was a baby, and the places I had performed. We drove to Reno and I showed her the home in Sparks we had brought the twins home to when she was born. We meandered back to California and ended up in San Diego to spend another summer in Del Mar.

CHAPTER FIFTY-FIVE
Returning to Headliner Music Production

Tad with the Righteous Brothers 1998

Fantasy Springs Casino in Indio, California, promoted Headliner concerts. The person they had in charge of producing the concerts was acting against their interests, skimming off of the top to keep extra money. One of my friends was a casino boss and he recommended me for the position.

Over the course of the next year or two, in 1997 and 1998, I produced a number of Headliner events at Fantasy Springs from the ground up, including *Earth, Wind & Fire, Los Lobos, The Righteous Brothers and Lou Rawls.* It was kind of bizarre because they were in the process of building their showroom through that time period, so the concerts were held in a huge parking lot outside behind the casino. I dealt with staging and security along with booking the events and handling all of the details of bringing in big artists. I enjoyed the process and I got to meet some amazing people.

When we brought in *Earth, Wind and Fire,* the tribe that owned the casino was pushing a measure in the State of California that would allow for more gaming machines, so the General Manager of the casino asked me to call them and suggest that the group mention the upcoming election while they were onstage doing the concert, and tell the audience, "Vote Yes on 'A'".

I called *Earth, Wind and Fire's* management and they put me with Maurice White. He told me that the band had decided early on in their career to stay apolitical, and he respectfully declined. That made a lot of sense to me, and from that point forward I thought I would adopt the same policy for myself.

The moment you become a political spokesman for anything, you've just lost half of your audience and half of your friends too.

Of course, I had strong opinions on political subjects. It's a wonderful thing to live in a free society where you can express your opinions openly. Being able to do this is rare in the history of mankind. But when you take your strong opinions, turn them into policy and impose them upon other people who do not agree, against their will, you've just taken away a little piece of their freedom. We must be careful not to allow our basic freedoms to continue to erode until there is nothing left. It is also dangerous to believe that you have the moral high ground in your beliefs. There are two interesting sides to every story. Let's all take the best of both sides and make it into something we can all appreciate, without stripping each other of sacred, hard-fought liberty.

Progress is inevitable. Society changes; manners and mores change through time, but values are the glue that holds a society together. We must never lose our values, or we will lose our freedoms, slowly but surely.

On the night of the *Earth, Wind & Fire* concert, my friend Gary Bias was on stage performing on tenor saxophone with the band, and they were gracious and kind. Gary had recorded often in my studio, and it was cool to see him with an outstanding band. A huge windstorm overwhelmed the venue on that night, and blowing sand filled the arena as they were performing. The elements were ridiculous and it was virtually ruining the concert. The band stayed totally professional in spite of the heavy wind and the sandstorm that was saturating their voices, instruments and equipment; they rocked through their incredible R&B hits and put on an incredible show. They joked that we certainly provided the Earth and Wind for them, and they were going to give us the Fire of their performance!

Shortly after that event, Gary Bias called me, mentioned that a position was opening up for a keyboardist in the band and he wanted me to come in and talk to them about it. I would have loved to tour with *EWF*, but my first priority was my children and I couldn't leave them to go on tour, especially after they had lost their mother.

The whole experience with *Fantasy Springs* was an eye opener. I learned how Native American casinos work behind the scenes, and I got insight into working with all of the top agents at *William Morris, CAA*, and the other big dogs. They are mostly overworked bears; very curt and short with you; when you get them on the phone, you really have to be prepared with all of the information they need in advance. And, they are always pushing an artist or two, so you can sometimes get a good deal on a large act in order to add a smaller one…or, if an artist is already in the area on one date, you can usually get them cheaper if you book them the following night or the night before.

•••••

Somewhere around this time, the State of California outlawed smoking in bars and most public places (with the exception of Indian Casinos on Native American land). This was truly a game changer for me. Up until this point, people would come in and chain smoke all night, blowing cigarette smoke in my face while I gasped to take breaths singing all night. My closet had smelled like cigarettes for twenty years. I could finally breathe.

My sister Kathy could not breathe. She found out that her mitral valve on her heart was failing from a childhood illness. Kathy was rushed into open-heart surgery in New York. Immediately, I flew into *JFK* airport and went to the hospital.

As I rushed into the hospital just hours after her surgery, I came around the corner towards her hospital room. Kathy was just awakening from her surgery and I was stunned to see an apparition of my deceased Grandmother Audrey hovering near Kathy, comforting her. I kid you not. It was surreal. As I walked into the room, Audrey smiled at me and disappeared. Kathleen had her guardian angel watching over her, and I witnessed it with my own two eyes.

I stayed for a week in Brooklyn, patiently helping Kathy, pushing the fluid from her feet from swelling edema, feeding her and loving her. Each of my sisters came for a week following until Kathy began to improve. Following her surgery, she did get better, although her heart would slip into fibrillation on occasion and she would have to be cardioverted.

•••••

In the mid-1990's, John Phillips, the great singer-songwriter of *The Mamas and the Papas* fame moved to Palm Springs following a liver transplant. He had some basement tapes that he had recorded several years back with the *Rolling Stones* and he wanted them transferred from two-inch reels to ADAT digital tape. We planned for him to come into Hillery Johnson's studio, and Jeff Edwards was to do the engineering on the session. When John was wheeled in by his manager, he looked yellow and close to death from the effects of the transplant, almost like an old version of Howard Hughes. He hardly muttered a word as these amazing tapes were transferred over.

As John recovered, we became great friends. He would come in regularly to *Club 340* or somewhere else I was performing in Palm Springs. John always wanted to hear his own music performed by me, and that was a bit intimidating, but also very cool! I would play *California Dreaming* or *Monday Monday*, or any other of his famous hits.

Once, at John's house, he pulled out a cassette tape of a song he had just written. It was just his vocal and guitar, singing a song called *Kokomo.* John mentioned that he was going to give it to the *Beach Boys*, and we laughed! They hadn't had a hit in over twenty years! Nevertheless, he did get the song to them and it became a smash hit! John was a very kind, very giving person.

I remember after the film *Forrest Gump* was released, after Stephanie and I took the twins to see it, I saw John Phillips one evening, and congratulated him on several of his songs being in this hit movie. He shrugged his shoulders as if he had no clue and he said, "Oh, that must be why my royalty checks are so big this quarter!" Unbelievable, it was, but I really don't think he cared too much about anything other than enjoying life at that point. Unfortunately, he died of a heart attack on March 18, 2001. It was a blessing in my life to know this iconic musician and songwriter.

•••••

On January 5, 1998, my friend Sonny Bono died in a skiing accident in Lake Tahoe. He had been elected to the *United States Congress* just four years before the accident.

I was already booked to perform at Tim Blixseth's house in Rancho Mirage for an event just two weeks later with my band. A grieving Mary Bono was at the event. Mary came up to me and we hugged. She knew I had gone through the death of my wife just three years before, and we now had this terrible thing in common.

For years after this night, whenever I saw her, we would stop and chat for a few minutes. I also spoke with her son later when he was a young teenager, just to give him a vibe and remind him that his father was a great man.

But, on this night, just two weeks after Sonny's death, I was standing in a small group with former President Gerald Ford, Tim Blixseth, Mary Bono and Jack Kemp. They were all trying to convince her in a loving way to run for Sonny's Congressional seat. They felt that she could carry on his vision like no one else. She agreed and was elected just a few months later. She served for many years afterwards as a Congresswoman, representing Sonny's district.

•••••

On January 25, 1998, I attended my first Super Bowl with Tracy. We watched John Elway and the *Denver Broncos* beat Brett Favre and the *Green Bay Packers* at the Charger's *Qualcomm* stadium in San Diego. Following the game, I performed with my band at an event for Jack Kemp at the *Horton Grand* hotel downtown.

Being an ex-NFL championship winning quarterback, Jack Kemp was at every Super Bowl and his parties were full of celebrities and Hall of Famers. It was really exciting to work for him and he was as gracious and kind as you would expect.

Even through these exciting times, being with Tracy was a struggle for me always. She could be kind and generous and giving, but I always felt like, underneath it all, she was just tolerating me. She actually told me that she wanted a prince and got a pauper instead, implying that I wasn't good enough for her (little did she know that I'm a descendant of Hungarian royalty!). Once the passion of our early relationship ebbed, there wasn't much there. I felt like I was the only one who wanted the relationship, and I wondered why I even did.

Be careful whom you choose as a life companion. Once the early passion has ebbed, you'd better have a compatible friend beneath the lover or you'll live a miserable life.

In early 1998, Rachel and Taddy were Juniors in High School. One night, Rachel wanted to go to the Homecoming dance, which was important to her, and Tracy wanted her to stay home and babysit. I sided with Rachel, of course, and allowed her to go, and Tracy was so angry that she literally physically hit me. I was trained very young to never, ever hit a woman, and although I tried to restrain her, the outburst caused some bruises on me.

I still don't understand why I stayed with her through it all. As I mentioned, I just felt that I had made my bed, and now I had to lie in it. We were not happy, but still she relied upon me and I was still in the cycle of trying to 'fix' her, as I had tried with my mother, and Carol, and Stephanie. Also, Red Tracton was becoming very ill and I felt that I owed him loyalty for his kindness. And, I had bonded hugely with Tracy's kids, especially Spencer and Blaire.

Tracy did have her generous and kind moments. My son Kevin agonized still from his brief marriage to Amber when they were so young. Tracy offered to pay for his annulment, and followed through on her promise to him. Kevin was grateful to finally wrap up that confusing chapter of his life, and I was grateful for her kindness towards him.

•••••

Red Tracton 1997

When we went to San Diego, I would have long talks with Red. He had a fiery personality that matched the color of his red hair when he was younger, but he was like a mentor to me. We had a mutual respect, and I knew he was grateful that I came into his grandchildren's lives when they needed security and sanity.

Red told me sensational stories of when he was young; he owned the *Cal Neva* resort briefly in the 1950's and he told me a confidential story about how he bought the resort, and then sold it to Frank Sinatra.

He told me that once he had a piano player at his restaurant. Although the guy was highly recommended, he wasn't working out so Red waited until the end of the night and gave the pianist his notice.

The piano player got angry and said, "No, wait a minute, we had an agreement." So, Red said, "Okay." The next night when the guy came in to play, the piano was not in the restaurant. He asked Red, "Where's the piano?" Red had moved it literally into the men's restroom! He informed the pianist that he would be playing in there from now on. At that point, the pianist quit and stormed out in anger. Red had his ways to win, and he wasn't going to be pushed around by anyone, ever.

He would tell me that many times he had mobsters on one side of his restaurant and the FBI on the other side. He knew who they all were, and he never got involved in any of it.

In fact, in the late 1960's, a man kidnapped a banker's son in Los Angeles. The kidnapper contacted Red, hearing about his reputation, to spell out his demands. The police asked Red for help and he somehow negotiated the boy's release for a cash settlement. Red was to take the money and get the boy. As helicopters swarmed overhead and police followed him at a distance, ready to swoop in and save the boy when the exchange happened, Red was nervous. He had a million dollars in cash sitting on the seat next to him. Red wanted a cigarette and realized that he had forgotten his cigarettes. He reached in his pocket and realized he didn't have any money either! So, he reached over to the briefcase and pulled a hundred dollar bill out to go and buy cigarettes! When he pulled over to a convenience store, he was the most protected man in Los Angeles! He did end up saving the boy, and the kidnapper was caught.

Loyalty is a rare commodity; it must be regarded highly and equally reciprocated always.

Red was a colorful character. As he aged, he had lost most of his hair and he walked carefully, almost hunched over at times. He reminded me of *Yoda* from *Star Wars*, and he certainly gave me loads of wisdom that I greatly needed at that moment in time. More importantly, his gracious understanding of my severe financial condition after Stephanie died, and his generosity in allowing me to pay what I could, instilled a strong loyalty to him within me. He was a loyal man as well. I wasn't going to let him down, because he soon confided in me that he needed my strength.

Tracy decided to move to San Diego to be close to Red. One night during the summer of 1998, we attended Tracy's stepsisters wedding. I sat with Red and his wife Carolyn. Red confided in me that he was declining. He compared himself to a racehorse that was rounding the stretch for the finish line. He knew he was dying and he wanted me to take care of his daughter. He didn't want me to talk to Tracy about it, because he knew she wouldn't be able to handle it. He just wanted me to know and he asked me for my strength and help through the process. So, we found a house in Encinitas and moved to San Diego, still maintaining the condo in Palm Springs. I took him to every doctor's appointment, holding on to him and walking him in while he could still walk; sometimes cleaning him up in the restroom as he began to lose his faculties.

I would not pull my twins out of their school, so I went back and forth each week from San Diego to Palm Springs, depending upon my work schedule. My twins were responsible individuals, which helped.

•••••

Jeff Edwards had gotten into composing music for television. He was working with another composer on two TV series, *Renegade* and *Silk Stalkings*, both on the *USA Network*. Jeff had a falling out with the other composer, and although they were still working together, their relationship was icy and they worked from separate facilities.

Jeff asked me if I wanted to rent a room from him at his studio in Burbank. I had finally paid off every musician I owed. It had taken me three years, but in small increments, I had paid back thousands of dollars and squared up with each musician. I was prepared to start building my studio.

Jeff was upgrading his main mixing board, so he sold me his old *Soundcraft* mixer, and I pulled together some other equipment and set up my first studio in Burbank. I bought a *Tascam DA-88* digital tape machine so I could be compatible with his set-up.

I also purchased *Roland* and *Akai* samplers, which gave me access to libraries of high quality, sampled instruments. It was a huge learning curve for me, but I loved it. My main challenge was just getting there to Burbank on a weekly basis. Now I was literally driving in a triangle every week, spending a couple days in Burbank, a couple days in San Diego and the rest of the time in Palm Springs with my twins.

I was a quick study and I began to learn the emotional impact of underscore. There is a certain kind of finesse to composing underscore for film and television. You can work with or against the vibe to create an emotion. Many times, you create a 'theme' for each character, which may appear throughout the film whenever they appear, in the form of a melody or even a particular sound.

•••••

Jeff and Andrew Fraga, Jr. had put together a little group of dance tracks; the music was placed on the *Jenny Jones* show on daytime network television. Through about a month of regular usages in a large marketplace, they made almost $100,000.00 between the two of them on the project. I was floored and I wanted to get in on this production music thing.

Jeff had other projects that he needed help with, in addition to the two series, so I composed music for the *Famous Families* series on *Foxstar*, and a few other film projects. Jeff insisted on keeping all of the composing and publishing on everything I did, stating that he didn't want his clients to see anyone else's name on the cue sheets but his. Later on, I realized how shady that was, but I willingly went along with it, in order to better learn the craft of composing. So, for years afterwards, Jeff earned royalties on much of my work and I didn't. I did get a solid education on music composition and production for television, however.

Red Tracton's cousin Jonathan Sanger was a film producer in Los Angeles. He was working with Tom Cruise at *Cruise/Wagner Productions,* and Jeff and I did some innovative script treatments for a handful of scripts that they were trying to develop. It was actually a cool concept. We would approach the script as if it was a finished film, do mock 'cue sheets' with song and musical theme suggestions, basically spotting it in advance with ideas for score and music supervision. Jon loved the concept, and the script from one of our treatments went on to become the feature film *Suspect Zero.*

In June of 1998, Jeff picked up an extra television series that paid low money, and he asked me if I would quit my performance job and take the lead on the series for him. The racetrack was going to open in Del Mar in a month, and I told him I would do the gig, but I would not give up my performance gig. It's a good thing I didn't, because a week later his other series fell through and he took the job back before I could write a note of music.

The awful part of it, though, was that in the interim, I went back to tell Tracy about the project, and she got so upset that she assaulted me again, literally on the night of my fortieth birthday. Again, I restrained her and calmed her down, but not before she bruised me badly. I was living with yet another unstable woman. I felt like a shell of a man through all of this, but still I had a loyalty to Red and he was becoming very ill.

•••••

I maintained my studio in Burbank for about a year, and then it became too difficult to continue to travel and still accomplish what I needed to. Besides that, Jeff was becoming more and more difficult to work with, as he had been in the past, and I decided to bow out gracefully.

Sometimes you need to give a lot of yourself in the beginning, in order to learn a new craft or to get in on something meaningful. You will know when you have reached a point of progress where you can stand on your own, and after that point, you must not continue to allow yourself to be taken advantage of.

Three huge things I learned from working with Jeff through this period were essential to the production music I did later. First, most of what Jeff and I produced had a bit more flair than you might expect. It was all almost "over the top", so it got noticed. Second, I learned to be unpredictable in my beginnings and endings, when writing a cue or a song. Don't do the traditional stuff, or what anyone might expect. Even if you just change it up a little bit, it's unique. Third, I learned how to break production music into sections, building and changing it up regularly to make it interesting.

•••••

In the late summer of 1998, my mother, now living in Palm Desert in a manufactured home, went to the pool in her complex to relax and swim. It was a blistering August day in the desert, and the temperature was above one hundred and fifteen degrees. She sat on a lawn chair in the quiet complex and when she went to get up, her sandal caught on the chair and she fell, breaking her hip and several bones in her hand and arm.

My poor mother lay out on the hot concrete screaming for help for almost an hour before someone heard her. She was rushed to Eisenhower Medical Center, severely dehydrated, burned and in incredible pain. I dropped everything and made it to the hospital quickly. Her bones had become brittle with calcium deficiency and the doctors performed surgery immediately.

Because of the nature of the injury, Elaine was never able to play piano again, which was a tragedy to me, not only because I loved my mother, but also because I had always dreamed of recording her. She was truly the finest classical pianist I had ever heard, hands down.

After a month or so in a rehabilitation facility, she was allowed to return home, and she learned to walk again with a walker very quickly. My mother had always been so vivacious and energetic, and she wasn't about to let this injury slow down her schedule. I was proud of her for getting right back out there and figuring out how to continue to do most of what she wanted to do, in spite of her injuries. I also kept an eye on her, and shortly thereafter she moved into a condo in Palm Desert, which was an easier place for her to maneuver around. She was very hard on herself, though. She couldn't believe she had been so careless. Accidents can happen, no matter how careful you may be.

At the end of 1998, I relocated my studio, renting a bedroom of my friend Tammy Neeley's house in Encinitas, close to our rental house in North County San Diego. I set it up as a one-room project center.

•••••

Right around this time, Red passed away and Tracy went into a deep depression. She was beside herself with grief. Her mother had died when we first met, and Tracy was raised as an only child. All she had left was her father, and Tracy did not get along at all with Carolyn, his wife. She had a nominal relationship with Carolyn's daughters, her stepsisters.

In his will, Red left the restaurant to Tracy and Carolyn equally, and left it up to them to fight it out. Carolyn never set foot in the restaurant after Red died, but she would occasionally call in a stupor and fire people randomly. My friend John Smith was now managing the restaurant, and he would simply rehire them on the spot.

Tracy wanted to just let go of the entire business and move on. Carolyn offered her $2,000.00 a month for life if she would leave, and John and I pleaded with her not to take the deal. John found an investor about a month later and bought out Carolyn's stake in the restaurant. So now, John and Tracy were co-owners and business partners.

•••••

Shortly after Red died, I got a call from Jack Kemp. Tim Blixseth had offered to fly my band to Miami for the Super Bowl on January 31, 1999. I took Tracy with me, and she stayed pretty much wasted through the entire trip. The game was exciting, though, and the band went with us this time to the

Tad with Glen Myerscough and Steve Neilen 1998

game at the stadium in Miami.

We watched John Elway's last game ever, with the Denver Broncos, as he beat Chris Chandler and the Atlanta Falcons. *Big Bad Voodoo Daddy*, Stevie Wonder and Gloria Estefan performed at the halftime show. My female vocalist, Paula Stapleton, was from Canada and she knew nothing about football! There were millions of people who would have done anything to have her seat at the Super Bowl. But, Paula was great, and she was fun to hang out with. She was an amazing singer. I relied on her, everyone loved her on stage, and we became very close friends through these years of traveling and gigs. Paula had short, dark hair and a cute persona. She was fun!

While we were in Miami, I took off for an afternoon and went alone to visit my first girlfriend Carol. She was remarried and living up in Margate, Florida, just north of Miami with her husband and her cats. We spent a couple hours together reminiscing. It was actually great to see her, and it felt good to know that she still cared for me. We would always be friends from then on. Long ago, I had let go of my anguish from our teenage relationship, and I had been through far worse than that since.

After the game, my band and me rushed to the hotel to perform for Jack Kemp's after-party. As we waited for the people to arrive from the game, a nice man named Bill walked in and came up to talk with the band. As band members will sometimes do, we were telling dirty jokes and laughing, and Bill was a regular guy who seemed to enjoy it all. Later that evening, when the band took a quick break, Jack Kemp came to the microphone, and introduced Bill. He said, "Ladies and Gentlemen, it's my pleasure to introduce the new Governor of Colorado, Mr. Bill Owens!" The entire band was in shock! We had just been telling dirty jokes and cutting up with this guy. We had no idea he was the Governor of Colorado!

Following the event, we stayed in Miami for a couple days and enjoyed the landmarks and beaches before we flew back to California. I thought that the trip would help Tracy, but she was out of control.

I was pleased to find out during this time that my sister Suzy's son Charles and his wife Margaret produced a son, Gregory… and Suzanne's other son, Michael and his wife Christina gave birth to their first son Josh, on May 20, 1999. Just a year later, Michael had another son, Joey, born on May 18, 2000.

Michael, Charles, Suzanne, Wendy and Lori

•••••

Throughout this period, Tracy was lost in pills and alcohol. It wasn't a secret. She would be the first to tell you that she had a problem, and it was obvious because she was falling around the place all the time. She was grieving the death of her father, and escaping. She was also changing, becoming even more full of herself and even more emotionally unavailable.

John Smith took the reins and kept the restaurant going through the transition. But, something really ugly was emerging within Tracy. As soon as she inherited the restaurant, she became a different person. I took over the full-time job performing at Tracton's, and within a year, we had tripled the bar business. But, it meant nothing to her. She would look at me in disdain and tell me that Tracton's had always been a dinner house, and the bar didn't matter.

If you're with someone who does not recognize or appreciate the value of your contribution to their life, you need to move on.

John Smith felt otherwise. My formula of performing at high energy without taking a lot of breaks had increased their bar sales by $1.5 million dollars within a couple years, and continued to rise. I hadn't yet learned a very important lesson that I would later hang on to for the rest of my life. If you're with someone who does not recognize or appreciate the value of your contribution to their life, you need to move on.

CHAPTER FIFTY-SIX
Returning to my Childhood Home of San Diego

In June of 1999, my darling twins Rachel and Taddy graduated from Palm Springs High School. For years when they were growing up, I always had this idea that one day my kids would grow up and I would have more freedom. When it actually happened, I cried and cried, knowing how much I would miss them being there every day with me. I loved my children with all my heart, and we had clung together, all of us, after they lost their mother. We would continue to be a close-knit family forever, but the day they went off to college was one of the most bittersweet days of my life.

Rachel, Kevin, Taddy, Regina and Tad
Twins High School Graduation - 1999

Even still, Rachel moved to San Diego to study psychology at *California State University, San Marcos*. For a few months, she stayed at Tammy Neeley's house, and then when she moved out I used that room at Tammy's place for my recording studio. Rachel wanted to move in with her boyfriend, Robert Barone.

Robert was a couple years older than Rachel. They had met at a party while Rachel was a Senior in High School and had been pretty much inseparable since. Robert was a student at the *University of California, San Diego*, and they were intent on being together, so I gave her my blessing.

Rachel with Robert Barone
1999

Rachel had already gone up to Canada with Robert for almost a month during that summer. Robert's parents owned a campground on the lake in Westbank, near Kelowna, British Columbia. Rachel went with Robert and worked the campground store through the summer. His mother was kind to Rachel and it meant a lot to her to have a sense of family, although it was difficult for us to be away from each other for almost an entire month. It was the longest we had ever been apart since she was born.

Robert was a handsome kid, half Italian, half French Canadian, intelligent, with dark hair and a solid frame. He was very respectful and kind, and I could tell that he really loved Rachel. She was happy and that meant everything to me.

It was great to have Rachel still close to me in San Diego, going to college, although I missed coming home to her at night. The love I got from Spencer and Blaire helped a lot, but it didn't completely make up for the emptiness I felt, missing my original family.

Taddy had enrolled in film school at *California State University, Northridge*, in the San Fernando Valley just north of Los Angeles. My other son Kevin was also attending college in Los Angeles. Taddy lived in the dorms for a year, doing the work-study program to make extra money, cleaning dorm rooms. I sent him some money to live on, and yet I'm sure he ate a lot of *Top Ramen* and Peanut Butter sandwiches during that year. He never complained.

At the end of the school year, Taddy and Kevin decided to get an apartment together, and they remained inseparable for many years following that. Kevin moved over to *Cal State Northridge* and switched his major to film. As they went to college, they waited tables and bartended together, first at *Black Angus* and then at *PF Changs* in Burbank. I was glad Taddy had his older brother close to him. Kevin was a loving, hardworking young man, and he watched over his younger brother. I was proud of them both.

•••••

In the early summer of 1999, Shari Kelley booked my band to play for the groundbreaking ceremonies of the *Yellowstone Club* in Big Sky, Montana. Tim Blixseth owned a huge mountain in Montana and he was building an exclusive, private ski and golf resort.

With Paula Stapleton, Glen Myerscough, Gary Hartman, Michael Higgins and Steve Neilen, I flew into Bozeman, Montana. We rented a *Chevrolet Suburban* SUV and drove the hour drive into Big Sky. Tim put us up in a nice hotel and rented all of our backline equipment for the gig.

This would be the first of many times we made this trip as *Yellowstone Club* grew and came together. On this first trip, we drove up a hairline cliff trail on a dirt road in the *Suburban* to the top of the mountain. It was scary! When we got up to the summit, we set up on a stage of plywood atop bales of hay. Generators were brought in for power and we had to wear bear mace on our belts in case we saw a Grizzly Bear! I'm absolutely sure it was the most remote gig I will ever do in my life! Even the band was wondering if I was just taking them out into the middle of nowhere as a joke. But, it was an amazing experience. And, many powerful people were there on the top of that mountain with us; Senators, Governors and Statesmen hobnobbed with developers and dignitaries.

At one point, Tim took me aside, standing on the hill and he said, "Look around as far as you can see in every direction, I own it all." And, he was humble about it, he wasn't bragging. It was as if he couldn't believe it himself. Tim had been a welfare baby who made his enormous fortune with hard work and opportunity.

At the same time, I couldn't help but imagine an Indian Chief on horseback in the same place, hundreds of years beforehand, saying, "Look around as far as you can see in every direction, this is my land." It's all-relative.

Within ten years, after so much hard work, Tim lost billions in the recession of 2007, but during these brief, shining years, it was an incredible thing to be able to be a part of his dream. You can't take it with you anyways, but what a way to go!

Even the greatest pinnacles of success are fleeting. Nothing lasts forever. All that matters in the end is family, friendship and love.

After an amazing weekend of horseback riding, having great conversations with fascinating people, and performing, we flew back to our normal lives.

Around this time, I began to realize how fortunate I was to have worked with so many great musicians, each lending a little bit of their soul and perspective to my own style. More so, it was the life lessons that I learned from each one along the way that shaped my character in ways I never would have imagined.

Glen Myerscough, by his actions alone, always reminded me of the value of being a good person and living a Christian example. His exemplary musicianship was trumped by his graciousness as he guided me to be a better musician and a better person.

Steve Neilen's struggle with his degenerative disc disease, yet still showing up and performing through all the pain reminded me once again of the value of persistence in the face of agonizing odds. I appreciated his loyalty and cherished his friendship.

Chuck Buffamonte, in spite of the problems he brought into my life, nevertheless was a great musician and helped to bring my performance to a different level. He was enjoyable to work with, until he turned on me. And, we had been very close friends for a time. Chuck's example reminded me of how important it is to remember to be moderate in anything you do. I also became a stronger person, and much wiser, not allowing betrayal to negatively impact my character. One of my favorite sayings is, "I used to get angry; now I get amused." We all must learn to let go.

Tad with Michael Higgins 2004

Michael Higgins would always be a gem in my life. His guitar performance far exceeded that of anyone else I had worked with. He could follow me anywhere in an arrangement and make it sound like we had rehearsed it a thousand times. Michael was a kind, dedicated friend who always gave his all to every situation, and I loved hanging out with him too!

Paula Stapleton 2017

Paula Stapleton relied upon my strength to get through her travails at times, but in return, she reminded me of the strength that comes in passion for your art and for your friends and loved ones. She was all heart. I loved her dearly.

I couldn't even begin to list the musicians I've worked with and the influence each and every one of them had on me. Most importantly, after weeding through musicians who had problems with attitudes and emotions or drugs or relationships or reliability issues or whatever, to find that core group of performers I cherished, I found that it was the friendships far more than the music that I would carry in my heart forever.

There is a lesson in everything, if you're open enough to find it.

Racetrack season at Del Mar is a spectacle every year. A whole culture of people moves from racetrack to racetrack; jockeys, trainers, owners, gamblers, bookies, all frequented *Red Tracton's* during racing season, which lasted from late July until early September every year. I now held the full-time, five nights a week gig at *Red Tracton's.*

During racing season of 1999, business tripled and we had an insane six weeks, full of party animals. Frank Hamblen was the assistant coach of the *Chicago Bulls* team of the *National Basketball Association*, working with the legendary head coach, Phil Jackson. Frank and Phil had just won two championships in a row with the Bulls, and Phil was getting ready to take over the *Los Angeles Lakers*, with Frank at his side once again.

Frank and Uta Hamblen

Frank Hamblen and his wife Uta were in *Tracton's* practically every night during racetrack season, and we began a friendship that lasted for many years. Frank was a big, imposing man with a low voice, intense on the basketball court but when he came in to see me he always had a huge grin on his face. He loved good piano music; in fact, Frank was a piano player himself.

He would ask for Jerry Lee Lewis music, or Frank Sinatra's *My Way*. We had some nights of heavy drinking, and Frank & Uta were about as down-to-earth people as you can find. Dr. Jerry Buss was the owner of the *Lakers*. Jerry Buss and I had become friends over the years. Dr. Buss owned the *Ocotillo Lodge* in Palm Springs, and he had sat at my piano bar many, many times with his entourage (usually consisting of young *Laker's* cheerleaders). He was always very kind and generous to me, and I was thrilled that he hired Phil Jackson and Frank Hamblen to coach the *Lakers*. At the same time, *Staples Center* had just been built in Los Angeles, and on the day it opened, Phil and Frank were coaching the team to what would end up being five more championships over the next ten years.

They had the luxury of coaching amazing players like Kobe Bryant, Shaquille O'Neill, Derek Fisher,

Karl Malone and Pau Gasol, but, even still, *NBA* seasons are grueling, and a championship team is hard to build. So, by the time Frank got to my piano bar on off-season, he was ready to party.

Tad with Junior Seau

Also, during that period, I met Junior Seau, the great *San Diego Chargers* linebacker. Junior frequented *Tracton's* quite a bit. He was another extremely generous person, not only to me, but also in giving of himself to his fans and friends. He was always eager to take a photo with anyone. He was so humble and kind, you would never have guessed his ferocity on the field if you didn't know him. Frank Hamblen was the same way, always patient and kind to fans. These men were great examples.

Junior Seau was huge but gentle. He always asked me to play Lionel Richie songs for him. His favorite was *Sail On*. Junior had a few friends who I also met during that period.

Richard Doan was a local developer who was always at Junior's table. Richard was assertive, sometimes brash, and very tall with striking blonde hair. He was cool to me.

Tad with Lawson Brown - 2008

Lawson Brown was a pilot who owned *Executive Charter Service*; his offices were based out of *Montgomery Field* in San Diego. Lawson was around my age, tall and sincere, with a large stomach that matched his kind grin under a gravelly beard, and it was always great to see him. We became fast friends and stayed that way from then on. Over time, he became one of my most dependable, loyal friends.

Ron Zagami owned *Clairemont Equipment* in San Diego with his brother Jerry, and he partied with Junior Seau quite a bit, too. Ron was an outgoing character of a man with a great personality and a love of people in general. He was the greatest salesman I had ever met. He could sell himself to practically any woman! By the end of the night, he would become friends with everyone in the room, and make them all feel better than when they came in. Ron had been a star pianist and *Hammond B3* organ player in the 1960's, recording at *Capitol Records* with Marvin Gaye, touring and recording with Frank Zappa and performing some late nights in Vegas with Frank Sinatra. Ron was a character, and he also became a lifetime friend. Many nights, Ron would get up on the piano and play *Georgia On My Mind* as I sang, or he would jump on the organ and perform along with me to *Route 66*. People would cheer whenever he got up and performed with me.

Ron Zagami with Robin Dougan

•••••

My friend Jim Vreeland owned a *Ford* dealership in central California. Since my *Plymouth Voyager* had caught on fire, I was literally driving either Tracy's *Chevrolet* minivan, or one of the cars that Red Tracton had leased for employees who had quit or been fired, making payments for Red to help him out, as he helped me out with a vehicle. Finally, the lease was up on the *Ford Expedition* I was driving. I was having trouble getting financed because I was still rebuilding my credit. Jim Vreeland leased me a really cool *Ford F150* crew cab truck, which was perfect for carrying equipment, and I kept it through the lease, for a couple years.

One night, in October of 1999, Tracy went out to party with her friends, Mark Piccone and Jim Grandison. She didn't come home that night at all. The next day, I announced to her that I couldn't take it anymore and I was going to leave her. After a day or two, she asked me to reconsider and apologized for her behavior. I fought within myself for weeks, knowing that the best thing I could do, would be to move on, but I relented and stayed with her. In fact, we actually bought a house in

La Costa Valley, in Carlsbad, at the end of 1999. That was not my finest hour or my best decision, deciding to stay with her and actually buy property together. All I was doing was prolonging the inevitable.

•••••

Towards the end of 1999, my oldest daughter Regina started dating Todd Phillips. Todd had a crush on Regina way back when they were in the seventh grade, and he was intent on marrying her. Soon after, they married. Todd was a good kid. He was a firefighter, and he had a business cleaning homes and washing windows on the side. Todd had a young son, Gage, and with Regina's daughter, Whitney, they began a new family life together.

Regina and Todd Phillips

Regina and Taddy 1998

Through all of this, I was still driving up to the desert at the break of dawn on Sunday mornings and showing up by eight o'clock to perform at the *Religious Science Church* in Palm Desert. Dr. Tom Costa's way of teaching, and the philosophy itself had become a cornerstone of my life at this point.

Although I was living a difficult life in so many ways, I was reminded to rejoice in each day I was given, and to be grateful for what I had. We would recite, "I am a very valuable, worthwhile person" every Sunday. Although a simple statement, it is important to remind yourself of that. I was reminded that jealousy or envy or anger all are wasted emotions. The biggest lesson, though, may have been this: What you think about, you bring about. What you dwell upon, you become (does that mean I'm going to become a vagina?) That's just a little joke but the message is true. I learned to focus on what's important and not to sweat the small stuff.

Elaine with Dr. Tom Costa 1997

At the church, I met Marcy Smothers. Her husband, Tommy Smothers was the great comedian who was one of my childhood favorites. He and his brother Dick had *The Smothers Brothers* show on prime-time television in the late 1960's. I watched that show religiously when I was a kid. Tom, Marcy and I became fast friends. He was hilarious, kind, and far more intelligent than he let on to in his routine with his brother.

CHAPTER FIFTY-SEVEN
Yamaha Corporation of America

I had a friend at the church named Mina Lewis. She was a kind elderly lady who was an usher at the church. Mina's daughter Cathy MacBride was a director in the *Musicsoft Department* at *Yamaha Corporation of America* in Buena Park, California. Mina was kind enough to arrange for me to meet with Cathy and her associate, Jim Leahy at *Yamaha*. *Yamaha* developers were creating musical content for their *Disklavier* pianos.

I met with Cathy and Jim at *Yamaha*, and they gave me a project to 'audition' with. I went back to my studio and created piano parts to sync with Carlos Santana's *Supernatural* album. It was an extremely cool new project that basically would have the piano play along to your favorite music album on compact disc. Nervously, I brought my work back up to *Yamaha*. When I arrived in their studio within the big complex, we made small talk for a few minutes.

Jim Leahy was a huge baseball fan, and he recognized my last name as the same name of the Hall of Famer George Sisler. He asked me if I was related, and I told him that George was a Great Uncle.

As if he didn't believe me, he went to his computer, did a *Google* search and pulled up a baseball card with George Sisler's picture on it. I looked strikingly like George in that photo, and Jim was instantly impressed! He told me that he was a big *Atlanta Braves* fan, and I was very much into baseball, so we had a lot to talk about regarding players and stats. Later, in appreciation, I found autographed photos of a handful of the great *Braves* pitchers and sent them to him.

I was sitting behind Cathy and Jim as they put my work up on their speakers and watched the piano play the parts in the other room. I couldn't see their faces, and my heart dropped. They weren't moving or reacting. They were just staring at the piano in the other room. When my first track was done, they both turned around, looked at each other, and Cathy said, "Welcome to *Yamaha*!"

Cathy got on the phone and ordered a *Disklavier* to be delivered to my new home in Carlsbad. I thought it would be a keyboard that I would be working with and it made me happy to be a part of this project. When it arrived, my eyes opened wide. The truck backed up into my driveway, and in the back of the truck was a gorgeous, brand new *Yamaha* C3 Conservatory Grand piano! It was the $50,000.00 version with all of the *Disklavier* hardware built into it, so I could play the piano through midi, and then fix the parts on the computer. I could put microphones on the piano and play back the parts I had just played, fixed perfectly, microphoned on a state-of-the-art piano!

I got to work on this project and worked my ass off for over two years, creating over one hundred albums of music. The project saved me, because our house was way out of our price range and it gave me the money to pay the payments and taxes. In fact, I cried when I got my first check. The money was great.

•••••

The bad news was that I had bought into a house with Tracy. She was making good money as the half-owner of *Tracton's*, even though they were paying back some debt, but she believed that the man should pay all the bills, so she paid the minimum of everything and left the burden to me.

At some point it got absolutely absurd. She wanted to take her kids to London, but she told me I couldn't afford to go with them because I had to pay all the bills. At the same time, she told me that maybe I should cancel my exercise classes because they were too expensive. Then, she got on a plane and traveled to Europe with her kids…

On the other hand, I was grateful to be in a house that I loved. I counted the times I had moved in my life, up to this point, and I had moved forty-one times in forty years. I lived in forty-one places in forty years! I had bounced from place to place my entire life, and my family was my only grounding force. Then, I watched my family go away, one by one. Left with Tracy and her kids, I vowed to make the best of it.

•••••

New Year's Eve 1999, moving forward into the year 2000, rang in a new millennium; my band performed up in downtown Palm Springs at the *Hyatt Regency*. Everyone was worried that the *Y2K Virus* would wipe out all of the computers because they couldn't handle the date change, but January 1, 2000 was just another day in our life. It was pretty cool, though, to be on the planet to witness the end of a thousand years and the beginning of another.

Tim Blixseth called Shari Kelley in early January of 2000, and booked my band to play at Jack Kemp's Super Bowl party in Atlanta, Georgia on January 30, 2000. By coincidence, *The Smothers Brothers* were performing at the Super Bowl.

Tracy came with us again to Atlanta, and again she was in party mode, but we still had a good time. I have to admit that we sometimes laughed a lot in-between the ugly, heavy moments.

I mentioned to Jack Kemp's secretary that Tom Smothers was my friend, and I asked her if she wouldn't mind if he and Marcy came by to say hello and to meet Jack and Joanna Kemp. Jack's secretary was a huge fan of the *Smothers Brothers* and she didn't believe me, so when Tom and Marcy arrived, everyone was pleasantly surprised! They were great and it was an amazing event.

My entire band got to go to the Super Bowl game yet again, this time at the *Georgia Dome*, and we were sitting on the end zone at the stadium. This was the big game between Dick Vermeil's *Saint Louis Rams* with Kurt Warner as quarterback, and the *Tennessee Titans*, led by Steve McNair and Eddie George.

The game was a nail-biter and I had to leave a couple minutes early to expedite the after-event at the hotel. I was on the bus going back to the hotel when, on the closed-circuit television I witnessed Kevin Dyson being tackled on the one-yard line, just feet from where the rest of my band was still sitting, to lose the game for the Titans. The band was ecstatic to see it up so closely, but I was already on the bus when it happened… oh well. But, the event went very well after the game. Jack Kemp was an amazing host and a great friend. It was surreal to be jet setting all over the country, going to the big game, and performing for celebrities with a great band.

Following the events, I flew to North Carolina to visit my sister Suzanne and her family. I hadn't been there for four years, so it was nice to see my nephews and nieces again, and their burgeoning offspring. Atlanta and North Carolina were absolutely freezing during the entire trip, and although I had a great time, it was great to be back in sunny Southern California again after the weekend.

•••••

My band went up to Montana again during the summers of 2001, 2002 and 2003. Tim Blixseth hosted "Camp Blixseth" at the *Yellowstone Club*, and we were the band for the events. Sometimes it was hilarious to us to see these hugely powerful people letting their hair down. Tim and Edra hosted a costume party one night, and we looked over and saw the Attorney General in a caveman costume!

The events were always full of activities, love and kindness. Mary Hart from *Entertainment Tonight* was generally in attendance, and we became friends. Vice President Dan Quayle and his wife attended the events, as did Jack Kemp. Pro golfer Tom Weiskopf was designing the golf courses at *Yellowstone* Club and he was gracious and kind to us.

Tim Blixseth was a songwriter. He worked with David Foster (and virtually anyone else he wanted to work with), and he had done some early recordings. Edra gave me the "45's", and I learned his songs to surprise him by performing his originals with the band. Tim was delighted!

•••••

In May of 2001, the lease was up on my *Ford F150* truck, and I bought a new *Ford Expedition* from Jim Vreeland. It was a great car, and I kept it for more than ten years.

Back in the desert, Tim Blixseth was building a huge compound with a mansion and his own golf course up against the mountain in Palm Desert. He casually mentioned to me in Montana that I should let him know when I'm available and he would show me the property.

Shortly before I pulled my studio out of Burbank, I was driving back into the desert one day from Los Angeles, so I called Tim's secretary and asked if that day would be a good time to tour the course. She got back on the line momentarily and gave me the go-ahead, along with directions.

As I pulled into the compound, expecting for a surrogate to give me the tour, I saw Tim waiting for me in a golf cart. He spent almost two hours taking me on a tour of each hole of the golf course, which all had indigenous plants from different parts of the world. He showed me the area on the property where they had spent three million dollars to ship huge rocks in, to build the course. Tim mentioned that he wasn't getting a good enough price on the plants for the golf course, so he just bought the chain of nurseries!

A homeowner close to his compound was complaining about the development, so Tim bought the guy out for double the price of his home. Even though Tim wielded so much power as a billionaire, he was truly the kindest, most down-to-earth guy you would ever meet. He invited me to fly on his private jet with his wife up to Montana. They were going to stop in Arizona to pick up Vice President Quayle and his wife. I couldn't do it, because I was booked on an event that I just couldn't get out of. Go figure.

•••••

Once, when I flew in to Bozeman, I was going to get my luggage and I heard a big, booming voice behind me calling my name. I looked back, and Jack Kemp was running over to give me a hug! I thought, "Here is a man who could be President of the United States, and he's chasing me through an airport, calling my name to hug me!"

I had a fantasy about the day he might become President, and we would be the house band at the White House. He would come to me on a break, and ask me what he should do with foreign policy, and I would change the course of world events with an idea! Of course, it was purely a dream, but Jack Kemp was a great man and I was grateful to be in his presence. He would have been a great President. He was an intense, but even-tempered and gracious man. He exuded goodness, and whether or not one agreed with his politics; he could win you over with his ideas and his charm. His wife, JoAnn, was equally as kind and open to sit and chitchat with us anytime.

•••••

The attacks by terrorists on September 11, 2001 changed the world forever. The images we saw on our televisions were terrifying. We were all in mourning when we saw the Twin Towers of the *World Trade Center* fall in New York, another plane crashing in Pennsylvania and yet another at the *Pentagon* in Washington. It was a dark time for America, and I hadn't felt this kind of sorrowful feeling permeating our country since I was a young boy when President Kennedy had been assassinated.

Security was tight at the airports in the winter of 2001 when my band flew to Montana again for a winter event at *Yellowstone Club.* Prime Minister Benjamin Netanyahu and his wife Sara were visiting from Israel. I had never really learned how to ski, but there was no better place on earth to learn than on these pristine ski trails up in Big Sky in this private resort. Tracy had taken me up to the mountains of Southern California a couple times with her kids, and I suffered through a few ski lessons, but in Big Sky, I had the luxury of learning from John Reveal. John was an expert skier; he was the cameraman who skied backwards in front of Warren Miller, holding a video camera, as Warren made his famous ski movies. John was patient and kind, and within a couple of days, I was attempting the intermediate slopes. He would make me sing the song *Raindrops Keep Falling on My Head* in order to get my mind off of my fear, and to relax into skiing. John was a great guy.

Israeli Prime Minister
Benjamin Netanyahu

But, on that first day of this trip, Mrs. Netanyahu was also learning to ski. They were still building the ski lifts, so when we skied down the slopes; we had to go back up the mountain in a big *Snow Cat* vehicle. As we went to approach the vehicle with Mrs. Netanyahu, someone got onto a walkie-talkie and asked if I was cleared with my guitarist Michael Higgins to go up in the vehicle with Mrs. Netanyahu. Due to security concerns, they wanted to make sure we were cool. I guess we got the approval, because they let us into the *Snow Cat* with this lovely, gracious woman.

As we went up the hill, two Israeli Secret Service agents rode with us, with their *Uzi's* trained on us, pointed directly at our heads! Mrs. Netanyahu was kind and chatty, but we were terrified that we might go over a rock or something and one of the guns would discharge! I guess you can't be too careful when you are high-profile Israelis. That night, we performed for the Prime Minister and his wife, and they enjoyed the event immensely.

•••••

Being around wealthy people or celebrities has never been a challenge for me. It is important that you treat them like the human beings they are, because most people don't. My experience all those years ago in Kansas City with Bill Dunphy is a good example of how important it is not to jump to conclusions about someone because of their status; I worked a year with him, not knowing he was a priest. I would have treated him entirely differently, and it's the same with celebrities; they want to be comfortable with you. It's also the same with extremely wealthy people. There are always people around them asking for something, or expecting something, or wanting something from them. People concoct schemes just to squeeze money from these people, so they are always relieved when they meet someone who wants nothing more from them than their friendship.

Only once did I unwittingly cross that line, and I regretted it. Jonathan Sanger, Red Tracton's cousin, the film producer I worked with briefly in Los Angeles, was putting together a film company to do *Surround 3D* filming of concerts, starting with an *NSync* band tour. He was looking for backing, and as a favor to him, I called Tim Blixseth to make an introduction. When Tim got on the phone, he asked me, "Did you get my song in that film?" He was referencing a song he had written entitled *Coyote Ugly*, and I had offside mentioned to him that a film by that title was about to be released.

At the moment Tim answered the phone, when I told him what I was really calling about, I could palpably hear the disappointment in his voice when he realized that I was 'representing' someone who wanted something from him. I would never make that mistake again, even though my intentions were pure, trying to help my friend Jonathan without any compensation for myself.

Comparison is the first step to unhappiness. If you can get past celebrity or social status of another, forgetting what they have that you don't, expecting nothing and appreciating their humanity, you've made a friend for life.

•••••

When I completed the engagement with my band in Montana, I flew to Memphis, and my dad picked me up in his new *Mercedes M550* SUV. He was proud of his SUV. Maynard drove back to Kennett, Missouri with me at night like a bat out of hell. We took Interstate 55 up to Blytheville, Arkansas, and then he cut across on a number of pitch-black two-lane roads through the middle of nowhere at eighty or ninety miles per hour. Maynard was almost eighty years old and it was a harrowing ride! But, we had bonded again after all of the insanity of my childhood.

When I got to Kennett, I was astounded to find all of Kimberley's furniture and possessions still in their living room and closets, ten years after her murder. I understood that Sandra could not let go, and I felt so deeply for her. She simply would never recover from the brutal loss of her only child. Once again, I quietly encouraged her to go through a couple chests of clothes and give them to family members or friends who could use them and would appreciate having something that belonged to Kimberley. It was a sensitive subject.

The winter mornings were biting as I took my walks in a freezing wind down the rural highway that bordered their Missouri home. Cotton fields were dormant, bare and dark. Occasionally, a farmer would drive by on a tractor and we would wave at each other, or a neighbor would look out and wave, surprised to see anyone. Dad and Sandra took me out to the local steak house and we said 'hello' to the locals.

One night, in keeping with our tradition, they would invite all of the family and some friends over to his living room, and I would entertain them by singing and performing on his old upright piano. Sandra would put on her best smile, doing what she could to hide her depression.

Another night, dad was pulling one of his regular 24-hour shifts at the Emergency Room at the *Twin Rivers* Hospital, and I went down and spent the night in the doctor's quarters with him. He introduced me to his staff, and they were all very kind and professional. I knew that he commanded the utmost of respect from these people, and he was a good teacher. Several trauma cases arrived while we were there, and he handled each one with expertise and expediency.

Dad had his "A Team" of nurses and orderlies. If he respected you and your work, it was a pleasure to work with him and you would learn so very much from this Renaissance man. If he didn't like or respect you, working with him could be pure hell.

After almost a week, I flew back home. It was a good visit, and I felt perhaps that I had helped Sandra a little in her grieving process, if there is any way to really do that after such a tragedy.

•••••

Back again in San Diego, at *Tracton's*, I was extremely happy to be working with Robin Dougan waitressing as I performed in the bar. Robin took really good care of me, but mostly she was kind and caring to me at a time when I was being tormented in my relationship with Tracy. Robin and I became close friends. I wasn't used to a normal, good-to-the-core woman showing me kindness and strength, listening when I had something important to say, and talking quite a bit about everything that mattered without drama. I realized that I was beginning to have feelings for her.

•••••

I met an old curmudgeon named Mac Roehm. He was a Vietnam War veteran, probably with PTSD and some anger issues, but he faithfully came to enjoy my music nightly at *Red's.* Mac stayed my friend until he died of cancer in 2015. He was a difficult person in the sense that he would come in, get in my face (like Jimmy McShane did), and stay in my face all night, asking for song after song after song, almost wanting to control the playlist of the evening. He was so persistent that it was hard to play requests or to play 'the room', picking songs that I knew the general public would like better.

Mac would ask for original songs, and he became a huge fan of my original music, pushing me to do an album of just the originals I wrote that he liked the most. Eventually, I recorded each song he liked, over again, in the style he suggested. Although he was a pain in the ass, he left a huge impact on my life ultimately.

Life can be like that when you perform in a lounge. Sometimes the personalities are overwhelming. A nice woman will get drunk and 'turn' her personality to the point that when you play a song she doesn't like, she will flail her arms in front of you and demand that you STOP playing that song NOW!... even if someone else right next to her requested it and is loving it. I've learned over the years to direct my attention elsewhere and not to be bothered or insulted by anyone who is inebriated and out of control.

Of course, it's not always that way; during some outstanding nights, I wish I could freeze my performance in time, or perhaps bottle and sell the crowd's reaction and interaction. I'm always aware that when I sing a song, it elicits an entirely different memory in every person that remembers it… some good, some bad, but always emotional. That's part of the magic of what I do. Looking into the wistful eyes of elderly people as I sang the standards of their generation made those tunes feel new to me and exciting to perform.

•••••

Tad with Rod Stewart

In February of 2002, Frank and Uta Hamblen invited us to see Rod Stewart perform at *Staples Center* in Los Angeles. They pulled some strings and we got into the after-party, where I hung with Rod Stewart for a few minutes. We chatted and took some photos together. He was very accommodating. It was cool for me because Rod's music was such a big part of my teenage years.

We also went to *Staples Center* many times to see the *Los Angeles Lakers* play. It was amazing to me, because s was an iconic coach. His players respected him, and standing next to Phil Jackson, he was an integral part of all of those championship wins. His defensive style was essential to the success of the teams he coached.

Yet, when I went to the games as his guest, he would search the stands to find us where we were sitting and he would wave at me as if I was the important one! Frank was generous of spirit; Uta was very kind to us and fun to party with, too. They would get us into the *Chairman's Room* after the games, to rub elbows with Jack Nicholson, Snoop Dogg, Jenna Elfman and other famous personalities. I would see my friend Dr. Jerry Buss, the owner of the *Lakers*, and he would hug me and smile.

Tad's Band with Mary Tyler Moore
Steve Alaniz, Jeri Lyne, Tad, MTM, Steve Nellen, Steve Madaio
2002

Also, in early 2002, in Solana Beach, CA, my band had the pleasure of performing at a private party for the celebrated, Emmy-winning television actress, Mary Tyler Moore. She was as gracious and kind as you would expect. I was a big fan, going all the way back to my childhood, watching the *Dick Van Dyke* show. I was fortunate enough to have Jeri Lyne as my female vocalist for this and many other gigs. She had been with the *Righteous Brothers* as a backup singer for much of her career, and she easily could have been a star in her own right, if the stars had aligned for her. Jeri was a good friend and her voice was golden. Also, performing on this gig was my friend Steve Madaio, the legendary trumpeter/arranger. Steve and I did a lot of gigs and recording together for twenty-five years, starting in 1994. At this point in time, I had no idea that I would eventually work with Steve, chronicling his amazing life story beginning at Woodstock with the *Butterfield Blues Band,* then with Stevie Wonder, the Rolling Stones, John Lennon and literally hundreds of other iconic artists. My saxophone player was Steve Alaniz. He was another great player and great guy, and he became the cornerstone of the soundtrack I did for *The Encore of Tony Duran* later, in 2011.

CHAPTER FIFTY-EIGHT
Dealing with More Dysfunction

As I mentioned before, I was never able to reach into Tracy's oldest son Mason's soul and help him to overcome his childhood anger and self-centeredness. As he became a teenager, he devolved into drug use and bad behavior. At one point, he started reading *Mein Kampf* by Adolf Hitler.

Mason liked the idea of being a skinhead. He wanted to cut off his hair and his mother said no, so he went into the bathroom defiantly with a razor blade and shaved his own hair off so he could look like a skinhead. He was completely out of control, and so was his mother.

Tracy would stay late at *Tracton's* even after I finished performing, just to sit at the bar and drink with Jimmy the bartender. I would beg her to go home with me and she would blow me off, so I would go home to her children, and look at their faces when they were disappointed again that their mother wasn't there. But I showed up and gave them love anyway. Mason wouldn't accept my love, though, and I couldn't discipline him in the way I had with my own children. He was angry about the fact that his mother was emotionally unavailable to him, and his father was generally absent during that period. When a child cries out for attention, he or she is going to get it, either positively or negatively.

I was disappointed in myself for my inability to reach through Mason's anger issues to help him to become a better human being. I prided myself on being a good stepfather. I was so very proud of my daughter Regina and my son Kevin. They had evolved into caring, strong adults with good moral compasses. Spencer and Blaire were my little loves, and they were also evolving into insightful, loving pre-teens. I just couldn't reach in and find Mason's soul, and it frustrated me. The wall was up. So, I gave him tough love. That was all I knew to do.

Some people are born into this world with unique personalities, attitudes and emotions. The environment in which they grow up may not be as strong of an influence as their inert nature will allow in order for them to thrive. Lessons are learned the hard way, and you can only hope that experience and circumstance will shape them to become functional adults.

Todd and Regina
2001

I kept my nose to the grindstone and did project after project for Yamaha, still performing full-time at *Tracton's* and doing three or four corporate gigs per month with my band. At some point in early 2002, I had made enough money to completely revamp my recording studio. My friend Scott Francisco came down and helped me install a new *Yamaha O2R96* digital mixer and a *Pro Tools HD* rig.

•••••

One day in 2002, my dad called me from Hawaii. He had gone to Oahu with Sandra and her nephew Devin, and a couple others, for one of his many vacations. My dad told me that he went to Pearl Harbor to pay his respects to his fellow World War II sailors who had made the ultimate sacrifice.

Maynard told me that he always felt guilty that he had never brought me to Pearl Harbor to experience it with him, so he had brought Devin instead to share the experience, I guess to make himself feel better. It was a weird comment. I wasn't jealous at all of Devin, and I was glad for my dad, but it was a reminder of how his actions (and inaction) had shaped my life. His selfishness and abandonment for so many years had cut to the core of my existence, and although I mostly ignored it or brushed it off, it ended up being a motivating force in my life, to show the world I could do it all without him. He sure did miss out on a lot of amazing moments with his actual son and family.

Maynard & Sandra
in Hawaii

•••••

I started to produce original music like mad. I brought in all of my friends who were amazing musicians, and during the next few years, we recorded hundreds of songs in practically every genre. We did public domain Americana songs. Andy Fraga, Jr. jumped in with me and we did techno-ambient electronica. I did country music with Bobby Furgo on fiddle, Gilbert Hansen on bass, Michael Higgins on Guitar and Steve Neilen on drums. We did rock and pop music. With Glen Myerscough and Gary Hartman, on sax and trumpet, I created jazz and classical music. We did a couple Christmas albums.

Paula Stapleton came in and did heartfelt vocals on many tracks. Her dream was to write songs, so I helped her with her ideas and created a couple originals with her. It was great to work and hang out with Paula. She had a beautiful soul. Later, we released an album for Paula from these sessions entitled *We're Making Love Tonight.*

I even flew my sister Kathy out from New York and we recorded some of her originals. This had been a dream for both of us, yet when Kathy first sat down in the tracking room with her guitar, she began to cry. She said, "I don't think I can do this!" Kathy had a meek soul and after so many years of wanting, she was afraid that she was incapable of making a good recording. I reassured her, reminding her that her soul was on fire with goodness and she had a lot to say musically to make this world a better place. I told her I would handle the technical part. All she had to do was to play and enjoy the experience. After that moment, Kathy nailed it and we recorded more than thirty-five songs together.

I was experiencing a renaissance at this time in my life, and as we compiled all of this music, I realized that I needed to put together my own company promoting production music for film and television.

I hadn't yet figured out how to release my own music to the marketplace since I left Hillery Johnson, but I still had all of these tracks on digital tape from that period, so I converted all of that music, updated and re-recorded much of it. At the end of it all, I ended up with a pretty large library of music to build upon.

•••••

In December of 2002, my band was again called to *Yellowstone Club* in Big Sky, Montana for a New Year's Eve event to ring in 2003. I booked *The Association* for Tim Blixseth's main event, and we were to perform after they were done. This was pretty cool; *The Association* was the first band I had ever seen in concert, in 1966!

A blinding winter storm enveloped Montana, so we were happy to arrive a couple days early to enjoy the ski slopes. I was getting bold as a skier, slamming down the intermediate slopes. Michael Higgins and Paula Stapleton skied with me. They were both experienced, and they laughed hysterically when I forced myself to go down a huge hill to meet them at the bottom and I sped by them, yelling, "Faaaaaaaaak!" I'm grateful that I didn't get hurt!

On New Year's Eve, though, Michael Higgins and I decided to ski together during the day. Michael hit an ice pocket and wiped out. He was delirious, so I somehow managed to get him down to the first responders, who took him to the hospital in Bozeman. I was worried about him and also upset because I needed my guitar player on New Year's Eve! But, his health was more important than all of that.

Meanwhile, *The Association* was having trouble getting into the *Yellowstone Club*, because the snowstorm was so bad they couldn't land in Bozeman until later in the evening. We made an executive decision to send Gary Hartman, the trumpeter, down in the *Suburban* to pick them up at the Bozeman airport. They were literally going to have to arrive and play the show without even a sound check, if they were going to pull it off. It was a scary day for me, wanting everything to work out.

Gary Hartman had confided in us that at one point in his life, he had a drug problem and had to quit performing for a few months while he worked it out. It was shocking to all of us, because we had never seen Gary at all out of control in any way. In fact, Gary was one of the most 'together' people I ever knew. He was a true professional, and an excellent player, and he was fun to hang out with! So, Gary drove through a snowstorm to get *The Association*, and then made his way gingerly up the hairline road on the edge of the cliff going up the mountain to the summit, where the event was to be held.

As he was carefully navigating the dirt road full of snow, one of the band members broke out some cocaine and started to cut it up on the door of the glove compartment. Gary looked over in horror! He told me later that he had trouble concentrating on the road, but, of course, he didn't partake. He was long over that! Anyway, *The Association* arrived at exactly their start time and jumped up onto the stage. The first two songs were horrible because they were stressed and still sound checking during performance. The vocals weren't harmonizing well and I was a little worried, but then they settled in and sounded great, and the guests loved them. They performed all of their hits, and they were a hit.

When *The Association* finished their show, it was time for my band to perform. Just as we started the first song, Michael Higgins stumbled in, grabbed his guitar and played his ass off all night! He had been released from the hospital in the nick of time, and although they suggested bed rest because he had suffered a concussion, he took an extra *Vicodin* and showed up for the gig! Michael was my hero that night.

I really loved performing with the band. Paula was a sensational vocalist and she was very dear to me. Steve Neilen was a solid drummer; he was really the best, and he was like a brother to me. Glen Myerscough was a great example to follow as a human being, and his nuances on saxophone and flute taught me so much about theory and harmony on a new level. Gary Hartman's harmonies on trumpet with Glen worked so well, and Gary couldn't have been a nicer person. And Michael Higgins… he was a great friend, a virtuoso on the guitar, and we ended up recording literally thousands of tracks together over the years.

Michael Higgins and I did a project of just solo classical and baroque guitar, and it sold like wildfire!

•••••

Jack Kemp was coming back to San Diego for the Super Bowl on January 26, 2003, and this time he asked me to perform as a solo for him at the *U.S. Grant Hotel* after the game. Also, my friend Mike Pegram, a racehorse owner, gave his Super Bowl tickets to Tracy and me.

The seats were literally on the third row up from the field on the fifty-yard line at *Qualcomm* stadium. Jon Gruden's *Tampa Bay Buccaneers* beat his former team, the *Oakland Raiders*, led by Bill Callahan, by a wide margin. Tracy was a huge Raider's fan and she was so upset by the score that she left and went up to the bar to drink. In spite of all of that, I loved the game, and I really loved my seat.

Tad, Lorenzo Lamas, A.J. Lamas and Tracy 2003

At the game, we spent some time with Lorenzo Lamas, the Emmy-Nominated television actor from *Renegade* and *Silk Stalkings.* It was a thrill for me because I had worked with Jeff Edwards on those shows just a handful of years back. Tracy's best friend Michelle had married Lorenzo years back, and their son, budding actor A.J. Lamas was there as well. Lorenzo was cool.

At halftime, the stage was literally twenty feet in front of me as Shania Twain, Gwen Stefani and *No Doubt*, and then Sting performed. It was cool! After the game, I rushed to the hotel and performed for Jack and Joanne Kemp once again. It was a more laid-back event, so my solo worked well, and as always, they were gracious and kind to me. Jack Kemp once said, "Democracy without morality is impossible", and he couldn't have been a more moral or compassionate human being. He would have made a great President, but perhaps he was a bit too kind and moral to endure the grind of a blistering, cutthroat campaign in these times.

•••••

One other winter day in February of 2003, I got the call to go alone to Big Sky, Montana to perform at the *Yellowstone Club* for one night only. They wanted me to basically commute for a quick turnaround, so I got on a plane, traveled for over two thousand miles, for hours and hours, got there right before the event, performed, slept, and came back to San Diego to work the next evening!

When I returned, Tracy wanted to go to Big Bear, in the mountains of Southern California, to take her children to ski. Going to the overcrowded slopes in Big Bear after skiing at *Yellowstone Club* was almost a joke. I was spoiled, but I was a good sport. At the bottom of a hill, I lost my balance and fell. I wasn't hurt, but a snowboarder behind me careened towards me and by some miracle, he stopped less than an inch from my head. Had he slammed into me, my skull would have been crushed. That incident pretty much cured me of skiing forever. Besides, lying out in the sun is much more comfortable, looking up at the snow-covered mountains in the distance.

•••••

In 2003, I incorporated a media corporation called *Mainstream Source,* and I started building a website and acquiring other production music to represent great composers from all over the world. Within five years, I had built up the collection to include thousands of tracks of quality production music. Many were our own tracks, but we also had music from composers from five continents. As I built the business, the nature of the industry changed, and the placements became harder to get. Later, streaming services killed the bulk of the money a composer or publisher could make on retail music. But, I had a strong collection to draw from whenever I did a film project, and my passion remained to create great music.

Work passionately, be motivated by your craft, your creativity and your talent; do what you do for the right reasons; success may not end up being what you expected it to be, but you will find more contentment along the way.

•••••

Makayla and Whitney 2004

In June of 2003, I became forty-five years old. In July, Regina gave birth to her second child, a daughter. She named this lovely girl Makayla, and the baby was adorable! In August, my father would be eighty, and the family planned a big reunion for his birthday. The family decided to come to San Diego, so we planned events for an entire weekend in August.

Since my parents still and always were not on speaking terms, we arranged for two separate main events. I planned one day to be a beach party with my mother attending. We rented Jet Skis down in Mission Bay and the entire family came, including my sisters and most of their children. My best friend, Eddie was there along with many friends from all over the country.

Suzanne, Kathy, Judy & Betsy 2000

My mother, using her walker, managed to get all the way on to the pier by the beach, and she was set up in the shade, holding court all day as the family played all around her.

Regina, Rachel and Taddy were enjoying riding the Jet Skis in the bay. My son Kevin didn't really like the ocean. He always mentioned to everyone that he didn't picture himself as shark food. My other kids convinced Kevin to ride a Jet Ski, and he actually enjoyed it. My sister Betsy's daughter Shana wanted to try to Jet Ski but she didn't want to go alone. Shana was a big girl and she asked if "Taddy's friend" Kevin would take her out. Even though Shana didn't remember Kevin as her cousin, he was a good sport. Kevin helped Shana onto the Jet Ski and took her out about one hundred feet where she promptly fell off the Jet Ski. She was paralyzed with fear, and Kevin could not persuade her to get back onto the ski. She told Kevin that she couldn't swim! So, he spent the next hour paddling back in, holding one side of the Jet Ski with her clinging to the other side. He was exhausted when he got back to the shore, and I don't think he

Mark, Judy, James, Shana, Betsy and Lucas 2003

Ted and Elaine - 2000

appreciated the fact that everyone was laughing hysterically at what he had just gone through!

Betsy's other son, David, who had been in the movie *Crisscross* with Goldie Hawn when he was a boy, was also there. David had spent a lot of time in and out of prison at this point, and he had a huge tattoo of a *swastika* on his chest. He proudly marched around shirtless on the beach as we all cringed. David had a girlfriend at the time; she was a *Disney* Princess. Really! She played the role of one of the Princesses at *Disneyland*. She was pretty and sweet and kind, and everyone loved her. David had an ex-girlfriend who heard about the event and showed up. She was obviously out of control, on some kind of drug. She marched in to the event and started to beat up the Disney Princess. We had to drag them off of each other. It was bizarre!

Even through all of that drama, it was a great day, and later that evening Tracy graciously hosted all of us for dinner at Tracton's, including my Uncles Ted and Gerry and their families. So, my mother was in all of her glory with her brothers, children and grandchildren all around her.

My Uncle Ted and his family had stayed available and close to mine through the years. Gerry, on the other hand, lived his life with minimal contact. He had become a successful attorney in Encino, CA, and coincidentally, he had lunched most days at *Red Tracton's* when it was located in Encino. He enjoyed the food at *Tracton's,* and I did see Gerry and Kathy a handful of times when I performed there, sometimes bringing his son Gerald, Jr. with him. I didn't really know my Uncle Gerry like I knew Ted. I guessed from comments he made after my mother passed away, later, that perhaps he had issues with her, and so, therefore, distanced himself from her side of the family. My mother could be combative at times, so I just shrugged it off, but really, I believe my Grandmother Gizella would have preferred it if he was more available and involved with us. Still, it was great to see Gerry and Ted together with my mom, this one last time.

My Uncle Gerry and his family 2019

•••••

2003
Teddy, Ted, Spencer, Maynard, Rachel, Blaire, Regina, Mckayla and Kevin

On the next day, we had a more subdued event with my father and his wife at the clubhouse of the community that I lived in, in La Costa Valley. In my recording studio at the house, my sisters all put their vocals on a song that my sister Kathy had written about Maynard's eighty years. The kids swam at the pool in the complex, and we all laughed, talked and played cards for hours. It was a wonderful time, and it would be the last time that my entire original family would be together in one weekend.

•••••

Through all of these experiences in my life, for all of these years, I had never taken time off from performing. I might have had a week or two here and there between gigs, but then the gigs would go on for years and years at a time. My life experience always revolved around my performance schedule, which was rarely less than five nights per week, and for many years, included daytime shifts as well.

My poolside gigs in the desert, in extreme conditions, had lasted for ten years…first at the *Marriott* in Palm Desert, through the *Desert Princess*, the *Riviera* hotel, the *Esmeralda* Resort, the *Hyatt Grand*

Champions and *La Quinta Resort*… through winters, summers, windstorms and sandstorms, bugs and intense heat and cold.

Through all the years of work, I had become a seasoned performer, and my repertoire became huge. My mother would come to see me perform, and she finally heaped praise on me, seeing how hard I had worked to improve. It meant the world to me. Even still, she would suggest a chord change here or there, and I gladly obliged. She was proud of me, as I had taken the talent I had inherited from her and made a life out of it.

My mom spent Thanksgiving and Christmas with us in 2003. My boys came down to my house in Carlsbad, California each time. Rachel and Robert would be there, along with Mason, Spencer and Blaire. Mom could be a bit difficult to hang out with even still! My kids and I would play a basketball game out in the front of my house in La Costa Valley, and the loser would have to go in and sit with Grandma Lainsie! But, my children were always gracious and gave her lots of love.

My mother was getting weaker. She walked with a walker; nevertheless, she stayed active at the church and other functions. Whenever I went to the desert, I would stop and spend time with her. I loved my mother with all my heart.

CHAPTER FIFTY-NINE
Drifting Apart from Tracy

I was really unhappy being with Tracy. I don't believe that she had ever really been happy being with me. Her addiction and alcoholism had gotten so far out of control that she was spending way too many nights hanging out at the bar at *Tracton's* when she should have been home with her children. I had my routine, though.

The *Yamaha* gig had morphed into a much more challenging and less lucrative project; at this point, I was creating songs from the ground up, for consumers to play on their sophisticated midi keyboards with lyrics scrolling. Nate Tschetter was my supervisor at *Yamaha*. He was truly a 'midi god' and he knew how to manipulate sound in a way I had never dreamed of. Through his patience and his long lists of errors we needed to correct, I became a more proficient programmer and editor. During the next three or four years, I would produce hundreds more songs for *Yamaha*. This was the period where I really learned how to produce music in a very technical way, superior to anything else I had ever done.

Andy Fraga, Jr. worked with me on this material, and his assistance was crucial to my success. I would literally touch each of the tens of thousands of notes of each instrument on each song at least

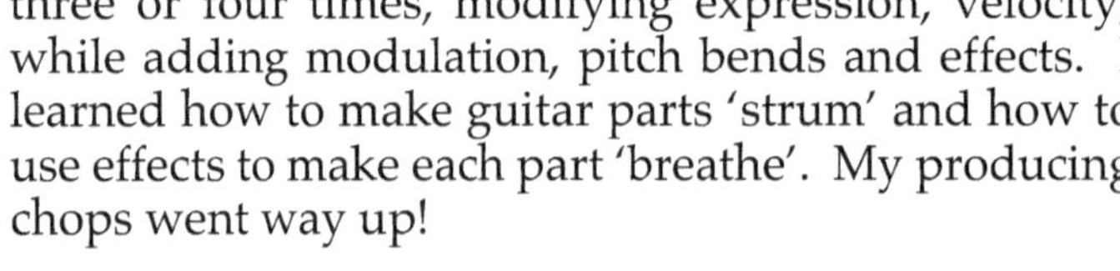
three or four times, modifying expression, velocity, duration and sustain while adding modulation, pitch bends and effects. I learned how to make guitar parts 'strum' and how to use effects to make each part 'breathe'. My producing chops went way up!

I was experiencing a renaissance in music production. During this year, I released several compact discs of music including a solo project entitled *We've Loved This Way Before*. I released two Christmas albums, *Peaceful Christmas* and *Christmas Rocks*, the latter of which actually was a hard-core techno rock instrumental album of Christmas music featuring Michael Higgins on guitars. I released a patriotic CD entitled, *The Spirit of America*. Andrew Fraga, Jr. and I produced a few new collections, including a cool African and East Indian collection. I completed Contemporary Jazz

and Smooth Jazz collections. We did this amazing hard rap, urban record with my old friend Lajuana Johnson, Hillery's daughter.

This and my performance nights kept me busy enough to stay the course for the time being. Working with Robin Dougan at *Tracton's* really helped. She was a grounded person and refreshingly sweet! On the nights when I would stay for a little bit after the gig, the staff would congregate in the back room and we would talk for a while, unwinding and joking with each other. Then, I would go into the bar and tell Tracy I was going home. I would ask her if she wanted to come with me, and she would say no, and then I would go home.

My relationship with Tracy was dying, although I really believe in retrospect that it never had a chance after Stephanie died. Something in me died when Stephanie died, at least for a while, and although any relationship in the beginning is full of lust and excitement, it all became like a bad version of reality after all these years. But, how was I going to get out of this? Tracy and I had bought the condo in Palm Springs from her father's estate and now I owned two properties with her. So, I kept working in my studio and performing at night, and then repeating the process for many months at a time.

•••••

In November of 2003, I performed for my friend Ric Mandelbaum's birthday at the *Palm Springs Air Museum* with my band. Ric owned a magazine and he had established some trade with the cruise lines, so he literally traded a stateroom with a balcony on a one-week cruise with me, in exchange for my band's performance at his event. The event was fun, and I made plans to take Tracy on a cruise from New Orleans to Jamaica in June of 2004. In my mind, I thought that if I took her somewhere alone for a week, it would be a last shot at seeing if this relationship had even the slightest chance to continue. The reality of the situation was that my heart wasn't in it anymore, and neither was hers. We were just going through the motions.

•••••

Tracy's son Mason was now entirely out of control. One night, he was so drugged out that he went into our laundry room thinking it was the bathroom, pulled down the dryer door, and defecated on it, stumbling back to bed. Ants were in his bathroom, so he burned them all the way up the wall with a cigarette lighter, almost setting the house on fire.

Mason was hiding drugs in his room through a hole he cut in the drywall, which was covered by a poster on the wall. One day, I got a call from the Academy where he was attending school. He had been detained in the office because he had pulled out a toy gun at the school and he was chasing another kid with it.

It had only been a handful of years since the terrible massacre at *Columbine High School* in Colorado, so the Academy had a zero-tolerance policy with weapons, even toy weapons.

I went into the office, and Mason was cursing at the principal and staff. They wanted to expel him from the school, and I completely understood, especially considering his behavior following the incident. He was not remorseful; he was combative, throwing F-bombs around with no respect for anyone in the room.

As I drove him home, Mason cursed at me the entire way to our house, calling me every name in the book and telling me how glad he was that his father had beaten me up all those years ago. I looked him straight in the eye and told him that I was not going to tolerate this any longer. He was a danger to himself and to this family, and he would no longer live at my house as long as I was in it.

I told Mason that I knew that neither of his parents had given him an ounce of discipline in his life, and this is what he became as a result of it, but I would not be a party to it any longer. I threw him out and sent him to live with his father in Palm Springs. Tough love is hard but it was entirely necessary in this case.

Years later, Mason would come back to me and thank me for doing what I did. He knew deep in his soul that he was out of control. Life at the house without Mason was mellower, for sure, but Tracy was consumed with guilt and sadness. She had temporarily put Mason into a treatment facility in Mexico several months before; she had tried to help him, but at that point, it obviously wasn't working.

•••••

Tad with Gayle Hall
Petco Park - 2009

On April 8, 2004, the *Major League Baseball* franchise *San Diego Padres* opened a new stadium, *Petco Park,* in downtown San Diego. I bought a couple commemorative bricks, located in the entry section of the park. One brick was dedicated to the memory of Red Tracton, and another brick simply said, "Thank you, God, for my children. Tad Sisler." Over the years since, I've taken my children to see the bricks as we went to baseball games. My friend Gayle Hall, who ran the *Winner's Circle* timeshare adjacent to *Red Tracton's* in Del Mar for so many years, would go to games with me all the time.

Only once every three or four years, the *New York Yankees* would come to town, and I always made a point of seeing my *Yankees* play, with the great Derek Jeter, Bernie Williams, Jorge Posada, Gary Sheffield and, of course, the great closer Mariano Rivera. The *Padres* were pretty good during that period too. I was able to see Tony Gwynn's final season at *Qualcomm Stadium* before the team moved into the new ballpark. It was cool.

•••••

In April of 2004, I took Tracy to see David Bowie in concert at the *Anaheim Pond*. The concert was amazing, and it brought me back to my teenage days when I had seen him perform on the *Ziggy Stardust* tour. Tracy was becoming more and more out of it as time went by, and Mason's departure did not help her state of mind one bit.

In June of 2004, Tracy and I drove to the San Diego airport to fly to New Orleans for our cruise trip. I was excited to take the trip. I had never been on a cruise. When we got to the airport, I got a call from an agent back in New York. He booked my band to perform in Maui in late July of 2004. I was ecstatic! I turned to Tracy and told her about the booking as we were waiting for our plane to fly out of San Diego. She said, "But that's the opening week of the *Del Mar Racetrack* season. You can't go."

I told her that was ridiculous, and that I would cover my shift for the first two days of track season with a great performer, but that I had already committed and I wasn't going to turn down an all-expense-paid trip to Hawaii, which also paid very well. I suggested that possibly Tracy could go, too, but that just made her angrier, because she wouldn't leave the restaurant on opening day of the racetrack.

So, Tracy decided at that moment that she was still going to get on the plane, but she was going to make me miserable for the entire cruise. She virtually ignored me for the first two days in New Orleans. I had gotten a room at the *Royal Sonesta.* I had gone so far out of my way to make this a special trip for her, and she wouldn't even talk to me.

We went out and ate at a couple places and went to a couple bars in the French Quarter, and during the whole time she was aloof to me. During the entire cruise, we hardly spoke to each other. She drank a lot of alcohol, and when we got to Jamaica, she somehow found a guy to sell her some kind of drugs. We took a bus for two hours to beautiful waterfalls in Jamaica, and she was cordial to me but distant. I was disgusted. I didn't even care about romance with her any more. I just wanted to enjoy this trip, and it was virtually impossible to do with her in this state of mind.

I had always wanted to take a cruise. I hadn't seen New Orleans since my parents took a trip with me when I was very small. I had never seen Jamaica before, and during the whole trip I was miserable… trying to stay optimistic and enjoy the sites and the experience, but being dragged down emotionally, the whole time.

Even after the whole week when we finally made it back home, Tracy stayed distant to me and basically mean.

•••••

July of 2004 came and I took the trip to Maui with the band. Paula, Michael, Steve, Glen (with his wife Lena), Gary and I went on a boat to an island off of Maui and went snorkeling one day. We all grabbed goggles, jumping into the water, and somehow, I had been given goggles for a person who is extremely nearsighted, so the ocean was all blurry to me. This was good, actually, because a great white shark swam right next to me as everyone else swam away, and I just calmly floated there until the shark left! But, we all laughed and had a wonderful time.

Michael Higgins, Paula Stapleton and Tad 2004

Tad with Glen Myerscough 2004

The promoter, who hired us for this gig, as it turned out, had hired us for a previous gig and he was extremely attracted to Paula. Of course, we didn't know this when we took the gig in Hawaii. One day, he asked Paula if she wanted to see the sights of Maui with him, and she obliged. He took her out on a road trip all day, all over Maui, and she had a great time. Later, he tried to 'put the moves' on her, and she politely rejected him. Paula stayed classy through the entire experience, but that was the last time the band flew to Hawaii for that client! We had a great gig, though, for a corporate client, and they loved the band. It was a much needed, amazing experience with close friends, after that cruise I had endured with Tracy.

•••••

When I flew back into San Diego, I walked into the house and Tracy was very ill, in our bedroom upstairs. She told me that she had consumed tons of alcohol and some pills and other drugs through the first few days of the racing season, and she was sick. She decided, finally, that she needed to go into treatment. I thought this was great and I told her that I would support her completely.

Foolishly, I again thought, as I had thought all those years ago about Stephanie, that maybe, just maybe this would make her okay. I was no longer emotionally attached to Tracy in any way. In fact, I was beginning to get more and more emotional support from my close friendship with Robin Dougan. We could talk about anything, and she actually liked me! But, I did care enough for Tracy that I wanted her to be okay. No matter what, I knew that I was again in a situation where I was watching someone slowly kill herself, and I was literally going out of my mind with her. So, I offered to drive her immediately into a treatment facility, but she said that she wanted to wait until the end of the six-week racing season before she checked herself in. I thought this was ridiculous, and typical of an addict to say you need treatment and then blow it off. But, she was adamant although she stayed very sick in bed for a few days. When she finally felt better, she went right back to drinking and drugging through the entire racetrack season, all the time swearing that she was going into treatment following. It was like a 'last hurrah.'

In September of 2004, Tracy checked herself into the *McDonald Center* at *Scripps Hospital* in La Jolla. It was like déjà vu to me. It was a brave move for her to do this, and she was scared, but I promised to support her through the process. I took very good care of Spencer and Blaire while she was in treatment, and we showed up faithfully every day, and to every class we were supposed to participate in.

After the month of treatment, Tracy came out and decided that she wanted to change everything in her life, which included me. It was like Chuck Buffamonte all over again; someone taking his or her sobriety to the limit with a different kind of addictive behavior; it was just sober addictive behavior. I had seen it before and it disgusted me. Even still, we continued to go through the motions for a month or two.

•••••

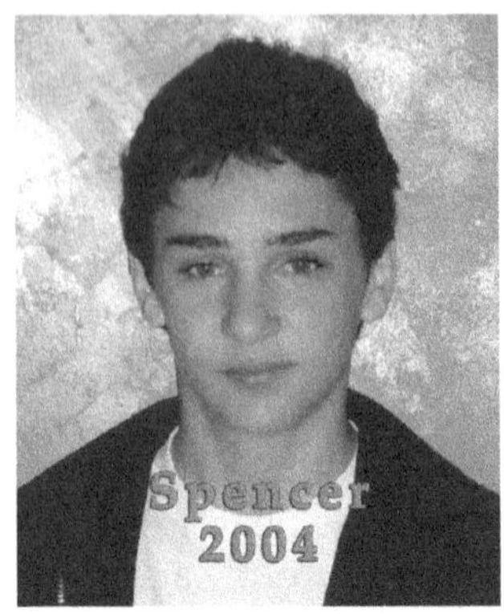

My mother came down for Thanksgiving in 2004, and the family had dinner at *Red Tracton's*. Elaine was delightful that day, and Rachel was at the restaurant with us along with Spencer and Blaire. Mom looked frail but I was glad she had a good time.

Around this time, Spencer was struggling with his older brother's departure. He was the oldest child at home now, and although he had been doing well in school and winning talent contests, he had some issues. One night, I asked him to do something and he defiantly said, "You're not my father."

I looked at him sternly and said, "You know what? You're right. I'm not your father, but in my heart, you've always been my son and I love you with all my heart. Now, get up to your room and don't ever talk to me like that again!" Later, we hugged, and from then on, we were always best friends. He never tested my love after that night, and I think it helped him to know that he was secure in my heart.

Blaire was my little darling. She had just turned eleven years old, and we were very close. Blaire would watch the film *Moulin Rouge* over and over again, and each time she would cry hysterically at the end of the film! She was an emotional girl.

I went up to Palm Desert to work at the church one Sunday in late 2004. I would work the early service and my mother would come to the later service. When I saw her, my heart sank. She looked frail and ill. We went to lunch afterwards, and she told me that she was not feeling well in general.

CHAPTER SIXTY
Losing My Mother

In the second week of January in 2005, I went to Palm Desert again to work the church and to see my mother. She didn't show up at the second service and I became concerned. Church meant everything to her, especially when I was performing. I called her after the service, and she told me she didn't feel well enough to come to church. She asked me if I would stop and get lunch for her and bring it to her. I got some Chinese food to go, and also went to the grocery store for her.

I called my sister Judy. She was in the Midwest. I asked her if she would consider coming to be with mother for a week or two. Judy had been honorably discharged from the Air Force, and she was on disability. Judy had her Master's Degree in nursing, so she was a perfect choice to get to the bottom of what was happening to our mother, and she agreed to come out.

When I brought the lunch to my mother's condo, I had no idea it would be the last time I would ever see my sweet mom Elaine.

She was still in her pajamas. She said that she didn't have much of an appetite. She had a rash on her back and the doctor had told her that it was likely *Herpes Zoster*. My mom always made lists to remind herself to talk to me about certain things. As she went down her current list, asking me questions about little things or asking me to change a light bulb for her, I listened dutifully. I prepared the table for us and opened up all of the food I had brought to her. She sat and picked at the food. The kitchen window was open, and she asked me to close it because she was cold.

All of a sudden, a magic moment happened. My mother Elaine recounted the night I was born, when she asked the nurse to open the window because she was so hot, and she saw me for the first time… we talked about my childhood and her life, and then I thanked her for everything she had done for me in my life.

I reminded my mother that she was the only one who ever did anything to help me when I needed it. I thanked her for co-signing on the cars and for the furniture she had given me when I was just starting out with my young family. When I thanked her for the furniture, she said, "The furniture, which disappeared!" I told her, well, yes, it disappeared after twenty more years of wear and tear after her twenty years of having it, and we laughed. Although I didn't have a clue this would be the last time I would visit with her, I couldn't have asked for a better last conversation, full of love and gratefulness.

I gave my mother hugs and kisses and told her I would be up to visit her on the following Sunday. She stood at the door holding on to her walker, waving at me as I drove away.

Judy arrived in the desert a couple days later. She was with my mother when Elaine went into congestive heart failure. Elaine was admitted to *Eisenhower Medical Center*. I spoke with my mother on the morning of her passing, and her thoughts were jumbled with confusion as she was fighting for life. I told her how much I loved her and asked her to hang in there. I told her I was going to work that night at *Red Tracton's*, and then drive up to see her afterwards.

My wonderful, talented mother Elaine died as I was performing, during my first set at the restaurant. Judy called me crying hysterically, and I left immediately and started driving. I cried all the way up to Palm Desert. When I arrived at the hospital two hours later, the nurses had allowed Judy to keep my mother in the hospital room until I made it there. Her skin was milky white, and her face radiated serenity I had never witnessed. I knew that her soul was no longer in her body, but still I felt her presence. I stroked her beautiful hair and kissed her on the cheek, and I told her I loved her. Judy and I held each other, crying, for a while until they took my mother's body away.

•••••

My Mother, Elaine
1945

All of my sisters flew in for my mother's funeral, and to help to clear out her condo. It was a profoundly sad time for all of us, going through all of her belongings and deciding what to do with them. We found shoeboxes full of photographs, and as I looked through them, I realized how much she had lived and experienced, and it made me feel a little better.

Elaine was a great woman and mother who cared to the core about her children. She wanted the best for us always. She was an extraordinary pianist who gave up her career for her family, resurrecting it later to a degree. I couldn't remember ever when I did not worry about her well-being, wanting her to overcome the pain she endured until the end from her divorce. Yes, she was always tortured in a sense, but my mother did what she could, when she could, always for her children. I knew she loved me with all her heart. Elaine still referred to Maynard as "my husband" until the end, even though he had moved on, long before.

Dr. Tom Costa had just been diagnosed with cancer, and he had retired from his ministry just months before Elaine's death, so another minister officiated at her memorial service. At Elaine's service, an elderly African-American lady from the church who had worked some events with my mother, summed her up in a couple sentences: "Elaine was a thorn in my side," she said dramatically, "but she always made sure that everything was done right and with a flair! She was a perfectionist and I loved that woman!"

Before my mom passed away, she was living in a condo complex right next to the *Sacred Heart Catholic Church* and school. She was informed about six months prior to her death that the school was going to expand and they were tearing down the condo she was living in. Although they offered to help her relocate, and possibly even allow her to move to another condo nearby that was identical, my mother was constantly worried about the possibility of having to move.

Don't worry until someone or something gives you a real reason to worry. Most of the time, nothing will come of it anyway.

We talked about it several times before she died and I hated to see her have so much anxiety about a move that never ended up happening. It reminded me of a saying I had heard: "If you're going to worry, don't pray, and if you're going to pray, don't worry."

As serendipity would have it, only a few years later my grandchildren would play on the playground at *Sacred Heart Elementary School* in the exact same location that had been created from the demolition of my mother's condo.

Aidan Phillips - 2006

Following a tumultuous couple of weeks dealing with my mother's affairs, tragedy turned temporarily to joy when my daughter Regina gave birth to a son, Aidan on February 22, 2005. He was a scrawny little guy but just adorable.

•••••

Shortly after my mother died, my father was forced to retire back in Kennett, Missouri, after fifty years of practicing medicine. He had remained in private practice, but due to his age he could no longer afford malpractice insurance, so he had closed his office a couple years back and he was limited to his emergency room shifts at the hospital, his patient load as a staff physician, and the occasional day of Medicare physicals, for which he would drive an hour north to Cape Girardeau, Missouri. At the age of eighty-two, Maynard was still doing 24-48 hour shifts in the Emergency Room, sleeping in the break room in-between trauma cases.

Maynard and Sandra Retirement Party 2004

He was also still teaching and administrating when the hospital board informed him that they could also no longer afford to pay the malpractice insurance of an eighty-two-year-old doctor. Maynard was devastated. Medicine was his life. He actually went on antidepressants for a while. The hospital staff threw him a retirement party and he put on his game face for the whole charade. Maynard was lost and miserable, all of a sudden. They took away his lifeblood.

Age should not become a cage, if you're still a master of your game. Never place a time limit upon excellence.

In Kennett, Maynard had worked hard for more than thirty years as a physician and as Chairman of the Board to transform a backwoods medical center into a thriving institution, through several different changes of ownership and corporate budget cuts. After the loss of his leadership, the hospital would eventually literally shut down all operations and close, just a handful of years after his death.

•••••

Frank and Uta Hamblen invited us to Los Angeles again to see the *Los Angeles Lakers* in early 2005. Rudy Tomjanovich had taken over the head coaching position after Phil Jackson left in 2004, and Frank had stayed on as assistant coach. Rudy suddenly resigned the position, and Dr. Jerry Buss

Tad with Frank Hamblen - 2002

named Frank head coach for the remainder of the season.

Dyan Cannon, the great actress, was at every *Laker's* game! On occasion, we would make small talk at the games. She was always gracious and kind to everyone. We took a photo together.

Tad with Dyan Cannon

The *Lakers* as a cohesive team were in disarray; Frank confided in me after the game. He said that he had initially attempted to decline the position as head coach, telling Dr. Buss that he didn't want to go down in history as the *Lakers* head coach with the most losses. Dr. Buss told Frank that it didn't matter to him, that the *Lakers* would be making money anyway through television revenues, and it would mean the world to him if Frank would coach the team through the season until they ironed out the problems associated with Mr. Tomjanovich's early departure.

As it turned out, Phil Jackson came back to the *Lakers*, and they continued to win championships after that year, but at that moment in time, Frank took one for the team. He put the team before himself, and coached to the best of his ability for the remainder of that season. It taught me a lesson in character and humility that I never forgot. Frank was a good man.

True character reveals itself in times of adversity. It's a rare individual who places a greater cause above his or her own personal good, knowing in advance that he or she will be portrayed unfavorably.

•••••

Through a mutual friend from Junior High School, I was put in touch again with my childhood crush, Sheryl Otte (now Sherry Coughlin). Her father had died within a day of my mother, and we emailed each other with condolences, and then began to catch up on each other's lives through email. I was delighted to find out that she had married a wonderful man who was good to her, and they had two grown sons.

Sheryl Otte Coughlin

Our friendship developed through the next year, and she actually became a sort of sounding board and voice of reason and compassion, as I went through the next fiasco in my life, the death of my relationship with Tracy. I was grateful for her quiet wisdom and Christian viewpoint on things.

Just to know that Sheryl cared after all those years helped me to put some of my childhood issues to rest. She had a little edge to her, with a little tattoo of a cross on her back, matching the tattoos her husband and sons had gotten. Sheryl will always stay pure in my heart. As much as I pined over her at the age of thirteen, we never actually were 'together' or had a real relationship to screw up in the first place, so we could remain close friends without any kind of a nasty old history. I will always love, cherish and appreciate her on an innocent level!

•••••

In April of 2005, my sister Kathy's heart began to fail quickly, and again, the doctors rushed her into cardiac surgery. Once again, the doctors repaired her mitral valve. Immediately, I dropped everything, flew back to New York and stayed with her again for a week while she recuperated. Following my visit, my sisters all came, one at a time, to help her recover.

Kathy was weak, and her heart would continue to slip into Atrial Fibrillation over the years following, until finally in 2017 she endured cardiac ablation, another surgical procedure where they spent eight hours removing scar tissue from the heart. Kathy was always a trooper. As weak and meek as she thought she was, in reality she was a fighter with a strong soul who just didn't know it.

CHAPTER SIXTY-ONE
My Relationship with Tracy Ends

Tracy had come out of rehab with a nervous determination to change everything in her life, which included me. As I mentioned before, it reminded me so much of Chuck Buffamonte's behavior when he came out of treatment all those years ago. It is as if the addictive behavior stays, takes on a different face and it rules the sobriety in a certain way.

A psychologist friend of mine said that a person who becomes sober after many years of addiction is usually the emotional age that they were when they became an addict. That made sense to me, because Tracy had admitted that she became addicted as a teenager. The thing is, I wanted her to be sober and be okay. I had just been hoping for all these years that maybe she would be a different person underneath it all. In fact, she was, but not the person I expected. She was a tormented child with loads of issues, and extremely self-centered. And, her disease had a totally different face on it than Stephanie's did, or even my father's.

Even though her counselors told her not to change anything drastically for at least a year until she became a whole person again, Tracy alienated the people who cared for her the most, with the exception of her children. She did not possess the same loyalty to others that her father had exhibited.

I had honestly tried very hard to make things right with her, but admittedly I brought way too much baggage myself into this relationship. I was fighting codependence and the need to 'fix' my significant other. In all fairness, we were both a mess at times. I just happened to be the consistent one who showed up and kept my shit together through it all.

Years before when Tracy and I had started dating, I was still wrapped up completely in my relationship with Stephanie, my wife of many years, worrying about her every day, still trying to guide her in the only way I knew how. Deep inside, I knew that my relationship with Tracy was doomed from the start, but especially at first it felt like love; there were many moments of closeness, laughter and life experience as you would expect would happen in every relationship. I never had the depth of relationship with her as I had with Stephanie, or I would have eventually with Robin.

When I met Tracy, she was a party girl, lost, with kids and no real direction in her life. She was fed up with her ex-husband's inability to get and keep a job (in defense of Rex, he had *Meniere's* disease, an affliction of the inner ear which causes vertigo and pain. Dealing with this disease threw off his career as a comedian and made it hard for him to concentrate, let alone work). Tracy had been basically estranged from her father for years, and Red was only slowly bringing her back into his realm when I entered the picture. Tracy changed when Red died. After he passed away, I never saw the Tracy again that I had been attracted to.

•••••

I worked hard to approach the situation with calmness and sincerity. I remained consistent in my behavior, not coming from anger or pain but from a willingness to help. I was shut down. When I offered to work through this with her, she called me codependent. When I mentioned that I had kept her children safe and loved while she went through treatment, she called me an enabler. When I stayed calm and kind but also drew a line with her behavior, refusing to allow her to emotionally abuse me anymore, she called me passive/aggressive. I realized I was in a completely losing situation.

Tracy demanded that I move out of our house. I had fought for us to keep the house for almost five years, putting over $400,000.00 of my own money into it, while she had contributed about $25,000.00

over the same time period. I decided that we should sell the house, and for the time being, I would start sleeping on a mattress in the corner of my recording studio that was built into the garage of the house. This went on for several months.

I remember driving to the beach in Cardiff-by-the-Sea, just a handful of miles west of my home in Carlsbad during the Labor Day weekend of 2005. I walked for miles along the ocean, watching families play together, while in my mind I was going over the choices I had made in the past and contemplating my future.

I wondered if Stephanie would have lived if I hadn't left her. I was still haunted by the ghosts of my past. I prayed that my children would always know that I did what I knew to do under the circumstances; whatever I did, whatever decisions I had made were never done with malice or to hurt anyone.

I worried what would happen to Spencer and Blaire after Tracy and I split up. I had been the only truly constant parent in their lives for the last ten years. They relied upon me. Would Tracy be able to actually rise to the task of parenting her children finally? Spencer was angry with his mother. He didn't want her to leave me. With all the love in my heart, I tried to guide him to understand the inevitable, and that it would ultimately all work out one way or the other.

Spencer and Blaire
2004

•••••

In December of 2005, the house had not yet sold, so Tracy moved out of the house and into her own rental condo. I had bought around $50,000.00 worth of high-end furniture for the house; she took it all, and I let her.

Once again, I found myself in the fetal position, crying my eyes out alone on the night she left with Spencer and Blaire. This time I wasn't crying because she left. We had already been done for a while at this point. I cried for the bad decisions I had made in my life, and the pain was palpable. I knew in my heart that I had tried so very hard. I sucked at picking women… at least until this point in my life. I wasn't going to make that mistake again.

Unfortunately, it took a year and a half to sell the house, so I remained working at *Red Tracton's* through it all. Twice, Tracy had lawyers write me letters demanding that I sell the house immediately! I would write them back, telling them that the house was indeed for sale at a fair price; from the beginning and even still, I was making all of the payments on the house until it sold, so if Tracy would like to contribute to the house payments in the meantime, that would be great. Otherwise, please tell your client to get off my back! And, they would leave me alone.

There is a general assumption about karma that resembles the Golden Rule. If you do something bad to another, the bad thing will come back and happen to you later. A more viable explanation may be that when you make a bad mistake, hurt someone or do a bad deed, perhaps you will have to come back at some point and experience a similar situation, to be given the opportunity to do the right thing this time, and then perhaps to repeat and repeat until you get it right and learn the lesson of doing the right thing, in order for your soul to progress. It's a gentler approach to karma than 'an eye for an eye.'

I quitclaimed the Palm Springs condo to her, even though I had paid to remodel it. In my heart, I told myself that it was my gift to Red Tracton for providing a shelter for my children and me when we needed it the most… and, it was originally his condo. I had only bought it back from the estate to save it for her anyway. I gave up practically everything we mutually owned, just to know in my heart I had done whatever I could to make it right. I could look myself in the mirror, knowing I did the right thing. Still, through it all, her narcissism and selfishness never ceased to amaze me. She really didn't care that she cleaned me out financially. I think she thought she deserved it all. I didn't care enough to fight it. I was glad to finally have some peace in my life.

Even though Tracy was horrible to me, I never wished ill or harm upon her. I knew she was a soul, struggling through life with many problems. I hoped that eventually she would figure it out, but I was ultimately relieved to move on to a new chapter in my own life.

CHAPTER SIXTY-TWO
An Angel Appears in my Life

Through this period following my breakup with Tracy, I remained in the Carlsbad house for a year and a half until it sold, paying all the bills on the property.

Robin Dougan was incredibly kind and loving to me. She was my saving grace and her kindness and compassion helped to heal my heart. She would bring me flowers and food when I worked my long hours in the studio, and when Tracy came back and took all the rest of the furniture out of the Carlsbad house, Robin offered to finance a houseful of furniture for me through the furniture company. So, we went and picked out new furniture for me, and I paid it off accordingly. It was a beautiful gesture on Robin's part, and I dearly appreciated her evenness and care.

One night, when things got really bad, Robin cried in my arms fearing that maybe too much baggage hung around my neck. Robin hardly ever cried, but in her eyes, I saw a sorrow arising from the thought that maybe we just had too much to overcome to be together. In that one moment, as I looked into her beautiful eyes, I saw more clearly than I had ever seen anything in my life. I knew that I needed to figure out a way to be with her, no matter what. Robin was an angel in my life, appearing at the perfect time when I needed her most; I would be the luckiest guy in the world if I could just figure out how to get through all of this and be with her. I knew it like I knew I was breathing.

The greatest sign of true love is when you cannot stand the thought of living your life without that person in it.

Most incredibly, I started to feel the dysfunction that I had carried from my childhood begin to disappear. My mother's passing had somehow freed me from the inner need to 'fix' whatever woman I was with, and I was starting to work my way into a normal, loving relationship with a normal woman. Robin was cool! She had that Midwestern charm and her values were obvious by her actions towards others. She would always pick up something nice for a friend if she saw it. She was just thoughtful, and I was so unused to a woman who thought of others before herself.

Even better, all of the labels that had been placed upon me through my years with addicts actually did not apply to me at all anymore. I had no need to enable, because I wasn't with an addict who might drag that behavior out of me. Codependency changed into a healthy interdependence. I was neither passive nor aggressive. I was just myself, and it was liberating.

•••••

After Tracy and I broke up, in the time before I sold the house and surrendered the condo to Tracy, my daughter Rachel's boyfriend Robert called and asked to meet me alone when I was out in Palm Springs. I thought it was odd but I agreed to meet him at the condo in Palm Springs. Robert and Rachel had been together since her senior year of high school in 1999.

When Robert showed up, he told me that he wanted to marry Rachel, and he asked me for my blessing. Robert was a good kid and I was grateful for the love he and his family had given to Rachel over the years. Of course, I said yes, but I also told him, "...On two conditions...first, I want you to promise that you will help her to finish her education, and second, don't ever, ever break her heart!" He agreed to both, and then promptly proposed to Rachel.

Still, I was trudging my way into *Red Tracton's* and performing full-time. I needed the paycheck along with my *Yamaha* money in order to keep paying the huge house payment until I could sell the house. Tracy treated me like dirt through the whole experience. All of a sudden, I had become 'just an employee' to her.

One night, I walked in to perform and she was sitting with a kind, elderly wealthy couple that I knew well. As I walked by the table, I said 'hello' to them and smiled. They were happy to see me and the man stood up and shook my hand. Tracy rushed over to the piano and asked me how dare I talk to other people while she was at their table? I looked at her in disbelief.

On another night, Tracy came in with a date and sat right in front of me having dinner with him as I performed. It was like she was flaunting herself in front of me, trying to make me miserable, or not caring about my feelings at all. Neither one worked; I was so over her. Many times, she would call me to tell me "You're fired!" ... And then John Smith would call me five minutes later and tell me to just ignore her. It was hell. I was just trying to make it through until the house sold. I was paying all of her bills and mine too.

They say that adversity builds character... and I say, "Lord, I have plenty of character now! Please, I don't need any more character!"

I even agreed to go to counseling with her, and that was a nightmare. She told the counselor that I was a con artist. I sat there in disbelief, thinking, "Oh, my God, I've given every ounce of myself and my money to this woman, and she's given hardly anything at all." In retrospect, I know now that she was very ill through that entire period and obviously not handling her sobriety very well, if she was even sober. I just kept on keeping on until the day would come that I didn't have to be in that situation any more. I was a tormented soul through that period.

My sister Kathy's son, my nephew Yash came to live with me during this period. Yash was cool. He was insecure and sometimes that would come out as ego, but in general, he was a mellow person to be around and he had amazing, untapped talent.

I let him loose in my studio, and many nights while I was performing at *Tracton's*, Yash would sit and record music in the studio. He was a cool little guitar player, and he turned me on to chill music, ambient music and a few genres I wasn't hip to. Kathy was staying in Los Angeles around this time, taking care of her husband's stepmother until she passed away later that year, so Kathy would come down on the train and stay with us, recording her music as well. It was great to have them with me as I was transitioning out of my life with Tracy.

Kathy

Yash came to me carrying a lot of unresolved issues from his childhood. I somehow could relate to him because of my own fractured childhood. We had some deep, long talks, but mostly I think it was what we didn't say that mattered. Just having an uncle who cared and opened up his heart might have been enough for Yash during that period.

Kevin, Mike Soffer, Tad, Yash, Taddy 2006

I don't think he worked through much of his childhood issues while he was with me. I know he carried a lot of baggage within his soul. But, we did accomplish some great music and camaraderie that meant a lot to me. I hope I made a positive impact on him during the seven months he lived with me.

•••••

In mid-2006, my sons Taddy and Kevin wanted to shoot their short Christmas comedy film entitled *'Tis The Season* at my house in Carlsbad. They brought a film crew and a few actors and actresses with them and spent about three days camping out. It was a great experience to watch my sons' talent come out. It was a darling little film and it ended up winning some Short Film Festival awards. Of course, I wrote the score to the film, and Yash assisted me.

•••••

On June 16, 2006, my daughter Rachel received her Bachelor's degree in Psychology from *California State University*. The ceremonies were held up in the Palm Springs area, and my children Regina (with her daughter Whitney and stepson, Gage, and her ex-husband, Gregory), Taddy and Kevin attended along with my best friend Eddie, Rachel's Aunt Denise, Rachel's cousin Hillery, and Rachel's best friend, Melissa.

I was sitting in the auditorium waiting for the ceremony, and I was unusually calm. I thought, "I'm actually not going to cry during this!" But, as soon as *Pomp and Circumstance* started, even before the graduates started walking in, I was sobbing! After everything we had been through as a family, it was amazing to see the first one of my children get a college degree. I was so very proud of my Rachel.

Taddy and Kevin had taken a couple years of college and not continued on. A couple years after this, my Regina would go on and get her High School diploma, having been denied it during her tumultuous eighteenth year. I was very proud of Regina also for following up on this after so many years.

But, for this moment, I felt that Stephanie would have been so proud, and I just loved that my Rachel had held her head high through it all and persevered.

•••••

Rachel went back to Canada with Robert again for the summer of 2006. I missed her terribly when she was gone for a month at a time, but big things were happening in Canada. Robert's parents had hired a developer, and they were turning their little campground into a condo complex called *Barona Beach*. They would make an enormous sum of money doing it, which ensured a lifetime of financial stability for Robert.

After college, Robert had been teaching Science full-time during the school year at a middle school in Indio, California Rachel would teach as a substitute to supplement their income. But, after *Barona Beach* was built, their lifestyle changed completely. Robert quit teaching and began to manage his parent's business affairs. Although Robert was always a good guy, I believe that when he began to work with his parents, he began to change; perhaps he lost some of the direction and personal ambition he had always had, at least for a time.

•••••

Towards the end of 2006, Andy Fraga, Jr. and I decided to pull together some jazz greats into my studio and do a *Jazz Masters* album. Andy's father, my friend Andy Fraga, Sr., had died suddenly of a heart attack, just months before, and we needed a welcome distraction from our respective crazy lives!

Andy's cousin Marty Morell had played drums with jazz legend Bill Evans for years, and he flew out from Florida. Marshall Hawkins, a great friend of Andy's dad and an iconic bass player who had performed and toured with Miles Davis and Shirley Bassey, agreed to play bass on the project. Michael Higgins, my dear friend who was my recording partner on so many tracks, and had performed on tour with Maynard Ferguson, did the guitar parts. I brought in accomplished recording artist and jazz pianist Larry

Tad with Pat Rizzo - 2017

Flahive, and he split the piano parts with me. Pat Rizzo, my dear friend who had performed on saxophone and flute for many greats including Sly and the Family Stone and Frank Sinatra, came in to do sax parts with Rod Kokolj. We also brought in Glen Myerscough, my other mentor who had toured with Andrae Crouch and the Disciples. Gary Hartman did all of the trumpet parts and wrote some amazing arrangements.

Between Marty Morell, Larry Flahive, Michael Higgins, Pat Rizzo, and myself we each chose two original songs to perform. Everyone came prepared with charts, except, of course, Pat. In his classic style, Pat was still writing and scribbling parts with Rod as we prepared to do the album. It came out great! We called it the *Barcelona Sessions* (Barcelona Road was the cross-street of my house in Carlsbad); the quality of the music and of the performers added to the profile of the *Mainstream Source* collection. For production value and quality of composition and performance, it was truly one of my greatest works to date. Of course, it was a collective effort and it was great to work with these outstanding performers.

•••••

My lovely little black kitty that I had since 1984 was becoming very ill. She was twenty-one years and seven months old. She couldn't bathe herself anymore, so I gave her a little bath one day, and she died in my arms shortly thereafter. I cried my heart out, holding her little body in my arms. She was the only thing I had left from my original family, and she had stayed with me through it all… through the death of my wife, through my children leaving home, through my mom's death and my splitting from Tracy and her kids. It was more than the death of an animal… it signaled the end of an era for me, and my heart was devastated.

A week or two later, Robin insisted that I get another kitten just to help to ease the pain. We went to the *Helen Woodward* shelter and found two kittens, a little grey boy and a beige boy cat that were brothers, huddled together in a cage. I brought them home and they hid behind the furniture for days. Yash and I named them "Chicken" and "Scaredy Cat."

•••••

In early December of 2006, my daughter Rachel and her Robert were married in Palm Springs. Robin and I were dating at this point, and our relationship was finally out in the open. We were committed to each other, and I couldn't be happier. In fact, I was ecstatic. Finally, I was in a calm, loving relationship with an amazing woman. Until now, I had only dreamed of this.

The wedding was not without incident. About a month before, Tracy had asked to meet with me. She told me that she wanted to go to the wedding but she didn't want to confront Robin or for them both to be there. This was totally weird to me because I knew that Rachel had a ton of issues with Tracy (especially after she witnessed how poorly Tracy had treated me during the last couple of years), and Rachel absolutely adored Robin.

I spoke with Rachel about it and we mutually decided that Robin should be a part of the wedding, but out of respect for the years that Tracy was a part of our lives, we would try to figure out a way to honor her wish. Robin absolutely did not want to cause or be a part of any controversy, knowing how much this day would mean to us. Rachel and I decided on a compromise. Although I wanted Robin at the ceremony and reception, Rachel asked Robin if she would come to the rehearsal dinner, the night before, and then Tracy would attend the wedding and reception.

So much of my family was coming out for the wedding. My father, my sister Kathy and her husband Steven, my sister Judy, my sister Betsy and her husband Mark, my Uncle Ted and Aunt Candy, my Uncle Gerry and Aunt Cathy, all of my children including Regina, Kevin, Taddy, Mason, Spencer and Blaire. Rex Meredith (Mason, Spencer and Blaire's dad) was invited.

The wedding would be at *St. Theresa Catholic Church* in Palm Springs, and we hosted the reception at *Indian Wells Country Club*. I hired my friend Larry Flahive to play piano for the early part of the reception, and my other friend Mike Capitanelli to DJ the reception.

On the night of the rehearsal dinner, Robin and I had a wonderful time with our families. It was a loving, close night and Rachel was excited and nervous about the next day.

Following the rehearsal dinner, Tracy called Rachel crying and accusing us of going against our word to have Robin there. Rachel began to cry and she was very upset, trying to explain to Tracy that Robin had gracefully bowed out of the reception the next day.

At this point, Robin was still waitressing at *Red Tracton's* and Tracy said she was going to fire Robin immediately when she returned. It was sad and disgraceful of Tracy to do this to Rachel. The really sad part was that Tracy did attend the wedding, but refused to attend the reception, and Robin had already driven back to San Diego, so she didn't go either. I was incensed about the whole thing, but I wanted Rachel to have a perfect day and I wasn't about to allow this to ruin it any more than it already had.

•••••

I prepared a speech, which I would read at the reception. The father-daughter dance would be *Rachel's Song*, the song I had written for my daughter at her birth. I prerecorded it with my voice; The DJ would play the track while we danced.

On the way to the wedding, Rachel and I rode alone in the limousine to the church. She looked stunningly beautiful in her wedding dress! I had prepared some very deep, important things I wanted to tell her at this special moment. As I began, Rachel said, "Daddy, please don't say anything! You'll just make me cry and mess up my makeup!" So, I sighed, took a deep breath and saved it all for later…

Dr. Tom Costa was present at the church along with all of our families and many of our friends, including Ron Zagami and Lawson Brown. The reception, *sans* Tracy went very well, and in spite of the fact that I missed having my Robin there, I will always cherish that night as one of the best of my life. It probably would have been weird with Tracy there anyway, in retrospect.

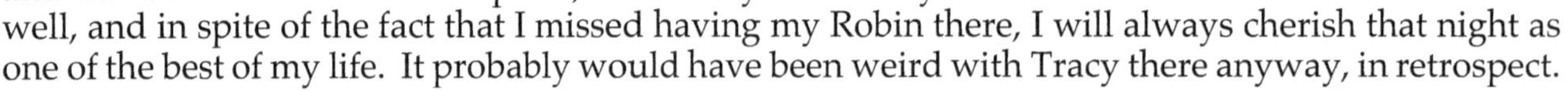

Father-Daughter Dance
Rachel's Wedding - 2006

My father rode in another limo with Robert's mother and father, and they became friends. I wished so much that my mother would have lived to see this day. Silently I prayed to her and to Stephanie, thanking them for the blessings they had brought to my life.

•••••

A few days later, when the wedding was said and done, Robin marched in to *Red Tracton's* and gave her two-week notice before Tracy could say a word. Robin had found an amazing job as a home health nurse.

For the next several years, Robin would drive all over San Diego healing wounds and treating patients. She was really good at it, and it was much better for her than waitressing after all. I missed so much working with Robin, but I was so glad for her. I was proud of her for holding her head up and not allowing anyone to manipulate or hurt her. Robin was a healer. She was now doing her life's work, using her amazing compassion to minister to many, many patients in her own way.

I still was stuck working at *Red Tracton's* until I could get the Carlsbad house sold. I needed the income since Tracy was not contributing at all to her half of the obligation. Walking away would destroy my credit, and I had vowed to never get into that ugly position again in my life.

•••••

In January of 2007, I got a call from the agent who was now booking the *Yellowstone Club* in Montana. He hired my band to come up one last time to perform. Tim and Edra Blixseth were becoming embroiled in lawsuits regarding the property, and they were divorcing at the same time. Neither of them was there for the event, which was weird to us after so many years of watching them work so hard to build up this amazing resort. But, *Yellowstone Club* was finally built almost to the point of completion. We had seen it at its inception, and the new *Warren Miller Lodge* was gorgeous. I was grateful for that one more trip to our getaway paradise, and my band performed at a high level.

Also, in early 2007, Ron Zagami flew Robin and I to Las Vegas in his corporate jet, along with his girlfriend Tina. A limo met us at the airport, and we stayed at the *Mirage* Resort. My dad and his wife Sandra met us there along with Sandra's sisters, Diane and Bonnie. Rachel and Robert flew out and met us there, and we had a warm, wonderful time. After a great dinner, Ron got us all in to the *Beatles Love Show* at the *Mirage*, and I sat next to my dad, holding his hand throughout the show. He was smiling and grateful, and he got along very well with Ron. It was great to spend this quality family time with my Robin, my Rachel and my dad, and our friends and family.

Maynard was introspective. He was slowing down after his forced retirement. I was grateful that he was still able to write his opinion pieces and his sonnets. This trip to Las Vegas meant a whole lot to both of us.

CHAPTER SIXTY-THREE
Reinventing Myself Once Again

Finally, In March of 2007, I sold the house in Carlsbad. We made a small profit, and although Tracy was not there to help me pay for the house, she was definitely there to claim her half of the profits. I could have fought her on it, but I just wanted to wash my hands of it. I had given her virtually everything she wanted, the Palm Springs condo, all of the furniture, and eleven years of my life. As I mentioned, I had continued to make all of the house payments in order to keep our credit intact, so I knew I could look myself in the mirror and know I did everything I could to be a good person, through it all.

I found a lovely little rental home overlooking the ocean on Cambridge Avenue in Cardiff-by-the-Sea, just a few blocks from Robin's house. Yash helped me with the move, and he stayed in the new place for about a month to paint the studio and help me with another project. He then made the decision to drive back home to New York, so we said our goodbyes, and I was alone in a house for the first time in my adult life.

Immediately, I stopped performing at *Red Tracton's* and cut off all ties with Tracy, except, of course, to stay in touch and as close as I could with Spencer and Blaire, under the circumstances. I saw Mason on occasion, and he was always cordial and kind to me. Ara Shamalyan hired me down the street to perform Thursdays, Fridays and Saturdays at *Scalini,* and I started my new life.

Ara Shamalyan
2016

I picked up Wednesdays at *Mille Fleurs* in Rancho Santa Fe, and although the *Scalini* gig only lasted a year until Ara closed the place, I continued to perform at *Mille Fleurs* on Wednesdays for many years.

•••••

Scalini was a bizarre place to work. It was off the beaten path and it had seen it's day. I had worked so hard to build up the business at *Tracton's* and as a result, we were usually busy when I performed at *Tracton's*. Ara was struggling to get people back in to his restaurant, and most nights business was very slow. This was a huge adjustment for me, but I was eternally grateful to Ara that he had brought me over directly to work; I was finally away from Tracy and her bullshit, and I hadn't yet missed a beat. I could always count on a handful of people to show up to *Scalini*.

Sheila and Peter Maglaque
2017

Peter and Sheila Maglaque would sit right outside at a bar table most nights. Sheila's sister Mistie had just moved to San Diego from Minnesota. They were really nice people and became good friends with Robin and myself. Lawson Brown was there with me most of the time after his long workday, and he struck up a strong friendship with Pete, Sheila and Mistie. Ron Zagami would frequent all of the places I performed on a regular basis, and so would Frank & Uta Hamblen when they were in town.

Tom Siegel was an aging bartender/musician who looked and dressed like Jimmy Buffet with a goatee. He was a super nice guy, and he introduced himself as Corky Siegel. The real Corky Siegel was a star blues musician back in the 1960's and '70's, and he was still touring. Corky wanted to pass himself off as the real Corky, and one night Ed Masterson 'outed' him. Although Corky became a close friend to me, he did have the tendency to tell 'tall-tales'. He was always telling me he had been hanging out with David Crosby or Gary Puckett or some other big star, and he always promised to bring them in to see me next time they were in town. Honestly, he meant no harm when he lied to people about his past.

Tom "Corky" Siegel
2008

As crazy as he seemed, Corky was always very kind to me. He was always bringing me a gift or some food, and he was very encouraging of my music. At first, I was so enamored by who I thought he was that I invited him into the studio to record a song with me. He was lost in the studio and I gently helped him through a song that went nowhere. But, I appreciated his friendship, and I was devastated when he died suddenly on Christmas day in 2010.

•••••

One of my kittens was hit by a car and killed a couple weeks after I moved in. That was tragic, and after that, the grey kitty alone kept me company.

Spencer, Blaire & Mason
2012

In my new life, I missed Spencer and Blaire a lot even still, but Spencer stayed close in touch with me, coming to visit me and doing some recordings with me. He was practicing his singing, and becoming a pretty good vocalist already. Spencer was already a great dancer. Blaire and I would get together here and there, and we always expressed our undying love for each other. She was my little sweetheart. Mason would get in touch with me on occasion, and he was always kind and grateful to me in our conversations. He was growing up.

Just a handful of years later, Mason would come in regularly to see me perform at *Manhattan of La Jolla*. One night, Mason came with his pregnant fiancé, to *Mille Fleurs* to see me on a Wednesday night. We talked about how much he had grown. He thanked me for the tough love I gave him, and told me I was the only one brave enough to do it when he needed it. My heart warmed in our conversation, as I winked, looked at his fiancé's belly and said, "Payback's a bitch!" We laughed. Since then, Mason and I still don't communicate much, but when we do, it's with love and kindness.

My sons Taddy and Kevin were doing pretty well in Los Angeles, bartending at *PF Changs* and working on their concepts for films. They had each other, and that meant a lot to me. Regina had Todd and her young children, and I loved them all. My daughter Rachel always stayed very close to me, and I cherished her love and friendship. When we weren't together, we always talked on the phone at least once or twice a day. The other kids would tease me and say that Rachel was my favorite. Rachel and I definitely remained inseparable in spirit throughout all of our lives.

Mary Wanner & Judy 2008

My sister Judy came out to visit often. She had reunited with Mary Wanner, a friend from her teenage years in San Diego. Mary and her husband Chewy would come over whenever I had events. They were sweet people, and I was glad Judy could meet with her friends when she came to see me.

•••••

The ocean breeze drifted through my open windows, allowing me to finally take deep breaths within my recently discovered serenity and solitude. As I continued my healing process in my new home in Cardiff, I began to put the past eleven years with Tracy into perspective. I realized that I had endured a rebound relationship that I allowed to continue for far too long.

It all wasn't bad. In the beginning, we laughed a lot. Although I should have never moved in with her, I was grateful that my children had a safe space to live during those years following their mother's tragic death, and it was gracious of Tracy to allow them to live in her house, although she did it kicking and screaming all the way! In all honesty, Stephanie's death put an enormous burden on Tracy. In her own way, she stepped up to the plate and helped me with my children, and for that, I would be eternally grateful. I also hoped that Tracy would forgive me for bringing my own baggage into her life. Losing Stephanie was devastating to myself and my children, but it also affected many other people around us as well. I certainly paid the price, putting up with Tracy's antics for eleven years, but even so, it was unfair for me to think that a relationship could survive such tragedy from the outset… and it was an outstanding gesture on her part to bring us into her home and her heart when we were at our worst.

Tracy was an only child from a broken home. I believe that she developed her narcissism in her childhood as a protective mechanism when her parents left her alone. I had learned so many coping mechanisms from my siblings, and I always had someone to turn to. Tracy had none of that. I also believe (and she admitted it at some point) that she was incapable of having a normal love-type relationship. As she admitted many times to me, her addictions were a devastating blow to any possibility of a semblance of normalcy in our lives, and I had still not learned to cope with addiction in others when we met (you would think that I would have, after a lifetime of dealing with addicts and alcoholics).

Rex Meredith with Tad 2017

Tracy had never developed her attitudes and emotions to the point of maturity, and everything in life boils down at some point to attitudes and emotions. I was in pain for some time because of the choices I had made. Tracy's actions and behavior had devastated me, as had Stephanie's. At some point, you have to turn inward and start wondering what's wrong with the choices you are making in your life.

Tracy's ex-husband Rex was a comedian. Rex and I had become good friends over the years, after all. He knew how much his children loved me, and I believe he was grateful that I was supportive of his desire to parent them, always encouraging them to be with him and to love him whenever they could. When Tracy and I broke up, a friend asked him if he might consider getting back with Tracy. In his comedic style, he said, "I would marry Tad!" Although funny, that comment validated my struggle in dealing with Tracy while helping her in her endeavors and raising her children for eleven years. Rex got it, and at least I knew he appreciated my love and care for his family.

•••••

I had attended some Al-Anon meetings back when Stephanie was in treatment, and I continued on for a while, while I was still with Tracy, to try to gain some coping mechanisms, but it was strange to me that, when the addicts in my life were no longer in my life, I no longer needed Al-Anon.

Al-Anon is a great concept; it is an essential tool for family members and friends of alcoholics and addicts to learn how to cope with the disease. But, what happens when you are finally free of the addicts that plagued your life, and you've worked through the confusion and despair that naturally comes with dealing with them? I had healed and grown so much from my experiences dealing first with my father (and mother to some extent), then Carol, Stephanie, Chuck Buffamonte, Tracy, and all the other addicts who affected my life.

In fact, I would regularly run into an older gentleman named Tom at the gym. He had attended Al-Anon meetings with me. A couple years after all of this, I saw him at the gym and he asked me if I was still going to Al-Anon. At first, I looked at him like he was crazy; it was almost like I had dealt with all of that in another life, and now it all seemed so foreign to me! I told Tom that Al-Anon had been essential to my healing, but now I was not being affected by any addicts or by their addictions. Robin was a functioning, caring person who brought a much-desired normalcy to my life that I greatly appreciated.

•••••

Now, I had to "own up" to my own dysfunction and to the baggage I carried into all of my relationships. As I moved through the greatest healing period of my life, I realized that, in all my relationships, for me it was more than just trying to 'fix' someone. I had a deep, inner need to be loved, wanted and needed. We all do, but we don't all realize how that adds to our insecurities and affects the decisions we make.

For those of us who are forced as little children to parent our own parents, we rise to the task and grow up too soon. But, deep inside each one of us festers a strong need to be wanted and cared about. So, for many of us who had to grow up too soon, when we become adults and get into a relationship, the moment it begins to feel safe, the child in us begins to come out and attempt to get the nurturing that we didn't get when we should have gotten it.

Particularly, when we marry someone who has so many of the good and bad qualities and attributes that our parents had, what starts out as a need to balance the child inside us turns into a dysfunctional relationship with consequences. And then, as we begin to outgrow the need, so we also outgrow the person we chose; we grow apart from the person with whom we became fixated, with dire consequences.

Some of us will cycle the same behavior into each new relationship. The enemy is always loneliness, isolation, being alone. It can become too much to bear for a little soul. This is the problem with so much of what goes on in the world. If people would just pay more attention to their children, to nurture them a little more, I believe that half of the world's problems would easily go away.

Forgiveness is essential in order to heal and move forward.

Some children naturally adapt, becoming their own best friend, finding optimism in every day, even creating imaginary playmates. But, even so, many children adapt so well that they put on a tough outer skin, preventing them later from allowing their inner selves to feel feelings that should be felt.

So, here I was, finally making sense of the choices I had made and of the women I had chosen to be my companions, and I realized that I was quite possibly equally as responsible as they were for the dysfunction and failure. I also began to forgive them and myself.

I filled the Cambridge house with plants. Every morning, the airflow from the beach wafted through my front windows and I breathed deeply, slowly healing one day at a time and becoming whole again. Robin came over daily to check on me, and her presence was like emotional salve to my heart. As busy as we both were, we found time to go on an occasional date, or just to be together here and there.

Robin and Tad 2007

Robin loved my home. She had a little getaway place to come to when her ex-husband had her kids for the day, or if she just wanted to come over for a few hours during the day or night. We hugged and kissed a lot! For the first time in many years, I felt hopeful for the future and I was starting to feel contentment in my life.

Tad's Recording Studio in Cardiff - 2008

I installed my recording studio into the back half of the Cambridge house. It was beautiful and effective. I had a tracking room and two recording suites. My lovely Yamaha C3 grand piano was the anchor in the tracking room, along with racks of keyboards and effects. I had room and space to create without much interruption for the first time in my life, and it was liberating! And, create, I did.

During this period, I delivered over a hundred projects for Yamaha, and I expanded our film music collection from around fifteen hundred tracks to over five thousand tracks. I produced a young Russian-American female vocalist. She was only fourteen when we started. Helene would come over every day with her father Vlad. Vlad spoke very little English, so Helene would translate between us, and in this manner, we co-wrote songs for her album. It was bizarre, but it worked, and they were nice people.

•••••

Robin and I hosted a few parties at my house. Ron Zagami would come in to the studio and play piano. Jesse Davis would sing, and everyone else would gather around and listen to the new tracks I was producing.

Christmas of 2007 was a warm, loving time for my family. On Christmas Eve, we all got together at Robin's house for her annual party. She had a Pomeranian dog named Callie who was a yapper dog, but she was a doll. Callie reminded me of Susie, Kirk Gentry's dog from when I was in first grade in Del Cerro.

Robin had a huge, old, archaic square television. HDTV was the new craze, and everyone was buying the flat screens. For Christmas, I bought her a new flat screen HDTV for her living room, and I promised to come over sometime after Christmas to hook it up for her.

•••••

In December of 2007, Ron Zagami invited Robin and me to go to Las Vegas for New Year's Eve. In my entire career, I had never taken a New Year's Eve off. Through all of the

Robin, Tammy Shulman, Jill Zagami and Tina
New Year's Eve, December 31, 2007

New Year's events I had performed, I never was able to enjoy the moment of midnight with a loved one because I WAS the party! We stayed at the *Mirage* with Ron and Tina, his brother Jerry and his wife Jill. Our friend, Matt Shulman was the VP of the *Mirage.* Matt and his wife Tammy joined us. We had an amazing dinner, and the culmination of the event was the very first performance at the *Mirage* by *America's Got Talent* winner, ventriloquist/puppeteer Terry Fator.

After Terry won *America's Got Talent* that year, he replaced impressionist Danny Gans in the showroom. Danny was a friend of mine. Stephanie had booked Danny Gans on some corporate events, some years back, and I was sad to see Danny leave the *Mirage.* Even sadder, just a year or so later I found out Danny had died in his hotel room in Vegas. He was a great talent and a good guy. Terry did a great show, though, and we enjoyed it immensely.

Afterwards, we went and watched as Ron Zagami played the draw poker machines in the High Roller room at the *Mirage.* Robin and I weren't big gamblers, but we dabbled on the machines. Ron was putting $100.00 bills in to the machines. He gave a few to Robin, and she was aghast! She couldn't bring herself to put that kind of money into the machines! Eventually, she played a couple hands next to him, but then we went over to the quarter machines for a while.

It was great, though, to have a break and such a nice vacation with my Robin, and I was so grateful to Ron for his kindness and generosity. He flew us both over and back in his private jet, and we were met at the airport by a limousine. The down side is that it kind of ruins your Vegas experience if you ever arrive any other way!

•••••

In January of 2008, I went to Robin's house to install the new television I had bought for her for Christmas. We had to roll up a large area rug three or four feet to pull the console out. I had been working out on a regular basis at the YMCA, so my muscles were pretty strong at that point, but as I went to pull out the old, very heavy square television to set down on the floor below, Callie came running under me and sat directly in the place I was going to put the TV. Not wanting to hurt her, I stumbled back and tripped over the rug… and the television came crashing down on me, crushing my leg at the ankle. My leg was severely broken. Both bones were practically severed, and a chip came off of my anklebone.

Robin rushed me to the emergency room, and I had to wait overnight for surgery. Rachel came down from Palm Springs to help to take care of me for a few days.

The surgeons did an excellent job repairing the bones in my lower leg with plates and screws. They reattached the chip onto the anklebone, which would take longer to heal, but it would eventually restore all movement to my foot and ankle. I woke up from the surgery in a daze, telling Rachel and Robin, "I remember the day I was born, it was raining," or something to that matter. I was out of it!

The pain was intense, reminding me again of what I had gone through at twelve years old when I broke my arm. This was a rough situation, because I was living alone. Just figuring out how to get my coffee from the kitchen to the living room so I could drink it, was a task… but Robin was very helpful. She cooked and did the dishes for a few days, and then she put a stool by the sink, and told me I was perfectly capable of doing it myself! She was right, and I needed someone to remind me that I would be fine.

•••••

My sister Judy came out from Texas to stay with me for a month. It was great to have Judy at my house. We bonded in a way we never had, and she was gracious and kind. Judy made lasagna and cookies, and she did her best to clean the house and take care of me as I was healing.

At some point, we invited Judy's ex-husband David and his brother Wes to come out and stay with us for a week or so. David and Wes were enmeshed in the Native American way, and part of that is taking care of family. They built a shed for me, and did minor repairs around the house. They were kind and light-hearted and it was great to have them there. They stayed for about a week.

Somehow, I continued to perform through my healing, going back to work just a couple days after my surgery. I would hobble in to *Scalini* or *Mille Fleurs* with my crutches, sit down and use my left foot to maneuver all of my pedals below. Although I was in pain, I did not like narcotics, so I would take Advil or Tylenol and just get through it. Robin's son, Kris, helped me to load in and out of *Mille Fleurs* every Wednesday. I was grateful for his kindness and assistance!

By March, I was in physical therapy and slowly taking my first steps within a walking boot. On the very first day, I drove down to the beach and walked so very slowly along the Pacific Coast Highway. I had a stupid grin on my face! I was going to somehow rehab and get back to normal. Judy went home, and I slowly continued to heal, finally removing my walking boot by June of 2008, just in time for my 50th birthday.

•••••

Around April of 2008, Ara Shamalyan lost the lease at *Scalini* where I had performed for a year after leaving *Red Tracton's*. I saw the writing on the wall, and moved on to perform at *Tuscany* in Carlsbad, and at *Delicias*, in Rancho Santa Fe, right down the street from my Wednesday gig at *Mille Fleurs.* I hadn't yet found a 'home' to perform in, as *Tracton's* had been for me for all those years. But, then again, I would tell people that *Tracton's* was the most expensive job I ever had in my life!

For a short period of time, I performed on Thursdays at the *La Costa* resort. The management in large corporate situations is always fickle. A new GM will come along and want to change everything, and the 'yes' men below him just go along with it without a fight. The manager of the restaurant jerked me around for a few weeks, and I just moved on. Thankfully, that kind of treatment hasn't happened to me much in my career.

As a performer, witnessing, enjoying and participating in the expression of talent with great artists is one of life's greatest joys. It gets even better when you realize that you are collaborating with great artists who are also incredible human beings.

I had a friend, Mike Labrador. He was an excellent guitarist, touring with Tom Jones and other greats. Mike would come and work corporate gigs with us in the late 1990's and early 2000's when he was off the road. He was a handsome Hawaiian man, very kind and an excellent performer. One night before the gig at *La Costa* ended, Mike drove out and worked with me. He had just been diagnosed with stage-four lung cancer. He was just about my age, and Mike died not long after the gig. His inner strength and optimism amazed me as he endured his battle with that ugly disease with a smile on his face… and he played his ass off that night.

•••••

On the day of my 50th birthday, June 28, 2008, we decided to have a party at Moonlight Beach in Encinitas, just a couple miles away from my house in Cardiff. My sister Suzanne came out from North Carolina with her daughter, my niece Lori. My sister Betsy and her husband Mark were there. My sister Judy came out. Kathy chose not to come out from the East coast because of her heart condition. My dad was supposed to be there, but he and Sandra bowed out at the last minute and promised to come later. My children were there, along with my Uncle Ted and Aunt Candy.

It was a great day… until Robin's mother had a stroke. Robin quickly made her way to the hospital and couldn't participate in the party. Robin's mother had cancer and although the stroke was minor, Robin stayed with her until the evening, when she stabilized, and then came to my house to join us all for the after-party.

•••••

Robin - 1970's

As I've already mentioned, Robin, to me, was an amazing person, full of compassion and always thinking of others.

She was born in Akron, Ohio on June 26, 1959. Her childhood wasn't great… her parents divorced when she was very young. She had an older brother, David, and a younger sister, Gina. When Robin was a young girl, her mother, Mary, left her father and married Jordan Christopher, an aspiring young singer. Mary and Jordan had a daughter, Jodi, Robin's other sister. For most of Robin's childhood, she was ushered back and forth, sometimes living with her Grandmother in Akron, Ohio, as all the other siblings were scattered to other relatives, and sometimes living with her mother and all of her siblings. They moved around a lot, from Florida to California.

Robin - 1970's

Robin was always responsible for her brother and sisters, and as a result of it she became a very strong and independent person. In her youth, Robin's mother bartended and drank a lot. Eventually, Jordan left Mary and ended up marrying Richard Burton's ex-wife, Sybil. So, when Jodi wasn't with her mom, she grew up spending a lot of time with the famous actor's family, which became an extension of her own family. Eventually, Robin's mother, Mary met a man named Steve Bache and they lived together from then on, adopting a child named Mary Kate and raising her into adulthood.

Robin and I figured out that, way back when I lived in Mission Beach when I was ten, Robin lived on the next block at age nine. We may have played on the beach together as children, for all we knew! And, during the same time period my father drank regularly at the bar where Robin's mother bartended. Small world.

Lynette (Friend), Robin's sisters Jodi and Gina, Robin, her mother Mary and stepfather Steve Circa 1980

•••••

At my Cambridge house in Cardiff during 2008, Robin's oldest, Sammi, would come over and help me do graphics for the *Mainstream Source* music collection on *Photoshop*. Sammi was actually Robin's niece, but Robin had pretty much raised her as a daughter from birth. Sammi was totally cool, a little eccentric, in her early twenties at that point. She could be at times negative, sarcastic or cynical, but she had a great sense of humor and we got along very well. At times, she would pour her heart out to me. My crazy brand of wisdom fit her well, and we bonded. She worked with me for several months on her spare time, mostly, until she moved up to San Francisco. I was glad for her help and to get to know her better.

Sammi with "Vinnie" - 2008

•••••

When I performed weekends at *Delicias* in Rancho Santa Fe for a short time, they had me located mostly on a patio that leaked when it rained, and I would be performing next to a waterfall which leaked all over my equipment, so it just wasn't working out. So, I continued to perform at *Tuscany*. It was usually packed there when I was performing, but it was a blue-collar crowd and the tips weren't great.

Miles Pelky and Larry Schmidtke ©2013

One night, Larry Schmitke and his brother Miles Pelky came into *Tuscany*. Larry and Miles had the same dad, but they had not met each other until a year or two before I met them. Larry was a big guy in his mid-fifties with red hair, an infectious smile, and a great singing voice. Miles was slightly younger with dark hair and a kind face. Larry got up to sing with me, and it became a regular thing. We became fast friends. Miles was a DJ and drummer, and he knew a few of the people I had worked with over the years.

•••••

In August of 2008, my father came out to San Diego to visit. He stayed at the *Four Seasons* with his wife, Sandra. They brought her sister, Bonnie and her nephew, Devin. Devin followed my dad and I as we walked on the beach, taking photos of us, which I cherished so much later after I lost my father.

Sandra wasn't feeling well. She had gone through so much losing Kimberley so terribly back in 1992, and she hadn't been well since. At some point, doctors had actually considered performing a heart transplant for her. She literally had a broken heart.

Maynard and Ted - August 2008

Sandra's heart had improved somewhat through the years, but she never felt completely well. We had a birthday party for my dad on August 12 while they were there. Frank and Uta Hamblen came along with Ron Zagami, Lawson Brown and some other friends and family.

Maynard wrote a sonnet for himself on that day. He had always written sonnets on most occasions, since I was very young, and when I was in high school, he would make me read them aloud, coaching me on pronunciation and inflection.

On this day in 2008, he asked me if I would read this sonnet aloud at his party, and I sighed affirmation. It was always uncomfortable for me to do this, but I thought that he would probably forget and not make me do it during the party.

When we brought out the cake, and sang "Happy Birthday" to him, he was elated! He cleared his voice, made a short speech and then said, "My son asked if he could read this little sonnet I wrote!" I laughed, and read it for the guests, who enjoyed it. That was my dad. Looking back, I wouldn't mind at all today reading one of his new sonnets if he were only still here with me.

If you find enough patience to indulge the harmless quirks and nuances of your loved ones, eventually you will thank yourself for putting up with it and making them happy. Isn't that what life's all about?

I'm guessing that, through my father's persistence in making me read and proofread his writings, perhaps it made me a better author.

•••••

Throughout the rest of 2008, I was busy in the studio doing more projects for *Yamaha's PSR* series of keyboards, producing a duet album for Jesse Davis and Darci Daniels, and doing karaoke projects with Chad Quist and Andrew Fraga, Jr. for a company that had contacted us to provide content. This karaoke company turned out to be a sham, and we had to fight for about a year to acquire back the rights to the songs we had given them. It all worked out in the end with a small out-of-court settlement and the release of the music back to us.

The catalog was expanding, and in addition to *Tadco Music Publishing (ASCAP)*, I expanded my publishing realm to include additional publishing companies. In 2008 Andrew Fraga, Jr. and I set up *Mainstream Global Publishing (ASCAP), Mainstream Worldwide Publishing (BMI) and Mainstream International Publishing (SESAC)* to handle music I had been acquiring from other composers. I also started *Tad Sisler Music (BMI).*

Around this time, my friend John Bergeson contacted me. He had a friend, Tommy Baker, who had produced a reality series about a motorcycle club, and they wanted some classic rock sound-alike tracks. Chad, Andy and I put together a great genre of classic rock, which I expanded upon later when Tommy hired me to do some music editing for the show. It almost made it onto several networks, and it ended up on iTunes in 2017 as *American MC*. We ended up placing over a hundred tracks into the series.

CHAPTER SIXTY-FOUR
Unexpected Cherished Moments with my Father and Sister

In January of 2009, my sister Judy drove from San Antonio, Texas to San Diego to visit me. I hadn't seen her for almost a year since she helped me heal from my broken leg. It was always great to see Judy. She had a calming influence on any situation, and I always knew how very much she loved me. She was a caring, devoted sister.

Judy was going to stay for about a week. One morning, we walked on the beach, and as always, we had a deep, philosophical talk. Judy and I were very close, and I was always grateful for her lightness and wisdom.

On the way back from the beach, we went to walk over the railroad tracks, as I have done almost every day for many years. Judy guided me up a little steeper of a slope than I normally took to get up there, and on the way back down she lost her footing on the rocks and fell. Judy screamed out in pain! She had broken her leg! I called 9-1-1 from my cell phone and paramedics arrived almost immediately.

As they took her in the ambulance, I ran all the way home and grabbed my SUV to drive to the hospital. It was a pretty bad break and she would require surgery. So, the tables were turned. Almost exactly a year to the day after I had broken my leg, I was taking care of my sister now for the same problem! Judy would need to stay with me for several months, and although she was in pain particularly during the first couple weeks, it was really great to have this special time with her. It was something I would cherish forever.

•••••

Just a couple days after Judy broke her leg, my father called one morning, sobbing. He was choking back tears as he told me what had just happened at his home in Kennett, Missouri. He had brought a cup of coffee into Sandra that morning. She was on the phone talking to her sister. All of a sudden, the sister heard a gasp. When my father walked back into the bedroom, Sandra had died of a heart attack. It was a real shock to all of us.

Maynard and Sandra

Sandra was only fifty-nine years old. Dad was eighty-three, and nobody on the planet would have guessed that she would go before him. Sandra truly had a broken heart after her Kimberley had been murdered so viciously. Really, she gave up on life in so many ways after Kimberley died.

She had won a huge settlement but the money meant nothing to her, so she squandered it on items from *QVC* or stores that were going out of business, or anything that caught her fancy, and then she hoarded it all.

Dad and Sandra had bought a couple of investment houses to rent to others in Kennett, but they never rented out the properties because the homes were filled to the brim with stuff Sandra had purchased.

I couldn't make it to her funeral because I was taking care of Judy, but my dad decided to come out to San Diego to be with us for a week following the services. My sister Kathy also flew out to San Diego from New Jersey.

Sandra's sister Diane really stepped up to the plate and began to take care of my dad and all of his affairs. The family filled the *Armory* in Kennett, Missouri with all of the items Sandra had bought, and they sold it all at fire sale prices. Their home had become so cluttered that they could barely make it from one room to another. For years, Sandra couldn't bear to get rid of any of Kimberley's stuff, and the mess just got bigger and bigger from there. Diane patiently and painstakingly went from room to room, removing and selling or donating everything that wasn't needed. She brought my dad lunch and dinner most days when he was home. He was family to them. I was grateful for Diane's love and care to my dad. He was grieving and she came through for him.

Kenny and Diane Johnson with Maynard

•••••

When my dad arrived in San Diego, he was depressed and in shock. I think my presence and Judy's calmness really helped him. When Kathy arrived, it was nice for us all to be together, but then Kathy went in to A-Fib and her heart needed to be cardioverted, so she went home a little earlier than expected. For a minute I gently chaffed them all that I was running an orthopedic, geriatric, psychiatric heart institute over here!

After my dad went home, during the course of the next few months, I began to develop the relationship with Maynard that I had always prayed for. He called me most days. After Judy healed and went home in May, I made plans to go back to visit him in Kennett for a week. I repeated that a couple of times over the next couple years, and he came out to see me for a week or two a couple times as well.

We got to say the things we always needed to say to each other. One day he asked me, "Do you still hate me for what I did to you when you were young?" I told him that the fifteen-year-old in me still had issues, but the parent I became made some terrible mistakes of my own that continue to haunt me, and the fifty-two-year-old me understood so much more about life that I had forgiven him long ago.

Of course, I had issues with him. For years, I held on to enormous issues as a result a lot of tragic things that happened to me as a child. But, I firmly believe that it is essential to our progress to learn how to let go, in order to move forward with our spiritual growth. My long talks with my father and his openness were the impetus for enormous healing within me, within both of us really, and it mirrored the experience I had with my mother prior to her death, just five years before.

Maynard was human and flawed. He was also a beautiful man underneath all of the addiction and bad behavior of his younger years. And, he had conquered it all and prevailed. But, at this point, he was depressed, no longer practicing medicine and having lost his wife. And,

When the tables turn, be prepared to lead.

for once, he needed my wisdom.

Uta, Robin, Tad and Veronica Lawlor 2009

In late March of 2009, my sons Kevin and Tad, Robin and I joined my now very pregnant daughter Rachel and her husband Robert in Los Angeles for Robert's thirtieth birthday. We went to a *Laker's* game. Frank Hamblen was coaching and Uta was a gracious hostess to us. We went to the *Chairman's Room* and to the *Lexus Club* at halftime. They put "Happy 30th Birthday Robert Barone" up in lights at *Staples Center*.

Thanks to Uta directing the cameraman to us, Robin and I got caught on the *JumboTron* on the "Kiss Cam." I wasn't looking at her, I was cheering at the game, and everybody 'booed' me because I didn't kiss Robin! But I didn't see it, so I made up for it all night by kissing her a lot! She said, "enough already!" with a big smile on her face. It was a warm and fun night.

We always seemed to run into celebrities when we went to the games. Uta knew everybody, and they all seemed to love her! We ran into Khloe Kardashian and she took a photo with us.

We all went to the *Harbor Room*, a little dive in Playa Del Rey, when the game was over, and stumbled into our hotel rooms afterwards. Rachel was the only sober one, now six months pregnant with my grandson!

•••••

Robin suggested that we all go on a cruise, to help my dad start to work on overcoming his grief from having lost his wife. Robin and her kids Danielle and Beau went on the cruise with her mother Mary, Mary's husband Steve, Robin's friend Judy, her boyfriend Chris and Judy's son, Jacob. Dad and I shared a room on the cruise.

It was still very soon after Sandra died, and I noticed that dad was projecting a lot onto Sandra's sister, Diane. He would call her several times a day, asking about any little thing he could think of. He was taking antidepressants, which was unlike him, and he was lethargic. Robin and I strongly suggested that he wean himself off of the medicine, which he did after the cruise.

When he got the antidepressants out of his system, he became very much back to his old self again. Maynard continued to write, and although his eyes were failing and his hands shook from *Parkinson's* disease, he managed to continue to read the classics.

On another trip that Maynard made to San Diego, I took him downtown to tour the *U.S.S. Midway*, a huge aircraft carrier from the Vietnam War era. Although it was commissioned slightly after World War II, Maynard was quite comfortable on the big ship as we toured. Although he was in his mid-eighties, he somehow scaled the steep stairwells into the bowels of the ship. He pointed out all of the archaic medical supplies, X-Ray and EKG machines in the sick bay, noting that he had participated in the progress of medical care from a time when polio ravaged youth, through the advent of antibiotics, to modern-day care. He was proud of his many years of service in the Navy and as an outstanding physician. I was proud of him, too.

•••••

I continued to perform at *Tuscany* in Carlsbad, but the owner was inconsistent and although I packed the place, they were constantly trying to pay me less and just basically messing with me. I was unhappy, but I stayed at *Tuscany* for a couple years.

Tuscany had an animated bartender named Howie Oveida, and my friend Paulie Alfano waited tables there. Paulie had worked with me at *Scalini*, and he was very supportive of me, particularly when the management messed with me. Somehow, I made it through that time financially, mostly by picking up outside projects.

I completed Jesse Davis and Darci Daniel's duets album comprised of mostly standards, in my studio. The album came out great. I did a project with Teri Krul, a jazz singer. Teri was an amazing singer and the tracks came out great, but she was a perfectionist, and I don't think she ever released the album. She would take it to different studios after we completed it, and get them to mix and remix the album.

I understand and admire perfectionism, but at some point, you need to let go of a product and give it the life it deserves.

In May of 2009, I got the news that my friend Jack Kemp had died of cancer. It was the end of an era for us. Jack had been so gracious, kind and generous to me and to my entire band, through the years. I grieved for his family.

My recording studio at the Cambridge house was kicking ass! I produced many outside projects and continued to develop our catalog of music for film, television and advertising. *Mainstream Source* was slowly growing into an entity of its own.

When we had parties, people would gather in the studio and listen to some of my new tracks. It was a great time in my life. Robin had insisted that I live on my own for a while in order to make sure I was whole again before we moved in together. I stayed in the Cambridge house in Cardiff for four years, until later in April of 2011, when I moved a couple blocks down to Montgomery Avenue in Cardiff to live with my Robin.

I was on a roll! After moving so much in my early life, I had managed to live in just two homes in nine years! My life would continue to become more secure, as I would live with Robin happily in the Montgomery home for many more years to come. But, that was not to happen for a couple more years. For the remaining time I had in the Cambridge house, I continued to heal my spirit and work hard to create content.

Cardiff was cool. At *Encinitas Acupuncture and Massage*, I would go to an amazing chiropractor named Mark Rosenberg. Mark did his adjustments by feel, unlike my mother's ex-husband Bart had. He was an artist and he would readjust me perfectly. Then I would go to Francine Chandler and get a massage. She was amazing, doing the deep tissue massages with essential oils. I went once every month or two, and it was always a healing experience.

Robin and Tad - 2009

Robin and I cuddled together when we were together. When I reached for her hand it was always there to grab mine back. She was solid and compassionate. I had never experienced this kind of love. It was a safe love. I wasn't afraid to express myself, or afraid of what she would say or think if I said the wrong thing. I wasn't worried about what drama was lurking around the corner, or what hell I was going to have to put up with because of someone's bad behavior.

•••••

A gentleman named David Kellough had written some country lyrics and wanted me to write the music and produce it out. The music evolved pretty well, although David had a particular vision of how he wanted tempos to go, and his rigidity made it difficult for me to complete the project in the way I would have done it on my own.

David later came to me after working with someone else in another studio, and apologized for his rigidity. He had lived and learned, but it all worked out well. The music was good enough.

•••••

Giorgio, ten days old

On Wednesday, June 17, 2009, my Rachel went into labor. She was at *JFK Hospital* in Indio. I was scheduled to work at *Mille Fleurs* that night. When I arrived at *Mille Fleurs*, I began to perform and I made it through about forty-five minutes before I looked at my friend Ron Zagami and said, "I can't just sit here! I have to go to the desert and experience the birth of my grandson!" Ronnie agreed, and offered to sit down and play piano for me for the rest of the evening. Ron was a good friend.

I took off, and made it to Indio just as the nurses were bringing Giorgio Douglas Barone in to Rachel's hospital room. She had given birth, and the nurses had cleaned the baby. After Rachel and Robert held him, they put him into my arms, and I had the same intense feeling that I had all those years ago when my own twins were born. He was a beautiful boy! I was ecstatic.

4 Generations
Taddy, Tad, Giorgio and Maynard
2009

Rachel and Robert were good young parents, and they brought Giorgio down for my big birthday celebration when he was about ten days old! He already had awareness in his eyes when he looked up at his grandfather Tad and grandmother Robin, and over the course of his first year, we spent whatever time we could with our little good boy.

•••••

In July of 2009 I finally made my way up to Westbank, British Columbia, Canada to see my Rachel. Robert's parents had taken the property where their summer campground had been located for twenty-five years, and hired a developer to turn it into condos. It was a beautiful resort on the lake in Westbank, across from Kelowna, called *Barona Beach*.

They owned a dock containing several boats. We would take the boats onto the glassy lake on the beautiful summer days. It was paradise. I enjoyed the experience immensely and Rachel was so happy to have her dad there finally after so many summers with none of her family up there throughout the long summer season!

•••••

In the late summer of 2009, Mitchell Cohen and Fred Sayeg approached Andrew Fraga, Jr. and me. They were producing a feature film entitled *The Encore Of Tony Duran,* loosely based on the life of our friend Gene Pietragallo. Gene was to star in the film. It was a story of hitting rock bottom, and finding redemption. I made a deal with them to compose and score all the music for the film.

During filming, there were a few live scenes where Gene performed. One was to be in a nursing home, where Gene sang *The Curtain Falls* live. The producers cast Elliot Gould, the great actor, in the film. It was amazing to work on the set with Elliot. He was the consummate professional, always prepared; always perfect in the emotional impact he brought to the scene.

I set up a mobile *Pro Tools* rig and recorded Gene singing as a lady pretended to play piano. I was playing piano for him on my keyboard off set into his headphones, and later I went to my studio and built the track, tuning his vocals and using my amazing Yamaha C3 grand piano on the track. It played to perfection in this emotional scene, where Gene cried as he sang.

Gene was supposed to lose forty pounds after the first scenes were shot, and then we would film the final scene after the weight was lost. Apparently, Gene went through a rough patch, and the producers wondered if he would be able to finish the film. I wrote a number of songs based on different scenarios… if they 'killed him off' I had a song that his son would sing in the finale… if they kept him alive and he pulled off the weight loss, we would do a full orchestral version of *Mack The*

Knife for him to sing during the final scene.

•••••

Betsy, Tad, Daniel, Kathy
Maynard, Suzanne and Judy
2010

Meanwhile, my father wanted to bring my sisters and I together for a family reunion in Kennett, Missouri in January of 2010. He and Sandra's sister Diane had worked hard to restore his house after Sandra's passing. Suzanne came out from North Carolina. Judy drove from Oklahoma. Kathy came from New Jersey, and Betsy came from Colorado. We had an amazing three or four days together.

My stepsister Leandra from my dad's second marriage was there. Although I had fond memories of Leann when she was a little girl, I had trouble getting along with her abrasive personality as an adult. But, I still gave her love and care. She mentioned her mother, Sandy, and told me that Sandy said 'hello'. I was cordial about Sandy, but I let Leann in on what had happened to me in Kansas City after High School, when Sandy basically emptied my father's accounts of all of my college money. I was never thrilled about Sandy or how she treated me, anyway. Leann was surprised, but very defensive of her mother, which I understood. I surmised that I would most likely not have much of a relationship with Leann after this reunion based upon our parents' history along with Leandra's own attitudes and emotions.

Suzy, Judy, Kathy, Maynard, Betsy, Tad, Leandra
01/15/2010

My sisters, dad and I brought out the playing cards and played endless games of Bridge. We helped Maynard set up his new *iMac* computer. We created a *Facebook* account for him, and he was delighted. Diane went out of her way to stock his refrigerator with supplies, and she dropped by several times a day to make sure we had what we needed. Somehow, we all realized that this would most likely be the last time we would all be together, and we were correct. It was a bittersweet day when we parted. I will always cherish that very last time all my sisters, my dad and myself were able to spend time together.

•••••

In March of 2010, I drove up to Los Angeles, and my son Kevin and I went with my son Taddy as he got a *Lasik* procedure on his eyes. Taddy had pretty bad eyesight before the procedure, and he was blown away to see so well afterwards! I was so happy for him.

Kevin, Robert, Taddy, Giorgio, Rachel & Maynard
Giorgio's Baptism 2010

In May of 2010, my dad once again flew out to San Diego to spend some time with me and to attend my grandson Giorgio's baptism in Palm Desert. It was amazing to me to witness my father holding his great grandson. Following that trip, Maynard wrote a special sonnet to Giorgio, which we framed and hung in Rachel and Robert's house.

In the first week of June in 2010, Frank and Uta Hamblen invited Robin and I up to Los Angeles to see a championship *NBA* game between the *Los Angeles Lakers* and the *Boston Celtics*. We arrived at the game with Frank and Uta, driving into the back of *Staples Center*, through security and into the garages by the training facility and locker rooms, as we had done with them in the past, but this time was
different.

Legions of press were waiting in the catacombs from all over the world, edging towards Frank in hopes of getting even a brief interview. As always, he was cordial to everyone, and Robin and I felt like stars walking with him to the locker room.

Tad with Snoop Dogg 2010

The game was amazing, and to see the *Lakers* win the championship that year was just wonderful. The energy level was equal to the Super Bowls I had attended, and Frank & Uta partied with us afterwards. We all ended up back at the *Harbor Room* in Playa Del Rey when it was all said and done.

Tad with Cloris Leachman 2010

In March of 2010, I performed at an event for Shari Kelley in Palm Springs at the home of Mr. and Mrs. Houston, owners of a local television station and philanthropists. I opened for Jennifer Hudson, the singer/actress of *American Idol* and *Dreamgirls* fame. We spoke briefly; she was distracted but nice. I was able to spend some quality time at the event with *Academy Award* winning actress Cloris Leachman. She was delightful and very animated. We took a photo together at the event.

•••••

In June of 2010, I went up to Kelowna, British Columbia, Canada again to visit Rachel and Robert, and Giorgio. Giorgio was just a year old and it was delightful playing with him throughout the week I was there. Rachel was just pregnant with her second child, and she was happy to have me there with her.

Kevin and Tad - Kelowna, BC Canada 2010

Through all of these summers she had spent in Kelowna, Rachel had never had any of her family members with her, and as a result, the summers felt way too long for her. This time, my sons Taddy and Kevin were there with us. We had a magical week playing on the lake. Robert's dad had bought the *Atlantis Waterpark* about an hour's drive from Kelowna, so we went to the waterpark and enjoyed that, too, while we were there. I was so glad to see the beauty of British Columbia and sad to leave!

•••••

When I returned to San Diego, a month or so later Rachel and Robert left Giorgio with me for a couple days while they attended a wedding in Orange County. This was the first time Rachel had been away from Giorgio, and she was nervous.

2010 Tad and Giorgio

While they were gone, Giorgio and I had the most wonderful time together! We laughed just about every moment, he slept right by my side at night, and I taught him how to walk! I set up pillows on all sides and he would walk a couple steps and then fall on to the pillows and laugh! It was just a great couple of days! When Rachel ran up the stairs to hug her boy when they got back from the wedding, Giorgio looked up at her like, "I'm cool here with Grandpa!"

Actually, Rachel was happy that Giorgio was always so comfortable with me. Robin and I were the only people he wanted to stay with, other than his parents. As he was learning to talk, he would call her "Ra", and then "Rara" and that name stuck! From then on, all my grandchildren called my Robin "Rara."

•••••

Tad and Robin - Thanksgiving 2009

On Thanksgiving Day, 2010, I invited the entire family to my house in Cardiff for a big Thanksgiving dinner. Robin was there with her mother Mary and Mary's husband Steve. Robin's kids Kris, Danielle and Beau were there. My daughters Rachel and Regina were there, along with their husbands and children.

At some point, I gathered everyone around the room and told them that a tradition in my family was for everyone to give thanks for something, and we would go around the room and let everyone say what they were thankful for. It was a bit awkward for some people, but we had a lot of laughs doing it, and I was the last one to give thanks.

Instead of giving thanks, I pulled a ring out of my pocket and asked Robin to marry me in front of everyone there! It was a beautiful moment, and of course, she said, "yes." So, began the longest engagement on record… but, I truly felt in my heart that from that moment on, we were married, and for so long already before that, I knew how lucky I was that I had found the woman who was entirely right for me. My heart would never stop beating for Robin. She and I had been through so much in our previous relationships. We were so glad to have calmness and compassion and no drama! Our birthdays were only two days apart, as well. We were compatible in almost every way.

•••••

Tad with Elliott Gould and Andrew Fraga, Jr. 2011

I continued to work on the film, *The Encore of Tony Duran*. As it turned out, Gene Pietragallo stepped up to the plate, lost the weight, and we filmed an amazing final scene of the film in the ballroom of the *Riviera Hotel* in Palm Springs, using the Ted Herman Orchestra.

Ted's orchestra pretended to play the track of *Mack The Knife* that I had pre-recorded with a full orchestra in my studio, and it worked flawlessly! I spent the entire day on stage as the pianist, working with Elliot Gould and Gene Pietragallo to make the scene work. They also brought in *Esteban*, a great guitarist, with his group. *Esteban* had a few minor *Billboard* hits, but he was mostly known for selling guitars on television. He was a gentleman and we became fast friends.

Tad with Esteban 2011

By the time we got the film into post-production, it was already the winter of 2010. I worked feverishly (literally!) on the score over the Christmas break, with a really bad case of pneumonia. Fred and Mitchell had entered the film into the prestigious *Palm Springs Film Festival*, and we needed a complete copy by January 1, 2011. Although I was extremely ill, I loved composing the music, and it was very well received when the film premiered at the festival.

Robin and I went out to Palm Springs with our friends Lawson Brown and his girlfriend Julie Mills to see the premiere of the film at the festival. We met my children, and my best friends Eddie and Kurt. The premiere was exciting, and during the film people actually cheered in all of the right spots.

The music brought the film to a higher level, and Elliot Gould complemented me personally on the score. Afterwards, they had a Q&A session with Elliot Gould, William Katt and Cody Kasch, the lead actors on the film along with Gene Pietragallo and the producers.

After the premiere, we all went over to *Tony's Pasta Mia* and I introduced my San Diego friends to my old friend Tony Prenesti. It was an enjoyable weekend, and when we returned home, I went back to work.

Following the release of *The Encore of Tony Duran* to film festivals, the film won many awards and was finally released on *Amazon Prime* in 2018. I went back to work on our production music, completing a *Western* collection and *Media* collection with Chad and Andy.

•••••

As we were all preparing to watch the Super Bowl on February 6, 2011, Rachel was ready to have her second child. It was a bizarre week for me, because the sixth of February was exactly sixteen years to the day that Stephanie had died. Rachel went into labor on the sixth, and on February 7, 2011, Stefani Elaine Barone was born.

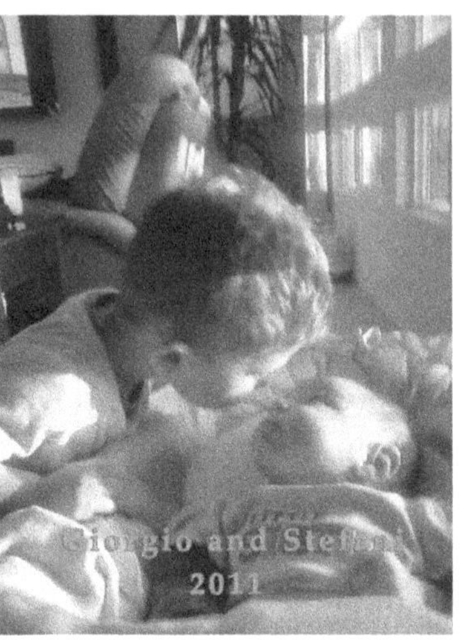

Giorgio and Stefani 2011

Stefani Barone

I went to the desert to stay at Rachel and Robert's house in La Quinta for a few days and to take care of Giorgio while she was in the hospital. Giorgio and I had a wonderful time together, and I was there to watch him see his baby sister for the very first time.

It was amazing for me to experience the circle of life. Almost sixteen years to the day after my Stephanie died, her namesake Stefani was born. And she was adorable. She would quickly steal my entire heart, and become another great love of my life.

God has amazing ways of soothing deep, old scars, if you are fortunate enough to live long enough to experience it.

•••••

Throughout this period, I was generally not thrilled with the places I was performing. *Tuscany* might have been fine if the management were more consistent. For a short period, if people got up to dance, a staff member would run up to them and make them stop, telling them that we didn't have a cabaret license and they weren't allowed to dance! It upset quite a few people, and it was ridiculous. I understand the laws of liquor licenses, but when an occasional couple dances, the 'dance police' generally don't come out and stop them!

Mille Fleurs Wednesdays were consistent enough, but around this time, a great tragedy occurred. The owner's son committed suicide out of the blue, and a pallor came over the establishment. Many of his friends stopped coming in, and it was a very sad period. Really, business on my Wednesday's never recovered from that period, even though I continued working Wednesday's at *Mille Fleurs* until 2019.

Bing Crosby's was a chain of restaurants, the closest located in Fashion Valley, a mall complex in San Diego. I found that I needed to go through their corporate offices to pick up a night or two. They were based in San Francisco, so I sent promo and waited about a month before I was given the go-ahead to work a couple of nights to supplement my schedule.

Bing Crosby's had a stage, which doesn't really work well in a large well-lit lounge in a mall setting. In a dive bar or concert setting, stages are excellent, but it almost felt as if I was removed from the audience. I was told to only do songs from *The Great American Songbook*, basically just standards reminiscent of the era of Bing Crosby. I knew hundreds of standards, so that wasn't a problem, but at some point, people would ask me for requests of current music that I knew, and I felt weird playing their requests.

Back in the 1990's my band would do 'theme' events for corporate parties. Sometimes, for instance, we would be an Arabian band for their "Arabian Nights" parties (until Desert Storm and 9/11 pretty much killed that idea!). We would play Arabian-sounding music for part of our first set to establish the theme, dressed in our Arabian costumes, and then we would break into whatever music we felt was appropriate for the crowd we had, and it always worked. I suggested this approach to the management of *Bing Crosby's*, but they were pretty resistant to the idea of me performing anything other than standards.

At some point, the chain started to move towards bankruptcy, and I heard that people weren't being paid for their services. One night, at the end of my night performing, the General Manager, who liked me and my performance, came up and told me that they had not received anyone's check from the corporate offices, so he went into the register and paid me with a huge stack of one-dollar bills! I saw the writing on the wall and moved on…

•••••

My sister Judy's ex-husband had a cousin who was a sweet lady. She was a shy Native American woman with long dark hair, brown eyes and a huge smile. She would come down to San Diego to visit on occasion, and she always brought these huge ball jars full of great weed for me.

The supply she brought to me would last for almost a year, and I was grateful, because I was still partaking in it. I really wasn't an alcohol drinker, so I went to marijuana for release, for inspiration to get through tedious editing, or just to relax after work. One time she brought me this huge jar full of 'butter', which was this *THC* compound used in baking. She didn't mention too much about it. She just put it in my refrigerator and told me to just use a little whenever I wanted to.

One Monday morning I was going to be off that night from performing and I had a huge task of editing some music on the computer during the day, which was going to take hours to do.

I never really got high during the day, but I thought, well, I would just see what this 'butter' is all about… so I went and made some toast, and spread some of it on the toast and ate it. I went into the studio to work. After about an hour, I thought, wow, this isn't doing anything at all… and then about ten minutes later it hit me like a ton of bricks!

I literally fell to the floor drooling and crawled into my bedroom. Eight hours later it was already getting dark outside. Robin had been trying to call and text me and I wasn't responding, which was unusual. She drove by my house and it was entirely dark but my car was in front. Right about this time, I was coherent enough to crawl back to the studio to get my phone, and I made it back to bed with the phone but I was unable to dial.

About fifteen minutes later, Robin (who had a key) helped herself in and found me in my bed. I kept saying over and over again, "I'm sorry, I messed up; I had no idea about this stuff!" After a while, I began to come out of it, but literally for days afterwards, I felt like a zombie. I honestly didn't know why I was still partaking of any of that stuff since Tracy and I had broken up. I rarely did it during the sixteen years I was with Stephanie. It was like a bad habit at this point.

Never in my life had I ever been out of control until this day although it was unintentional. I learned a tough, valuable lesson about how important it is for us to take care of ourselves. You only have one body and mind in this life. You'd better take care of it.

•••••

Anthony Robbins, the great motivational speaker, says that if you really want to get rid of a habit, you need to begin to start to associate more pain than pleasure with it. This experience was a really good motivator for that!

I had just been through a huge bout with pneumonia, and I was regularly getting bronchitis, which was affecting my singing voice. I never, ever got stoned while performing or when I was working outside of the studio in any capacity. The couple times I had done that when I was much younger, I… forgot the words… got cotton-mouth… got really paranoid because everyone was staring at me… and couldn't concentrate on the perfection of the performance I had worked so hard to attain.

Robin was cool about the fact that I smoked a little pot. She had never 'partaken' with me, but she allowed me to do whatever I wanted without giving me any grief about it. She did say once or twice that doing it made people 'stupid', and she was right. Also, although it produced a great feeling during the first few minutes, as it dragged on, I became tired and a bit disoriented. Why would anyone want to do that every day?

I also read somewhere that, every seven years, the cells in your body completely regenerate. So, I thought that if I got through seven years without any of that in my system, my body would completely heal from it. Even when I cleaned my smoking pipes, the heavy resin was almost impossible to remove. That was the same stuff that was settling into my lungs.

So, I committed to stop smoking or ingesting any drug ever again (other than an occasional drink of alcohol here and there in great moderation), and on April 8, 2011, I stopped and never looked back. Seven years later, I was still as committed as I became that day, and it was a great feeling to know that my body had healed. It was obvious to me, as I noticed after about a year that the bronchitis went almost completely away. My breathing and singing were stronger than ever. And… we laughed about the 'butter' experience whenever I told the story, but it was part of what 'cured' me from all of that!

If you wake up each morning with purpose, you will accomplish great things. Don't slow yourself down with anything that affects your physical or mental clarity.

I also read somewhere that the reason people begin to turn to alcohol or drugs is usually because they are trying to escape a reality in which they are not happy. That was true of me years ago when I started all of that, but I had grown from all of that. What reason was I left with, now? Release, perhaps… Boredom? Never! Unhappiness? Absolutely not!

I started to adapt my thinking to something I had never thought of when I was younger… getting 'straight'! Hey man, let's get straight! The world around us is full of amazing things to experience and appreciate without the need to enhance it with temporary pleasures that make you sick and tired later. Although I grew up in a drug culture, which was normalized by mass consumption by youths in my generation, I did not need to perpetuate that reality any longer within my own life experience.

My *Yamaha* gig pretty much wrapped-up by the end of 2010. The projects from *Yamaha* had been coming fewer and farther-between for a while. At this point, they were farming out most of the work to European and Japanese developers. Still, I was working hard on the *Mainstream Source* catalog of music, and recording new tracks like mad. I did an electronica album under the surname *Maynard Of Goth.* I increased the *Mainstream Source* production music catalog to almost seven thousand tracks. I did a "Classic Blues" collection of original blues music with Chad Quist and Andrew Fraga, Jr. We completed a "Motivational" collection with Scott Francisco. We followed that up with a cool "Modern Classic Soul" collection, featuring great horns by Steve Madaio and Steve Alaniz. I released one cut as a single from this project, *Bad Ass Funk,* and it was in Grammy consideration during that year. My renaissance of content creation continued.

CHAPTER SIXTY-FIVE
Evolving into a New Life with Robin

Robin and I had been talking about finally moving in together. After four years at the Cambridge house, on April 9, 2011, I moved in to Robin's house. This was also significant, because April 9 was Stephanie's birthday. I believe in my heart that Stephanie would have whole-heartedly approved of Robin, knowing that she could not be here herself to influence her children and grandchildren. Robin was a friend and confidant to my children, and she was the perfect grandmother to my grandkids. I truly believed that she was 'sent by the Angels' to my family.

Whenever the anniversary of Stephanie's tragic death happened, or when her birthday came, I would always say a silent prayer of thanks. Time had lessened the jagged edges of grief and guilt, and I was working to replace those heavy weights on my soul with gratitude and love.

I was going to move in to Robin's home on April 1, but we weren't done painting her house and preparing it for my furniture to be integrated with hers. It was a big move really for both of us, because Robin parted with much of her belongings in order to fit my furniture into her house. Of course, I also let go of a lot of stuff too.

We decided to build a building above her rental house, and I made a deal with Robin's sister Jodi's husband, Kenny, a licensed contractor. I offered to produce an entire CD for Jodi and Kenny's son Jordan, an aspiring young songwriter and rock musician, in exchange for Kenny building the building for my studio.

I had a blast with Jordan and his high school buddies producing the music for his band *Creative Conspiracy*, and we released it just in time for the move. Unfortunately, the City of Encinitas made us tear my studio building down to a ten-by-twelve-foot structure, and with my baby grand piano in the room, it turned into a one-man operation.

I sold off a lot of my equipment, but I was still able to produce my music, so it all worked out. Eventually, I also put together a mobile *Pro Tools* rig, so I could go off-site and record guitars, or horns, vocals or whatever I needed for a project. I learned to adapt, and it was great to live with Robin. The four years on Cambridge had allowed me to heal properly and to become whole again, and we were both ready to share a life together.

It's great to have someone behind you all the way. It's even better to know someone is beside you all the way.

Of course, Robin still had two children at home, and we also had a 'revolving kid bedroom' that was frequented at all times by either Sammi, Kris or Taddy… so I went from living alone to being back into a family situation. Given my history, it didn't take much for me to slip right in to the new routine. I finally had a companion who was independent, strong and hardworking; a woman who supported me with love and kindness and encouraged healthy behavior. We were interdependent but not codependent. We lived a life with no drama between us. We both craved serenity.

In early 2011, we had planned to fly my dad back out to San Diego to stay another week with me and to meet my new little granddaughter. Dad was pleased that they had given Stefani my mother Elaine's name as a middle name (Elaine was also Robert's mother's name, so they made both families happy!) Dad had come out twice already for a week and stayed in my guest bedroom on Cambridge, and it was great. When he had been able to get to San Diego in the past couple of years since Sandra died, I was able to cook him breakfast and dinner, and he watched me produce my music. We talked for hours and hours at a time and I cherished that time with Maynard. But, this time, he was too frail

Maynard and Tad
2011

to make the trip. I made plans to go to Kennett in May, and when I flew back, I stayed with him for a week.

In Kennett, I noticed that my father's health was deteriorating. I gave him breathing treatments and checked his oxygen levels daily. He was becoming incontinent. I called Robin and she came to the rescue. She got on the phone and worked it out to get his nurses to order medical supplies including a comfortable chair, which would automatically rise up to help him get up when he was ready to leave the chair.

He loved to read but he couldn't see the small type any longer and it was becoming increasingly harder for him to hold a book, so we got him a *Kindle* reader and finally an *iPad*. Even still, he had too much difficulty working the devices. We would watch television or talk, but I knew he was getting weaker. I vowed to come back in October after the summer season.

•••••

Brian and Nancy O'Donnell
2015

In May of 2011, I was performing at *Mille Fleurs* one Wednesday night, and Brian and Nancy O'Donnell approached me. Brian was the attorney for the restaurant *Manhattan Of La Jolla*, and they had bought an ownership stake into the restaurant. I had eaten at *Manhattan* several times over the years; in fact, Robin and I had taken my father to eat there during his previous trip to San Diego.

Brian and Nancy were remodeling the restaurant, which had been in that location in the *Empress Hotel* in La Jolla for over thirty years. Brian wanted to put a piano bar into the lounge, and he had seen me when I was performing at *Tracton's.*

One Monday, Robin and I went down to have dinner with them at *Manhattan* and I told him that I would be delighted to do the gig. I told him that I had a strategy that I always use when I come into a lounge. At *Tracton's* when I started performing, there were maybe three or four people still at the bar around ten at night after the dinner rush. By the time I left *Tracton's*, we had increased the business by $1.5 million per year and the bar was packed most of the time. I told Brian that if he would just let me 'do my thing' and implement my strategy, that I would triple his business. I asked for a good salary and Brian accepted it. Shortly after my birthday in 2011, I began to perform at *Manhattan* and I found my new performance 'home' in La Jolla.

CHAPTER SIXTY-SIX
Losing My Father

In October of 2011, I went back to Kennett, Missouri to stay with my dad for another week. He was failing physically. When he became incontinent, I would go into the shower and clean him. Although at the time I thought it was a disgusting job to do, I was so grateful to do it; in retrospect, I consider it one of the holy things I was able to do in my life, to take care of my father.

I wished he lived closer so I could have been with him more, but during that week we held each other and loved each other deeply. Although he had never met my granddaughter Stefani, we 'FaceTimed' with Rachel, in order for him to see her on the *iPad*. One day while I was there, my father slowly walked into his home office and opened a drawer. Inside the drawer were a few keepsakes, photos and letters to him from Sandra. It was important to him to show them to me. Shuffling through each item gingerly with his shaking fingers, Maynard cried quietly and deeply, knowing that the life he had made was ending.

No matter how long I live, I believe that when it is done it will feel like it was done too soon. This is what I saw in my father's eyes.

The *Saint Louis Cardinals* were my dad's baseball team. They had been my Grandma Sisler's baseball team. While I was in Kennett in October of 2011, they won the World Series and my dad was ecstatic! We shared in a few wonderful private moments that week. He had a swinging bench outside his front door that we sat on, looking out at the cotton fields once again turning brown and bare, anticipating the upcoming winter months. We watched the sun set as I held his frail, big trembling hand.

My father looked at me, eyes twinkling, and said, "I've gotten to the point in my life where any damn fool thing I say, they think it's wisdom!" Maynard never lost his sense of humor.

On the morning that I left him to go home, I held his head in my hands and kissed his forehead. Maynard's tired old eyes looked into mine, and I think we both realized this was the last time we would see each other. I loved him so very much, and my heart hurt deeply as I drove away from his house. I hated to leave him.

Even still, after I got home, we spoke every day on the phone. As Maynard sat on his rocking bench outside his home in Kennett overlooking the fields and radio tower adjacent to his property, he would share with me whatever the temperature and wind speed was at any given moment, or the condition of the cotton fields around his home. He found some solace in that, in the rhythm of the planet, as his life ebbed. Maynard feared he had outlived his usefulness, but I never saw it that way. His mind and his intellect were intact, and I gleaned so much knowledge and wisdom from him in his final days.

He had been given a 'loaner' companion dog since his beloved dog *Twocents* had passed just a year before. He missed his dog terribly, but dutifully fed and loved the new dog. Maynard was no longer able to walk the dog around his property. Diane would be at his house religiously, two or three times a day, watching over him and helping him as he declined. My heart broke for my dad, yet he retained his optimism throughout his final days.

•••••

In March of 2012, my dad could no longer swallow food. He went in to the hospital for a procedure to put in a feeding tube. When he woke up from the procedure, he asked for a cup of coffee, and they told him he wasn't allowed to have any coffee.

Coffee had been our mutual addiction. I had been drinking coffee with my dad since he made me my 'little boy's coffee' when I was so small. He probably thought, "Screw it, if I can't have my coffee, I'm checking out."

My sister Suzanne and her daughter Lori drove out from North Carolina to be with him. On the afternoon following his surgery, Suzanne was sitting on the chair visiting with Maynard, and the nurse came in to get him to do some physical therapy. In his classic form, he flipped the nurse off with his middle finger and smiled at my sister.

Suzy called me and told me that she thought he might be improving. I wanted to fly out immediately, but she thought that maybe I should wait until he got out of the hospital when he needed help at home. I wouldn't have made it there on time to see him anyway.

On the morning of March 7, 2012, Suzanne was sitting next to our father, quietly reading, when he took his last breath. When she called me, I was just devastated.

My entire family arranged to fly out to Kennett for the funeral. My daughter Regina brought her husband Todd.

You can spend half of your life hating a parent, or working to overcome whatever they did to harm you, but if you're lucky, you can repair that relationship to the point that when they leave the planet, you will grieve like you just lost your best friend ever.

Rachel and Robert brought Giorgio and Stefani. My sons Kevin and Taddy came along with Robin and me.

All of my sisters came for the funeral. Suzanne brought her daughter Wendy, and her grandchild Jim and his fiancée. Betsy brought her husband Mark. Judy and Kathy were there. It was a bittersweet couple of days as we went through the funeral, burial and reception. My dad had full military honors at his burial, and they handed the flag to my oldest sister Suzanne as we looked on. A bugler played *Taps.* We all cried hard.

Maynard Sisler circa 1950

It was bizarre to witness the dichotomy between my sister's and my own memories of my father's younger years, against the memories of all of the people in Kennett who adored him in his later years. Of course, we knew and experienced his struggle with alcoholism and his Jekyll & Hyde personality while drinking… knowing how his addiction had destroyed his original family, and yet seeing the faces of these people who came to memorialize him, we realized that Maynard had become almost a god to many of them.

In the last thirty-five years of Maynard's life, he had been sober, living a Christian example and healing all of these people. They really thought of him as a saint, and although we knew better, we were grateful for the outpouring of emotion and love. He had redeemed himself in the only way he could.

You can't change the past. You can absolutely change the present, and in doing so, hope for a better future with those you may have transgressed. Redemption comes gradually, in a series of small acts of goodness.

I had lived in Kennett for a couple years in high school, so I had many friends there, and the people of the town generally accepted me. Dad had asked me to write a eulogy and to describe him, warts and all, and so I lovingly and carefully revealed his true-life story to all of these people with respect and care not to tarnish his image. I cried several times while delivering it, and when I was finished, there was not a dry eye in the mortuary. It was a healing experience, I believe, for all of us. I ended, of course, with our signature line to each other from all those years ago… "Say a prayer for me…I always do."

•••••

On the following day after the services, my sisters and I were called in to dad's attorney's office. Wendell Crow, the great entertainer Sheryl Crow's father was dad's attorney. They had advised my father to leave us nothing in his will so that none of us could go after what he had, which was a little weird to all of us. He did, however, include a letter saying that he wanted to 'gift' us all ten thousand dollars each.

Sandra's family would keep the house, sell it, and divide the money between them. It was fine with my sisters and me; at the same time, it left us all with a sad feeling about my father and his trust issues. He just handled it in a way that made us all feel like he thought we'd be sleazy and try to go after his estate.

Also, he left an equal ten thousand dollars to our stepsister Leandra, who had been in our lives for a total of about three years way back in the 1970's, had massive issues with my father and Sandra, and, in my humble opinion, only seemed to come back around when she wanted something.

Suzanne was confused because my dad had told her several times that he was going to leave her his house in his will. Sandra's sister Diane had been a great caretaker to my dad, and she had never accepted a dime during the three years she watched completely over him. Dad left the house to Diane, and after deducting the money he allotted to us; she divided the assets from the sale amongst all of her family. Sandra had owned half the house, after all, and I believed that my dad was as fair to us all as he knew how to be.

Dad left me his car, which was a ten-year-old *Mercedes ML500* SUV. I was grateful for the car and for the money, and mostly I just missed my dad. I drove the car from Missouri back to California and took it into a mechanic, who told me I should sell it immediately because the hoses were all decomposing from the years it sat outside in the frigid winters and hot summers without being driven. So, I sold it pretty soon after I got home.

As time goes by, I notice that I have so many mannerisms that my dad had. Little things, really, like vocal inflections or physical movements, are what I notice the most. The knowledge he passed on to me, nuances of thought and memories of the deep conversations we had… all of these things stay with me in my everyday life. His puns, and his bad jokes too are subtleties I have adopted and with which I can chide my own progeny.

If you can see the good qualities of your parents in yourself, then you'll know that in a sense they accomplished their job as parents.

I knew that my sisters were struggling in their own ways to overcome their childhoods, just as I had. I reached out to my sister Kathy. I told her that when I stopped thinking of Maynard as the father who had given me such a shitty childhood, and started thinking of him as a soul who had come onto this planet and had his own set of issues and dealt with them in the way he knew how, making mistakes as we all do, it helped me to release the pain. Taking the label of 'father' out of the equation helps you to humanize the person and the problem. It's a good exercise for anyone. I think it helped her to put it all into perspective. I know she worked hard to heal, as we all did.

And, I was lucky to have become best friends with him again before he died.

•••••

Home again, I was back into work mode, building the collection more and working on producing more of our *Mainstream Source Pro Karaoke* brand of Karaoke music.

My sister Judy drove out to spend a couple weeks with me in early June of 2012, and on June 8 we drove to Temecula to witness my oldest daughter Regina finally get her High School Diploma. I cried remembering how Regina had been ripped from us in her senior year of High School, and it meant so much to Regina to finally go back, twenty years later, and complete the task. I was so proud of her, and grateful that Judy took the trip with Robin and me to see Regina graduate. My sister and I had closeness and a calmness that I loved, as long as we were together. Judy was the one family member who would go way out of her way to participate in your life, whenever she could.

Judy, Regina, Tad, Whitney Aidan and Makayla Regina's Graduation 2012

•••••

In September of 2012, I was called back to Kennett, Missouri to speak at an event. My dad had been posthumously nominated and selected to be in the *Hall of Honor* for Dunklin County, Missouri, and they asked me to fly back and speak on his behalf. I was honored to do it.

When I flew into Memphis, I realized that, for the first time in my life, I would probably have no reason to fly into Memphis anymore. My grandparents and cousins had lived there since my birth, until my dad moved to Kennett, and Memphis was always the closest airport to fly into when visiting him.

Memphis held deep memories for me, some very dark. My lovely cousins Dylan and Dixie had died in a house fire there when I was just five. Kimberley had been murdered there when I was thirty-three. Two of my grandparents were buried there. My Uncle Jack had built skyscrapers that still dotted the skyline of Memphis when I flew in on that muggy day.

I decided to drive to the house at 267 Rose Road that I lived in when I was four and five years old. I had not seen the house in fifty years. When I pulled up to the house, for a moment I didn't recognize it. It looked smaller than I remembered. But then, as I saw the circular driveway and the detached garage, memories flooded back. The tree that my parents had planted in my name was now over a hundred feet tall. A young family was playing in the yard. I only stayed for a few minutes, parked across the street, and respectfully drove away without bothering anyone. My heart became heavy.

Next, I drove to the apartment on Tutwiler and McLean that my grandparents had lived in for so many years. I cried, remembering the love that my grandmother had given me. Walking around the back, I smelled the same smells I remembered from my childhood. The drugstore across the street was long gone. I said a prayer for my grandparents, and moved on.

In Kennett, the ceremony was also emotional. Several people spoke on my dad's behalf, before I made my speech. They created a display case with some of his medals from the war, his *Freedom's Foundation* awards, and other memorabilia. For a moment, I thought, "This is what we are all reduced to in time... a few memories of scattered accomplishments. But, we are all so much more than that."

Someone once told me that, even after we die, we remain alive as long as someone still alive remembers us. There's truth to that. I've looked at photos of my Grandfather Ted, who I never met, so many times, and tried hard to picture what kind of person he was. I imagined a thick accent, a kind smile or wink, but that was all it was... imagination. But, to my mother, he was everything. He was absolutely a love of her life that had died too soon.

This day, though, was all about my dad, and it was wonderful again to see the outpouring of emotion and love for him. Diane was great; she was very accommodating to me on the trip. I stayed at Maynard's house for the last time, in my father's bed, and although it was quiet, I felt his presence. While I was there, I went to church with Diane and Kenny, and visited the gravesite of my dad, Sandra and Kimberley.

The very same memory can haunt you or fill you with joy – or both - at any given moment.

Sandra's sister Diane was so very kind to me. She tried to accommodate me in any way she could, and she remained in touch with me after this event for many years. I had a greater connection to Kennett, Missouri than my sisters did, having lived there and experienced life with the people who lived there. I was grateful for Diane's love and kindness, and I believe that she did the best she could to honor my dad's wishes. I also believe that my dad wished for her to have whatever she wanted, based upon his love for Sandra, his closeness with Diane and the way she cared for him in his final days. She had to weigh her family against ours and do what she felt was right. You can't please all the people all the time. You just do the best you can.

CHAPTER SIXTY-SEVEN
Work is Fulfilling - Family is Life

Aidan and Makayla Phillips 2013

Returning again to San Diego, I plunged myself back into production. Around this time, we began to see my granddaughter Makayla's musical talent blossom. Regina had enrolled her into drama classes, the *Hollywood Launch* program and private music lessons as she homeschooled her youngest two children.

Little Aidan was a darling little budding young actor, with his glasses and bowtie, getting some commercial roles and a few acting roles as well. In fact, in 2015 Aidan was featured in an online commercial for *Tropicana* orange juice and he got almost a million views!

Makayla, though, was something special although she was very raw at first, a little pitchy and trying a little too hard to hit ALL the notes. It was amazing watching her mature into a great performer as time went on. She entered the *Temecula Idol* competition, and worked her way from placing in the top five to winning two years in a row. Robin and I went to all of the performances!

•••••

Ermanno and Giorgio - 2009

Robert's dad, Ermanno Barone, had briefly bought a western town movie set in Tyndall, Manitoba, outside of Winnipeg in Canada. He hired a crew to shoot a kid's mystery film in the town, which they originally entitled *Cowboy Dreams*. When the film crew flaked out on Ermanno, he inherited the footage and gave it to me to sort out. I bought *Avid Media Composer* software and began to learn video editing on my own. I was a pro at music and audio, but this was a whole new world to me.

Unfortunately, shortly after I acquired the film, Ermanno became gravely ill and died of Pancreatic cancer in early 2013. The film was caught up in probate, and didn't resurface until 2017 when Robert and I bought the rights from the writer and I began to work to release it to the film festival circuit in 2018 as *The Ghosts of Brewer Town*.

Ermanno's death was tough on Robert. He was an only child and his parents had divorced when he was young. His father was an Italian Canadian, with mannerisms from the old country. He was hard on Robert much of the time, and Robert had quit teaching and taken over his parents' businesses, so they had worked hand-in-hand for the last few years. Robert inherited the water park, but his father had been generous and liberal with his money, and left his estate in a shambles. Fortunately, Robert's mother was the exact opposite and she conservatively invested. After a few years, Robert worked through the problems of the estate, but Ermanno's passing was hard on him.

Through this period, I produced an album entitled *Waiting in the Wings* with the Tad Sisler Orchestra, gleaning some original tracks I had produced for earlier projects with instrumentalists from the *San Diego Symphony*, other tracks using great studio musicians and a handful of new songs. It was exciting to put out an album with strings and horns throughout, using all of my own arrangements.

•••••

Stefani's Baptism - May 2, 2013

On May 2, 2013, my darling granddaughter Stefani was baptized at Sacred Heart Church in Palm Desert, California. I drove up early on that Sunday morning with Danielle and Beau. Robin couldn't attend because she was working that weekend in San Diego.

We met Regina and Todd with their kids Whitney, Makayla and Aidan. Robert's mom Elaine and her husband Ray were there, along with some other friends and family. My sister Judy drove with her friend Curtis Spottedcorn, all the way from Oklahoma, just to attend the baptism.

Judy arrived late night on May 1, and on May 2 she proudly sat next to me as our little Stefani was baptized. When they called for the grandparents to come up to the front, Judy grabbed my hand and went up with me to 'stand up' for Stefani. At first, I hesitated, because Judy was not a grandparent. But, then, I remembered her mentioning that in Native American culture, every family member is a brother, sister, father, mother, aunt, uncle or grandparent. I grabbed her hand right back, and we proudly marched up to the altar. It was a very holy moment. As I looked over into my sister's eyes they were filled with love and happiness. Little Stefani cried for a moment when they poured water over her head, but then she composed herself and smiled up at her grandfather and her great aunt. Stefani was my little sweetheart.

Judy 2013

After the baptism, we went to Rachel and Robert's house for a little reception, and I sat again with Judy for a while that day. Judy and Curtis had driven a truck from Oklahoma. They were going to go to get items of Judy's out of a storage facility in Northern California following the baptism. When we left, I guided their truck to the freeway as they followed my SUV. When we got to the freeway, we waved and blew kisses to each other and they drove on to their destination as I drove back to San Diego. Little did I know, that wave would be the last time I would ever see my sister Judy. Had I known, I would have held onto her like mad and never let go.

•••••

Beau and Danielle 2012 High School Graduation

In late June of 2013, Robin wanted to go back to a family reunion in Ohio. We took Beau and Danielle back to see her father, Tony, his wife Maureen, and her uncles and aunts. Tony's brothers and sisters were all approaching their nineties, and it was important to Robin to spend some time with her dad, aunts and uncles while she could.

We flew into Cleveland and spent the first night at Robin's stepsister Donna's house. Donna was very accommodating to us. When I woke up the next morning, I took off to walk for an hour through their neighborhood, in the suburbs of Cleveland. It was a gorgeous summer day, and I found a trail to walk, which made its way to a high school sports field and then through a medical center lot, back to the trail and back to Donna's house.

As I walked, I put my *Bluetooth* into my ear and called my sister Judy. Judy, at this point, was preparing to go to the *Sun Dance* in Wyoming, that great Native American festival that I had attended with her when I was a teenager. Judy and I talked on the phone for almost an hour, about everything.

We talked about the changes that had happened in our lives since our father died. I told her about the projects I was involved in, and what I was going to do while in Ohio. Judy was in so many ways my best friend. She had always been a calm voice in my life, always listening and understanding, and sharing her great wisdom. In the past few years, we had finally come together, sometimes for months at a time, and spent quality time loving and learning from each other. Even though she was ten years older than me, she always treated me like an equal, and I was so grateful for her, in so many ways.

•••••

The Ohio trip was eventful. Donna's husband David took me to the *Pro Football Hall of Fame* in Canton, Ohio. I had always wanted to do that, and it was as cool as I had dreamed it would be. David was a huge *Cleveland Indians* baseball fan, and another dream I had was to go to as many baseball stadiums to see Major League games around the country as possible. I offered to take David to a game, and he gleefully agreed.

On the way to the stadium, David told me that many times he had gone to this stadium in Cleveland as a kid with his father to see the games. They always sat in the nosebleed sections of the field. I knew David was struggling for money, and he and Donna had been so hospitable to Robin and me.

When we got to the ticket booth, I bought the two best available tickets left on field level. He had never sat so close to the team before! There was only one downside; on the field that day we sat in the sun and it was an extremely hot and humid day. I was used to the heat from my years performing at poolside in the desert, but clearly David was not. As the game progressed, I was amazed to see a mixture of joy and agony on his face! He drank a lot of fluids and made it through the game, and it was a great experience for both of us ultimately.

When we made it to Robin's father's house, his wife Maureen mentioned to me that, by coincidence, *Sisler Park* was a quarter mile down the highway near Massillon where my father was born. Robin and I drove down to the park. A huge plaque stood at the entrance to the park honoring my great uncle George Sisler. Truly, we all live in a small world!

On the next day Robin's uncle hosted their big family reunion. Robin's uncle Abe owned a huge farm with an enormous farmhouse out in the country outside of Akron. It was a perfect location for a large event. It was lovely, but hot and humid, and we fought off mosquitos all day. In the evening, fireflies lit up the thick air around the farmhouse, and we continued our warm conversations with interesting people.

Robin's stepmother Maureen, Beau, Danielle, Robin's uncle Mike, Robin and her father Tony 2013

Robin's family embraced me as one of their own, and we immensely enjoyed our time with them that day. Beau and Danielle reconnected with their cousins, aunts, uncles and grandparents, and we all played cards in-between all of the cooking and cleaning. A large Italian family eats! Following a wonderful trip, we returned to San Diego, and I went back to work.

CHAPTER SIXTY-EIGHT
My Sister Dies Suddenly

I reached out to my sister Judy to see how the *Sun Dance* was, and she never responded. After a few days, I began to worry about her. On July 6, she called me from a hospital in Oklahoma. She was very ill, and they couldn't figure out what was wrong with her. They had given her an antibiotic but it wasn't working. Judy called me from the ICU at *Yukon Hospital* on July 7, and told me that while she was in Wyoming a tick had bitten her; they were beginning to think that she contracted *Rocky Mountain Spotted Fever*. Only one antibiotic works for that illness, and they had given her the wrong one. Her organs quickly began to fail, and on the morning of July 8, 2013, my lovely sister Judy died suddenly.

I was devastated. My grandchildren were visiting me on that day, and it took everything out of me not to just sob in front of them. I had scheduled a recording session for that day for a commercial project I was doing with Andy and Michael Kennedy; Andy drove down immediately and handled the vocal session for me.

I was beside myself with grief. When you lose a parent, it's a life-changing experience and it's never good, but there is almost a circle of life feeling of succession to it. Losing a sibling is entirely different. I grew up as one of the 'fingers on a hand'. There were five of us, always, and no matter what terrible stuff happened around us, we always had each other. My sisters were always my saving grace, and Judy was so deeply and dearly important to me. Losing a sibling reminds you of your own mortality in ways you never thought of before.

As memories of Judy flooded through me, I became so grateful for the time we had spent together in later life.

Judy was not yet even sixty-five years old, and she was probably the healthiest of all of my sisters, yet she left the planet first. Her Native American family had a celebration of life for her in Oklahoma, and we planned another one for those of us, who couldn't attend, to happen in August of 2013.

Every moment is important. It may not seem that way while you're experiencing the moment, but later you will be shocked at the importance of moments that seemed trivial at the time.

•••••

On the night that Judy died, I got a strange call from one of my sister Kathy's friends, a clairvoyant. I remembered her from when I was younger. We had met a couple of times, years ago. When she called me on that night of my sister Judy's death, she told me, "I spoke to your sister today." I mentioned that I had also talked to Kathy, and she said, "No, I spoke to Judy."

I asked her if she knew Judy had died, and she said, "Yes, she contacted me and wanted me to tell you that she was okay, that she was spiraling overhead with the souls of the people she loved on the other side, and that she was okay. She told me to tell you that she saw her body and realized that she would not be able to live a healthy life based upon the illness, so she went to the other side, but she wants you to know that she loves you and that she will be with you always... all you need to do is just to call her by name and she will be there with you." I was dumbfounded. My sister Betsy had just arrived from Colorado, and I said, "Would you mind repeating this to my other sister?" ... just so Betsy would know I wasn't crazy!

It's funny in life... we all ask for a 'sign', but when we get one, we think, "Oh, that's ridiculous! I don't believe it!" I decided to take this one at face value and accept it as truth. It wasn't going to hurt me either way, and it was comforting to believe that Judy was, and is, there with me when I need her.

Still, I will always miss her soft voice, her gentle touch and her laughter. Judy was amazing; she was superbly intelligent. She had secured a *Master's Degree* in nursing, and she was a walking medical textbook. She was a skilled artisan, crafting jewelry and beaded purses that would stand up to any of the best ever made throughout history. She was a mother and grandmother. Judy had been awaiting the birth of her first granddaughter, Aria. She had already bought a card to give to her son Brian and daughter-in-law Jenna celebrating her birth. Aria was born about two weeks after Judy died. Again, the circle of life reminded us that there is promise in every new day.

Judy had been an outstanding mother to her children. Although her Native American son Abraham would spend years finding himself, he had love in his heart and a strong sense of family. All three of her children had achieved their own *Master's Degrees*. Her son Brian had gotten his *Masters* at the age of twenty-one, and shortly thereafter began an outstanding career, beginning with an excellent job at *Microsoft*. Judy and her daughter Jenny were inseparable. They would sit quietly and giggle together, more comfortable with each other than anyone else in the world. Judy had moved to Pittsburgh at some point to see Jenny through her Master's program after Jenny graduated from *Hampshire*. While she was alive, Judy immersed herself fully into family and friends, and I deeply mourned her passing.

•••••

My Aunt Candace had become a minister, and she offered to officiate for Judy's memorial service. We secured a lovely area at a park in Cardiff by my house. My sister Kathy's boyfriend from high school, Andy Robinson, came and played the dulcimer and led a drum circle in her honor. My uncle Ted was with us, along with Judy's children and my children, Robin and her children, Betsy and her family and my sister Suzy with her daughter Lori. It was a beautiful ceremony and we laughed and cried a lot as we eulogized her. Judy was a saint on Earth in so many ways, and we knew she would watch over us.

On the morning of the ceremony, my sisters Suzanne and Betsy went down before dawn to the park to secure the area. I walked down to relieve them shortly after sunrise, and on the way, a thousand birds were singing… 'coo' and 'cheep' sounded like Ju-dy to me… it felt like the universe was singing her name.

On the next day, we had an event at the beach in Judy's honor. Almost a hundred people attended, including most of our family and so many close friends. I swam in the ocean with my nephew, Judy's son Abraham. It was a beautiful summer day. Because Judy had been with me so much in the last few years, most of my friends knew her well and loved her.

Abraham Pedro and Tad - 2013

As I bonded with Abraham really for the first time in his life, I wondered how he had dealt with the experience of being an interracial child. Most mothers expect that both races will embrace their interracial children, but often both races reject them, unfortunately. In Abraham's case, his Native American relatives embraced him, and I could tell that his affinity was to the Native American family that accepted him unconditionally. Our part of his family had not completely accepted him, mostly because of geographical distance, but also because he had anger issues as a child, and his relationship with Judy's husband George was strained. It was tragic to me. Abraham was a beautiful man, and I loved him dearly. He was an extension of my beloved sister. He was carrying a lot of baggage in his soul, though. Abraham had two beautiful sons back in Oklahoma, Winter Hawk and Oh Hey Mo, and he did his best to stay in their lives despite his estrangement from their mother. Judy loved those boys and she had been with them whenever she could be, as long as she was alive.

As a child, you cannot choose whether or not to be a victim. You have no power over that. As an adult survivor, you must choose to no longer have a victim's mentality.

The next morning, Judy's children, my sisters and I walked down to the beach and spread some of Judy's ashes into the Pacific Ocean. I've walked past that point countless times since, and each time I've said a prayer for Judy, as I do when I walk over the railroad tracks in the spot she fell and broke her leg. When I walk past that spot where we gave a small amount of Judy to the vast ocean, I know that there are still some molecules of her essence there, but what I really know is that she lives on in me. The heavy weight of grief once again enveloped my soul.

Abraham Pedro

When we lose someone, it is a life-changing experience. As you go through all the stages of grief, working your way towards acceptance, you still must go on. My mother always said, "Life is meant for the living."

CHAPTER SIXTY-NINE
New Projects and Opportunities

If you're still here, you must have a purpose. It is right and proper to remember and grieve, but at some point, you must stand up, brush yourself off, move on and discover that purpose.

I had been beating my head against the wall building this enormous catalog of music for film and television applications. In the process of producing thousands of songs and getting them in to every marketplace over a period of several years, I made my climb to the middle.

But, the industry changed in ten years, and streaming of music was taking over CD sales and downloads. At this point in time, very few artists were making any money off of streaming recordings; the big winners were the companies that stream the music. It's a tragedy for composers. I began to think about changing my business model to perhaps create entire film projects, and sell them, using our music as underscore.

My sons Kevin and Taddy had bartended at *PF Changs* for many years in Burbank. Kevin began to fly all over the world to open up new *PF Changs* and set up their bars. He did some domestic openings, and also went to Istanbul, Turkey, as well as to Puerto Rico and the Philippines.

Taddy was going through a rough patch, I think maybe having a bit of an identity crisis. Kevin was being offered many opportunities within the corporation and Taddy was happy for his brother, but I think probably he was feeling a bit left behind. Kevin was traveling so much, he didn't want to keep paying rent on their two-bedroom apartment, and he was talking about having Taddy move into his own place or possibly find another roommate.

As Kevin was contemplating taking a full-time management position in Canada opening multiple *PF Changs* throughout the country, Taddy went into the hospital. I believe it was a mixture of anxiety and perhaps a little depression that put him in, but I immediately drove to Los Angeles to be by his side.

While I was there, I had a long talk with Kevin about his options and I was worried about Taddy. None of us had completely gotten over the death of Taddy's mom (or probably ever would), but we all agreed that Taddy took it the hardest. A culmination of years of stress and struggle had brought Taddy to this point. After talking with Robin, we decided to ask Taddy if he would consider moving in with us in San Diego, and transferring to a *PF Changs* down in our area.

Kevin decided to take the Canada job, promising to have Taddy join him as part of his staff as it all unfolded. *PF Changs* had a policy of allowing training bartenders to retain their jobs when they went off to open new restaurants, so Taddy moved down to Cardiff.

I have to say, I was delighted, just delighted to have my son back living with me after so many years. He had left me at age eighteen to go off to college, and now he was in his early thirties. At times, I forgot he had grown into a man and I reverted to treating him as I had when he was eighteen... still attempting to coddle and console him and to ask him if he was okay. And... I had envisioned him waking up with me and taking long walks with me as I do every morning, forgetting that he had been a night owl since he was young. But, as we evolved into our new relationship, Robin and I began to watch Taddy heal on new levels. Kevin made good on his promise and flew Taddy to Toronto to open two new restaurants, and then to Montreal for another opening. At some point, Taddy flew by himself to Beirut, Lebanon to open a new *PF Changs* there. He was coming into his own, and I was so proud of him.

After a little more than a year in the job, Kevin realized that the company he had gotten involved in was not going to open any more *PF Changs* in Canada, at least not for a long while. He was devastated, because he had turned down other options and had specifically picked this one believing that his future was to grow and become an executive in the company.

They wanted to break his contract and he could have sued them, but he chose to be cool, stay with the company and they relocated him to the only viably available *PF Changs* in Southern California, the one in Beverly Hills. They kept him at his salary, which basically made him, all of a sudden, the best-paid assistant manager in the business.

•••••

At that point, Taddy and Kevin decided to move back in together, and Taddy found a great apartment for them in Valley Village, a suburb of Los Angeles. At first, Taddy relocated to a *PF Changs* in Los Angeles that wasn't one of the best stores, but then he got a call to work at *Mastro's* in Beverly Hills, the premiere restaurant and bar in Los Angeles. He jumped at the position, and it was amazing to see how it transformed his entire persona.

We all knew Taddy was always a very hard-working, valuable performer in the business, and finally he was reaping the benefits of his hard work with an excellent position. Eventually, Kevin would find his way into *Mastro's*, and again they were working and living together in Los Angeles. I was so grateful that my boys were always best friends, and also that they watched out for each other.

Mostly, I finally saw them both evolve into amazing, kind, functional adults. Taddy had become extremely self-sufficient. Over a period of time, he began building his credit up and paying off his student debts. He leased a beautiful new car. The job at *Mastro's* helped both of my sons to overcome really most of the baggage they had carried for so long. I loved my sons with all my heart and I couldn't have been prouder of them.

•••••

While Kevin was still in Canada, my sons and I talked a lot about their dream to make films, and to start by finishing a feature film version of *Tis' The Season*, the short film they had shot at my house in Carlsbad back in 2006. Over a period of several years, they pulled their hair out looking for someone to back them, or invest in their project to no avail. I told them, "What is keeping you from doing this film on your own?"

I invited Kevin and Taddy to a Major League Baseball game between the *New York Yankees* and the *Los Angeles Angels* at Anaheim stadium, in Orange County, California. As we sat watching the game, I asked them what they needed in order to move forward on producing their film.

They told me, basically, that they needed a good camera and some professional lighting. I told them I would finance that for them, and they could start filming immediately if they wanted. They were delighted, and began to pull a cast together and rewrite the story of *Tis' The Season* as one that could be filmed on a low budget. I ended up purchasing two great Canon DSLR cameras, and later two Sony 4K Pro Video cameras along with professional lighting. I already pretty much had the sound equipment covered.

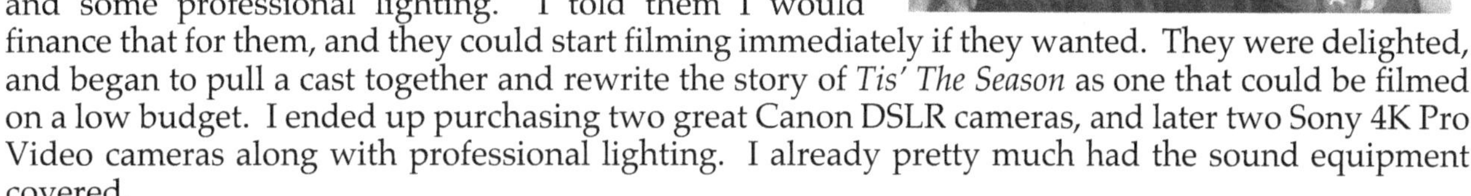

You can beat your head against the wall for years looking for someone to help you or invest in you, or you can make it happen on your own in an instant. Anyone is capable of this with thought, persistence and just a little opportunity.

•••••

They would shoot some scenes at Rachel & Robert's house in Rancho Mirage, and they pulled together a couple apartments, including their own, as other locations. Some of the original cast, including Walter Pena would get involved. They asked me to play the part of Mr. Baxter, and I agreed. Robert would be the FBI agent. After beginning filming, the protagonist, Mike, dropped out of the film, so Kevin told Taddy that he would have to play the protagonist, and it was a great choice. Taddy was perfect for the role that he, himself had written with his brother.

They got Regina's ex-husband Gregory involved in the beginning with his pro camera and audio, but working with him was arduous and slow, so when we purchased the lights, they decided to continue with the film on their own. The film unfolded over a three-year period following, and it was a great experience as well as a learning experience for them both. I was glad to be a part of it, working with audio and underscore as well as my little part in the film.

My company, *Mainstream Source*, was getting placements for our library catalog music.

Because my friend Scott Francisco was the music editor on the show and he needed a track at the last minute, we placed a song on *In The Motherhood* on *ABC*. I was delighted, and I contacted *ABC* asking to be on their preferred vendors list. I immediately got 'cease and desist' letters back from *Disney's* lawyers (the parent company of *ABC*). I get it… I know many people who came before me had looked for any reason to sue *Disney*, so the company put up a firewall against everyone who wasn't handpicked. But, it was extremely disconcerting after years of single-handedly building the collection of music for film and television, to be shot down, especially after we had already contracted with them for the placement we had.

I had decided years ago to be a righteous businessman, and I have no intentions of screwing anybody out of anything, ever. But, over time, we did get the occasional placement. One of our songs was used on an episode of the *Today Show* on *NBC*. Later, in 2015 and 2016 I placed a number of tracks on *The Librarians* on *TNT*, and made a little money from that. And, another track was picked up on *The Tonight Show with Jimmy Fallon.*

In general, though, it became apparent that the investment I had made in time and effort into the production music collection was not necessarily going to pay off in the way I hoped. Still, I've persisted, and creating my own film projects has helped through time to place more of the music. We revamped the website in 2018 and early 2019 to make it current, and pressed on attempting to market music in the industry. While I was making my long climb to the middle, I was creating an enormous amount of great content with talented people.

CHAPTER SEVENTY
Life and Friends in San Diego

Frank Hamblen retired from the *NBA* following the 2011 season with the *Lakers*. He and Uta bought a beautiful home on the hill in Rancho Santa Fe, CA, right above Del Mar. For a moment, a couple years later, it looked like Phil Jackson might go back to the *Lakers*, and Frank would have gone back with him, but as it turned out, Frank never went back to coaching.

At first, it seemed so wonderful to have them both down in San Diego with us, but quickly we began to find out that the marriage was troubled. Frank had traveled with different *NBA* teams for over forty years, and he was really ready to settle down. His ideal day consisted of waking up, going down to *Red Tracton's* for lunch and a few drinks, going home for a nap, and going back to *Red's* to sit at Jimmy's Bar until bedtime. This was pretty much all he did, every day, when they moved down, and Uta went with him every day until she started getting tired of that routine.

I believe that Uta had a different idea of what his retirement would look like. I imagine that she thought they would travel, maybe go on a few cruises together; something, anything above and beyond going back and forth to *Tracton's.* Uta became disillusioned and started coming to see me every night at *Mille Fleurs* or *Manhattan of La Jolla.* Uta and I were close, like a brother and sister, and she had been so good to Robin and me throughout the years. She was fun, but not as carefree as she had been for so long, and I could tell she was very unhappy.

I had seen this scenario so many times, as I performed in the bars for most of my adult life, but this one really hurt, because I loved both Uta and Frank. It wasn't long before they were separated, and Uta got together with Miles Pelky, who happened to be hanging out a lot with (and without) his brother Larry wherever I worked.

Needless to say, Frank was devastated, and they soon divorced. It took him a couple years to become himself again. He had a couple of rebound relationships, but none seemed to do more than temporarily fill the void. He had worked hard his whole life to get to retirement, and he and Uta simply didn't see eye-to-eye on what that actually meant.

Robin and I tried not to judge either of them, and we remained friends with both of them. We would try to choose evenly between them when inviting people to special events, but after a while, it seemed like Frank was the one who would be at our Thanksgiving or Christmas parties, or Super Bowl events. He liked the warmth of our house. Having been raised in Ohio, Robin had that Midwestern quality that Frank grew up knowing, being that he was from Terre Haute, Indiana, and she had made our home very comfortable and unassuming... so he felt comfortable with us.

Uta bought a home and began her new life, and we did continue to get together with her here and there too; it was never the same as it was when we all were together, and we always felt that Frank and Uta were great together. They both had great hearts. Nothing lasts forever. Truly, in my heart, I wanted them both to be happy, and after my own relationship experiences, I understood that sometimes it's best to move on and create a new life.

•••••

I had never met Robin's brother, David. He was schizophrenic, probably induced by heavy early drug use and a troubled childhood. By the time I came into the picture, David was a transient, wandering the streets of any given city for years at a time. This troubled my Robin to no end because she loved her brother with all her heart, and she had tried several times to help him, getting him housing and furniture more than once. He would seem to improve, and then he would run off again.

Robin and her brother David
1980's

David impregnated a girl in a facility he was staying, and the baby boy was put up for adoption at birth. Little David was given to a wonderful Midwestern couple, and they stayed in touch with Robin and her family throughout the years, even bringing him out several times to get to know his biological family. Knowing that she had a little nephew who was intelligent and being raised well, made Robin feel a little better about everything.

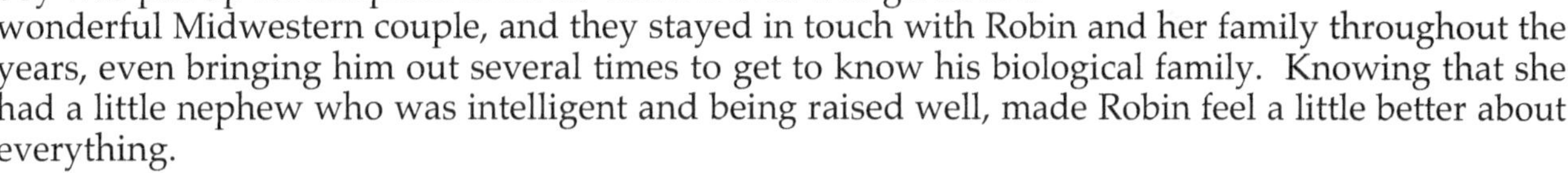

In December of 2013, Robin was devastated to find out that her brother David had been hit by a car and killed while wandering through Phoenix. In so many ways you could say that he may have gone to a better place, but my Robin's pain was real and I grieved for her. We had both lost a cherished sibling within six months of each other.

•••••

Getting together with family for the holidays always soothes the soul. Robin was famous for her Christmas Eve events, and in 2013 we had the whole family together for Thanksgiving as well. My grandchildren always warmed my heart. My favorite times have always been when I can just hug my loved ones!

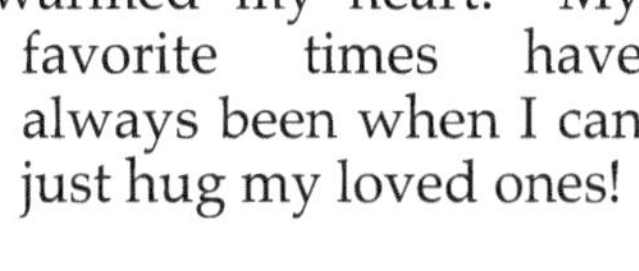

Beau, Danielle, Kris and Sammi
Christmas 2013

Tad and Trini Lopez

My friend Darci Daniels was putting together a fund-raiser for *Well in The Desert,* a local charity in Palm Springs. I helped her put together the first CD for their fundraiser, and I contributed my famous Palm Springs song, *I've Learned Just What It Means (To Love Palm Springs),* which I had recently re-recorded. At the fundraiser in January of 2014, I met up with my old friend Trini Lopez. Trini was still a huge star, particularly in Europe and

South America, and he always was the kindest man to me, sitting in and singing with me on many gigs through the years.

•••••

One of my greatest regrets was that I was never able to record my mother, Elaine, playing piano. By the time I had my studio in place, she had broken her hand and could not play anymore. I also had many friends, great musicians who died without much of a record of who they were or how talented they were.

I began to conceive the idea of creating a documentary series entitled *Legends Among Us,* which would chronicle the lives and music of people from all rungs of success. First, I had to put together a nonprofit 501 C (3) corporation. Over the course of several months, I conceived and incorporated the nonprofit *Foundation For Arts & Music Preservation, Inc.,* which would be a vehicle for us to raise money to chronicle the lives of legendary artists, sports figures, actors, medical pioneers and virtually anyone who had lived an extraordinary life and contributed to their profession or art form. We would also work to raise money for school music programs, with proceeds from our documentaries. This would take several years to get off the ground, but I began working on the concept immediately.

I started with my friend Jesse Davis, compiling a huge amount of information about him, interviewing him on camera several times, and cutting together a one-hour documentary with my limited knowledge of video editing.

I also interviewed Pat Rizzo but I was unhappy with the material I got from him. I didn't feel like he was totally in to the concept, and it fell short.

I then went to my friend Steve Madaio. Steve was a legend if there ever was one. He was on stage at Woodstock in 1969 with the *Butterfield Blues Band.* He recorded and toured with Stevie Wonder, The Rolling Stones, John Lennon, and so very many others.

When I went to interview Steve, he began to talk. Six hours later I had run out of memory on my video cards. So, I went back again, and again, and altogether I had over twenty-four hours of his recollections. I spent some time cutting together a documentary on him, but the footage we got was not visually good enough. So, I transcribed the interviews and started to write his biography.

I mentioned to Steve that he should look for old photos, so he began to call around to people he had worked with. He reached out to Veronique Sanson, a legendary French artist he had worked with in the 1970's and 1980's. She invited him to go back and work with her, so for years afterwards he flew back and forth to France and toured with her all over Europe, just because of our little book concept. When he was home, Steve and I worked on completing the book and an accompanying audiobook. We also worked on a podcast with the help of my good friend Jimi "Fitz" Fitzgerald, an iconic DJ and producer friend, as narrator. So, the concept of *Legends Among Us* began to grow.

•••••

Tad with Hall of Fame MLB Pitcher Trevor Hoffman 2015

I met Louie Stevens, a film producer, at the *YMCA* gym, and we began to talk about my concept. Over the next year or two, Louie and I morphed the *Legends Among Us* concept into a different idea called *Journey to an Extraordinary Life*.

We interviewed Frank Hamblen, Jesse Davis and Steve Madaio. I reached out to my friend Trevor Hoffman, the legendary *San Diego Padres* pitcher (and later Hall of Famer), and he gave us a great interview. Through Jesse and Diane Davis, I met Carol Conners. Carol had a *Billboard #1* Hit in 1958, and went on to write more hits as well as co-writing the theme from the movie *Rocky*, a smash hit. She gave us a great interview.

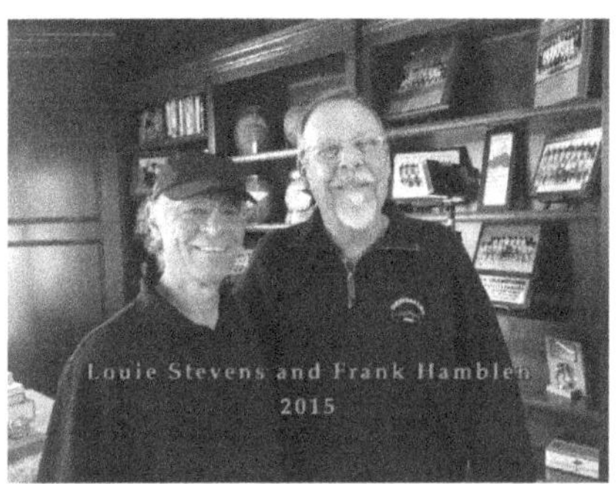
Louie Stevens and Frank Hamblen 2015

Louie had a friend he had mentored; she was now a huge Broadway star, performing as the lead in *Miss Saigon*. Dee Dee Magno, and her husband, Cliffton Hall, *Skyped* us from a hotel room on the road and we cut their interview along with the others into a thirteen-minute promotional film attempting to sell the series. It turned out to be more of a motivational film, and it was great, but I began to think later that I had perhaps gotten too far away from my original *Legends Among Us* concept. So, now I had two great concepts to expand upon.

•••••

Robin and Sammi 2017

Robin and I still had the 'revolving kid door' going on at our house. For a time, her Sammi moved back. Sammi had been in San Francisco, and in mid-2014 Robin and I went to visit her a month or two before she moved home. Sammi had gotten her *Bachelor's Degree* in SF and she was working at *Nordstrom's* selling shoes. She was actually making good money, but she was getting burnt out on being up there, and wanted a change. She stayed with us for a short time until she found another place to stay. Eventually, Sammi moved to New York for a long period.

•••••

Larry Schmidtke 2013

Uta and Miles had settled down and weren't frequenting my gigs as much, but Miles' brother Larry would come in and see me once or twice a week. We had become very close friends. When Larry got up to sing with me, everyone cheered.

Larry began to complain about a backache in January of 2014, and it kept getting worse and worse. He finally went to get it checked out and found out that he had stage four Cancer. Larry was dying. He was only fifty-nine years old.

As his illness progressed, I went to visit him at his home in La Mesa. Strangely enough, his house was directly across the street from the house my mother and sisters had lived in, back in 1969. Larry was perhaps in denial of the finality of his prognosis and he kept hope alive until he couldn't. When Larry was finally admitted into the hospital, Robin and I went to visit him several times. We were there with him during the last days, and it was so sad to see him go so quickly. Larry and I had only been friends for maybe four years, but his life and death left a huge impact on me.

Larry had no children, and I remember thinking how grateful I was to have made the decision to have children when I was young. Of course, life was a struggle because of it. But, the rewards so outweighed the struggle; I couldn't have made a better decision. Even so, Larry didn't die alone. Friends surrounded him as he took his last breaths. I did think it was weird though, at his memorial service. Miles did not show; he had another commitment, and Larry's other brother was out of the country. I sang *The Dance* by Garth Brooks, a cappella, to a small group of congregants and friends. Larry deserved better than that. Admittedly, they were all there for him as much as they knew how, when he was still alive, though.

I was working two or three jobs while raising my children as a very young man, sacrificing while many of my friends were partying through their twenties and thirties. Although it was the road less travelled (and a hard and bumpy road at that), the reward of having adult children and grandchildren who loved and cared for me, while I was still young enough to appreciate it, became priceless.

Dr. Tom used to say that, just as there are waiting hands for us when we are born, we must believe that there are waiting hands for us when we pass on. Still, it is a sad thought to die alone.

•••••

In September of 2014, my buddy Ron Zagami took Robin and me along with his girlfriend Heloa to see Paul McCartney perform at *Petco Park* in San Diego. I had already seen Paul twice… not to mention the time he 'opened' for me at *Delicias*! Yes, one night a billionaire in Rancho Santa Fe hired Paul McCartney to do a solo for a party for a million dollars before I performed, so technically, he opened for me!

It was still amazing to see one of my childhood idols, already in his seventies, performing with gusto with still an amazing voice. Although I always worked towards not needing to perform to make a living into my old age, I realized that I could probably continue doing my live shows full-time at least into my seventies.

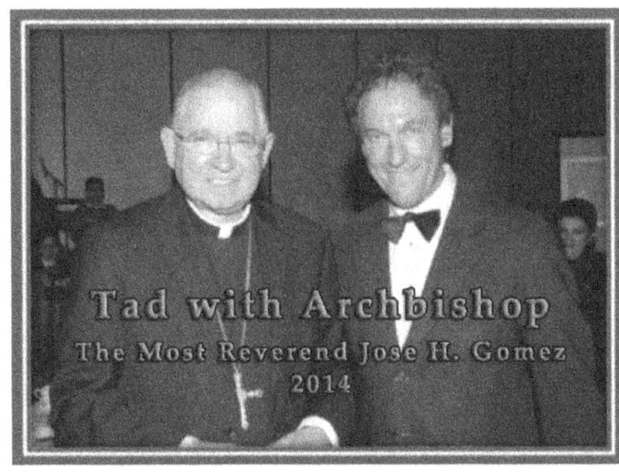
Tad with Archbishop
The Most Reverend Jose H. Gomez
2014

I did a pretty cool gig for my friend Adrienne Selekman in mid-2014. I called my friend Chad Quist, the great guitarist-vocalist, to do the gig with me. It was for a Catholic Charity, and we performed for an Archbishop, The Most Reverend Jose Gomez. He was actually cool. The Archbishop was a member of *Opus Dei,* an offshoot of the Catholic church from which Stephanie's uncle Gregory Haddock was also a lifetime member. Gregory had been a priest in Toronto his entire life, and although aging, we still corresponded regularly for many, many years after Stephanie died. It felt good to know that Gregory was praying for my children's health and safety, and it was nice to relate all of this to the Archbishop. He knew Father Gregory, and it was a warm and friendly event.

•••••

I continued to work hard to stay current, not only in the recording studio with techniques and updated instruments and sounds, but also as a live performer. I was always adding songs to my repertoire, not only filling out my catalogue with classic music, but also learning current tunes as well.

The biggest challenge of my career was keeping up with the times. I had been involved in the business since the advent of the personal computer, and this was truly a renaissance age of computing, with speeds and bit-rates and new technology improving at a furious pace.

I had bought an *Apple Mac Pro* desktop computer for my studio in 2009, loading it up, and it lasted until 2018. Even with all of the improvements and upgrades I had made to the computer, after nine years when I moved on to a new *iMac Pro,* I was stunned by the improvement in speed and capability. All of a sudden, we were working in 4K, and then 8K, with 3D capabilities as well. I'm sure that future generations will laugh at these breakthroughs, but at this time, working with this new technology, we felt like we were on the cutting edge!

Giorgio Barone
2015

Much of my off time during this period was spent traveling to and from Palm Springs and Temecula, watching my grandkids play football, soccer or baseball, and showering them with love. I was always at my happiest with my kids and grandkids. I was grateful for the entire early struggle, to have evolved to a place in life with so much love around me.

I continued to write, embarking on creating a couple screenplays. One, entitled *Please Don't Forget* was loosely based upon the tragedy I endured with Stephanie. I didn't humanize her enough in the story, so I vowed to go back and give it another try at a later date. Another screenplay I wrote was a great political story based upon the idea of what Benjamin Franklin would think if he were exposed to life as it is in America today. The screenplay is entitled *The Incredible spark of Franklin Benjamin* and I began to shop it in late 2018.

Giorgio and Stefani Barone
2014

•••••

Rachel's husband Robert had a Fantasy Football league, and the whole family participated in it. My team, the *San Diego Fourskins,* won multiple championships, and it was a fun way for us to stay connected. During this period, the *National Football League* had grown larger than *Major League Baseball,* and when both seasons were on, there was usually a game in the background on the television while I was working; some Sundays were devoted to watching multiple games with my family.

Family Christmas - December 2014

Every once in a while, Robin and I would go to *Qualcomm Stadium* and take in a *San Diego Chargers* game. San Diego was collectively devastated when the owner of the *Chargers,* Dean Spanos, decided to move the team to Los Angeles in 2016. Dean was a friend of mine, and I understood it from a business point of view. He had tried for decades to get a new stadium built, albeit not giving much on his end to complete the plan. Even so, his decision to move the team had made him a pariah in San Diego.

•••••

In January of 2015, Robin and I brought her daughter Danielle and her niece Malia to Hawaii for a week vacation. Danielle and Malia were young adults, and they enjoyed each other's company as Robin and I had some quiet time together from our busy lives.

Tad, Robin, Danielle and Malia
Oahu, Hawaii - 2015

We stayed on the West shore of Oahu in a timeshare, and drove all over the island, going to a *Luau,* snorkeling, eating from the food trucks as the girls went zip lining, and visiting Robin's mother's old home from years before, on a beautiful beach on the East shore.

Hawaii remained my favorite destination throughout my life. Living in San Diego, I always told people, "When you already live in paradise, you can go anywhere else and enjoy it." But, Hawaii was a step above everywhere I had been. It was tropical, laid-back and gorgeous.

We went to Pearl Harbor, which was a profoundly spiritual and emotional experience for me. Standing in the memorial above the *USS Arizona* reminded me again about how fortunate I was to have been born into liberty, and to be free because of other's ultimate sacrifices. It also made me sad that I never had been able to experience this with my father. It would have meant more in a way to stand there holding his hand as he remembered the actual experience of fighting in that war. It was his loss, too, to not have taken the time to bring me to this hallowed place. But now, none of that really mattered. I said a prayer for him, as I always do…

•••••

When we returned to San Diego, we all went to a Bruno Mars concert. Bruno was truly the "Michael Jackson" of this era. He had figured out a way to take all of the great elements of old soul and R&B tunes, and remake them into modern classics. His choreography, dance routines, and his amazing musicianship, not only as a vocalist but also as a drummer, made him one of the great talents of this generation, and deservedly so.

I remember talking to my father about all of the great music of his era. I had gotten in on the tail end of it… The Glenn Miller Orchestra, Tommy Dorsey with Frank Sinatra, Billie Holliday, Louis Armstrong and all the other greats, not to mention the great songwriters, Rodgers and Hart, and then Hammerstein; Cahn and Van Heusen, Jule Styne, Johnny Mercer and so many more.

He had seen so many of these musicians, experiencing them 'live' when he was young, and how I would have loved to be in on all of that! I had met and worked with quite a few of these iconic musicians as old men, and they had many great stories of their heyday. But, here we were in this era; experiencing new great talent, and watching music expand into areas we had never dreamed of. I felt important in a way to be a small part of it, producing my own music and offering it to the world.

•••••

Around this time, I became a voting member of the *Academy of Recording Arts & Sciences*, using my own voice and vote to choose *Grammy* award winners. It was exciting to have risen to the level where my opinion actually really did mean something in helping other artist's careers to get to a new level as *Grammy* winners. I was grateful for the status and the opportunity. This was a big step in my long climb to the middle!

During this time, I began to work on several classical piano album projects, releasing them over the course of the next two years. It was great, going back to my roots. It was much easier too, because I could fix all of my mistakes within Pro Tools and then record the live pianos, perfectly with my Yamaha C3 grand piano, which was also a Disklavier. I was grateful for my equipment. The piano was the crown jewel of my studio.

I also recorded new versions of two cover songs with Chad Quist. One was the old Cream hit *White Room.* I did a cool new dance version of that under my surname *Maynard of Goth.* Chad and I also released a morphed version of Elton John's *Bennie and the Jets* with Queen's *We Will Rock You.* Both songs got a lot of hits in the retail market for quite some time afterwards.

•••••

2015
Robin's Uncles Abe & Mike, Father Isaac (Tony), Aunts Ann & Martha

Robin found out in early 2015 that her father Isaac (Tony) was dying of cancer. She flew back to Ohio and found him in bad shape. Robin got him into the hospital, and then got on the phone and got him everything he would need at home for comfort care, as she had done for my father just a handful of years back. The weather was terrible back in Ohio in February and March, but she arranged for a hospital bed in his home, oxygen and other medical supplies to help him.

Family members surrounded him every day, even playing cards with them as he found it hard to continue breathing until his last day on earth. Shortly before he died, he was baptized. It was something he had wanted to do since his youth. Tony was very close with his brother Abe. Along with his sisters Martha and Ann, and his other brother Mike, they stayed close to Tony and his wife Maureen as he deteriorated.

It's always so tragic when we lose one we love, but it is also an amazing part of life to be able to be surrounded by the people we love the most when we need them the most.

Isaac (Tony) and Maureen Digildo
Robin's dad and stepmother

•••••

In May of 2015, I flew to Denver, Colorado, for a reunion with my sisters at Betsy's house. This was the first time the four of us had gotten together since we lost my sister Judy. Although Betsy and Mark had lived in Colorado for more than ten years, I had never made the trip to see their house until this time.

Kathy, Tad, Suzanne and Betsy - 2015

It was an emotional few days. Mostly, we played cards and other games. One morning, we drove to Boulder and experienced a huge *Tea House* restaurant for lunch. We spent a lot of time reminiscing about our Judy, and giving thanks that we still had each other. Our lives journeys had taken many turns. We were all so different as individuals, but the common thread of our history and combined memories made it a joyful and healing occasion, whenever we got together. I was glad to see that Betsy and Mark had made a good life for themselves in Colorado.

•••••

On my birthday, June 28, 2015, my friend Ron Zagami rented a limousine, and a group of us went to Los Angeles to *Mastro's Restaurant* in Beverly Hills to have dinner and see my sons at work. Frank Hamblen came with us, along with his current girlfriend Debbie. Lawson Brown and his girlfriend Michele were in the limo as well. Michele and Lawson were a good couple. Michele was generous in spirit, baking goodies for all of our events for years to come. On that evening, we celebrated both Robin's and my own birthdays, as they were only two days apart.

Lawson & Michele, Tad & Robin, Frank & Debbie, Ron
2015

We had a great dinner, and my sons Taddy and Kevin were attentive and so glad to see us! Frank was always classy, but at some point, he decided he had enough and it was time to go home, so we cut the night a bit earlier than expected and headed back to San Diego.

Ron became inebriated on the way up to Beverly Hills, and somehow, he met a woman outside and invited her in for dinner. He brought her down to San Diego later that week, and that relationship lasted about another week before they both mutually agreed they had nothing in common. Ron truly was the greatest salesman in the world, and I always believed he could sell himself to anyone, given enough time and effort! He was a good friend to Robin and me.

•••••

Shana Moura

During the summer of 2015, my sister Betsy's daughter Shana came to visit us in California. She had asked me when I was up in Colorado if I would bring her on as an intern for a short period of time during the summer for school credits, and I agreed. Shana was an extremely talented artist, and she was going to graphic design school. I had some projects lined up for her to assist me with, but she wasn't serious about interning, and she ran off to see the sights in San Diego instead. Nevertheless, we had a nice visit.

Steve and Mistie McDougall with Frank Hamblen August, 2015

In August of 2015, our friend Mistie Breen married a really good guy, Steve McDougall. Robin and I, along with her daughter Danielle, attended the wedding at a resort in Carlsbad with Frank and Debbie. Mistie chose my song, *You're My World*, to walk down the aisle. I was honored. Shortly after the wedding, I released my CD entitled *Feel Free*, which contained Mistie's wedding song. This was the song that Barbara Sinatra loved all those years ago.

Feel Free
Tad Sisler

•••••

My daughter Rachel's husband Robert had an idea for a game called *Pongolf*. It was sort of a morph between table tennis and golf, using little table tennis balls on a round table to try to get into the middle hole. As he patented his idea, I employed my friend Worthington Foster, along with a master carpenter, to build two prototype *Pongolf* tables. We were always trying something new… I always believed that if you throw enough at the wall, some of it is bound to stick. And… the game was fun! We had many ideas for marketing, but it languished in limbo for several years after we came up with the concept.

•••••

At the end of September in 2015, my sister Kathy's and brother-in-law Steven's son Mike and his wife Alex had a son. They named him Elliott in honor of Steve's childhood friend who died as a young adult somewhere in the Bermuda Triangle. Kathy finally had a grandchild, and she was delighted!

Mike, Elliott & Alex Soffer 2018

I had traveled to Asheville, North Carolina a couple years before to witness Mike and Alex's wedding. It was a fun and loving event with my sister Kathy and her family, along with my sister Suzanne, her husband Carey and her family traveling from Greensboro. Mike had a high-powered job in New York City, and I was glad that he was doing so well. Shortly after Elliott was born, Mike and Alex would move to Nashville to be closer to Alex's family, as her father was ill. Mike always seemed to go with the flow and adjust to whatever he was given. He was easygoing and charming, with sleepy eyes and an infectious smile.

In early 2019, Mike and Alex had a second child, a beautiful little girl named Penelope.

•••••

In October of 2015, a group of my songs went into *Grammy* consideration for the first time. Five of my songs from the *Feel Free* album and a couple of singles, including *Bad Ass Funk* featuring Steve Madaio, were in consideration in multiple categories.

It was exciting, although as time has gone by and I've been able to get much more of my music into consideration, I've found that the Grammy process can be political. Some of the more aggressive entrants hound you and shower you with gifts so you'll vote for them even though it's against the rules; the main categories are rumored to be 'owned' by major label artists and the labels that represent them. Still, it's a thrill to be part of the process and to have a voice in *Grammy* voting, through my membership in the *Recording Academy of Arts and Sciences.*

•••••

At the end of October in 2015, Robin's stepsister Donna came out from Ohio with her longtime husband David. She confided in us privately that she was going to break up with David following the trip. Needless to say, it was a weird week with them! I love Donna, but it was kind of like a "farewell, thanks for everything, I love you but I'm out" kind of send-off without him knowing until the end of the trip. Who am I to judge after everything I've done?

What is it within us, causing us to feel morally superior to those we don't agree with, as if we have a lock on all the answers or the truth? It's okay to agree to disagree. It's also okay to have a different opinion. Most importantly, we need to let people live their own lives.

CHAPTER SEVENTY-ONE
Detached Retina

Something terribly wrong was happening with my left eye. One day in October of 2015, I walked out of my studio into the sunny morning and I experienced a million "floaters" in my eye, blocking much of my vision.

Immediately. I went to an ophthalmologist at Kaiser and told him of my family history of detached retinas. I was sure that my retina was detached, but he looked in my eye and said nothing was wrong. He sent me in for some random eye tests and I got a letter from the doctor saying that my eye was fine. I believed strongly that something major was wrong, but I thought, well, maybe it will just go away like they said it would in a few months.

•••••

Through the Thanksgiving and Christmas season of 2015, my family remained close. Rachel and Robert and their babies came down to be with us on Thanksgiving along with Robin's family, and we had a very loving time together. We had a wonderful family Christmas party about a week early at Rachel and Robert's house in Rancho Mirage with Regina, Todd and their children along with Dennis Burge, my wife Stephanie's first husband and Kevin's and Regina's 'first' father. Following that event, Robin again hosted her big Christmas Eve party at our house, and Frank Hamblen attended.

Dennis Burge, my son Kevin's natural father had always remained a good guy, and in his own way, he was there for his children, and even for me at times. He was a Christian man with values that emanated from his quiet soul. Even though he had only lived with Regina for maybe two years when she was two and three years old, he continued to keep a strong bond with Regina and Kevin throughout his life, always available with open arms and a calm demeanor. Dennis eventually remarried and had two lovely daughters, Kevin's half-sisters, Sarah and Lauren.

Robin and Tad - 2015

•••••

Each day brings its own challenges, but if you approach life with optimism and keep your expectations low, you may be pleasantly surprised. Optimism lays the path to happiness.

Life in my late fifties was generally good. I had gone through the fire and emerged with my battle scars, yet still intact. I had an amazing relationship with my Robin. Our closeness meant the world to me. I would tell people, "Robin works days and I work nights. We hardly ever see each other, and so we always miss each other!" Is that the secret to a great relationship?

•••••

Underneath the façade of my daughter Rachel's perfect family brewed a deep unhappiness, which I had not only witnessed here and there throughout the years, but about which Rachel also confided in me.

Kevin, Rachel, Tad, Regina, Taddy
January 2016

Robert was a good guy, but mistakes can be made in a marriage, and when you marry so young, the odds are against you. Even still, on January 3, 2016, all four of my original children and I met at Rachel & Robert's house to go to the *Palm Springs Film Festival* Gala.

When I'm with my core family, the children that I raised, I am always filled with so much joy to see them. We always held each other so close in our hearts. Sometimes, as individuals, they would struggle and other times they would thrive, but always we knew that we had each other, and that meant the world to me. I was behind each of them one hundred percent, and they could always confide in me if they needed me.

I had just performed a New Year's Eve gig with my band for the Chairman of the *Palm Springs Film Festival*, and we dressed up and went in a limo to the event. Robert's dad, Ermanno, had been a big supporter of the *Palm Springs Film Festival*, and, as I had mentioned, my band had actually performed for one of the early events when Sonny Bono founded the Festival in the late 1980's. Robert continued to purchase a table after his father passed, and we had a wonderful time at the event.

Andrew Fraga, Jr. - 2014

Andrew Fraga, Jr., my drummer and business associate, was the drummer for the orchestra, and Chad Quist was playing guitar that night. It was fun to be with movie stars, but mostly to see my children happy together.

•••••

Taddy and Kevin had entered an early version of their feature film, *'Tis the Season* into the *Idyllwild Film Festival*. Taddy had to work, so I drove to Idyllwild with Kevin and Walter Pena, a good friend of the family who was a lead actor in the film. They had submitted a rough cut to get into the festival, and sent a more complete version later with music and fixes.

Tad, Walter Pena and Kevin
2018

When we got to Idyllwild, we found that they weren't screening the film in a theatre, but rather in some multi-purpose room, off the beaten path on a portable screen and projector. There were only about eight people in the room (including the three of us and the projectionist). When they started to roll the film, we were extremely disappointed because they hadn't bothered to use the more completed version, but instead screened the rough cut.

Kevin and Walter were embarrassed, but the bright spot was that we received some encouraging feedback from a reviewer and the couple of other people who showed up and watched the film. Kevin was also delighted when they laughed at the right times in the film, and we knew that they had something here which just needed to be polished. But, also, Kevin and Walter learned that it is extremely important not to release anything into the world that is not complete, regardless of whether you think you're going to be able to replace it later.

Always put your best foot forward. Mostly, don't be in a rush, but rather, be patient and do it right. That way, you'll only have to do it once.

•••••

In late January of 2016, we went to *Staples Center* to see the *Lakers* play basketball with our friends Pete & Sheila, Mistie & Steve, Lawson & Michele. Veronica Lawlor was one of the big bosses with the *Laker's* organization and she had become a dear friend of ours, initially through our association with Frank Hamblen. Frank didn't like going to the games much. He preferred to watch them from the comfort of his home in Del Mar. Frank was concerned that the media would give attention to him and take it away from the people who deserved it. He was a selfless man.

Tad with MLB All-Star Yasiel Puig
2016

Veronica arranged for tickets for all of us, and a trip to the *Chairman's Room* following the game, as we had done so many times with Frank and Uta through the years. I met and spoke with the great *Los Angeles Dodgers* All-star baseball player Yasiel Puig. He didn't speak much English, but he was very kind and accommodating to the people around him. I was a big fan.

Robin and I also had a chance to sit and chat with the great actress Jenna Elfman. I told her that I was a huge fan of her uncle, composer Danny Elfman. She was sweet, and very down to earth.

It was great to be with friends, but through it all, my eyesight was deteriorating.

•••••

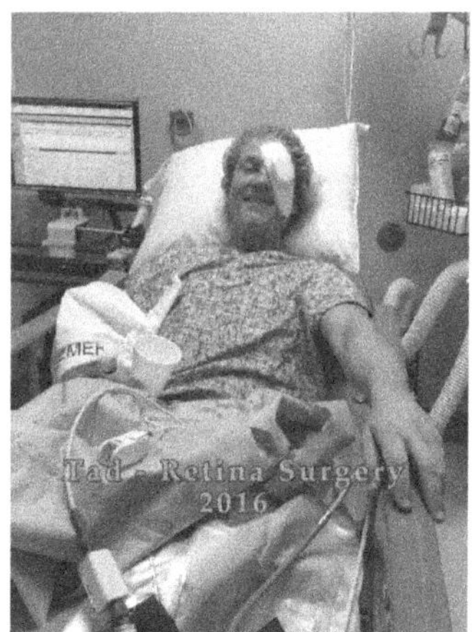
Tad - Retina Surgery
2016

At the end of March, my left eye began to project a circular glow, like the outline of the Sun within my eyesight. A few days into the experience, everything within the circle went dark. I was blind in my left eye with the exception of some peripheral vision. Immediately, I went back to the ophthalmologist who had misdiagnosed me, and they sent me directly to a retina specialist. I made it home driving with one eye, and Robin left work immediately to drive me down to the specialist.

Dr. Dick was a graduate of *Harvard* and *Johns Hopkins*. He was an excellent eye surgeon. He immediately diagnosed a detached retina. I had laser surgery on my left eye on April 1, 2016. Because the retina had been in various stages of detachment since October, I had two holes and four tears in the retina. It was a catastrophic detachment.

Fortunately, the two holes in the retina were outside my line of sight, but when Dr. Dick repaired the retina, my vision in that eye became distorted.

For six weeks I had oil in my eye socket, keeping the retina in place as it healed, and when they removed the oil through another surgery, I realized that my vision in that eye would never be the same. It was as if everything was thinner when I looked out of that eye. The full moon looked like an egg. And, there was a wavy perception in my vision, almost like looking through a heat wave on a summer day, where everything didn't quite line up and almost seemed to move around in my sight. Somehow, through it all, I still had 20/25 Vision in that eye when I stopped and concentrated on an image.

The human brain is an amazing thing. Whether to simply accomplish the proper dissemination of information or even to protect a child against the horrors of war, abuse or torture, the brain will compensate with outstanding speed and clarity.

The eye surgeon wanted to make sure my other retina did not detach, so he scheduled a painful laser session with me. I had to keep my eye completely open and not blink either eye as he shot hundreds of pulses of laser light all around the retina in my right eye. It was a deeply difficult experience, and I had to literally 'go somewhere else' in my mind while he was doing the procedure.

A couple months later, he repeated the Laser procedure in a corner of my eye that was still beginning to detach. So, my eyesight has never been the same, although I was able to completely function in every normal activity. Interestingly enough, Dr. Dick mentioned to me that the brain would compensate for the distortion, and he was entirely right.

•••••

In June of 2016, iconic recording artist Billy Joel came in to *Manhattan of La Jolla* where I was performing. He was staying at the *La Valencia Hotel* in La Jolla with his wife in La Jolla.

Ron Zagami and Tad, Jamming! 2015

One Thursday night, he came in and sat in the back quietly while I was performing. It was a fun night, with Jesse Davis sitting in on vocals for a couple songs, and Ron Zagami playing organ while I sang and played piano, keyboards and bass. None of us knew he was there, but on the next night, he came back in for dinner with his wife.

They were sitting at a booth across the room and Billy had just finished his dinner when I began to play. I was well aware that he was there, but I didn't want to make him uncomfortable. I had remembered an interview I had seen of Billy Joel from years ago, when he mentioned that one of his favorite songs he wrote was *Everybody Has A Dream,* off of *The Stranger* album. It was the soft dinner set, so I did a quiet, heartfelt version of the song.

Aidan, Tad, Makayla Stefani & Giorgio 2017

Although I had the oil in my eye from my retina surgery, but I could still see him approaching me at the piano when I finished the song. He came up and said a few words to me, and told me I was good. I said, "I love you, man!" and he put $100.00 in my tip jar. It was cool meeting someone who had so very much influenced my career without even knowing it. I did have a fleeting thought.... "Hmm, that $100.00 bill is like Billy Joel giving me a nickel for every time I had played *Piano Man!"*

CHAPTER SEVENTY-TWO
Guiding my Children and Grandchildren

On August 28, 2016, our Makayla won her first *Temecula Idol*

Stefani, Giorgio and Tad 2016

competition. She was becoming an outstanding vocalist and her stage presence was improving vastly. Winning this competition put her on the radar for shows like *American Idol, The Voice* and *America's Got Talent.* Robin and I were immensely proud of her.

As my Stefani started her first day of Kindergarten and Giorgio went into second grade, I went to Palm Springs to walk them in to the school with their parents, and it felt good.

•••••

Rachel, Kevin, Tad and Taddy 2016

In September of 2016, my friend Steve Cantore flew me back to Pennsylvania to perform for his son's wedding. Steve took really good care of me and I loved the experience. The wedding was at a winery overlooking a river on a beautiful late summer day. Steve had remained a good friend to me through all the years. He always seemed to 'show up' wherever I lived. He was kind and supportive always to my family, and I appreciated him.

Tad with Steve Cantore - 2017

While I was in Pennsylvania, I went to Gettysburg to see the Civil War battleground and cemetery and to pay my respects. It was a profound experience, to stand in the spot where Lincoln gave his *Gettysburg Address* and to imagine the carnage and sacrifice that so
many young men gave in such a dark period of our history.

Following the wedding, I drove over to see my friend Gayle Hall. Gayle was dear to me from all the *San Diego Padres* games we attended together and for all the times she helped us with rooms at the *Winners Circle* when she ran the timeshare next to *Red Tracton's.*

Gayle had moved back home to be with family in a small town near Philadelphia, and she had recently had a bad fall, so she was glad to see me. Although it was about an hour out of my way, I spent the afternoon with her and really enjoyed taking the time to see my dear old friend.

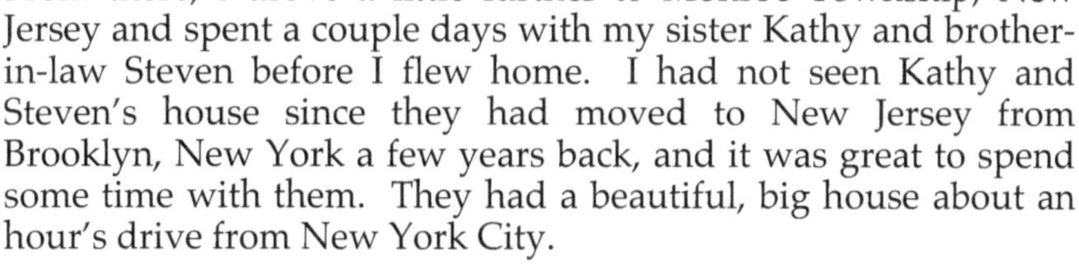

From there, I drove a little further to Monroe Township, New Jersey and spent a couple days with my sister Kathy and brother-in-law Steven before I flew home. I had not seen Kathy and Steven's house since they had moved to New Jersey from Brooklyn, New York a few years back, and it was great to spend some time with them. They had a beautiful, big house about an hour's drive from New York City.

Steven and Kathy Soffer 2017

Kathy's heart would still act up on occasion and she would have to get cardio version. Steven was still practicing his nutrition and holistic medicine, and he took me to his office and performed some tests on me to see what I was lacking in nutrition. His suggestions were invaluable and helped me to live a healthier life when I returned to San Diego. I was sad that we didn't live closer so I could see them more often. I knew that Kathy could get lonely and sad, missing her family, although her life was full. They had a new grandson now, and that helped her a lot.

•••••

Returning home, I continued to perform full-time, as I always had. In October of 2016 around Blaire's birthday, I took her to lunch. My little stepdaughter had grown into a lovely, 23-year-old woman. She had a boyfriend, and she was working a full-time job. We had a deep soul connection

Blaire

from her early childhood, and I was grateful to spend time with her whenever I could. Although I didn't see her often, she would make a point of coming to our holiday events, and it meant the world to me.

During Christmas of 2016 we all converged at Rachel & Robert's house in Rancho Mirage for a warm family gathering, and then we had Robin's traditional Christmas Eve party at our house in San Diego with the rest of the family.

Frank Hamblen with Robin
Christmas 2016

As 2017 unfolded, I had yet another eye surgery to 'clean up' my left eye. It didn't do much good; my vision in that eye remained the same. I was grateful to still have one good eye at this point.

•••••

In March of 2017, I did an outside gig with my band in an amphitheater at a country club in Palm Desert overlooking the beautiful desert below, where I had raised my children and spent so many years.

Tad and Spencer
2018

This gig was special, however, because I hired my son Spencer to sing with the band. He and a female vocalist fronted my band, and they were excellent. I was so proud of Spencer for becoming such a great stage performer. His voice was excellent, and mostly he was a kind, loving person. He would tell me how grateful he was that I came into his life and helped to shape him into the adult he had become. Truly, he had come so far, and I was grateful that he recognized the value of my contribution to his life. I loved my Spencer! We continued to perform together, here and there, after that event.

Through this period, I continued to record amazing music in the studio. I resurrected and released a collection of my original country music tracks under the surname *Maynard Lee*. I did another *Maynard of Goth* album, which I released in 2018. I completed more Christmas and Patriotic music for the collection and for worldwide retail distribution.

•••••

Around April 1, 2017, Robert called me and asked me to come up to the desert to talk with Rachel. They were having major problems in their relationship, and he felt like I needed to talk to her to 'fix' it. Rachel and I had always been so very close and we had no real secrets between each other.

I went up to talk with her, but not for Robert's reasons. I felt like she needed her dad, and I wanted to know how she really was feeling. I opened up my heart and finally admitted to her the affair I had with Monica all those years ago, and I told her that I had come around to the realization, at that moment in time, that staying in my marriage and with my children would benefit my kids more than if I split up with their mom at that point in our young lives. Of course, my life didn't end up working out the way I hoped it would when I made that decision, and I've laid out the tragedy in this book.

Rachel was determined to end her marriage. She was unhappy for many reasons. Robert had made some errors in judgment, and Rachel felt that he had not grown up, really. He was still partying, going to concerts with his friends, and misbehaving. Also, they were together all day, every day; they had not had a break from each other at any point. Robert seemingly was codependent upon her for everything, she felt he was not taking his role seriously as a father and husband, and she just couldn't do it anymore.

It was devastating to all of us because from the outside they really did have a fairy-tale marriage. I had grown to love Robert like a son. Giorgio and Stefani were my loves of my life, and I didn't want them to endure pain ever, but I also knew from my own experience that there can be greater pain within a dysfunctional marriage for everyone involved than if people just move on and live a new life. The only thing I could really tell Rachel was that I would be there for her as I always had, and whatever she needed, I would back her up.

Makayla, Aidan
Stefani & Giorgio
Giorgio's First Communion 2017

Through all of this, my grandson Giorgio was given his First Communion at *Sacred Heart Catholic Church* in Palm Desert. At this point, it was kind of awkward to be around Robert and his mother, but Giorgio was beaming with pride as he marched to the altar with the other children. I was so proud of that boy, and really of all of my grandchildren for the good people they were, to the core.

Tad, Robin, Frank & Jane
April 2017

•••••

In mid-April of 2017, Robin and I threw a big party for Frank Hamblen to celebrate his 70th birthday, at *Manhattan of La Jolla*. The room was packed with his friends, and the former *NBA* coach was in his element. He was happier than we had seen him in years.

Kristin and Andrew Mardis
2018

Frank had a new girlfriend, Jane, who was very attentive to him. Jane was a wealthy woman, and Frank had plenty of money, so he knew her affection was genuine, and not based on wanting more from him than his love and attention. Frank had known Jane since he was a junior coach for the *San Diego Rockets* in the late 1960's (before they moved to Houston). At that time, by Frank's recollection, Jane was a gorgeous, hot young girl who wouldn't give him the time of day back then, so he was especially happy to have her as his girlfriend all these years later. They bantered back and forth in their conversations, which was cute, and his family was so grateful that Frank was happy again.

Regina, Rachel, Kevin and Taddy
2017

Frank's nephew Andrew and his wife Kristin came down from Los Angeles for the party. We had become close with Andrew throughout the years, and I had performed at his wedding to Kristin as a favor to Frank for all of the wonderful things he had done for us over the years. Later, Andrew had given me some money for my performance; it was appreciated but not wanted or expected.

Kevin, Taddy, Tad, Regina
Spencer, Rachel and Todd - 2017

Towards the end of April in 2017, I celebrated my ten-year anniversary performing on Wednesdays at Mille Fleurs in Rancho Santa Fe. A large crowd came to celebrate with me, including my children and many friends. It was a great evening!

•••••

In June of 2017, Robin's daughter Danielle graduated with a Bachelor's Degree in Biology from *University of California, Davis.* Robin and I went up to Sacramento to attend the graduation, and for the first time I got to know her ex-husband, Kevin, a little more. Kevin was a good guy. I knew he had struggled a lot in life, as we all have, and we got along pretty well. He was concerned about his children, and I understood it. I believe that he was happy that if he couldn't be around them as much as he wanted to, that he knew I was trying to be a good influence on them.

Tad, Danielle & Robin
UC Davis Graduation

Kris and Tad
Petco Park 2016

I had bonded with Robin's kids in the years I lived in the house. Through the revolving 'kid' door, her son Kris had come back to live with us for a while. Kris was a good young adult, and we became very close. We shared a love of sports, and I was grateful for all of his help around the house, and for his love and concern for his mother's well-being. He was always watching out for her, even though she was independent and fine.

Kris was finding his way through life. He hadn't yet settled on what he wanted to do, but whatever he did, he worked hard and he had loyal friends. Kris co-owned a fishing boat with a couple friends, and fishing off the coast of San Diego was his passion. He would bring in big hauls of fresh Yellow Fin, Yellow Tail, Halibut and Mahi-Mahi on a regular basis. We would come up with new recipes and feast!

Danielle moved back home after she graduated, so now we had a house full again with Robin's kids Danielle, Kris and Beau. Danielle went back into babysitting, and she had some wealthy clients, once even being flown to Europe to babysit two babies on the famous yacht *Christina O.* She was a go-getter, and she had grown up into a compassionate, kind young woman with an edge similar to her mom's. She was plotting her next move, possibly becoming a nurse or physician's assistant. I knew she would be fine.

Kris, Danielle and Robin
2017

Beau - 2017

Beau was still navigating his way through life, starting college slowly after graduating High School in 2016. He could be opinionated and strong-willed, and sometimes I didn't like how he treated his mom, but I knew he was young and would outgrow many of these characteristics. He loved playing his video games. We would hear him in his room laughing with his online friends as he played late into the night at times.

Beau kept to himself; we would laugh when we had a Beau "sighting." He was a good kid, extremely intelligent and I believed that if he applied himself, he could literally be whatever he wanted to be in life. My role in parenting had switched to mentoring when I could, listening a lot and doing my best to be a good influence. In Beaus case, I had learned enough to know that I might be able to guide him with a suggestion here and there, but mostly I had to leave it up to his mother to help him to be a functioning adult. I knew he would be fine.

Ron Zagami would laugh and tell people I had eleven kids! In a sense, I guess he was right, with my original four, Tracy's three and Robin's four. I have to admit that it did come naturally to me at this point!

Ron would also joke with me. We bantered when he came to watch me perform. He would say, "You're pretty good; have you considered doing this for a living?" And, I would answer, "No, it doesn't pay enough!" People still loved it when he came up to play his excellent jazz piano, and I stood up and sang *Georgia on My Mind* or *You Don't Know Me* with him.

Ron Zagami with Robin 2017

During my years performing at *Manhattan Of La Jolla,* I met many great musicians. Some, like Floyd A. Smith, would sit in and wow the crowd. Mike Laz was a great bassist/vocalist who had a successful band in San Diego during the 1960's and 1970's. Although he was semi-retired, Mike still coached basketball locally in La Jolla, and his voice was still very resonant. We would do a resounding duet of *You've Lost That Loving Feeling.* Mike actually looked a little bit like Bill Medley from the *Righteous Brothers,* so I would introduce him as "Mike Medley" when he sang. Mike actually acquired a little following of people who regularly asked him to sing with me, and that was always nice. Mike was a huge fan of Frank Hamblen, being involved in a local level in basketball himself, so I always let him know when Frank was coming in. Frank was a big fan of 1950's and 1960's music anyway, so they became fast friends! It was always great to see Mike.

2016 Mike "Medley" (Laz) with Frank Hamblen

Mike "Medley" (Laz) with Ron Zagami 2016

My gig at *Manhattan of La Jolla* continued to be a blessing. I met and became friends with many influential people, along with the regular crowd that I appreciated so very much. Floyd A. Smith brought in David Meece, the great Christian *Billboard Top 100* artist. Andrew Mardis brought in Mark Redman, the MLB All-Star pitcher who won the World Series with the Florida Marlins. On another evening, I was blessed to meet the esteemed Senator Dennis DeConcini and his wife. These people had fame, but so many other people who lived their own extraordinary lives had an equal impact on my own.

Tad with Mark Redman MLB All-Star World Series Winning Pitcher 2017

Tad with Senator Dennis DeConcini 2018

•••••

Tad with Floyd A. Smith and David Meece - 2016

The next few months were difficult. Rachel moved out of her house and found a rental home for herself and the children, around the first of August. They were embroiled in divorce and custody issues. At first, Robert insisted on revisiting the marriage after six months of separation, but a very short time afterward, he was already engaged to another woman, which threw us all for a loop.

My sons had initially appeared to take Robert's side, in a sense. After all, they had all been like brothers for many years, and Rachel had initiated the separation. But, after a period of time, they came around to understanding that the situation was far more complicated and unraveled than they had known, and eventually they came around to supporting Rachel completely, once again. Meanwhile, Rachel was hurt without the support of her family, and even though it was temporary, I always wanted her to know that I was there for her. I knew everyone would come back around. It was my mission in life at this point to do whatever I could to keep my family together. Our bond was our strength.

Everybody loved Rachel and Robert, and I believe my sons looked at Rachel and Robert's life as the ideal life, the one they too had strived for, so when it fell apart, it was hard on them too. But, as time went by, Rachel became more whole again.

Nobody wants a breakup to happen. And, nobody wants to take sides, but support for your own is essential. Sometimes people just grow apart, but it doesn't mean they stop loving each other. Love and happiness are two distinctly different emotions, and they don't always go hand in hand.

She was working hard on her *Master's* program, and my grandchildren were amazingly strong through the transition. My heart broke for them all for a while, but I had to keep the faith that this too would pass and they would all get through it and become better people, hopefully.

Tad and Rachel 2017

Just like I had witnessed with my parents, and just like I had experienced with Stephanie, I knew that Rachel and Robert loved each other and will always love each other. How can you not, after sharing so much for so many years? But, as my father said to me once when I asked him why my parents seemed to hate each other so much... You can dislike a person today, and yet still love that person for everything you shared, for every experience that was a part of shaping you into who you are today. Sometimes you just grow apart.

Time and experience have blurred the lines that were so massive to me then. I use the analogy of my original songs. I am so very proud of some of them, and others were products of a time or fad or a bizarre idea that I put into music. If you look at a single song, or a single moment in a life, you can draw all kinds of conclusions about what kind of person I am... but, I sincerely hope, when all is said and done, that when people look at my body of work, they will have a much more complete picture. It is the same with life experience.

Hopefully, eventually you can look back at a failed relationship that produced beautiful children or shaped you positively in many ways, and say, "hey, we had a good run there, and I'm ultimately so very grateful for what we had." Everything is temporary. I experienced a wealth of growth, finding strength and learning many life lessons in my turbulent relationships with Carol, Stephanie and Tracy.

Mostly, I was so very proud of how my Rachel handled life. Even in single motherhood, she maintained her poise and elegance. Her children's kindness and compassion were a direct reflection of their parenting, and Rachel was maintaining her strength, somehow, through this very difficult time. I loved her with all my heart, and I knew she would ultimately rise above all of this.

Rachel met a new man, Leo, who had two lovely children, Jaxson and Daisy. His kids were close to Giorgio and Stefani's age, and he seemed to be very good to her. It was good to have someone watching over them, and Rachel seemed happy, as she began to navigate her way through life after Robert.

Stefani, Tad & Giorgio 2017

The best part of it all, if there is such a thing, is that I made a point of driving up to the desert more often to spend time with my grandchildren and they always embraced my love and attention when I was there.

As time went on, Giorgio became an amazing athlete, winning track and field championships, scoring multiple touchdowns in football games, hitting home runs in baseball, and scoring many goals in soccer. He was an outstanding student, winning the prestigious "Gold Leaf" award in Elementary school. He was my shining light.

Stefani was equally as intelligent; she was also very competitive in sports; her awareness and compassion were beyond her years. I was blessed with yet another sweetheart in my life. I cherished her love and the closeness we had, and I just couldn't wait to see her again when we were apart.

•••••

Not that I needed excuses to drive all the way from San Diego to the desert to see my grandkids, but it worked out well because throughout this period, I began to work on Steve Madaio's audiobook with him. I would go to his house and he would narrate the book I had written and derived from his interviews.

We would get through about twenty pages at a time before he got tired, so I made several trips to the desert to make it happen. I would set up my mobile *Pro Tools* rig in his house, and he would dictate the book into a microphone until his voice got a little scratchy and his lungs were tired.

Since Steve had COPD, it took months for me to edit what ended up being over five hours of audio, carefully removing each breath from between words to make sure that it flowed without the distraction of the heavy breathing, but Steve did an amazing job of narrating his life story, in-between his trips to France to tour with Veronique Sanson. He was a pretty amazing dude, touring in huge arenas into his seventies.

•••••

At the end of July in 2017, my sister Judy's son Brian and his lovely wife Jenna gave birth to their second child, August. He was a beautiful baby. Several months later, they came to visit us and I was amazed by his agility and awareness at such a young age. I also grieved for my sister missing another grandchild's birth. I knew she was watching over them. I vowed to keep her memory alive with all of her grandchildren.

August & Aria Kane
Judy's Grandchildren
2018

•••••

On the early morning of September 30th, 2017, we got a frantic call from Frank Hamblen's girlfriend, Jane. Frank had suffered a heart attack in bed, and although he was rushed to the hospital, he did not survive. We were devastated. Robin and I went immediately to the house; Frank's nephew Andrew and his wife Kristin drove down from Los Angeles and arrived within a couple of hours. Frank's sister Susan immediately came out.

Frank was not just an icon in the basketball community; he was our dear friend, and probably the most real, normal, kind, humble person of his stature that I have ever met. Frank was always genuinely concerned about everyone in your family and all of your friends that he knew. He took a real interest in people. Robin and I had been there with him through the best years, the playoffs, through his marriage and divorce with Uta and his ensuing depression. We had laughed and cried with him, and we all grieved.

Frank and Robin
August 2017

A couple weeks later, his family held a memorial in Los Angeles for him. I performed *My Way* and I also backed up Frank's sister Susan as she sang a beautiful religious song. Kobe Bryant gave an impassioned eulogy, among other giants in the industry and childhood friends of Frank. We followed the service with a wake for him at a local hotel. I performed with my trio, and a couple hundred people came for the event to toast Frank.

•••••

Way back when I was in High School, my dad had written a book entitled, *But, What About the People?* ...He had given me his scribbled manuscripts when I was a teenager, and for months, when I was fifteen and sixteen, I sat at his desk in his medical office on a typewriter, typing them into a book for him.

As I went through a stack of papers I had been given after his passing, I found the manuscript and decided that it was time to move forward on publishing it, forty years later. It was an interesting read, because it had been written at a pivotal time in American History when *Roe vs. Wade* had recently been decided by the Supreme Court, and President Richard Nixon had recently resigned from office.

I worked hard to update some of the passages and add some private thoughts of my own, and then I sent the manuscript to my sister Suzanne to review. Suzanne had just been diagnosed with *Parkinson's* disease, and I thought it would be a good distraction for her. She decided to painstakingly go through some other writings that he had, and the process went on and on, without a publishing date set, so I moved on to other projects. I knew it would evolve accordingly.

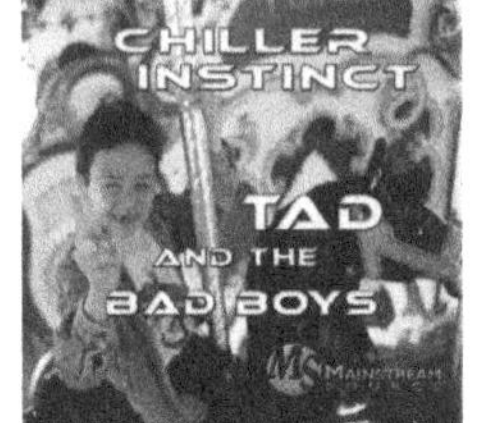

I did a "vocal and guitar duets" album of jazz standards and originals with Michael Higgins; in the style of the Joe Pass-Ella Fitzgerald album that Bill Hawkins had turned me on to so many years ago. It was a labor of love, and Michael's guitar parts were just excellent. Later, in 2018, I released a "Chill" collection of music under the surname *Tad and the Bad Boys.*

My friend Floyd A. Smith, an amazing bass singer with the Grammy-winning *Fifth Dimension,* came into my studio and sang one of my originals, *We're Making Love Tonight.* We released it as a single and submitted it for Grammy consideration.

In late 2017, a woman approached me regarding a manuscript she had written. It happened to involve her own true story of having been raped by a young mafioso and raising his child alone. I happened to know the man who did this to her. He had already died. Although her story was not very well written, I thought it was compelling enough to release as I wanted to start to expand the "publishing arm" of *Mainstream Source.* I spent several months grammatically correcting, rewriting and adding to her manuscript. She wanted to remain anonymous because of the sensitivity of the material. We released it in mid-2018 under the title "Mafia Baby!" and her pseudonym Megan Cain. I didn't expect the book to sell much, but I felt as if we told an important story, and I knew it would impact the people who did read it.

•••••

Robin and I hosted our traditional Christmas Eve event in December of 2017. Although it was warm and full of laughter, we missed Frank's presence, as he had made it his own tradition to attend our parties every Christmas for several years. My Uncle Ted and Aunt Candy came with my cousin Warren and his

Life goes on. Although our contributions may be significant, they all end up as part of the collective consciousness. We are only alive as long as someone who knew and loved us remains on the planet. We then live on as a footnote to history, no matter how famous or important we became.

Tad with Uncle Ted 2017

beautiful wife and kids. Rachel was there with Giorgio and Stefani. Robin's sister Gina's husband Pepe put up a Piñata outside, and the kids squealed with delight as it was pounded into shreds with candy falling everywhere.

•••••

In early 2018, Robin and I went to a *Laker's* game in honor of Frank. Our friend Veronica Lawlor set it up for us and then spent a couple hours with us reminiscing after the game. It was bizarre to see a new *Laker's* coaching staff, with new coaches (many of whom Frank had trained).

•••••

Makayla's Golden Buzzer Moment
America's Got Talent 2018
with Heidi Klum

In March of 2018, my granddaughter Makayla auditioned for *America's Got Talent* on *NBC*. She walked out in front of the judges, Simon Cowell, Mel B, Howie Mandel and Heidi Klum, and sang *Warrior* by *Demi Lovato.*

Makayla gave a powerful performance and Heidi gave her the "golden buzzer", which put her directly through to the live shows, to the quarterfinals! Although we knew about it, the show didn't air until July of 2018, so we had to keep it to ourselves for four months! It was excruciating but so exciting for our little girl!

Mostly, I was so very proud of my daughter Regina, and of her work ethic and devotion to her family. Maybe in some ways she was living vicariously through Makayla's success, but I knew that Regina was one hundred percent behind her children, and she was a strong, loving influence on them. In addition to running Makayla and Aidan all over creation to auditions and film dates, she was a talent manager with *Dream Talent*, handling the careers of dozens of others. She had so many of the great qualities of her mother in her. Also, her husband Todd, Makayla's father, was a great provider. He was a firefighter, rising to the ranks of Captain, and his work ethic was admirable, to say the least.

Tad and Makayla
June 2018

•••••

In May of 2018 I got a call from a huge communications company we had worked with in the past on some commercial spots and live events. They were hosting a large convention in Las Vegas to be held during the first week of June 2018. They asked me to put together a utility band to play walk-on and walk-off cues, as well as to put together elaborate skits for the executives to perform in which would include band members.

At first, they asked for classic rock cues, and as the event loomed closer they changed their focus to contemporary cues. I was stressed but I stayed on top of the whole process. During the process, however, I had a rare recurrence of my childhood *Herpes Zoster* (Shingles) on my face. It was excruciating, burning my face and causing splitting headaches for the entire month as I was preparing for Vegas. It may have been brought on by the stress, but it was bizarre, literally fifty-six years later, for this thing inside me to recur which had laid dormant in me for so long. I was miserable!

Tad's Band in Las Vegas - June 2018
with Chad Quist, Steve Alaniz,
Andrew Fraga, Jr. and Steve Madaio

The illness had just started to subside when I arrived in Las Vegas on the second of June. I had a great band with me, including Steve Madaio on trumpet, Steve Alaniz on sax, Andrew Fraga, Jr. on drums and Chad Quist on guitar and vocals. We picked up a competent local bass player in Las Vegas. These were highly trained professionals, and although it was an intense few days with early calls, a ballroom with around 5,000 people attending every day, and hundreds of immediate cues, it went off without a hitch and we nailed it. It reminded me of how valuable experience is, over anything else.

Steve Madaio
June 2018

Education is essential, but it pales in comparison to life experience.

It was such a pleasure to work with this group of great musicians. Steve Madaio had sprained his foot just a few days before the gig, so his companion Eileen Collins pushed him in a wheelchair through the miles of convention space to the ballroom at the *Aria.* He never complained of the pain, and during virtually every cue, he stood up to perform, even though this went on for hours, and then days. He was a true professional. Chad Quist had become a very close friend to me. In addition to his excellent guitar and vocal performance, he had great stage presence and he calmly offered his services to be on-camera through many of the client's skits. I loved recording with Chad, and performing with him was an even greater blessing. Andy was solid as always on drums. I had watched him develop from the little boy in eighth grade banging the cymbal in band, to a world-class drummer, now performing with elite musicians in huge venues. Steve Alaniz was always on-point and tasty in his approach to the saxophone. He used effects to double or add an octave to his sound, so he was able to sound like a section. He was also always great to hang out with. I was blessed to have a great experience on the Vegas gig.

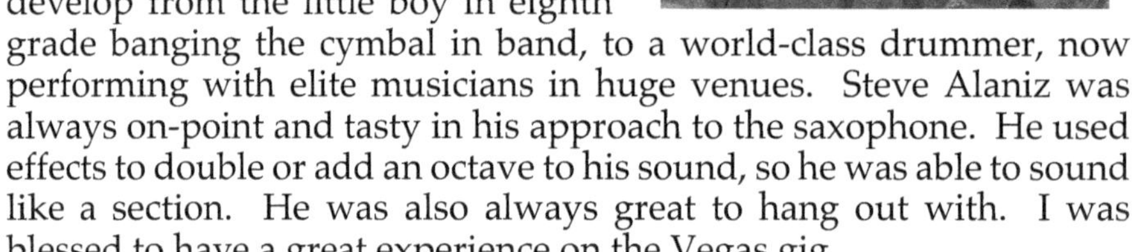

Chad Quist
June 2018

Andrew Fraga, Jr.
June 2018

•••••

June 28, 2018 was my sixtieth birthday. That was a strange milestone for me, because I felt so very much younger than that, and as I looked around at other people my age, I realized that thankfully I was aging gracefully and perhaps slower than many of my peers.

The important thing is that I maintained the energy of a thirty-five-year-old. I was on a vitamin regimen, which included many herbs and supplements. I needed to drop fifteen pounds, so during the month of July I went on a crash diet and did just that.

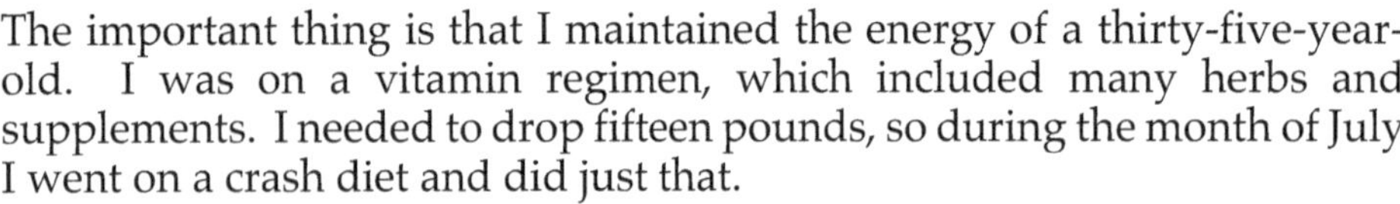

Steve Alaniz
November 2018

I remembered my beloved grandmother Audrey when she was ninety, telling me that she swore to me that she felt eighteen inside. Now, I knew and understood exactly what she meant, all those years ago.

On June 23, 2018, my family and friends threw me a huge birthday party at our friend's Peter and Sheila's home in San Diego.

My sister Betsy, with her husband Mark arrived from Colorado, and Betsy's son Lucas came down from Oregon with his family. Lucas and his wife Julieann had two boys and a girl. They were lovely kids. Lucas was very tall and always smiling. I was always glad to spend time with my good nephew. Betsy's other son James was also there. James lived close to us in San Diego but we rarely saw him. He was quiet but kind, and I knew he was superbly intelligent, observing everything around him

without missing a beat. James had lost a couple hundred pounds, and he looked great.

My sister Suzanne came out from North Carolina for the events; Suzy brought my niece Wendy for the event. As I mentioned, Suzanne had been diagnosed with *Parkinson's Disease*, and I could tell that she had slowed down greatly in the two years since I had seen her last.

I loved her with all my heart and the selfish part of me wanted her to always be young and healthy, but the main thing was that she showed up! It was great to have my children and grandchildren, cousins, nephews and nieces with me, and so many of my dear friends. My Robin organized the entire event; Robin, Sheila and her sister Mistie worked extremely hard to make that day one of the greatest days of my life.

•••••

When my old computer died and I upgraded to the *iMac Pro* in June of 2018, I realized that I had to upgrade everything in my studio, because all of the bit rates had changed, and even the connectors had changed from *firewire* to *thunderbolt*. The expense was ridiculous, and it took me literally almost until the end of July 2018 to purchase and set up all of the different new components.

While I was at it, I had a few classic pieces of outboard equipment rebuilt or repaired, and as of August 1, 2018, I was rocking on a much higher level in the studio. I continued to work on the Steve Madaio audiobook, beginning a series of podcasts with Steve and Jimi (Fitz) Fitzgerald, and prepared for several future projects.

•••••

Once again, at the end of August of 2018, I had a retinal detachment, this time in my right eye. Even though the surgeon had lasered the eye to prevent it, the retina still detached and I was rushed into surgery.

Through the process of all of the surgeries and complications with my eyes, I became so grateful to have the gift of sight, and I learned more about the human eye than I ever wanted to know! The eye is a universe of its own; it is so complicated and intricate; understanding this small piece of our enormous universe brought me closer to God.

Everyone is entitled to their beliefs and opinions, but frankly, it makes no sense to me why some people are atheists. Creation is so vast; only a small portion of it is revealed to us. To me, it's insanity to not believe or understand that the Universe is too intricate to not have had a Master Planner. I know many people have different concepts of God; call It what you want, but in my humble opinion there would be no Creation without a Creator.

•••••

Our Makayla moved on to the quarterfinals and then the semifinals of *America's Got Talent*. Robin and I were there at the quarterfinals with the entire family and some friends. It was held at the *Dolby* Theatre in Hollywood, and I literally cried like a baby when she made it through to the semifinals.

It was amazing to see the outpouring of affection and support for her from millions of people watching on *NBC*. Her performances were flawless. In one week after the first episode aired, she was the number one trending person in the world on

YouTube for a short period. She had over ten million views of her first video, and the entire process was amazing.

AGT Quarterfinals 2018

I kidded with my friends that I had been in the business for forty years, working with amazing people including Frank Sinatra, and yet, forevermore I would be known as "Makayla Phillip's grandfather!" And, that was okay with me.

One major thing that stood out to me was the closeness Makayla had with her family, especially with her sister, my first granddaughter Whitney. My Whitney had grown up into a lovely, caring woman. She was now twenty—three years old, kind and sweet to everyone, and her sister's biggest supporter. Whitney looked so very much like her grandmother Stephanie, and surely, she had many of Steph's good qualities. Whitney was wise beyond her years.

Whitney

As a result of my eye surgery, I was not able to attend the semifinals of *America's Got Talent* to see our Makayla perform at the *Dolby Theatre* in Los Angeles with Robin. I had a gas bubble in my eye and I was forced to lie on my left side ninety percent of the time without moving for ten days. That part of my healing, just allowing the eye to heal without moving too much, was excruciating because I am generally a person who never stops. I've been blessed with energy, vitality and stamina for my entire life, and I generally don't stop doing something, except to rest.

You can't hit a moving target!

Although Makayla didn't make it into the finals, her path was set. Her social media fingerprint had become huge, and soon, she would be getting offers from huge management companies. I was confident that she would make it to the top! I could certainly help to boost her from my place in the middle!

Tad on the L.A. Lakers Bench with Magic Johnson 2018

•••••

At the end of September, 2018, the *Los Angeles Lakers* were playing a pre-season game in San Diego at the *Valley View Center.* It happened to be on the exact one-year anniversary of Frank Hamblen's passing. Veronica Lawlor came down along with Andrew Mardis, Frank's nephew, and we brought a large group to the game, including Frank's girlfriend Jane, Ron Zagami, Lawson Brown and Michele Ebbert, my Robin, Ron's daughter Michelle and her young son. I was able to sit on the bench next to Magic Johnson and enjoy the game courtside. I continued to count my blessings. Frank's sister Susan Mardis had become a close friend of ours, and she would remain so for life. Frank's family was now our family; it was as simple as that.

The Mardis Family 2018

Tad with Eddie 2017

Through all of the trials and tribulations of my life, I was grateful for the lifetime friendships I had gained from so many amazing people. Friends make you rich in spirit. Of all of my friends, my best friend Eddie kept showing up and caring, not only for me but for my children and grandchildren.

I am eternally grateful for Eddie's kindness and calm, deep but understanding demeanor, always. We should all be so lucky to have a friend like Eddie.

•••••

Towards the end of 2018, my daughter Rachel's ex-husband Robert was moving towards marrying his fiancé, and he decided that he wanted an annulment of his marriage to Rachel in the Catholic Church so he could marry the new girl in the Catholic Church. I thought this was absurd for him to even consider this after a twenty-year relationship and two kids, and I was sure the Catholic Church that I knew and grew up in, would turn him down.

Somehow, the church actually gave him the annulment. I was disgusted, mainly because Giorgio and Stefani deserved more than that from their father. An annulment is supposed to be allowed after a mistake that lasted only briefly. I wondered how Robert could say whatever he had to say to get the annulment, and how that would look in the eyes of God.

I didn't want to judge Robert for his actions. I knew he was devastated about his divorce, but I really felt that this was a classless act from a really good but misguided man. I was told that he used the reasoning that he never really loved Rachel and he made a mistake marrying her. I knew that wasn't true firsthand, as I remembered him coming to me personally and asking for my daughter's hand in marriage. Nevertheless, it was Rachel who asked for the divorce, and I understand first-hand the pain of losing a marriage, but, an annulment? Really? I think it also affected me more so because of my memory of my mother's experience with the Catholic priest after her divorce, where he promptly excommunicated her and threw her out of the church. My, how times had changed in just a few years. It shook the core of everything I had been taught in Catechism when I was young. I just hoped that my grandchildren wouldn't be too affected by this decision over time. I pray every day for the health and safety of my loved ones, all of them!

My sister Judy once told me that everyone is just trying to figure out their lives, and to live their lives in the only way they know how. So, I've learned to let go and to attempt to start with forgiveness. It's a tough task, but nobody completely understands the challenges another person has, and what coping mechanisms they have to deal with them. Forgiveness is essential.

•••••

Steve Madaio

I woke up on Wednesday, January 16, 2019 to find out that my dear friend Steve Madaio had passed away of congestive heart failure, the night before. I had spent an enormous amount of time with Steve from 2015 through 2018, working on his life story book, audiobook and podcasts. We never know when our day will come, and I was grateful to have helped him to leave a legacy behind that went beyond his talent and his music, to his philosophy and the lessons he learned, in order to help others.

I am able to look back with clarity on my life and give thanks for the lessons I've learned, too. My father imparted his intellect and wit; somehow Maynard mostly maintained a strong connection with me throughout all of his travails. My mother gave me her talent and reminded me that against all odds, you can keep moving forward in life. From my sisters: Suzanne was like a second mother, always optimistic and caring when I needed her the most. Judy was the philosopher and traveler who first opened up my eyes to accepting new cultures and new ideas, and she left the planet first, to pave the way for all of the rest of us to meet up with her on her latest journey. Kathleen was the spiritual seeker, reminding me always to breathe and be grateful for each moment. When Betsy was at a lifetime low, she reinvented herself and found success in her own life, reminding me to never give up. I learned great lessons from each of my children and grandchildren as I evolved through my own life, counting my blessings always. Robin's example reminded me that you don't need to wait for a holiday or special occasion to do something nice for someone else. With her, I finally had found a truly reciprocal relationship, based upon love, goodness and strength.

CHAPTER SEVENTY-THREE
Grateful for Life Experience

In the end, the only thing left will be love, I promise.

I wrote this book in my sixtieth year of life on Earth. The year 2019 would mark my fortieth year as a professional performer. Who knows? The Lord may call me home tomorrow, or with not-yet-discovered advances in medical science, I might live yet another sixty years. In that case, a sequel would be in order, hopefully filled with much more joy than sorrow. Regardless of what happens, I am amazed about the complexity of life on this planet, about everything I've learned and for the love I've found, and I pray each day to be a better person than I was the day before.

I hope my story influences the reader in a positive way, to look at your own life perhaps a bit deeper, and to know that life lessons can be derived from virtually every one of your experiences, if you look deep enough.

In 2017, the population of the Earth was estimated at 7.5 billion people. Mine is one small story in a vast sea of triumph and tragedy. Climbing to the middle in America is like being beyond the stratosphere in most of the rest of the world. Even with advances in science and engineering, much of our planet is ravaged with war, poverty, disease and famine. Yes, mankind continues to make major strides, but even in America, opioid abuse remains rampant, homelessness and crime are prevalent in many cities, and we still have much work to do. It must be noted that I am quite aware that my climb to the middle in America, although beset with struggle and tragic circumstance, was filled with blessings other people could only imagine. I remain grateful every day and I believe strongly: As long as you're alive, you can make a difference.

As I continue to perform and produce content, and to move forward with my life, I look around me and I am eternally grateful for the life I have lived to this point. Life is difficult at times, but as long as you're in the game, you have a chance to better yourself.

I wanted to change the world with my music, with my talent and my songs. In a small way, I succeeded. Throughout my long career as a performer, thousands of people would come to me and tell me how touched they were by a lyric I wrote or a song I sang, or how profoundly their lives were impacted by the way I communicate through my music.

On a greater scale, when I was finally able to release my music to the world through all the platforms available to me in the early 21st century, I would look at the long reports of music downloads and streams from all over the world and marvel at how far and wide it reached. People were downloading my music in New Zealand, Russia, South Africa, Japan, Europe, North America and practically everywhere else in the world.

Hundreds of thousands of people had their own experiences with my music, and I would never have a clue about those experiences or how it impacted their moments. Although, at the point of this writing I never had a 'hit' song, I had produced and composed thousands of songs, which were being heard everywhere, and that was heartwarming. Making it to the middle wasn't so bad after all.

•••••

As I outlined in this book, I have experienced profound tragedies and amazing triumphs as well. I have languished in the depths of despair and also, I've felt intense joy. Such is life. I look around at some of the people I've met… the billionaire grocery-store heiress who is lost in addiction; the trust-fund son who drinks himself silly because he never earned the privilege he has gained; the wealthy Arab horse owner with the ditzy young blond at his side, throwing money around like it is dirt… I've never been envious about what they have and what I don't have. In fact, it's been the opposite.

Dr. Tom Costa used to ask people, "Would you give up your arm for a million dollars? How about a leg?" Of course, the answer would be 'no'. So, we are all millionaires in our own right. And, way more importantly, my joy has come from raising children who became amazing adults, with compassion, strength, a work ethic, and a great understanding of how important it is to treat others as you would like to be treated. My joy has also come from my work ethic, and from all of the people, family, friends and others, who made an impact on my life.

More so, as time goes by I try to be a little easier on myself. As humans (as I mentioned in the prologue to this book), we are really half-animal and half-god. I believe that all good people strive towards their god-self, and yet we are all imbued with primordial impulses, which ebb over time.

Looking back, I believe that many of the transgressions that other people committed against me originated from desperation, in desperate circumstances. Overcoming the pain that naturally occurred as a result of these transgressions was difficult for me, and lasted for years. But, it was easier to forgive, understanding that much of what was done to me was done more from desperation, or addictive behavior (or both) rather than from outright malice. And, again, forgiving myself was critical to my healing and to my survival.

At times, I myself had acted out of desperation, having been backed up against a wall or forced to my knees by circumstance. It's an awful place to be. I honestly never intended or wanted to hurt anyone, ever, and I lived the *Golden Rule* as much as I knew how. Because of that, it's easier to let go of pain, and when it rears its ugly head, I deal with it, and try not to beat myself up any longer.

If we all lived our lives as Christ had done, we would not need Him or His example.

Having said that, some wounds last forever. Understanding that fact is a strong step towards releasing the pain just enough to be able to cope, and continue to move forward in life. Unquestionably, I was a completely different person before and after Stephanie died. Kimberley's brutal murder had the same effect upon me. What do you do? You do your best to work through posttraumatic stress. You embrace and protect the loved ones in your charge. You try not to live a life of regret. If you do the work, you might emerge a deeper and stronger person.

•••••

Our hormones play a large part in our youth. How we are parented and guided through our childhood plays a huge part in what we become. Teaching simple things like the *Golden Rule* can make such a difference in a child's life. Learning the importance of faith and hope, and having something to look forward to always, can lead us from depression and self-doubt. Delayed gratification; learning to get the hard things done before we play, can add to our contentment. Managing temptation, allowing the god-side to pull us away from the animal side of ourselves, is important to strive towards. Forgiving others and forgiving ourselves is essential. As I mentioned earlier, jealousy, greed, envy and anger are all acids that eat their own containers.

The *Optimists Creed* leads with a statement, "To be so strong that nothing can disturb your peace of mind." One of the *Four Agreements* states that we should not take anything personally. None of us is truly strong enough to follow these guidelines always, every day, but these are tools for our arsenal of striving towards happiness and contentment.

Companionship with the right person can be huge. It took me a few times before I found a companion who was capable of loving me unconditionally (and could also put up with me at the same time!) ... I loved and lost, loved and lost, loved and lost, and then loved again; most importantly, I never gave up.

When the Lord calls me home, I fully expect to leave this world and enter the next with an intense feeling of love and gratefulness. Yes, there were times when I cursed the darkness, when I questioned everything because life seemed so cruel at that moment.

There were other times when I felt the sting of unrequited love, the pain of rejection, rage that came from people deceiving me, the uncontrollable sadness from losing a loved one. But, as I've already said, with each new day, with each new opportunity to wake up and experience this big, beautiful world, we have a new opportunity to reinvent ourselves.

My Uncle Bill used to say that for every youthful year he lived hard, partied hard and squeezed two years into one, little did he know that he was just subtracting a year from the end of his life.

Be good to yourself. Take care of your body. Most things (not everything) in moderation are okay. Learn to love yourself. Honor your parents and the wisdom of those who came before you. Wisdom generally comes from hard experience.

In the depths of winter, you must always reach deep within yourself to find that invincible summer.

If you can't point to something tragically heartbreaking or something breathtakingly amazing that happened to you in your life, you haven't completely lived.

Make sure you're insulated with a network of caring people around you, and turn to them when you need to. Life is difficult and you may feel unworthy or unjustly treated by others, but as long as the fire of life is within you, you can overcome anything. Mind over matter is real.

Always remember, you are a very valuable, worthwhile person.

Love your children (and grandchildren), if you're lucky enough to have any. If you nurture them, in the end, you will know absolutely that they were the greatest gifts of your lifetime.

Yes, it was a long climb to the middle! It was the journey that mattered, not the destination. Every day I have left to breathe, to continue to do my life's work and mostly to love my family… is a good day.

•••

A NOTE FROM THE AUTHOR:

The stories in this book are reconstructed from memory. Other people may remember experiences differently. Events in the book were based off of events that happened in the real world, but all of the real-world participants were replaced with newly written characters. As a result, all characters appearing in this work are fictitious. As a result, any resemblance to real persons, living or dead, is purely coincidental.

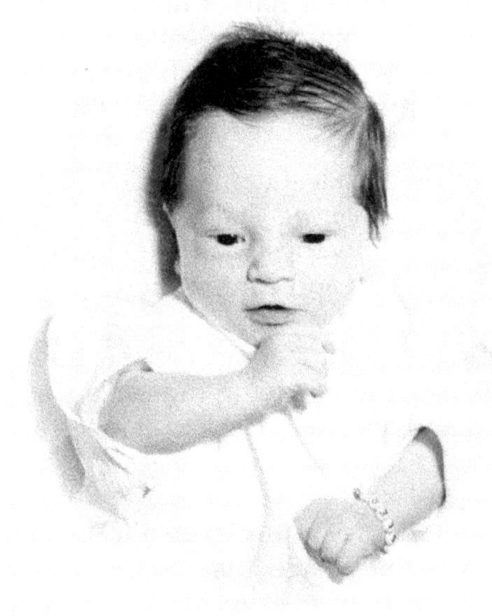

By: Tad Sisler

Post Office Box 400
Cardiff, CA 92007
(818) 845-6700

ISBN: 978-1-966258-45-2

www.ingramcontent.com/pod-product-compliance
Lightning Source LLC
LaVergne TN
LVHW081401110826
845149LV00010B/1630
9781966258452